M: Finance 6e

THE MCGRAW HILL Series in Finance, Insurance, and Real Estate

M: Finance 6e

Marcia Millon Cornett
Bentley University

Troy A. Adair Jr.
Lehigh University

John Nofsinger
University of Alaska Anchorage

M: FINANCE, SIXTH EDITION

Published by McGraw Hill LLC, 1325 Avenue of the Americas, New York, NY 10019. Copyright ©2024 by
McGraw Hill LLC. All rights reserved. Printed in the United States of America. Previous editions ©2022, 2019,
and 2016. No part of this publication may be reproduced or distributed in any form or by any means, or stored in
a database or retrieval system, without the prior written consent of McGraw Hill LLC, including, but not limited
to, in any network or other electronic storage or transmission, or broadcast for distance learning.

Some ancillaries, including electronic and print components, may not be available to customers outside the
United States.

This book is printed on acid-free paper.

1 2 3 4 5 6 7 8 9 LMN 28 27 26 25 24 23

ISBN 978-1-264-41275-4 (bound edition)
MHID 1-264-41275-4 (bound edition)
ISBN 978-1-266-82787-7 (loose-leaf edition)
MHID 1-266-82787-0 (loose-leaf edition)

Portfolio Manager: *Becky Olson*
Product Developer: *Barb Hari*
Marketing Manager: *Sarah Hurley*
Content Project Managers: *Melissa M. Leick/Katie Reuter*
Manufacturing Project Manager: *Laura Fuller*
Content Licensing Specialists: *Melissa Homer/Karyn Morrison*
Cover Image: *Shutterstock Images, LLC*
Compositor: *Straive*

All credits appearing on page or at the end of the book are considered to be an extension of the copyright page.

Library of Congress Control Number: 2022947971

The Internet addresses listed in the text were accurate at the time of publication. The inclusion of a website does
not indicate an endorsement by the authors or McGraw Hill LLC, and McGraw Hill LLC does not guarantee the
accuracy of the information presented at these sites.

mheducation.com/highered

about the
authors

Courtesy of Marcia Million Cornett

Marcia Millon Cornett *Robert A. and Julia E. Dorn Professor of Finance at Bentley University.* She received her BS degree in economics from Knox College in Galesburg, Illinois, and her MBA and PhD degrees in finance from Indiana University in Bloomington, Indiana. Dr. Cornett has written and published several articles in the areas of bank performance, bank regulation, corporate finance, and investments. Articles authored by Dr. Cornett have appeared in such academic journals as the *Journal of Finance; Journal of Money, Credit, and Banking; Journal of Financial Economics; Financial Management;* and *Journal of Banking and Finance.* She was recently ranked the 124th most published out of more than 17,600 authors and the number five female author in finance literature over the last 50 years. Along with Anthony Saunders and Otgontsetseg Erhemjamts, Dr. Cornett has recently completed work on the tenth edition of *Financial Institutions Management* (McGraw Hill Education) and the seventh edition of *Financial Markets and Institutions* (McGraw Hill Education). Professor Cornett serves as an associate editor for the *Journal of Banking and Finance, Journal of Financial Services Research, Review of Financial Economics, Financial Review,* and *Multinational Finance Journal.* Dr. Cornett has served as a member of the board of directors, the executive committee, and the finance committee of the SIU Credit Union. Dr. Cornett has also taught at Southern Illinois University at Carbondale, the University of Colorado, Boston College, and Southern Methodist University. She is a member of the Financial Management Association, the American Finance Association, and the Western Finance Association.

Troy Alton Adair, Jr.

Troy Alton Adair Jr. *Professor of Practice at Lehigh University and Founder and CEO of dataDicts, Inc.* He received his BS degree in computers/information science from the University of Alabama at Birmingham, his MBA from the University of North Dakota, and his PhD in finance from Indiana University. Dr. Adair serves Lehigh as the Co-Director of the Computer Science and Business (CSB) Program, the FinTech Minor, and the Business Analytics Certificate Program. He also manages a data science consulting business specializing in providing customized data analytics assessments and training. He previously managed research computing infrastructure and support services for Harvard Business School and has written articles on bank regulator self-interest, analyst earnings per share forecasting, and capital budgeting in continuous time. He is the author of *Corporate Finance Demystified, Excel Applications in Corporate Finance,* and *Excel Applications in Investments* (all McGraw Hill Education). He has also served as a consultant on financial data information systems and business intelligence to a number of international banks and insurance companies and as the faculty representative to the board of trustees investments committee at Alma College. Dr. Adair has also taught at the University of Michigan, Alma College, Hofstra University, Indiana University, and the University of North Carolina at Chapel Hill. He is a member of the Financial Management Association, the American Finance Association, and the Southern Finance Association.

John R. Nofsinger

John Nofsinger *Dean, Professor, and William H. Seward Endowed Chair of International Finance at the University of Alaska Anchorage.* He earned his BS degree in electrical engineering from Washington State University, his MBA degree from Chapman University, and his PhD degree in finance from Washington State University. Dr. Nofsinger has written over 70 articles in the areas of investments, corporate finance, and behavioral finance. These papers have appeared in the scholarly journals, including *Journal of Finance, Journal of Business, Journal of Financial and Quantitative Analysis, Financial Management, Journal of Corporate Finance, Journal of Banking and Finance,* and *Journal of Behavioral Decision Making.* Dr. Nofsinger has also authored (or coauthored) 14 trade books, scholarly books, and textbooks that have been translated into 11 different languages. The most prominent of these books is the industry book *The Psychology of Investing.* Dr. Nofsinger is a leading expert in behavioral finance and is a frequent speaker on this topic at industry conferences, universities, and academic conferences. He is frequently quoted or appears in the financial media, including *The Wall Street Journal, Financial Times, Fortune, Bloomberg Business Week, Smart Money, The Washington Post,* and *CNBC,* and other media from *The Dolans* to *The Street.com.*

a note from the
authors

"There is a lot to cover in this course so I focus on the core concepts, theories, and problems."

"I like to teach the course by using examples from their own individual lives."

"My students come into this course with varying levels of math skills."

How many of these quotes might you have said while teaching the undergraduate corporate finance course? Our many years of teaching certainly reflect such sentiments, and, as we prepared to write this book, we conducted many market research studies that confirm just how much these statements—or ones similar— are common across the country. This critical course covers so many crucial topics that instructors need to focus on core ideas to ensure that students are getting the preparation they need for future classes—and for their lives beyond college.

We did not set out to write this book to change the way finance is taught, but rather to parallel and support the way that instructors from across the country currently teach finance. Well over 600 instructors teaching this course have shared their class experiences and ideas via a variety of research methods that we used to develop the framework for this text. We are excited to have authored a book that we think you will find fits your classroom style perfectly.

KEY THEMES

This book's framework emphasizes three themes. See the next section in this preface for a description of features in our book that support these themes.

- **Finance is about connecting core concepts.** We all struggle with fitting so many topics into this course, so this text strives to make it easier for you by getting back to the core concepts, key research, and current topics. We realize that today's students expect to learn more in class from lectures than in closely studying their textbooks, so we've created brief chapters that clearly lead students to crucial material that they need to review if they are to understand how to approach core financial concepts. The text is also organized around learning goals, making it easier for you to prep your course and for students to study the right topics.

- **Finance can be taught using a personal perspective.** Most long-term finance instructors have often heard students ask "How is this course relevant to me?" on the first day of class. We no longer teach classes dedicated solely to finance majors; many of us now must teach the first finance course to a mix of business majors. We need to give finance majors the rigor they need while not overwhelming class members from other majors. For years, instructors have used individual examples to help teach these concepts, but this is the first text to integrate this personal way of teaching into the chapters.

- **Finance focuses on solving problems and decision making.** This isn't to say that concepts and theories aren't important, but students will typically need to solve some kind of mathematical problem—or at least understand the impact of different numerical scenarios—to make the right decision on common finance issues. If you, as an instructor, either assign problems for homework or create exams made up almost entirely of mathematical material, you understand the need for good problems (and plenty of them). You also understand from experience the number of office hours you spend tutoring students and grading homework. Students have different learning styles, and this text aims to address that challenge to allow you more time in class to get through the critical topics.

changes in the
sixth edition

The global pandemic greatly impacted business and global trade. As a financial response, central banks around the world eased monetary policy and made money more easily available. The resulting impact on a firm's cost of capital affected the estimation of project cash flows, valuations, and more. As capital budgeting is an important part of this book, we have quickly incorporated the new environment into our theory and applications. In addition, we have updated every chapter. Below are the changes we made for this sixth edition, broken out by chapter.

OVERALL

- Increased the number of spreadsheet-oriented end-of-chapter problems
- Updated data, company names, and scenarios to reflect the latest available data and real-world changes
- Removed the "twin" problems in the end-of-chapter problem sets as they duplicate online assessment assignments

chapter one
INTRODUCTION TO FINANCIAL MANAGEMENT

- Updated the Personal Application with information on firms that have filed for bankruptcy more recently
- Updated the data in Example 1-2 on executive compensation
- Edited Section 1.7: Big Picture Environment to discuss the ramifications of COVID-19 and the Tax Cuts and Jobs Act of 2017

chapter two
REVIEWING FINANCIAL STATEMENTS

- Added Excel to some examples
- Added Excel problems
- Deleted the second twin in the Problems

chapter three
ANALYZING FINANCIAL STATEMENTS

- Added Excel problems
- Deleted the second twin in the Problems

chapter four
TIME VALUE OF MONEY 1: ANALYZING SINGLE CASH FLOWS

- Updated the data in Figure 4.5 on gold prices
- Increased the number of Excel problems and added Excel to Examples
- Included a short paragraph to mention the TVM tables
- Deleted the second twin in the Problems

chapter five
TIME VALUE OF MONEY 2: ANALYZING ANNUITY CASH FLOWS

- Added Excel to examples and in text
- Updated Finance at Work box
- Added Excel problems
- Deleted the second twin in the Problems

chapter six
UNDERSTANDING FINANCIAL MARKETS AND INSTITUTIONS

- Increased the number of Excel problems and added Excel to examples
- Updated Figures 6.4, 6.5, 6.8, 6.9, 6.13, 6.14
- Deleted the second twin in the Problems

chapter seven
VALUING BONDS

- Updated Figures 7.1–7.5 on bond issuance, interest rate path, yield to maturities, new bond quotes, and a summary of the bond market
- Updated Table 7.2, Time Out 7.2, and associated discussions
- Changed the subject of a Finance at Work box to negative interest rates
- Changed the subject of a Finance at Work box to COVID-19 and the credit market
- Increased the number of Excel problems and added Excel to examples
- Deleted the second twin in the Problems

chapter eight
VALUING STOCKS

- Updated all table and figure values in the body of the chapter
- Rewrote the introduction of the Variable-Growth Technique section
- Updated market and stock index discussions
- Changed Finance at Work box on psychology to focus on the GameStop event
- Revised examples to include new McDonald's and Coca-Cola's firm data and figures
- Increased the number of Excel problems and added Excel to examples
- Deleted the second twin in the Problems

chapter nine
CHARACTERIZING RISK AND RETURN

- Updated all table and figure values in the body of the chapter
- Updated Time Out 9.1 and 9.2
- Added ETF popularity discussion to motivate diversification
- Updated the International Finance at Work box
- Updated the Google and GE text running examples
- Increased the number of Excel problems and added Excel to examples
- Deleted the second twin in the Problems

chapter ten
ESTIMATING RISK AND RETURN

- Updated values and data in Tables 10.1 to 10.3
- Changed discussion and Figure 10.2
- Added discussion in Behavioral Finance section about market reaction and COVID-19
- Increased the number of Excel problems and added Excel to examples
- Deleted the second twin in the Problems

chapter eleven
CALCULATING THE COST OF CAPITAL

- Updated Viewpoints example to use a streaming device rather than MP3
- Increased the number of Excel problems and added Excel to most examples
- Deleted the second twin in the Problems

chapter twelve
ESTIMATING CASH FLOWS ON CAPITAL BUDGETING PROJECTS

- A majority of the Problems were turned into Excel problems

chapter thirteen
WEIGHING NET PRESENT VALUE AND OTHER CAPITAL BUDGETING CRITERIA

- Added Excel to most of the examples
- Deleted the second twin in the Problems and added more Excel problems

chapter fourteen
WORKING CAPITAL MANAGEMENT AND POLICIES

- Added Excel to the examples
- Deleted the second twin in the Problems and added more Excel problems

supplements

INSTRUCTOR LIBRARY

A wealth of information is available online through McGraw Hill Connect. In the Connect Instructor Library, you will have access to supplementary materials specifically created for this text, such as:

- **Test Bank** Revised by Leslie Rush, University of Hawaii West O'ahu, the test bank contains hundreds of questions that complement the material presented in the book. The Test Bank is tagged by level of difficulty, learning goal, AACSB knowledge categories, and Bloom's taxonomy—making it easy for instructors to customize exams to reflect the material stressed in class. The test bank is available in Word files, and tests can also be created in Test Builder.

- **Solutions Manual** Developed by authors Marcia Cornett, Troy Adair, and John Nofsinger, this resource contains the worked-out solutions to all the end-of-chapter problems, in the consistent voice and method of the book. The solutions have been class-tested and checked by multiple instructors to ensure accuracy.

- **PowerPoint Presentations** The PowerPoint presentations have been carefully updated for the sixth edition by Courtney Baggett. These slides contain lecture notes, which closely follow the book content, enhanced with the tables and figures from the chapters. Several chapters are also supplemented with additional presentations that contain notes and examples using financial calculators. Instructors can easily customize these slides to suit their classroom needs and various presentation styles.

REMOTE PROCTORING & BROWSER-LOCKING CAPABILITIES

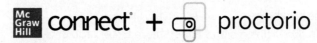

New remote proctoring and browser-locking capabilities, hosted by Proctorio within Connect, provide control of the assessment environment by enabling security options and verifying the identity of the student.

Seamlessly integrated within Connect, these services allow instructors to control students' assessment experience by restricting browser activity, recording students' activity, and verifying students are doing their own work.

Instant and detailed reporting gives instructors an at-a-glance view of potential academic integrity concerns, thereby avoiding personal bias and supporting evidence-based claims.

ASSURANCE OF LEARNING

Many educational institutions today are focused on the notion of assurance of learning, an important element of some accreditation standards. *M: Finance* is designed specifically to support your assurance of learning initiatives with a simple, yet powerful, solution.

Each test bank and end-of-chapter question for *M: Finance* maps to a specific chapter learning goal listed in the text. You can use the test bank software to easily query for learning goals that directly relate to the learning objectives for your course. You can then use the reporting features of the software to aggregate student results in a similar fashion, making the collection and presentation of assurance of learning data simple and easy.

AACSB STATEMENT

McGraw Hill is a proud corporate member of AACSB International. Understanding the importance and value of AACSB accreditation, *M: Finance* has sought to recognize the curricula guidelines detailed in the AACSB standards for business accreditation by connecting selected questions in the test bank to the general knowledge and skill guidelines found in the AACSB standards.

The statements contained in *M: Finance* are provided only as a guide for the users of this text. The AACSB leaves content coverage and assessment within the purview of individual schools, the mission of the school, and the faculty. While *M: Finance* and the teaching package make no claim of any specific AACSB qualification or evaluation, we have, within *M: Finance,* labeled selected questions according to the six general knowledge and skills areas.

STUDENT STUDY CENTER

In Connect, students will receive access to all of their assignments, the eBook, and McGraw Hill's adaptive study tools in SmartBook. The Connect Student Study Center is the place for students to access additional resources. Students will have access to study materials specifically created for this text, such as:

Instructors have access to all the material that students can view but will also have password-protected access to the teaching support materials.

MCGRAW HILL CUSTOMER CARE CONTACT INFORMATION

At McGraw Hill, we understand that getting the most from new technology can be challenging. That's why our services don't stop after you purchase our products. You can e-mail our Product Specialists 24 hours a day to get product training online. Or you can search our knowledge bank of Frequently Asked Questions on our support website.

For Customer Support, call **800-331-5094** or visit www.mhhe.com/support. One of our Technical Support Analysts will be able to assist you in a timely fashion.

FOR MORE INFORMATION ABOUT CONNECT AND ITS AVAILABLE RESOURCES, REFER TO THE PAGES THAT FOLLOW.

SUPPORT AT *every step*

Students
Get Learning that Fits You

Effective tools for efficient studying

Connect is designed to help you be more productive with simple, flexible, intuitive tools that maximize your study time and meet your individual learning needs. Get learning that works for you with Connect.

Study anytime, anywhere

Download the free ReadAnywhere® app and access your online eBook, SmartBook® 2.0, or Adaptive Learning Assignments when it's convenient, even if you're offline. And since the app automatically syncs with your Connect account, all of your work is available every time you open it. Find out more at **mheducation.com/readanywhere**

"I really liked this app—it made it easy to study when you don't have your text-book in front of you."

- Jordan Cunningham,
  Eastern Washington University

iPhone: Getty Images

Everything you need in one place

Your Connect course has everything you need—whether reading your digital eBook or completing assignments for class, Connect makes it easy to get your work done.

Learning for everyone

McGraw Hill works directly with Accessibility Services Departments and faculty to meet the learning needs of all students. Please contact your Accessibility Services Office and ask them to email accessibility@mheducation.com, or visit **mheducation.com/about/accessibility** for more information.

acknowledgments

Development of the first edition of this book series started with a course survey that was completed by 400 instructors across the country. The following is a list of the reviewers that became part of the many review stages, focus groups, and class-testing for the revisions that followed—all of which were invaluable to us during the development of this book.

Rebecca Abraham
Nova Southeastern University

Benjamin Abugri
Southern Connecticut State University

Paul Adams
University of Cincinnati

Pankaj Agrrawal
University of Maine

Aigbe Akhigbe
University of Akron

Mfon Akpan
Methodist University

Anne Anderson
Lehigh University

Murat Aydogdu
Bryant University

Robert Balik
Western Michigan University

Marvin Ball
East Oregon University

Brian Barczyk
University of Akron

Laura Beal
University of Nebraska, Omaha

Jaclyn Beierlein
East Carolina University

Ronald Benson
University of Maryland University College

Eli Beracha
East Carolina University

Robert Boldin
Indiana University of Pennsylvania

Denis Boudreaux
University of Louisiana

David Bourff
Boise State University

Lyle Bowlin
Southeastern University

Walter Boyle
Fayetteville Tech Community College

Joe Bracato
Tarleton State University

Ileana Brooks
Aurora University

Cheryl A. Broyler
Preston University

Celso Brunetti
Johns Hopkins University

Sarah K. Bryant
Shippensburg University

James Buck
East Carolina University

Steven Burris
Kennedy-King College

Steven Byers
Idaho State University

Cynthia Campbell
Iowa State University

Stephen Caples
University of Houston, Clear Lake

Bob Castaneda
Robert Morris University

Su-Jane Chen
Metro State College of Denver

Samuel Chinnis
Guilford Tech Community College

Andreas Christofi
Monmouth University

Ting-Heng Chu
East Tennessee State University, Johnson City

Cetin Ciner
University of North Carolina, Wilmington

Thomas Coe
Quinnipiac University

Bob Curtis
Biola University

Julie Dahlquist
University of Texas, San Antonio

Kenneth Daniels
Virginia Commonwealth University

Maria De Boyrie
Florida International University, Miami

Natalya Delcoure
Sam Houston State University

James DeLoach
Troy University

Michael Devaney
Southeast Missouri State University

Anne Drougas
Dominican University

David Dumpe
Kent State University

Alan Eastman
Indiana University of Pennsylvania

Scott Ehrhorn
Liberty University

Zekeriya Eser
Eastern Kentucky University

Angelo Esposito
University of North Florida

Omar Esqueda
Tarleton State University

Joe Farinella
University of North Carolina, Wilmington

John Farlin
Ohio Dominican University

John Fay
Santa Clara University

David Fehr
Southern New Hampshire University

Calvin Fink
Bethune-Cookman College

Barbara Fischer
Cardinal Stritch University

Susan Flaherty
Towson University

Frank Flanegin
Robert Morris University

Sharon Garrison
University of Arizona

Victoria Geyfman
Bloomsburg University

Charmaine Glegg
East Carolina University

Cameron Gordon
University of Canberra

Ed Graham
University of North Carolina, Wilmington

Greg Gregoriou
SUNY, Plattsburgh

Richard Gregory
East Tennessee State University, Johnson City

Keshav Gupta
Kutztown University

Neeraj Gupta
Elon University

Matthew Haertzen
Northern Arizona University

Christine Harrington
State University of New York, Oneonta

James Harriss
Campbell University

Travis Hayes
Chattanooga State University

Susan He
Washington State University, Pullman

Heikki Heino
Governors State University

Susan Hendrickson
Robert B. Miller College

Steve Henry
Sam Houston State University

Rodrigo Hernandez
Radford University

James Howard
University of Maryland

Bharat Jain
Towson University

Joel Jankowski
University of Tampa

Jeff Jewell
Lipscomb University

Domingo Joaquin
Illinois State University

Steve Johnson
Sam Houston State University

Jacqueline Griffith Jonnard
Berkeley College

Daniel Jubinski
Saint Joseph's University

Dongmin Ke
Kean University

Jaemin Kim
San Diego State University

Marek Kolar
Trine University

Lynn Kugele
University of Mississippi

Francis E. Laatsch
Bowling Green State University

Stephen Lacewell
Murray State University

Miranda Lam
Salem State University

Baeyong Lee
Fayetteville State University

Adam Lei
Midwestern State University

Fei Leng
University of Washington, Tacoma

Denise Letterman
Robert Morris University

Quin Li
Midwestern State University

Ralph Lim
Sacred Heart University

Bing-Xuan Lin
University of Rhode Island

Leng Ling
Georgia College and State University

Scott W. Lowe
James Madison University

Davinder Malhotra
Philadelphia University

Balasundram Maniam
Sam Houston State University

Kelly Manley
Gainesville State College

Peter Martino
Johnson & Wales University

Mario Mastrandrea
Cleveland State University

Leslie Mathis
University of Memphis

Christine McClatchey
University of Northern Colorado

Jennifer McCune
Western Iowa Tech
Community College

Bruce L. McManis
Nicholls State University

Kathleen S. McNichol
LaSalle University

James A. Milanese
University of North Carolina,
Greensboro

William Miller
Dallas Baptist University

Banamber Mishra
McNeese State University

Helen Moser
St. Cloud State University

Anastasios Moysidis
Florida International
University

Tarun Mukherjee
University of New Orleans

Elisa Muresan
Long Island University

James Nelson
East Carolina University

Tom Nelson
University of Colorado,
Boulder

Terry Nixon
Miami University of Ohio,
Oxford

Vivian Okere
Providence College

Brett Olsen
University of Northern
Iowa

Jennifer O'Sullivan
Hardin-Simmons
University

Elisabeta Pana
Illinois Wesleyan University

Jeff Parsons
California State University,
Fullerton

Robert Pavlik
Elon University

Ivelina Pavlova
University of Houston, Clear
Lake

Anil Pawar
San Diego State University

Glenn Pettengill
Grand Valley State
University

Ted Pilger
Southern Illinois University,
Carbondale

Wendy Pirie
Valparaiso University

Gary E. Porter
John Carroll University

Franklin Potts
Baylor University

Eric Powers
University of South
Carolina

Robert Prati
East Carolina University

Lora Reinholz
Marquette University

Nivine Richie
University of North Carolina,
Wilmington

Tammy Rogers
University of Central
Arkansas

Philip Romero
University of Oregon

Gerald Root
Lake Superior State
University

Philip Russel
Philadelphia University

Benito Sanchez
Kean University

Atul Saxena
Georgia Gwinnett College

Victoria Scalise
University of Pittsburgh,
Johnstown

Oliver Schnusenberg
University of North Florida

Andrew Spieler
Hofstra University

Jim Sprow
Corban College

Martin S. St. John
Westmoreland County
Community College

Tanja Steigner
Emporia State University

Gikenn L. Stevens
Franklin & Marshall College

Gordon Stringer
University of Colorado,
Colorado Springs

Don Stuhlman
Wilmington University

Mike Sullivan
University of Nevada, Las
Vegas

Janikan Supanvanji
St. Cloud State University

Arun Tandon
University of South Florida,
Lakeland

Heidi Toprac
University of Texas, Austin

Kudret Topyan
Manhattan College

Michael Toyne
Northeastern State University

Anca Traian
East Tennessee State
University

Bill Trainor
East Tennessee State
University, Johnson City

Jack Trifts
Bryant University

Gary Tripp
Southern New Hampshire
University

Demetri Tsanacas
William Paterson University

Kuo-Cheng Tseng
California State University,
Fresno

James A. Turner
Weber State University

Arun Upadhyay
Florida International
University, Miami

John Upstrom
Loras College

Victor Wakeling
Kennesaw State
University

Michael C. Walker
University of Cincinnati

Kainan Wang
University of Toledo

Peggy Ward
Wichita State University

Gwendolyn Webb
Baruch College

Paul Weinstock
The Ohio State University

Kyle Wells
University of New Mexico

John B. White
Georgia Southern
University

Susan White
University of Maryland

David J. Wozniak
University of North Texas,
Dallas

Mela Wyeth
Charleston Southern
University

George Young
Liberty University

Nafeesa Yunus
University of Baltimore

Zhong-Guo Zhou
California State University,
Northridge

Feifei Zhu
Hawaii Pacific University,
Honolulu

Emily Norman Zietz
Middle Tennessee State
University

We are also indebted to the talented staff at McGraw Hill for their expertise and guidance, specifically Christina Kouvelis, senior product developer; Chuck Synovec, portfolio director; Sarah Hurley, executive marketing manager; and Melissa Leick and Katie Reuter, content and assessment project managers. We would also like to thank Blerina Reca, Weicheng Wang, and Hongyan Fang.

We hope you like the outcome of this text. Research and development is always ongoing, and we are interested in your feedback on how this text has worked for you!

Marcia Millon Cornett

Troy A. Adair Jr.

John Nofsinger

brief contents

contents

introduction to
financial management

Sebastiaan Blockmans/Alamy Stock Photo

chapter one

finance The study of applying specific value to things we own, services we use, and decisions we make.

financial management The process for and the analysis of making financial decisions in the business context.

D o you know: What finance entails? How does financial management function within the business world? Why you might benefit from studying financial principles? This chapter is the ideal place to get answers to those questions. **Finance** is the study of *applying specific value* to things we own, services we use, and decisions we make. Examples are as varied as shares of stock in a company, payments on a home mortgage, the purchase of an entire firm, and the personal decision to retire early. In this text, we focus primarily on one area of finance, **financial management,** which concentrates on valuing things from the perspective of a company or firm.

Financial management is critically important to the success of any business organization, and, throughout the text, we concentrate on describing the key financial concepts in corporate finance. As a bonus, you will find that many tools and techniques for handling the financial management of a firm also apply to broader types of financial problems, such as personal financial decisions.

In finance, *cash flow* is the term that describes the process of paying and receiving money. It makes sense to start our discussion of finance with an illustration of various financial cash flows. We use simple graphics to help explain the nature of finance and to demonstrate the different *subareas* of the field of finance.

continued on p. 4

LEARNING GOALS

LG1-1 Define the major areas of finance as they apply to corporate financial management.

LG1-2 Show how finance is at the heart of sound business decisions.

LG1-3 Learn the financial principles that govern your personal decisions.

LG1-4 Examine the three most common forms of business organization in the United States today.

LG1-5 Distinguish among appropriate and inappropriate goals for financial managers.

LG1-6 Identify a firm's primary agency relationship and discuss the possible conflicts that may arise.

LG1-7 Discuss how ethical decision making is part of the study of financial management.

LG1-8 Describe the complex, necessary relationships among firms, financial institutions, and financial markets.

LG1-9 Understand how the new tax law impacts financial decision making.

»viewpoints

business APPLICATION

Caleb has worked very hard to create and expand his juice stand at the mall. He has finally perfected his products and feels that he is offering the right combination of juice and food. As a result, the stand is making a nice profit. Caleb would like to open more stands at malls all over his state and eventually all over the country.

Caleb knows he needs more money to expand. He needs money to buy more equipment, buy more inventory, and hire and train more people. How can Caleb get the capital he needs to expand? **(See the solution at the end of the book.)**

continued from p. 3

After we have an overall picture of finance, we will discuss three important variables in the business environment that can and do have a significant impact on the firm's financial decisions. These are (1) the organizational form of the business, (2) the agency relationship between the managers and owners of a firm, and (3) the ethical considerations as finance is applied in the real world. ■

1.1 • FINANCE IN BUSINESS AND IN LIFE LG1-1

If your career leads you to make financial decisions, then this book will be indispensable. But even if your career takes a different path, it is still likely that your activities in a business will involve interacting with the finance functions. After all, the important investments of a firm involve capital and, therefore, finance. Expanding marketing channels, developing new products, and upgrading a factory all cost money. A firm spends its capital on these projects to foster growth. Understanding how finance professionals evaluate those projects will help you to be successful in your business focus. In addition, everyone will benefit in their personal life from learning finance and understanding financial decisions.

And what exactly makes up this engine of financial decision making? Successful application of *financial theories* helps money flow from individuals who want to improve their financial future to businesses that want to expand the scale or scope of their operations. These exchanges lead to a growing economy and more employment opportunities for people at all income levels. So, two important things result from this simple exchange: The economy will be more productive, and individuals' wealth will grow into the future.

In this first section, we develop a comprehensive description of finance and its subareas, and we look at the specific decisions that professionals in each subarea must make. As you will see, all areas of finance share a common set of ideas and application tools.

What Is Finance?

To get the clearest possible picture of how finance works, let's begin by grouping all of an economy's participants along two dimensions. The first dimension is made up of those who may have "extra" money (i.e., money above and beyond their current spending needs) for investment. The second dimension is made up of those who have the ability to develop

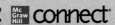
viable business ideas and a sense of business creativity. Both money and ideas are fuel for the financial engine. In our simple model, these two dimensions result in four groups representing economic roles in society, as shown in Figure 1.1. Of course, people can move from one group to another over time.

Type 1 people in our model do not lend significant sums of money (*capital*) or spend much money in a business context, so they play no direct role in **financial markets,** the mechanisms by which capital is exchanged. Although these people probably play indirect roles by providing labor to economic enterprises or by consuming their products, for simplicity, we are going to focus on those who play direct roles. Therefore, type 1 participants will be asked to step aside.

Type 4 people use financial tools to evaluate their own business concepts and then choose the ideas with the most potential. From there, they create their own enterprises to implement their best ideas efficiently and effectively. Type 4 individuals, however, are self-funded and do not need financial markets. The financial tools they use and the types of decisions they make are narrowly focused or specific to their own purposes. For our discussion, then, type 4 individuals also are asked to move to the sidelines.

Now for our financial role players, the type 2 and type 3 people. Financial markets and financial institutions allow these people to participate in a mutually advantageous exchange. Type 2 people temporarily lend their money to type 3 people, who put that money to use with their good business ideas, and who then turn around and (hopefully) repay the type 2 people, plus interest.

financial markets The arenas through which funds flow.

▼**FIGURE 1.1** Participants in Our Hypothetical Economy

	No Extra Money	Extra Money
No Economically Viable Business Ideas	Type 1: No money and no ideas	Type 2: Money but no ideas
Economically Viable Business Ideas	Type 3: No money but ideas	Type 4: Both money and ideas

Four groups form according to the availability of money and ideas.

investors Those who buy securities or other assets in hopes of earning a return and getting more money back in the future.

retained earnings The portion of company profits that are kept by the company rather than distributed to the stockholders as cash dividends.

In most developed economies, type 2 participants are usually individual **investors.** *You will likely be an individual investor for most of your life.* Each of us separately may not have a lot of extra money at any one time, but by aggregating our available funds, we can provide sizable amounts for investment.

Type 3 participants, the idea generators, may be individuals, but they are more commonly corporations or other types of companies with research and development (R&D) departments dedicated to developing innovative ideas. It's easy to see that investors and companies can help one another. If investors lend their "extra" capital to companies, as shown in Figure 1.2, then companies can use this capital to fund expansion projects. Economically successful projects will eventually be able to repay the money (plus profit) to investors, as Figure 1.3 shows.

Of course, not all of the cash will return to the investors. In reality, sources of friction arise in this system, and the amount of capital returned to investors is reduced. Two primary sources of friction are **retained earnings,** which are basically funds the firm keeps for its ongoing operations, and *taxes,* which the government imposes on the company and individuals to help fund public services.

▼**FIGURE 1.2** Capital Flow from Investors to Companies

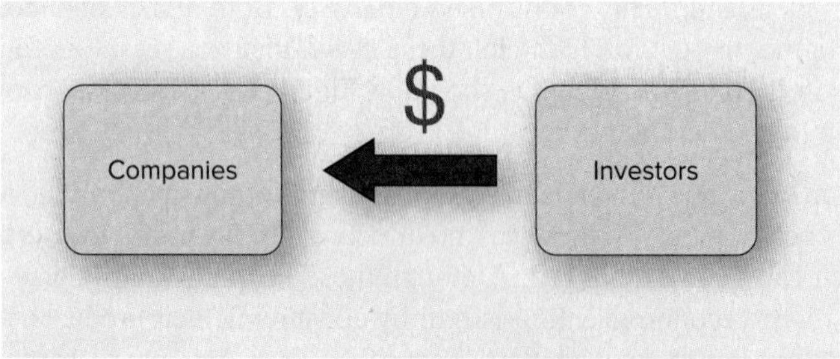

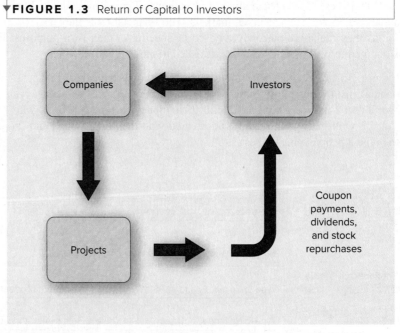

Investors are people or groups who need ideas to make more money, and companies are groups who need money to develop the ideas they do have.

▼**FIGURE 1.3** Return of Capital to Investors

In this basic process, the company can expand its business, hire more employees, and create a promising future for its own growth. Meanwhile, the investor can increase wealth for the future.

As described at the end of this chapter, tax laws in the United States underwent massive changes as a result of the Tax Cuts and Jobs Act (TCJA) signed into law by President Trump in 2017. As we'll discuss, many of these changes have significant impacts on the financial decisions of the firm.

Figure 1.4 shows an analysis of cash flows with the associated retained earnings and tax payments. In a very simple way, this figure provides an intuitive overall explanation of finance and of its major subareas. For example, individuals must assess which investment opportunities are right for their needs and risk tolerance; financial institutions and markets must efficiently distribute the capital; and companies must evaluate their potential projects and wisely decide which projects to fund, what kind of capital to use, and how much capital to return to investors. All of these types of decisions deal with the basic cash flows of finance shown in Figure 1.4, but from different perspectives.

Subareas of Finance

Investments is the subarea of finance that involves methods and techniques for making decisions about what kinds of *securities* to own (e.g., bonds or stocks), which firms' securities to buy, and how to pay the investor back in the form that the investor wishes (e.g., the timing and certainty of the promised cash flows). Figure 1.5 models cash flows from the investor's perspective. The concerns of the investments subarea of finance are shown (with the movement of red arrows) from the investor's viewpoint (seen as the blue box).

Financial management is the subarea that deals with a firm's decisions in acquiring and using the cash that is received from investors or from retained earnings. Figure 1.6 depicts the financial management process very simply. As we know, this text focuses primarily on financial management. We'll see that this critical area of finance involves decisions about

- How to organize the firm in a manner that will attract capital.

- How to raise capital (e.g., bonds versus stocks).

- Which projects to fund.

investment The analysis and process of choosing securities and other assets to purchase.

▼**FIGURE 1.4** The Complete Cash Flows of Finance

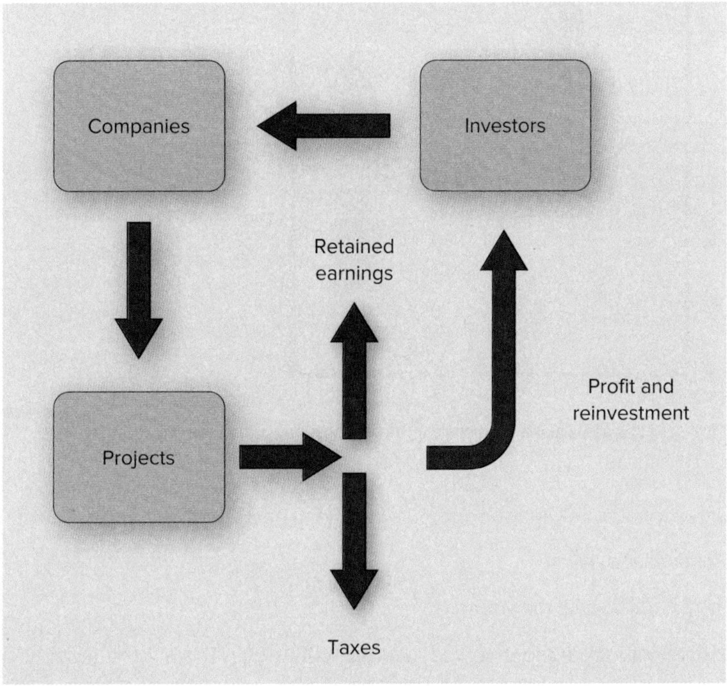

All the subareas of the financial system interact, with retained earnings and taxes playing a role in the flows.

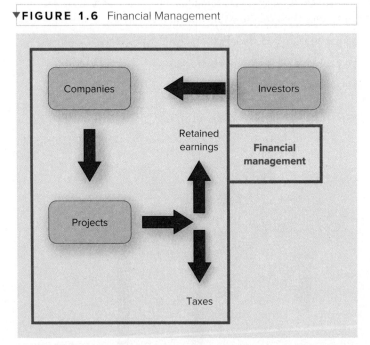

▼FIGURE 1.5 Investments

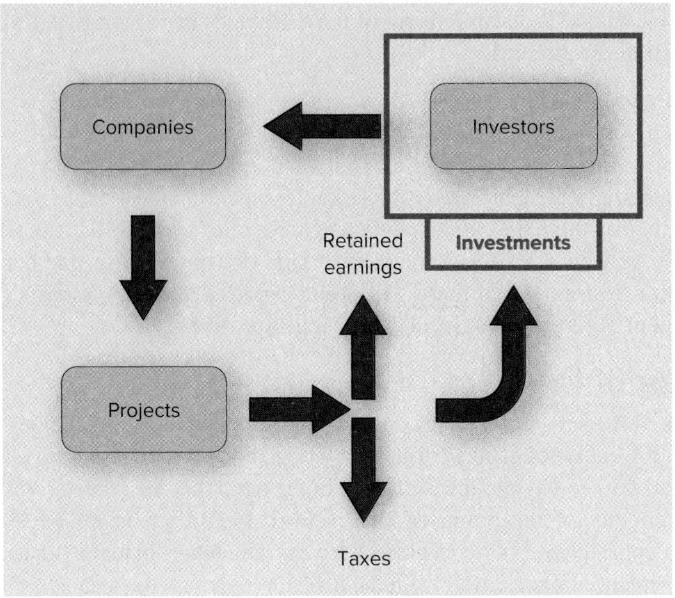

Companies

Investors

Retained earnings

Investments

Projects

Taxes

Investors mark the start and end of the financial process; they put money in and reap the rewards (or take the risk).

▼FIGURE 1.6 Financial Management

Companies

Investors

Retained earnings

Financial management

Projects

Taxes

Financial managers make decisions that should benefit both the company and the investor.

- How much capital to retain for ongoing operations and new projects.
- How to minimize taxation.
- How to pay back capital providers.

All of these decisions are quite involved, and we will discuss them throughout later chapters.

Financial institutions and markets make up another major subarea of finance. These two dynamic entities work in different ways to facilitate capital flows between investors

financial institutions and markets The organizations that facilitate the flow of capital between investors and companies.

and companies. Figure 1.7 illustrates the process in which the firm acquires capital and investors take part in ongoing securities trading to increase that capital. Financial institutions, such as banks and pension administrators, are vital players that contribute to the dynamics of interest rates.

International finance is the final major subarea of finance we will study. As the world has transformed into a global economy, finance has had to become much more innovative and sensitive to changes in other countries. Investors, companies, business operations, and capital markets may all be located in different countries. Adapting to this environment requires understanding of international dynamics, as Figure 1.8 shows. In the past, international

▼**FIGURE 1.7** Financial Institutions and Markets

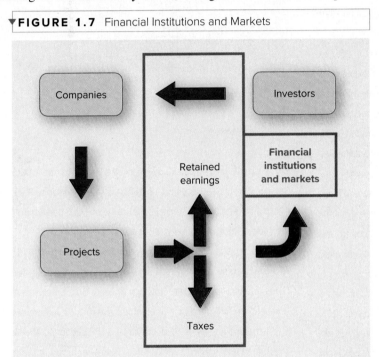

Financial institutions and markets facilitate the flow of money between investors and companies.

▼**FIGURE 1.8** International Finance

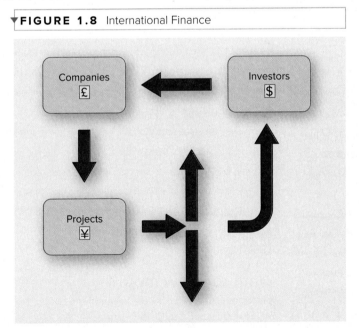

Laws, risks, and business relationships are variable across different countries but can interact profitably.

finance at work //:markets

Quantitative Easing in the United States and Around the World

The Financial Crisis of 2007 to 2008 led to a global recession that ended in the United States in 2009. The severe recession is often referred to as the "Great Recession" to give it a Great Depression flavor. However, the ensuing economic recovery was slow. It did not have the typical bounce-back that often occurs after an acute recession.

To foster economic growth and give the financial sector time to recover, the U.S. Federal Reserve embarked on a grand experiment called *quantitative easing (QE)*. QE is a monetary policy designed to increase the money supply in the economy through buying securities in the market and lowering short-term interest rates. The first round of QE involved the Fed buying potentially toxic mortgage-backed securities (see Chapter 7), primarily from banks. This removed the suspect securities from the banks' balance sheets and allowed them time to get financially stronger. Also, the *federal funds rate,* the interest rate at which banks and other depository institutions lend reserve balances to one another overnight, and which heavily influences other short-term rates, was cut to zero.

This initial round of QE ended in early 2010 after the Fed had purchased $1.25 trillion of mortgage-backed securities. Chapter 6 discusses QE's impact on the financial system. By the end of 2010, the economy was still not as strong as desired. The Fed's mission has been to foster maximum employment in an environment of 2 percent inflation. But the employment market was still lackluster and inflation was near zero in 2010.

In the fourth quarter of 2010, the Fed began QE 2, in which it bought $600 billion of long-term U.S. Treasury securities over the ensuing nine months. This was an attempt to lower long-term interest rates. It did not have the desired impact on long-term rates, so QE 3 was implemented in late 2012 and continued through 2013. For QE 3, the Fed sold short-term bonds in order to purchase more long-term securities. Short-term interest rates were kept near zero. The low-interest rates had profound impacts on the bond market (see Chapter 7) and companies' cost of capital (see Chapter 11).

Instead of ending QE 3, the Fed decided to reduce its purchases each month through most of 2014. This QE taper was an attempt to wean the economy from the constant Fed influence. QE 3 finally tapered out at the end of 2014. Speculation then grew about when the Fed would start raising interest rates. The Fed finally raised its key interest rate to 0.25 percent on December 16, 2015. It was the first rate hike in nearly 10 years.

DAJ/Getty Images

Subsequently, the Fed continued to raise the Fed funds rate in 0.25 percent increments, until, by December of 2018, the rate had risen to 2.50 percent. This put the rate in the historical target range of 2 to 5 percent preferred by the Federal Reserve, but still at the low end of that range.

Amid signs that U.S. economic growth was slowing in 2019, the Fed reversed course and enacted several small decreases in the federal funds rate during that year, moving it down to 2.25 percent in August of that year, to 2.00 percent in September, and to 1.75 percent in October.

These moves were in accordance with economic theories stating that, when the Fed cuts its rates, borrowing costs in the economy decrease, and this prompts businesses to take out loans to hire more people and expand production.

However, the start of the COVID-19 pandemic in early 2020 prompted the Fed to take even more drastic action to try and help counter the economic effects of shutdowns and stay-at-home orders on the economy. They dropped the federal funds rate to 1.25 percent in early March of 2020, and then dropped it yet again to 0.25 percent on March 16, where it has stayed up to the date of the writing of this text in July 2021.

As we are still in the midst of the COVID-19 pandemic and economic recovery, it is impossible to say how long this most recent quantitative easing is likely to stay in effect. It is worth noting, however, that, if the QE associated with the Great Recession stayed in effect for almost 10 years, there is a very good chance that this round of QE will last as long, if not longer.

Want to know more?

Key Words to Search for Updates: **quantitative easing, zero rate environment, QE taper, COVID-19**

financial decisions were considered to be a straightforward application of the other three financial subareas. But experience has shown that the uncertainty about future exchange rates, political risk, and changing business laws across the globe adds enough complexity to these decisions to classify international finance as a subarea of finance in its own right.

Application and Theory for Financial Decisions

Cash flows are neither instantaneous nor guaranteed. We need to keep this in mind as we begin to apply finance theory to real decisions. Future cash flows are uncertain in terms of both timing and size, and we refer to this uncertainty as **risk.** Investors experience risk about the return of their capital. Companies experience risk in funding and operating their business projects. Most financial decisions involve comparing the rewards of a decision to the risks that decision may generate.

Comparing rewards with risks frequently involves assessing the value today of cash flows that we expect to receive in the future. For example, the price of a **financial asset,** something worth money, such as a stock or a bond, should depend on the cash flows you expect to receive from that asset in the future. A stock that's expected to deliver high cash flows in the future will be more valuable today than a stock with low expected future cash flows. Of course, investors would like to buy stocks whose market prices are currently lower than their actual values. They want to get stocks on sale! Similarly, a firm's goal is to fund projects that will give them more value than their costs.

Financial assets are normally grouped into **asset classes** according to their risk and return characteristics. The most commonly accepted groups of asset classes are stocks, bonds, money market instruments, real estate, and derivative securities, all of which we will discuss in more detail later in the book. As the risk and return profiles of each of these asset classes differ widely between classes, the mathematical models, terminology, and expertise of each class tend to be very specialized and trading tends to happen in distinct, separate financial markets for each asset class.

Risk tolerance varies among individuals.
Purestock/SuperStock

Despite the large number of stories about investors who've struck it rich in the stock market, it's actually more likely that a firm will find "bargain" projects, projects that may yield profit for a reasonable investment than investors will find underpriced stocks. Firms can find bargains because business projects involve **real assets** trading in **real markets** (markets in tangible assets). In the real environment, some level of monopoly power, special knowledge, and expertise possibly can make such projects worth more than they cost. Investors, however, are trading financial assets in financial markets, where the assets are more likely to be worth, on average, exactly what they cost.

The method for relating expected or future cash flows to today's value, called *present value,* is known as **time value of money (TVM).** Chapters 4 and 5 cover this critical financial concept in detail and apply it to the financial world (as well as daily life). Since the expected cash flows of either a business project or an investment are likely to be uncertain, any TVM analysis must account for both the timing and the risk level of the cash flows.

Finance versus Accounting

In most companies, the financial function is usually closely associated with the accounting function. In a very rough sense, the accountant's job is to keep track of what happened *in the past* to the firm's money, while the finance job uses these historical figures with current information to determine what should happen *now and in the future* with the firm's

risk A potential future negative impact to value and/or cash flows. It is often discussed in terms of the probability of loss and the expected magnitude of the loss.

financial asset A general term for securities like stocks, bonds, and other assets that represent ownership in a cash flow.

asset classes A group of securities that exhibit similar characteristics, behave similarly in the marketplace, and are subject to the same laws and regulations.

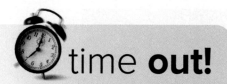

1-1 What are the main subareas of finance and how do they interact?

real assets Physical property like gold, machinery, equipment, or real estate.

real markets The places and processes that facilitate the trading of real assets.

time value of money (TVM) The theory and application of valuing cash flows at various points in time.

defined benefit plan A retirement plan in which the employer funds a pension generally based on each employee's years of service and salary.

defined contribution plan A retirement plan in which the employee contributes money and directs its investment. The amount of retirement benefits is directly related to the amount of money contributed and the success of its investment.

401k plan A defined contribution plan that is sponsored by corporate employers.

Individual Retirement Account (IRA) A self-sponsored retirement program.

time **out!**

1-2 How might the application of finance improve your professional and personal decisions?

money. The results of financial decisions will eventually appear in accounting statements, so this close association makes sense. Nevertheless, accounting tends to focus on and characterize the past, whereas finance focuses on the present and future.

1.2 • THE FINANCIAL FUNCTION LG1-2

As we said previously, this text focuses primarily on financial management, so we will discuss the particular functions and responsibilities of the firm's financial manager. We will also explain how the financial function fits in and interacts with the other areas of the firm. Finally, to make this study as interesting and as relevant as possible, we will make the connections that allow you to see how the concepts covered in this book are important in your own personal finances.

The Financial Manager

The firm's highest-level financial manager is usually the chief financial officer or CFO. Both the company treasurer and the controller report to the CFO. The treasurer is typically responsible for

- Managing cash and credit.

- Issuing and repurchasing financial securities such as stocks and bonds.

- Deciding how and when to spend capital for new and existing projects.

- Hedging (reducing the firm's potential risk) against changes in foreign exchange and interest rates.

In larger corporations, the treasurer may also oversee other areas, such as purchasing insurance or managing the firm's pension fund investments. The controller oversees the accounting function, usually managing the tax, cost accounting, financial accounting, and data processing functions.

Finance in Other Business Functions

Although the CFO and treasurer positions tend to be the firm's most visible finance-related positions, finance affects the firm in many ways and throughout all levels of a company's organizational chart. Finance permeates the entire business organization, providing guidance for both strategic and day-to-day decisions of the firm and collecting information for control and feedback about the firm's financial decisions.

Operational managers use finance daily to determine how much overtime labor to use, or to perform cost/benefit analysis when they consider new production lines or methods. Marketing managers use finance to assess the cost-effectiveness of doing follow-up marketing surveys. Human resource managers use finance to evaluate the company's cost for various employee benefit packages. No matter where you work in business, finance can help you do your job better.

Finance in Your Personal Life LG1-3

Finance can help you make good financial decisions in your personal life. Consider these common activities you will probably face in your life:

- Borrowing money to buy a new car.

- Refinancing your home mortgage at a lower rate.

- Making credit card or student loan payments.

- Saving for retirement.

You will be able to perform all of these tasks better after learning about finance. Recent changes throughout our economy and the U.S. business environment make knowledge of finance even more valuable to you than before. For example, most companies have

Finance Applications LG1-3

Chloe realizes how important finance will be for her future business career. However, some of the ways that she will see financial applications seem way off in the future. She is curious about how the theory applies to her personal life, both in the near term and in the long term.

SOLUTION:

Chloe will quickly find that her financial health now and in the future will depend upon many decisions she makes as she goes through life—starting now! For example, she will learn that the same tools that she applies to a business loan analysis can be applied to her own personal debt. After this course, Chloe will be able to evaluate credit card offers and select one that could save her hundreds of dollars per year. When she buys a new car and the dealership offers her a low-interest-rate loan or a higher-rate loan with cash back, she will be able to pick the option that will truly cost her the least. Also, when Chloe gets her first professional job, she will know how to direct her retirement account so that she can earn millions of dollars for her future. (Of course, inflation between now and when she retires will imply that Chloe's millions won't be worth as much as they would today.)

switched from providing **defined benefit** retirement plans to employees to offering **defined-contribution** plans (such as **401k plans**) and self-funded plans like **Individual Retirement Accounts (IRAs)**. Tax changes in the early 1980s made this switch more or less inevitable. It appears that each of us will have to ensure adequate funds for our own retirement—much more so than previous generations.

1.3 • BUSINESS ORGANIZATION LG1-4

In the United States, people can structure businesses in any of several ways; the number of owners is the key to how business structures are classified. Traditionally, single owners, partners, and corporations operate businesses. We can express the advantages and disadvantages of each organizational form through several dimensions:

- Who controls the firm.
- Who owns the firm.
- What are the owners' risks.
- What access to capital exists.
- What are the tax ramifications.

Recently, small businesses have adopted hybrid structures that capture the benefits from multiple organizational forms. We'll discuss those hybrid structures after we cover the more common, traditional types of business organizations.

Sole Proprietorships

The **sole proprietorship** represents, by far, the most common type of business in the United States.[1] A sole proprietorship is defined as any unincorporated business owned by a single individual.[2] Perhaps these businesses are so popular because they are relatively easy to start, and they're subject to a much lighter regulatory and paperwork burden than other business forms. The owner, or sole proprietor, of the business has complete control of the firm's activities. The owner also receives all of the firm's profits and is solely responsible for all losses.

The biggest disadvantage that sole proprietorships carry relative to other organizational forms is that they have **unlimited liability** for their companies' debts and actions. The owner's personal assets may be confiscated if the business fails. The law recognizes no

sole proprietorship A business entity that is not legally separate from its owner.

unlimited liability A situation in which a person's personal assets are at risk from a business liability.

Venture capital helped Starbucks become a success story.
John Flournoy/McGraw-Hill Education

distinction between the owner's business assets and personal assets. The income of the business is also added to the owner's personal income and taxed by the government at the appropriate personal tax rate. Finally, sole proprietors have a difficult time obtaining capital to expand their business operations. Banks and other lenders are not typically interested in lending much money to sole proprietors because small firms have only one person liable for paying back the debt. A sole proprietor could raise capital by issuing **equity** to another investor. **Angel investors** and **venture capitalists** exchange capital for ownership in a business. But this requires reforming the business as a partnership and the sole proprietor must give up some of the ownership (and thus control) of the firm. Table 1.1 summarizes sole proprietorships' characteristics, along with those of the three other business organizations we will study.

equity An ownership interest in a business enterprise.

angel investors Individuals who provide small amounts of capital and expert business advice to small firms in exchange for an ownership stake in the firm.

venture capitalists Similar to angel investors except that they are organized as groups of investors and can provide larger amounts of capital.

general partnership A form of business organization where the partners own the business together and are personally liable for legal actions and debts of the firm.

Partnerships

A **general partnership,** or as it is more commonly known, a *partnership,* is an organizational form that features multiple individual owners. Each partner can own a different percentage of the firm. Firm control is typically determined by the size of partners' ownership stakes. Business profits are split among the partners according to a prearranged agreement, usually by the percentage of firm ownership. Received profits are added to each partner's personal income and taxed at personal income tax rates.

The partners jointly share unlimited personal liability for the debts of the firm and all are obligated for contracts agreed to by any one of the partners. Banks are more willing to lend to partnerships than to sole proprietorships because all partners are liable for repaying the debt. Partners would have to give up some ownership and control in the firm to raise more equity capital. In order to raise enough capital for substantial growth, a partnership often changes into a public corporation.

Corporations

A **public corporation** is a legally independent entity entirely separate from its owners. This independence dramatically alters the firm's characteristics. Corporations hold many rights and obligations of individual persons, such as the ability to own property, sign binding contracts, and pay taxes. Federal and state governments tax corporate income once at

▼ **TABLE 1.1** Characteristics of Business Organization

	Ownership	Control	Ownership Risk	Access to Capital	Taxes
Sole Proprietor	Single individual	Proprietor	Unlimited liability	Very limited	Paid by owner
Partnership	Multiple people	Shared by partners	Unlimited liability	Limited	Paid by partners
Corporation	Public investors who own the stock	Company managers	Stockholders can only lose their investment in the firm	Easy access	Corporation pays income tax and stockholders pay taxes on dividends
Hybrids: S corp, LLP, LLC, LP	Partners or shareholders	Shared	Mostly limited	Limited by firm size restrictions	Paid by partners or shareholders

finance at work //:corporate

More Beer

In November 2015, Anheuser-Busch InBev NV agreed to buy SABMiller for $104 billion. AB InBev produces the popular beer brands Budweiser, Corona, Stella Artois, Beck's, Hoegaarden, and Leffe. SABMiller is known for Miller, Foster's, and Grolsch, among others. These are the two largest brewing companies in the world. The combined firm would produce nearly a third of the beer worldwide.

InBev paid 45 pounds sterling ($59) in cash per share for a majority of SABMiller shares. This was a 50 percent increase, or premium, over the market price of SABMiller stock. This merger raised many interesting finance questions. For example, why did InBev believe that SABMiller should be valued at least 50 percent more than the market does? Why were they paying cash for the shares instead of exchanging their stock for SABMiller stock? What are the business opportunities and cost-cutting cash flows of the combined firm that were not available as separate firms?

This book describes the theories and tools needed to make these judgments. The practice of finance isn't just about numbers; it's about real valuation and cash flow—the results of the financial analysis are very dynamic and exciting!

This proposed merger will have significant hurdles to overcome in order to be completed. Governments regulate mergers to ensure competition in consumer markets. For example, in many regions of the United States, Budweiser and Miller together make up a high percentage of the market. Thus, if one firm owned both brands, a near monopoly would occur. The U.S. regulatory system would not allow that. So to prevent this objection, SABMiller is selling its stake in this brand to Molson

scukrov/123RF

Coors Brewing for $12 billion. Other countries had similar concerns. This megamerger took nearly a year to gain the needed shareholder approval and regulatory approval around the world. The deal finally closed and the two firms became one in October of 2016.

Want to know more?

Key Words to Search for Updates: **InBev, SABMiller, beer**

---

the corporate level. Then shareholders pay taxes again at the personal level when corporate profits are paid out as dividends. This practice is generally known as **double taxation.**

Corporate owners are stockholders, also called *shareholders.* Public corporations typically have thousands of stockholders. The firm must hire managers to direct the firm since thousands of individual shareholders could not direct day-to-day operations under any sort of consensus. As a result, managers control the company. Strong possibilities of conflicts of interests arise when one group of people owns the business, but another group controls it. We'll discuss conflicts of interest and their resolution later in the chapter.

As individual legal entities, corporations assume liability for their own debts, so the shareholders have only **limited liability.** That is, corporate shareholders cannot lose more money than they originally paid for their shares of stock. This limited liability is one reason that many people feel comfortable owning stock. Corporations are thus able to raise incredible amounts of money by selling stock (equity) and borrowing money. The largest businesses in the world are organized as corporations.

public corporation A company owned by a large number of stockholders from the general public.

double taxation A situation in which two taxes must be paid on the same income.

limited liability Limitation of a person's financial liability to a fixed sum or investment.

1-3 Why must an entrepreneur give up some control of the business as it grows into a public corporation?

1-4 What advantages does the corporate form of organization hold over a partnership?

hybrid organizations Business forms that have some attributes of corporations and some of proprietorships/partnerships.

maximization of shareholder wealth A view that management should first and foremost consider the interests of shareholders in its business decisions.

stakeholder A person or organization that has a legitimate interest in a corporation.

invisible hand A metaphor used to illustrate how an individual pursuing his own interests also tends to promote the good of the community.

Hybrid Organizations

To promote the growth of small businesses, the U.S. government allows for several types of business organizations that simultaneously offer limited personal liability for the owners *and* provide a pass-through of all firm earnings to the owners, so that the earnings are subject only to single taxation.

Hybrid organizations offer single taxation and limited liability to all owners. Examples are *S corporations, limited liability partnerships (LLPs)*, and *limited liability companies (LLCs)*. Others, called *limited partnerships (LPs)*, offer single taxation and limited liability to the *limited partners,* but also have *general partners,* who benefit from single taxation but also must bear personal liability for the firm's debts.

The U.S. government typically restricts hybrid organization status to relatively small firms. The government limits the maximum number of shareholders or partners involved,[3] the maximum amount of investment capital allowed, and the lines of business permitted. These restrictions are consistent with the government's stated reason for allowing the formation of these forms of business organization—to encourage the formation and growth of small businesses.

1.4 • FIRM GOALS LG1-5

Tens of thousands of public corporations operate in the United States. Many of them are the largest business organizations in the world. Because U.S. corporations are so large and because there are so many of them, corporations have a tremendous impact on society. Given the power that these huge firms wield, many people question what the corporate goals should be. Two different, well-developed viewpoints have arisen concerning what the goal of the firm should be. The owners' perspective holds that the only appropriate goal is to **maximize shareholder wealth.** The competing viewpoint is from the **stakeholders'** perspective, which emphasizes social responsibility over profitability. This view maintains that managers must maximize the total satisfaction of all stakeholders in a business. These stakeholders not only include the owners and shareholders, but also include the business's customers, employees, and local communities.

While strong arguments speak in favor of both perspectives, financial practitioners and academics now tend to believe that the manager's primary responsibility should be to maximize shareholder wealth and give only secondary consideration to other stakeholders' welfare. One of the first, and most well-known, proponents of this viewpoint was Adam Smith, an 18th-century economist who argued that, in capitalism, an individual pursuing his own interests tends also to promote the good of his community.[4]

Smith argued that the **invisible hand** of the market, acting through competition and the free price system, would ensure that only those activities most efficient and beneficial to society as a whole would survive in the long run. Thus, those same activities would also profit the individual most. When companies try to implement a goal other than profit maximization, their efforts tend to backfire. Consider the firm that tries to maximize employment. The high number of employees raises costs. Soon the firm will find that its costs are too high to allow it to compete against more efficient firms, especially in a global business environment. When the firm fails, all employees are let go and employment ends up being minimized, not maximized.

Regardless of whether you believe Smith's assertion or not, a more pragmatic reason supports the argument that maximizing owners' wealth is an admirable goal. As we will discuss, the owners of the firm hire managers to work on their behalf, so the manager is morally, ethically, and legally required to act in the owners' best interests. Any relationships between the manager and other firm stakeholders are necessarily secondary to the goal that shareholders give to their hired managers.

Maximizing owners' equity value means carefully considering

- How best to bring additional funds into the firm.

- Which projects to invest in.

- How best to return the profits from those projects to the owners over time.

For corporations, maximizing the value of owners' equity can also be stated as *maximizing the current value per share, or* **stock price,** *of existing shares.* To the extent that the current stock price can be expected to include the present value of any future expected cash flows accruing to the owners, the goal of maximizing stock price provides us with a single, concrete, measurable gauge of value. You may be tempted to choose several other potential goals over maximizing the value of owners' equity. Common alternatives are

- Maximizing net income or profit.

- Minimizing costs.

- Maximizing market share.

Although these may look appealing, each of these goals has some potentially serious shortcomings. For example, net income is measured on a year-by-year or quarter-by-quarter basis. When we say that we want to maximize profits, to *which* net income figure are we referring? We can maximize this year's net income in several legitimate ways, but many of these ways impose costs that will reduce future income. Or current net income can be pushed into future years. Neither of these two extremes will likely encourage the firm's short-term and long-term stability. One more likely goal would be to maximize today's value of *all* future years of net income. Of course, this possible goal is very close to maximizing the current stock price, without the convenient market-oriented measure of the stock price. Another problem with considering maximizing all future profits as the goal is that net income (for reasons we'll go into later) does not really measure how much money the firm is actually earning.

Minimizing costs and *maximizing market share* also have fundamental problems as potential goals. Certainly minimizing costs would not make some stakeholders, such as employees, very happy. In addition, without spending the money on R&D and new product development, many companies would not survive long in the ever-evolving economy without improving their products. A firm can always increase market share by lowering price. But if a firm loses money on every product sold, then selling more products will simply drive the firm into fiscal distress.

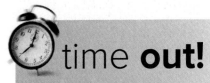

time **out!**

1-5   Describe why the primary objective of maximizing shareholder value may actually be the most beneficial for society in the long run.

1.5 • AGENCY THEORY LG1-6

Whenever one party (the *principal*) hires someone else (the *agent*) to work for him or her, their interaction is called an *agency relationship.* The agent is always supposed to act in the principal's best interests. For example, an apartment complex manager should ensure that tenants aren't doing willful damage to the property, that fire codes are enforced, and that the vacancy rate is kept as low as possible because these are best for the apartment owner.

Agency Problem

In the context of a public corporation, we have already noted that stockholders hire managers to run the firm. Ideally, managers will operate the firm so that the shareholders realize maximum value for their equity. But managers may be tempted to operate the firm to serve their own best interests. Managers could spend company money to improve their own lifestyle

Perks can range from extra vacation to private transportation.
Philip Nealey/Photodisc/Getty Images

instead of earning more profits for shareholders. Sometimes the manager's best interest does not necessarily align with shareholder goals. This creates a situation that we refer to as the **agency problem.**

For example, suppose it is time to buy a new corporate car for the firm's **chief executive officer (CEO).** Assuming that the CEO has no extraordinary driving requirements, shareholders might wish for the CEO to buy a nice, conservative domestic sedan. But suppose that the CEO demands the newest, biggest luxury car available. It's tempting to say that the shareholders could just tell the CEO which car to buy. But remember, the CEO has most of the control in a public corporation. Organizational behavior specialists have identified three basic approaches to minimize this conflict of interest. First, ignore it. If the amount of money involved is small enough relative to the firm's cash flows, or if the suitability of the purchase in question is ambiguous enough, shareholders might be best served to simply overlook the problem. A good deal of research literature suggests that allowing the manager a certain amount of such **perks (perquisites)** might actually enhance owner value, in that such items may boost managers' productivity.[5]

The second approach to mitigating this conflict is to monitor managers' actions. Monitoring at too fine a level of detail is probably counterproductive and prohibitively expensive. However, major firm decisions are usually monitored at least roughly through the accounting auditing process.

In addition, concentrated ownership in the firm by large stakeholders such as financial institutions, investment companies, individual block holders, or debt holders gives those large stakeholders increased incentives to monitor the activities of management. These incentives are often driven both by **economies of scale** in monitoring and by the claim of the stakeholder having a different risk/return profile than the claim of other stakeholders.

To see the impact of economies of scale in monitoring costs, consider a simple example: Suppose that it costs $3 each way (i.e., $6 round-trip) for a shareholder in a firm to hop on the subway and ride down to the firm's offices in order to go through the firm's financial statements, and that the most savings to shareholders that could possibly result from this monitoring would be $5 per share. Would anyone owning a single share ever take the ride to check up on the firm? No, because it would cost a certain $6 in order to save a possible $5. However, someone owning 100 shares in the firm would find it worthwhile to pay for the subway ride, assuming that the chance of saving $5 × 100 = $500 is large enough.

To envision the effect of one stakeholder having a different claim than others, consider the position of a bondholder in a firm where there isn't much free cash flow in the firm above and beyond that which is needed to make the interest payments on her bond. If the manager of the firm is going to spend an extra $20,000 to buy an unnecessarily luxurious company car, that $20,000 is very likely to come out of the bondholder's pocket, so she will definitely have a heightened incentive to monitor the manager's company car purchase. On the other hand, if the firm had so much free cash flow available that the expenditure of the extra $20,000 is unlikely to affect the payment of the bond interest, then the bondholder would have much less incentive to monitor.[6]

The final approach for aligning managers' personal interests with those of owners is to make the managers owners—that is, to offer managers an equity stake in the firm so that management participates in any equity value increase. Many corporations take this approach, either through explicitly granting shares to managers, by awarding them **options** on the firm's stock, or by allowing them to purchase shares at a subsidized price through an **employee stock option plan (ESOP).** When firm managers are also firm owners, their incentives are more likely to align with stockholders' best interests.

Corporate Governance

We refer to the process of monitoring managers and aligning their incentives with shareholder goals as **corporate governance.** Theoretically, managers work for shareholders.

In reality, because shareholders are usually inactive, the firm actually seems to belong to management. Generally speaking, the investing public does not know what goes on at the firm's operational level. Managers handle day-to-day operations, and they know that their work is mostly unknown to investors. This lack of supervision demonstrates the need for monitors. Figure 1.9 shows the people and organizations that help monitor corporate activities.

The monitors inside a public firm are the **board of directors,** who are appointed to represent shareholders' interests. The board hires the CEO, evaluates management, and can also design compensation contracts to tie management's salaries to firm performance.

The monitors outside the firm include auditors, analysts, investment banks, and credit rating agencies. **Auditors** examine the firm's accounting systems and comment on whether financial statements fairly represent the firm's financial position. **Investment analysts** follow a firm, conduct their own evaluations of the company's business activities, and report to the investment community. **Investment banks,** which help firms access capital markets and advise managers about how to interact with those capital markets, also monitor firm performance. **Credit analysts** examine a firm's financial strength for its debt holders. The government also monitors business activities through the Securities and Exchange Commission (SEC) and the Internal Revenue Service (IRS).

board of directors The group of directors elected by stockholders to oversee management in a corporation.

auditor A person who performs an independent assessment of the fairness of a firm's financial statements.

investment analyst A person who analyzes a company's business prospects and gives opinions about its future success.

investment banks Banks that help companies and governments raise capital.

credit analyst A person who analyzes a company's ability to repay its debts and reports the findings as a grade.

▼**FIGURE 1.9** Corporate Governance Monitors

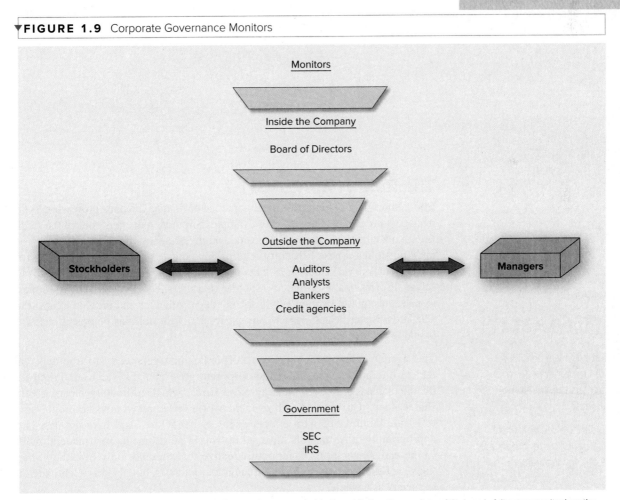

Corporate governance balances the needs of stockholders and managers. Inside the public firm, the members of the board of directors monitor how the firm is run. Outside the firm, auditors, analysts, investment banks, and credit rating agencies act as monitors.

For interactive versions of this example, log in to Connect or go to mhhe.com/Cornett6e.

Executive Compensation LG1-6

In 2017, the median CEO compensation of the largest 100 firms in terms of sales was $15.7 million—a 5 percent increase over the previous year. As per a U.S. Securities and Exchange Commission rule that went into effect in 2017 requiring publicly traded companies to release a ratio of what their CEOs make in comparison to their median paid worker, the median ratio of CEO-to-median-worker-salary for these 100 largest companies was 235-to-one. Every year, the controversy over CEO pay arises again. What arguments could be made for each side?

SOLUTION:

Many people believe that CEOs are paid too much for the services they provide. They receive compensation that is far higher than workers' pay within their firms. Over the years, executive compensation has also increased at a faster rate than has the value of the stockholders' wealth. For example, the Economic Policy Institute reports that after adjusting for inflation, CEO pay increased nearly 1,000 percent between 1978 and 2014. As a comparison, the typical worker's inflation-adjusted pay increased less than 11 percent during the same period. Each firm's board of directors sets CEO compensation. However, CEOs may have undue influence over director selection, tenure, and committee assignments—even over selecting the compensation advisors. This practice creates an unhealthy conflict of interest.

Others believe that a skilled CEO can positively affect company performance and that, therefore, the firm needs to offer high compensation and a bundle of perquisites to attract the best talent. To overcome agency problems, managers must be given incentives that pay very well when the company performs very well. If CEOs create a substantial amount of shareholder wealth, then who is to say that they are overpaid?

ethics The study of values, morals, and morality.

fiduciary A legal duty between two parties where one party must act in the interest of the other party.

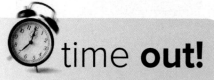

time out!

1-6 What unethical activities might managers engage in because of the agency problem?

1-7 Explain how the corporate governance system reduces the agency problem.

The Role of Ethics LG1-7

Ethics must play a strong role in any practice of finance. Finance professionals commonly manage other people's money. For example, corporate managers control the stockholder's firm, bank employees manage deposits, and investment advisors manage people's investment portfolios. These **fiduciary** relationships create tempting opportunities for finance professionals to make decisions that either benefit the client or benefit the advisors themselves. Professional associations (such as treasurers, bank executives, investment professionals, etc.) place a strong emphasis on ethical behavior and provide ethics training and standards. Nevertheless, as with any profession with millions of practitioners, a few are bound to act unethically.

The agency relationship between corporate managers and stockholders can create ethical dilemmas. Sometimes the corporate governance system has failed to prevent unethical managers from stealing from firms, which ultimately means stealing from shareholders. Governments all over the world have passed laws and regulations meant to ensure compliance with ethical codes of behavior.[7] And if professionals don't act appropriately, governments have set up strong punishments for financial malfeasance. In the end, financial managers must realize that they not only owe their shareholders the very best decisions to further shareholder interests, but also have a broader obligation to society as a whole.

finance at work //:corporate

The Amazing Story of Apple Inc. and Steve Jobs

Steven Jobs and Stephen Wozniak started Apple Computer in 1976 as an equal partnership. Together, they built 50 computers in a garage using money borrowed from family, the proceeds from the sale of a VW bus, and credit from the parts distributor.

Jobs and Wozniak then designed the Apple II computer. But a higher production level to make more than 50 computers required more space and employees. They needed much more capital. They could not get a loan until angel investor Mike Markkula (an Intel executive) became a partner in the firm. He invested $92,000, and his personal guarantee induced a bank to loan Apple $250,000. As production ramped up in 1977, Apple Computer incorporated. Most shares were owned by Jobs, Wozniak, and Markkula, but the principals made some shares available to employees. They also hired an experienced manager (Mike Scott) to be the CEO and run the firm. Note that as the firm expanded, Jobs's ownership level and control got diluted. By 1980, Apple Computer had sold a total of 121,000 computers—against a potential demand of millions more. Apple needed even more capital.

At the end of 1980, Apple became a public corporation and sold $65 million worth of stock to public investors. Steve Jobs, cofounder of Apple, still owned more shares than anyone else (7.5 million), but he owned less than half of the firm. He gave up a great deal of ownership to new investors in exchange for the capital to expand the firm. Unhappy with Mike Scott's leadership, Steve Jobs also became CEO of Apple.

After a couple of years, Apple's board of directors felt that Jobs was not experienced enough to steer the firm through its rapid expansion. They hired John Sculley as CEO in 1983. In 1985, a power struggle ensued for control of the firm, and the board backed Sculley over Jobs. Jobs was forced out of Apple and no longer had a say in business operations, even though he was the largest shareholder and an original cofounder of the firm.

Christopher Kerrigan/McGraw Hill

So, Steve Jobs bought Pixar in 1986 for $5 million and founded NeXT Computer. Over the next 10 years, Jobs's Pixar produced mega hit movies like *Toy Story, A Bug's Life,* and *Monsters, Inc.* This time, he kept 53 percent ownership of Pixar to ensure keeping full control. In the meantime, Apple Computer began to struggle, with losses of $800 million in 1996 and $1 billion in 1997. To get Steve Jobs back into the firm, Apple bought NeXT for $400 million and hired him as Apple's CEO. Over the next few years, Jobs introduced the iMac, iPod, and iTunes, and Apple became very profitable again! Jobs was given the use of a $90 million Gulfstream jet as a perk. To realign his incentives, he became an Apple owner again via compensation that included options on 10 million shares of stock and 30 million shares of **restricted stock.** Then in 2006, Disney bought Pixar by swapping $7.4 billion worth of Disney stock for Pixar stock. When the deal closed, Steve Jobs became the largest owner of Disney stock (7 percent) and joined Disney's board of directors.

Wow! What a story of accessing capital, business organizational form, company control, and corporate governance.

Want to know more?

Key Words to Search for Updates: **Steve Jobs, Apple Computer, Pixar**

1.6 • FINANCIAL MARKETS, INTERMEDIARIES, AND THE FIRM LG1-8

> **restricted stock** A special type of stock that is not transferable from the current holder to others until specific conditions are satisfied.

Astute readers will note that our emphasis on the role of financial markets and intermediaries grew throughout this chapter. This emphasis is intentional, as we feel that you must understand the role and impact of these institutions on the firm if you are to grasp the context in which professionals make financial management decisions.

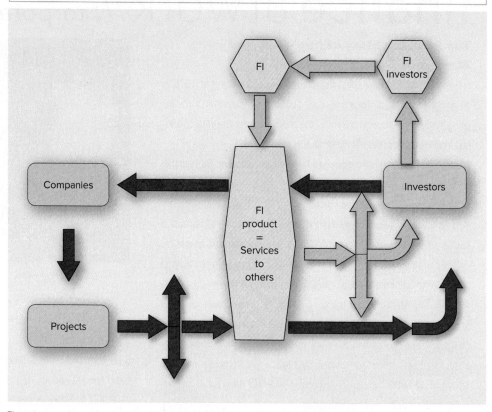

The unique services and products that financial institutions provide allow them to make money.

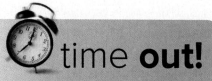

time out!

1-8 What is the role of financial institutions in a capitalist economy?

We want to emphasize one other important point about these financial institutions (FI). Very astute readers may wonder how, if financial markets are competitive, investment banks and other financial institutions are able to make such impressive profits. Although FIs assist others with transactions involving financial assets in the financial markets, they do so as paid services. Successful execution of those services takes unique assets and expertise. As shown in Figure 1.10, it's the use of those unique assets and expertise that provides financial institutions with their high-profit margins.

1.7 • BIG PICTURE ENVIRONMENT LG1-9

The business world is constantly changing. Companies must constantly adapt in order to succeed. These changes and adaptations include the field of finance. For example, when interest rates increase in an economy, then the cost of capital increases for companies. This could make some projects that were worthy of corporate investment become too costly. In other words, changes in interest rates directly lead to changes in the amount of expansion projects taken on by companies. Similarly, changes in currency exchange rates between countries directly impact the attractiveness of expansion into foreign markets. Therefore, while managers often direct most of their focus to their own firms, it is useful to keep an eye on the big picture.

Two of the biggest recent factors affecting the business environment in the United States are the Tax Cuts and Jobs Act (TCJA) of 2017 and the COVID-19 pandemic of 2020.

As discussed in more detail below, the net effect of the TCJA was to reduce effective tax rates for most individuals and corporations. In a reprise of the arguments used to support President Ronald Reagan's Economic Recovery Tax Act of 1981, supporters of the TCJA argued that the resulting corporate tax cuts would eventually "trickle down" to workers' wages. Preliminary studies of the effect of the TCJA on the economy have been inconclusive, but almost all of the provisions of the TCJA are set to expire after 2025.

The economic effects of the COVID-19 pandemic are likely to greatly reduce the chances of the TCJA being extended past 2025, and may, in fact, result in many of them being reversed even sooner. The demand shock resulting from quarantine, unemployment, and business closures that took effect in March 2020 dealt a blow to consumer services industries, while lockdown measures and social distancing also reduced the economy's capacity to produce goods and services by those businesses that remained open. As a result, federal, state, and local governments all saw massive declines in tax revenues at the same time that the demand for their services and for economic assistance skyrocketed.

Looking ahead, it seems inevitable that both corporate and personal income tax rates will have to rise to help keep governments themselves running and to help provide funding for ongoing assistance payments to both individuals and small businesses that are likely to suffer long-term effects from the pandemic. As of the writing of this text, however, TCJA is still in effect, so it makes sense to discuss the changes and implications of the TCJA in the context of a comparison with the economic situation prior to its passing.

People and companies try to legally minimize their tax bill, so changes in tax law can lead to different financial decisions than previously made. For example, the new law reduces the amount of debt interest that can be deducted. Therefore, companies are likely to use more equity financing and less debt financing in the future.

We will examine the specific impact of each of the major tax law changes in more detail later in the text, but, for now, our discussion will merely touch upon the general impact expected on financial decisions.

Reductions in Individual Income Tax Rates

Tables 1.2 and 1.3 show the "break point" brackets for both individual tax filers and married households have changed, with the net effect that most taxpayers will be subject to lower tax rates.

▼ **TABLE 1.2** Single Filer Tax Rates, 2021

Prior Law		Current Law	
Tax Rate	Income Range	Tax Rate	Income Range
10%	$0–$9,525	10%	$0–$9,950
15%	$9,526–$38,700	12%	$9,951–$40,525
25%	$38,701–$93,700	22%	$40,526–$86,375
28%	$93,701–$195,450	24%	$86,376–$164,925
33%	$195,451–$424,950	32%	$164,926–$209,425
35%	$424,951–$426,700	35%	$209,426–$523,600
39.6%	$426,701+	37%	$523,601+

▼ **TABLE 1.3** Married Filing Jointly Tax Rates, 2021

Prior Law		Current Law	
Tax Rate	Income Range	Tax Rate	Income Range
10%	$0–$19,050	10%	$0–19,900
15%	$19,051–$77,400	12%	$19,901–$81,050
25%	$77,401–$156,150	22%	$81,051–$172,750
28%	$156,151–$237,950	24%	$172,751–$329,850
33%	$237,951–$424,950	32%	$329,851–$418,850
35%	$424,951–$480,050	35%	$418,851–$628,300
39.6%	$480,051+	37%	$628,301+

However, TCJA eliminated or restricted many itemized deductions beginning in 2018, and raised the standard deduction, implying that fewer taxpayers are likely to itemize. The major relevant changes include

- The state and local tax deduction is now capped at $10,000.

- Mortgage interest is still deductible, but, for mortgages taken out after December 14, 2017, only the interest on the first $750,000 of mortgage debt is deductible. This may not be a factor where housing prices are relatively low and mortgages are below this limit. However, a mortgage greater than $750,000 is common in locations with high residential real estate costs. For example, the median home price in San Francisco is $1.5 million.

- Interest on home equity loans will no longer be deductible after 2017.

In general, we expect the net impact of the reduction in individual income tax rates to result in more free cash for expenditures on the part of consumers, more potential savings on the part of investors, and a slight downward pressure on housing sales in high-value markets.

Corporate Tax Rates Reduced

Under previous tax law, corporations paid graduated federal income-tax rates of 15 percent, 25 percent, 34 percent, and 35 percent, while personal service corporations (PSCs) paid a flat 35 percent rate. The TCJA establishes a flat 21 percent corporate rate, and that reduced rate also applies to PSCs.

One effect of the reduced corporate tax rates should be for U.S. corporations to bring profits earned overseas back to the United States. Previously, companies did not want to pay the high U.S. marginal tax rate on these funds, so they left the cash in overseas locations. After TCJA, U.S. companies are more likely to "bring home" these foreign profits. That should spur corporate investment within the United States. Indeed, foreign companies may also find the new U.S. tax rates an attractive environment for investment.

New Deduction for "Pass-Through" Business Income

Under previous tax law, net taxable income from so-called pass-through business entities (meaning sole proprietorships, partnerships, LLCs that are treated as sole proprietorships or as partnerships for tax purposes, and S corporations) was simply passed through to owners and taxed at the owner level at standard rates.

TCJA establishes a new deduction based on a noncorporate pass-through entity owner's qualified business income (QBI). This break is available to eligible individuals, estates, and trusts. The deduction generally equals 20 percent of QBI, subject to restrictions that can apply at higher income levels. The QBI deduction is not allowed in calculating the noncorporate owner's adjusted gross income (AGI), but it reduces taxable income. In effect, it is treated the same as an allowable itemized deduction.

We expect the net effect of this deduction to roughly equate the effective tax rate paid by pass-through business entities to that paid by corporations.

Liberalized Asset Expensing and Depreciation Provisions

Under the TCJA, for qualifying property placed in service in tax years beginning after December 31, 2017, the maximum Section 179 deduction is increased to $1 million (up from $510,000).

The first-year bonus depreciation percentage is increased to 100 percent (up from 50 percent). The 100 percent deduction is allowed for both new and used qualifying property. In later years, the first-year bonus depreciation deduction is scheduled to be reduced as follows:

- 80 percent for property placed in service in calendar year 2023.

- 60 percent for property placed in service in calendar year 2024.

- 40 percent for property placed in service in calendar year 2025.

- 20 percent for property placed in service in calendar year 2026.

For new or used passenger vehicles that are placed in service after December 31, 2017, and used over 50 percent for business, the maximum annual depreciation deductions allowed under the TCJA are as follows:

- $10,000 for Year 1.

- $16,000 for Year 2.

- $9,600 for Year 3.

- $5,760 for Year 4 and thereafter until the vehicle is fully depreciated.

Under the old law, these were $11,160 for Year 1 for a new car or $3,160 for a used car, $5,100 for Year 2, $3,050 for Year 3, and $1,875 for Year 4 and thereafter.

We expect the net effect of these liberalized expensing provisions to be an increase in companies' expenditures on depreciable assets.

New Limits on Business Interest Deductions

Subject to some restrictions and exceptions, prior law generally allowed full deductions for interest paid or accrued by a business. Under the TCJA, affected corporate and non-corporate businesses generally cannot deduct interest expense in excess of 30 percent of "adjusted taxable income." For S corporations, partnerships, and LLCs that are treated as partnerships for tax purposes, this limitation is applied at the business level rather than at the owner level.

For tax years beginning in 2018–2021, adjusted taxable income was calculated by adding back allowable deductions for depreciation, amortization, and depletion. After 2021, these amounts are not added back in calculating adjusted taxable income.

Business interest expense that is disallowed under this limitation is treated as business interest arising in the following taxable year. Amounts that cannot be deducted in the current year can generally be carried forward indefinitely.

Overall, we expect this change to effectively limit the amount of debt financing in many industries.

Stricter Rules for Deducting Losses

For business net operating losses (NOLs) that arise in tax years ending after December 31, 2017, the maximum amount of taxable income that can be offset with NOL deductions is generally reduced from 100 percent to 80 percent. In addition, NOLs incurred in those years can no longer be carried back to an earlier tax year (except for certain farming losses). Affected NOLs can be carried forward indefinitely.

Since the net effect of these changes will be to effectively delay when NOLs can be used to shelter income from taxes, we expect firms to be even more motivated to avoid having "paper losses."

Reduced or Eliminated Deductions for Business Entertainment and Some Employee Fringe Benefits

Under prior law, taxpayers could generally deduct 50 percent of expenses for business-related meals and entertainment. Meals provided to an employee for the convenience of the employer on the employer's business premises were 100 percent deductible by the employer and tax-free to the recipient employee. Various other employer-provided fringe benefits were also deductible by the employer and tax-free to the recipient employee.

Under the TCJA, deductions for business-related entertainment expenses are completely disallowed. However, meal expenses incurred while traveling on business are still 50 percent deductible.

The TCJA also disallows employer deductions for the cost of providing commuting transportation to an employee (such as hiring a car service), unless the transportation is necessary for the employee's safety. TCJA also eliminates employer deductions for the cost of providing qualified employee transportation fringe benefits (e.g., parking, mass transit passes, and van pooling), but those benefits are still tax-free to recipient employees.

The net effect of all these changes will obviously be to reduce employers' incentives to provide business-related entertainment or to subsidize employee commuting expenses.

Change to R&D Expense Deduction

Specified R&D expenses must be capitalized and amortized over five years, or 15 years if the R&D is conducted outside the United States, instead of being deducted as under current tax law.

We expect the net effect of this change will be to slightly reduce the amounts spent on R&D by U.S. businesses.

Get Online

mhhe.com/CornettM6e

for study materials including quizzes,
iPod downloads, and video

Jamie Grill/JGI/Blend Images LLC

Your Turn...

Questions

1. Describe the type of people who use the financial markets. *(LG1-1)*

2. What is the purpose of financial management? Describe the kinds of activities that financial management involves. *(LG1-1)*

3. What is the difference in perspective between finance and accounting? *(LG1-2)*

4. What personal decisions can you think of that will benefit from your learning finance? *(LG1-3)*

5. What are the three basic forms of business ownership? What are the advantages and disadvantages to each? *(LG1-4)*

6. Among the three basic forms of business ownership, describe the ability of each form to access capital. *(LG1-4)*

7. Explain how the founder of a business can eventually lose control of the firm. How can the founder ensure this will not happen? *(LG1-4)*

8. Explain the shareholder wealth maximization goal of the firm and how it can be measured. Make an argument for why it is a better goal than maximizing profit. *(LG1-5)*

9. Name and describe as many corporate stakeholders as you can. *(LG1-5)*

10. What conflicts of interest can arise between managers and stockholders? *(LG1-6)*

11. Figure 1.9 shows firm monitors. In your opinion, which group is in the best position to monitor the firm? Explain. Which group has the potential to be the weakest monitor? Explain. *(LG1-6)*

12. In recent years, governments all over the world have passed laws that increased the penalties for executives' crimes. Do you think this will deter unethical corporate managers? Explain. *(LG1-6)*

13. Every year, the media report on the vast amounts of money (sometimes hundreds of millions of dollars) that some CEOs earn from the companies they manage. Are these CEOs worth it? Give examples. *(LG1-6)*

14. Why is ethical behavior so important in the field of finance? *(LG1-7)*

15. Does the goal of shareholder wealth maximization conflict with behaving ethically? Explain. *(LG1-7)*

16. Describe how financial institutions and markets facilitate the expansion of a company's business. *(LG1-8)*

Notes

CHAPTER 1

1. According to the Small Business Administration, over 70 percent of all businesses in the United States were sole proprietorships.

2. However, if you are the sole member of a domestic limited liability company, you are not a sole proprietor if you elect to treat the LLC as a corporation.

3. For example, current federal regulations limit the number of shareholders in an S corporation to no more than 100.

4. See Book IV of his *The Wealth of Nations.*

5. See, for example, Raghuram Rajan and Julie Wulf, "Are Perks Really Managerial Excess?" *Journal of Financial Economics* 79(1), 2006, 1–33.

6. In case you are wondering why the stockholders—who would be the eventual recipients of such "extra" free cash flow—wouldn't then have increased incentives to monitor, they would. But considering that the typical bond sells for $1,000 or more while the typical share of stock sells for much less, and taking into account that bond ownership tends to be much more concentrated than stock ownership in many firms, ask yourself whether bondholders or stockholders are more likely to enjoy economies of scale in monitoring.

7. The Sarbanes-Oxley Act of 2002 was passed in response to a number of recent major corporate accounting scandals including those affecting Enron, Tyco International, and WorldCom. The goal of the act was to make the accounting and auditing procedures more transparent and trustworthy.

Design elements: (Clock) Floortje/Getty Images; (Referee) Richard Ransier/Getty Images

Corporate managers must issue many reports to the public. Most stockholders, analysts, government entities, and other interested parties pay particular attention to annual reports. An annual report provides four basic *financial statements:* the balance sheet, the income statement, the statement of cash flows, and the statement of retained earnings. A **financial statement** provides an accounting-based picture of a firm's financial condition.

Whereas accountants use reports to present a picture of what happened in the past, finance professionals use financial statements to draw inferences about the future. The four statements function to provide key information to managers, who make financial decisions, and to investors, who will accept or reject possible future investments in the firm. When you

two

reviewing
financial
statements

part two

encountered these four financial statements in accounting classes, you learned how they function to place the right information in the right places. In this chapter, you will see how understanding these statements, which are the "right places" for crucial information, creates a solid base for your understanding of decision-making processes in managerial finance.

Financial statements of publicly traded firms can be found in a number of places. For example, all quarterly and annual financial statements can be found on a firm's website (often under a section titled "investor relations"). Financial statements of publicly traded companies are reported to the Securities and Exchange Commission (SEC), which makes them publicly available on their website (www.sec.gov); annual reports are listed under the term 10-K, and quarterly financial statements are listed as 10-Qs. Finally, a number of websites exist (e.g., finance.yahoo.com) where one can view and download financial statements of publicly traded companies. Nonpublic firms are not required to submit financial statements to the SEC. Thus, it can be quite difficult to find detailed financial

continued on p. 31

LEARNING GOALS

LG2-1 Recall the major financial statements that firms must prepare and provide.

LG2-2 Differentiate between book (or accounting) value and market value.

LG2-3 Explain how taxes influence corporate managers' and investors' decisions.

LG2-4 Differentiate between accounting income and cash flows.

LG2-5 Demonstrate how to use a firm's financial statements to calculate its cash flows.

LG2-6 Observe cautions that should be taken when examining financial statements.

>>viewpoints

business APPLICATION

The managers of DPH Tree Farm, Inc., believe the firm could double its sales if it had additional factory space and acreage. If DPH purchased the factory space and acreage in 2025, these new assets would cost $27 million to build and would require an additional $1 million in cash, $5 million in accounts receivable, $6 million in inventory, and $4 million in accounts payable. In addition to accounts payable, DPH Tree Farm would finance the new assets with the sale of a combination of long-term debt (40 percent of the total) and common stock (60 percent of the total). Assuming all else stays constant, what will these changes do to DPH Tree Farm's 2025 balance sheet assets, liabilities, and equity? (See 2024 balance sheet in Table 2.1.) **(See the solution at the end of the chapter.)**

financial statement
Statement that provides an accounting-based picture of a firm's financial position.

balance sheet The financial statement that reports a firm's assets, liabilities, and equity at a particular point in time.

continued from p. 30

information about these firms. This is one reason why some large firms (Cargill, Aldi, State Farm) hesitate to become publicly traded; they prefer to keep their financial statement information private.

It should also be noted that this chapter presents a basic set of financial statements—enough so that, from a financial manager's viewpoint, we can identify the basic categories on each statement and relationships across statements. Individual firms' financial statements may look different from those presented in the chapter, depending on the level of detail and accounting methods used. Further, financial statements may be presented in various formats, for example, in a pdf file or in an Excel spreadsheet.

This chapter examines each statement to clarify its major features and uses. We highlight differences between the accounting-based (book) value of a firm (reflected in these statements) and the true market value of a firm, which we will come to understand more fully. We also make a clear distinction between accounting-based income and actual cash flows, a topic further explored in Chapter 3, where we see how important cash flows are to the study of finance.

We also open a discussion in this chapter about how firms choose to represent their earnings. We'll see that managers have substantial discretion in preparing their firms' financial statements, depending on strategic plans for the organization's future. This is worth looking into as we keep the discipline of finance grounded in a real-world context. Finally, leading into Chapter 3, we discuss some cautions to bear in mind when reviewing and analyzing financial statements. ■

2.1 • BALANCE SHEET LG2-1

The **balance sheet** reports a firm's assets, liabilities, and equity at a particular point in time. It is a picture of the assets the firm owns and who has claims on these assets as of a given date, for example, December 31, 2024. A firm's assets must equal (balance) the liabilities and equity used to purchase the assets (hence the term *balance sheet*):

$$\text{Assets} = \text{Liabilities} + \text{Equity} \tag{2-1}$$

Figure 2.1 illustrates a basic balance sheet and Table 2.1 presents a simple balance sheet for DPH Tree Farm, Inc., as of December 31, 2024 and 2023. The left side of the balance

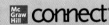
sheet lists assets of the firm and the right side lists liabilities and equity. Both assets and liabilities are listed in descending order of **liquidity,** that is, the time and effort needed to convert the accounts to cash. The most liquid assets—called *current assets*—appear first on the asset side of the balance sheet. The least liquid assets, called *fixed assets,* appear last. Similarly, current liabilities—those obligations that the firm must pay within a year—appear first on the right side of the balance sheet. Stockholders' equity, which never matures, appears last on the balance sheet.

Assets

Figure 2.1 shows that assets fall into two major categories: current assets and fixed assets. **Current assets** will normally convert to cash within one year. They include cash and **marketable securities** (short-term, low-rate investment securities held by the firm for liquidity purposes), accounts receivable, and inventory. **Fixed assets** have a useful life exceeding one year. This class of assets includes physical (tangible) assets, such as net plant and equipment, and other, less tangible, long-term assets, such as patents and trademarks. We find the value of net plant and equipment by taking the difference between gross plant and equipment (or the fixed assets' original value) and the depreciation accumulated against the fixed assets since their purchase.

Liabilities and Stockholders' Equity

Lenders provide funds, which become **liabilities,** to the firm. Liabilities fall into two categories as well: current or long-term. **Current liabilities** constitute the firm's obligations due within one year, including accrued wages and taxes, accounts payable, and notes payable. **Long-term debt** includes long-term loans and bonds with maturities of more than one year.

The difference between total assets and total liabilities of a firm is the stockholders' (or owners') equity. The firm's preferred and common stock owners provide the funds known as **stockholders' equity. Preferred stock** is a hybrid security that has characteristics of both long-term debt and common stock. Preferred stock is similar to common stock in that it represents an ownership interest in the issuing firm but, like long-term debt, it pays a fixed periodic (dividend) payment. Preferred stock appears on the balance sheet as the cash proceeds when the firm sells preferred stock in a public offering. **Common stock and paid-in surplus** are the fundamental ownership claim in a public or private company.

liquidity The ease with which an asset can be converted into cash.

current assets Assets that will normally convert to cash within one year.

marketable securities Short-term, low-rate investment securities held by the firm for liquidity purposes.

fixed assets Assets with a useful life exceeding one year.

liabilities Funds provided by lenders to the firm.

current liabilities Obligations of the firm that are due within one year.

long-term debt Obligations of the firm that are due in more than one year.

▼**FIGURE 2.1** The Basic Balance Sheet

Total Assets	Total Liabilities and Equity
Current assets	Current liabilities
Cash and marketable securities	Accrued wages and taxes
Accounts receivable	Accounts payable
Inventory	Notes payable
Fixed assets	Long-term debt
Gross plant and equipment	Stockholders' equity
Less: Accumulated depreciation	Preferred stock
Net plant and equipment	Common stock and paid-in surplus
Other long-term assets	Retained earnings

	2024	2023		2024	2023
DPH TREE FARM, INC. Balance Sheet as of December 31, 2024 and 2023 (in millions of dollars)					
Assets			**Liabilities and Equity**		
Current assets			Current liabilities		
Cash and marketable securities	$ 24	$ 25	Accrued wages and taxes	$ 20	$ 15
Accounts receivable	70	65	Accounts payable	55	50
Inventory	111	100	Notes payable	48	45
Total	$205	$190	Total	$123	$110
Fixed assets			Long-term debt	192	190
Gross plant and equipment	$368	$300	Total debt	315	300
Less: Accumulated depreciation	53	40	Stockholders' equity		
Net plant and equipment	$315	$260	Preferred stock (5 million shares)	$ 5	$ 5
Other long-term assets	50	50	Common stock and paid-in surplus (20 million shares)	40	40
			Retained earnings	210	155
Total	$365	$310	Total	$255	$200
Total assets	$570	$500	Total liabilities and equity	$570	$500

The proceeds from common stock and paid-in surplus appear as the other component of stockholders' equity. If the firm's managers decide to reinvest cumulative earnings (recorded on the firm's income statement) rather than pay the dividends to stockholders, the balance sheet will record these funds as **retained earnings.**

Managing the Balance Sheet

Managers must monitor a number of issues underlying items reported on their firms' balance sheets. We examine these issues in detail throughout the text. In this chapter, we briefly introduce them. These issues include the

- Accounting method for fixed asset depreciation.

- Level of net working capital.

- Liquidity position of the firm.

- Method for financing the firm's assets—equity or debt.

- Difference between the book value reported on the balance sheet and the true market value of the firm.

Accounting Method for Fixed Asset Depreciation Managers can choose the accounting method they use to record depreciation against their fixed assets. Recall from accounting that *depreciation* is the charge against income that reflects the estimated dollar cost of the firm's fixed assets. The straight-line method and the MACRS (modified accelerated cost recovery system) are two choices. Companies commonly choose MACRS when computing the firm's taxes and the straight-line method when reporting income to the firm's stockholders. The MACRS method accelerates depreciation, which results in higher depreciation expenses and lower taxable income, and thus lower taxes, in the early years of a project's life. Regardless of the depreciation method used, over time both the straight-line and MACRS methods result in the same amount of depreciation and therefore tax (cash) outflows. However, because the MACRS method defers the payment of taxes to later periods, firms often favor it over the straight-line method of depreciation.

Since 2001, businesses have had the ability to immediately deduct a percentage of the acquisition cost of qualifying assets as "bonus depreciation." This additional depreciation deduction was allowed to encourage business investment. However, bonus depreciation was a temporary provision; the rate would have been 50 percent in 2017, 40 percent in 2018, and 30 percent in 2019, before phasing out in 2020. The Tax Cuts and Jobs Act of 2017 temporarily modified and extended bonus depreciation, allowing businesses to immediately deduct 100 percent of the cost of eligible property in the year it is placed into service, through 2022. The amount of allowable bonus depreciation will then be phased down over four years: 80 percent will be allowed for property placed in service in 2023, 60 percent in 2024, 40 percent in 2025, and 20 percent in 2026. MACRS, or straight-line depreciation, is applied to any costs that do not qualify for bonus depreciation. We discuss these issues further in Chapter 12.

net working capital The difference between a firm's current assets and current liabilities.

financial leverage The extent to which debt securities are used by a firm.

Net Working Capital We arrive at a **net working capital** figure by taking the difference between a firm's current assets and current liabilities.

$$\text{Net working capital} = \text{Current assets} - \text{Current liabilities} \qquad (2\text{-}2)$$

So, clearly, net working capital is positive when the firm has more current assets than current liabilities. Table 2.1 shows the 2024 and 2023 year-end balance sheets for DPH Tree Farm, Inc. At year-end 2024, the firm had $205 million of current assets and $123 million of current liabilities. So the firm's net working capital was $82 million. A firm needs cash and other liquid assets to pay its bills as expenses come due. As described in more detail in Chapter 14, liability holders monitor net working capital as a measure of a firm's ability to pay its obligations. Positive net working capital values are usually a sign of a healthy firm.

Liquidity As we noted previously, any firm needs cash and other liquid assets to pay its bills as debts come due. Liquidity actually refers to two dimensions: the ease with which the firm can convert an asset to cash and the degree to which such a conversion takes place at a fair market value. You can convert any asset to cash quickly if you price the asset low enough. But clearly, you will wish to convert the asset without giving up a great portion of its value. So a highly liquid asset can be sold quickly at its fair market value. An illiquid asset, on the other hand, cannot be sold quickly unless you reduce the price far below fair value.

Current assets, by definition, remain relatively liquid, including cash and assets that will convert to cash within the next year. Inventory is the least liquid of the current assets. Fixed assets, then, remain relatively illiquid. In the normal course of business, the firm would have no plans to liquefy or convert these tangible assets such as buildings and equipment into cash.

Liquidity presents a double-edged sword on a balance sheet. The more liquid assets a firm holds, the less likely the firm will be to experience financial distress. However, liquid assets generate little or no profits for a firm. For example, cash is the most liquid of all assets, but it earns little, if anything, for the firm. In contrast, fixed assets are illiquid but provide the means to generate revenue. Thus, managers must consider the trade-off between the advantages of liquidity on the balance sheet and the disadvantages of having money sitting idle rather than generating profits.

Debt Versus Equity Financing You learned in your high school physics class that levers are very useful and powerful machines—given a long enough lever, you can move almost anything. **Financial leverage** is likewise very powerful. Leverage in the financial sense refers to the extent to which a firm chooses to finance its ventures or assets by issuing debt securities. The more debt a firm issues as a percentage of its total assets, the greater its financial leverage. We discuss in later chapters why financial leverage can greatly magnify the firm's gains and losses for the firm's stockholders.

When a firm issues debt securities—usually bonds—to finance its activities and assets, debt holders usually demand first claim to a fixed amount of the firm's cash flows.

Their claims are fixed because the firm must only pay the interest owed to bondholders and any principal repayments that come due within any given period. Stockholders—who buy equity securities or stocks—claim any cash flows left after debt holders are paid. When a firm does well, financial leverage increases shareholders' rewards because the share of the firm's profits promised to debt holders is set and predictable.

However, financial leverage also increases risk. Leverage can create the potential for the firm to experience financial distress and even bankruptcy. If the firm has a bad year and cannot make its scheduled debt payments, debt holders can force the firm into bankruptcy. As described in more detail in Chapter 16, managers often walk a fine line as they decide upon the firm's **capital structure**—the amount of debt versus equity financing held on the balance sheet—because it can determine whether the firm stays in business or goes bankrupt.

Book Value Versus Market Value LG2-2 Beginning finance students usually have already taken accounting, so they are familiar with the accounting point of view. For example, a firm's balance sheet shows its **book (or historical cost) value** based on generally accepted accounting principles (GAAP). Under GAAP, assets appear on the balance sheet at what the firm paid for them, regardless of what those assets might be worth today if the firm were to sell them. Inflation and market forces make many assets worth more now than they were worth when the firm bought them. So in many cases, book values differ widely from **market values** for the same assets—the amount that the assets would fetch if the firm actually sold them. For the firm's current assets—those that mature within a year—the book value and market value of any particular asset will remain very close. For example, the balance sheet lists cash and marketable securities at their market value. Similarly, firms acquire accounts receivable and inventory and then convert these short-term assets into cash fairly quickly, so the book value of these assets is generally close to their market value.

The "book value versus market value" issue really arises when we try to determine how much a firm's fixed assets are worth. In this case, book value is often very different from

---

EXAMPLE 2-1

For interactive versions of this example, log in to Connect or go to mhhe.com/Cornett6e.

Calculating Book versus Market Value LG2-2

EZ Toy, Inc., lists fixed assets of $25 million on its balance sheet. The firm's fixed assets were recently appraised at $32 million. EZ Toy, Inc.'s balance sheet also lists current assets at $10 million. Current assets were appraised at $11 million. Current liabilities' book and market values stand at $6 million and the book and market value of the firm's long-term debt is $15 million. Calculate the book and market values of the firm's stockholders' equity. Construct the book value and market value balance sheets for EZ Toy, Inc.

SOLUTION:

Recall the balance sheet identity in equation 2-1: Assets = Liabilities + Equity. Rearranging this equation: Equity = Assets − Liabilities. Thus, the balance sheets would appear as follows:

	A	B	C	D	E	F	G
1		Book Value	Market Value		Book Value	Market Value	
2	**Assets**			**Liabilities and Equity**			
3	Current assets	$10	$11	Current liabilities	$6	$6	
4	Fixed assets	25	32	Accrued wages and taxes	15	15	=E6-E3-E4
5				Stockholders' equity	14	22	=F6-F3-F4
6	Total =	$35	$43	Total =	$35	$43	
7		=10+25	=C3+C4		=$B$6	=C6	

Source: Microsoft Excel

Similar to Problems 2-17, 2-18, and Self-Test Problem 2.

The book value and market value of a classic car can be very different.
Sreedhar Yedlapati/Getty Images

market value. For example, if a firm owns land for 100 years, this asset appears on the balance sheet at its historical cost (of 100 years ago). Most likely, the firm would reap a much higher price on the land upon its sale than the historical price would indicate.

Again, accounting tools reflect the past: Balance sheet assets are listed at historical cost. Managers would thus see little relation between the total asset value listed on the balance sheet and the current market value of the firm's assets. Similarly, the stockholders' equity listed on the balance sheet generally differs from the true market value of the equity. In this case, the market value may be higher or lower than the value listed on the firm's accounting books. So financial managers and investors often find that balance sheet values are not always the most relevant numbers. The following example illustrates the difference between the book value and the market value of a firm's assets.

income statement Financial statement that reports the total revenues and expenses over a specific period of time.

gross profit Net sales minus cost of goods sold.

EBITDA Earnings before interest, taxes, depreciation, and amortization.

time out!

2-1 What is a balance sheet?

2-2 Which are the most liquid assets and liabilities on a balance sheet?

2.2 • INCOME STATEMENT LG2-1

You will recall that **income statements** show the total revenues that a firm earns and the total expenses the firm incurs to generate those revenues over a specific period of time, for example, the year 2024. Remember that while the balance sheet reports a firm's position at a point in time, the income statement reports performance over a period of time, for example, over the last year. Figure 2.2 illustrates a basic income statement and Table 2.2 shows a simple income statement for DPH Tree Farm, Inc., for the years ended December 31, 2024 and 2023. DPH's revenues (or net sales) appear at the top of the income statement. Net sales are defined as gross sales minus any discounts and/or returns. The income statement then shows various expenses (cost of goods sold [e.g., raw material costs], other operating expenses [e.g., utilities], depreciation, interest, and taxes) subtracted from revenues to arrive at profit or income measures.

The top part of the income statement reports the firm's operating income. First, we subtract the cost of goods sold (the direct costs of producing the firm's product) from net sales to get **gross profit** (so, DPH Tree Farm enjoyed gross profits of $155 million in 2023 and $184 million in 2024). Next, we deduct other operating expenses from gross profits to get earnings before interest, taxes, depreciation, and amortization (**EBITDA**); DPH Tree Farm's EBITDA was $140 million in

▼**FIGURE 2.2** The Basic Income Statement

Net sales	
Less: Cost of goods sold	
Gross profits	
Less: Other operating expenses	Operating income
Earnings before interest, taxes, depreciation, and amortization (EBITDA)	
Less: Depreciation and amortization	
Earnings before interest and taxes (EBIT)	
Less: Interest	
Earnings before taxes (EBT)	Financing and tax considerations
Less: Taxes	
Net income before preferred dividends	
Less: Preferred stock dividends	
Net income available to common stockholders	

▼ **TABLE 2.2** Income Statement for DPH Tree Farm, Inc.

DPH TREE FARM, INC. Income Statement Balance Sheet as of December 31, 2024 and 2023 (in millions of dollars)		
	2024	**2023**
Net sales (all credit)	$ 315	$ 275
Less: Cost of goods sold	131	120
Gross profits	$ 184	$ 155
Less: Other operating expenses	17	15
Earnings before interest, taxes, depreciation, and amortization (EBITDA)	$ 167	$ 140
Less: Depreciation and amortization	13	12
Earnings before interest and taxes (EBIT)	$ 154	$ 128
Less: Interest	16	18
Earnings before taxes (EBT)	$ 138	$ 110
Less: Taxes	29	23
Net income	$ 109	$ 87
Less: Preferred stock dividends	$ 10	$ 10
Net income available to common stockholders	$ 99	$ 77
Less: Common stock dividends	44	44
Addition to retained earnings	$ 55	$ 33
Per (common) share data:		
Earnings per share (EPS)	$4.95	$3.85
Dividends per share (DPS)	2.22	2.22
Book value per share (BVPS)	12.50	9.75
Market value (price) per share (MVPS)	17.25	15.60

2023 and $167 million in 2024. Other operating expenses include marketing and selling expenses as well as general and administrative expenses. Finally, we subtract depreciation and amortization from EBITDA to get operating income or earnings before interest and taxes (**EBIT**)[1] (so DPH Tree Farm's EBIT was $128 million in 2023 and $154 million in 2024). The EBIT figure represents the profit earned from the sale of the product without any financing cost or tax considerations.

The bottom part of the income statement summarizes the firm's financial and tax structure. First, we subtract interest expense (the cost to service the firm's debt) from EBIT to get earnings before taxes (**EBT**). So, as we follow our sample income statement, DPH Tree Farm had EBT of $110 million in 2023 and $138 million in 2024. Of course, firms differ in their financial structures and tax situations. These differences can cause two firms with identical operating income to report differing levels of net income. For example, one firm may finance its assets with only debt, while another finances with only common equity. The company with no debt would have no interest expense. Thus, even though EBIT for the two firms is identical, the firm with all-equity financing and no debt would report higher net income. We subtract taxes from EBT to get the last item on the income statement (the "bottom line"), or **net income.** DPH Tree Farm, Inc., reported net income of $87 million in 2023 and $109 million in 2024.

Below the net income, or bottom line, on the income statement, firms often report additional information summarizing income and firm value. For example, with its $109 million of net income in 2024, DPH Tree Farm, Inc., paid its preferred stockholders cash dividends of $10 million and its common stockholders cash dividends of $44 million, and added the remaining $55 million to retained earnings. Table 2.1 shows that retained earnings on the balance sheet increased from $155 million in 2023 to $210 million in 2024. Other items reported below the bottom line include:

$$\text{Earnings per share}\,(EPS) = \frac{\text{Net income available to common stockholders}}{\text{Total shares of common stock outstanding}} \qquad (2\text{-}3)$$

$$\text{Dividends per share}\,(DPS) = \frac{\text{Common stock dividends paid}}{\text{Number of shares of common stock outstanding}} \qquad (2\text{-}4)$$

$$\text{Book value per share}\,(BVPS) = \frac{\text{Common stock} + \text{Paid-in surplus}}{\text{Number of shares of common stock outstanding}} \qquad (2\text{-}5)$$

$$\text{Market value per share}\,(MVPS) = \text{Market price of the firm's common stock} \qquad (2\text{-}6)$$

We discuss these items further in Chapter 3.

Debt versus Equity Financing

As mentioned earlier, when a firm issues debt to finance its assets, it gives the debt holders first claim to a fixed amount of its cash flows. Stockholders are entitled to any residual cash flows, or net income. Thus, when a firm alters its capital structure to include more or less debt (and, in turn, less or more equity), it impacts the residual cash flows available for the stockholders, that is, the numerator of the EPS equation. Further, as the firm alters its capital structure, it will issue more shares of stock when it increases equity to reduce debt, or it will buy back shares of stock when it decreases equity to increase debt, that is, the denominator of the EPS equation. Thus, a change in capital structure will cause a firm's stockholders' EPS to change. The question is: Will the reduction (increase) in financial distress and bankruptcy risk from the reduction (increase) in financial leverage appease the stockholders who have lost (gained) earnings per share, and ultimately, how will the change affect stockholder wealth?

EXAMPLE 2-2

For interactive versions of this example, log in to Connect or go to mhhe.com/Cornett6e.

Impact of Capital Structure on a Firm's EPS LG2-1

Consider a firm with an EBIT of $750,000. The firm finances its assets with $1,600,000 debt (costing 5 percent and all is tax deductible) and 200,000 shares of stock selling at $6.00 per share. To reduce the firm's risk associated with this financial leverage, the firm is considering reducing its debt by $600,000 by selling an additional 100,000 shares of stock. The firm's tax rate is 21 percent. The change in capital structure will have no effect on the operations of the firm. Thus, EBIT will remain at $750,000. Calculate the dilution in the firm's EPS from this change in capital structure.

SOLUTION:

The EPS before and after this change in capital structure is illustrated below:

Change	Before Capital Structure Change		After Capital Structure Change	
EBIT		$750,000		$750,000
Less: Interest	($1,600,000 × 0.05)	80,000	($1,000,000 × 0.05)	50,000
EBT		$670,000		$700,000
Less: Taxes (21%)		140,700		147,000
Net income		$529,300		$553,000
Divided by # of shares		200,000		300,000
EPS		$ 2.65		$ 1.84

The change in capital structure would dilute the stockholders' EPS by $0.81.
Similar to Problems 2-5, 2-22, and 2-31.

Corporate Income Taxes LG2-3

Firms pay out a large portion of their earnings in taxes. For example, in 2020, Walmart had EBT of $20.12 billion. Of this amount, Walmart paid $4.92 billion (nearly 25 percent of EBT) in taxes. Firms may also defer taxes; for example, in 2020, Walmart listed deferred taxes of $12.96 billion on its balance sheet. Deferred taxes occur when a company postpones paying taxes on profits earned in a particular period. For example, some expenses, such as those associated with research and development or incurred in mergers, may be written off over a fixed number of years. In these cases, the firm's current year profits for tax purposes would be lower than the profits computed for accounting purposes. Thus, the company ends up postponing part of its tax liability on this year's profits to future years.

EXAMPLE 2-3

For interactive versions of this example, log in to Connect or go to mhhe.com/Cornett6e.

Calculation of Corporate Taxes LG2-3

Indian Point Kennels, Inc.'s 2024 Income Statement is reported below (in millions of dollars). Determine the firm's tax liability, net income, average tax rate, and marginal tax rate.

Indian Point Kennels, Inc., Income Statement (in Millions of Dollars)	
Net Sales (all credit)	$475
Less: Cost of Goods Sold	245
Gross Profits	$230
Less: Other Operating Expenses	110
EBITDA	$120
Less: Depreciation and Amortization	12
Earnings before Interest and Taxes (EBIT)	$108
Less: Interest	38
Earnings before Taxes (EBT)	$ 70
Less: Taxes	
Net Income	$___

SOLUTION:

With $120,000,000 of EBITDA, Indian Point Kennels is allowed to deduct only $36,000,000 ($120,000,000 × 30 percent) of its $38,000,000 in net interest expense. Thus,

Taxable income = EBIT − Allowable interest deduction
        = $108,000,000 − $36,000,000 = $72,000,000
    Tax liability = 0.21 × *Taxable income*
        = 0.21($72,000,000) = $15,120,000

The 30 percent cap on the allowable interest deduction results in an increase in Indian Point Kennels's tax liability of $420,000 [0.21($38,000,000 − $36,000,000)].

Net Income = EBT − Tax Liability
        = $70,000,000 − $15,120,000 = $54,880,000

The average tax rate for Indian Point Kennels, Inc., comes to:

$$\text{Average tax rate} = \frac{\text{Tax liability}}{\text{Taxable income}}$$
        = $15,120,000/$72,000,000 = 21.0%

If Indian Point Kennels earned $1 more of taxable income, it would pay 21 cents (its tax rate of 21 percent) more in taxes. Thus, the firm's marginal tax rate is 21 percent.

Similar to Problems 2-6, 2-7, 2-13, 2-23, and Self-Test Problem 3.

EXAMPLE 2-4

Corporate Taxes with Interest and Dividend Income LG2-3

 For interactive versions of this example, log in to Connect or go to mhhe.com/Cornett6e.

In the previous example, suppose that in addition to the items listed on the income statement, Indian Point Kennels, Inc., received $400,000 of interest on state-issued bonds and $1,000,000 of dividends on common stock it owns in DPH Tree Farm, Inc. How do these items affect Indian Point Kennels's tax liability, average tax rate, and marginal tax rate?

SOLUTION:

In this case, interest on the state-issued bonds is not taxable and should not be included in taxable income. Further, the first 50 percent of the dividends received from DPH Tree Farm is not taxable. Thus, only the remaining 50 percent of the dividends received are taxed, so:

Taxable income = (EBIT − Allowable interest deduction + 0.50 (dividend income))

$$= (\$108,000,000 - \$36,000,000 + (0.50)\,\$1,000,000) = \$72,500,000$$

Now Indian Point Kennels's tax liability will be:

Tax liability = 0.21 × taxable income

$$= 0.21 \times \$72,500,000 = \$15,225,000$$

The $1,000,000 of dividend income increased Indian Point Kennels's tax liability by $105,000. Indian Point Kennels, Inc.'s resulting average tax rate is now:

Average tax rate = $15,225,000/$72,500,000 = 21.0%

Finally, if Indian Point Kennels earned $1 more of taxable income, it would still pay 21 cents (based upon its marginal tax rate of 21 percent) more in taxes.

The spreadsheet solution is:

	A	B	C
1	**Indian Point Kennels, Inc.'s 2024 Income Statement**		
2	**(in millions)**		
3	Net Sales	$475	
4	Less: Cost of Goods Sold	245	
5	Gross Profits	$230	
6	Less: Other Operating Expenses	110	
7	EBITDA	$120	
8	Less: Depreciation and Amortization	12	
9	EBIT	$108	
10	Less: Interest	38	
11	Taxable Income	$72.5	=B9-B15+0.5*B16
12	Less: Taxes	$15.23	=0.21*B11
13	Net Income	$57.28	
14			
15	Max Interest Deduction	$36	
16	Dividend Income	$1	
17			
18	Average Tax Rate	21.00%	=B12/B11
19	Marginal Tax Rate	21.00%	

Microsoft Excel

Similar to Problems 2-13 and 2-23.

Congress oversees the U.S. tax code, which determines corporate tax obligations. Corporate taxes can thus change with changes of administration or other changes in the business or public environment. As you might expect, the U.S. tax system is extremely complicated, so we do not attempt to cover it in detail here. However, firms recognize taxes as a major expense item and many financial decisions arise from tax considerations. In this section, we provide a general overview of the U.S. corporate tax system.

EXAMPLE 2-5

Effect of Debt-versus-Equity Financing on Funders' Returns LG2-1

For interactive versions of this example, log in to Connect or go to mhhe.com/Cornett6e.

Suppose that you are considering a stock investment in one of two firms (AllDebt, Inc., and AllEquity, Inc.), both of which operate in the same industry and have identical EBITDA of $6.2 million and operating incomes of $5 million. AllDebt, Inc., finances its $12 million in assets with $11 million in debt (on which it pays 10 percent interest, or interest payments are $1.1 million) and $1 million in equity. With $6.2 million of EBITDA, AllDebt, Inc., may deduct up to $1.86 million ($6.2 × 30 percent) of interest expense for tax purposes. Thus, AllDebt, Inc., is allowed to deduct all of its interest expense. AllEquity, Inc., finances its $12 million in assets with no debt and $12 million in equity. Both firms pay 21 percent tax on their taxable income. Calculate the income that each firm has available to pay its debt and stockholders (the firms' asset funders) and the resulting returns to these asset funders for the two firms.

SOLUTION:

	AllDebt	AllEquity
EBITDA	$6.200m	$6.200m
Less: Depreciation and amortization	$1.200m	$1.200m
Operating income (EBIT)	$5.000m	$5.000m
Less: Interest	1.100m	0.000m
Taxable income	$3.900m	$5.000m
Less: Taxes (21%)	0.819m	1.050m
Net income	$3.081m	$3.950m
Income available for asset funders (= Operating income − Taxes)	$4.181m	$3.950m

Return on asset-funders' investment $4.181m/$12.00m = 34.84% $3.950m/$12.00m = 32.92%

By financing most of its assets with debt and receiving the associated tax benefits from the interest paid on this debt, All Debt, Inc., is able to pay more of its operating income to the funders of its assets, that is, its debt holders and stockholders, than All Equity, Inc.

Similar to Problem 2-19

The Tax Cut and Jobs Act (TCJA) of 2017 is the most recent revision of corporate tax laws and represents one of the most significant changes in more than 30 years. The act permanently lowers corporate taxes from a progressive schedule that saw tax rates as high as 35 percent to a flat 21 percent starting in 2018. Further, prior corporate tax laws generally allowed full deduction of interest paid or accrued by businesses. The TCJA contains a new limitation on the deductibility of net interest expense (interest expense minus interest income) that exceeds 30 percent of a firm's "adjusted taxable income" starting in 2018. For tax years beginning before January 1, 2022, "adjustable taxable income" is measured as a business's EBITDA. For subsequent tax years, "adjusted taxable income" is measured as EBIT, no longer including an add-back for depreciation and amortization. Thus, beginning in 2022, the new limitation becomes more severe.

In addition to calculating their tax liability, firms also want to know their **average tax rate** and **marginal tax rate.** You can figure the average tax rate as the percentage of each dollar of taxable income that the firm pays in taxes.

average tax rate The percentage of each dollar of taxable income that the firm pays in taxes.

marginal tax rate The amount of additional taxes a firm must pay out for every additional dollar of taxable income it earns.

$$\text{Average tax rate} = \frac{\text{Tax liability}}{\text{Taxable income}} \tag{2-7}$$

From your economics classes, you can probably guess that the firm's marginal tax rate is the amount of additional taxes a firm must pay out for every additional dollar of taxable income it earns.

Interest and Dividends Received by Corporations Any interest that corporations receive is taxable, although a notable exception arises: Interest on state and local government bonds is exempt from federal taxes. The U.S. tax code allows this exception to encourage corporations to be better community citizens by supporting local governments. Another exception of sorts arises when one corporation owns stock in another corporation. Fifty percent of any dividends received from other corporations is tax exempt. Only the remaining 50 percent is taxed at the receiving corporation's tax rate.[2]

Interest and Dividends Paid by Corporations Corporate interest payments appear on the income statement as an expense item, so we deduct the allowable portion of interest payments from operating income when the firm calculates taxable income. But any dividends paid by corporations to their shareholders are not tax deductible. This is one factor that encourages managers to finance projects with debt financing rather than to sell more stock. Suppose one firm uses mainly debt financing and another firm, with identical operations, uses mainly equity financing. The equity-financed firm will have very little interest expense to deduct for tax purposes. Thus, it will have higher taxable income and pay more taxes than the debt-financed firm. The debt-financed firm will pay fewer taxes and be able to pay more of its operating income to asset funders, that is, its bondholders and stockholders. So, all else constant, as long as interest on debt is under the 30 percent allowable cap for tax deduction, even stockholders prefer that firms finance assets primarily with debt rather than with stock. However, as mentioned earlier, increasing the amount of debt financing of the firm's assets also increases risks. So these effects must be balanced when selecting the optimal capital structure for a firm. The debt-versus-equity financing issue is called *capital structure,* which we address more fully in Chapters 16–18.

time out!

2-3 What is an income statement?

2-4 When a corporation owns stock in another corporation, what percentage of dividends received on the stock is taxed?

2.3 • STATEMENT OF CASH FLOWS LG2-4

Income statements and balance sheets are the most common financial documents available to the public. However, managers who make financial decisions need more than these two statements—reports of past performance—on which to base their decisions for today and into the future. A very important distinction between the accounting point of view and the finance point of view is that financial managers and investors are *far more interested in actual cash flows* than in the backward-looking profit listed on the income statement.

The **statement of cash flows** is a financial statement that shows the firm's cash flows over a given period of time. This statement reports the amounts of cash the firm has generated and distributed during a particular time period. The bottom line on the statement of cash flows—the difference between cash sources and uses—equals the change in cash and marketable securities on the firm's balance sheet over a period of time. That is, the statement of cash flows reconciles noncash balance sheet items and income statement items to show changes in the cash and marketable securities account on the balance sheet over the particular analysis period.

To clarify why this statement is so crucial, it helps to understand that figures on an income statement may not represent the actual cash inflows and outflows for a firm during a given period of time. There are two main issues: GAAP accounting principles and noncash income statement entries.

GAAP Accounting Principles

Company accountants must prepare firm income statements following GAAP principles. GAAP procedures require that the firm recognize revenue at the time of sale. But sometimes the company receives the cash before or after the time of sale. Likewise, GAAP counsels the firm to show production and other expenses on the income statement as the sales of those goods take place. So production and other expenses associated with a particular product's sale appear on the income statement (e.g., cost of goods sold) only

statement of cash flows
Financial statement that shows the firm's cash flows over a period of time.

when that product sells. Of course, just as with revenue recognition, actual cash outflows incurred with production may occur at a very different point in time—usually much earlier than GAAP principles allow the firm to formally recognize the expenses.

Noncash Income Statement Entries

Further, income statements contain several noncash entries, the largest of which is depreciation. Depreciation attempts to capture the noncash expense incurred as fixed assets deteriorate from the time of purchase to the point when those assets must be replaced.

Let's illustrate the effect of depreciation: Suppose a firm purchases a machine for $100,000. The machine has an expected life of five years and at the end of those five years, the machine will have no expected salvage value. The firm incurs a $100,000 cash outflow at the time of purchase. But the entire $100,000 does not generally appear on the income statement in the year that the firm purchases the machine—in accounting terms, the machine is not expensed in the year of purchase. Rather, ignoring the temporary allowance of bonus depreciation, if the firm's accounting department uses the straight-line depreciation method, it deducts only $100,000/5, or $20,000, each year as an expense. This $20,000 equipment expense is not a cash outflow for the firm. The person in charge of buying the machine knows that the cash flow occurred at the time of purchase—and it totaled $100,000 rather than $20,000.

In conclusion, even though a company may report a large amount of net income on its income statement during a year, the firm may actually receive a positive, negative, or zero amount of cash. For example, DPH Tree Farm, Inc., reported net income of $109 million on its income statement (in Table 2.2), yet reported a net change in cash and marketable securities of –$1 million on its balance sheet (in Table 2.1). Accounting rules under GAAP create this sense of discord: Net income is the result of accounting rules, or GAAP, that do not necessarily reflect the firm's cash flows. Finance professionals know that the firm needs cash, not accounting profits, to pay the firm's obligations as they come due, to fund the firm's operations and growth, and to compensate the firm's ultimate owners: its shareholders. While the income statement shows a firm's accounting-based income, the statement of cash flows more often reflects reality today and is thus more important to managers and investors as they seek to answer such important questions as

- Does the firm generate sufficient cash to pay its obligations, thus avoiding financial distress?

- Does the firm generate sufficient cash to purchase assets needed for sustained growth?

- Does the firm generate sufficient cash to pay down its outstanding debt obligations?

Sources and Uses of Cash LG2-5

In general, some activities increase cash (cash sources) and some decrease cash (cash uses). Figure 2.3 classifies the firm's basic cash sources and uses. Cash sources include decreasing noncash assets or increasing liabilities (or equity). For example, a drop in accounts receivable means that the firm has collected cash from its credit sales—a cash source. Likewise, if a firm sells new common stock, the firm has used primary markets to raise cash. In contrast, a firm uses cash when it increases noncash assets (buying inventory) or decreases a liability (paying off a bank loan). The statement of cash flows separates these cash flows into four categories or sections:

▼FIGURE 2.3 Sources and Uses of Cash

Sources of Cash	Uses of Cash
Net income	Net losses
Depreciation	Increase a noncash current asset
Decrease a noncash current asset	Increase a fixed asset
Decrease a fixed asset	Decrease a current liability
Increase a current liability	Decrease long-term debt
Increase long-term debt	Repurchase common or preferred stock
Sell common or preferred stock	Pay dividends

1. Cash flows from operating activities.

2. Cash flows from investing activities.

3. Cash flows from financing activities.

4. Net change in cash and marketable securities.

The basic setup of a statement of cash flows is shown in Figure 2.4, and a more detailed statement of cash flows for DPH Tree Farm for the year ending December 31, 2024, appears as Table 2.3.

Cash flows from operations (Section A in Figure 2.4 and Table 2.3) are those cash inflows and outflows that result directly from producing and selling the firm's products over a period of time. These cash flows include

> **cash flows from operations**
> Cash flows that are the direct result of the production and sale of the firm's products.

- Net income (adding back depreciation,[3] a noncash expense item that is included in net income).

- Change in working capital accounts other than cash and operations-related short-term debt.

Most finance professionals consider this top section of the statement of cash flows to be the most important. It shows quickly and compactly the firm's cash flows generated by and used for the production process. For example, DPH Tree Farm, Inc., generated $116 million in cash flows from its 2024 production. That is, producing and selling the firm's product resulted in a net cash inflow for the firm. Managers and investors look for positive cash flows from operations as a sign of a successful firm—positive cash flows from the firm's operations are precisely what gives the firm value. Unless the firm has a stable, healthy pattern in its cash flows from operations, it is not financially healthy no matter what its level of cash flow from investing activities or cash flows from financing activities.

FIGURE 2.4 The Statement of Cash Flows

Section A. Cash flows from operating activities

Net income

Additions:

  Depreciation

  Decrease in noncash current assets (e.g., decrease in accounts receivable)

  Increase in accrued wages and taxes

  Increase in accounts payable

Subtractions:

  Increase in noncash current assets (e.g., increase in inventory)

  Decrease in accrued wages and taxes

  Decrease in accounts payable

Section B. Cash flows from investing activities

Additions:

  Decrease in fixed assets

  Decrease in other long-term assets

Subtractions:

  Increase in fixed assets

  Increase in other long-term assets

Section C. Cash flows from financing activities

Additions:

  Increase in notes payable

  Increase in long-term debt

  Increase in common and preferred stock

Subtractions:

  Decrease in notes payable

  Decrease in long-term debt

  Decrease in common and preferred stock

  Dividends paid

Section D. Net change in cash and marketable securities

TABLE 2.3 Statement of Cash Flows for DPH Tree Farm, Inc.

DPH TREE FARM, INC. Statement of Cash Flows for Year Ending December 31, 2024 (in millions of dollars)	2024
Section A. Cash flows from operating activities	
Net income	$109
Additions:	
Depreciation	13
Increase in accrued wages and taxes ($20 − $15)	5
Increase in accounts payable ($55 − $50)	5
Subtractions:	
Increase in accounts receivable ($65 − $70)	−5
Increase in inventory ($100 − $111)	−11
Net cash flow from operating activities	$116
Section B. Cash flows from investing activities	
Subtractions:	
Increase in fixed assets ($300 − $368)	−$ 68
Increase in other long-term assets ($50 − $50)	0
Net cash flow from investing activities	−$ 68
Section C. Cash flows from financing activities	
Additions:	
Increase in notes payable ($48 − $45)	$ 3
Increase in long-term debt ($192 − $190)	2
Increase in common and preferred stock ($40 − $40) + ($5 − $5)	0
Subtractions:	
Preferred stock dividends paid	−10
Common stock dividends paid	−44
Net cash flow from financing activities	−$ 49
Section D. Net change in cash and marketable securities	−$ 1

cash flows from investing activities Cash flows associated with the purchase or sale of fixed or other long-term assets.

cash flows from financing activities Cash flows that result from debt and equity financing transactions.

net change in cash and marketable securities The sum of the cash flows from operations, investing activities, and financing activities.

Cash flows from investing activities (Section B in Figure 2.4 and Table 2.3) are cash flows associated with the buying or selling of fixed or other long-term assets. This section of the statement of cash flows shows cash inflows and outflows from changes in long-term investing activities—most significantly the firm's investment in fixed assets. For example, DPH Tree Farm, Inc., used $68 million in cash to purchase fixed and other long-term assets in 2024. DPH funded this $68 million cash outflow with the $116 million cash surplus DPH Tree Farm produced from its operations.

Cash flows from financing activities (Section C in Figure 2.4 and Table 2.3) are cash flows that result from changes in debt and equity financing. These include raising cash by

- Issuing short-term debt

- Issuing long-term debt

- Issuing stock

or using cash to

- Pay dividends

- Pay off debt

- Buy back stock

In 2024, DPH Tree Farm, Inc.'s financing activities produced a net cash outflow of $49 million. As we saw with cash flows from financing activities, this $49 million cash outflow was funded (at least partially) with the $116 million cash surplus DPH Tree Farm produced from its operations. Managers, investors, and analysts normally expect the cash flows from financing activities to include small amounts of net borrowing along with dividend payments. If, however, a firm is going through a major period of expansion, net borrowing could reasonably be much higher.

Net change in cash and marketable securities (Section D in Figure 2.4 and Table 2.3), the bottom line of the statement of cash flows, shows the sum of cash flows from operations, investing activities, and financing activities. This sum will reconcile to the net change in cash and marketable securities account on the balance sheet over the period of analysis. For example, the bottom line of the statement of cash flows for DPH Tree Farm is −$1 million. This is also the change in the cash and marketable securities account on the balance sheet (in Table 2.1) between 2023 and 2024 ($24 million − $25 million = −$1 million). In this case, the firm's operating, investing, and financing activities combined to produce a net drain on the firm's cash during 2024—cash outflows were greater than cash inflows, largely because of the $68 million investment in long-term and fixed assets. Of course, when the bottom line is positive, a firm's cash inflows exceed cash outflows for the period.

When evaluating the statement of cash flows, the overall change in the cash account should be evaluated with care. For example, a negative cash flow could be the result when a growing firm invests in new fixed assets, inventory, and so on. Cash expenditures used to expand firm capacity would drain cash during the expansion period. However, if utilized efficiently, they would result in increases in cash flows through time. Thus, the cash flow statement assists financial professionals

DPH Tree Farm reported net income of $90 million yet reported a net change in cash and marketable securities of -$1 million on its statement of cash flows.
Photo courtesy of USDA Natural Resources Conservation Service

to identify where cash is generated and where cash is disbursed over a time period. These cash inflows and outflows should then be evaluated based on how they added to the value of the firm to its stockholders.

free cash flows The cash that is actually available for distribution to the investors in the firm after the investments that are necessary to sustain the firm's ongoing operations are made.

net operating profit after taxes (NOPAT) Net profit a firm earns after taxes but before any financing costs.

2.4 • FREE CASH FLOW LG2-5

The statement of cash flows measures net cash flow as net income plus noncash adjustments. However, to maintain cash flows over time, firms must continually replace working capital and fixed assets and develop new products. Thus, firm managers cannot use the available cash flows any way they please. Specifically, the value of a firm's operations depends on the future expected **free cash flows,** defined as after-tax operating profit minus the amount of new investment in working capital, fixed assets, and the development of new products. Thus, free cash flow represents the cash that is actually available for distribution to the investors in the firm—the firm's debt holders and stockholders—after the investments that are necessary to sustain the firm's ongoing operations are made.

To calculate free cash flow (FCF), we use the mathematical equation that appears below:

$$
\begin{aligned}
FCF &= [EBIT\,(1 - \text{Tax rate}) + \text{Depreciation}] - [\Delta\text{Gross fixed assets} \\
&\quad + \Delta\text{Net operating working capital}] \\
&= [NOPAT + \text{Depreciation}] - \text{Investment in operating capital} \\
&= \text{Operating cash flow} - \text{Investment in operating capital}
\end{aligned}
\tag{2-8}
$$

Notice from this equation that free cash flow merges information from the income statement (performance) with information from the balance sheet (resources used to produce performance).

To calculate free cash flow, we start with operating cash flow. Firms generate operating cash flow (OCF) after they have paid necessary operating expenses and taxes. This **net operating profit after taxes (NOPAT)** is the net profit a firm earns after taxes but before any financing costs. It is the profit available for debt holders and stockholders if the firm does not replace existing or invest in new working capital or fixed assets. Depreciation, a noncash charge, is added back to NOPAT to determine total OCF. We add other relevant noncash charges, such as amortization and depletion, back as well. Firms either buy physical assets or earmark funds for eventual equipment replacement to sustain firm operations; this is called *investment in operating capital* (*IOC*). In accounting terms, IOC includes the firm's gross investments (or changes) in fixed assets, current assets, and spontaneous current liabilities (such as accounts payable and accrued wages). Thus, free cash flow measures how well managers utilize the resources of the company to increase firm performance and, thus, enhance shareholder wealth.

Like the bottom line shown on the statement of cash flows, the level of free cash flow can be positive, zero, or negative. A positive free cash flow value means that the firm may distribute funds to its investors (debt holders and stockholders). When the firm's free cash flows come in as zero or negative, however, the firm's operations produce no cash flows available for investors. Of course, if free cash flow is negative because operating cash flow is negative, investors are likely to take up the issue with the firm's management. Negative free cash flows as a result of negative operating cash flows generally indicate that the firm is experiencing operating or managerial problems. A firm with positive operating cash flows, but negative free cash flows, however, is not necessarily a poorly managed firm. Firms that invest heavily in operating capital to support growth often have positive operating cash flows but negative free cash flows. But in this case, the negative free cash flow will likely result in growing future profits.

EXAMPLE 2-6

Calculating Free Cash Flow LG2-5

From Tables 2.1 and 2.2, in 2024, DPH Tree Farm, Inc., had EBIT of $154 million, a tax rate of 21 percent ($29m/$138m), and depreciation expense of $13 million. Therefore, DPH Tree Farm's operating cash flow was

$OCF = EBIT$ (1 − Tax rate) + Depreciation

$= \$154m\ (1 − 0.21) + \$13m = \$134.66m$

DPH Tree Farm's gross fixed assets increased by $68 million between 2023 and 2024. The firm's current assets increased by $15 million and spontaneous current liabilities increased by $10 million ($5 million in accrued wages and taxes and $5 million in accounts payable). Therefore, DPH's investment in operating capital for 2024 was

$IOC = \Delta$Gross fixed assets + ΔNet operating working capital

$= \$68m + (\$15m − \$10m) = \$73m$

Accordingly, what was DPH Tree Farm's free cash flow for 2024?

SOLUTION:

$FCF =$ Operating cash flow − Investment in operating capital

$= \$134.66m − \$73m = \$61.66m$

In other words, in 2024, DPH Tree Farm, Inc., had cash flows of $61.66 million available to pay its stockholders and debt holders.

Similar to Problems 2-9, 2-10, and Self-Test Problem 4.

time out!

2-5 What is a statement of cash flows?

2-6 What are the main sections on the statement of cash flows?

statement of retained earnings Financial statement that reconciles net income earned during a given period and any cash dividends paid with the change in retained earnings over the period.

2.5 • STATEMENT OF RETAINED EARNINGS LG2-1

The **statement of retained earnings** provides additional details about changes in retained earnings during a reporting period. This financial statement reconciles net income earned during a given period and any cash dividends paid within that period on one side with the change in retained earnings between the beginning and ending of the period on the other. Table 2.4 presents DPH Tree Farm, Inc.'s statement of retained earnings as of December 31, 2024. The statement shows that DPH Tree Farm brought in a net income of $109 million during 2024. The firm paid out $10 million in dividends to preferred stockholders and another $44 million to common stockholders. The firm then had $55 million to reinvest back into the firm, which shows as an increase in retained earnings. Thus, the retained earnings account on the balance sheet (Table 2.1) increased from $155 million at year-end 2023 to $210 million at year-end 2024.

Increases in retained earnings occur not just because a firm has net income, but also because the firm's common stockholders agree to let management reinvest net income back into the firm rather than pay it out as dividends. If the shareholders disagreed with the firm's policy, they would simply sell their shares. Reinvesting earnings is less expensive than raising capital from outside sources (equity markets). Further, reinvesting net income into retained earnings allows the firm to grow by providing additional funds that can be spent on plant and equipment, inventory, and other assets needed to generate even more profit. So, retained earnings represent a claim against all of the firm's assets and not against a particular asset.

EXAMPLE 2-7

For interactive versions of this example, log in to Connect or go to mhhe.com/Cornett6e.

Statement of Retained Earnings LG2-1

Indian Point Kennels, Inc., earned net income in 2024 of $10.78 million. The firm paid out $1 million in cash dividends to its preferred stockholders and $2.5 million in cash dividends to its common stockholders. The firm ended 2023 with $135.75 million in retained earnings. Construct a statement of retained earnings to calculate the year-end 2024 balance of retained earnings.

SOLUTION:

The statement of retained earnings for 2024 is as follows:

	A	B	C	D	E
1	Statement of Retained Earnings				
2	Starting Balance of Retained Earnings			$135.75	
3	Plus: Net Income			10.78	
4	Less: Cash Dividends Paid				
5	Preferred Stock	$1.00			
6	Common Stock	2.50			
7	Total Cash Dividends Paid			$3.50	=B5+B6
8	Ending Balance of Retained Earnings			$143.03	=D2+D3-D7

Microsoft Excel

Similar to Problems 2-12, 2-14, and Self-Test Problem 1.

▼ **TABLE 2.4** Statement of Retained Earnings for DPH Tree Farm, Inc.

DPH TREE FARM, INC. Statement of Retained Earnings as of December 31, 2024 (in millions of dollars)		
Balance of retained earnings, December 31, 2023		$155
Plus: Net income for 2024		109
Less: Cash dividends paid		
Preferred stock	$10	
Common stock	44	
Total cash dividends paid		54
Balance of retained earnings, December 31, 2024		$210

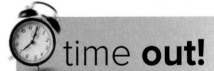

time out!

2-7 What is a statement of retained earnings?

2-8 If, during a given period, a firm pays out more in dividends than it has net income, what happens to the firm's retained earnings?

2.6 • CAUTIONS IN INTERPRETING FINANCIAL STATEMENTS LG2-6

As we mentioned earlier in the chapter, firms must prepare their financial statements according to GAAP. GAAP provides a common set of standards intended to produce objective and precise financial statements. But recall also that managers have significant discretion over their reported earnings. Managers and financial analysts have recognized for years that firms use considerable latitude in using accounting rules to manage their reported earnings in a wide variety of contexts. Indeed, within the GAAP framework, firms can "smooth" earnings. That is, firms often take steps to over- or understate earnings at various times. Managers may choose to smooth earnings to show investors that firm assets are growing steadily. Similarly, one firm may be using straight-line depreciation for its fixed

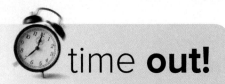

earnings management The process of controlling a firm's earnings.

Sarbanes-Oxley Act of 2002 Requires that a firm's senior management must sign off on the financial statements of the firm, certifying the statements as accurate and representative of the firm's financial condition during the period covered.

assets, while another is using a modified accelerated cost recovery method (MACRS), which causes depreciation to accrue quickly. If the firm uses MACRS accounting methods, its managers write fixed asset values down quickly; assets will thus have lower book values than if the firm used straight-line depreciation methods. Managers' choices in these areas make comparisons of such measures as EPS and BVPS across firms difficult.

This process of controlling a firm's earnings is called **earnings management.** At the extreme, earnings management has resulted in some widely reported accounting scandals involving Enron, Merck, WorldCom, and other major U.S. corporations that tried to artificially influence their earnings by manipulating accounting rules. Congress responded to the spate of corporate scandals that emerged after 2001 with the **Sarbanes-Oxley Act,** passed in June 2002. Sarbanes-Oxley requires public companies to ensure that their corporate boards' audit committees have considerable experience applying generally accepted accounting principles (GAAP) for financial statements. The act also requires that a firm's senior management must sign off on the financial statements of the firm, certifying the statements as accurate and representative of the firm's financial condition during the period covered. If a firm's board of directors or senior managers fail to comply with Sarbanes-Oxley (SOX), the firm may be delisted from stock exchanges.

In June 2020, Luckin Coffee was issued a delisting notice from NASDAQ for failure to comply with regulatory financial disclosure requirements, including various quarterly and annual reports, after financial fraud accusations. Congress's goal in passing SOX was to prevent deceptive accounting and management practices and to bring stability to jittery stock markets battered in 2002 by accounting and managerial scandals that cost employees their life savings and harmed many innocent shareholders as well. See also the discussion of the role of ethics in finance in Chapter 1.

finance at work//:markets

Luckin Coffee Delisted from NASDAQ

On June 29, 2020, the United States' NASDAQ Stock Market officially delisted controversial company Luckin Coffee, which effectively suspends trading of the stock on the NASDAQ capital market. Luckin Coffee is China's home-grown answer to Starbucks Coffee. Its business model was to offer low-priced coffee for takeout and delivery through an app. It argued that the app aspect made it a disrupter tech firm. Founded in 2017, the firm quickly opened 5,000 locations throughout China. It announced plans to operate 10,000 locations by the end of 2021. The firm listed on NASDAQ in May 2019 through an initial public offering (IPO) at $17 per share. The enthusiasm for the Chinese growth stock eventually pushed the stock to $51 per share in January 2020. But shares quickly plummeted after allegations of accounting fraud. The Securities and Exchange Commission investigated reports that showed Luckin fabricated revenue by $2.2 billion yuan (the equivalent of $310 million). It was delisted for failure to comply with regulatory financial disclosure requirements, including various quarterly and annual reports. Chinese regulators subsequently investigated Luckin Coffee and leveled fines for its financial fraud.

jmiks/Getty Images

Want to know more?

Key Words to Search for Updates: **stock delistings, Sarbanes-Oxley Act of 2002, mislead investors**

Get Online

mhhe.com/CornettM6e

for study materials including
quizzes, iPod downloads,
and video

JGI/Jamie Grill/Getty Images

Your Turn...

Questions

1. List and describe the four major financial statements. *(LG2-1)*

2. On which of the four major financial statements (balance sheet, income statement, statement of cash flows, or statement of retained earnings) would you find the following items? *(LG2-1)*

   a. Earnings before taxes.

   b. Net plant and equipment.

   c. Increase in fixed assets.

   d. Gross profits.

   e. Balance of retained earnings, December 31, 2024.

   f. Common stock and paid-in surplus.

   g. Net cash flow from investing activities.

   h. Accrued wages and taxes.

   i. Increase in inventory.

3. What is the difference between current liabilities and long-term debt? *(LG2-1)*

4. How does the choice of accounting method used to record fixed asset depreciation affect management of the balance sheet? *(LG2-1)*

5. What is bonus depreciation? How did the Tax Cuts and Jobs Act of 2017 temporarily extend and modify bonus depreciation? *(LG2-3)*

6. What are the costs and benefits of holding liquid securities on a firm's balance sheet? *(LG2-1)*

7. Why can the book value and market value of a firm differ? *(LG2-1)*

8. From a firm manager's or investor's point of view, which is more important—the book value of a firm or the market value of the firm? *(LG2-2)*

9. How did the Tax Cuts and Jobs Act of 2017 change corporate tax laws? *(LG2-3)*

10. What is the difference between an average tax rate and a marginal tax rate? *(LG2-3)*

11. How did the Tax Cuts and Jobs Act of 2017 change the tax deductibility of corporate interest on debt? *(LG2-3)*

12. How does the payment of interest on debt affect the amount of taxes the firm must pay? *(LG2-4)*

13. The income statement is prepared using GAAP. How does this affect the reported revenue and expense measures listed on the balance sheet? *(LG2-4)*

14. Why do financial managers and investors find cash flows to be more important than accounting profit? *(LG2-4)*

15. Which of the following activities result in an increase (decrease) in a firm's cash? *(LG2-5)*

    a. Decrease fixed assets.

    b. Decrease accounts payable.

    c. Pay dividends.

    d. Sell common stock.

    e. Decrease accounts receivable.

    f. Increase notes payable.

16. What is the difference between cash flows from operating activities, cash flows from investing activities, and cash flows from financing activities? *(LG2-5)*

17. What are free cash flows for a firm? What does it mean when a firm's free cash flow is negative? *(LG2-5)*

18. What is earnings management? *(LG2-6)*

19. What does the Sarbanes-Oxley Act require of firm managers? *(LG2-6)*

Problems

BASIC PROBLEMS

2-1 **Balance Sheet** You are evaluating the balance sheet for Goodman Bees Corporation. From the balance sheet you find the following balances: cash and marketable securities = $400,000, accounts receivable = $1,200,000, inventory = $2,100,000, accrued wages and taxes = $500,000, accounts payable = $800,000, and notes payable = $600,000. Calculate Goodman Bees' net working capital. *(LG2-1)*

2-2 **Balance Sheet** Casello Mowing & Landscaping's year-end balance sheet lists current assets of $435,200, fixed assets of $550,800, current liabilities of $416,600, and long-term debt of $314,500. Calculate Casello's total stockholders' equity. *(LG2-1)*

2-3 **Income Statement** The Fitness Studio, Inc.'s income statement lists the following income and expenses: EBITDA = $650,000, EBIT = $538,000, interest expense = $63,000, and net income = $435,000. Calculate the taxes reported on the income statement. *(LG2-1)*

2-4 **Income Statement** The Fitness Studio, Inc.'s income statement lists the following income and expenses: EBITDA = $923,000, EBIT = $773,500, interest expense = $100,000, and taxes = $234,500. The firm has no preferred stock outstanding and 100,000 shares of common stock outstanding. Calculate the earnings per share. *(LG2-1)*

2-5 **Income Statement** Consider a firm with an EBIT of $850,000. The firm finances its assets with $2,500,000 debt (costing 7.5 percent and is all tax deductible) and 400,000 shares of stock selling at $5.00 per share. To reduce the firm's risk associated with this financial leverage, the firm is considering reducing its debt by $1,000,000 by selling an additional 200,000 shares of stock. The firm's tax rate is 21 percent. The change in capital structure will have no effect on the operations of the firm. Thus, EBIT will remain at $850,000. Calculate the change in the firm's EPS from this change in capital structure. *(LG2-1)*

2-6 **Corporate Taxes** Oakdale Fashions, Inc.'s income statement is reported below.

Oakdale Fashions, Inc., Income Statement	
Net sales (all credit)	$565,000
Less: Cost of goods sold	215,000
Gross profits	$350,000
Less: Other operating expenses	90,000
EBITDA	$260,000
Less: Depreciation and amortization	15,000
EBIT	$245,000
Less: Interest	80,000
EBT	$165,000
Less: Taxes	
Net income	$

Determine the firm's tax liability, net income, average tax rate, and marginal tax rate. *(LG2-3)*

2-7 **Corporate Taxes** Hunt Taxidermy, Inc., is concerned about the taxes paid by the company. In addition to $42.4 million of taxable income, the firm received $2,975,000 of interest on state-issued bonds and $1,000,000 of dividends on common stock it owns in Oakdale Fashions, Inc. Calculate Hunt Taxidermy's tax liability, average tax rate, and marginal tax rate. *(LG2-3)*

2-8 **Corporate Taxes** Chapman & Power, Inc., is concerned about the taxes paid by the company. In addition to $135,000,000 of taxable income, the firm received $15,500,000 of interest on state-issued bonds and $12,000,000 of dividends on common stock it owns in Hunt Taxidermy. Calculate Chapman & Power's tax liability, average tax rate, and marginal tax rate. *(LG2-3)*

2-9 **Statement of Cash Flows** Ramakrishnan, Inc., reported 2024 net income of $15 million and depreciation of $2,650,000. The top part of Ramakrishnan, Inc.'s 2024 and 2023 balance sheets is reproduced below *(in millions of dollars):*

	2024	2023		2024	2023
Current assets:			Current liabilities:		
Cash and marketable securities	$ 20	$ 15	Accrued wages and taxes	$ 19	$ 18
Accounts receivable	84	75	Accounts payable	51	45
Inventory	121	110	Notes payable	45	40
Total	$225	$200	Total	$115	$103

Calculate the 2024 net cash flow from operating activities for Ramakrishnan, Inc. *(LG2-4)*

2-10 **Statement of Cash Flows** Usher Sports Shop had cash flows from investing activities of −$4,364,000 and cash flows from financing activities of −$5,880,000. The balance in the firm's cash account was $1,615,000 at the beginning of the year and $1,742,000 at year-end. Calculate Usher Sports Shop's cash flow from operations. *(LG2-4)*

2-11 **Free Cash Flow** You are considering an investment in Fields and Struthers, Inc., and want to evaluate the firm's free cash flow. From the income statement, you see that Fields and Struthers earned an EBIT of $62 million and had a tax rate of 21 percent; its depreciation expense was $5 million. Fields and Struthers's gross fixed assets increased by $32 million from last year to this year. The firm's current assets increased by $20 million and spontaneous current liabilities increased by $12 million. Calculate Fields and Struthers's NOPAT, operating cash flow, investment in operating capital, and free cash flow. *(LG2-5)*

2-12 **Statement of Retained Earnings** Mr. Husker's Tuxedos Corp. began the year with $256 million in retained earnings. The firm earned net income of $33 million and paid dividends of $5 million to its preferred stockholders and $10 million to its common stockholders. What is the year-end balance in retained earnings for Mr. Husker's Tuxedos? *(LG2-1)*

 2-13 **Spreadsheet Problem: Corporate Taxes** Everybody's Fitness's income statement is reported below *(in millions of dollars).*

	A	B
1	Everybody's Fitness Income Statement (in millions of dollars)	
2		
3	Net sales (all credit)	$ 885
4	Less: Cost of goods sold	440
5	Gross profits	445
6	Less: Other operating expenses	215
7	Earnings before interest, taxes, depreciation, and amortization (EBI	230
8	Less: Depreciation and amortization	52
9	Earnings before interest and taxes (EBIT)	178
10	Less: Interest	75
11	Earnings before taxes (EBT)	103
12	Less: Taxes	
13	Net income	$

Microsoft Excel

Determine the firm's tax liability, net income, average tax rate, and marginal tax rate. *(LG2-3)*

2-14 Spreadsheet Problem: Statement of Retained Earnings Use the following information to find dividends paid to common stockholders during 2024. *(LG2-1)*

	A	B	C
1	(in millions)		
2	Balance of retained earnings, December 31, 2023		$462
3	Plus: Net income for 2024		15
4	Less: Cash dividends paid		
5	Preferred stock	$1	
6	Common stock		
7	Total cash dividends paid		
8	Balance of retained earnings, December 31, 2024		$470

Microsoft Excel

INTERMEDIATE PROBLEMS

2-15 Balance Sheet Mikey's Bar and Grill has total assets of $15 million, of which $5 million are current assets. Cash makes up 10 percent of the current assets and accounts receivable makes up another 40 percent of current assets. Mikey's gross plant and equipment has a book value of $11.5 million, and other long-term assets have a book value of $500,000. Using this information, what is the balance of inventory and the balance of depreciation on Mikey's Bar and Grill's balance sheet? *(LG2-1)*

2-16 Balance Sheet Sophie's Tobacco Shop has total assets of $91.8 million. Fifty percent of these assets are financed with debt, of which $28.9 million is current liabilities. The firm has no preferred stock, but the balance in common stock and paid-in surplus is $20.4 million. Using this information, what is the balance for long-term debt and retained earnings on Sophie's Tobacco Shop's balance sheet? *(LG2-1)*

2-17 Market Value versus Book Value Muffin's Masonry, Inc.'s balance sheet lists net fixed assets as $14 million. The fixed assets could currently be sold for $19 million. Muffin's current balance sheet shows current liabilities of $5.5 million and net working capital of $4.5 million. If all the current accounts were liquidated today, the company would receive $7.25 million cash after paying the $5.5 million in current liabilities. What is the book value of Muffin's Masonry's assets today? What is the market value of these assets? *(LG2-2)*

2-18 Market Value versus Book Value Ava's SpinBall Corp. lists fixed assets of $12 million on its balance sheet. The firm's fixed assets have recently been appraised at $16 million. Ava's SpinBall Corp.'s balance sheet also lists current assets at $5 million. Current assets were appraised at $6 million. Current liabilities' book and market values stand at $3 million, and the firm's book and market values of long-term debt are $7 million. Calculate the book and market values of the firm's stockholders' equity. Construct the book value and market value balance sheets for Ava's SpinBall Corp. *(LG2-2)*

2-19 Debt versus Equity Financing You are considering a stock investment in one of two firms (NoEquity, Inc., and NoDebt, Inc.), both of which operate in the same industry and have identical EBITDA of $37.7 million and operating income of $32.5 million. NoEquity, Inc., finances its $65 million in assets with $64 million in debt (on which it pays 10 percent interest annually) and $1 million in equity. NoDebt, Inc., finances its $65 million in assets with no debt and $65 million in equity. Both firms pay a tax rate of 21 percent on their taxable income. Calculate the net income and return on assets—funders' investments—for the two firms. *(LG2-1)*

2-20 Income Statement You have been given the following information for Corky's Bedding Corp.:

a. Net sales = $11,250,000.

b. Cost of goods sold = $7,500,000.

c. Other operating expenses = $250,000.

d. Addition to retained earnings = $1,000,000.

e. Dividends paid to preferred and common stockholders = $817,000.

f. Interest expense = $850,000, all of which is tax deductible.

The firm's tax rate is 21 percent. Calculate the depreciation expense for Corky's Bedding Corp. *(LG2-1)*

2-21 Income Statement You have been given the following information for Moore's HoneyBee Corp.:

a. Net sales = $32,000,000.

b. Gross profit = $18,700,000.

c. Other operating expenses = $2,500,000.

d. Addition to retained earnings = $6,343,000

e. Dividends paid to preferred and common stockholders = $2,900,000.

f. Depreciation expense = $2,800,000.

The firm's tax rate is 21 percent. The firm's interest expense is all tax deductible. Calculate the cost of goods sold and the interest expense for Moore's HoneyBee Corp. *(LG2-1)*

2-22 Income Statement Consider a firm with an EBITDA of $1,100,000 and an EBIT of $1,000,000. The firm finances its assets with $4,500,000 debt (costing 8 percent, all of which is tax deductible) and 200,000 shares of stock selling at $16.00 per share. To reduce risk associated with this financial leverage, the firm is considering reducing its debt by $2,500,000 by selling additional shares of stock. The firm's tax rate is 21 percent. The change in capital structure will have no effect on the operations of the firm. Thus, EBIT will remain at $1,000,000. Calculate the change in the firm's EPS from this change in capital structure. *(LG2-1)*

2-23 Corporate Taxes The Dakota Corporation had a 2021 taxable income of $33,365,000 from operations after all operating costs but before (1) interest charges of $8,500,000, all of which is tax deductible; (2) dividends received of $750,000; (3) dividends paid of $5,250,000; and (4) income taxes. The firm's tax rate is 21 percent. *(LG2-3)*

a. Calculate Dakota's income tax liability.

b. What are Dakota's average and marginal tax rates on taxable income?

2-24 Statement of Cash Flows Use the balance sheet and income statement below to construct a statement of cash flows for Clancy's Dog Biscuit Corporation. *(LG2-5)*

CLANCY'S DOG BISCUIT CORPORATION
Balance Sheet as of December 31, 2024 and 2023
(in millions of dollars)

Assets	2024	2023	Liabilities and Equity	2024	2023
Current assets:			**Current liabilities:**		
Cash and marketable securities	$ 5	$ 5	Accrued wages and taxes	$ 10	$ 6
Accounts receivable	20	19	Accounts payable	16	15
Inventory	36	29	Notes payable	14	13
Total	$ 61	$ 53	Total	$ 40	$ 34
Fixed assets:			Long-term debt:	$ 57	$ 53
Gross plant and equipment	$ 106	$ 88			
Less: Accumulated depreciation	15	11	**Stockholders' equity:**		
	$ 91	$ 77	Preferred stock (2 million shares)	$ 2	$ 2
Net plant and equipment			Common stock and paid-in surplus (5 million shares)	11	11
			1. Numbered list		
			2. Numbered list		
			3. Numbered list		
Other long-term assets	15	15	Retained earnings	57	45
Total	$ 106	$ 92	Total	$ 70	$ 58
Total assets	$ 167	$ 145	Total liabilities and equity	$ 167	$ 145

CLANCY'S DOG BISCUIT CORPORATION
Income Statement for Years Ending December 31, 2024 and 2023
(in millions of dollars)

	2024	2023
Net sales	$ 76	$ 80
Less: Cost of goods sold	38	35
Gross profits	$ 38	$ 45
Less: Other operating expenses	6	5
Earnings before interest, taxes, depreciation, and amortization (EBITDA)	$ 32	$ 40
Less: Depreciation	4	4
Earnings before interest and taxes (EBIT)	$ 28	$ 36
Less: Interest	5	5
Earnings before taxes (EBT)	$ 23	$ 31
Less: Taxes	5	7
Net income	$ 18	$ 24
Less: Preferred stock dividends	$ 1	$ 1
Net income available to common stockholders	$ 17	$ 23
Less: Common stock dividends	5	5
Addition to retained earnings	$ 12	$ 18
Per (common) share data:		
Earnings per share (EPS)	$ 3.00	$ 4.20
Dividends per share (DPS)	$ 1.00	$ 1.00
Book value per share (BVPS)	$13.60	$11.20
Market value (price) per share (MVPS)	$14.25	$14.60

2-25 **Statement of Cash Flows** Chris's Outdoor Furniture, Inc., has net cash flows from operating activities for the last year of $340 million. The income statement shows that net income is $315 million and depreciation expense is $46 million. During the year, the change in inventory on the balance sheet was $38 million, change in accrued wages and taxes was $15 million, and change in accounts payable was $20 million. At the beginning of the year, the balance of accounts receivable was $50 million. Calculate the end-of-year balance for accounts receivable. *(LG2-5)*

2-26 **Statement of Cash Flows** Dogs 4 U Corporation has net cash flow from financing activities for the last year of $34 million. The company paid $178 million in dividends last year. During the year, the change in notes payable on the balance sheet was $39 million and change in common and preferred stock was $0. The end-of-year balance for long-term debt was $315 million. Calculate the beginning-of-year balance for long-term debt. *(LG2-5)*

2-27 **Free Cash Flow** The income statement for Duffy's Pest Control shows that depreciation expense was $197 million, EBIT was $440 million, and the tax rate was 21 percent. At the beginning of the year, the balance of gross fixed assets was $1,562 million and net operating working capital was $417 million. At the end of the year, gross fixed assets were $1,803 million. Duffy's free cash flow for the year was $424 million. Calculate the end-of-year balance for net operating working capital. *(LG2-5)*

2-28 **Free Cash Flow** The income statement for Egyptian Noise Blasters shows that depreciation expense is $85 million and NOPAT is $246 million. At the end of the year, the balance of gross fixed assets was $655 million. The change in net operating working capital during the year was $73 million. Egyptian's free cash flow for the year was $190 million. Calculate the beginning-of-year balance for gross fixed assets. *(LG2-5)*

2-29 **Statement of Retained Earnings** Thelma and Louie, Inc., started the year with a balance of retained earnings of $543 million and ended the year with retained earnings of $589 million. The company paid dividends of $35 million to the preferred stockholders and $88 million to common stockholders. Calculate Thelma and Louie's net income for the year. *(LG2-1)*

2-30 **Statement of Retained Earnings** Jamaica Tours, Inc., started the year with a balance of retained earnings of $1,780 million. The company reported net income for the year of $284 million and paid dividends of $17 million to the preferred stockholders and $59 million to common stockholders. Calculate Jamaica Tour's end-of-year balance in retained earnings. *(LG2-1)*

 2-31 **Spreadsheet Problem: Income Statement** Consider a firm with an EBITDA of $13,000,000 and an EBIT of $10,500,000. The firm finances its assets with $50,000,000 debt (costing 6.5 percent, all of which is tax deductible) and 10,000,000 shares of stock selling at $10.00 per share. The firm is considering increasing its debt by $25,000,000, using the proceeds to buy back shares of stock. The firm's tax rate is 21 percent. The change in capital structure will have no effect on the operations of the firm. Thus, EBIT will remain at $10,500,000. Calculate the change in the firm's EPS from this change in capital structure. *(LG2-1)*

	A	B	C	D	E	F
1		*Before capital structure change*			*After capital structure change*	
2	EBIT		$10,500,000			$10,500,000
3	Less: Interest	$50,000,000 x 0.065 =	3,250,000		$75,000,000 x 0.065 =	4,875,000
4	EBT					
5	Less: Taxes (21%)					
6	Net income					
7	Divide by # of shares					
8	EPS					

Microsoft Excel

2-32 **Spreadsheet Problem: Statement of Cash Flows** Use the balance sheet and income statement below to construct a statement of cash flows for Valium's Medical Supply Corporation. *(LG2-5)*

	A	B	C	D	E	F	G
1	VALIUM'S MEDICAL SUPPLY CORPORATION Balance Sheet as of December 31, 2024 and 2023						
2	(in millions of dollars)						
3		2024	2023			2024	2023
4	Assets				Liabilities and Equity		
5	Current Assets				Current liabilities		
6	Cash and marketable Securities	$ 74	$ 73		Accrued wages and taxes	$ 58	$ 45
7	Accounts receivable	199	199		Accounts payable	159	145
8	Inventory	322	291		Notes payable	131	131
9	Total	$ 595	$ 553		Total	$ 348	$ 321
10	Fixed Assets				Long-term debt	$ 565	$ 549
11	Gross plant and equipment	1,084	886		Stockholders' equity		
12	Less: Accumulated depreciation	153	116		Preferred stock (6 thousand shares)	$ 6	$ 6
13	Net plant and equipment	$ 931	$ 770		Common stock and paid-in surplus (100,000 shares)	120	120
14	Other long-term assets	130	130		Retained earnings	617	457
15	Total	$ 1,061	$ 900		Total	$ 743	$ 583
16	Total Assets	$ 1,656	$ 1,453		Total liabilities and equity	$ 1,656	$ 1,453

Microsoft Excel

	A	B	C
1	Valium's Medical Supply Corporation		
2	Income Statement for Years Ending December 31, 2024 and 2023		
3	(in millions of dollars)	2024	2023
4	Net sales	$888	$798
5	Less: Cost of goods sold	387	350
6	Gross profits	$501	$448
7	Less: Other operating expenses	48	42
8	Earnings before interest, taxes, depreciation, and amortization (EBITDA)	$453	$406
9	Less: Depreciation and amortization	37	35
10	Earnings before interest and taxes (EBIT)	$416	$371
11	Less: Interest	46	40
12	Earnings before taxes (EBT)	$370	$331
13	Less: Taxes	78	70
14	Net income	$292	$261
15	Less: Preferred stock dividends	$6	$6
16	Net income available to common stockholders	$286	$255
17	Less: Common stock dividends	126	126
18	Addition to retained earnings	$160	$129
19			
20	Per (common) share data:		
21	Earnings per share (EPS)	$2.86	$2.55
22	Dividends per share (DPS)	$1.26	$1.26
23	Book value per share (BVPS)	$7.37	$5.77
24	Market value (price) per share (MVPS)	$8.40	$6.25

Microsoft Excel

ADVANCED PROBLEMS

2-33 **Income Statement** Listed below is the income statement for Tom and Sue Travels, Inc. *(LG2-5)*

TOM AND SUE TRAVELS, INC. Income Statement for Year End (in millions of dollars)	
Net sales	$16.500
Less: Cost of goods sold	7.100
Gross profits	$ 9.400
Less: Other operating expenses	3.200
Earnings before interest, taxes, depreciation, and amortization (EBITDA)	$ 6.200
Less: Depreciation	2.900
Earnings before interest and taxes (EBIT)	$ 3.300
Less: Interest	0.950
Earnings before taxes (EBT)	$ 2.350
Less: Taxes	0.495
Net income	$ 1.855

The CEO of Tom and Sue's wants the company to earn a net income of $2.250 million next year. Cost of goods sold is expected to be 60 percent of net sales, depreciation and other operating expenses are not expected to change, interest expense is expected to increase to $1.050 million, and the firm's tax rate will be 21 percent. Calculate the net sales needed to produce net income of $2.250 million. *(LG2-1)*

2-34 Income Statement You have been given the following information for Patty-Cake's Athletic Wear Corp. for the year:

a. Net sales = $38,250,000.

b. Cost of goods sold = $22,070,000.

c. Other operating expenses = $5,300,000.

d. Addition to retained earnings = $2,195,500.

e. Dividends paid to preferred and common stockholders = $1,912,000.

f. Interest expense = $1,785,000.

g. The firm's tax rate is 21 percent.

Next year:

h. Net sales are expected to increase by $9.75 million.

i. Cost of goods sold is expected to be 60 percent of net sales.

j. Depreciation and other operating expenses are expected to be the same as in the last year.

k. Interest expense is expected to be $2,004,367.

l. The tax rate is expected to be 21 percent of EBT.

m. Dividends paid to preferred and common stockholders will not change.

Calculate the addition to retained earnings expected next year. *(LG2-1)*

 2-35 Spreadsheet Problem: Free Cash Flow Rebecky's Flowers 4U, Inc., had free cash flows during 2024 of $43 million, NOPAT of $85 million, and depreciation of $14 million. Using this information, fill in the blanks on Rebecky's balance sheet below. *(LG2-5)*

	A	B	C	D	E	F	G
1				Rebecky's Flowers 4U, Inc.			
2			Balance Sheet as of December 31, 2024 and 2023				
3				(in millions of dollars)			
4		2024	2023			2024	2023
5	**Assets**				**Liabilities and Equity**		
6							
7	Current assets:				Current liabilities		
8	Cash and marketable securities	$ 28	$ 25		Accrued wages and taxes	$ 17	$ 15
9	Accounts receivable	75	65		Accounts payable		50
10	Inventory	118	100		Notes payable	45	45
11	Total	$ 221	$ 190		Total		$ 110
12					Long-term debt:		$ 190
13	Fixed assets:						
14	Gross plant and equipment	$ 333	$ 300		Stockholders' equity:		
15	Less: Accumulated depreciation	54	40		Preferred stock (5 million shares)	$ 5	$ 5
16	Net plant and equipment	$ 279	$ 260		Common stock and paid-in surplus	40	40
17	Other long-term assets	50	50		(20 million shares)		
18	Total	$ 329	$ 310		Retained earnings	192	155
19					Total	$ 237	$ 200
20	Total assets	$ 550	$ 500		Total liabilities and equity	$ 550	$ 500

Microsoft Excel

2-36 **Spreadsheet Problem: Free Cash Flow** Vinny's Overhead Construction had free cash flow of $25.4 million. The change in gross fixed assets on Vinny's balance sheet was $7.0 million, the change in net operating working capital was $8.4 million, and the firm's tax rate was 21 percent. Using this information, fill in the blanks on Vinny's income statement below. *(LG2-5)*

◢	A	B
1	**Vinny's Overhead Construction, Corp.**	
2	**Income Statement for Year**	
3	**(in millions of dollars)**	
4	Net sales	
5	Less: Cost of goods sold	116.10
6	Gross profits	$ 66.00
7	Less: Other operating expenses	
8	Earnings before interest, taxes, depreciation, and amortization (EBITDA)	
9	Less: Depreciation	10.20
10	Earnings before interest and taxes (EBIT)	
11	Less: Interest	
12	Earnings before taxes (EBT)	
13	Less: Taxes (21% from above)	
14	Net income	$ 27.65

Microsoft Excel

Notes

CHAPTER 2

1. Technically, operating income and EBIT are different. Specifically, operating income is considered an official financial measure under GAAP, while EBIT is a non-GAAP measure. EBIT makes adjustment for items that are not accounted for in operating income. In a majority of cases, these differences are minimal and not crucially important to individual investors who are reviewing financial statements. As a result, operating income and EBIT are used interchangeably across much of the accounting and finance world.

2. This tax code provision prevents or reduces any triple taxation that could occur. Income could be taxed at three levels: (1) on the income from the dividend-paying firm, (2) as income for the dividend-receiving firm, and (3) finally, on the personal income of stockholders who receive dividends.

3. Any other noncash expense (e.g., amortization) would also be added back to net income and any noncash revenue would be subtracted.

Design elements: (Clock) Floortje/Getty Images; (Referee) Richard Ransier/Getty Images

Zigzag Mountain Art/Shutterstock

chapter three

analyzing
financial statements

We reviewed the major financial statements in Chapter 2. These financial statements
provide information on a firm's financial position at a point in time or its operations
over some past period of time. But the real value of these financial statements lies in
the fact that managers, investors, and analysts can use the information the statements contain to
analyze the current financial performance or condition of the firm. More importantly, managers can
use this information to plan changes that will improve the firm's future performance and, ultimately,
its market value. Managers, investors, and analysts universally use ratios to evaluate financial
statements. **Ratio analysis** involves calculating and analyzing financial ratios to assess a firm's
performance and to identify actions that could improve firm performance. The most frequently
used ratios fall into five groups: (1) liquidity ratios, (2) asset management ratios, (3) debt management ratios, (4) profitability ratios, and (5) market value ratios. Each of the five groups focuses on a
specific area of the financial statements that managers, investors, and analysts assess.

continued on p. 64

LEARNING GOALS

LG3-1 Calculate and interpret major liquidity ratios.

LG3-2 Calculate and interpret major asset management ratios.

LG3-3 Calculate and interpret major debt management ratios.

LG3-4 Calculate and interpret major profitability ratios.

LG3-5 Calculate and interpret major market value ratios.

LG3-6 Recognize how various ratios relate to one another.

LG3-7 Understand the differences between time series and cross-sectional ratio analyses.

LG3-8 Explain cautions that should be taken when examining financial ratios.

»viewpoints

business APPLICATION

The managers of DPH Tree Farm, Inc., have released public statements that the firm's performance surpasses that of other firms in the industry. They cite the firm's liquidity and asset management positions as particularly strong. DPH's superior performance in these areas has resulted in superior overall returns for their stockholders. What are the key financial ratios that DPH Tree Farm, Inc., needs to calculate and evaluate in order to justify these statements? **(See the solution at the end of the chapter.)**

ratio analysis The process of calculating and analyzing financial ratios to assess a firm's performance and to identify actions needed to improve firm performance.

liquidity ratios Measure the relationship between a firm's liquid (or current) assets and its current liabilities.

continued from p. 63

In this chapter, we review these ratios, describe what each ratio means, and identify the general trend (higher or lower) that managers and investment analysts look for in each ratio. Note as we review the ratios that the number calculated for a ratio is not always good or bad and that extreme values (either high or low) can be a bad sign for a firm. We will discuss how a ratio that seems too good can actually be bad for a company. We will also see how ratios interrelate—how a change in one ratio may affect the value of several ratios. It is often hard to make sense of a set of performance ratios. Thus, when managers or investors review a firm's financial position through ratio analysis, they often start by evaluating trends in the firm's financial ratios over time and by comparing their firm's ratios with those of other firms in the same industry. Finally, we discuss cautions that you should take when using ratio analysis to evaluate firm performance. As we go through the chapter, we show sample ratio analysis using the financial statements for DPH Tree Farm, Inc., listed in Tables 2.1 and 2.2. ■

3.1 • LIQUIDITY RATIOS LG3-1

As we stated in Chapter 2, firms need cash and other liquid assets (or current assets) to pay their bills (or current liabilities) as they come due. **Liquidity ratios** measure the relationship between a firm's liquid (or current) assets and its current liabilities. The three most commonly used liquidity ratios are the current ratio, the quick (or acid-test) ratio, and the cash ratio.

$$\text{Current ratio} = \frac{\text{Current assets}}{\text{Current liabilities}} \qquad (3\text{-}1)$$

The broadest liquidity measure, the current ratio, measures the dollars of current assets available to pay each dollar of current liabilities.

$$\text{Quick ratio (acid-test ratio)} = \frac{\text{Current assets} - \text{Inventory}}{\text{Current liabilities}} \qquad (3\text{-}2)$$

Inventories are generally the least liquid of a firm's current assets. Further, inventory is the current asset for which book values are the least reliable measures of market value. In practical terms, what this means is that if the firm must sell inventory to pay upcoming bills, the firm will most likely have to discount inventory items in order to liquidate them, and thus they are the current assets on which losses are most likely to occur. Therefore, the quick (or acid-test) ratio measures a firm's ability to pay off short-term obligations without

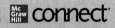
relying on inventory sales. The quick ratio measures the dollars of more liquid assets (cash and marketable securities and accounts receivable) available to pay each dollar of current liabilities.

$$\text{Cash ratio} = \frac{\text{Cash and marketable securities}}{\text{Current liabilities}} \qquad (3\text{-}3)$$

If the firm sells accounts receivable to pay upcoming bills, the firm must often discount the accounts receivable to sell them—the assets once again bring less than their book value. Therefore, the cash ratio measures a firm's ability to pay short-term obligations with its available cash and marketable securities.

Of course, liquidity on the balance sheet is important. The more liquid assets a firm holds, the less likely the firm is to experience financial distress. Thus, the higher the liquidity

EXAMPLE 3-1   Calculating Liquidity Ratios

For interactive versions of this example, log in to Connect or go to mhhe.com/Cornett6e.

Use the balance sheet (Table 2.1) for DPH Tree Farm, Inc., to calculate the firm's 2024 values for the liquidity ratios.

SOLUTION:

The liquidity ratios for DPH Tree Farm, Inc., are calculated as follows. The industry average is reported alongside each ratio.

$$\text{Current ratio} = \frac{\$205m}{\$123m} = 1.67 \text{ times} \qquad \text{Industry average} = 1.50 \text{ times}$$

$$\text{Quick ratio (acid-test ratio)} = \frac{\$205m - \$111m}{\$123m} = 0.76 \text{ times} \qquad \text{Industry average} = 0.50 \text{ times}$$

$$\text{Cash ratio} = \frac{\$24m}{\$123m} = 0.20 \text{ times} \qquad \text{Industry average} = 0.15 \text{ times}$$

All three liquidity ratios show that DPH Tree Farm, Inc., has more liquidity on its balance sheet than the industry average (we discuss the process used to develop an industry average in Section 3.8). Thus, DPH Tree Farm has more cash and other liquid assets (or current assets) available to pay its bills (or current liabilities) as they come due than does the average firm in the tree farm industry.

Similar to Problems 3-1, 3-13, and Self-Test Problem 1.

time out!

3-1 What are the three major liquidity ratios used in evaluating financial statements?

3-2 How do the three major liquidity ratios used in evaluating financial statements differ?

3-3 Does a firm generally want to have high or low liquidity ratios? Why?

ratios, the less liquidity risk a firm has. But as with everything else in business, high liquidity represents a painful trade-off for the firm. Liquid assets generate little, if any, profits for the firm. In contrast, fixed assets are illiquid but generate revenue for the firm. Thus, extremely high levels of liquidity guard against liquidity crises, but at the cost of lower returns on assets. High liquidity levels may actually show bad or indecisive firm management. Thus, in deciding the appropriate level of current assets to hold on the balance sheet, managers must consider the trade-off between the advantages of being liquid versus the disadvantages of reduced profits. Note that a company with very predictable cash flows can maintain low levels of liquidity without incurring much liquidity risk.

3.2 • ASSET MANAGEMENT RATIOS LG3-2

Asset management ratios measure how efficiently a firm uses its assets (inventory, accounts receivable, and fixed assets), as well as how efficiently the firm manages its accounts payable. The specific ratios allow managers and investors to evaluate whether a firm is holding a reasonable amount of each type of asset and whether management uses each type of asset to effectively generate sales. The most frequently used asset management ratios are listed in the following sections, grouped by type of asset.

Inventory Management

As they decide the optimal inventory level to hold on the balance sheet, managers must consider the trade-off between the advantages of holding sufficient levels of inventory to keep the production process going versus the costs of holding large amounts of inventory. Two frequently used ratios are the inventory turnover and days' sales in inventory.

$$\text{Inventory turnover} = \frac{\text{Sales or Cost of goods sold}}{\text{Inventory}} \qquad (3\text{-}4)$$

The inventory turnover ratio measures the number of dollars of sales produced per dollar of inventory. Cost of goods sold is used in the numerator when managers want to emphasize that inventory is listed on the balance sheet at cost, that is, the cost of sales generated per dollar of inventory.

$$\text{Days' sales in inventory} = \frac{\text{Inventory} \times 365 \text{ days}}{\text{Sales or Cost of goods sold}}$$
$$= \frac{365 \text{ days}}{\text{Inventory turnover}} \qquad (3\text{-}5)$$

The days' sales in inventory ratio measures the number of days that inventory is held before the final product is sold.

In general, a firm wants to produce a high level of sales per dollar of inventory; that is, it wants to turn inventory over (from raw materials to finished goods to sold goods) as quickly as possible. A high level of sales per dollar of inventory implies reduced warehousing, monitoring, insurance, and any other costs of servicing the inventory. So, a high inventory turnover ratio or a low days' sales in inventory is generally a sign of good management.

However, if the inventory turnover ratio is extremely high and the days' sales in inventory is extremely low, the firm may not be holding sufficient inventory to prevent running out (or stocking out) of the raw materials needed to keep the production process going. Thus, production and sales stop, which wastes the firm's fixed resources. So, extremely high levels for the inventory turnover ratio and low levels for the days' sales in inventory ratio may

The inventory turnover ratio measures the number of dollars of sales produced per dollar of inventory.
Ryan McVay/Getty Images

actually be a sign of bad firm or production management. Note that companies with very good supply chain relations can maintain lower levels of inventory without incurring as much risk of stockouts.

Accounts Receivable Management

As they decide the level of accounts receivable to hold on the firm's balance sheet, managers must consider the trade-off between the advantages of increased sales by offering customers better terms versus the disadvantages of financing large amounts of accounts receivable. Two ratios used here are the accounts receivable turnover and average collection period.

$$\text{Accounts receivable turnover} = \frac{\text{Credit sales}}{\text{Account receivable}} \qquad (3\text{-}6)$$

The accounts receivable turnover measures the number of dollars of sales produced per dollar of accounts receivable.

$$\begin{aligned} \text{Average collection period } (ACP) &= \frac{\text{Accounts receivable} \times 365 \text{ days}}{\text{Credit sales}} \\ &= \frac{365 \text{ days}}{\text{Accounts receivable turnover}} \end{aligned} \qquad (3\text{-}7)$$

The average collection period (ACP) measures the number of days accounts receivable are held before the firm collects cash from the sale. This ratio is also sometimes termed the days' sales outstanding (DSO).

In general, a firm wants to produce a high level of sales per dollar of accounts receivable; that is, it wants to collect its accounts receivable as quickly as possible to reduce any cost of financing accounts receivable, including interest expense on liabilities used to finance accounts receivable and defaults associated with accounts receivable. In general, a high accounts receivable turnover or a low ACP is a sign of good management, which is well aware of financing costs and customer remittance habits.

However, if the accounts receivable turnover is extremely high and the ACP is extremely low, the firm's accounts receivable policy may be so strict that customers prefer to do business with competing firms. Firms offer accounts receivable terms as an incentive to get customers to buy products from their firm rather than a competing firm. By offering customers the accounts receivable privilege, management allows them to buy (more) now and pay later. Without this incentive, customers may choose to buy the goods from the firm's competitors who offer better credit terms. So extremely high accounts receivable turnover levels and low ACP levels may be a sign of bad firm management.

Accounts Payable Management

As they decide the accounts payable level to hold on the balance sheet, managers must consider the trade-off between maximizing the use of free financing that raw material suppliers offer versus the risk of losing the opportunity to buy on account. Two ratios commonly used are the accounts payable turnover and average payment period.

$$\text{Account payable turnover} = \frac{\text{Cost of goods sold}}{\text{Accounts payable}} \qquad (3\text{-}8)$$

The accounts payable turnover ratio measures the dollar cost of goods sold per dollar of accounts payable.

$$\begin{aligned} \text{Average payment period } (APP) &= \frac{\text{Accounts payable} \times 365 \text{ days}}{\text{Cost of goods sold}} \\ &= \frac{365 \text{ days}}{\text{Accounts payable turnover}} \end{aligned} \qquad (3\text{-}9)$$

The average payment period (APP) measures the number of days that the firm holds accounts payable before it has to extend cash to pay for its purchases.

In general, a firm wants to pay for its purchases as slowly as possible. The slower the firm pays for its supply purchases, the longer it can avoid obtaining other costly sources of financing such as notes payable or long-term debt. Thus, a low accounts payable turnover or a high APP is generally a sign of good management.

However, if the accounts payable turnover is extremely low and the APP is extremely high, the firm may be abusing the credit terms that its raw materials suppliers offer. At some point, the firm's suppliers may revoke its ability to buy raw materials on account and the firm will lose this source of free financing. If this situation is developing, extremely low levels for the accounts receivable turnover and high levels for the APP may point to bad firm management.

Fixed Asset and Working Capital Management

Two ratios that summarize the efficiency in a firm's overall asset management are the fixed asset turnover and sales to working capital ratios.

$$\text{Fixed asset turnover} = \frac{\text{Sales}}{\text{Net fixed assets}} \qquad (3\text{-}10)$$

The fixed asset turnover ratio measures the number of dollars of sales produced per dollar of net fixed assets.

$$\text{Sales to working capital} = \frac{\text{Sales}}{\text{Working Capital}} \qquad (3\text{-}11)$$

Similarly, the sales to working capital ratio measures the number of dollars of sales produced per dollar of net working capital (current assets minus current liabilities).

In general, the higher the level of sales per dollar of fixed assets and working capital, the more efficiently the firm is being run. Thus, high fixed asset turnover and sales to working capital ratios are generally signs of good management. However, if either the fixed asset turnover or sales to working capital ratio is extremely high, the firm may be close to its maximum production capacity. If capacity is hit, the firm cannot increase production or sales. Accordingly, extremely high fixed asset turnover and sales to working capital ratio levels may actually indicate bad firm management if managers have allowed the company to approach maximum capacity without making any accommodations for growth.

Note a word of caution here. The age of a firm's fixed assets will affect the fixed asset turnover ratio level. A firm with older fixed assets, listed on its balance sheet at historical cost, will tend to have a higher fixed asset turnover ratio than will a firm that has just replaced its fixed assets and lists them on its balance sheet at a (most likely) higher value. Accordingly, the firm with newer fixed assets would have a lower fixed asset turnover ratio. But this is because it has updated its fixed assets, while the other firm has not. It is not correct to conclude that the firm with new assets is underperforming relative to the firm with older fixed assets listed on its balance sheet. Similarly, for firms that are in an expansion phase, a lower fixed asset turnover is actually a good sign. It is not correct to conclude that a firm with expanding assets is underperforming relative to a firm with no growth.

Total Asset Management

The final two asset management ratios put it all together. They are the total asset turnover and capital intensity ratios.

$$\text{Total asset turnover} = \frac{\text{Sales}}{\text{Total assets}} \qquad (3\text{-}12)$$

The total asset turnover ratio measures the number of dollars of sales produced per dollar of total assets.

$$\text{Capital intensity} = \frac{\text{Total assets}}{\text{Sales}} \qquad (3\text{-}13)$$

Similarly, the capital intensity ratio measures the dollars of total assets needed to produce a dollar of sales.

In general, a well-managed firm produces many dollars of sales per dollar of total assets, or uses few dollars of assets per dollar of sales. Thus, in general, the higher the total asset

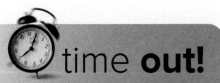

time out!

3-4 What are the major asset management ratios?

3-5 Does a firm generally want to have high or low values for each of these ratios?

3-6 Explain why many of these ratios are mirror images of one another.

EXAMPLE 3-2

Calculating Asset Management Ratios LG3-2

 For interactive versions of this example, log in to Connect or go to mhhe.com/Cornett6e.

Use the balance sheet (Table 2.1) and income statement (Table 2.2) for DPH Tree Farm, Inc., to calculate the firm's 2024 values for the asset management ratios.

SOLUTION:

We calculate the asset management ratios for DPH Tree Farm, Inc., as follows. The industry average is reported alongside each ratio.

i. Inventory turnover $= \dfrac{\$315m}{\$111m} = 2.84$ times Industry average $= 2.15$ times

ii. Days' sales in inventory $= \dfrac{\$111m \times 365 \text{ days}}{\$315m}$

$= \dfrac{365 \text{ days}}{2.84 \text{ times}} = 129$ days Industry average $= 170$ days

iii. Accounts receivable turnover $= \dfrac{\$315 m}{\$70 m} = 4.50$ times Industry average $= 3.84$ times

iv. Average collection period $= \dfrac{\$70m \times 365 \text{ days}}{\$315m}$

$= \dfrac{365 \text{ days}}{4.50 \text{ times}} = 81$ days Industry average $= 95$ days

v. Accounts payable turnover $= \dfrac{\$131m}{\$55m} = 2.38$ times Industry average $= 3.55$ times

vi. Average payment period $= \dfrac{\$55m \times 365 \text{ days}}{\$131m}$

$= \dfrac{365 \text{ days}}{2.38 \text{ times}} = 153$ days Industry average $= 102$ days

vii. Fixed asset turnover $= \dfrac{\$315m}{\$315m} = 1.00$ times Industry average $= 0.85$ times

viii. Sales to working capital $= \dfrac{\$315m}{\$205m - \$123m} = 3.84$ times Industry average $= 3.20$ times

ix. Total assets turnover $= \dfrac{\$315m}{\$570m} = 0.55$ times Industry average $= 0.40$ times

x. Capital intensity $= \dfrac{\$570m}{\$315m} = 1.81$ times Industry average $= 2.50$ times

In all cases, asset management ratios show that DPH Tree Farm, Inc., is outperforming the industry average. The firm is turning over its inventory faster than the average firm in the tree farm industry, thus producing more dollars of sales per dollar of inventory. It is also collecting its accounts receivable faster and paying its accounts payable slower than the average firm. Further, DPH Tree Farm is producing more sales per dollar of fixed assets, working capital, and total assets than the average firm in the industry.

Similar to Problems 3-2, 3-3, and Self-Test Problem 1.

turnover and lower the capital intensity ratio, the more efficient the overall asset management of the firm will be. However, if the total asset turnover is extremely high and the capital intensity ratio is extremely low, the firm may actually have an asset management problem. As described above, inventory stockouts, capacity problems, or tight account receivables policies can all lead to a high total asset turnover and may actually be signs of poor firm management.

3.3 • DEBT MANAGEMENT RATIOS LG3-3

As we discussed in Chapter 2, financial leverage refers to the extent to which the firm uses debt securities in its capital structure. The more debt a firm uses as a percentage of its total assets, the greater is its financial leverage. **Debt management ratios** measure the extent to which the firm uses debt (or financial leverage) versus equity to finance its assets as well as how well the firm can pay off its debt. The specific ratios allow managers and investors to evaluate whether a firm is financing its assets with a reasonable amount of debt versus equity financing, as well as whether the firm is generating sufficient earnings or cash to make the promised payments on its debt. The most commonly used debt management ratios are listed in the following sections.

Debt versus Equity Financing

Managers' choice of **capital structure**—the amount of debt versus equity to issue—affects the firm's viability as a long-term entity. In deciding the level of debt versus equity financing to hold on the balance sheet, managers must consider the trade-off between maximizing cash flows to the firm's stockholders versus the risk of being unable to make promised debt payments. Ratios that are commonly used are the debt ratio, debt-to-equity, and equity multiplier.

$$\text{Debt ratio} = \frac{\text{Total debt}}{\text{Total assets}} \tag{3-14}$$

The debt ratio measures the percentage of total assets financed with debt.

$$\text{Dept-to-equity} = \frac{\text{Total dept}}{\text{Total equity}} \tag{3-15}$$

The debt-to-equity ratio measures the dollars of debt financing used for every dollar of equity financing.

$$\text{Equity multiplier} = \frac{\text{Total assets}}{\text{Total equity}} \text{ or } \frac{\text{Total assets}}{\text{Common stockholders' equity}} \tag{3-16}$$

The equity multiplier ratio measures the dollars of assets on the balance sheet for every dollar of equity (or just common stockholders' equity) financing.

As you might suspect, all three measures are related.[1] Specifically,

$$\text{Debt ratio} = 1 - \frac{1}{\text{Equity multiplier}} = \frac{1}{(1/\text{Debt-to-equity}) + 1}$$

$$\text{Debt-to-equity} = \frac{1}{(1/\text{Debt ratio}) - 1} = \text{Equity multiplier} - 1$$

$$\text{Equity multiplier} = \frac{1}{(1 - \text{Debt ratio})} = \text{Debt-to-equity} + 1$$

Notice in all three ratios, the less debt (and more equity) a firm uses, the lower the value of the ratio. Conversely, the lower the debt, debt-to-equity, or equity multiplier, the less debt and more equity the firm uses to finance its assets (i.e., the bigger the firm's equity cushion).

When a firm issues debt to finance its assets, it gives the debt holders first claim to a fixed amount of its cash flows. Stockholders are entitled to any residual cash flows—those left after debt holders are paid. When a firm does well, financial leverage increases the reward to shareholders because the amount of cash flows promised to debt holders is constant and capped. So when firms do well, financial leverage creates more cash flows to share with stockholders—it magnifies the return to the stockholders of the firm (recall Example 2-5). This magnification is one reason that stockholders encourage the use of debt financing.

However, financial leverage also increases the firm's potential for financial distress and even failure. If the firm has a bad year and cannot make promised debt payments, debt holders can force the firm into bankruptcy. Thus, a firm's current and potential debt holders (and even stockholders) look at equity financing as a safety cushion that can absorb fluctuations in the firm's earnings and asset values and guarantee debt service payments. Clearly, the larger the fluctuations or variability of a firm's cash flows, the greater the need for an equity cushion.

The Tax Cuts and Jobs Act of 2017 contains a new limitation on the deductibility of net interest expense (interest expense − interest income) that exceeds 30 percent of a firm's adjusted taxable income, starting in 2018. For tax years beginning before January 1, 2022, adjusted taxable income is measured as a business's EBITDA. For subsequent tax years, adjusted taxable income is measured as EBIT, no longer including an add-back for depreciation and amortization. Thus, beginning in 2022, the new limitation will become more severe. Prior corporate tax laws generally allowed full deduction of interest paid or accrued by businesses. As a result, once a firm issues enough debt such that interest payments are no longer deductible, the tax benefits of additional debt do not apply, causing debt to no longer be an attractive option from stockholders' viewpoint.

EXAMPLE 3-3

For interactive versions of this example, log in to Connect or go to mhhe.com/Cornett6e.

Calculating Debt Management Ratios LG3-3

Use the balance sheet (Table 2.1) and income statement (Table 2.2) for DPH Tree Farm, Inc., to calculate the firm's 2024 values for the debt management ratios.

SOLUTION:

The debt management ratios for DPH Tree Farm, Inc., are calculated as follows. The industry average is reported alongside each ratio.

i. Debt ratio $= \dfrac{\$123m + 192m}{\$570m} = 55.26\%$ Industry average = 68.50%

ii. Debt-to-equity $= \dfrac{\$123m + 192m}{\$255m} = 1.24$ times   Industry average = 2.17 times

iii. Equity multiplier $= \dfrac{\$570m}{\$255m} = 2.24$ times   Industry average = 4.10 times

or $\dfrac{\$570m}{\$255m - \$5m} = 2.28$ times   Industry average = 4.14 times

iv. Times interest earned $= \dfrac{\$154m}{\$16m} = 9.62$ times   Industry average = 5.15 times

v. Fixed-charge coverage $= \dfrac{\$154m}{\$16m} = 9.62$ times   Industry average = 5.70 times

vi. Cash coverage $= \dfrac{\$154m + \$13m}{\$16m} = 10.44$ times   Industry average = 7.78 times

In all cases, debt management ratios show that DPH Tree Farm, Inc., holds less debt on its balance sheet than the average firm in the tree farm industry. Further, the firm has more dollars of operating earnings and cash available to meet each dollar of interest obligations (there are no other fixed charges listed on DPH Tree Farm's income statement) on the firm's debt. This lack of financial leverage decreases the firm's potential for financial distress and even failure, but may also decrease equity shareholders' chance for magnified earnings. If the firm has a bad year, it has promised relatively few payments to debt holders. Thus, the risk of bankruptcy is small. However, when DPH Tree Farm, Inc., does well, the low level of financial leverage dilutes the return to the stockholders of the firm. This dilution of profit is likely to upset common stockholders of the firm.

Similar to Problems 3-4, 3-5, and Self-Test Problem 1.

Coverage Ratios

Three additional debt management ratios are the times interest earned, fixed-charge coverage, and cash coverage ratios. These ratios are different measures of a firm's ability to meet its debt obligations.

$$\text{Times interest earned} = \frac{EBIT}{\text{Interest}} \qquad (3\text{-}17)$$

The times interest earned ratio measures the number of dollars of operating earnings available to meet each dollar of interest obligations on the firm's debt.

$$\text{Fixed-charge coverage} = \frac{\text{Earnings available to meet fixed charges}}{\text{Fixed charges}} \qquad (3\text{-}18)$$

The fixed-charge coverage ratio measures the number of dollars of operating earnings available to meet the firm's interest obligations and other fixed charges.

$$\text{Cash coverage} = \frac{EBIT + \text{Depreciation}}{\text{Fixed charges}} \qquad (3\text{-}19)$$

The cash coverage ratio measures the number of dollars of operating *cash* available to meet each dollar of interest and other fixed charges that the firm owes.

With the help of the times interest earned, fixed-charge coverage, and cash coverage ratios, managers, investors, and analysts can determine whether a firm has taken on a debt burden that is too large. These ratios measure the dollars available to meet debt and other fixed-charge obligations. A value of one for these ratios means that $1 of earnings or cash is available to meet each dollar of interest or fixed-charge obligations. A value of less (greater) than one means that the firm has less (more) than $1 of earnings or cash available to pay each dollar of interest or fixed-charge obligations.[2] Further, the higher the times interest earned, fixed-charge coverage, and cash coverage ratios, the more equity and less debt the firm uses to finance its assets. Thus, low levels of debt will lead to a dilution of the return to stockholders due to increased use of equity as well as to not taking advantage of the tax deductibility of interest expense.

time out!

3-7 What are the major debt management ratios?

3-8 Does a firm generally want to have high or low values for each of these ratios?

3-9 What is the trade-off between using too much financial leverage and not using enough leverage? Who is likely to complain the most in each case?

3.4 • PROFITABILITY RATIOS LG3-4

The liquidity, asset management, and debt management ratios examined so far allow for an isolated or narrow look at a firm's performance. **Profitability ratios** show the combined effects of liquidity, asset management, and debt management on the overall operating results of the firm. Profitability ratios are among the most watched and best known of the financial ratios. Indeed, firm values (or stock prices) react quickly to unexpected changes in these ratios. The most commonly used profitability ratios are listed below.

$$\text{Gross profit margin} = \frac{\text{Sales} - \text{Cost of goods sold}}{\text{Sales}} \qquad (3\text{-}20)$$

The gross profit margin is the percent of sales left after costs of goods sold are deducted.

$$\text{Operating profit margin} = \frac{EBIT}{\text{Sales}} \qquad (3\text{-}21)$$

The operating profit margin is the percent of sales left after all operating expenses are deducted.

$$\text{Profit margin} = \frac{\text{Net income available to common stockholders}}{\text{Sales}} \qquad (3\text{-}22)$$

The profit margin is the percentage of sales left after all firm expenses are deducted. Thus, this ratio provides the net profit margin of the firm, as opposed to the gross profit or operating profit margin.

A company's profit margin is inversely related to its sales.
B.O'Kane/Alamy Stock Photo

$$\text{Basic earnings power } (BEP) = \frac{EBIT}{\text{Total assets}} \qquad (3\text{-}23)$$

The basic earnings power ratio measures the operating return on the firm's assets, regardless of financial leverage and taxes. This ratio measures the operating profit (EBIT) earned per dollar of assets on the firm's balance sheet.

$$\text{Return on assets } (ROA) = \frac{\text{Net income available to common stockholders}}{\text{Total assets}} \qquad (3\text{-}24)$$

Return on assets (ROA) measures the overall return on the firm's assets, including financial leverage and taxes. This ratio is the net income earned per dollar of assets on the firm's balance sheet.

$$\text{Return on equity } (ROE) = \frac{\text{Net income available to common stockholders}}{\text{Common stockholders' equity}} \qquad (3\text{-}25)$$

EXAMPLE 3-4

For interactive versions of this example, log in to Connect or go to mhhe.com/Cornett6e.

Calculating Profitability Ratios

Use the balance sheet (Table 2.1) and income statement (Table 2.2) for DPH Tree Farm, Inc., to calculate the firm's 2024 values for the profitability ratios.

SOLUTION:

The profitability ratios for DPH Tree Farm, Inc., are calculated as follows. The industry average is reported alongside each ratio.

i. Gross profit margin $= \dfrac{\$184m}{\$315m} = 58.41\%$ industry average $= 56.65\%$

ii. Opening profit margin $= \dfrac{\$154m}{\$315m} = 48.89\%$ industry average $= 46.88\%$

iii. Profit margin $= \dfrac{\$99m}{\$315m} = 31.43\%$ industry average $= 28.25\%$

iv. Basic earnings power $(BEP) = \dfrac{\$154m}{\$570m} = 27.02\%$ industry average $= 22.85\%$

v. Return on assets $(ROA) = \dfrac{\$99m}{\$570m} = 17.37\%$ industry average $= 11.30\%$

vi. Return on equity $(ROE) = \dfrac{\$99m}{\$40m + \$210m} = 39.60\%$ industry average $= 46.78\%$

vii. Dividend payout $= \dfrac{\$44m}{\$99m} = 44.44\%$ industry average $= 43.00\%$

These ratios show that DPH Tree Farm, Inc., is more profitable than the average firm in the tree farm industry. The profit margin, gross profit margin, operating profit margin, BEP, and ROA are all higher than industry figures. Despite this, the ROE for DPH Tree Farm is much lower than the industry average. DPH's low debt level and high equity level relative to the industry are the main reason for DPH's strong figures relative to the industry. As we mentioned above, DPH's managerial decisions about capital structure dilute its returns, which will likely upset its common stockholders. To counteract common stockholders' discontent, DPH Tree Farm pays out a slightly larger percentage of its income to its common stockholders as cash dividends. Of course, this slightly high dividend payout ratio means that DPH Tree Farm retains less of its profits to reinvest into the business. A profitable firm that retains its earnings increases its equity capital level as well as its own value.

Similar to Problems 3-6, 3-7, and Self-Test Problem 1.

market value ratios Ratios that relate a firm's stock price to its earnings and book value.

Return on equity (ROE) measures the return on the common stockholders' investment in the assets of the firm. ROE is the net income earned per dollar of common stockholders' equity. The value of a firm's ROE is affected not only by net income, but also by the amount of financial leverage or debt that firm uses. As stated previously, financial leverage magnifies the return to the stockholders of the firm. However, financial leverage also increases the firm's potential for financial distress and even failure. Generally, a high ROE is considered to be a positive sign of firm performance. However, if performance comes from a high degree of financial leverage, a high ROE can indicate a firm with an unacceptably high level of bankruptcy risk as well.

$$\text{Dividend payout} = \frac{\text{Common stock dividends}}{\text{Net income available to common stockholders}} \tag{3-26}$$

Finally, the dividend payout ratio is the percentage of net income available to common stockholders that the firm actually pays as cash to these investors.

For all but the dividend payout, the higher the value of the ratio, the higher the profitability of the firm. But just as has been the case previously in this chapter, high profitability ratio levels may result from poor management in other areas of the firm as much as superior financial management. A high profit (and gross profit or operating profit) margin means that the firm has low expenses relative to sales. The BEP reflects how much the firm's assets earn from operations, regardless of financial leverage and taxes. It follows logically that managers, investors, and analysts find BEP a useful ratio when they compare firms that differ in financial leverage and taxes. In contrast, ROA measures the firm's overall performance. It shows how the firm's assets generate a return that includes financial leverage and tax decisions made by management.

ROE measures the return on common stockholders' investment. Because managers seek to maximize common stock price, managers, investors, and analysts monitor ROE above all other ratios. The dividend payout ratio measures how much of the profit the firm retains versus how much it pays out to common stockholders as dividends. The lower the dividend payout ratio, the more profits the firm retains for future growth or other projects. A profitable firm that retains its earnings increases its level of equity capital as well as its own value.

time out!

3-10 What are the major profitability ratios?

3-11 Does a firm generally want to have high or low values for each of these ratios?

3-12 What are the trade-offs to having especially high or low values for ROE?

3.5 • MARKET VALUE RATIOS LG3-5

As noted, ROE is the most important financial statement ratio for managers and investors to monitor. Generally, a high ROE is considered to be a positive sign of firm performance. However, if a high ROE results from a highly leveraged position, it can signal a firm with a high level of bankruptcy risk. While ROE does not directly incorporate this risk, for publicly traded firms, market prices of the firm's stock do. (We look at stock valuation in Chapter 8.) Since the firm's stockholders earn their returns primarily from the firm's stock market value, ratios that incorporate stock market values are equally, and arguably more, important than other financial statement ratios.

The final group of ratios is market value ratios. **Market value ratios** relate a firm's stock price to its earnings and its book value. For publicly traded firms, market value ratios measure what investors think of the company's future performance and risk.

$$\text{Market-to-book ratio} = \frac{\text{Market price per share}}{\text{Book value per share}} \tag{3-27}$$

The market-to-book ratio measures the amount that investors will pay for the firm's stock per dollar of equity used to finance the firm's assets. Book value per share is an accounting-based number reflecting the firm's assets' historical costs, and hence historical value. The market-to-book ratio compares the market (current) value of the firm's equity to its historical cost. In general, the higher the market-to-book ratio, the better the firm. If liquidity, asset management, debt management, and accounting profitability are good for a firm,

EXAMPLE 3-5

For interactive versions of this example, log in to Connect or go to mhhe.com/Cornett6e.

Calculating Market Value Ratios

Use the balance sheet (Table 2.1) and income statement (Table 2.2) for DPH Tree Farm, Inc., to calculate the firm's 2024 values for the market value ratios.

SOLUTION:

The market value ratios for DPH Tree Farm, Inc., are calculated as follows. The industry average is reported alongside each ratio.

i. Market-to-book ratio $= \dfrac{\$17.25}{\$12.50} = 1.38$ times   Industry average $= 2.15$ times

ii. Price-earnings (*PE*) ratio $= \dfrac{\$17.25}{\$4.95} = 3.48$ times   Industry average $= 5.25$ times

These ratios show that DPH Tree Farm's investors will not pay as much for a share of DPH's stock per dollar of book value and earnings as the average for the industry. DPH's low leverage level and high reliance on equity relative to the industry are likely the main reason for investors' disinterest. As mentioned previously, DPH's seemingly intentional return dilution will likely upset the firm's common stockholders. Accordingly, stockholders lower the amount they are willing to invest per dollar of book value and EPS.

Similar to Problems 3-8 and Self-Test Problem 1.

then the market-to-book ratio will be high. A market-to-book ratio greater than one (or 100 percent) means that stockholders will pay a premium over book value for their equity investment in the firm.

$$\text{Price-earnings } (PE) \text{ ratio} = \frac{\text{Market price per share}}{\text{Earnings per share}} \qquad (3\text{-}28)$$

One of the best-known and most often-quoted figures, the price-earnings (or PE) ratio measures how much investors are willing to pay for each dollar the firm earns per share of its stock. PE ratios are often quoted in multiples—the number of dollars per share—that fund managers, investors, and analysts compare within industry classes. Managers and investors often use PE ratios to evaluate the relative financial performance of the firm's stock. Generally, the higher the PE ratio, the better the firm's performance. Analysts and investors, as well as managers, expect companies with high PE ratios to experience future growth, to have rapid future dividend increases, or both, because retained earnings will support the company's goals. However, for value-seeking investors, high PE firms indicate expensive companies. Further, higher PE ratios carry greater risk because investors are willing to pay higher prices today for a stock in anticipation of higher earnings in the future. These earnings may or may not materialize. Low PE firms are generally companies with little expected growth or low earnings. However, note that earnings depend on many factors (such as financial leverage or taxes) that have nothing to do directly with firm operations.

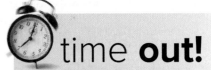

time out!

3-13 What are the major market value ratios?

3-14 Does a firm generally want to have high or low values for each of these ratios?

3-15 Discuss the price-earnings ratio and explain why it assumes particular importance among all of the other ratios we have presented.

3.6 • DUPONT ANALYSIS LG3-6

Table 3.1 lists the ratios we discuss; their values for DPH Tree Farm, Inc., as of 2021; and the corresponding values for the tree farm industry. The value of each ratio for DPH Tree Farm is highlighted in green if it is generally stronger than the industry and is highlighted in red if it is generally a negative sign for the firm. As we noted in this chapter's

	Value for DPH Tree Farm, Inc.	Value for the Tree Farm Industry
Liquidity ratios:		
Current ratio $= \dfrac{\text{Current assets}}{\text{Current liabilities}}$	1.67 times	1.50 times
Quick ratio (acid-test ratio) $= \dfrac{\text{Current assests} - \text{Inventory}}{\text{Current liabilities}}$	0.76 times	0.50 times
Cash ratio $= \dfrac{\text{Cash and marketable Securities}}{\text{Current liabilities}}$	0.20 times	0.15 times
Asset management ratios:		
Inventory turnover $= \dfrac{\text{Sales or cost of goods sold}}{\text{Inventory}}$	2.84 times	2.15 times
Days' sales in inventory $= \dfrac{\text{Inventory} \times 365 \text{ days}}{\text{Sales or Cost of goods sold}}$	129 days	170 days
Accounts receivable turnover $= \dfrac{\text{Credit sales}}{\text{Accounts receivable}}$	4.50 times	3.84 times
Average collection period $= \dfrac{\text{Accounts receivable} \times 365 \text{ days}}{\text{Credit sales}}$	81 days	95 days
Accounts payable turnover $= \dfrac{\text{Cost of goods sold}}{\text{Accounts payable}}$	2.38 times	3.55 times
Average payment period (APP) $= \dfrac{\text{Acconts payable} \times 365 \text{ days}}{\text{Cost of goods sold}}$	153 days	102 days
Fixed asset turnover $= \dfrac{\text{Sales}}{\text{Net fixed assets}}$	1.00 times	0.85 times
Sales to working capital $= \dfrac{\text{Sales}}{\text{Working capital}}$	3.84 times	3.20 times
Total assets turnover $= \dfrac{\text{Sales}}{\text{Total assets}}$	0.55 times	0.40 times
Capital intensity $= \dfrac{\text{Total assets}}{\text{Sales}}$	1.81 times	2.50 times
Debt management ratios:		
Debt ratio $= \dfrac{\text{Total debt}}{\text{Total assets}}$	55.26%	68.50%
Debt-to-equity $= \dfrac{\text{Total dept}}{\text{Total equity}}$	1.24 times	2.17 times
Equity multiplier $= \dfrac{\text{Total assets}}{\text{Total equity}}$	2.24 times	4.10 times
or $\dfrac{\text{Tota assets}}{\text{Common stockholders' equity}}$	2.28 times	4.14 times
Times interest earned $= \dfrac{EBIT}{\text{Interest}}$	9.62 times	5.15 times
Fixed-charge coverage $= \dfrac{\text{Earnings available to meet fixed charges}}{\text{Fixed charges}}$	9.62 times	5.70 times
Cash coverage $= \dfrac{EBIT + \text{Depreciation}}{\text{Fixed charges}}$	10.44 times	7.78 times

Profitability ratios:

Gross profit margin $= \dfrac{\text{Sales } - \text{ Cost of goods sold}}{\text{Sales}}$	58.41%	56.65%
Operating profit margin $= \dfrac{EBIT}{\text{Sales}}$	48.29%	46.88%
Profit margin $= \dfrac{\text{Net income available to common stockholders}}{\text{Sales}}$	31.43%	28.25%
Basic earning power $= \dfrac{EBIT}{\text{Total assets}}$	27.02%	22.85%
Return on assets $= \dfrac{\text{Net income available to common stockholders}}{\text{Total Sales}}$	17.37%	11.30%
Return on equity $= \dfrac{\text{Net income available to common stockholders}}{\text{Common stockholders' equity}}$	39.60%	46.78%
Divident payout $= \dfrac{\text{Common stock dividends}}{\text{Net income available to common stockholders}}$	44.44%	43.00%

Market value ratios:

Market-to-book ratio $= \dfrac{\text{Market price per share}}{\text{Earnings per share}}$	1.38 times	2.15 times
Price-earnings ratio $= \dfrac{\text{Market price per share}}{\text{Earnings per share}}$	3.48 times	5.25 times

introduction, many of the ratios we have discussed thus far are interrelated, so a change in one ratio may well affect the value of several ratios. Often these interrelations can help evaluate firm performance. Managers and investors often perform a detailed analysis of ROA (return on assets) and ROE (return on equity) using the **DuPont system of analysis**. Popularized by the DuPont Corporation, the DuPont system of analysis uses the balance sheet and income statement to break the ROA and ROE ratios into component pieces.

> **DuPont system of analysis**
> An analytical method that uses the balance sheet and income statement to break the ROA and ROE ratios into component pieces.

The basic DuPont equation looks at ROA as the product of the profit margin and the total asset turnover ratios:

$$ROA \quad = \quad \text{Profit margin} \quad \times \text{ Total asset turnover}$$

$$\frac{\text{Net income available to common stockholders}}{\text{Total assets}} = \frac{\text{Net income available to common stockholders}}{\text{Sales}} \times \frac{\text{Sales}}{\text{Total assets}} \quad (3\text{-}29)$$

The basic DuPont equation looks at the firm's overall profitability as a function of the profit the firm earns per dollar of sales (operating efficiency) and the dollar of sales produced per dollar of assets on the balance sheet (efficiency in asset use). With this tool, managers can see the reason for any changes in ROA in more detail. For example, if ROA increases, the DuPont equation may show that the net profit margin was constant, but the total asset turnover (efficiency in using assets) increased, or that total asset turnover remained constant, but profit margins (operating efficiency) increased. Managers can identify the reasons for an ROA change more specifically by using the ratios described above to further break down operating efficiency and efficiency in asset use.

FIGURE 3.1 DuPont System Analysis Breakdown of ROA and ROE

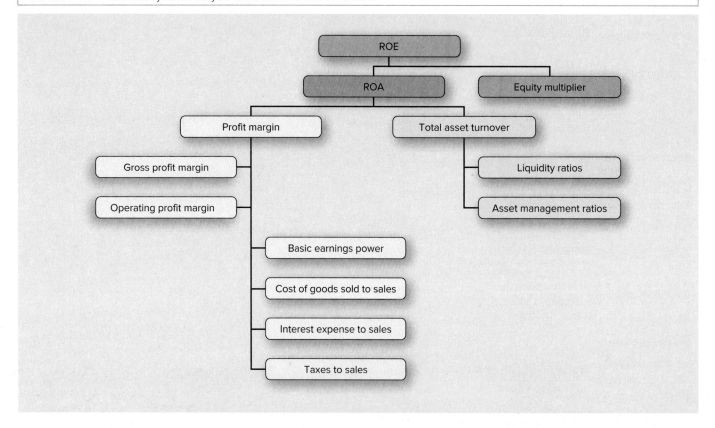

Next, the DuPont system looks at ROE as the product of ROA and the equity multiplier.

$$ROE = ROA \times \text{Equity multiplier}$$

$$\frac{\text{Net income available to common stockholders}}{\text{Common stockholders' equity}} = ROA \times \frac{\text{Total assets}}{\text{Common stockholders' equity}} \qquad (3\text{-}30)$$

Notice that this version of the equity multiplier uses the return to common stockholders (the firm's owners) only. So the DuPont equity multiplier uses common stockholders' equity only, rather than total equity (which includes preferred stock).

Taking this breakdown one step further, the DuPont system breaks ROE into the product of the profit margin, the total asset turnover, and the equity multiplier.

$$ROE = \text{Profit margin} \times \text{Total asset turnover} \times \text{Equity multiplier}$$

$$\frac{\text{Net income available to common stockholders}}{\text{Common stockholders' equity}} = \frac{\text{Net income available to common stockholders}}{\text{Sales}} \times \frac{\text{Sales}}{\text{Total assets}} \times \frac{\text{Total assets}}{\text{Common stockholders' equity}} \qquad (3\text{-}31)$$

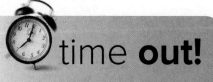

time **out!**

3-16 What are the DuPont ROA and ROE equations?

3-17 How does each of these equations help to explain firm performance and pinpoint areas for improvement?

This presentation of ROE allows managers, analysts, and investors to look at the return on equity as a function of the net profit margin (profit per dollar of sales from the income statement), the total asset turnover (efficiency in the use of assets from the balance sheet), and the equity multiplier (financial leverage from the balance sheet). Again, we can break these components down to identify possible causes for an ROE change more specifically. Figure 3.1 illustrates the DuPont system of analysis breakdown of ROA and ROE. The figure highlights how many of the ratios discussed in this chapter are linked.

Application of DuPont Analysis LG3-6

For interactive versions of this example, log in to Connect or go to mhhe.com/Cornett6e.

Use the balance sheet (Table 2.1) and income statement (Table 2.2) for DPH Tree Farm, Inc., to calculate the firm's 2024 values for the DuPont equations.

SOLUTION:

The ROA and ROE DuPont equations for DPH Tree Farm, Inc., are calculated as follows. The industry average is reported below for each ratio.

i.
$$ROA = \text{Profit margin} \times \text{Total asset turnover}$$
$$17.37\% = 31.428571\% \times 0.55263 \text{ times}$$
$$\text{Industry average: } 11.30\% = 28.25\% \times 0.40 \text{ times}$$

$$\frac{\text{Net income available to common stockholders}}{\text{Total assets}} = \frac{\text{Net income available to common stockholders}}{\text{Sales}} \times \frac{\text{Sales}}{\text{Total assets}}$$

$$\frac{\$99m}{\$570m} = \frac{\$99m}{\$315m} \times \frac{\$315m}{\$570m}$$

ii.
$$ROE = \text{Profit margin} \times \text{Total asset turnover} \times \text{Equity multiplier}$$
$$39.60\% = 31.428571\% \times 0.55263 \text{ times} \times 2.28 \text{ times}$$
$$\text{Industry average: } 46.78\% = 28.25\% \times 0.40 \text{ times} \times 4.14 \text{ times}$$

$$\frac{\text{Net income available to common stockholders}}{\text{Common stockholders' equity}} = \frac{\text{Net income available to common stockholders}}{\text{Sales}} \times \frac{\text{Sales}}{\text{Total assets}} \times \frac{\text{Total assets}}{\text{Common stockholders' equity}}$$

$$\frac{\$99m}{\$40m + \$210m} = \frac{\$99m}{\$315m} \times \frac{\$315m}{\$570m} \times \frac{\$570m}{\$40m + \$210m}$$

As we saw with profitability ratios, DPH Tree Farm, Inc., is more profitable than the average firm in the tree farm industry when it comes to overall efficiency expressed as return on assets, or ROA. The DuPont equation highlights that this superior performance comes from both profit margin (operating efficiency) and total asset turnover (efficiency in asset use). Despite this, the ROE for DPH Tree Farm lags the average industry ROE. The DuPont equation highlights that this inferior performance is due solely to the low level of debt and high level of equity used by DPH Tree Farm relative to the industry.

Similar to Problems 3-9 and 3-10.

3.7 • OTHER RATIOS LG3-6

Spreading the Financial Statements

In addition to the many ratios listed, managers, analysts, and investors can also compute additional ratios by dividing all balance sheet amounts by total assets and all income statement amounts by net sales. These calculations, sometimes called *spreading the financial statements,* yield what we call **common-size financial statements** that correct for sizes. Year-to-year growth rates in common-size balance sheets and income statement balances provide useful ratios for identifying trends. They also allow for an easy comparison of balance sheets and income statements across firms in the industry. Common-size financial statements may provide quantitative clues about the direction that the firm (and perhaps the industry) is moving. They may thus provide roadmaps for managers' next moves.

common-size financial statements Dividing all balance sheet amounts by total assets and all income statement amounts by net sales.

Internal and Sustainable Growth Rates

Remember again that any firm manager's job is to maximize the firm's market value. The firm's ROA and ROE can be used to evaluate the firm's ability to grow and its market value to be maximized. Specifically, managers, analysts, and investors use these ratios to calculate two growth measures: the internal growth rate and the sustainable growth rate.

The **internal growth rate** is the growth rate a firm can sustain if it uses only internal financing—that is, retained earnings—to finance future growth. Mathematically, the internal growth rate is

$$\text{Internal growth rate} = \frac{ROA \times RR}{1 - (ROA \times RR)} \qquad (3\text{-}32)$$

where RR is the firm's earnings retention ratio. The retention ratio represents the portion of net income that the firm reinvests as retained earnings:

$$\text{Retention ration } (RR) = \frac{\text{Addition to retained earnings}}{\text{Net income available to common stockholders}} \qquad (3\text{-}33)$$

Because a firm either pays its net income as dividends to its stockholders or reinvests those funds as retained earnings, the dividend payout and the retention ratios must always add to one:

$$\text{Retention ratio} = 1 - \text{Dividend payout ratio} \qquad (3\text{-}34)$$

EXAMPLE 3-7

For interactive versions of this example, log in to Connect or go to mhhe.com/Cornett6e.

Calculating Internal and Sustainable Growth Rates LG3-6

Use the balance sheet (Table 2.1) and income statement (Table 2.2) for DPH Tree Farm, Inc., to calculate the firm's 2024 values for the internal and sustainable growth rates.

SOLUTION:

The internal and sustainable growth rates for DPH Tree Farm, Inc., are calculated as follows. The industry average is reported alongside each ratio.

$$\text{Retention rate } (RR) = \frac{\$210m - \$155m}{\$99m}$$
$$= 0.5556 \text{ or } 55.56\%$$

$$\text{Industry RR} = 1 - \text{Industry dividend payout ratio}$$
$$= 1 - 0.43112 = 0.56888$$

i. $\text{Internal growth rate} = \frac{0.1737 \times 0.5556}{1 - (0.1737 \times 0.5556)}$
$$= 0.1068 \text{ or } 10.68\%$$

Industry average/
$$\text{internal growth rate} = \frac{0.1130 \times 0.56888}{1 - (0.1130 \times 0.56888)}$$
$$= 0.0687 \text{ or } 6.87\%$$

ii. $\text{Sustainable growth rate} = \frac{0.3960 \times 0.5556}{1 - (0.3960 \times 0.5556)}$
$$= 0.2821 \text{ or } 28.21\%$$

Industry average sustainable growth rate $= \frac{0.4678 \times 0.56888}{1 - (0.4678 \times 0.56888)}$
$$= 0.3626, \text{ or } 36.26\%$$

These ratios show that DPH Tree Farm, Inc., can grow faster than the industry if the firm uses only retained earnings to finance the growth. However, if DPH grows while keeping the debt ratio constant (e.g., both debt and retained earnings are used to finance the growth), industry firms can grow much faster than DPH Tree Farm. Once again, DPH's low debt level and high equity level relative to the industry create this disparity. Therefore, DPH Tree Farm limits its growth as a result of its managerial decisions.

Similar to Problems 3-11, 3-12, and Self-Test Problem 2.

the
Math Coach on...

66 When putting values into the equation, enter them in decimal format, not percentage format:
CORRECT: 1 − (0.1737 × 0.5556)
NOT CORRECT: 1 − (17.37 × 55.56) 99

A problem arises when a firm relies only on internal financing to support asset growth: Through time, its debt ratio will fall because as asset values grow, total debt stays constant—only retained earnings finance asset growth. If total debt remains constant as assets grow, the debt ratio decreases. As we noted above, shareholders often become disgruntled if, as the firm grows, a decreasing debt ratio (increasing equity financing) dilutes their return. So as firms grow, managers must often try to maintain a debt ratio that they view as optimal. In this case, managers finance asset growth with new debt *and* retained earnings. The maximum growth rate that can be achieved this way is the **sustainable growth rate**. Mathematically, the sustainable growth rate is

$$\text{Sustainable growth rate} = \frac{ROE \times RR}{1 - (ROE \times RR)} \qquad (3\text{-}35)$$

Maximizing the sustainable growth rate helps firm managers maximize firm value. When applying the DuPont ROE equation (3-31) here (i.e., ROE = Profit margin × Total asset turnover × Equity multiplier), notice that a firm's sustainable growth depends on four factors:

1. The profit margin (operating efficiency).

2. The total asset turnover (efficiency in asset use).

3. Financial leverage (the use of debt versus equity to finance assets).

4. Profit retention (reinvestment of net income into the firm rather than paying it out as dividends).

Increasing any of these factors increases the firm's sustainable growth rate and hence helps to maximize firm value. Managers, analysts, and investors will want to focus on these areas as they evaluate firm performance and market value.

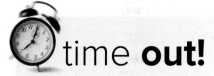

time **out!**

3-18 What does "spreading the financial statements" mean?

3-19 What are retention rates and internal and sustainable growth rates?

3-20 What factors enter into sustainable growth rates?

3.8 • TIME SERIES AND CROSS-SECTIONAL ANALYSES LG3-7

We have explored many ratios that allow managers and investors to examine firm performance. But to really analyze performance in a meaningful way, we must interpret our ratio results against some kind of standard or benchmark. To interpret financial ratios, managers, analysts, and investors use two major types of benchmarks: (1) performance of the firm over time (**time series analysis**) and (2) performance of the firm against one or more companies in the same industry (**cross-sectional analysis**).

Analyzing ratio trends over time, along with absolute ratio levels, gives managers, analysts, and investors information about whether a firm's financial condition is improving or deteriorating. For example, ratio analysis may reveal that the days' sales in inventory is increasing. This suggests that inventories, relative to the sales they support, are not being used as well as they were in the past. If this increase is the result of a deliberate policy to increase inventories to offer customers a wider choice and if it results in higher future sales volumes or increased margins that more than compensate for increased capital tied up in inventory, the increased relative size of the inventories is good for the firm. Managers and investors should be concerned, on the other hand, if increased inventories result from declining sales but steady purchases of supplies and production.

Looking at one firm's financial ratios, even through time, gives managers, analysts, and investors only a limited picture of firm performance. Ratio analysis almost always includes a comparison of one firm's ratios relative to the ratios of other firms in the industry, or cross-sectional analysis. The key to cross-sectional analysis is identifying similar firms that compete in the same markets, have similar asset sizes, and operate in a similar manner to the firm being analyzed. Because no two firms are identical, obtaining such a comparison group is no easy task. Thus, the choice of which companies to use in a cross-sectional analysis is at best subjective. Note that as we calculated the financial ratios for DPH Tree Farm, Inc., throughout the chapter, we compared them to the industry average. Comparative ratios that can be used in cross-sectional analysis are available from many sources. For example, Value Line Investment Surveys (www.valueline.com), Risk Management Association (www.rmahq.org/who-we-are), Hoover's Online (at www.hoovers.com), and MSN Money (at msn.com/en-us/money) are examples of four major sources of financial ratios for numerous industries that operate within the United States and worldwide.

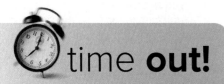

time out!

3-21 What is time series analysis of a firm's operations?

3-22 What is cross-sectional analysis of a firm's operations?

3-23 How do time series and cross-sectional analyses differ, and what information would you expect to gain from each?

3.9 • CAUTIONS IN USING RATIOS TO EVALUATE FIRM PERFORMANCE LG3-8

Financial statement analysis allows managers, analysts, and investors to better understand a firm's performance. However, data from financial statements should not be received without certain cautions. These include

1. Financial statement data are historical. Historical data may not reflect future performance. While we can make projections using historical data, we must also remember that projections may be inaccurate if historical performance does not persist.

2. As we discussed in Chapter 2, firms use different accounting procedures. For example, inventory methods can vary. One firm may use FIFO (first-in, first-out), transferring inventory at the first purchase price, while another uses LIFO (last-in, first-out), transferring inventory at the last purchase price. Likewise, the depreciation method used to value a firm's fixed assets over time may vary across firms. One firm may use straight-line depreciation, while another may use an accelerated depreciation method (e.g., MACRS). Particularly when reviewing cross-sectional ratios, differences in accounting rules can affect balance sheet values and financial ratios. It is important to know which accounting rules the firms under consideration are using before making any conclusions about their performance from ratio analysis.

3. Similarly, a firm's cross-sectional competitors may often be located around the world. Financial statements for firms based outside the United States do not necessarily conform to GAAP. Even beyond inventory pricing and depreciation methods, different accounting standards and procedures make it hard to compare financial statements and ratios of firms based in different countries.

4. Sales and expenses vary throughout the year. Managers, analysts, and investors need to note the timing of these fund flows when performing cross-sectional analysis. Otherwise they may draw conclusions from comparisons that are actually the result of seasonal

cash flow differences. Similarly, firms end their fiscal years at different dates. For cross-sectional analysis, this complicates any comparison of balance sheets during the year. Likewise, one-time events, such as a merger, may affect a firm's financial performance. Cross-sectional analysis involving these events can result in misleading conclusions.

5. Large firms often have multiple divisions or business units engaged in different lines of business. In this case, it is difficult to truly compare a set of firms with which managers and investors can perform cross-sectional analysis.

6. Firms often window-dress their financial statements to make annual results look better. For example, to improve liquidity ratios calculated with year-end balance sheets, firms often delay payments for raw materials, equipment, loans, and so on to build up their liquid accounts and thus their liquidity ratios. If possible, it is often more accurate to use something other than year-end financial statements to conduct ratio analysis.

7. Individual analysts may calculate ratios in modified forms. For example, one analyst may calculate ratios using year-end balance sheet data, while another may use the average of the beginning- and end-of-year balance sheet data. If the firm's balance sheet has changed significantly during the year, this difference in the way the ratio is calculated can cause large variations in ratio values for a given period of analysis and large variations in any conclusions drawn from these ratios regarding the financial health of the firm.

Financial statement ratio analysis is a major part of evaluating a firm's performance. If managers, analysts, or investors ignore the issues noted here, they may well draw faulty conclusions from their analysis. However, used intelligently and with good judgment, ratio analysis can provide useful information on a firm's current position and hint at future performance.

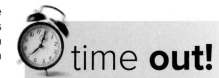

time out!

3-24 What cautions should managers and investors take when using ratio analysis to evaluate a firm?

Get Online

mhhe.com/CornettM6e

for study materials including quizzes, iPod downloads, and video

JGI/Jamie Grill/Getty Images

Your Turn...

Questions

1. Classify each of the following ratios according to a ratio category (liquidity ratio, asset management ratio, debt management ratio, profitability ratio, or market value ratio). *(LG3-1 through LG3-5)*

   a. Current ratio
   b. Inventory turnover
   c. Return on assets
   d. Average payment period
   e. Times interest earned
   f. Capital intensity
   g. Equity multiplier
   h. Basic earnings power

2. For each of the following actions, determine what would happen to the current ratio. Assume nothing else on the balance sheet changes and that net working capital is positive. *(LG3-1)*

   a. Accounts receivable are paid in cash.
   b. Notes payable are paid off with cash.
   c. Inventory is sold on account.
   d. Inventory is purchased on account.
   e. Accrued wages and taxes increase.
   f. Long-term debt is paid with cash.
   g. Cash from a short-term bank loan is received.

3. Explain the meaning and significance of the following ratios. *(LG3-1 through LG3-5)*

   a. Quick ratio
   b. Average collection period
   c. Return on equity
   d. Days' sales in inventory
   e. Debt ratio
   f. Profit margin
   g. Accounts payable turnover
   h. Market-to-book ratio

4. A firm has an average collection period of 10 days. The industry average ACP is 25 days. Is this a good or poor sign about the management of the firm's accounts receivable? *(LG3-2)*

5. A firm has a debt ratio of 20 percent. The industry average debt ratio is 65 percent. Is this a good or poor sign about the management of the firm's financial leverage? *(LG3-3)*

6. A firm has an ROE of 20 percent. The industry average ROE is 12 percent. Is this a good or poor sign about the management of the firm? *(LG3-4)*

7. Why is the DuPont system of analysis an important tool when evaluating firm performance? *(LG3-6)*

8. A firm has an ROE of 10 percent. The industry average ROE is 15 percent. How can the DuPont system of analysis help the firm's managers identify the reasons for this difference? *(LG3-6)*

9. What is the difference between the internal growth rate and the sustainable growth rate? *(LG3-6)*

10. What is the difference between time series analysis and cross-sectional analysis? *(LG3-7)*

11. What information do time series and cross-sectional analyses provide for firm managers, analysts, and investors? *(LG3-7)*

12. Why is it important to know a firm's accounting rules before making any conclusions about its performance from ratios analysis? *(LG3-8)*

13. What does it mean when a firm window-dresses its financial statements? *(LG3-8)*

Problems

BASIC PROBLEMS

3-1 Liquidity Ratios You are evaluating the balance sheet for SophieLex's Corporation. From the balance sheet you find the following balances: cash and marketable securities = $400,000; accounts receivable = $1,200,000; inventory = $2,100,000; accrued wages and taxes = $500,000; accounts payable = $800,000; and notes payable = $600,000. Calculate SophieLex's current ratio, quick ratio, and cash ratio. *(LG3-1)*

3-2 Asset Management Ratios Tater and Pepper Corp. reported sales of $23 million. Tater and Pepper listed $5.6 million of inventory on its balance sheet. Using a 365-day year, how many days did Tater and Pepper's inventory stay on the premises? How many times per year did Tater and Pepper's inventory turn over? *(LG3-2)*

3-3 Asset Management Ratios Mr. Husker's Tuxedos Corp. ended the year with an average collection period of 32 days. The firm's credit sales were $56.1 million. What is the year-end balance in accounts receivable for Mr. Husker's Tuxedos? *(LG3-2)*

3-4 Debt Management Ratios Tiggie's Dog Toys, Inc., reported a debt-to-equity ratio of 1.75 times at the end of 2024. If the firm's total debt at year-end was $25 million, how much equity does Tiggie's have on its balance sheet? *(LG3-3)*

3-5 Debt Management Ratios You are considering a stock investment in one of two firms (LotsofDebt, Inc., and LotsofEquity, Inc.), both of which operate in the same industry. LotsofDebt, Inc., finances its $30 million in assets with $29 million in debt and $1 million in equity. LotsofEquity, Inc., finances its $30 million in assets with $1 million in debt and $29 million in equity. Calculate the debt ratio, equity multiplier, and debt-to-equity ratio for the two firms. *(LG3-3)*

3-6 Profitability Ratios Maggie's Skunk Removal Corp.'s income statement listed net sales of $12.5 million, gross profit of $6.9 million, EBIT of $5.6 million, net income available to common stockholders of $3.2 million, and common stock dividends of $1.2 million. The year-end balance sheet listed total assets of $52.5 million and common stockholders' equity of $21 million with 2 million shares outstanding. Calculate the gross profit margin, operating profit margin, profit margin, basic earnings power, ROA, ROE, and dividend payout. *(LG3-4)*

3-7 Profitability Ratios Jake's Jamming Music, Inc., announced an ROA of 8.56 percent, ROE of 14.5 percent, and profit margin of 20.5 percent. The firm had total assets of $9.5 million at year-end 2024. Calculate the values of net income available to common stockholders, common stockholders' equity, and net sales for Jake's Jamming Music, Inc. *(LG3-4)*

3-8 Market Value Ratios You are considering an investment in Roxie's Bed & Breakfast Corp. During the last year, the firm's income statement listed an addition to retained earnings of $4.8 million and common stock dividends of $2.2 million. Roxie's year-end balance sheet shows common stockholders' equity of $35 million with 10 million shares of common stock outstanding. The common stock's market price per share was $9.00. What are Roxie's Bed & Breakfast's book value per share and earnings per share? Calculate the market-to-book ratio and PE ratio. *(LG3-5)*

3-9 **DuPont Analysis** If Silas 4-Wheeler, Inc., has an ROE of 18 percent, equity multiplier of 2, and profit margin of 18.75 percent, what are the total asset turnover and the capital intensity? *(LG3-6)*

3-10 **DuPont Analysis** Last year, Hassan's Madhatter, Inc., had an ROA of 7.5 percent, a profit margin of 12 percent, and sales of $25 million. Calculate Hassan's Madhatter's total assets. *(LG3-6)*

3-11 **Internal Growth Rate** Last year, Lakesha's Lounge Furniture Corporation had an ROA of 7.5 percent and a dividend payout ratio of 25 percent. What is the internal growth rate? *(LG3-6)*

3-12 **Sustainable Growth Rate** Last year Lakesha's Lounge Furniture Corporation had an ROE of 17.5 percent and a dividend payout ratio of 20 percent. What is the sustainable growth rate? *(LG3-6)*

3-13 **Spreadsheet Problem: Liquidity Ratios** The top part of Ramakrishnan, Inc.'s 2024 and 2023 balance sheets is listed below *(in millions of dollars)*. Calculate Ramakrishnan, Inc.'s current ratio, quick ratio, and cash ratio for 2024 and 2023. *(LG3-1)*

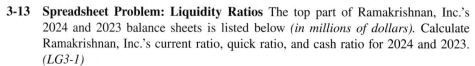

◢	A	B	C	D	E	F	G	H
1			**2024**	**2023**			**2024**	**2023**
2		**Assets**				**Liabilities & Equity**		
3	Current assets					Current liabilities		
4		Cash and marketable securities	$ 34	$ 25		Accrued wages and taxes	$ 32	$ 31
5		Accounts receivable	143	128		Accounts payable	87	75
6		Inventory	206	187		Notes payable	76	68
7		Total	$ 383	$ 340		Total	$ 195	$ 175

Microsoft Excel

INTERMEDIATE PROBLEMS

3-14 **Liquidity Ratios** Brenda's Bar and Grill has current liabilities of $15 million. Cash makes up 10 percent of the current assets and accounts receivable makes up another 40 percent of current assets. Brenda's current ratio is 2.1 times. Calculate the value of inventory listed on the firm's balance sheet. *(LG3-1)*

3-15 **Liquidity and Asset Management Ratios** Mandesa, Inc., has current liabilities of $8 million, current ratio of 2 times, inventory turnover of 12 times, average collection period of 30 days, and credit sales of $64 million. Calculate the value of cash and marketable securities. *(LG3-1, LG3-2)*

3-16 **Asset Management and Profitability Ratios** You have the following information on Els' Putters, Inc.: Sales to working capital is 4.6 times, profit margin is 20 percent, net income available to common stockholders is $5 million, and current liabilities are $6 million. What is the firm's balance of current assets? *(LG3-2, LG3-4)*

3-17 **Debt Management Ratios** Tiggie's Dog Toys, Inc., reported a debt-to-equity ratio of 1.75 times at the end of the year. If the firm's total assets at year-end were $25 million, how much of its assets are financed with debt and how much with equity? *(LG3-3)*

3-18 **Debt Management Ratios** Calculate the times interest earned ratio for LaTonya's Flop Shops, Inc., using the following information. Sales are $1.5 million, cost of goods sold is $600,000, depreciation expense is $150,000, other operating expenses are $300,000, addition to retained earnings is $176,625, dividends per share is $1, tax rate is 21 percent, and number of shares of common stock outstanding is 90,000. LaTonya's Flop Shops has no preferred stock outstanding. *(LG3-3)*

3-19 Profitability and Asset Management Ratios You are thinking of investing in Nikki T's, Inc. You have only the following information on the firm at year-end: Net income is $250,000, total debt is $2.5 million, and debt ratio is 55 percent. What is Nikki T's ROE for next year? *(LG3-2, LG3-4)*

3-20 Profitability Ratios Rick's Travel Service has asked you to help piece together financial information on the firm for the most current year. Managers give you the following information: Sales are $8.2 million, total debt is $2.1 million, debt ratio is 40 percent, and ROE is 18 percent. Using this information, calculate Rick's ROA. *(LG3-4)*

3-21 Market Value Ratios Leonatti Labs' year-end price on its common stock is $35. The firm has total assets of $50 million, debt ratio of 65 percent, no preferred stock, and 3 million shares of common stock outstanding. Calculate the market-to-book ratio for Leonatti Labs. *(LG3-5)*

3-22 Market Value Ratios Leonatti Labs' year-end price on its common stock is $15. The firm has a profit margin of 8 percent, total assets of $42 million, a total asset turnover of 0.75, no preferred stock, and 3 million shares of common stock outstanding. Calculate the PE ratio for Leonatti Labs. *(LG3-5)*

3-23 DuPont Analysis Last year, Stumble-on-Inn, Inc., reported an ROE of 18 percent. The firm's debt ratio was 55 percent, sales were $15 million, and the capital intensity was 1.25 times. Calculate the net income for Stumble-on-Inn last year. *(LG3-6)*

3-24 DuPont Analysis You are considering investing in Nuran Security Services. You have been able to locate the following information on the firm: Total assets are $24 million, accounts receivable are $3.3 million, ACP is 25 days, net income is $3.5 million, and debt-to-equity is 1.2 times. Calculate the ROE for the firm. *(LG3-6)*

3-25 Internal Growth Rate Dogs R Us reported a profit margin of 10.5 percent, total asset turnover of 0.75 times, debt-to-equity of 0.80 times, net income of $500,000, and dividends paid to common stockholders of $200,000. The firm has no preferred stock outstanding. What is Dogs R Us's internal growth rate? *(LG3-6)*

3-26 Sustainable Growth Rate You have located the following information on Webb's Heating & Air Conditioning: Debt ratio is 54 percent, capital intensity is 1.10 times, profit margin is 12.5 percent, and the dividend payout is 25 percent. Calculate the sustainable growth rate for Webb. *(LG3-6)*

Use the following financial statements for Lake of Egypt Marina, Inc., to answer Problems 3-27 through 3-30.

			2024	2023						2024	2023
						Lake of Egypt Marina, Inc.					
						Balance Sheet					
						(in millions of dollars)					
	Assets					**Liabilities & Equity**					
Current assets:						Current liabilities					
	Cash and marketable securities		$ 75	$ 65			Accrued wages and taxes			$ 40	$ 43
	Accounts receivable		115	110			Accounts payable			90	80
	Inventory		200	190			Notes payable			80	70
		Total	390	365				Total		210	193
Fixed assets:						Long-term debt:				192	190
	Gross plant and equipment		580	471		Total debt:				300	280
	Less: Depreciation		110	100		Stockholders' equity:					
	Net plant and equipment		470	371			Preferred stock (5 million shares)			5	5
	Other long-term assets		50	49			Common stock and paid-in surplus			65	65
		Total	520	420		Retained earnings				330	242
							Total			400	312
Total assets			$ 910	$ 785		Total liabilities and equity				$ 910	$ 785

Microsoft Excel

◢	A	B	C	D	E	F	G	H
22			Lake of Egypt Marina, Inc.					
23			Income Statement					
24			(in millions of dollars)					
25							**2024**	**2023**
26	Net sales (all credit)						$ 515	$ 432
27	Less: Cost of goods sold						230	175
28	Gross profits						285	257
29	Less: Other operating expenses						30	25
30	Earnings before interest, taxes, depreciation and amortization (EBITDA)						255	232
31	Less: Depreciation and amortization						22	20
32	Earnings before interest and taxes (EBIT)						233	212
33	Less: Interest						33	30
34	Earnings before taxes (EBT)						200	182
35	Less: Taxes						57	55
36	Net income						$ 143	$ 127
37								
38	Less: Preferred stock dividends						$ 5	$ 5
39	Net income available to common stockholders						$ 138	$ 122
40	Less: Common stock dividends						$ 65	$ 65
41	Addition to retained earnings						$ 73	$ 57
42	Per (common) share data:							
43		Earnings per share (EPS)					$ 2.123	$ 1.877
44		Dividends per share (DPS)					$ 1.000	$ 1.000
45		Book value per share (BV)					$ 6.077	$ 4.723
46		Market value (price) per share (MV)					$ 14.750	$ 12.550

Microsoft Excel

3-27 **Spreadsheet Problem: Spreading the Financial Statements** Spread the balance sheets and income statements of Lake of Egypt Marina, Inc., for 2024 and 2023. *(LG3-6)*

3-28 **Spreadsheet Problem: Calculating Ratios** Calculate the following ratios for Lake of Egypt Marina, Inc., as of year-end. *(LG3-1 through LG3-5)*

Lake of Egypt Marina, Inc.	Industry
a. Current ratio	2.00 times
b. Quick ratio	1.20 times
c. Cash ratio	0.42 times
d. Inventory turnover	3.60 times
e. Days' sales in inventory	101.39 days
f. Average collection period	32.50 days
g. Average payment period	45.00 days
h. Fixed asset turnover	1.25 times
i. Sales to working capital	4.25 times
j. Total asset turnover	0.85 times
k. Capital intensity	1.18 times
l. Debt ratio	62.50%
m. Debt-to-equity	1.67 times

Lake of Egypt Marina, Inc.	Industry
n. Equity multiplier (total equity)	2.67 times
o. Times interest earned	8.50 times
p. Cash coverage	8.75 times
q. Profit margin	30.75%
r. Gross profit margin	56.45%
s. Operating profit margin	46.78%
t. Basic earnings power	32.50%
u. ROA	19.75%
v. ROE	51.35%
w. Dividend payout	35.00%
x. Market-to-book ratio	2.55 times
y. PE ratio	15.60 times

3-29 **Spreadsheet Problem: DuPont Analysis** Construct the DuPont ROA and ROE breakdowns for Lake of Egypt Marina, Inc. *(LG3-6)*

3-30 **Spreadsheet Problem: Internal and Sustainable Growth Rates** Calculate the internal and sustainable growth rates for Lake of Egypt Marina, Inc. *(LG3-6)*

ADVANCED PROBLEMS

3-31 **Ratio Analysis** Use the following information to complete the balance sheet below. *(LG3-1 through LG3-5)* Current ratio = 2.5 times

Profit margin = 10%

Sales = $1,200m

ROE = 20%

Long-term debt to long-term debt and equity = 55%

Current assets	$ ____	Current liabilities	$ 210
Fixed assets	____	Long-term debt	____
		Stockholders' equity	____
Total assets	$ ____	Total liabilities and equity	$ ____

3-32 **DuPont Analysis** Last year, K9 WebbWear, Inc., reported an ROE of 20 percent. The firm's debt ratio was 55 percent, sales were $20 million, and the capital intensity was 1.25 times. Calculate the net income and profit margin for K9 WebbWear last year. This year, K9 WebbWear plans to increase its debt ratio to 60 percent. The change will not affect sales or total assets; however, it will reduce the firm's profit margin to 11 percent. By how much will the change in K9 WebbWear's debt ratio affect its ROE? *(LG3-6)*

3-33 **DuPont Analysis** You are considering investing in Dakota's Security Services. You have been able to locate the following information on the firm: Total assets are $32 million, accounts receivable are $4.4 million, ACP is 25 days, net income is $4.66 million, and debt-to-equity is 1.2 times. All sales are on credit. Dakota's is considering loosening its credit policy such that ACP will increase to 30 days. The change is expected to increase credit sales by 5 percent. Any change in accounts receivable will be offset with a change in debt. No other balance sheet changes are expected. Dakota's profit margin will remain unchanged. How will this change in accounts receivable policy affect Dakota's net income, total asset turnover, equity multiplier, ROA, and ROE? *(LG3-6)*

3-34 Internal Growth Rate Last year, Marly Brown, Inc., reported an ROE of 20 percent. The firm's debt-to-equity was 1.50 times, sales were $20 million, the capital intensity was 1.25 times, and dividends paid to common stockholders were $1,000,000. The firm has no preferred stock outstanding. This year, Marly Brown plans to decrease its debt-to-equity ratio to 1.20 times. The change will not affect sales, total assets, or dividends paid; however, it will reduce the firm's profit margin to 9.85 percent. Use the DuPont equation to determine how the change in Marly Brown's debt ratio will affect its internal growth rate. *(LG3-6)*

3-35 Sustainable Growth Rate You are considering investing in Annie's Eatery. You have been able to locate the following information on the firm: Total assets are $40 million, accounts receivable are $6.0 million, ACP is 30 days, net income is $4.75 million, debt-to-equity is 1.5 times, and dividend payout ratio is 45 percent. All sales are on credit. Annie's is considering loosening its credit policy such that ACP will increase to 35 days. The change is expected to increase credit sales by 5 percent. Any change in accounts receivable will be offset with a change in debt. No other balance sheet changes are expected. Annie's profit margin and dividend payout ratio will remain unchanged. Use the DuPont equation to determine how this change in accounts receivable policy will affect Annie's sustainable growth rate. *(LG3-6)*

3-36 Spreadsheet Problem: Ratio Analysis Use the following information to complete the balance sheet below. *(LG3-1 through LG3-5)*

Current ratio = 2.20 times

Credit sales = $1,200m

Average collection period = 60 days

Inventory turnover = 1.50 times

Total asset turnover = 0.75 times

Debt ratio = 60%

	A	B	C	D	E
1	Cash	$			
2	Accounts receivable			Current liabilities	$500
3	Inventory			Long-term debt	
4	Current assets	$		Total debt	$
5	Fixed assets			Stockholders' equity	
6	Total assets	$		Total liabilities & equity	$

Microsoft Excel

Notes

CHAPTER 3

1. To see this remember the balance sheet identity is Assets (A) = Debt (D) + Equity (E). Dividing each side of this equation by assets, we get A/A = D/A + E/A. Rearranging this equation, D/A = A/A − E/A = 1 − E/A = 1 − [1/(A/E)]. Also, D/A = (A − E)/A = 1/[A/(A − E)] = 1/[(A − E + E)/(A − E)] = 1/[(E/(A − E) + (A − E)/(A − E)] = 1/[E/D + 1] = 1/[1/(D/E) + 1]. Dividing each side of the balance sheet identity equation by equity, we get A/E = D/E + E/E, or A/E = D/E + 1. Also, rearranging this equation, D/E = A/E − 1.

2. The fixed-charge and cash coverage ratios can be tailored to a particular firm's situation, depending on what really constitutes fixed charges that must be paid. One version of it follows: (EBIT + Lease payments)/[Interest + Lease payments + Sinking fund/$(1 - t)$], where t is the firm's marginal tax rate. Here, it is assumed that sinking fund payments must be made. They are adjusted by the division of $(1 - t)$ into a before-tax cash outflow so they can be added to other before-tax cash outflows.

Design elements: (Clock) Floortje/Getty Images; (Referee) Richard Ransier/Getty Images

four

time value of money 1: analyzing single cash flows

In business and personal life, cash flows of different types are paid and received in the future. Your company can contract to build and ship its product to a foreign buyer for a $10 million single payment in two years. You may have a car loan and a $300 per month level payment over the next four years. It may be that you will pay a series of uneven tuition payments over the next couple of years as tuition changes. Whether the future entails single, level, or uneven **cash flows,** we need a method for comparing them when paid at different points in time.

Both this chapter and the next illustrate time value of money (TVM) calculations, which we will use throughout the rest of this book. We hope you will see what powerful tools they are for making financial decisions. Whether you're managing the financial or other functional area of a business or making decisions in your personal life, being able to make TVM calculations will help you make financially sound decisions.

This background will also allow you to understand why CEOs, CFOs, and other professionals make the decisions that they do. Together, this chapter and the next will present all aspects of TVM. Since some students find this topic intimidating, we split the topic into two chapters as a way of providing more examples and practice opportunities. As you see the examples and work the practice problems, we believe that you will find that TVM is not difficult.

Factors to consider when making time value of money decisions include

- Size of the cash flows.
- Time between the cash flows.
- Rate of return we can earn.

> **cash flow** The net amount of money being paid or received.

continued on p. 94

LEARNING GOALS

LG4-1 Create a cash flow time line.

LG4-2 Compute the future value of money.

LG4-3 Show how the power of compound interest increases wealth.

LG4-4 Calculate the present value of a payment made in the future.

LG4-5 Move cash flows from one year to another.

LG4-6 Apply the Rule of 72.

LG4-7 Compute the rate of return realized on selling an investment.

LG4-8 Calculate the number of years needed to grow an investment.

»viewpoints

business APPLICATION

As the production manager of Head Phone Gear, Inc., you have received an offer from the supplier who provides the wires used in headsets. Due to poor planning, the supplier has an excess amount of wire and is willing to sell $500,000 worth for only $450,000. You already have one year's supply on hand. It would cost you $2,000 to store the wire until Head Phone Gear needs it next year. What implied interest rate would you be earning if you purchased and stored the wire? Should you make the purchase? **(See the solution at the end of the chapter.)**

continued from p. 93

time line A graphical representation showing the size and timing of cash flows through time.

inflow Cash received, often from income or sale of an investment.

outflow Cash payment, often a cost or the price of an investment or deposit.

interest rate The cost of borrowing money denoted as a percent.

The title of this chapter refers to the time value of money. But why might money change values, and why does it depend on time? The term "time value of money" really refers to the difference in buying power for a dollar over time. Consider that $100 can buy you an assortment of food and drinks today. Will you be able to buy those same items in five years with the same $100? Probably not. Inflation might cause these items to cost $120. If so, in terms of buying "stuff," the dollar would have lost value over the five years. If you don't need to spend your money today, putting it in your mattress will only cause it to lose value over time. Instead, there are banks that would like to use your money and pay you back later, with interest. This interest is your compensation to offset the money's decline in value. Each dollar will be worth less in the future, but you'll get more dollars, so you'll be able to buy the same items as before.

The basic idea behind the time value of money is that $1 today is worth more than $1 promised next year. But how much more? Is $1 today worth $1.05 next year? $1.08? $1.12? The answer varies depending on current interest rates. This chapter describes the time value of money concept and provides the tools needed to analyze single cash flows at different points in time. ■

4.1 • ORGANIZING CASH FLOWS LG4-1

Managing cash flow timing is one of the most important tasks in successfully operating a business. A helpful tool for organizing our analysis is the **time line,** which shows the magnitude of cash flows at different points in time, such as monthly, quarterly, semiannually, or yearly. Cash we receive is called an **inflow,** and we denote it with a positive number. Cash that leaves us, such as a payment or contribution to a deposit, is an **outflow,** designated with a negative number.

Here's a simple example: Suppose you deposit $100 at a bank and allow the bank to rent your $100 for a year at a cost of 5 percent, or $5. This cost is known as the **interest rate.** The following time line illustrates that $100 deposit made at the bank that pays 5 percent interest. In one year, the $100 has become $105. *Given that interest rate,* having $100 now (in year 0) has the same value as having $105 in one year.

Period	0	5%	1	2 years
Cash flow	−100		105	

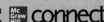

Interest rates will affect you throughout your life, both in business and in your personal life. Companies borrow money to build factories and expand into new locations and markets. They expect the future revenues generated by these activities to more than cover the interest payments and repay the loan. People borrow money on credit cards and obtain loans for cars and home mortgages. They expect their purchases to give them the satisfaction in the future that compensates them for the interest payments charged on the loan. Understanding the dynamics between interest rates and cash inflows and outflows over time is key to financial success. The best place to start learning these concepts lies in understanding how money grows over time.

> **future value (FV)** The value of an investment after one or more periods.
>
> **present value (PV)** The amount a future cash flow is worth today.

4.2 • FUTURE VALUE LG4-2

The $105 one-time cash flow that your bank credits to your account in one year is known as a **future value (FV)** of $100 in one year at a 5 percent annual interest rate. If interest rates were higher than 5 percent, then the future value of your $100 would also be higher. If you left your money in the bank for more than one year, then its future value would continue to grow over time. Let's see why.

Single-Period Future Value

Computing the future value of a sum of money one year from today is straightforward: Add the interest earned to today's cash flow. In this case

$$\text{Value in 1 year} = \text{Today's cash flow} + \text{Interest earned}$$
$$\$105 = \$100 + \$5$$

We computed the $5 interest figure by multiplying the interest rate by today's cash flow ($100 × 5%). Note that in equations, interest rates appear in decimal format, so we use 0.05 for 5 percent:

$$\$100 + (\$100 \times 0.05) = \$105$$

Note that this is the same as

$$\$100 \times (1 + 0.05) = \$105$$

We need the 1 in the parentheses to recapture the original deposit and the 0.05 is for the interest earned. We can generalize this computation to any amount of today's cash flow. In the general form of the future value equation, we call cash today **present value**, or **PV.** We compute the future value one year from now, called FV_1, using the interest rate i:

$$\text{Value in 1 year} = \text{Today's value} \times (1 + \text{Interest rate})$$
$$FV_1 = PV \times (1 + i) \qquad (4\text{-}1)$$

> **⏰ time out!**
>
> **4-1** Why is a dollar worth more today than a dollar received one year from now?
>
> **4-2** Drawing on your past classes in accounting, explain why time lines must show one negative cash flow and one positive cash flow.
>
> **4-3** Set up a time line, given a 6 percent interest rate, with a cash inflow of $200 today and a cash outflow of $212 in one year.

▼ **TABLE 4.1** Higher Interest Rates and Cash Flows Lead to Higher Future Values

	A	B	C	D
1	Higher Interest Rates Lead to Higher Future Values			
2	Today's Cash Flow	Interest Rate	Interest Earned	Next Year's Future Value
3	$100.00	5%	$5.00	$105.00
4	$100.00	6%	$6.00	$106.00
5	$15,000.00	5%	$750.00	$15,750.00
6	$15,000.00	6%	$900.00	$15,900.00
7				
8	Higher Cash Flows Today Lead to Higher Future Values			
9	Today's Cash Flow	Interest Rate	Interest Earned	Next Year's Future Value
10	$500.00	7.50%	$37.50	$537.50
11	$750.00	7.50%	$56.25	$806.25

Microsoft Excel

Notice that this is the same equation we used to figure the future value of your $100. We've simply made it generic so we can use it over and over again. The 1 subscript means that we are calculating for only one period—in this case, one year. If interest rates were 6 percent instead of 5 percent per year, for instance, we could use equation 4-1 to find that the future value of $100 in one year is $106[= $100 \times (1 + 0.06)]$.

Of course, the higher the interest rate, the larger the future value will be. Table 4.1 shows the interest earned and future value for a sample of different cash flows and interest rates. Notice from the first two lines of the table that, while the difference in interest earned between 5 percent and 6 percent ($1) doesn't seem like much on a $100 deposit, the difference on a $15,000 deposit (the following two lines) is substantial ($150).

Compounding and Future Value LG4-3

After depositing $100 for one year, you must decide whether to take the $105 or leave the money at the bank for another year to earn another 5 percent (or whatever interest rate the bank currently pays). In the second year at the bank, the deposit earns 5 percent on the $105 value, which is $5.25(= $105 \times 0.05)$. Importantly, you get more than the $5 earned the first year, which would be a simple total of $110. The extra 25 cents earned in the second year is interest *on interest that was earned in the first year.* We call this process of earning interest both on the original deposit and on the earlier interest payments **compounding.**

So, let's illustrate a $100 deposit made for two years at 5 percent in the following time line:

Period   0   5%   1   5%   2 years

Cash flow   PV = −100   FV = ?

LG4-1

The question mark denotes the amount we want to solve for. As with all TVM problems, we simply have to identify what element we're solving for; in this case, we're looking for the FV. To compute the two-year compounded future value, simply use the one-year equation 4-1 twice.

$$\$100 \times (1 + 0.05) \times (1 + 0.05) = \$110.25$$

So the future value of $100 deposited today at 5 percent interest is $110.25 in period 2. You can see that this represents $10 of interest payments generated from the original $100 ($5 each year) and $0.25 of interest earned in the second year on previously earned interest payments. The $5 of interest earned every year on the original deposit is called **simple interest.** Any amount of interest earned above the $5 in any given year comes from compounding. Over time, the new interest payments earned from compounding can become substantial. The multiyear form of equation 4-1 is the future value in year N, shown as:

Future value in N years = Present value
$$\times \text{ Growth for } N \text{ years of compounding} \qquad (4\text{-}2)$$
$$FV_N = PV \times (1 + i)^N$$

We can solve the two-year deposit problem more directly using equation 4-2 as $\$110.25 = \$100 \times (1.05)^2$. Here, solving for FV in the equation requires solving for only one unknown. In fact, all TVM equations that you will encounter only require figuring out what is unknown in the situation and solving for that one unknown factor.

We can easily adapt equation 4-2 to many different future value problems. What is the future value in 30 years of that $100 earning 5 percent per year? Using equation 4-2, we see that the future value is $\$100 \times (1.05)^{30} = \$432.19$. The money has increased substantially! You have made a profit of $332.19 over and above your original $100. Of this profit, only $150(= \$5 \times 30\text{years})$ came from simple interest earned on the original deposit. The rest, $\$182.19(= \$332.19 - \$150)$, is from the compounding effect of earning interest on previously earned interest.

Remember that the difference between earning 5 percent and 6 percent in interest on the $100 was only $1 the first year. So what is the future value difference after 15 years? Is it $15? No, as Figure 4.1 shows, the difference in future value substantially increases over time. The difference is $31.76 in year 15 and $142.15 in year 30.

The Power of Compounding LG4-3 Compound interest is indeed a powerful tool for building wealth. Albert Einstein, the German-born American physicist who developed the special and general theories of relativity and won the Nobel Prize for Physics in 1921, is supposed to have said, "The most powerful force in the universe is compound interest."[1] Figure 4.2 illustrates this point. It shows the original $100 deposited, the cumulative interest earned on that deposit, and the cumulative interest-on-interest earned. By the 27th year, the money from the interest-on-interest exceeds the interest earned on the original deposit. By the 40th year, interest-on-interest contributes more than double the interest on the deposit. The longer money can earn interest, the greater the compounding effect.

▼**FIGURE 4.1** The Future Value of $100

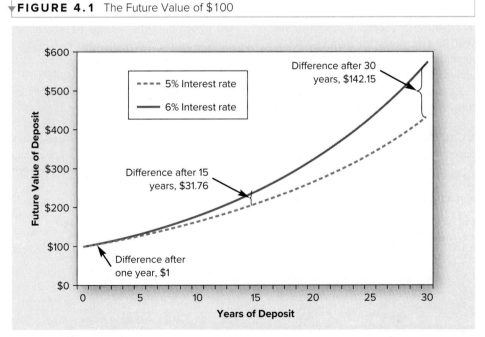

Small differences in interest rates can really add up over time!

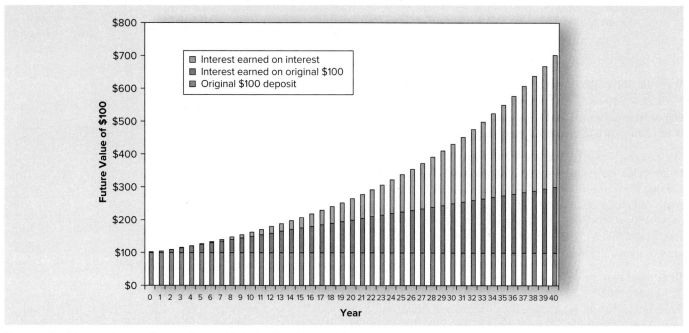

The money from interest-on-interest will eventually exceed the interest from the original deposit.

Earning higher interest rates on the investment for additional time periods magnifies compounding power. Consider the future value of $100 deposited at different interest rates and over different time periods as shown in Table 4.2. The future value of $100 earning 5 percent per year for five years is $127.63, for a gain of $27.63. Would you double your gain by simply investing that same $100 at double the interest rate, 10 percent? No, because compounding changes the nature of the investment so that your money grows exponentially, not in a simple linear relationship. The future value of $100 in five years at 10 percent is $161.05. The $61.05 gain is *more* than double the gain of $27.63 earned at 5 percent. Tripling the interest rate to 15 percent shows a gain of $101.14, which is nearly *quadruple* the gain earned at 5 percent.

The same effect occurs when we increase the time. When the deposit earns 10 percent per year for five years, the gain is $61.05. When we double the amount of time to 10 years, the gain more than doubles to $159.37. If we double the time again to 20 years, the gain increases not to just $318.74(= $159.37 × 2) but to $572.75. At 10 percent for 30 years, the gain on $100 is a whopping $1,644.94. Interest rates and time *are both* important factors in compounding! These relationships are illustrated in Figure 4.3.

Compounding at Different Interest Rates Over Time+   LG4-4   Interest rates have varied over time. In the past half-century, banks have offered depositors rates lower than 1 percent and as high as double digits. They've also charged interest from about 5.5 percent

▼ **TABLE 4.2**   Compounding Builds Wealth over Time

	A	B	C	D	E	F
1	Future value of $100 deposited at 5%, 10%, and 15% interest rates.					
2						
3			Future Value			
4	**Interest Rate Earned**	**5 years**	**10 years**	**20 years**	**30 years**	
5	5%	$127.63	$162.89	$265.33	$432.19	
6	10%	$161.05	$259.37	$672.75	$1,744.94	
7	15%	$201.14	$404.56	$1,636.65	$6,621.18	
8		=FV(A7,5,0,-100)			=FV(A6,30,0,-100)	

Microsoft Excel

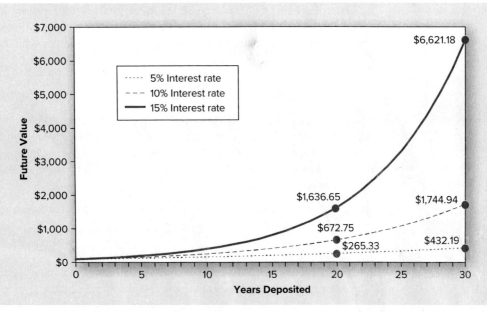

Future value of $100 deposited at 5%, 10%, and 15% interest rates: The future value differences between compounding interest rates expand exponentially over time.

EXAMPLE 4-1

For interactive versions of this example, log in to Connect or go to mhhe.com/Cornett6e.

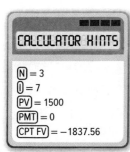

Graduation Celebration Loan LG4-3

Dominic is a fourth-year business student who wants to go on a graduation celebration/vacation in Mexico, but he has no money to pay for the trip. After the vacation, Dominic will start his career. His job will require moving to a new town and buying professional clothes. He asked his parents to lend him $1,500, which he figures he will be able to pay back in three years. His parents agree to lend him the money, but they will charge 7 percent interest per year. What amount will Dominic need to pay back? How much interest will he pay? How much of what he pays is interest-on-interest?

SOLUTION:

Dominic will have to pay:

$$FV_3 = \$1,500 \times (1.07)^3 = \$1,500 \times 1.225 = \$1,837.56$$

Of the $1,837.56 he owes his parents, $337.56(= \$1,837.56 − \$1,500) is interest. We can illustrate this time-value problem in the following time line.

The spreadsheet solution is:

	A	B	C	D
1	PV	i	N	FV
2	$1,500	7%	3	-$1,837.56
3				=FV(B2,C2,0,A2)

Microsoft Excel

Compare this compound interest with simple interest. Simple interest would be 7 percent of $1,500 (which is $105) per year. The three-year cost would then be $315(= 3 × $105). The difference between the compound interest of $337.56 and the total simple interest of $315 is the interest-on-interest of $22.56.

Similar to Problems 4-2, 4-3, 4-13, 4-21, Self-Test Problem 1

to 21.6 percent to consumers for various kinds of loans. Let's look at how to compute future value when rates change, so that money earns interest at multiple interest rates over time. In our first example in this chapter, your deposit of $100 earned 5 percent interest. Now consider the future value when the bank announces it will pay 6 percent interest in the second year. How much will you earn now? We can illustrate the question with this time line:

Period	0	5%	1	6%	2 years
Cash flow	PV = −100				FV = ?

We already know that the $100 deposit will grow to $105 at the end of the first year. This $105 will then earn 6 percent in the second year and have a value of $111.30 (= $105 × 1.06). If we put the two steps together into one equation, the solution appears as $111.30 = $100 × 1.05 × 1.06. From this you should not be surprised that a general equation for future value of multiple interest rates is

Future value in N periods = Today's value × Each period's compounding

$$FV_N = PV \times (1 + i_{\text{period 1}}) \times (1 + i_{\text{period 2}}) \tag{4-3}$$
$$\times (1 + i_{\text{period 3}}) \times \ldots \times (1 + i_{\text{period } N})$$

Note that the future value equation 4-2 is a special case of the more general equation 4-3. If the interest rate every period is the same, we can write equation 4-3 as equation 4-2.

time **out!**

4-4 How does compounding help build wealth (or increase debt) over time?

4-5 Why does doubling the interest rate or time quickly cause more than a doubling of the future value?

EXAMPLE 4-2

For interactive versions of this example, log in to Connect or go to mhhe.com/Cornett6e.

Celebration Loan with Payback Incentive LG4-4

Reexamine the loan Dominic was seeking from his parents in the previous example. His parents want to give him an incentive to pay off the loan as quickly as possible. They structure the loan so they charge 7 percent interest the first year and increase the rate 1 percent each year until the loan is paid. How much will Dominic owe if he waits three years to pay off the loan? Say that in the third year he considers whether to pay off the loan or wait one more year. How much more will he pay if he waits one more year?

SOLUTION:

For a payment in the third year, Dominic will pay interest of 7 percent the first year, 8 percent the second year, and 9 percent the third year. He will have to pay

$$FV_3 = \$1,500 \times 1.07 \times 1.08 \times 1.09 = \$1,500 \times 1.2596 = \$1,889.41$$

The cash flow time line is

Period	0	7%	1	8%	2	9%	3 years
Cash flow	PV = 1,500						FV = −1,889.41

Even worse, if he waits until the fourth year, he will pay one year of interest at 10 percent. The total payment will be

$$FV_4 = \$1,889.41 \times 1.10 = \$2,078.35$$

The spreadsheet solution uses the FVSCHEDULE(principal, schedule) function. Use a cell range to highlight the scheduled interest rates.

Because of both the escalating interest rate and the compounding effect, Dominic must make timely and increasing payments the

	A	B	C
1	PV	$ 1,500	
2	i_1	7.0%	
3	i_2	8.0%	
4	i_3	9.0%	
5	i_4	10.0%	
6			
7	FV_3	$1,889.41	=FVSCHEDULE(B1,B2:B4)
8	FV_4	$ 2,078.35	=FVSCHEDULE(B1,B2:B5)

Microsoft Excel

longer he delays in paying off the loan. Deciding in the third year to put off the payment an extra year would cost him an additional $188.94(= $2,078.35 − $1,889.41).

Similar to Problems 4-4, 4-12

the
Math Coach on...

Using a Financial Calculator

Financial, or business, calculators are programmed to perform the time value of money (TVM) equations we develop in this chapter and the next. The two most common types of inexpensive financial calculators that can perform such functions are the Hewlett-Packard 10B II Business Calculator and the Texas Instruments BA II (Plus or Professional). Among many useful financial shortcuts, these calculators have five specific financial buttons. The relevant financial buttons for TVM calculations are listed below. The HP 10B II calculator buttons look like this:

McGraw Hill

1. N (for the number of periods),
2. I/YR (for the interest rate),
3. PV (for present value),
4. PMT (for a constant payment every period), and
5. FV (for future value).

Texas Instruments, Inc.

Notice that the TI BA II Plus financial calculator buttons appear to be very similar:

To get to the TVM menu, select APPLICATIONS and then choose FINANCE, and finally 1 TVM SOLVER on the previous screens.

A common, more sophisticated and expensive calculator is the TI-83. This calculator has a menu system that includes the financial functions as shown:

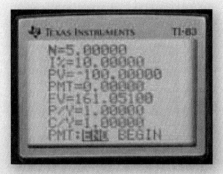

Texas Instruments, Inc.

Setting up Your Calculator

These calculators come from the factory with specific settings. You will find it useful to change two of them. The first is to set the number of digits shown after the decimal point on the calculator display. The factory setting is for two digits. However, consider a problem in which we use a 5.6 percent interest rate. The decimal version of this percentage is 0.056, which a two-digit display would round to 0.06. It's less worrisome to set the calculator to display the number of digits necessary to show the right number; this is called a *floating point display.* To set a floating point display for the HP calculator, press the color button, then the DISP button, and finally the decimal (.) button. To set the display for a floating point decimal on the TI calculator, push the 2ND button, followed by the FORMAT button, followed by the 9 button, and finally the ENTER button.

The second change you'll want to make is to set the number of times the calculator compounds each period. The settings may be preset to 12 times per period. Reset this to one time per period. To change the HP calculator to compound once per period, push the 1 button, then the color button, and finally the P/YR button. On the TI calculator, simply push the 2ND button, the P/Y button, the number one, and the ENTER button. These new settings will remain in the calculator until you either change them or remove the calculator's batteries.

Using Your Calculator

The calculators compute time-value problems in similar ways. Enter the cash flows into the time-value buttons (PV, PMT, and FV) consistent with the way they are shown in a time line. In other words, cash inflows should be positive and cash outflows negative. Thus, PV and FV cash flows are nearly always opposite in sign. Enter interest rates (I) in the percentage form, not the decimal form. Also enter the number of periods in the problem (N).

Consider our earlier example of the $100 deposit for two years earning a 5 percent interest rate.

1. To set the number of years, press 2 and then the N button.
2. To set the interest rate, press 5 and then the I button. (Note that interest rates are in percentage format for using a financial calculator and in decimal format for using the equations.)
3. To enter the current cash flow, press 100; then make it negative by pressing the +/− button; then press the PV button.

4. We won't use the PMT button, so enter 0 and then the PMT button.

5. To solve for future value, press the compute button (CPT) [for the TI] and then the FV button [press the FV button only for the HP].

6. Solution: the display should show $FV = 110.25$.

Note that the answer is positive, consistent with an inflow and the time line diagram. These values remain in the TVM registers even after the calculator is turned off. So when you start a new problem, you should clear out old values first. For the HP calculator, clear the registers by pressing the shift/orange key before pressing C. You can clear the BAII Plus calculator using 2ND and CLR TVM.

You'll notice that throughout this book, we use the equations in the main text to solve time value of money problems. We provide the calculator solutions in the margins.

4.3 • PRESENT VALUE LG4-4

We asked earlier what happens when you deposit $100 cash in the bank to earn 5 percent interest for one year—the bank pays you a $105 future value. However, we could have asked the question in reverse. That is, if the bank will pay $105 in one year and interest rates are 5 percent, how much would you be willing to deposit now to receive that payment in a year? Here, we start with a future value and must find the present value—a different kind of calculation called discounting.

Discounting

While the process of a present value growing over time into the future is called *compounding,* the process of figuring out how much an amount that you expect to receive in the future is worth today is **discounting.** Just as compounding significantly increases the present value into the future, discounting significantly decreases the value of a future amount to the present. Since discounting is the reverse of compounding, we can rearrange equation 4-1 to solve for the present value of a cash flow received one year in the future.

How much would you be willing to deposit now to receive a certain payment in a year?
Ryan McVay/Getty Images

Present value of next period's cash flow = Next period's value
÷ One period of
discounting

$$PV = \frac{FV_1}{(1 + i)} \qquad (4\text{-}4)$$

Suppose the bank is going to pay $105 in one year and interest rates are 5 percent. Then the present value of the payment is $105/1.05 = $100. Present values are always smaller than future values (as long as interest rates are greater than zero!), and the difference between what an investment is worth today and what it's worth when you're supposed to redeem it gets larger as the interest rate increases. Likewise, if the amount of time until the expected payment date increases, the difference will also increase in value.

Discounting Over Multiple Periods Discounting over multiple periods is the reverse process of compounding over multiple periods. Knowing this, we can find the general equation for present value by rearranging the terms in equation 4-2 to form:

PV of cash flow made in N years = Cash flow in year N
÷ Decline for N years of discounting

$$PV = \frac{FV_N}{(1 + i)^N} \qquad (4\text{-}5)$$

The interest rate, i, which we use to calculate present value, is often referred to as the **discount rate.** How much is a $100 payment to be received in the future worth today? Of course, it depends on how far into the future you expect to receive the payment and the discount rate used. If you receive a $100 cash flow in five years, then its present value is $78.35, discounted at 5 percent:

$$PV = \$100/(1.05)^5 = \$100/1.2763 = \$78.35$$

The time line looks like this:

Period	0	5%	1	5%	2	5%	3	5%	4	5%	5 years
Cash flow	PV = −78.35										FV = 100

If the discount rate rises to 10 percent, the present value of our $100 to be paid to us in five years is only $62.09 today. At a 15 percent interest rate, the present value declines to less than half the future cash flow: $49.72. Higher interest rates discount future cash flows more quickly and dramatically. You can see this principle illustrated in Figure 4.4.

Moving right from point A in Figure 4.4, notice that if interest rates are 0 percent, the present value will equal the future value. Also note from the curved lines that when the discount rate is greater than zero, the discounting to present value is not linear through time. The higher the discount rate, the more quickly the cash flow value falls. If the discount rate is 10 percent, a $100 cash flow that you would receive in 25 years is worth less than $10 today, as shown at point B in the figure. With a 15 percent discount rate, the $100 payment to be received in 33 years, at point C, is worth less than $1 today.

LG4-1

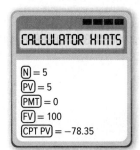

CALCULATOR HINTS

N = 5
PV = 5
PMT = 0
FV = 100
CPT PV = −78.35

the
Math Coach on...

❝When using a financial calculator, be sure to either clear the time value of money buttons or enter a zero for the factors that you won't use to solve the problem. ❞

▼**FIGURE 4.4** Present Value of a $100 Cash Flow Made in the Future

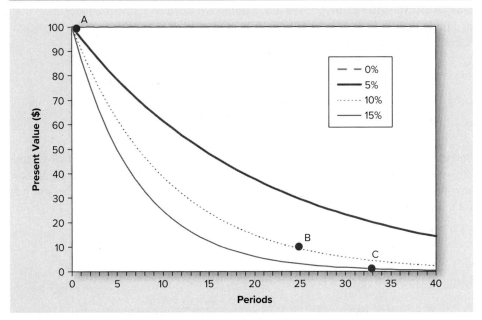

The higher the discount rate, the more quickly the cash flow value falls.

EXAMPLE 4-3

For interactive versions
of this example, log in to
Connect or go to
mhhe.com/Cornett6e.

Buy Now and Don't Pay for Two Years LG4-4

Suppose that a marketing manager for a retail furniture company proposes a sale. Customers can buy now but don't have to pay for their furniture purchases for two years. From a time value of money perspective, selling furniture at full price with payment in two years is equivalent to selling furniture at a sale, or discounted, price with immediate payment. If interest rates are 7.5 percent per year, what is the equivalent sale price of a $1,000 sleeper-sofa when the customer takes the full two years to pay for it?

SOLUTION:

The time line for this problem is:

Period	0	7.5%	1		2 years
Cash flow	PV = ?				FV = 1,000

Using equation 4-5, the present value computation is

$$PV = \frac{FV_N}{(1 + i)^N} = \frac{\$1,000}{1.075^2} = \frac{\$1,000}{1.1556} = \$865.33$$

In this case, the marketing proposal for delaying payment for two years is equivalent to selling the $1,000 sleeper-sofa for a sale price of $865.33, or a 13.5 percent discount. When stores promote such sales, they often believe that customers will not be able to pay the full amount at the end of the two years and then must pay high interest rate charges and late fees. Customers who do pay on time are getting a good deal.

The spreadsheet solution is:

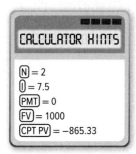

	A	B	C	D
1	FV	i	N	PV
2	$1,000	8%	2	$865.33
3				=PV(B2,C2,0,-A2)

Microsoft Excel

Similar to Problems 4-5, 4-6, and Self-Test Problem 2.

Discounting with Multiple Rates LG4-4

We can also discount a future cash flow at different interest rates per period. We find the general form of the equation for present value with multiple discount rates by rearranging equation 4-3:

Present value with different discount rates = Future cash flow

÷ Each period's discounting

$$PV = \frac{FV_N}{\left(1 + i_{\text{period 1}}\right) \times \left(1 + i_{\text{period 2}}\right) \times \left(1 + i_{\text{period 3}}\right) \times \cdots \times \left(1 + i_{\text{period } N}\right)} \quad (4\text{-}6)$$

Suppose that we expect interest rates to increase over the next few years, from 7 percent this year, to 8 percent next year, to 8.5 percent in the third year. In this environment, how would we work out the present value of a future $2,500 cash flow in year 3? The time line for this problem is

Period	0	7%	1	8%	2	8.5%	3 years
Cash flow	PV = ?						FV = 2,500

Using equation 4-6 shows that the present value is $1,993.90:

$$PV = \frac{\$2,500}{1.07 \times 1.08 \times 1.085} = \frac{\$2,500}{1.2538} = \$1,993.90$$

LG4-1

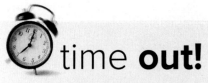

time out!

4-6 How are interest rates in the economy related to the way people value future cash payments?

4-7 Explain how discounting is the reverse of compounding.

4.4 • USING PRESENT VALUE AND FUTURE VALUE LG4-5

Rule of 72 An approximation for the number of years needed for an investment to double in value.

Moving Cash Flows

As managers analyze investment projects, debt management, and cash flows, they frequently find it useful to move cash flows to different points in time. While you may be planning to keep money deposited in the bank for three years when you will buy a car, life often has a way of altering plans. What type of car might you purchase if the money earns interest for only two years, or for four years? How is a corporate financial forecast affected if the firm needs to remodel a factory two years sooner than planned? Moving cash flows around in time is important to businesses and individuals alike for sound financial planning and decision making.

Moving cash flows from one point in time to another requires us to use both present value and future value equations. Specifically, we use the present value equation for moving cash flows to an *earlier* point in time, and the future value cash flows for moving cash flows to a *later* point in time. For example, what's the value in year 2 of a $200 cash flow to be received in three years, when interest rates are 6 percent? This problem requires moving the $200 payment in the third year to a value in the second year, as shown in the time line:

Period	0	1	2	6%	3 years
Cash flow			$PV_2 = ?$		$FV = 200$

LG4-1

Since the cash flow is to be moved one year *earlier* in time, we use the present value equation:

$$PV_2 = FV_3/(1 + i)^1 = \$200/(1.06)^1 = \$188.68$$

When interest rates are 6 percent, a $188.68 payment in year 2 equates to a $200 payment in year 3.

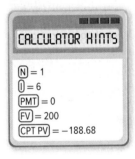

What about moving the $200 cash flow to year 5? Since this requires moving the cash flow later in time by two years, we use the future value equation. In this case, the equivalent of $200 in the third year is a fifth-year payment of:

$$FV_5 = PV_3/(1 + i)^2 = \$200 \times (1.06)^2 = \$200 \times 1.1236 = \$224.72$$

Table 4.3 illustrates how we might move several cash flows. At an 8 percent interest rate, a $1,000 cash flow due in year 5 compounded to year 10 equals $1,469.33. We could also discount that same $1,000 cash flow to a value of $793.83 in year 2. At an 8 percent interest rate, the three cash flows ($793.83 in year 2, $1,000 in year 5, and $1,469.33 in year 10) become equivalent. Table 4.3 illustrates the movement of other cash flows given different interest rates and time periods.

Moving cash flows from one year to another creates an easy way to compare or combine two cash flows. Would you rather receive $150 in year 2 or $160 in year 2? Because both cash flows occur in the same year, the comparison is straightforward. But we can't directly add or compare cash flows in different years until we consider their time value. We can compare cash flows in different years by moving one cash flow to the same time as the other using the present value or future value equations. Once you have the value of each cash flow in the same year, you can directly compare or combine them.

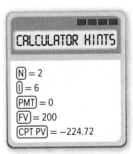

Rule of 72 LG4-6 Albert Einstein is also credited with popularizing compound interest by introducing a simple mathematical approximation for the number of years required to double an investment. It's called the **Rule of 72.**

$$\text{Approximate number of years to double an investment} = \frac{72}{\text{Interest rate}} \quad (4\text{-}7)$$

▼ TABLE 4.3 Equivalent Cash Flows in Time

When Interest Rates Are	A Cash Flow of	In Year	Can be Moved to Year	With Equation	Equivalent Cash Flow
Moving Later versus Moving Earlier					
8%	$1,000	5	10	$FV_{10} = PV_5 \times (1 + i)^5 = \$1{,}000 \times (1.08)^5 =$	$1,469.33
8	1,000	5	2	$PV_2 = FV_5/(1 + i)^3 = \$1{,}000 \times (1.08)^3 =$	793.83
Moving Earlier					
10	500	9	8	$PV_8 = FV_9/(1 + i)^1 = \$500/(1.10)^1 =$	454.55
10	500	9	0	$PV_0 = FV_9/(1 + i)^9 = \$500/(1.10)^9 =$	212.05
Moving Later					
12	100	4	20	$FV_{20} = PV_4 \times (1 + i)^{16} = \$100 \times (1.12)^{16} =$	613.04
12	100	4	30	$FV_{30} = PV_4 \times (1 + i)^{26} = \$100 \times (1.12)^{26} =$	1,904.01

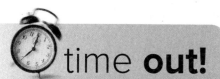

time out!

4-8 In Example 4-4, could Timber, Inc., have performed its analysis by moving the $175,000 to year 2 and comparing? Would the firm then have made the same decision?

4-9 At what interest rate (and number of years) does the Rule of 72 become too inaccurate to use?

The Rule of 72 illustrates the power of compound interest. How many years will it take to double money deposited at 6 percent per year? Using the Rule of 72, we find the answer is 12 years(=72/6). A higher interest rate causes faster increases in future value. A 9 percent interest rate allows money to double in just eight years (=72/9). Remember that this rule provides only a mathematical approximation. It's more accurate with lower interest rates. After all, with a 72 percent interest rate, the rule predicts that it will take one year to double the money (=72/72). However, we know that it actually takes a 100 percent rate to double money in one year.

We can also use the Rule of 72 to approximate the interest rate needed to double an investment in a specific amount of time. What rate do we need to double an investment in five years? Rearranging equation 4-7 shows that the rate needed is 14.4 percent (= 72/5) per year.

EXAMPLE 4-4

For interactive versions of this example, log in to Connect or go to mhhe.com/Cornett6e.

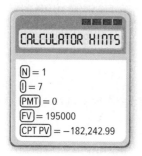

CALCULATOR HINTS

$N = 1$
$I = 7$
$PMT = 0$
$FV = 195000$
$CPT\ PV = -182{,}242.99$

Pay Damages or Appeal? LG4-5

Timber, Inc., lost a lawsuit in a business dispute. The judge ordered the company to pay the plaintiff $175,000 in one year. Timber's attorney advises Timber to appeal the ruling. If so, Timber will likely lose again and will still have to pay the $175,000. But by appealing, Timber moves the $175,000 payment to year 2, along with the attorney fee of $20,000 for the extra work. The interest rate is 7 percent. What decision should Timber make?

SOLUTION:
Timber executives must decide whether to pay $175,000 in one year or $195,000 in two years. To compare the two choices more directly, move the payment in year 2 to year 1 and then compare it to $175,000. Timber should choose to make the smaller payment. The computation is

$$PV_1 = FV_2/(1 + i)^1 = \$195{,}000/(1.07)^1 = \$182{,}242.99$$

The value in year 1 of a year 2 payment of $195,000 is $182,242.99, which is clearly more than the $175,000 year 1 payment. So Timber should *not* appeal and should pay the plaintiff $175,000 in one year (and may want to look for another attorney).

Similar to Problems 4-14, 4-15, 4-16, 4-25

finance atwork //:investments

4.5 • COMPUTING INTEREST RATES LG4-7

Time value of money calculations come in handy when we know two cash flows and need to find the interest rate. The investment industry often uses this analysis. Solving for the interest rate, or rate of return,[2] can answer questions like, "If you bought a gold coin for $350 three years ago and sell it now for $475, what rate of return have you earned?" The time line for this problem looks like this:

Period	0	1	?	2	3 years
Cash flow	PV = −350				FV = 475

In general, computing interest rates is easiest with a financial calculator. To compute the answer using the time-value equations, consider how the cash flows fit into the future value equation 4-2:

LG4-1

$$FV_N = PV \times (1 + i)^N$$
$$\$475 = \$350 \times (1 + i)^3$$

the
Math Coach on...

Rearranging gives

$$\$475/\$350 = (1 + i)^3, \text{ or } 1,357 = (1 + i)^3$$

To solve for the interest rate, i, take the third root of both sides of the equation. To do this, take 1.357 to the 1/3 power using the y^x button on your calculator.[3] Doing this leads to.

$$1.107 = (1 + i), \text{ or } i = 0.107 = 10.7\%$$

If you buy a gold coin for $350 and sell it three years later for $475, you earn a 10.7 percent return per year.

The spreadsheet solution is:

CALCULATOR HINTS

$N = 3$
$PV = -350$
$PMT = 0$
$FV = 475$
$CPT\ I = 10.716$

	A	B	C	D	E
1	PV	FV	N	i	
2	$350	$475	3	10.72%	
3				=RATE(C2,0,-A2,B2)	

Microsoft Excel

LG4-6 Time is an important factor in computing the return that you're earning per year. Turning a $100 investment into $200 is a 100 percent return. If your investments earn this much in two years, then they earned a 41.42 percent rate of return per year $[\$100 \times (1.4142)^2 = \$200]$. Table 4.4 shows the annual interest rate earned for doubling an investment over various

▼ **TABLE 4.4** Interest Rate per Year to Double an Investment

	A	B	C
1	Number of Years to Double Investment	Precise Annual Interest Rate	Rule of 72 Interest Rate Estimate
2	1	100.00%	72.00%
3	2	41.42%	36.00%
4	3	25.99%	24.00%
5	4	18.92%	18.00%
6	5	14.87%	14.40%
7	6	12.25%	12.00%
8	7	10.41%	10.29%
9	8	9.05%	9.00%
10	9	8.01%	8.00%
11	10	7.18%	7.20%
12	15	4.73%	4.80%
13	20	3.53%	3.60%
14	25	2.81%	2.88%
15	30	2.34%	2.40%
16			
17		=RATE(A9,0,−1,2)	

time periods. Notice how compounding complicates the solution: It's not as simple as just dividing by the number of years. Getting a 100 percent return in two years means earning 41.42 percent per year, not 50 percent per year. Table 4.4 also shows the Rule of 72 interest rate estimate.

Return Asymmetries

Suppose you bought a gold coin for $700 last year and now the market will pay you only $350. Clearly, the investment earned a negative rate of return. Use a financial calculator or a time-value equation to verify that this is a return of −50 percent. You lost half your money! So, in order to break even and get back to $700, you need to earn a positive 50 percent, right? Wrong. Note that to get from $350 to $700, your money needs to double! You need a 100 percent return to make up for a 50 percent decline. Similarly, you need a gain of 33.33 percent to make up for a 25 percent decline. If your investment declines by 10 percent, you'll need an 11.11 percent gain to offset the loss. In general, only a higher positive return can offset any given negative return.

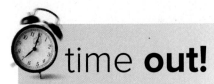

time out!

4-10 Say you double your money in three years. Explain why the rate of return is NOT 33.3 percent per year.

4-11 Show that you must earn a 25 percent return to offset a 20 percent loss.

4.6 • SOLVING FOR TIME LG4-8

Sometimes you may need to determine the time period needed to accumulate a specific amount of money. If you know the starting cash flow, the interest rate, and the future cash flow (the amount you will need), you can solve the time-value equations for the

---

EXAMPLE 4-5

For interactive versions of this example, log in to Connect or go to mhhe.com/Cornett6e.

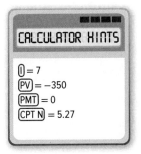

CALCULATOR HINTS

I = 7
PV = −350
PMT = 0
CPT N = 5.27

Growth in Staffing Needs LG4-8

Say that you are the sales manager of a company that produces software for human resource departments. You are planning your staffing needs, which depend on the volume of sales over time. Your company currently sells $350 million of merchandise per year and has grown 7 percent per year in the past. If this growth rate continues, how long will it be before the firm reaches $500 million in sales? How long before it reaches $600 million?

SOLUTION:

You could set up the following time line to illustrate the problem:

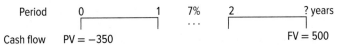

Period	0		1	7%	2		? years
Cash flow	PV = −350			. . .			FV = 500

As shown in the time line, $350 million of sales growing at 7 percent per year will reach $500 million in five years and three months. To reach $600 million will take just two weeks short of eight years.

The spreadsheet solution is:

	A	B	C	D	E
1	PV	FV	i	N	
2	$350	$500	7%	5.271683	
3				=NPER(C2,0,-A2,B2)	
4			Years =	5	
5			Months =	3.26	
6				=(D2-D4)*12	
7					
8	PV	FV	i	N	
9	$350	$600	7%	7.96641	
10				=NPER(C9,0,-A9,B9)	

Microsoft Excel

Similar to Problem 4-18, Self-Test Problem 4

number of years that you will need to accumulate that money. Just as with solving for different interest rates, solving for the number of periods is complicated and requires using natural logarithms.[4] Many people prefer to use a financial calculator to solve for the number of periods.

LG4-7 When interest rates are 9 percent, how long will it take for a $5,000 investment to double? Finding the solution with a financial calculator entails entering

- $I = 9$
- $PV = -5,000$
- $PMT = 0$
- $FV = 10,000$

The answer is 8.04 years, or eight years and two weeks. The Rule of 72 closely approximates the answer, which predicts eight years ($=72/9$).

Using TVM Tables

time out!

4-12 In Example 4-5, how long will it take your company to double its sales?

4-13 In what other areas of business can these time-value concepts be used?

Chapters 4 and 5 describe how to solve TVM problems using equations, a TVM calculator, and spreadsheets. There is a fourth method—using TVM tables. TVM tables are a series of tables that can be used to easily calculate present or future values by showing "factors" for various interest rates and numbers of periods. To compute the future value, use a Future Value Table, locate the interest rate needed in the first column, and locate the number of periods in the first row. The factor in the intersecting row and column is used to multiply by the cash flow in the problem to compute the future value. Where do these factors come from? They come directly from the TVM equations. Note that the future value equation is $FV = PV \times (1 + i)^N$. The future value factor for interest rate i and number of periods N is $(1 + i)^N$. Essentially, the TVM tables compute most of the TVM equations for you, leaving just multiplying the appropriate factor by the cash flow in the problem for the solution.

Get Online

mhhe.com/CornettM6e

for study materials including
quizzes, iPod downloads,
and video

Your Turn. . .

Questions

1. List and describe the purpose of each part of a time line with an initial cash inflow and a future cash outflow. Which cash flows should be negative and which positive? Why? *(LG4-1)*

2. How are the present value and future value related? *(LG4-2)*

3. Would you prefer to have an investment earning 5 percent for 40 years or an investment earning 10 percent for 20 years? Explain. *(LG4-3)*

4. How are present values affected by changes in interest rates? *(LG4-4)*

5. What do you think about the following statement? "I am going to receive $100 two years from now and $200 three years from now, so I am getting a $300 future value." How could the two cash flows be compared or combined? *(LG4-5)*

6. Show how the Rule of 72 can be used to approximate the number of years to quadruple an investment. *(LG4-6)*

7. Without making any computations, indicate which of each pair has a higher interest rate: *(LG4-7)*

    a. $100 doubles to $200 in five years *or* seven years.

    b. $500 increases in four years to $750 *or* to $800.

    c. $300 increases to $450 in two years *or* increases to $500 in three years.

8. A $1,000 investment has doubled to $2,000 in eight years because of a 9 percent rate of return. How much longer will it take for the investment to reach $4,000 if it continues to earn a 9 percent rate? *(LG4-8)*

Problems

BASIC PROBLEMS

4-1   **Time Line** Show the time line for a $500 cash inflow today, a $605 cash outflow in year 2, and a 10 percent interest rate. *(LG4-1)*

4-2   **One Year Future Value** What is the future value of $500 deposited for one year earning an 8 percent interest rate annually? *(LG4-2)*

4-3   **Multiyear Future Value** How much would be in your savings account in 11 years after depositing $150 today if the bank pays 8 percent per year? *(LG4-3)*

4-4   **Compounding with Different Interest Rates** A deposit of $350 earns the following interest rates:

   a. 8 percent in the first year.

   b. 6 percent in the second year.

   c. 5.5 percent in the third year.

   What would be the third year future value? *(LG4-3)*

4-5   **Discounting One Year** What is the present value of a $350 payment in one year when the discount rate is 10 percent? *(LG4-4)*

4-6   **Present Value** What is the present value of a $1,500 payment made in nine years when the discount rate is 8 percent? *(LG4-4)*

4-7   **Present Value with Different Discount Rates** Compute the present value of $1,000 paid in three years using the following discount rates: 6 percent in the first year, 7 percent in the second year, and 8 percent in the third year. *(LG4-4)*

4-8   **Rule of 72** Approximately how many years are needed to double a $100 investment when interest rates are 7 percent per year? *(LG4-6)*

4-9   **Rule of 72** Approximately what interest rate is needed to double an investment over five years? *(LG4-6)*

4-10   **Rates over One Year** Determine the interest rate earned on a $1,400 deposit when $1,800 is paid back in one year. *(LG4-7)*

 4-11   **Spreadsheet Problem: Compounding with Different Interest Rates** A deposit of $750 earns interest rates of 9 percent in the first year and 12 percent in the second year. What would be the second year future value? *(LG4-3)*

	A	B	C	D
1	PV	i1	i2	FV
2	$750	9%	12%	

Microsoft Excel

 4-12   **Spreadsheet Problem: Rates over One Year** Determine the interest rate earned on a $2,300 deposit when $3,500 is paid back in three years. *(LG4-7)*

	A	B	C	D
1	PV	FV	N	i
2	$2,300	$3,500	3	

Microsoft Excel

4-13 **Interest-on-Interest** Consider a $2,000 deposit earning 8 percent interest per year for five years. What is the future value, and how much total interest is earned on the original deposit versus how much is interest earned on interest? *(LG4-3)*

4-14 **Comparing Cash Flows** What would be more valuable, receiving $500 today or receiving $625 in three years if interest rates are 7 percent? Why? *(LG4-5)*

4-15 **Moving Cash Flows** What is the value in year 3 of a $700 cash flow made in year 6 if interest rates are 10 percent? *(LG4-5)*

4-16 **Moving Cash Flows** What is the value in year 10 of a $1,000 cash flow made in year 3 if interest rates are 9 percent? *(LG4-5)*

4-17 **Solving for Rates** What annual rate of return is earned on a $1,000 investment when it grows to $1,800 in six years? *(LG4-7)*

4-18 **Solving for Time** How many years *(and months)* will it take $2 million to grow to $5 million with an annual interest rate of 7 percent? *(LG4-8)*

4-19 **Spreadsheet Problem: Solving for Rates** You invested $3,000 in the stock market one year ago. Today, the investment is valued at $3,750. What return did you earn? What return would you suffer next year for your investment to be valued at the original $3,000? *(LG4-7)*

	A	B	C	D
1	PV	FV	N	i
2	$3,000	$3,750	1	
3				
4				
5	PV	FV	N	i
6	$3,750	$3,000	1	
7				

Microsoft Excel

4-20 **Spreadsheet Problem: Solving for Rates** What annual rate of return is implied on a $2,500 loan taken next year when $3,500 must be repaid in year 4? *(LG4-7)*

	A	B	C	D	E
1	PV	Year	FV	Year	i
2	$2,500	1	$3,500	4	

Microsoft Excel

4-21 **Future Value** At age 30 you invest $1,000 that earns 8 percent each year. At age 40 you invest $1,000 that earns 12 percent per year. In which case would you have more money at age 60? *(LG4-2)*

4-22 **Solving for Rates** You invested $2,000 in the stock market one year ago. Today, the investment is valued at $1,500. What return did you earn? What return would you need to get next year to break even overall? *(LG4-7)*

4-23 **Solving for Rates** What annual rate of return is earned on a $4,000 investment made in year 2 when it grows to $6,500 by the end of year 7? *(LG4-7)*

4-24 **General TVM** Ten years ago, Hailey invested $2,000 and locked in a 9 percent annual interest rate for 30 years *(ending 20 years from now)*. Aidan can make a 20-year investment today and lock in a 10 percent interest rate. How much money should he invest now in order to have the same amount of money in 20 years as Hailey? *(LG4-2, LG4-4)*

4-25 **Moving Cash Flows** You are scheduled to *receive* a $500 cash flow in one year, a $1,000 cash flow in two years, and *pay* an $800 payment in three years. If interest rates are 10 percent per year, what is the combined present value of these cash flows? *(LG4-5)*

 4-26 **Spreadsheet Problem: Growth Rates** Oil prices have increased a great deal in the last decade. The following table shows the average oil price for each year since 1949. Many companies use oil products as a resource in their own business operations *(like airline firms and manufacturers of plastic products).* Managers of these firms will keep a close watch on how rising oil prices will impact their costs. The interest rate in the PV/FV equations can also be interpreted as a growth rate in sales, costs, profits, and so on (see Example 4-5).

a. Using the 1949 oil price and the 1969 oil price, compute the annual growth rate in oil prices during those 20 years.

b. Compute and compare the annual growth rate between 1969 and 1989 and between 1989 and 2020.

c. Given the average price of oil in 2020 and your computed growth rate between 1989 and 2020, compute the estimated future price of oil in 2023 and 2028.

	A	B	C	D	E	F	G	H
1				Average Oil Prices				
2								
3	Year	per barrel	Year	per barrel	Year	per barrel	Year	per barrel
4	1949	$2.54	1969	$3.09	1989	$15.86	2009	$53.48
5	1950	$2.51	1970	$3.18	1990	$20.03	2010	$71.21
6	1951	$2.53	1971	$3.39	1991	$16.54	2011	$87.04
7	1952	$2.53	1972	$3.39	1992	$15.99	2012	$93.02
8	1953	$2.68	1973	$3.89	1993	$14.25	2013	$97.91
9	1954	$2.78	1974	$6.87	1994	$13.19	2014	$93.26
10	1955	$2.77	1975	$7.67	1995	$14.62	2015	$48.69
11	1956	$2.79	1976	$8.19	1996	$18.46	2016	$43.14
12	1957	$3.09	1977	$8.57	1997	$17.23	2017	$50.88
13	1958	$3.01	1978	$9.00	1998	$10.87	2018	$65.23
14	1959	$2.90	1979	$12.64	1999	$15.56	2019	$56.99
15	1960	$2.88	1980	$21.59	2000	$26.72	2020	$39.23
16	1961	$2.89	1981	$31.77	2001	$21.84		
17	1962	$2.90	1982	$28.52	2002	$22.51		
18	1963	$2.89	1983	$26.19	2003	$27.54		
19	1964	$2.88	1984	$25.88	2004	$38.93		
20	1965	$2.86	1985	$24.09	2005	$46.47		
21	1966	$2.88	1986	$12.51	2006	$58.30		
22	1967	$2.92	1987	$15.40	2007	$64.67		
23	1968	$2.94	1988	$12.58	2008	$91.48		

Microsoft Excel

4-27 **Spreadsheet Problem: Future Sales** Consider that you are the marketing manager of a firm. You need to have approximately one additional salesperson for every $10 million in sales. You currently have $50 million in sales and have five employees handling the sales accounts. In order to plan ahead, you want to get an idea of when you may need to hire more salespeople. Build a table that shows the sales for each of the next 10 years for sales growth of 5 percent, 10 percent, 15 percent, and 20 percent *(see Example 4-5).*

	A	B	C	D	E	F	G	H	I	J	K	L
1	Growth Rate	Today	Year 1	Year 2	Year 3	Year 4	Year 5	Year 6	Year 7	Year 8	Year 9	Year 10
2	5%	$50	$52.50									
3	10%	$50	$55.00									
4	15%	$50	$57.50									
5	20%	$50	$60.00									

Microsoft Excel

Comment on when new sales staff should be hired for each growth rate.

Notes

CHAPTER 4

1. No one seems to know exactly what he said, when he said it, or to whom. Similar statements commonly attributed to Einstein are (1) compound interest is the greatest wonder of the universe, (2) compound interest is the ninth wonder of the world, and (3) it is the greatest mathematical discovery of all time. If he did not say any of these things, he (or someone else) should have!

2. The terms *interest rate* and *rate of return* are referring to the same thing. However, it is a common convention to refer to interest rate when you are the one paying the cash flows and to rate of return when you are the one receiving the cash flows.

3. The general equation for computing the interest rate is

   $$i = (FV_N/PV)^{\frac{1}{N}} - 1.$$

4. The equation for solving for the number of periods is

   $$N = \frac{\ln\left(\frac{FV_N}{PV}\right)}{\ln(1 + i)}.$$

Design elements: (Clock) Floortje/Getty Images; (Referee) Richard Ransier/Getty Images

five

time value of money 2:
analyzing annuity cash flows

We explained basic time-value computations in the previous chapter. Those TVM equations covered moving a single cash flow from one point in time to another. While this circumstance does describe *some* problems that businesses and individuals face, most debt and investment applications of time value of money feature multiple cash flows. In fact, *most* situations require many equal payments over time. Since these situations require a bit more complicated analysis, this chapter continues the TVM topic for applications that require many equal payments over time. For example, car loans and home mortgage loans require the borrower to make the same monthly payment for many months or years. People save for the future through monthly contributions to their pension portfolios. People in retirement must convert their savings into monthly income. Companies also make regular payments. Johnson & Johnson (ticker: JNJ) will pay level semiannual interest payments through 2033 on money it borrowed. The Boeing Company (ticker: BA) paid a $2.055 per share quarterly dividend to stockholders in 2020, an increase from the $1.71 quarterly dividend paid in 2018. These examples require

continued on p. 118

LEARNING GOALS

LG5-1 Compound multiple cash flows to the future.

LG5-2 Compute the future value of frequent, level cash flows.

LG5-3 Discount multiple cash flows to the present.

LG5-4 Compute the present value of an annuity.

LG5-5 Figure cash flows and present value of a perpetuity.

LG5-6 Adjust values for beginning-of-period annuity payments.

LG5-7 Explain the impact of compound frequency and the difference between the annual percentage rate and the effective annual rate.

LG5-8 Compute the interest rate of annuity payments.

LG5-9 Compute payments and amortization schedules for car and mortgage loans.

LG5-10 Calculate the number of payments on a loan.

»viewpoints

continued from p. 117

payments (and compounding) over different time intervals (monthly for car loans and semiannually for company debt). How are we to value these payments into common or comparable terms? In this chapter, we illustrate how to value multiple cash flows over time, including equal and uneven payments, and how to incorporate different compounding frequencies. ∎

5.1 • FUTURE VALUE OF MULTIPLE CASH FLOWS LG5-1

Chapter 4 illustrated how to take single payments and compound them into the future. To save enough money for a down payment on a house or for retirement, people typically make many contributions over time to their savings accounts. We can add the future value of each contribution together to see what the total will be worth at some future point in time—such as age 65 for retirement or in two years for a down payment on a house.

Finding the Future Value of Several Cash Flows

Consider the following contributions to a savings account over time. You make a $100 deposit today, followed by a $125 deposit next year, and a $150 deposit at the end of the second year. If interest rates are 7 percent, what's the future value of your deposits at the end of the third year? The time line for this problem is illustrated as

Period	0	1	7%	2	3 years
Cash flow	−100	−125		−150	FV = ?

Note that the first deposit will compound for three years. That is, the future value in year 3 of a cash flow in year 0 will compound $3(= 3 - 0)$ times. The deposit at the end of the first year will compound twice $(= 3 - 1)$. In general, a deposit in year m will compound $N - m$ times for a future value in year N. We can find the total amount at the end of three years by computing the future value of each deposit and then adding them together. Using the future value equation from Chapter 4, the future value of today's deposit is $100 \times (1 + 0.07)^3 = 122.50. Similarly, the future value of the next two deposits are $125 \times (1 + 0.07)^2 = 143.11 and $150 \times (1 + 0.07)^1 = 160.50, respectively.

Putting these three individual future value equations together would yield

$$FV_3 = \$100 \times (1 + 0.07)^3 + \$125 \times (1 + 0.07)^2$$
$$+ \$150 \times (1 + 0.07)^1 = \$426.11$$

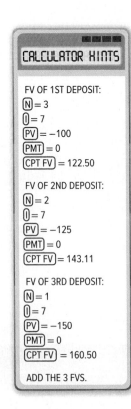

CALCULATOR HINTS

FV OF 1ST DEPOSIT:
N = 3
I = 7
PV = −100
PMT = 0
CPT FV = 122.50

FV OF 2ND DEPOSIT:
N = 2
I = 7
PV = −125
PMT = 0
CPT FV = 143.11

FV OF 3RD DEPOSIT:
N = 1
I = 7
PV = −150
PMT = 0
CPT FV = 160.50

ADD THE 3 FVS.

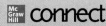
A spreadsheet solution can use the TVM future value function multiple times. Chapter 4 shows that function to be FV(rate,nper,pmt,pv,type). In the spreadsheet, you can add the three future value functions together in one cell.

	A	B	C	D	E	F	G	H
1	Year	0	1	2	3			
2	Cash Flow	-$100	-$125	-$150	$426.12			
3	Rate	7%			=FV(B3,3,0,B2)+FV(B3,2,0,C2)+FV(B3,1,0,D2)			

Microsoft Excel

> **annuity** A stream of level and frequent cash flows paid at the end of each time period—often referred to as an *ordinary annuity.*

The general equation for computing the future value of multiple and varying cash flows (or payments) is

$$FV_N = \text{Future value of first cash flow} + \text{Future value of second cash flow}$$

$$+ \cdots + \text{Future value of last cash flow}$$

$$= PMT_m \times (1+i)^{N-m} + PMT_n \times (1+i)^{N-n} + \cdots$$

$$+ PMT_p \times (1+i)^{N-p}$$

(5-1)

In this equation, the letters *m, n,* and *p* denote when the cash flows occur in time, so $N - m$ and so on represent the length of time that the respective cash flow will get to earn compound interest. Each deposit can be different from the others.

Future Value of Level Cash Flows LG5-2

Now suppose that each cash flow is the same and occurs every year. Level sets of frequent cash flows are common in finance—we call them **annuities.** The first cash flow of an annuity occurs at the end of the first year (or other time period) and continues every year to the last year. We derive the equation for the future value of an annuity from the general equation for future value of multiple cash flows, equation 5-1. Since each cash flow is the same, and the cash flows are every period, the equation appears as

$$FVA_N = \text{Future value of first payment} + \text{Future value of second payment}$$

$$+ \cdots + \text{Last payment}$$

$$= PMT \times (1+i)^{N-1} + PMT \times (1+i)^{N-2} + PMT \times (1+i)^{N-3}$$

$$+ \cdots + PMT(1+i)^0$$

EXAMPLE 5-1

For interactive versions
of this example, log
in to Connect or go to
mhhe.com/Cornett6e.

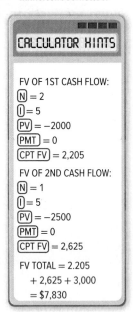

CALCULATOR HINTS

FV OF 1ST CASH FLOW:

$\boxed{N} = 2$

$\boxed{I} = 5$

$\boxed{PV} = -2000$

$\boxed{PMT} = 0$

$\boxed{CPT\ FV} = 2,205$

FV OF 2ND CASH FLOW:

$\boxed{N} = 1$

$\boxed{I} = 5$

$\boxed{PV} = -2500$

$\boxed{PMT} = 0$

$\boxed{CPT\ FV} = 2,625$

FV TOTAL = 2.205
+ 2,625 + 3,000
= $7,830

Saving for a Car LG5-1

Say that, as a freshman in college, you will be working as a house painter for each of the next three summers. You intend to set aside some money from each summer's paycheck to buy a car for your senior year. If you can deposit $2,000 at the end of the first summer, $2,500 at the end of the second summer, and $3,000 at the end of the last summer, how much money will you have to buy a car at the end of the last summer if interest rates are 5 percent?

SOLUTION:

The time line for the forecast is

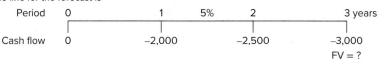

Period	0	1	5%	2		3 years
Cash flow	0	−2,000		−2,500		−3,000
						FV = ?

The first cash flow, which occurs at the end of the first year, will compound for two years. The second cash flow will be invested for only one year. The last contribution will not have any time to grow before the purchase of the car. Using Equation 5-1, the solution is

$$FV_3 = \left[\$2,000 \times (1+0.05)^{3-1}\right] + \left[\$2,500 \times (1+0.05)^{3-2}\right] + \left[\$3,000 \times (1+0.05)^{3-3}\right]$$
$$= (\$2,000 \times 1.1025) + (\$2,500 \times 1.05) + (\$3,000 \times 1) = \$7,830$$

You will have $7,830 in cash to purchase a car for your senior year.

The spreadsheet solution is:

⊿	A	B	C	D	E	F	G	H
1	Year	0	1	2	3	Future money for car		
2	Deposit	$0	$2,000	$2,500	$3,000	$7,830.00		
3	Rate	5%				=FV(B3,2,0,-C2)+FV(B3,1,0,-D2)+E2		

Microsoft Excel

Similar to Problems 5-1, 5-12, and 5-28.

The term *FVA* is used to denote that this is the future value of an annuity. Factoring out the common level cash flow, PMT, we can summarize and reduce the equation as

Future value of an annuity = Payment × Annuity compounding

$$FVA_N = PMT \times \frac{(1+i)^N - 1}{i} \qquad (5\text{-}2)$$

Suppose that $100 deposits are made at the end of each year for five years. If interest rates are 8 percent per year, the future value of this annuity stream is computed using equation 5-2 as

$$FVA_5 = \$100 \times \frac{(1+0.08)^5 - 1}{0.08} = \$100 \times 5.8666 = \$586.66$$

The spreadsheet function for the future value of an annuity is the same TVM future value function used before, FV(rate,nper,pmt,pv,type). The annuity is denoted with the *pmt* input. For this illustration, −100 is the annual cash flow, so =FV(0.08,5,−100,0) = $586.66.

We can show these deposits and future value on a time line as

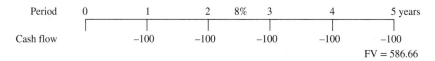

Period	0	1	2	8%	3	4	5 years
Cash flow		−100	−100		−100	−100	−100
							FV = 586.66

Five deposits of $100 each were made, so the $586.66 future value represents $86.66 of interest paid. As with almost any TVM problem, the length of time of the annuity and the interest rate for compounding are very important factors in accumulating wealth within the annuity. Consider the examples in Table 5.1. A $50 deposit made every year for 20 years will grow to $1,839.28 with a 6 percent interest rate. Doubling the annual deposits to $100 also doubles the future value to $3,678.56. However, making $100 deposits for *twice* the amount of time, 40 years, more than *quadruples* the future value to $15,476.20! Longer time periods lead to more total compounding and much more wealth. Interest rates also have this effect. Doubling the interest rate from 6 to 12 percent on the 40-year annuity results in nearly a fivefold increase in the future value to $76,709.14. Think about it: Depositing only $100 per year (about 25 lattes per year) can generate some serious money over time. See Figure 5.1. How much would $2,000 annual deposits generate?

the
Math Coach on...

Annuities and the Financial Calculator

66 In the previous chapter, the level payment button (PMT) in the financial calculator was always set to zero because no constant payments were made every period. We use the PMT button to input the annuity amount. For calculators, the present value is of the opposite sign (positive versus negative) from the future value. This is also the case with annuities. The level cash flow will be of the opposite sign as the future value, as the time line presented earlier shows.

You would use the financial calculator to solve the problem of depositing $100 for five years via the following inputs: N = 5, I = 8, PV = 0, PMT = −100. In this case, the input for present value is zero because no deposit is made today. The result of computing the future value is 586.66. 99

Future Value of Multiple Annuities

At times, multiple annuities can occur in both business and personal life. For example, you may find that you can increase the amount of money you save each year because of a promotion or a new and better job. As an illustration, reconsider the annual $100 deposits made for five years at 8 percent per year. This time, the deposit can be increased to $150 for the fourth and fifth years. How can we use the annuity equation to compute the future value when we have two levels of cash flows? In this case, the cash flow can be categorized as two annuities. The first annuity is a $100 cash flow for five years. The second annuity is a $50 cash flow for two years. We demonstrate this as

Period	0	1	2	8%	3	4	5 years
Cash flow	0	−100	−100		−100	−100	−100
						−50	−50
							FV = ?

▼ **TABLE 5.1** Magnitude of Periodic Payments, Number of Years Invested, and Interest Rate on FV of Annuity

	A	B	C	D
1	**Annuity Cash Flow**	**Number of Years**	**Interest Rate**	**Future Value**
2	$ 50	20	6%	$ 1,839.28
3	100	20	6%	3,678.56
4	100	40	6%	15,476.20
5	100	40	12%	76,709.14
6				
7			=FV(C5, B5, −A5, 0)	

Microsoft Excel

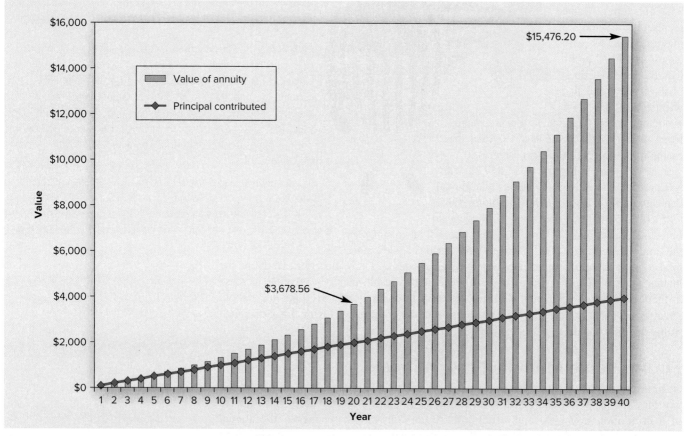

Longer time periods lead to more total compounding and much more wealth.

To determine the future value of these two annuities, compute the future value of each one separately, and then simply add them together. The future value of the $100 annuity is the same as computed before, $586.66. The future value of the $50 annuity, using the TVM equation for the future value of a cash stream, is

$$FVA_N = \$50 \times \frac{(1 + 0.08)^2 - 1}{0.08}$$
$$= \$50 \times 2.08 = \$104$$

the
Math Coach on...

Solving Multiple Annuities

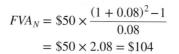 The trick to solving multiple annuity problems is to disentangle cash flows into groups of level payments ending in the future value year that we've designated. 🙶🙶

So, the future value of both of the annuities is $690.66 (= $586.66 + $104).

Use a similar procedure to solve multiple annuities in a spreadsheet. Use the FV function for each annuity and add them together:
=FV(0.08,5,−   100,0)
+FV(0.08,2,− 50,0) =
$586.66 + $104.00 =
$690.66.

finance at work //: personal

Who Will Save for their Future?

Though it seems way too early for you to think about planning for your "golden years," financially wise people realize that it's never too early to start. Unfortunately, most people save little for their retirement years. Twenty-nine percent of households age 55 and older have no pension or retirement savings. About 20 percent have no savings but do have a pension. Of the 52 percent that have retirement savings, the median amount is $109,000. How far does that get you? Using a 6 percent investment return, $109,000 can generate a monthly income of only $653.51 for 30 years, at which time it is used up. That is less than $8,000 per year! The average Social Security monthly benefit is just over $1,318 per month, or about $15,816 per year. It appears that the millennial generation is not doing any better. Two-thirds of working millennials have nothing saved for retirement. Only half of this generation that has a retirement plan at work are contributing to it. Few people will have the lifestyle they wanted in their retirement years. However, that doesn't have to be true for you if you start saving early!

This chapter illustrates that much higher amounts of wealth can be accumulated if you start early. One easy way to do this is through a retirement plan at work. Most company and government employers offer their employees defined contribution plans. (The corporate version is called a 401(k) plan; a nonbusiness plan is usually referred to as a 403(b) plan—both named after the legislation that created the plans.) These plans place all of the responsibility on employees to provide for their retirement. Employees contribute from their own paychecks and decide how to invest. Employees' decisions about how much to contribute and how early to start contributing have a dramatic impact on retirement wealth.

Consider employees who earn $50,000 annually for 40 years and then retire. Note that if the employees contribute for 40 years, they must start by age 25 or so—starting early is vitally important! Contributing 5 percent of their salaries ($2,500) to the 401(k) plan every year and having it earn a 4 percent return will generate $237,564 for retirement. A 10 percent contribution ($5,000) would create

Chris Ryan/AGE Fotostock

$475,128 for retirement. Finally, investment decisions that yield an 8 percent return would yield $1.3 million with a 10 percent contribution. This is quite a range of retirement wealth generated from just three important decisions each employee must make—how much to contribute, how to invest the funds, and when to start! Unfortunately, too many people make poor decisions. Their first mistake is to start making 401(k) contributions too late to allow the funds to generate significant compounding.

Saving and investing money through a defined contribution plan is a good way to build wealth for retirement. But you must follow these rules: Start early, save much, and don't touch!

Want to know more?

Key Words to Search for Updates: **Employee Benefit Research Institute (go to www.ebri.org), retirement income**

Sources: "Retirement Security: Most Households Approaching Retirement Have Low Savings, an Update," Government Accountability Office, GAO-15-419, March 26, 2019, www.gao.gov/products/GAO-19-442R; and Jennifer Erin Brown, "Millennials and Retirement: Already Falling Short," National Institute on Retirement Security Report, February 2018.

In the same way, we could easily compute the future value if the last two cash flows are $50 *lower* ($50 each), instead of $50 higher ($150 each). To solve this alternative version, we would simply *subtract* the $104 future value instead of adding it.

Saving in the Company Pension Plan LG5-2

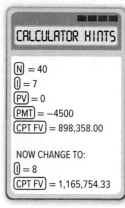
You started your first job after graduating from college. Your company offers a retirement plan for which the company contributes 50 percent of what you contribute each year. So, if you contribute $3,000 per year from your salary, the company adds another $1,500. You get to decide how to invest the total annual contribution from several portfolio choices that the plan administrator provides. Suppose that you pick a mixture of stocks and bonds that is expected to earn 7 percent per year. If you plan to retire in 40 years, how big will you expect that retirement account to be? If you could earn 8 percent per year, how much money would be available?

SOLUTION:

Every year, you and your employer will set aside a total of $4,500 for your retirement. Using Equation 5-2 shows that the future value of this annuity is

$$FVA_{40} = \$4,500 \times \frac{(1 + 0.07)^{40} - 1}{0.07} = \$4,500 \times 199.6351 = \$898,358.00$$

Note that you can build a substantial amount of wealth ($898,358) through your pension plan at work. If you can earn just 1 percent more each year, 8 percent total, you could be a millionaire!

$$FVA_{40} = \$4,500 \times \frac{(1 + 0.08)^{40} - 1}{0.08} = \$4,500 \times 259.0565 = \$1,165,754.33$$

The spreadsheet solution is:

	A	B	C	D	E
1	**Using 7% Annual Return**			**Using 8% Annual Return**	
2	PMT	$ 4,500		PMT	$ 4,500
3	i	7.00%		i	8.00%
4	N	40		N	40
5					
6	FV_{40}	$898,358.00		FV_{40}	$1,165,754.33
7		=FV(B3,B4,-B2,0)			=FV(E3,E4,-E2,0)

Microsoft Excel

Similar to Problems 5-2, 5-9, Self-Test Problem 1

Growing Retirement Contributions LG5-2

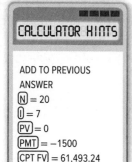
In the previous example, you are investing a total of $4,500 per year for 40 years in your employer's retirement program. You believe that with raises and promotions, you will eventually be able to contribute more money each year. Consider that halfway through your career, you are able to increase your investment in the retirement program to $6,000 per year (your contribution plus the company match). What would be the future value of your retirement wealth from this program if investments are compounded at 7 percent?

SOLUTION:

You can compute the future value using two annuities. The first annuity is one with payments of $4,500 that lasts 40 years. The second is a $1,500 (= $6,000 − $4,500) annuity that lasts only 20 years. We already computed the future value of the first annuity in the previous example: $898,358. The future value of the second annuity is

$$FVA_{20} = \$1,500 \times \frac{(1 + 0.07)^{20} - 1}{0.07} = \$1,500 \times 40.9955 = \$61,493.24$$

So, your retirement wealth from this program would be $959,851 (= $898,358 + $61,493).

The spreadsheet solution is:

	A	B	C	D	E	F	G	H	I
1	**First Annuity**			**Second Annuity**					
2	PMT$_A$	$	4,500	PMT$_B$	$	1,500		**Or solve with one cell**	
3	i		7.00%	i		7.00%			
4	N$_A$		40	N$_B$		20	$959,851.24		
5	FV$_{40}$	$898,358.00		FV$_{40}$	$61,493.24		=FV(0.07,40,-4500,0)+FV(0.07,20,-1500,0)		
6		=FV(B3,B4,-B2)			=FV(E3,E4,-E2)				
7									
8				Total =	$959,851.24				
9					=B5+E5				

Microsoft Excel

Similar to Problems 5-13, 5-27, Self-Test Problem 1

5.2 • PRESENT VALUE OF MULTIPLE CASH FLOWS LG5-3

The future value concept is very useful to understand how to build wealth for the future. The present value concept will help you most particularly for personal applications such as evaluating loans (like car and mortgage loans) and business applications (like determining the value of business opportunities).

Finding the Present Value of Several Cash Flows

Consider the cash flows that we showed at the very beginning of the chapter: You deposit $100 today, followed by a $125 deposit next year, and a $150 deposit at the end of the second year. In the previous situation, we sought the future value when interest rates are 7 percent. Instead of future value, we compute the present value of these three cash flows. The time line for this problem appears as

Period	0		1	7%	2 years
Cash flow	−100		−125		−150
	PV = ?				

The first cash flow is already in year zero, so its value will not change. We will discount the second cash flow one year and the third cash flow two years. Using the present value equation from the previous chapter, the present value of today's payment is simply $100 ÷ (1 + 0.07)^0 = 100. Similarly, the present value of the next two cash flows are $125 ÷ (1 + 0.07)^1 = 116.82 and $150 ÷ (1 + 0.07)^2 = 131.02, respectively. Therefore, the present value of these cash flows is $347.84 (= $100 + $116.82 + $131.02)$.

Putting these three individual present value equations together would yield

$$PV = \left[\$100 \div (1 + 0.07)^0\right] + \left[\$125 \div (1 + 0.07)^1\right]$$
$$+ \left[\$150 \div (1 + 0.07)^2\right]$$
$$= \$347.84$$

A spreadsheet solution can use the TVM present value function multiple times. Chapter 4 shows the function to be PV(rate,nper,pmt,fv,type). In the spreadsheet, you can add the three present value functions together in one cell.

time **out!**

5-1 Describe how compounding affects the future value computation of an annuity.

5-2 Reconsider your original retirement plan in Example 5-3 to invest $4,500 per year for 40 years. Now consider the result if you don't contribute anything for four years (years 19 to 22) while your child goes to college. How many annuity equations will you need to find the future value of your 401(k) in this situation?

The general equation for discounting multiple and varying cash flows is

$$PV = \text{Present value of first cash flow} + \text{Present value of second cash flow}$$

$$+ \cdots + \text{Present value of last cash flow}$$

$$= \frac{PMT_m}{(1 + i)^m} + \frac{PMT_n}{(1 + i)^n} + \cdots + \frac{PMT_p}{(1 + i)^p} \tag{5-3}$$

In this equation, the letters m, n, and p denote when the cash flows occur in time. Each deposit can differ from the others in terms of size and timing.

Present Value of Level Cash Flows LG5-4

You will find that this present value of an annuity concept will have many business and personal applications throughout your life. Most loans are set up so that the amount borrowed (the present value) is repaid through level payments made every period (the annuity). Lenders will examine borrowers' budgets and determine how much each borrower can afford as a payment. The maximum loan offered will be the present value of that annuity payment. The equation for the present value of an annuity can be derived from the general equation for the present value of multiple cash flows, equation 5-3. Since each cash flow is the same, and the borrower pays the cash flows every period, the present value of an annuity, PVA, can be written as

$$\text{Present value} = \text{Payment} \times \text{Annuity discount}$$

$$PVA_N = PMT \times \left[\frac{1 - \frac{1}{(1 + i)^N}}{i} \right] \tag{5-4}$$

Suppose that someone makes $100 payments at the end of each year for five years. If interest rates are 8 percent per year, the present value of this annuity stream is computed using equation 5-4 as

$$PVA_5 = \$100 \times \left[\frac{1 - \frac{1}{(1 + 0.08)^5}}{0.08} \right] = \$100 \times 3.9927 = \$399.27$$

The spreadsheet function for the present value of an annuity is the same TVM present value function used before, PV(rate,nper,pmt,fv,type). The annuity is denoted with the *pmt* input. For this illustration, −100 is the annual cash flow, so =PV(0.08,5,−100,0) = $399.27.

The time line for these payments and present value appears as

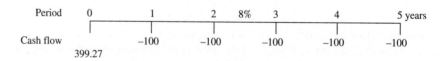

Notice that although five payments of $100 each were made, $500 total, the present value is only $399.27. As we've noted previously, the span of time over which the borrower pays the annuity and the interest rate for discounting strongly affect present value computations. When you borrow money from the bank, the bank views the amount it lends as the present value of the annuity it receives over time from the borrower. Consider the examples in Table 5.2.

A $50 deposit made every year for 20 years is discounted to $573.50 with a 6 percent discount rate. Doubling the annual cash flow to $100 also doubles the present value to $1,146.99. But extending the time period does not impact the present value as much as you might expect. Making $100 payments for twice the amount of time—40 years—does not double the present value. As you can see in Table 5.2, the present value increases less than 50 percent to only $1,504.63! If the discount rate increases from 6 percent to 12 percent on the 40-year annuity, the present value will shrink to $824.38.

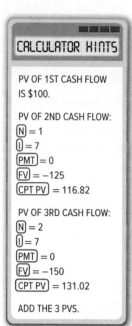

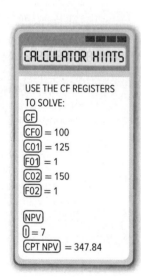

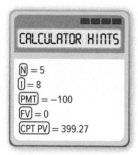

	A	B	C	D
1	**Annuity Cash Flow**	**Number of Years**	**Interest Rate**	**Present Value**
2	$ 50	20	6%	$573.50
3	100	20	6%	$1,146.99
4	100	40	6%	$1,504.63
5	100	40	12%	$824.38
6				
7			=PV(C5, B5, −A5, 0)	

Microsoft Excel

The present value of a cash flow made far into the future is not very valuable today, as
Figure 5.2 illustrates. That's why doubling the number of years in the table from 20 to
40 only increased the present value by approximately 30 percent. Notice how the present
value of $100 annuity payments declines for the cash flows made later in time, especially
at higher discount rates. The $100 cash flow in year 20 is worth less than $15 today if we
use a 10 percent discount rate; they're worth more than double, at nearly $38 today, if we
use a discount rate of 5 percent. The figure also shows how quickly present value declines
with a higher discount rate relative to a lower rate. As we showed above, the present values
of the annuities in the figure are the sums of the present values shown. Because the present values for the 10 percent discount rate are smaller, the present value of an annuity is
smaller as interest rates rise.

Present Value of Multiple Annuities

Just as we can combine annuities to solve various future value problems, we can also combine annuities to solve some present value problems with changing cash flows. Consider
David Price's Major League Baseball contract signed in 2015 with the Boston Red Sox.

▼**FIGURE 5.2** Present Value of Each Annuity Cash Flow

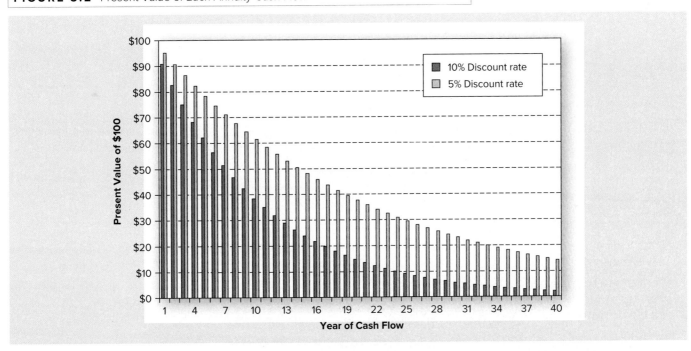

the
Math Coach on...

Using a Financial Calculator—Part 2

The five TVM buttons/functions in financial calculators have been fine, so far, for the types of TVM problems we've been solving. Sometimes we had to use them two or three times for a single problem, but that was usually because we needed an intermediate calculation to input into another TVM equation.

Luckily, most financial calculators also have built-in worksheets specifically designed for computing TVM in problems with multiple nonconstant cash flows.

To make calculator worksheets as flexible as possible, they are usually divided into two parts: one for input, which we'll refer to as the CF (cash flow) worksheet, and one or more for showing the calculator solutions. We'll go over the conventions concerning the CF worksheet here, and we'll discuss the output solutions in Chapter 13.

The CF worksheet is usually designed to handle inputting sets of multiple cash flows as quickly as possible. As a result, it normally consists of two sets of variables or cells—one for the cash flows and one to hold a set of frequency counts for the cash flows, so that we can tell it we have seven $1,500 cash flows in a row instead of having to enter $1,500 seven times.

Using the frequency counts to reduce the number of inputs is handy, but you must take care. Frequency counts are only good for embedded annuities of identical cash flows. You have to ensure that you don't mistake another kind of cash flow for an annuity.

Also, using frequency counts will usually affect the way that the calculator counts time periods. As an example, let's talk about how we would put the set of cash flows shown here into a CF worksheet:

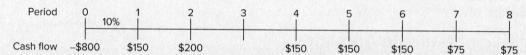

Period	0	1	2	3	4	5	6	7	8
	10%								
Cash flow	–$800	$150	$200		$150	$150	$150	$75	$75

To designate which particular value we'll place into each particular cash flow cell in this worksheet, we'll note the value and the cell identifier, such as CF0, CF1, and so forth. We'll do the same for the frequency cells, using F1, F2, and so on, to identify which CF cell the frequency cell goes with. (Note that, in most calculators, CF0 is treated as a unique value with an unalterable frequency of 1; we're going to make the same assumption here so you'll never see a listing for F0.) For this sample time line, our inputs would be

–$800	[CF0]		
$150	[CF1]	1	[F1]
$200	[CF2]	1	[F2]
$ 0	[CF3]	1	[F3]
$150	[CF4]	3	[F4]
$ 75	[CF5]	2	[F5]

To compute the present value of these cash flows, use the NPV calculator function. The NPV function computes the present value of all the future cash flows and then adds the year 0 cash flow. Then, on the NPV worksheet, you would simply need to enter the interest rate and solve for the NPV:

10%	[I]
[CPT]	[NPV] = –$144.61

Note a few important things about this example:

1. We had to manually enter a value of $0 for CF3. If we hadn't, the calculator wouldn't have known about it and would have implicitly assumed that CF4 came one period after CF2.

2. Once we use a frequency cell for one cash flow, all numbering on any subsequent cash flows that we enter into the calculator is going to be messed up, at least from our point of view. For instance, the first $75 isn't what we would call "CF5," is it? We'd call it "CF7" because it comes at time period 7; but calculators usually treat CF5 as "the fifth set of cash flows," so we'll just have to try to do the same to be consistent.

3. If we really don't need to use frequency cells, we will usually just leave them out of the guidance instructions in this chapter to save space.

EXAMPLE 5-4

Value of Payments LG5-4

For interactive versions of this example, log in to Connect or go to mhhe.com/Cornett6e.

Your firm needs to buy additional physical therapy equipment that costs $20,000. The equipment manufacturer will give you the equipment now if you will pay $6,000 per year for the next four years. If your firm can borrow money at a 9 percent interest rate, should you pay the manufacturer the $20,000 now or accept the four-year annuity offer of $6,000?

SOLUTION:

We can find the cost of the four-year, $6,000 annuity in present value terms using equation 5-4:

$$PVA_4 = \$6,000 \times \left[\frac{1 - \dfrac{1}{(1 + 0.09)^4}}{0.09} \right] = \$6,000 \times 3.2397 = \$19,438.32$$

The cost of paying for the equipment over time is $19,438.32. This is less, in present value terms, than paying $20,000 cash. The firm should take the annuity payment plan.

The spreadsheet solution is:

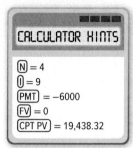

CALCULATOR HINTS

N = 4
I = 9
PMT = −6000
FV = 0
CPT PV = 19,438.32

	A	B	C	D
1	PMT	i	N	
2	$6,000	9.00%	4	
3				
4	PV =	$19,438.32	=PV(B2,C2,-A2)	

Microsoft Excel

Similar to Problems 5-4, 5-10, and Self-Test Problem 2.

This was the largest contract for a pitcher ever. It was reported as having a $217 million value. The contract was structured so that the Red Sox paid Price $30 million per year in 2016 through 2018, $31 million in 2019, and $32 million per year in 2020 through 2022.[1] However, we know that future cash flows have lower present values. So, using a 5 percent discount rate, what is the present value of Price's contract?

We begin by showing the salary cash flows with the time line

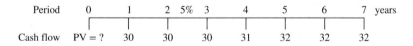

Period	0	1	2	5%	3	4	5	6	7	years
Cash flow	PV = ?	30	30		30	31	32	32	32	

First create a $32 million, seven-year annuity. Here are the associated cash flows:

Period	0	1	2	5%	3	4	5	6	7	years
Cash flow	PV = ?	32	32		32	32	32	32	32	
		−2	−2		−2	−1				

Now create a −$1 million, four-year annuity:

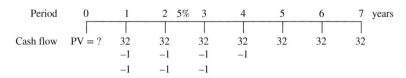

Period	0	1	2	5%	3	4	5	6	7	years
Cash flow	PV = ?	32	32		32	32	32	32	32	
		−1	−1		−1	−1				
		−1	−1		−1					

The reported value for many sports contracts may be misleading in present value terms.

Akihiro Sugimoto/Aflo/age fotostock

Notice that creating the −$1 million annuity also resulted in the third annuity of −$1 million for three years. This time line shows three annuities. If you add the cash flows in any year, the sum is Price's salary for that year. Now we can find the present value of each annuity using equation 5-4 three times.

$$PVA_7 = \$32m \times \left[\frac{1 - \frac{1}{(1+0.05)^7}}{0.05} \right]$$

$$= \$32m \times 5.7864 = \$185.16 \text{ million}$$

$$PVA_4 = -\$1m \times \left[\frac{1 - \frac{1}{(1+0.05)^4}}{0.05} \right]$$

$$= -\$1m \times 3.5460 = -\$3.55 \text{ million}$$

$$PVA_3 = -\$1m \times \left[\frac{1 - \frac{1}{(1+0.05)^3}}{0.05} \right]$$

$$= -\$1m \times 2.7232 = -\$2.72 \text{ million}$$

Adding the value of the three annuities reveals that the present value of Price's salary was $178.89 million (= $185.16m − $3.55m − $2.72m). So, the present value of Price's contract turns out to be quite considerable, but it is not the $217 million contract value advertised!

Use a similar procedure to solve multiple annuities in a spreadsheet. Use the PV function for each annuity and add them together: = PV (0.05,7,−32,0) + PV (0.05,4,1,0) + PV (0.05,3,1,0) = $185.16 − $3.55 − $2.72 = $178.89 million.

Perpetuity—A Special Annuity LG5-5

A perpetuity is a special type of annuity with a stream of level cash flows that are paid forever. These arrangements are called **perpetuities** because payments are perpetual. Assets that offer investors perpetual payments are preferred stocks and British 2½% Consolidated Stock, a debt referred to as **consols**.

The value of an investment like this is the present value of all future annuity payments. As the cash flow continues indefinitely, we can't use equation 5-4. Luckily, mathematicians have figured out that when the number of periods, *N*, in equation 5-4 goes to infinity, the equation reduces to a very simple one:

Present value of a perpetuity = Payment ÷ Interest rate

$$PV \text{ of a perpetuity} = \frac{PMT}{i} \qquad (5\text{-}5)$$

For example, the present value of an annual $100 perpetuity discounted at 10 percent is $1,000 (= $100 − 0.10). Compare this to the present value of a $100 annuity of 40 years as shown in Table 5.2. The 40-year annuity's value is $977.91. You'll see that extending the payments from 40 years to an infinite number of years adds only $22.09 (= $1,000 − $977.91) of value. This demonstrates once again how little value today is placed on cash flows paid many years into the future.

5.3 • ORDINARY ANNUITIES VERSUS ANNUITIES DUE LG5-6

So far, we've assumed that every cash flow comes in at the *end* of every period. But in many instances, cash flows come in at the *beginning* of each period. An annuity in which the cash flows occur at the beginning of each period is called an **annuity due.**

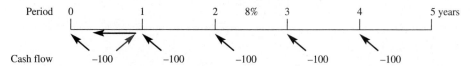

Period   0   1   2   8%   3   4   5 years

Cash flow   −100   −100   −100   −100   −100

Consider the five-year $100 annuity due. The cash flow in the beginning of year 1 looks like it's actually a cash flow today. Annuity due moved the cash flow from the end of the year to the beginning, which looks like the end of the previous year.

Note that these five annuity-due cash flows are essentially the same as a payment today and a four-year ordinary annuity.

Future Value of an Annuity Due So, how do we calculate the future value of the five-year annuity due shown in the time line? The first cash flow of an ordinary five-year annuity can compound for four years. The last cash flow does not compound at all. From the time line, you can see that the first cash flow of the annuity due essentially occurs in year zero, or today. So the first cash flow compounds for five years. The last cash flow of an annuity due compounds one year. The main difference between an annuity due and an ordinary annuity is that all the cash flows of the annuity due compound one more year than the ordinary annuity. The future value of the annuity due will simply be the future value of the ordinary annuity multiplied by $(1 + i)$:

$$\text{Future value of an annuity due} = \text{Future value of an annuity}$$
$$\times \text{One year of compounding} \quad (5\text{-}6)$$
$$FVA_N \text{ due} = FVA_N \times (1 + i)$$

Earlier in the chapter, the future value of this ordinary annuity was shown to be $586.66. Therefore, the future value of the annuity due is $633.59 (= $586.66 × 1.08).

To compute the future value of an annuity due using the spreadsheet function FV(rate,nper,pmt,pv,type), set *type* equal to 1. So for this annuity due, = FV(0.08,5,−100,0,1) = $633.59.

Present Value of an Annuity Due What is a five-year annuity due, shown previously, worth today? Remember that we discount the first cash flow of an ordinary five-year annuity one year. We discount the last cash flow for the full five years. But because the first cash flow of the annuity due is already paid today, we don't discount it at all. We discount the last cash flow of an annuity due only four years. Indeed, we discount all the cash flows of the annuity due one year less than we would

time out!

5-3 How important is the magnitude of the discount rate in present value computations? Do significantly higher interest rates lead to significantly higher present values?

5-4 Reconsider the physical therapy equipment example. If interest rates are only 7 percent, should you pay the up-front fee or the annuity?

perpetuity An annuity with cash flows that continue forever.

consols Investment assets structured as perpetuities.

annuity due An annuity in which cash flows are paid at the beginning of each time period.

the Math Coach on...

Setting Financial Calculators for Annuity Due

❝ Financial calculators can be set for beginning-of-period payments. Once set, you compute future and present values of annuities due just as you would the ordinary annuity. To set the HP calculator, press the color button followed by the BEG/END button. To set the TI calculator for an annuity due, push the 2ND button, followed by the BGN button, followed by the 2ND button again, followed by the SET button, and followed by the 2ND button a third time, and finally the QUIT button. To set the HP and TI calculators back to end-of-period cash flows, repeat these procedures. ❞

finance at work //: behavioral

Take Your Lottery Winnings Now Or Later?

On January 22, 2021, one lottery ticket won a massive Mega Millions jackpot of $1.05 billion. The winner had two choices for payment: They could take a much-discounted lump-sum cash payment immediately or take 30 annuity payments (one immediately and then one every year for 29 years, which is a 30-year annuity due). The annuity payment would be $35 million (= $1.05 billion ÷ 30) for 30 years. The alternative immediate lump sum was $776.6 million before taxes. One way to decide between the two alternatives would be to use the time value of money concepts. The winner might have computed the present value of the annuity and compared it to the lump-sum cash payment.

At the time, long-term interest rates were 1.8 percent. The present value of the annuity offered was $820.37 million per winning ticket. (Compute this yourself.) Notice that winning $1.05 billion does not deliver $1.05 billion of value! If the decision was made from this perspective, the winner should choose to take the annuity because it has more value than the lump-sum alternative. Most winners take the lump sum. Financial advisors tend to recommend that lottery winners take the lump sum because they believe that the money can earn a higher return than the 1.8 percent interest rate. Of course, you pay income taxes too. The 39.6 percent federal tax rate brings the lump-sum payment down to $469.1 million.

Good reasons arise for taking the annuity, however. To earn the higher return on the lump sum, the advisor (and the group of owners) would have to take risks. In addition, most of the lump sum would have

McGraw Hill

to be invested. But most people who choose the lump sum end up spending much of it in the first couple of years. Stories abound about lottery winners who declare bankruptcy a few years after receiving their money. Choosing the annuity helps instill financial discipline since the winners can't waste money today that they won't receive for years.

Want to know more?

Key Words to Search for Updates: **Powerball winners (go to www.powerball.com)**

Source: "Historic Mega Millions Jackpot Won in Michigan!" *Mega Millions,* January 23, 2021, www.megamillions.com/News/2021/Historic-Mega-Millions-Jackpot-Won-in-Michigan!.aspx.

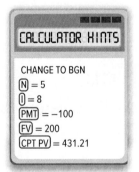

CALCULATOR HINTS

CHANGE TO BGN
N = 5
I = 8
PMT = −100
FV = 200
CPT PV = 431.21

discount the ordinary annuity. Therefore, the present value of the annuity due is simply the present value of the ordinary annuity multiplied by $(1 + i)$:

$$PVA_N \text{ due} = PVA_N \times (1 + i) \qquad (5\text{-}7)$$

Earlier in the chapter, we discovered that the present value of this ordinary annuity was $399.27. So the present value of the annuity due is $431.21 (= $399.27 × 1.08).

To compute a present value annuity due using the spreadsheet function, PV(rate,nper,pmt,fv,type), set *type* equal to 1. So for this annuity due, = PV(0.08,5,−100,0,1) = $431.21.

Interestingly, we make the same adjustment, $(1 + i)$, to both the ordinary annuity present value and future value to compute the annuity due value.

5.4 • COMPOUNDING FREQUENCY LG5-7

So far, all of our examples and illustrations have used annual payments and annual compounding or discounting periods. But many situations that use cash flow time-value-of-money analysis require more frequent or less frequent time periods than simple yearly entries. Bonds make semiannual interest payments; stocks pay quarterly dividends. Most consumer loans require monthly payments. Monthly payments require monthly compounding. In this section, we'll discuss the implications of compounding more than once a year.

Effect of Compounding Frequency

Consider a $100 deposit made today with a 12 percent annual interest rate. What's the future value of this deposit in one year? Equation 4-2 from the previous chapter shows that the answer is $112. What would happen if the bank compounded the interest every six months instead of at the end of the year? Halfway through the year, the bank would compute that the deposit has grown 6 percent (half the annual 12 percent rate) to $106. At the end of the year, the bank would compute another 6 percent interest payment. However, this 6 percent is earned on $106, not the original $100 deposit. The end-of-year value is therefore $112.36 (= $106 × 1.06). By compounding twice per year instead of just once, the future value is $0.36 higher. Though this amount may seem negligible, you might be surprised to see how quickly the difference becomes significant.

Instead of compounding annually or semiannually, what might happen if compounding were quarterly? Since each year contains four quarters, the interest rate per quarter would be 3 percent (= 12 percent ÷ 4 quarters). The future value in one year, compounded quarterly, is $112.55 (= $100 × 1.03^4). Again, the compounding frequency increased and so did the future value.

Table 5.3 shows the effect of various compounding frequencies. We'd like to draw your attention to two important points in the table. First, the higher the compound frequency, the higher the future value will be. Second, the relative increase in value from increasing compounding frequency seems to diminish with increasing frequencies. For example, increasing frequency from annual to semiannual increased the future value by 36 cents. However, increasing frequency from daily to hourly compounding increases the future value by only 0.1 cent.[2]

When we work with annuity cash flows, the compound frequency used is the same as the timing of the cash flows. When annuity cash flows are paid monthly, then interest is also compounded monthly, as seen in Examples 5-5 and 5-6.

EARs and APRs If you borrowed $100 at a 12 percent interest rate, you would expect to pay $112 in one year. If the loan compounded monthly, then you would owe $112.68 at the end of the year, as Table 5.3 shows. So a 12 percent loan compounded monthly means that you really pay more than 12 percent. In fact, you would pay 12.68 percent. In this example, the 12 percent rate is called the **annual percentage rate (APR)**. The 12.68 percent is called the **effective annual rate (EAR)**—a more accurate measurement of what you will actually pay.

time out!

5-5 In what situations might you need to use annuity due analysis instead of an ordinary annuity analysis?

5-6 Reconsider your retirement plan earlier in this chapter. What would your retirement wealth grow to be if you started contributing today?

annual percentage rate (APR) The interest rate per period times the number of periods in a year.

effective annual rate (EAR) An interest rate that reflects annualizing with compounding figured in.

▼ **TABLE 5.3** Future Value in One Year and Compounding Frequency of $100 at 12 percent

	A	B	C	D
1	**Frequency**	**Period Interest Rate**	**Future Value Equation**	**Future Value**
2	Annual	12%	$100 × 1.12^1	$112.00
3	Semiannual	6	$100 × 1.06^2	112.36
4	Quarterly	3	$100 × 1.03^4	112.55
5	Monthly	1	$100 × 1.01^{12}	112.68
6	Daily	0.032877	$100 × 1.00032877^{365}	112.748
7	Hourly	0.00136986	$100 × 1.0000136986^{8760}	112.749

The higher the compound frequency, the higher the future value will be.
Microsoft Excel

EXAMPLE 5-5

For interactive versions of this example, log in to Connect or go to mhhe.com/Cornett6e.

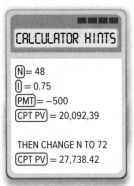

CALCULATOR HINTS

$N = 48$
$I = 0.75$
$PMT = -500$
$CPT\ PV = 20,092.39$

THEN CHANGE N TO 72
$CPT\ PV = 27,738.42$

Car Loan Debt LG5-4

Now you would like to buy a car. You have reviewed your budget and determined that you can afford to pay $500 per month as a car payment. How much can you borrow if interest rates are 9 percent and you pay the loan over four years? How much could you borrow if you agree to pay for six years instead?

SOLUTION:

The loan amount is the present value of the 48-month, $500 annuity. Note that the loan term will be 48 (= 4 × 12) months and the interest rate is 0.75 (= 9 ÷ 12) percent. Using equation 5-4, you discover that you can borrow up to $20,092 to buy a car:

$$PVA_{48} = \$500 \times \left[\frac{1 - \frac{1}{(1 + 0.0075)^{48}}}{0.0075} \right] = \$500 \times 40.1848 = \$20,092.39$$

If you are willing to borrow money for six years instead of four, the small change to the equation results in your ability to borrow $27,738. Although this would allow you to buy a more expensive car, it would also require two more years of $500 payments (an additional $12,000 of payments!). The spreadsheet solution is:

	A	B	C	D	E	F	G	H	I
1	PMT	i	N			PMT	i	N	
2	$500	9.00%	4			$500	9.00%	6	
3									
4	Loan Amount =	$20,092.39	=PV(B2/12,C2*12,-A2)			Loan Amount =	$27,738.42	=PV(G2/12,H2*12,-F2)	

Microsoft Excel

Similar to Problem 5-16, Self-Test Problem 4.

EXAMPLE 5-6

For interactive versions of this example, log in to Connect or go to mhhe.com/Cornett6e.

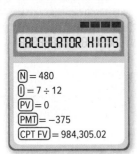

CALCULATOR HINTS

$N = 480$
$I = 7 \div 12$
$PV = 0$
$PMT = -375$
$CPT\ FV = 984,305.02$

Making Monthly Pension Contributions LG5-7

Reexamine your original plan to contribute to your company retirement plan. Instead of a total contribution of $4,500 per year for 40 years, you are able to contribute monthly. Given your expected 7 percent per year investment return, how much money can you expect in your retirement account?

SOLUTION:

Now your total monthly contribution will be $375 (= $4,500 ÷ 12), which will continue for 480 months and earn a 0.58333 (= 7 ÷ 12) percent monthly return. The results of equation 5-2 show that the future value of this annuity is

$$FVA_{40} = \$375 \times \left[\frac{[1 + (0.07/12)]^{480} - 1}{0.07/12} \right] = \$375 \times 2,624.8135 = \$984,305.02$$

The spreadsheet solution is:

	A	B	C	D
1	PMT	i	N	
2	$375	7.00%	40	
3				
4	FV =	$984,305.02	=FV(B2/12,C2*12,-A2)	

Microsoft Excel

When you made contributions annually, the future value was $898,358 (Example 5-2). By changing to monthly contributions, your retirement nest egg increased by nearly $86,000 to $984,305!

Similar to Problems 5-51, 5-52, Self-Test Problem 3

Lenders are legally required to show potential borrowers the APR on any loan offered. While the difference in APR and EAR is not that large in this example, it's interesting that the law requires only the less accurate (and lower) one to be shown. Since the EAR is a more accurate measure of what you will pay, it's useful to know how to convert a stated APR to an EAR. Equation 5-8 shows this conversion with a compounding frequency of *m* times per year:

the
Math Coach on...
Common Mistakes

66 As you figure present and future values of annuity cash flows, check that all terms are consistent: The number of payments, interest rate, and payment size all need to use common terms. If your payments are monthly, then the number of payments must reflect the number of months; the interest rate must be stated as a per-month rate, and the payment register must reflect that monthly payment. 99

$$EAR = \left(1 + \frac{APR}{m}\right)^m - 1 \qquad (5\text{-}8)$$

To compute the EAR using a spreadsheet, use the EFFECT(nominal_rate,npery) function, where nominal_rate is the APR and npery is the number of compounding periods per year.

Table 5.4 shows various EAR conversions. If compounding occurs annually, you will see that the EAR and the APR will be the same. If compounding happens more than once a year, then the EAR will be higher than the APR. The table also demonstrates that the

---

EXAMPLE 5-7

For interactive versions of this example, log in to Connect or go to mhhe.com/Cornett6e.

Evaluating Credit Card Offers LG5-7

As a college student, you probably receive many credit card offers in the mail. Consider these two offers. The first card charges a 16 percent APR. An examination of the footnotes reveals that this card compounds monthly. The second credit card charges 15.5 percent APR and compounds weekly. Which card has a lower effective annual rate?

SOLUTION:

Compute the EAR of each card to compare them in common (and realistic) terms. The first card has an EAR of

$$EAR = \left(1 + \frac{0.16}{12}\right)^{12} - 1 = 0.1732, \text{ or } 17.23\%$$

The EAR of the second card is

$$EAR = \left(1 + \frac{0.155}{52}\right)^{52} - 1 = 0.1674, \text{ or } 16.74\%$$

You should pick the second credit card because it has a lower effective annual rate. But note also that you will always be better off if you pay your credit card balance whenever the bill comes due.

The spreadsheet solution is:

	A	B	C	D	E	F
1		Card 1			Card 2	
2	APR	16.00%			15.50%	
3	Compounding Periods	12			52	
4						
5	EAR	17.23%			16.74%	
6		=EFFECT(B2,B3)			=EFFECT(E2,E3)	

Microsoft Excel

Similar to Problems 5-15, 5-16, Self-Test Problem 3.

	A	B	C	D
1	**APR**	**Compounding Periods**	**Equation**	**= EAR**
2	Varying the Compounding Periods			
3	5%	1	$(1 + 0.05/1)^1 - 1$	5.00%
4	5	4	$(1 + 0.05/4)^4 - 1$	5.09
5	5	12	$(1 + 0.05/12)^{12} - 1$	5.12
6	Varying APR and Compounding Periods			
7	9	4	$(1 + 0.09/4)^4 - 1$	9.31
8	9	12	$(1 + 0.09/12)^{12} - 1$	9.38
9	12	4	$(1 + 0.12/4)^4 - 1$	12.55
10	12	12	$(1 + 0.12/12)^{12} - 1$	12.68

Note: This compound frequency effect grows substantially for higher interest rates or longer-term loans.
Microsoft Excel

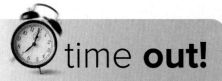

time **out!**

5-7 Why is EAR a more accurate measure of the rate actually paid than APR?

5-8 What would have a smaller present value: a future sum discounted annually or one discounted monthly?

compound frequency effect grows substantially for higher interest rates or longer-term loans. Compounded quarterly, the EAR is hardly different at all from a 5 percent APR: 5.09 percent versus 5 percent. The difference is larger when the APR is 12 percent. Compounded quarterly, the EAR is higher at 12.55 percent.

5.5 • ANNUITY LOANS LG5-8

In this chapter, we've focused on computing the future and present value of annuities. But in many situations, these values are already known and what we really need to compare are the payments or implied interest rate—usually, the highest interest rate offered.

What Is the Interest Rate?

Many business and personal applications already state the cost of an investment, as well as the annuity cash flows and time period. We need, then, to solve for the implied interest rate of this investment. Unfortunately, we have no general, easy equation to solve for the interest rate. Even financial calculators use an iterating process, which causes them to "think" a little longer before displaying the estimated interest rate result.

Consider the plight of a manager of a small doctor's office who has the opportunity to buy a piece of imaging equipment for $100,000. The equipment will allow the office to generate $25,000 in profits for six years, at which time the equipment will be worn out and without value in the United States. What rate of return does this purchase offer the doctor's office? The time line for this problem appears as

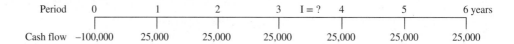

For the financial calculator solution, input N = 6, PV = −100000, PMT = 25000, and FV = 0. The interest rate result is then 12.98 percent. So, if this is a high enough return relative to other uses of the $100,000, the doctor's office should seriously consider purchasing the imaging machine.

To solve for the interest rate using a spreadsheet use the RATE(nper,pmt,pv,fv,type) function. For this problem, the function would appear as RATE(6,25000,-100000,0) and generate an answer of 12.98 percent.

EXAMPLE 5-8

For interactive versions of this example, log in to Connect or go to mhhe.com/Cornett6e.

Computing Interest Rate Needed LG2-2

After saving diligently throughout your entire career, you and your spouse are finally ready to retire with a nest egg of $800,000. You need to invest this money in a mix of stocks and bonds that will allow you to withdraw $6,000 per month for 30 years. What interest rate do you need to earn?

SOLUTION:

Use a financial calculator and input N = 360, PV = −800000, PMT = 6000, and FV = 0. The interest rate result is 0.6860 percent. But remember, because the periods and payments are in months, the interest rate is too. It is customary to report this as an APR: 8.23 percent (= 0.6860 percent × 12). However, the EAR more accurately reflects the true interest rate, 8.55 percent $(= 1.00686^{12} − 1)$. In order for your money to last for 30 years while funding a $6,000 per month income, you must earn at least an 8.23 APR per year return.

If you have uneven cash flows, use the calculator CF worksheet and then solve with the IRR function.

The spreadsheet solution is:

	A	B	C	D
1	PV	PMT	N	
2	$800,000	$6,000	30	
3				
4	i =	0.69%	=RATE(C2*12,-B2,A2,0)	
5	APR	8.23%	=B4*12	

Microsoft Excel

Similar to Problems 5-20, 5-21

Finding Payments on an Amortized Loan LG5-9

Many consumers and small business owners already know how much money they want to borrow and the level of current interest rates. Usually, they need to translate this information into the actual payments to determine if they can really afford the purchase. A loan structured for annuity payments that completely pay off the debt is called an **amortized loan.** To compute the annuity cash flow of an amortized loan, rearrange the present value of an annuity formula, Equation 5-4, to solve for the payment:

> **amortized loan** A loan in which the borrower pays interest and principal over time.

Payment = Present value × Amortization

$$PMT_N = PV \times \left[\frac{i}{1 - \dfrac{1}{(1+i)^N}} \right]$$ (5-9)

Most car loans require monthly payments for three to five years. Assume that you need a $10,000 loan to buy a car. The loan is for four years and interest rates are 9 percent per year APR. To implement Equation 5-9, use an interest rate of 0.75 percent (= 9 percent/12) and 48 periods (= 4 × 12) as

$$PMT_{48} = \$10,000 \times \left[\frac{0.0075}{1 - \dfrac{1}{(1+0.0075)^{48}}} \right] = \$10,000 \times 0.024885 = \$248.85$$

So, when interest rates are 9 percent, it takes monthly payments of $248.85 to pay off a $10,000 loan in four years.

Phillip Spears/Getty Images

the
Math Coach on...

Common Mistakes

❝ As we noted in Chapter 4, when computing the interest rate, make sure that the present value and the annuity payments are of different signs (positive versus negative). Otherwise, the calculator will show an error. ❞

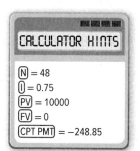

CALCULATOR HINTS

Ⓝ = 48
Ⓘ = 0.75
ⓅⓋ = 10000
ⒻⓋ = 0
CPT PMT = −248.85

loan principal The balance yet to be paid on a loan.

amortization schedule A table detailing the periodic loan payment, interest payment, and debt balance over the life of the loan.

To solve for the payment using a spreadsheet, use the PMT(rate,nper,pv,fv,type) function. For this problem, the function would appear as PMT(0.09/12,4*12, −10000,0) and generate an answer of $248.85.

Interest rate levels and loan length strongly affect how large your payments will be. Table 5.5 shows the monthly payments needed to pay off a mortgage debt at various interest rates and lengths of time. (Try computing the payments yourself!) Note that as the interest rate declines, the monthly payment also declines. This is why people rush to refinance their mortgages after interest rates fall. A decline of 1 or 2 percent can save a homeowner hundreds of dollars every month. You will also see from the table that paying off a mortgage in only 15 years requires larger payments, but generally saves thousands in interest.

Amortized Loan Schedules When you pay a car loan or home mortgage, you will often find it useful to know how much of the debt, or **loan principal**, you still owe. For example, consider a case wherein you bought a car two years ago using a four-year loan. In order to sell the car now, the loan balance will have to be paid off. Being able to compute this principal balance may influence your chances of selling the car.

An interest-only loan allows the borrower to make payments that consist totally of interest payments, so none of the debt is reduced. A $10,000 interest-only loan with a 9 percent APR paid monthly will cost $75 per month (= $10,000 × 0.09 ÷ 12). Amortizing this loan over four years requires monthly payments of $248.85 (see earlier car loan problem). The difference in the first month's payment on the two loans is $173.85 (= $248.85 − $75) and represents the amount of the regular amortized loan's payment that goes to reducing the principal balance. So after the first month's payment, the amortized loan's balance has fallen to $9,826.15, while the interest-only loan still has a balance of $10,000.

In the second month, the interest incurred on the regular amortized loan is $73.70 (= $9,826.15 × 0.09 ÷ 12), so the $248.85 second-month payment represents principal payment of $175.15. These numbers are shown in the **amortization schedule** of Table 5.6. The table will show you that the early payments on a car loan go mostly to

▼ **TABLE 5.5** Monthly Payments on a $225,000 Loan

	A	B	C
1	**Annual Percentage Rate (APR)**	**Years to Repay Loan**	**Monthly Payment**
2	*30-Year Mortgage*		
3	10%	30	$1,974.54
4	8%	30	1,650.97
5	7%	30	1,496.93
6	6%	30	1,348.99
7	*15-Year Mortgage*		
8	8%	15	2,150.22
9	7%	15	2,022.36
10	6%	15	1,898.68
11			
12		=PMT(A10/12,B10*12,−225000,0)	

Microsoft Excel

▼ TABLE 5.6 Amortization Schedule over Four Years (9 Percent APR)

	A	B	C	D	E	F	G	H	I	J	K	L
1	Month	Beginning Balance	Total Payment	Interest Paid	Principal Paid	Ending Balance	Month	Beginning Balance	Total Payment	Interest Paid	Principal Paid	Ending Balance
2	1	$10,000.00	$248.85	$75.00	$173.85	$9,826.15	25	$5,447.13	$248.85	$40.85	$208.00	$5,239.14
3	2	9,826.15	248.85	73.70	175.15	9,651.00	26	5,239.14	248.85	39.29	209.56	5,029.58
4	3	9,651.00	248.85	72.38	176.47	9,474.53	27	5,029.58	248.85	37.72	211.13	4,818.45
5	4	9,474.53	248.85	71.06	177.79	9,296.74	28	4,818.45	248.85	36.14	212.71	4,605.74
6	5	9,296.74	248.85	69.73	179.12	9,117.61	29	4,605.74	248.85	34.54	214.31	4,391.43
7	6	9,117.61	248.85	68.38	180.47	8,937.15	30	4,391.43	248.85	32.94	215.91	4,175.52
8	7	8,937.15	248.85	67.03	181.82	8,755.32	31	4,175.52	248.85	31.32	217.53	3,957.99
9	8	8,755.32	248.85	65.66	183.19	8,572.14	32	3,957.99	248.85	29.68	219.17	3,738.82
10	9	8,572.14	248.85	64.29	184.56	8,387.58	33	3,738.82	248.85	28.04	220.81	3,518.01
11	10	8,387.58	248.85	62.91	185.94	8,201.64	34	3,518.01	248.85	26.39	222.46	3,295.55
12	11	8,201.64	248.85	61.51	187.34	8,014.30	35	3,295.55	248.85	24.72	224.13	3,071.41
13	12	8,014.30	248.85	60.11	188.74	7,825.56	36	3,071.41	248.85	23.04	225.81	2,845.60
14	13	7,825.56	248.85	58.69	190.16	7,635.40	37	2,845.60	248.85	21.34	227.51	2,618.09
15	14	7,635.40	248.85	57.27	191.58	7,443.81	38	2,618.09	248.85	19.64	229.21	2,388.88
16	15	7,443.81	248.85	55.83	193.02	7,250.79	39	2,388.88	248.85	17.92	230.93	2,157.94
17	16	7,250.79	248.85	54.38	194.47	7,056.32	40	2,157.94	248.85	16.18	232.67	1,925.28
18	17	7,056.32	248.85	52.92	195.93	6,860.40	41	1,925.28	248.85	14.44	234.41	1,690.87
19	18	6,860.40	248.85	51.45	197.40	6,663.00	42	1,690.87	248.85	12.68	236.17	1,454.70
20	19	6,663.00	248.85	49.97	198.88	6,464.12	43	1,454.70	248.85	10.91	237.94	1,216.76
21	20	6,464.12	248.85	48.48	200.37	6,263.75	44	1,216.76	248.85	9.13	239.72	977.04
22	21	6,263.75	248.85	46.98	201.87	6,061.88	45	977.04	248.85	7.33	241.52	735.51
23	22	6,061.88	248.85	45.46	203.39	5,858.49	46	735.51	248.85	5.52	243.33	492.18
24	23	5,858.49	248.85	43.94	204.91	5,653.58	47	492.18	248.85	3.69	245.16	247.02
25	24	5,653.58	248.85	42.40	206.45	5,447.13	48	247.02	248.87	1.85	247.02	0.00
26												
27		=F24	=B25*0.09/12		=C25-D25	=B25-E25		Total interest paid =		$1,944.82		

Microsoft Excel

paying the interest rather than reducing the principal. That interest component declines over time, and then the principal balance declines.

The amortization schedule shows that if you wish to sell the car after two years, you will have to pay the loan company a car loan (principal) debt of $5,447.13. Of course, if you had an interest-only loan, you would still owe the full principal of $10,000 after two years. Amortization schedules are also useful for determining other things, like the total amount of interest that you will pay over the life of the loan. In this case, if you take a regular loan in which you pay both principal and interest, you pay $10,000 in principal and nearly $1,945 in interest during the four years of the loan. The interest component is an even larger component of longer-term loans, like 30-year mortgages. Depending on the interest rate charged, the first payment in a mortgage consists of 75 percent to 95 percent interest. The home mortgage principal balance falls very slowly in the first years of the loan.

We construct amortization schedules by showing the loan's principal balance at the beginning of the month. This is the same as the balance at the end of the previous month (except for the very first payment). Then we compute the interest owed on that balance for the month. After paying that interest, what's left of the monthly payment reduces the loan balance for the next month. Because of these repetitive computations, spreadsheets make amortization schedules easy to construct.

Compute the time Period You might also find it useful to know how long it will take to pay off a loan with specific annuity payments. To find the number of periods, you can solve equation 5-9 for N—the number of payments—but the equation becomes

time out!

5-9 How might credit card companies keep their cardholders in debt for a long time? What payment do the credit card companies expect your friend to make so that he never pays down the debt?

5-10 Can you find the interest rate if you know the annuity payments and a future value? Under what circumstances might you want to solve this kind of problem? Which equation would you use?

EXAMPLE 5-9

Monthly Mortgage Payments LG5-9

For interactive versions of this example, log in to Connect or go to mhhe.com/Cornett6e.

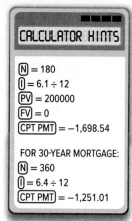

CALCULATOR HINTS

N = 180
I = 6.1 ÷ 12
PV = 200000
FV = 0
CPT PMT = −1,698.54

FOR 30-YEAR MORTGAGE:
N = 360
I = 6.4 ÷ 12
CPT PMT = −1,251.01

Say that you have your heart set on purchasing a beautiful, old Tudor-style house for $250,000. A mortgage broker says that you can qualify for a mortgage for 80 percent (or $200,000) of the price. If you get a 15-year mortgage, the interest rate will be 6.1 percent APR. A 30-year mortgage costs 6.4 percent. One of the factors that will help you decide which mortgage to take is the magnitude of the monthly payments. What will they be?[3]

SOLUTION:

To pay off the mortgage in only 15 years, the payments would have to be larger than for the 30-year mortgage. The higher payment will be eased somewhat because the interest rate is lower on the 15-year mortgage. The interest rate would be $i = 0.061 \div 12 = 0.0050833$, or 0.50833% per month. The payment for the 15-year mortgage is

$$PMT_{180} = \$200,000 \times \left[\frac{0.0050833}{1 - \frac{1}{(1 + 0.0050833)^{180}}} \right] = \$200,000 \times 0.0084927 = \$1,698.54$$

The payment for the 30-year mortgage would be

$$PMT_{360} = \$200,000 \times \left[\frac{0.0053333}{1 - \frac{1}{(1 + 0.0053333)^{360}}} \right] = \$200,000 \times 0.00625506 = \$1,251.01$$

The spreadsheet solution is:

	A	B	C	D
1		**15-Year Mortgage**		**30-Year Mortgage**
2	Home Price	250,000		250,000
3	Amount Financed	200,000		200,000
4	APR	6.10%		6.40%
5	N	15		30
6				
7	PMT =	$1,698.54		$1,251.01
8		=PMT(B4/12,B5*12,-B3)		=PMT(D4/12,D5*12,-D3)

Microsoft Excel

So, the payments on the 15-year mortgage are nearly $450 more each month than the 30-year mortgage payments. You must decide whether the cost of paying the extra $450 each month is worth it to own the house with no debt 15 years sooner. The decision would depend on your financial budget and the strength of your desire to be debt free.

Similar to Problem 5-13, Self-Test Problems 1 and 4

---

add-on interest A calculation of the amount of interest determined at the beginning of the loan and then added to the principal.

quite complicated.[4] Many people just use a financial calculator or spreadsheet. We can check to see if the $248.85 monthly payment would indeed pay off the $10,000, 9 percent car loan in four years. Finding the solution with a financial calculator entails entering I = 0.75, PV = 10000, PMT = −248.85, and FV = 0. The answer is 48 months. To solve for the number of periods using a spreadsheet use the NPER(rate,pmt,pv,fv,type) function. For this problem, the function would appear as =NPER(0.09/12,−248.85,10000,0) and generate an answer of 48 months.

Add-On Interest One method of calculating payments of a loan that is popular in payday lending is called **add-on interest.** This method computes the amount of the interest payable at the beginning of the loan, which is then added to the principal of the loan. This total is then divided into the number of payments to be made. Consider a loan of $1,000 to be paid with 9 percent add-on interest and repaid in six monthly payments.

the Math Coach on...

Using the AMORT Function in TVM Calculators

❝ TVM calculators have preprogrammed functions to compute the amount of principal paid part way through a mortgage. For example, if you took out a 30-year, $200,000 mortgage at a 6 percent APR, how much principal have you paid after five years? How much do you still owe? How much interest have you paid?

To answer these questions, first enter the mortgage information to compute the monthly payments. Then use the AMORT function. This example uses the Texas Instruments BA II+ as an example. The Hewlett-Packard and other TVM calculators have similar functions. The AMORT function allows you to compute the loan balance at any time during the mortgage period. It also computes the amount of principal and interest that has been paid during any time period. To answer the questions above,

1. Press 2nd AMORT and P1 = 1 appears. (This refers to the first payment of the mortgage.)

2. Press the down arrow ↓; P2 = appears. (This refers to the last payment made.)

3. The question refers to 5 years of payments, which is 60 months. Enter 60 and press ENTER.

   The calculator has now computed the loan balance after the 60th payment and the amount of principal and interest that have been paid between the 1st and the 60th payments.

4. Press the down arrow ↓; displayed is BAL = 186,108.71, which is the loan balance.

5. Press the down arrow ↓; displayed is PRN = 13,891.29, which is the principal paid in the first five years.

6. Press the down arrow ↓; displayed is INT = −58,054.78, which is the interest paid in the first five years.

   Note that in the beginning of a mortgage, far more interest is paid than principal. ❞

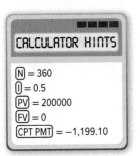

CALCULATOR HINTS

N = 360
I = 0.5
PV = 200000
FV = 0
CPT PMT = −1,199.10

EXAMPLE 5-10

For interactive versions of this example, log in to Connect or go to mhhe.com/Cornett6e.

Time to Pay Off a Credit Card Balance LG5-10

Through poor financial management, your friend has racked up $5,000 in debt on his credit card. The card charges a 19 percent APR and compounds monthly. His latest bill shows that he must pay a minimum of $150 this month. At this rate, how long will it take your friend to pay off his credit card debt?

SOLUTION:

Using the financial calculator, input I = 1.58333(= 19/12), PV = 5000, PMT = −150, FV = 0. The answer is 48 months, or 4 years. If the friend pays the minimum payment, then it will be a long time before he will be out of debt. The credit card company is very content to continue to earn the high return for many years—essentially, the interest on the loan and a very small portion of the principal. Your friend should pay more than the minimum charge to reduce his debt quicker.

Similar to Problems 5-41, 5-42, Self-Test Problem 4

The total interest for this loan is computed as 9 percent of $1,000 for six months, or $45 (= 0.09 × $1,000 × ½). This is added to the principal for a total of $1,045. Each of the six monthly payments is then $1,045 ÷ 6 = $174.17. Be alert that the add-on interest method seriously understates the real interest rate that is being paid! If you borrow $1,000 and repay a $174.17 monthly annuity for six months, the monthly interest rate is 1.27 percent. This is a 15.27 percent APR (= 1.27% × 12) and a 16.39 percent EAR (= 1.0127^{12} − 1)—both much higher than the advertised 9 percent interest rate of this loan.

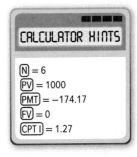

CALCULATOR HINTS

N = 6
PV = 1000
PMT = −174.17
FV = 0
CPT I = 1.27

Get Online

mhhe.com/CornettM6e

for study materials including
quizzes, iPod downloads,
and video

JGI/Jamie Grill/Getty Images

Your Turn...

Questions

1. How can you add a cash flow in year 2 and a cash flow in year 4? In year 7? *(LG5-1)*

2. People can become millionaires in their retirement years quite easily if they start saving early in employer 401(k) or 403(b) programs (or even if their employers don't offer such programs). Demonstrate the growth of a $250 monthly contribution for 40 years earning 9 percent APR. *(LG5-2)*

3. When you discount multiple cash flows, how does the future period that a cash flow is paid affect its present value and its contribution to the value of all the cash flows? *(LG5-3)*

4. How can you use the present value of an annuity concept to determine the price of a house you can afford? *(LG5-4)*

5. Because perpetuity payments continue forever, how can a present value be computed? Why isn't the present value infinite? *(LG5-5)*

6. Explain why you use the same adjustment factor, $(1 + i)$, when you adjust annuity due payments for both future value and present value. *(LG5-6)*

7. Use the idea of compound interest to explain why EAR is larger than APR. *(LG5-7)*

8. Would you rather pay $10,000 for a five-year, $2,500 annuity or a 10-year, $1,250 annuity? Why? *(LG5-8)*

9. The interest on your home mortgage is tax deductible. Why are the early years of the mortgage more helpful in reducing taxes than in the later years? *(LG5-9)*

10. How can you use the concepts illustrated in computing the number of payments in an annuity to figure how to pay off a credit card balance? How does the magnitude of the payment impact the number of months? *(LG5-10)*

Problems

5-1   **Future Value** Compute the future value in year 9 of a $2,000 deposit in year 1 and another $1,500 deposit at the end of year 3 using a 10 percent interest rate. *(LG5-1)*

5-2   **Future Value of an Annuity** What is the future value of a $900 annuity payment over five years if interest rates are 8 percent? *(LG5-2)*

5-3   **Present Value** Compute the present value of a $2,000 deposit in year 1 and another $1,500 deposit at the end of year 3 if interest rates are 10 percent. *(LG5-3)*

5-4   **Present Value of an Annuity** What's the present value of a $900 annuity payment over five years if interest rates are 8 percent? *(LG5-4)*

5-5   **Present Value of a Perpetuity** What's the present value, when interest rates are 7.5 percent, of a $50 payment made every year forever? *(LG5-5)*

5-6   **Present Value of an Annuity Due** If the present value of an ordinary, seven-year annuity is $6,500 and interest rates are 7.5 percent, what's the present value of the same annuity due? *(LG5-6)*

5-7   **Future Value of an Annuity Due** If the future value of an ordinary, seven-year annuity is $6,500 and interest rates are 7.5 percent, what is the future value of the same annuity due? *(LG5-6)*

5-8   **Effective Annual Rate** A loan is offered with monthly payments and a 10 percent APR. What's the loan's effective annual rate (*EAR*)? *(LG5-7)*

5-9   **Spreadsheet Problem: Future Values of an Ordinary Annuity and Annuity Due** What is the future value of a $100 annual payment over 10 years if interest rates are 4 percent using both end-of-year and beginning-of-year payments? *(LG5-6)*

5-10   **Spreadsheet Problem: Present Values of an Ordinary Annuity and Annuity Due** What is the present value of a $100 annual payment over 10 years if interest rates are 4 percent using both end-of-year and beginning-of-year payments? *(LG5-6)*

5-11   **Spreadsheet Problem: Effective Annual Rate** A loan is offered with twice-monthly payments (26 payments per year) and a 14 percent APR. What's the loan's effective annual rate (*EAR*)? *(LG5-7)*

5-12   **Future Value** Given a 4 percent interest rate, compute the year 6 future value of deposits made in years 1, 2, 3, and 4 of $1,100, $1,200, $1,200, and $1,500. *(LG5-1)*

5-13   **Future Value of Multiple Annuities** Assume that you contribute $200 per month to a retirement plan for 20 years. Then you are able to increase the contribution to $300 per month for another 30 years. Given a 7 percent interest rate, what is the value of your retirement plan after the 50 years? *(LG5-2)*

5-14   **Present Value** Given a 6 percent interest rate, compute the present value of payments made in years 1, 2, 3, and 4 of $1,000, $1,200, $1,200, and $1,500. *(LG5-3)*

5-15   **Present Value of Multiple Annuities** A small business owner visits her bank to ask for a loan. The owner states that she can repay a loan at $1,000 per month for the next three years and then $2,000 per month for two years after that. If the bank is charging customers 7.5 percent APR, how much would it be willing to lend the business owner? *(LG5-4)*

5-16   **Present Value** You are looking to buy a car. You can afford $450 in monthly payments for four years. In addition to the loan, you can make a $1,000 down payment. If interest rates are 5 percent APR, what price of car can you afford? *(LG5-4)*

5-17 **Present Value of a Perpetuity** A perpetuity pays $100 per year and interest rates are 7.5 percent. How much would its value change if interest rates increased to 9 percent? Did the value increase or decrease? *(LG5-5)*

5-18 **Future and Present Values of an Annuity Due** If you start making $50 monthly contributions today and continue them for five years, what's their future value if the compounding rate is 10 percent APR? What is the present value of this annuity? *(LG5-6)*

5-19 **Compound Frequency** Payday loans are very-short-term loans that charge very high interest rates. You can borrow $225 today and repay $300 in two weeks. What is the compounded *annual* rate implied by this 33.33 percent rate charged for only two weeks? *(LG5-7)*

5-20 **Annuity Interest Rate** What's the interest rate of a six-year, annual $5,000 annuity with present value of $20,000? *(LG5-8)*

5-21 **Annuity Interest Rate** What annual interest rate would you need to earn if you wanted a $1,000 per month contribution to grow to $75,000 in six years? *(LG5-8)*

5-22 **Add-on Interest Payments** To borrow $500, you are offered an add-on interest loan at 8 percent. Two loan payments are to be made, one at six months and the other at the end of the year. Compute the two equal payments. *(LG5-8)*

5-23 **Loan Payments** You wish to buy a $25,000 car. The dealer offers you a four-year loan with a 9 percent APR. What are the monthly payments? How would the payment differ if you paid interest only? What would the consequences of such a decision be? *(LG5-9)*

5-24 **Number of Annuity Payments** Joey realizes that he has charged too much on his credit card and has racked up $5,000 in debt. If he can pay $150 each month and the card charges 17 percent APR (*compounded monthly*), how long will it take him to pay off the debt? *(LG5-10)*

5-25 **Spreadsheet Problem: Annuity Interest Rate** What is the APR interest rate of a six-year, monthly $400 annuity with present value of $20,000? *(LG5-8)*

5-26 **Spreadsheet Problem: Number of Annuity Payments** You realize that you can retire when you have $1 million in assets. You currently have $500,000 in retirement assets and contribute $500 more each month? If your investment portfolio earns an 8 percent annual rate of return, how long will it be until you can retire? *(LG5-10)*

5-27 **Spreadsheet Problem: Future Value of Multiple Annuities** Assume that you contribute $150 per month to a retirement plan for 20 years. Then you can increase the contribution to $250 per month for another 20 years, and finally, $400 per month for the last 10 years. Given a 7 percent interest rate, what is the value of your retirement plan after the 50 years? *(LG5-2)*

	A	B	C	D
1	Time Period	Years	Rate	Monthly Contribution
2	1 to 20	20	7%	$150
3	21 to 40	20	7%	$250
4	41 to 55	10	7%	$400
5				
6				FV of Annuity 1 =
7				FV of Annuity 2 =
8				FV of Annuity 3 =
9				
10				Value of Retirement Assets =

Microsoft Excel

5-28 **Future Value** Given an 8 percent interest rate, compute the year 7 future value if deposits of $1,000 and $2,000 are made in years 1 and 3, respectively, and a withdrawal of $700 is made in year 4. *(LG5-10)*

5-29 **EAR of Add-on Interest Loan** To borrow $2,000, you are offered an add-on interest loan at 10 percent with 12 monthly payments. First compute the 12 equal payments and then compute the EAR of the loan. *(LG5-7, LG5-8)*

5-30 **Low Financing or Cash Back?** A car company is offering a choice of deals. You can receive $500 cash back on the purchase or a 3 percent APR, four-year loan. The price of the car is $15,000 and you could obtain a four-year loan from your credit union at 6 percent APR. Which deal is cheaper? *(LG5-4, LG5-9)*

5-31 **Amortization Schedule** Create the amortization schedule for a loan of $15,000, paid monthly over three years using a 9 percent APR. *(LG5-9)*

5-32 **Investing for Retirement** Monica has decided that she wants to build enough retirement wealth, if invested at 8 percent per year, to provide her with $3,500 of monthly income for 20 years. To date, she has saved nothing, but she still has 30 years until she retires. How much money does she need to contribute per month to reach her goal? *(LG5-4, LG5-9)*

5-33 **Loan Balance** Rachel purchased a $15,000 car three years ago using an 8 percent, four-year loan. She has decided that she would sell the car now, if she could get a price that would pay off the balance of her loan. What is the minimum price Rachel would need to receive for her car? *(LG5-9)*

5-34 **Teaser Rate Mortgage** A mortgage broker is offering a $183,900 30-year mortgage with a teaser rate. In the first two years of the mortgage, the borrower makes monthly payments on only a 4 percent APR interest rate. After the second year, the mortgage interest rate charged increases to 7 percent APR. What are the monthly payments in the first two years? What are the monthly payments after the second year? *(LG5-9)*

5-35 **Spreadsheet Problem: Investing for Retirement and Retirement Annuity** Consider a person who begins contributing to a retirement plan at age 25 and contributes for 40 years until retirement at age 65. For the first 10 years, she contributes $250 per month. She increases the contribution rate to $416.67 per month in years 11 through 20. This is followed by increases to $833.33 per month in years 21 through 30 and to $1,250 per month for the last 10 years. This money earns a 9 percent return. First compute the value of the retirement plan when she turns age 65. Then compute the monthly payment she would receive over the next 40 years if the wealth was converted to an annuity payment at 6 percent. *(LG5-2, LG5-9)*

	A	B	C	D
1	**Earning Years**			
2	**Time Period**	**Years**	**Rate**	**Monthly Contribution**
3	1 to 10	10	9%	$250.00
4	11 to 20	10	9%	$416.67
5	21 to 30	10	9%	$833.33
6	31 to 40	10	9%	$1,250.00
7				
8				
9				FV of Annuity 1 =
10				FV of Annuity 2 =
11				FV of Annuity 3 =
12				FV of Annuity 4 =
13				
14				Value of Retirement Assets =
15				
16	**Retirement Years**			
17	**Time Period**	**Years**	**Rate**	**Monthly Payment =**
18	1 to 40	40	6%	

Microsoft Excel

5-36   **Spreadsheet Problem: Extra Mortgage Payments** When paying off a home mortgage, extra principal payments can have a dramatic impact on the time needed to pay off the mortgage. *(LG5-9)*

     a. Create an amortization schedule for a $200,000, three-year mortgage, with a 6 percent APR.

     b. After the fifth year, add an extra $100 to each monthly payment. When is the loan paid off?

Combined chapter 4 and chapter 5 problems

4&5-1   **Future Value** Consider that you are 35 years old and have just changed to a new job. You have $80,000 in the retirement plan from your former employer. You can roll that money into the retirement plan of the new employer. You will also contribute $3,600 each year into your new employer's plan. If the rolled-over money and the new contributions both earn a 7 percent return, how much should you expect to have when you retire in 30 years?

4&5-2   **Future Value and Number of Annuity Payments** Your client has been given a trust fund valued at $1 million. He cannot access the money until he turns 65 years old, which is in 25 years. At that time, he can withdraw $25,000 per month. If the trust fund is invested at a 5.5 percent rate, how many months will it last your client once he starts to withdraw the money?

4&5-3   **Present Value and Annuity Payments** A local furniture store is advertising a deal in which you buy a $3,000 dining room set and do not need to pay for two years *(no interest cost is incurred)*. How much money would you have to deposit now in a savings account earning 5 percent APR, compounded monthly, to pay the $3,000 bill in two years? Alternatively, how much would you have to deposit in the savings account each month to be able to pay the bill?

4&5-4   **House Appreciation and Mortgage Payments** Say that you purchase a house for $200,000 by getting a mortgage for $180,000 and paying a $20,000 down payment. If you get a 30-year mortgage with a 7 percent interest rate, what are the monthly payments? What would the loan balance be in 10 years? If the house appreciates at 3 percent per year, what will be the value of the house in 10 years? How much of this value is your equity?

4&5-5   **Construction Loan** You have secured a loan from your bank for two years to build your home. The terms of the loan are that you will borrow $200,000 now and an additional $100,000 in one year. Interest of 10 percent APR will be charged on the balance monthly. Since no payments will be made during the two-year loan, the balance will grow at the 10 percent compounded rate. At the end of the two years, the balance will be converted to a traditional 30-year mortgage at a 6 percent interest rate. What will you be paying as monthly mortgage payments *(principal and interest only)*?

4&5-6   **Spreadsheet Problem: Construction Loan** You have secured a loan from your bank for two years to build your home. The terms of the loan are that you will borrow $100,000 now and an additional $50,000 in one year. Interest of 9 percent

APR will be charged on the balance monthly. Since no payments will be made during the two-year loan, the balance will grow. At the end of the two years, the balance will be converted to a traditional 15-year mortgage at a 7 percent interest rate. What will you pay as monthly mortgage payments *(principal and interest only)*?

	A	B	C
1	**Borrow Amount**	**Beginning Year**	**Rate**
2	$100,000	0	9%
3	$50,000	1	
4			
5		**Loan Balance after 2 years =**	
6			
7	**After converting loan to mortgage:**		
8	N	15	
9	i	7%	
10		**Monthly Payment =**	

Microsoft Excel

Notes

CHAPTER 5

1. The contract actually contains some complications like incentives to play well and salary deferral. We ignore those complicating factors here.

2. It is also possible to continuously compound. The future value of a continuously compounded deposit is $FV^N = PV \times e^{(i \times N)}$, where e has a value of 2.7183.

3. Most homeowners are actually most interested in their total payment, which will include hazard insurance for the home and property taxes. Such payments are referred to as PITI—principal, interest, taxes, and insurance. For simplicity, we use only PI payments here—principal and interest.

4. The equation for solving for the number of periods in an annuity is:

$$N = \frac{\ln (PMT/(PMT - PVA_N \times i))}{\ln (1 + i)}.$$

Design elements: (Clock) Floortje/Getty Images; (Referee) Richard Ransier/Getty Images

Tupungato/Shutterstock

part four

understanding financial markets and institutions

How do funds flow throughout the economy? How do financial markets operate and relate to one another? As an individual investor or a financial manager, you need to know. Your future decision-making skills depend on it. Investors' funds flow through financial markets such as the New York Stock Exchange and mortgage markets. Financial institutions—commercial banks (e.g., Bank of America), investment banks (e.g., Morgan Stanley), and mutual funds (e.g., Fidelity)—act as intermediaries to channel funds from individual savers or investors through financial markets. This chapter looks at the nature and operations of financial markets and discusses the financial institutions (FIs) that participate in those markets. Bonds, stocks, and other securities that trade in the markets are covered in Chapters 7 and 8. ∎

LEARNING GOALS

LG6-1 Differentiate between primary and secondary markets and between money and capital markets.

LG6-2 List the types of securities traded in money and capital markets.

LG6-3 Identify different types of financial institutions and the services that each provides.

LG6-4 Know the main suppliers and demanders of loanable funds.

LG6-5 Understand how equilibrium interest rates are determined.

LG6-6 Analyze specific factors that influence interest rates.

LG6-7 Offer different theories that explain the shape of the term structure of interest rates.

LG6-8 Demonstrate how forward interest rates derive from the term structure of interest rates.

»viewpoints

DPH Corporation needs to issue new bonds either this year or in two years. DPH Corp. is a profitable firm, but if the U.S. economy were to experience a downturn, the company would see a big drop in sales over the next two years as its products are very sensitive to changes in the overall economy. DPH Corp. currently has $10 million in public debt outstanding, but its bonds are not actively traded. What questions must DPH Corp. consider as its managers decide whether to issue bonds today or in two years? How can DPH Corp. get these bonds to potential buyers and thus raise the needed capital? **(See the solution at the end of the chapter.)**

---

financial markets The arenas through which funds flow.

primary markets Markets in which corporations raise funds through new issues of securities.

investment banks Banks that help companies and governments raise capital.

commercial banks Depository institutions whose major assets are loans and whose major liabilities are deposits.

6.1 • FINANCIAL MARKETS LG6-1

Financial markets exist to manage the flow of funds from investors to borrowers as well as from one investor to another. We generally differentiate financial markets by their primary financial instruments' characteristics (such as bond maturities) or the market's location. Specifically, we can distinguish markets along two major dimensions:

1. Primary versus secondary markets.
2. Money versus capital markets.

Primary Markets versus Secondary Markets

Primary Markets **Primary markets** provide a forum in which demanders of funds (e.g., corporations such as IBM or government entities such as the U.S. Treasury) raise funds by issuing new financial instruments, such as stocks and bonds. Corporations or government entities continually have new projects or expanded production needs but do not have sufficient internally generated funds (such as retained earnings) to support their capital needs. Thus, corporations and governments issue securities in external primary markets to raise additional funds. These entities sell the new financial instrument issues to initial fund suppliers (e.g., households) in exchange for the funds (money) that the issuer requires.

In the United States, financial institutions called **investment banks** arrange most primary market transactions for businesses. Some of the best-known examples of U.S. investment banks include Morgan Stanley, Goldman Sachs, or Merrill Lynch (owned by Bank of America, a **commercial bank**). These firms intermediate between issuing parties (fund demanders) and investors (fund suppliers). Investment banks provide fund demanders with a number of services, including advising the company or government agency about the securities issue (such as an appropriate offer price and number of securities to issue) and attracting initial public purchasers of the customer's securities offerings. Firms that need funds are seldom expert at raising capital themselves, so they avert risk and lower their costs by turning to experts at investment banks to issue their primary market securities.

The initial (or primary market) sale of securities occurs either through a public offering or as a private placement to a small group of investors. An investment bank serves as a security underwriter in a public offering. In a private placement, the security issuer engages the group of buyers (usually fewer than 10) to purchase the whole issue. Buyers are typically financial institutions. To protect smaller individual investors against a lack of disclosure, publicly traded securities must be registered with the Securities and Exchange Commission (SEC). Private placements, on the other hand, can be unregistered and resold to large,

John Adams wants to invest in one of two corporate bonds issued by separate firms. One bond yields 8.00 percent with a 10-year maturity; the other offers a 10.00 percent yield and a 9-year maturity. The second bond *seems* to be the better deal if one only looks at the interest rate. Is it necessarily the bond in which John should invest? Once he decides which bond represents the better investment, how can John go about buying the bond? **(See the solution at the end of the chapter.)**

Should John consider bonds from other countries?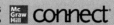

financially sophisticated investors only. Large investors supposedly possess the resources and expertise to analyze a security's risk. Privately placed bonds and stocks traditionally have been among the most illiquid securities in the securities markets; only the very largest financial institutions or institutional investors are able or willing to buy and hold them in the absence of an active secondary market. Issuers of privately placed securities tend to be less well known (e.g., medium-sized municipalities and corporations). Because of this lack of information and its associated higher risk, returns paid to holders of privately placed securities tend to be higher than those on publicly placed securities issues.

Figure 6.1 illustrates a time line for the primary market exchange of funds for a new issue of corporate bonds or equity. We will further discuss how companies, the U.S. Treasury, and government agencies that market primary government securities, such as Ginnie Mae and Freddie Mac, go about selling primary market securities in Chapter 8. Throughout this text, we focus on government securities from the *buyer's,* rather than the seller's, point of view. You can find in-depth discussions of government securities from the seller's point of view in a public finance text.

Primary market financial instruments include stock issues from firms initially going public (e.g., allowing their equity shares to be publicly traded on stock markets for the first time). We usually refer to these first-time issues as **initial public offerings (IPOs).** For example, on December 10, 2020, Airbnb conducted a $3.5 billion IPO of its common stock. Airbnb used several investment banks, including Morgan Stanley and Goldman Sachs, to underwrite the company's stock. Publicly traded firms may issue additional

> **initial public offerings (IPOs)**
> A first-time issue of stock by a private firm going public (e.g., allowing its equity, some of which was held privately by managers and venture capital investors, to be *publicly* traded in stock markets for the first time).

▼FIGURE 6.1 Primary Market Transfer of Funds

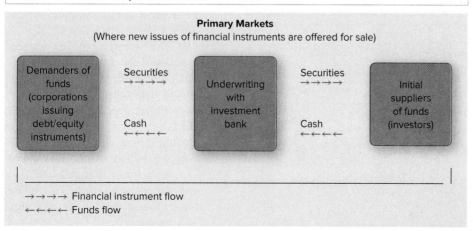

bonds or stocks as primary market securities. For example, on December 8, 2020, Tesla announced that it would sell an additional 7.8 million shares of common stock (at $641.00 per share) by selling shares directly on the stock exchange. The firm expected to use the net proceeds from the offering to strengthen its balance sheet, providing flexibility to fund its growth strategies. Specifically, Tesla was planning to build new factories in Germany and Texas.

Secondary Markets Once firms issue financial instruments in primary markets, these same stocks and bonds are then traded—that is, bought and resold—in **secondary markets.** The New York Stock Exchange (NYSE) and the NASDAQ are two well-known examples of secondary markets for trading stocks (see Chapters 7 and 8). In addition to stocks and bonds, secondary markets also exist for financial instruments backed by mortgages and other assets, foreign exchange, and futures and options (i.e., derivative securities, discussed later in the chapter).

Buyers find sellers of secondary market securities in economic agents that need funds (fund demanders). Secondary markets provide a centralized marketplace where economic agents know that they can buy or sell most securities quickly and efficiently. Secondary markets, therefore, save economic agents the search costs of finding buyers or sellers on their own. Figure 6.2 illustrates a secondary market transfer of funds. Secondary market buyers often use securities brokers such as Charles Schwab or other brokerage firms to act as intermediaries as they exchange funds for securities (see Chapter 8). An important note: The firm that originally issued the stock or bond is not involved in secondary market transactions in any way—no money accrues to the company itself when its stock trades in a secondary market.

Secondary markets offer benefits to both investors (fund suppliers) and issuers (fund demanders). Investors gain liquidity and diversification benefits (see Chapter 10). Although corporate security issuers are not directly involved in secondary market transactions, issuers do gain information about their securities' current market value. Publicly traded firms can thus observe how investors perceive their corporate value and their corporate decisions by tracking their firms' securities' secondary market prices. Such price information allows issuers to evaluate how well they are using internal funds as well as the funds generated from previously issued stocks and bonds and provides indications about how well any subsequent bond or stock offerings might be received—and at what price.

Secondary market **trading volume** can be quite large. Trading volume is defined as the number of shares of a security that are simultaneously bought and sold during a given period. Each seller and each buyer actually contract with the exchange's clearinghouse, which then matches sell and buy orders for each transaction. The clearinghouse is a company whose stock trades on the exchange, and the clearinghouse runs on a for-profit basis.

The exchange and the clearinghouse can process many transactions in a single day. For example, on October 28, 1997, NYSE trading volume exceeded 1 billion shares for the first time ever. On October 10, 2008 (at the height of the financial crisis), NYSE trading volume topped 7.3 billion shares, the highest level to date. The average trading volume on the NYSE in 2020 was 4.9 billion shares. In contrast, during the mid-1980s, an NYSE trading day during which 250 million shares traded was considered a high-volume day.

▼**FIGURE 6.2** Secondary Market Transfer of Funds

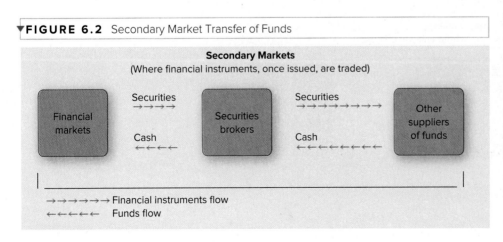

Money Markets versus Capital Markets

We noted that financial markets are differentiated in part by the maturity dates of the instruments traded. This distinction becomes important when we differentiate money markets from capital markets. Both of these markets deal in debt securities (capital markets also deal in equity securities); the question becomes one of when the securities come due.

Money Markets **Money markets** feature debt securities or instruments with maturities of one year or less (see Figure 6.3). In money markets, agents with excess short-term funds can lend (or supply) to economic agents who need (or demand) short-term funds. The suppliers of funds buy money market instruments and the demanders of funds sell money market instruments. Because money market instruments trade for only short periods of time, fluctuations in secondary-market prices are usually quite small. With less volatility, money market securities are thus less risky than longer-term instruments. In the United States, many money market securities do not trade in a specific location; rather, transactions occur via telephones, wire transfers, and computer trading. Thus, most U.S. money markets are said to be **over-the-counter (OTC) markets.**

Money Market Instruments LG6-2 Corporations and government entities issue a variety of money market securities to obtain short-term funds. These securities include

- Treasury bills.
- Federal funds and repurchase agreements.
- Commercial paper.
- Negotiable certificates of deposit.
- Banker's acceptances.

Table 6.1 lists and defines each money market security. Figure 6.4 graphically depicts the proportion of U.S. money market instruments outstanding across several decades. Notice that, in 2021, Treasury bills and federal funds and repurchase agreements commanded the highest dollar value of all money market instruments, followed by commercial paper and negotiable CDs.

Capital Markets **Capital markets** are markets in which parties trade equity (stocks) and debt (bonds) instruments that mature in more than one year (see Figure 6.3). Given their longer maturities, capital market instruments are subject to wider price fluctuations than are money market instruments (see the term structure discussion below and in Chapter 7).

money markets Markets that trade debt securities or instruments with maturities of less than one year.

over-the-counter (OTC) market Markets that do not operate in a specific fixed location—rather, transactions occur via telephones, wire transfers, and computer trading.

capital markets Markets that trade debt (bonds) and equity (stock) instruments with maturities of more than one year.

▼**FIGURE 6.3** Money versus Capital Market Maturities

	Capital Market Securities		
Money market securities	Notes and bonds	Stocks (equities)	Maturity
0	1 year to maturity	30 years to maturity	No specified maturity

▼ **TABLE 6.1** Money Market Instruments

Treasury bills: Short-term U.S. government obligations.

Federal funds: Short-term funds transferred between financial institutions, usually for no more than one day.

Repurchase agreements (repos): Agreements involving security sales by one party to another, with the promise to reverse the transaction at a specified date and price, usually at a discounted price.

Commercial paper: Short-term unsecured promissory notes that companies issue to raise short-term cash (sometimes called paper).

Negotiable certificates of deposit: Bank-issued time deposits that specify an interest rate and maturity date and are negotiable—that is, traded on an exchange. Their face value is usually at least $100,000.

Banker acceptances (BAs): Bank-guaranteed time drafts payable to a vendor of goods.

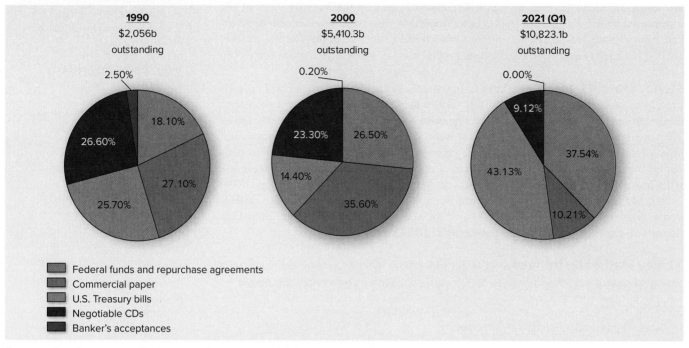

Here we see how the percentage of each money market instrument traded changes across several decades.

Source: Federal Reserve Board, "Financial Accounts of the United States," Statistical Releases, Washington, DC, various issues. www.federalreserve.gov.

foreign exchange markets
Markets in which foreign currency is traded for immediate or future delivery.

foreign exchange risk Risk arising from the unknown value at which foreign currency cash flows can be converted into U.S. dollars.

Capital Market Instruments Capital market securities include

- U.S. Treasury notes and bonds.
- U.S. government agency bonds.
- State and local government bonds.
- Mortgages and mortgage-backed securities.
- Corporate bonds.
- Corporate stocks.

Table 6.2 lists and defines each capital market security. Figure 6.5 graphically depicts U.S. capital market instruments outstanding over several decades. Note that corporate stocks (equities) represent the largest capital market instrument, followed by Treasury securities, and mortgages and mortgage-backed securities. The relative size of capital markets depends on two factors: the number of securities issued and their market prices. The 1990s saw consistently rising bull markets; hence the sharp increase in equities' dollar value outstanding. Stock values fell in the early 2000s as the U.S. economy experienced a downturn—partly because of 9/11 and partly because interest rates began to rise—and stock prices fell. Stock prices in most sectors subsequently recovered and, by 2007, even surpassed their 1999 levels. Stock prices fell precipitously during the financial crisis of 2008 and 2009. As of mid-March 2009, the Dow Jones Industrial Average (DJIA) had fallen in value 53.8 percent in less than 1½ years' time. This was greater than the decline during the market crash of 1937 and 1938, when it fell 49 percent. However, stock prices recovered along with the economy in the last half

▼ TABLE 6.2 Capital Market Instruments

Treasury notes and bonds: U.S. Treasury long-term obligations issued to finance the national debt and pay for other federal government expenditures.

U.S. government agency bonds: Long-term debt securities collateralized by a pool of assets and insured by agencies of the U.S. government.

State and local government bonds: Debt securities issued by state and local (e.g., county, city, school) governments, usually to cover capital (long-term) improvements.

Mortgages: Long-term loans issued to individuals or businesses to purchase homes, pieces of land, or other real property.

Mortgage-backed securities: Long-term debt securities that offer expected principal and interest payments as collateral. These securities, made up of many mortgages, are gathered into a pool and are thus "backed" by promised principal and interest cash flows.

Corporate bonds: Long-term debt securities issued by corporations.

Corporate stocks: Long-term equity securities issued by public corporations; stock shares represent fundamental corporate ownership claims.

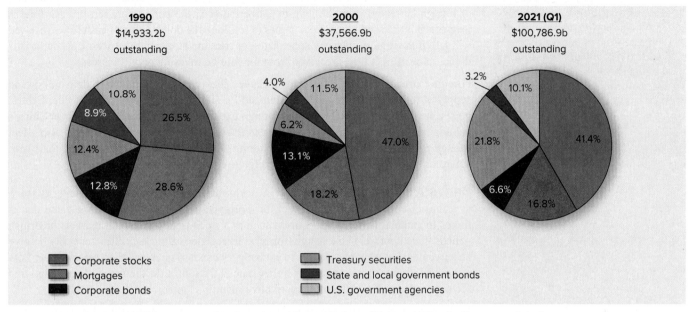

1990	2000	2021 (Q1)
$14,933.2b outstanding	$37,566.9b outstanding	$100,786.9b outstanding

1990
- 10.8%
- 26.5%
- 8.9%
- 12.4%
- 12.8%
- 28.6%

2000
- 4.0%
- 11.5%
- 6.2%
- 47.0%
- 13.1%
- 18.2%

2021 (Q1)
- 3.2%
- 10.1%
- 21.8%
- 41.4%
- 6.6%
- 16.8%

Legend:
- Corporate stocks
- Mortgages
- Corporate bonds
- Treasury securities
- State and local government bonds
- U.S. government agencies

Source: Federal Reserve Board, "Financial Accounts of the United States," Statistical Releases, Washington, DC, various issues. www.federalreserve.gov.

of 2009 and first half of 2010, rising 71.1 percent between March 2009 and April 2010. However, it took until March 5, 2013, for the DJIA to surpass its pre-crisis high of 14,164.53, closing at 14,253.77 for the day. Nevertheless, the DJIA continued its powerful rise to over 28,000 by the end of 2019. The stock market struggled in the early part of 2020 due to the pandemic. However, it had recovered to over 30,000 by the end of the year.

Other Markets

Foreign Exchange Markets Today, most U.S.-based companies operate globally. Competent financial managers understand how events and movements in financial markets in other countries can potentially affect their own companies' profitability and performance. Many U.S.-based companies receive a majority of their revenue from foreign sales. For example, oil companies like Exxon Mobil and Chevron and technology companies like Apple, IBM, and Intel receive most of their sales from overseas. Thus, changes in the dollar exchange rate with foreign currencies impact these firms' profits.

Foreign exchange markets trade currencies for immediate (also called "spot") or some future stated delivery. When a U.S. corporation sells securities or goods overseas, the resulting cash flows denominated in a foreign currency expose the firm to **foreign exchange risk.** This risk arises from the unknown value at which foreign currency cash flows can be converted into U.S. dollars. Foreign currency exchange rates vary day to day with worldwide demand and supply of foreign currency and U.S. dollars. Investors who deal in foreign-denominated securities face the same risk.

The actual number of U.S. dollars that a firm receives on a foreign investment depends on the exchange rate between the U.S. dollar and the foreign currency just as much as it does on the investment's performance. Firms will have to convert the foreign currency into

Jack Star/PhotoLink/Getty Images

derivative security A security formalizing an agreement between two parties to exchange a standard quantity of an asset at a predetermined price on a specified date in the future.

U.S. dollars at the prevailing exchange rate. If the foreign currency depreciates (falls in value) relative to the U.S. dollar (say from $0.1679 per unit of foreign currency to $0.1550 per unit of foreign currency) over the investment period (i.e., the period between when a foreign investment is made and the time it comes to fruition), the dollar value of cash flows received will fall. If the foreign currency appreciates, or rises in value, relative to the U.S. dollar, the dollar value of cash flows received from the foreign investment will increase.

Foreign currency exchange rates are variable. They vary day to day with demand for and supply of foreign currency and with demand for and supply of dollars worldwide. Central governments sometimes intervene in foreign exchange markets directly—such as China's valuing of the yuan at artificially high rates relative to the dollar. Governments also affect foreign exchange rates indirectly by altering prevailing interest rates within their own countries. You will learn more about foreign exchange markets in Chapter 19.

Derivative Securities Markets

A **derivative security** is a financial security (such as a futures contract, option contract, or mortgage-backed security) with a value that is linked to another, underlying security, such as a stock traded in capital markets or British pounds traded in foreign exchange (forex) markets. Derivative securities generally involve an agreement between two parties to exchange a standard quantity of an asset or cash flow at a predetermined price and at a specified date in the future. As the value of the underlying security changes, the value of the derivative security changes.

While derivative security contracts, especially for physical commodities like corn or gold, have existed for centuries, derivative securities markets grew increasingly popular in the 1970s, 1980s, and 1990s as traders, firms, and academics figured out how to spread risk for more and more underlying commodities and securities by using derivative contracts. Derivative contracts generally feature a high degree of leverage; that is, the investor only has to put up a very small portion of the underlying commodity or security's value to affect or control the underlying commodity or security.

Derivative securities traders can be either users of derivative contracts (for hedging and other purposes) or dealers (such as banks) that act as counterparties in customer trades for fees. An example of hedging involves commodities such as corn, wheat, or soybeans. For example, suppose you run a flour mill and will need to buy either soft wheat (Chicago) or hard red winter wheat (Kansas City) in the future. If you are concerned that the price of wheat will rise, you might lock in a price today to meet your needs six months from now by buying wheat futures on a commodities exchange. If you are correct and wheat prices rise over the six months, you may purchase the wheat by closing out your futures positions, buying the wheat at the futures price rather than the higher market price. Likewise, if you know that you will be delivering a large shipment to, say, Europe in three months, you might take an offsetting position in euro futures contracts to lock in the exchange rate between the dollar and the euro as it stands today—and (you hope) eliminate foreign exchange risk from the transaction.

Derivative securities markets are the newest—and potentially the riskiest—of the financial security markets. Losses associated with off-balance-sheet mortgage-backed securities created and held by FIs were at the very heart of the financial crisis. Signs of significant problems in the U.S. economy first appeared in late 2006 and early 2007 when home prices plummeted and defaults began to affect the mortgage lending industry as a whole, as well as other parts of the economy noticeably. Mortgage delinquencies, particularly on subprime mortgages, surged in the last quarter of 2006 through 2008 as homeowners who had stretched themselves to buy or refinance a home in the early 2000s fell behind on their loan payments. As mortgage borrowers defaulted, the financial institutions that held their mortgages and credit derivative securities (in the form of mortgage-backed securities) started announcing huge losses on them. These losses reached $700 billion worldwide by early 2009. The situation resulted in the failure, acquisition, or bailout of some of the largest FIs and a near meltdown of the world's financial and economic systems. More recently, as the Finance at Work box highlights, JPMorgan Chase experienced huge losses from positions in the derivative securities markets.

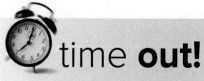

time out!

6-1 How do primary and secondary markets differ?

6-2 What are foreign exchange markets?

6-3 What are derivatives securities?

finance atwork //:markets

6.2 • FINANCIAL INSTITUTIONS LG6-3

Financial institutions (e.g., banks, thrifts, insurance companies, mutual funds) perform vital functions to securities markets of all sorts. They channel funds from those with surplus funds (suppliers of funds) to those with shortages of funds (demanders of funds). In other words, FIs operate financial markets. FIs allow financial markets to function by providing the least costly and most efficient way to channel funds to and from these markets. FIs play a second crucial role by spreading risk among market participants. This risk-spreading function is vital to entrepreneurial efforts, for few firms or individuals could afford the risk of launching an expensive new product or process by themselves. Individual investors take on pieces of the risk by buying shares in risky enterprises. Investors then mitigate their own risks by diversifying their holdings into appropriate portfolios, which we cover in Chapters 9 and 10. Table 6.3 lists and summarizes the various types of FIs.

financial institutions
Institutions that perform the essential function of channeling funds from those with surplus funds to those with shortages of funds.

▼ TABLE 6.3 Types of Financial Institutions

Commercial banks: Depository institutions whose major assets are loans and whose major liabilities are deposits. Commercial bank loans cover a broader range, including consumer, commercial, and real estate loans, than do loans from other depository institutions. Because they are larger and more likely to have access to public securities markets, commercial bank liabilities generally include more nondeposit sources of funds than do those of other depository institutions.

Thrifts: Depository institutions including savings associations, savings banks, and credit unions. Thrifts generally perform services similar to commercial banks, but they tend to concentrate their loans in one segment, such as real estate loans or consumer loans. Credit unions operate on a not-for-profit basis for particular groups of individuals, such as a labor union or a particular company's employees.

Insurance companies: Protect individuals and corporations (policyholders) from financially adverse events. Life insurance companies provide protection in the event of untimely death or illness, and help in planning retirement. Property casualty insurance protects against personal injury and liability due to accidents, theft, fire, and so on.

Securities firms and investment banks: Underwrite securities and engage in related activities such as securities brokerage, securities trading, and making markets in which securities trade.

Finance companies: Make loans to both individuals and businesses. Unlike depository institutions, finance companies do not accept deposits but instead rely on short- and long-term debt for funding, and many of their loans are collateralized with some kind of durable goods, such as washer/dryers, furnitures, and carpets.

Mutual funds: Pool many individuals' and companies' financial resources and invest those resources in diversified asset portfolios.

Pension funds: Offer savings plans through which fund participants accumulate savings during their working years. Participants then withdraw their pension resources (which have presumably earned additional returns in the interim) during their retirement years. Funds originally invested in and accumulated in a pension fund are exempt from current taxation. Participants pay taxes on distributions taken after age 55, when their tax brackets are (presumably) lower.

▼ FIGURE 6.6 Flow of Funds in a World without FIs

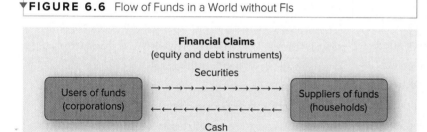

direct transfer The process used when a corporation sells its stock or debt directly to investors without going through a financial institution.

To understand just how important FIs are to the efficient operation of financial markets, imagine a simple world in which FIs did not exist. In such a world, suppliers of funds (e.g., households), generating excess savings by consuming less than they earn, would have a basic choice. They could either hold cash as an asset or invest that cash in the securities issued by users of funds (e.g., corporations, governments, or retail borrowers). In general, demanders (users) of funds issue financial claims (e.g., equity and debt securities) to finance the gap between their investment expenditures and their internally generated savings, such as retained earnings. As shown in Figure 6.6, in a world without financial institutions, we would have **direct transfers** of funds from fund suppliers to fund users. In return, financial claims would flow directly from fund users to fund suppliers.

In this economy without FIs, the amount of funds flowing between fund suppliers and fund users through financial markets would likely be quite low for several reasons:

- Once they have lent money in exchange for financial claims, fund suppliers would need to continually monitor the use of their funds. Fund suppliers must ensure that fund users neither steal the funds outright nor waste the funds on projects that have low or negative returns since either theft or waste would lower fund suppliers' chances of being repaid and/ or earning a positive return on their investments (such as through the receipt of dividends or interest). Monitoring against theft, misuse, or underuse of their funds would cost any given fund supplier a lot of time and effort, and of course each fund supplier, regardless of the dollar value of the investment, would have to carry out the same costly and time-consuming process. Further, many investors do not have the financial training to understand the necessary business information to assess whether a securities issuer is making the best use of their funds. In fact, so many investment opportunities are available to fund suppliers that even those trained in financial analysis rarely have the time to monitor how their funds are used in all of their investments. The resulting lack of monitoring increases the risk of directly investing in financial claims. Given these challenges, fund suppliers would likely prefer to delegate the task of monitoring fund borrowers to ensure good performance to others.

- Many financial claims feature a long-term commitment (e.g., mortgages, corporate stock, and bonds) for fund suppliers, but suppliers may not wish to hold these instruments directly. Specifically, given the choice between holding cash or long-term securities, fund suppliers may choose to hold cash for its **liquidity.** This is especially true if the suppliers plan to use their savings to finance consumption expenditures before their creditors expect to be repaid. Fund suppliers may also fear that they will not find anyone to purchase their financial claim and free up their funds. When financial markets are not very developed, or deep, in terms of the number of active buyers and sellers in the market, such liquidity concerns arise.

- Even though real-world financial markets provide some liquidity services by allowing fund suppliers to trade financial securities among themselves, fund suppliers face **price risk** when they buy securities—fund suppliers may not get their principal back, let alone any return on their investment. The price at which investors can sell a security on secondary markets such as the New York Stock Exchange (NYSE) or NASDAQ may well differ from the price they initially paid for the security. The investment community as a whole may change the security's valuation between the time the fund supplier bought it and the time the fund supplier sold it. Also, dealers, acting as intermediaries between buyers and sellers, charge transaction costs for completing a trade. So even if an investor bought a security and then sold it the next day, the investor would likely lose money from transaction and other costs.

Unique Economic Functions Performed by Financial Institutions

Because of (1) monitoring costs, (2) liquidity costs, and (3) price risk, most average investors may well view direct investment in financial claims and markets as an unattractive proposition and, as fund suppliers, they will likely prefer to hold cash. As a result, financial market activity (and therefore savings and investment) would likely remain quite low. However, the financial system has developed an alternative, indirect way for investors (or fund suppliers) to channel funds to users of funds: Financial intermediaries **indirectly transfer** funds to ultimate fund users. Because of monitoring, liquidity risk, and price risk costs, fund suppliers often prefer to hold financial intermediaries' financial claims rather than those directly issued by the ultimate fund users. Consider Figure 6.7, which more closely represents the way that funds flow in the U.S. financial system than does Figure 6.6. Notice how financial institutions stand—or intermediate—between fund suppliers and fund users. That is, FIs channel funds from ultimate suppliers to ultimate fund users. Fund suppliers and users use these FIs to channel funds because of financial intermediaries' unique ability to measure and manage risk, and thus reduce monitoring costs, liquidity costs, and price risk.

Monitoring Costs As we noted above, a fund supplier who directly invests in a fund user's financial claims faces a high cost of comprehensively monitoring the fund user's actions in a timely way. One solution to this problem is that a large number of small investors can group their funds together by holding claims issued by an FI. In turn, the FI will invest in direct financial claims that fund users issue. Financial institutions' aggregation of funds from fund suppliers resolves a number of problems:

- First, large FIs now have much greater incentive to collect information and monitor the ultimate fund user's actions because the FI has far more at stake than any small individual fund supplier would have.

- Second, the FI performs the necessary monitoring function via its own internal experts. In an economic sense, fund suppliers appoint the FI as a **delegated monitor** to act on their behalf. For example, full-service securities firms such as Bank of America Merrill Lynch carry out investment research on new issues and make investment recommendations for their retail clients (investors), while commercial

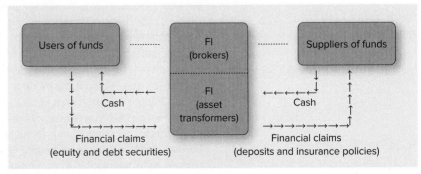

▼**FIGURE 6.7** Flow of Funds in a World with FIs

Financial institutions stand between fund suppliers and users.

banks collect deposits from fund suppliers and lend these funds to ultimate users, such as corporations. An important part of these FIs' functions is their ability and incentive to monitor ultimate fund users.

Liquidity and Price Risk In addition to providing more and better information about fund users' activities, financial intermediaries provide additional liquidity to fund suppliers, acting as **asset transformers** as follows: FIs purchase the financial claims that fund users issue—primary securities such as mortgages, bonds, and stocks—and finance these purchases by selling financial claims to household investors and other fund suppliers as deposits, insurance policies, or other **secondary securities.** The secondary securities—packages or pools of primary claims—that FIs collect and then issue are often more liquid than are the primary securities themselves. For example, banks and thrift institutions (e.g., savings associations) offer draft deposit accounts with fixed principal values and (often) guaranteed interest rates. Fund suppliers can generally access the funds in those accounts on demand. Money market mutual funds issue shares to household savers that allow the savers to maintain almost fixed principal amounts while earning somewhat higher interest rates than on bank deposits. Further, savers can also withdraw these funds on demand whenever the saver writes a check on the account. Even life insurance companies allow policyholders to borrow against their company-held policy balances with very short notice.

The Shift away from Risk Measurement and Management and the Financial Crisis

Certainly, a major event that changed and reshaped the financial services industry was the financial crisis of the late 2000s. As FIs adjusted to regulatory changes brought about in the 1980s and 1990s, one result was a dramatic increase in systemic risk of the financial system, caused in large part by a shift in the banking model from that of "originate and hold" to "originate to distribute." In the traditional model, banks take short-term deposits and other sources of funds and use them to fund longer-term loans to businesses and consumers. Banks typically hold these loans to maturity, and thus have an incentive to screen and monitor borrower activities even after a loan is made. However, the traditional banking model exposes the institution to potential liquidity, interest rate, and credit risk. In attempts to avoid these risk exposures and generate improved return–risk trade-offs, banks have shifted to an underwriting model in which they originate or warehouse loans, and then quickly sell them. Figure 6.8 shows the growth in bank loan secondary market trading from 1991 through 2019. Note the huge growth in bank loan trading even during the financial crisis of 2008 and 2009. When loans trade, the secondary market produces information that can substitute for the information and monitoring of banks. Further, banks may have lower incentives to collect information and monitor borrowers if they sell loans rather than keep them as part of the bank's portfolio of assets. Indeed, most large banks are organized as financial service holding companies to facilitate these new activities.

More recently activities of shadow banks, nonfinancial service firms that perform banking services, have facilitated the change from the "originate and hold" model of commercial banking to the "originate and distribute" banking model. Participants in the shadow banking system include structured investment vehicles (SIVs), special purpose vehicles (SPVs), asset-backed commercial paper (ABCP) conduits, limited-purpose finance companies, money market mutual funds (MMMFs), and credit hedge funds. In the shadow banking system, savers place their funds with money market mutual and similar funds, which invest these funds in the liabilities of other shadow banks. Borrowers get loans and leases from shadow banks such as finance companies rather than from banks. Like the traditional banking system, the shadow banking system intermediates the flow of funds between net savers and net borrowers. However, instead of the bank serving as the middleman, it is the nonbank financial service firm, or shadow bank, that intermediates. Further, unlike the traditional banking system, where the complete credit intermediation is performed by a single bank, in the shadow banking system it is performed through a series of steps involving many nonbank, unregulated financial service firms.

▼FIGURE 6.8 Bank Loan Secondary Market Trading

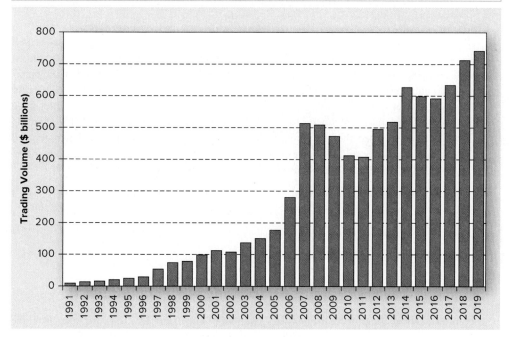

Bank loan sales have increased dramatically over the last several decades.

These innovations remove risk from the balance sheet of financial institutions and shift risk off the balance sheet and to other parts of the financial system. Since the FIs, acting as underwriters, are not exposed to the credit, liquidity, and interest rate risks of traditional banking, they have little incentive to screen and monitor activities of borrowers to whom they originate loans. Thus, FIs' role as specialists in risk measurement and management is reduced.

First, once they have lent money in exchange for financial claims, fund suppliers would need to continually monitor the use of their funds to guard against theft and waste. Second, many financial claims feature a long-term commitment (e.g., mortgages, corporate stock, and bonds) for fund suppliers, thus creating another disincentive for fund suppliers to hold direct financial claims that fund users may issue. Third, even though real-world financial markets provide some liquidity services by allowing fund suppliers to trade financial securities among themselves, fund suppliers face price risk when they buy securities—fund suppliers may not get their principal back, let alone any return on their investment.

The economy relies on financial institutions to act as specialists in risk measurement and management. The importance of this was demonstrated during the global financial crisis. When FIs failed to perform their critical risk measurement and management functions, a crisis of confidence that disrupted financial markets ensued. The result was a worldwide breakdown in credit markets, as well as an enhanced level of equity market volatility.

6.3 • INTEREST RATES AND THE LOANABLE FUNDS THEORY LG6-4

We often speak of "the interest rate" as if only one rate applies to all financial situations or transactions. In fact, we can list tens or hundreds of interest rates that are appropriate in various conditions or situations within the U.S. economy on any particular day. Let's explore a bit how the financial sector sets these rates and how the rates relate to one another. We actually observe **nominal interest rates** in financial markets—these are the rates most often quoted by financial news services. As we will see in Chapters 7 and 8, nominal interest rates (or, simply, interest rates) directly affect most tradable securities'

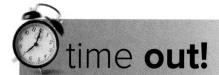
time **out!**

6-4 List the major types of financial institutions.

6-5 What three main issues would deter fund suppliers from directly purchasing securities?

6-6 What events resulted in banks' shift from the traditional banking model of "originate and hold" to a model of "originate and distribute"?

nominal interest rates The interest rates actually observed in financial markets.

value or price. Since any change in nominal interest rates has such profound effects on security prices, financial managers and individual investors spend a lot of time and effort trying to identify factors that may influence future interest rate levels.

Of course, interest rate changes influence investment performance and trigger buy or sell decisions for individual investors, businesses, and governmental units alike. For example, in 2008 and 2009, the Federal Reserve, in an effort to address the severe financial crisis, unexpectedly announced that it would drop its target fed funds rate to a range between 0 percent and 0.25 percent and lowered its discount window rate to 0.5 percent, the lowest level since the 1940s. These rates remained at historically low levels until December 2015 when the Federal Reserve raised the fed funds rate to a range of 0.25 percent to 0.5 percent and the discount window rate to 1 percent. This was the first interest rate increase since 2006. However, by 2019, the Federal Reserve was pushing down interest rates again.

Figure 6.9 illustrates the movement of the following key U.S. interest rates over the past 48 years:

- The prime commercial loan rate.

- The three-month T-bill rate.

- The home mortgage rate.

- The high-grade corporate bond rate.

Figure 6.9 shows how interest rates vary over time. For example, the prime rate hit highs of over 20 percent in the early 1980s, yet fell as low as 4.75 percent in the early 1970s. The prime rate stayed below 10 percent throughout much of the 1990s, fell back further

▼FIGURE 6.9 Key U.S. Interest Rates, 1972–2020

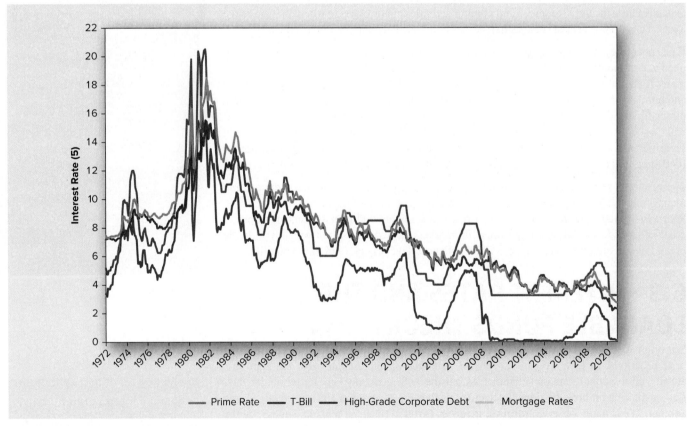

Loan rates tend to move together over time.

Source: Federal Reserve Board website, various dates. www.federalreserve.gov.

to 4.00 percent in the early 2000s, then rose to as high as 8.25 percent in the mid-2000s. During the financial crisis of 2008 and 2009, the Fed took aggressive actions to stimulate the economy, including dropping interest rates to historic lows. As a result, the prime rate fell to 3.25 percent and stayed there until December 2015. The pandemic in 2020 forced the Fed to lower the prime rate again. By the end of the year, it was back down to 3.25 percent.

Interest rates play a major part in the determination of the value of financial instruments. For example, in September 2015 the Federal Reserve unexpectedly announced that it would not raise interest rates. The financial markets reacted significantly: The Dow Jones Industrial Average declined almost 300 points, 1.75 percent in value; the interest rate on Treasury securities decreased (i.e., the yield on 10-year T-notes decreased 0.123 percent); gold prices increased 1.6 percent; and the U.S. dollar strengthened against foreign currencies. Given the impact a change in interest rates has on security values, financial institution and other firm managers spend much time and effort trying to identify factors that determine the level of interest rates at any moment in time, as well as what causes interest rate movements over time.

One model that is commonly used to explain interest rates and interest rate movements is the **loanable funds theory.** The loanable funds theory views the level of interest rates as resulting from factors that affect the supply of and demand for loanable funds. It categorizes financial market participants—consumers, businesses, governments, and foreign participants—as net suppliers or demanders of funds.

loanable funds theory A theory of interest rate determination that views equilibrium interest rates in financial markets as a result of the supply of and demand for loanable funds.

Supply of Loanable Funds LG6-4

The *supply of loanable funds* is a term commonly used to describe funds provided to the financial markets by net suppliers of funds. In general, the quantity of loanable funds supplied increases as interest rates rise. Figure 6.10 illustrates the supply curve for loanable funds.

Other factors held constant, more funds are supplied as interest rates increase (the reward for supplying funds is higher). Table 6.4 presents data on the supply of loanable funds from the various groups of market participants from U.S. flow of funds data as of 2020.

The household sector (consumer sector) is a large supplier of loanable funds in the United States—$98.71 trillion in 2020. Households supply funds when they have excess income or want to reallocate their asset portfolio holdings. For example, during times of high economic growth, households may replace part of their cash holdings with earning assets (i.e., by supplying loanable funds in exchange for holding securities). As the total wealth of a

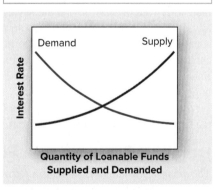

▼**FIGURE 6.10** Supply of and Demand for Loanable Funds

The demand for and supply of loanable funds varies with interest rates.

▼ **TABLE 6.4** Funds Supplied and Demanded by Various Groups (in trillions of dollars)

	Funds Supplied	Funds Demanded	Net Funds Supplied (Funds Supplied − Funds Demanded) (Equity)
Households	$ 98.71	$ 16.79	$ 81.92
Business—nonfinancial	28.97	40.68	−11.71
Business—financial	116.88	108.85	8.03
Government units	8.35	34.29	−25.94
Foreign participants	37.12	14.65	22.47

Source: Federal Reserve Board, "Flow of Fund Accounts," December 2020, www.federalreserve.gov.

consumer increases, the total supply of loanable funds from that consumer will also generally increase. Households determine their supply of loanable funds not only on the basis of the general level of interest rates and their total wealth, but also on the risk of securities investments. The greater the perceived risk of securities investments, the less households are willing to invest at each interest rate. Further, the supply of loanable funds from households also depends on their immediate spending needs. For example, near-term educational or medical expenditures will reduce the supply of funds from a given household.

Higher interest rates will also result in higher supplies of funds from the U.S. business sector ($28.97 trillion from nonfinancial business and $116.88 trillion from financial business in 2020), which often has excess cash, or working capital, that it can invest for short periods of time in financial assets. In addition to the interest rates on these investments, the expected risk on financial securities and their businesses' future investment needs will affect their overall supply of funds.

Loanable funds are also supplied by some governments ($8.35 trillion in 2020). For example, some governments (e.g., municipalities) temporarily generate more cash inflows (e.g., through local taxes) than they have budgeted to spend. These funds can be loaned out to financial market fund users until needed. During the recent financial crisis, the federal government significantly increased the funds it supplied to businesses and consumers as it attempted to rescue the U.S. economy from a deep economic recession.

Finally, foreign investors increasingly view U.S. financial markets as alternatives to their domestic financial markets ($31.12 trillion of funds were supplied to the U.S. financial markets in 2020). When interest rates are higher on U.S. financial securities than they are on comparable securities in their home countries, foreign investors increase their supply of funds to U.S. markets. Indeed the high savings rates of foreign households (such as Japanese households) have resulted in foreign market participants being major suppliers of funds to U.S. financial markets in recent years. Similar to domestic suppliers of loanable funds, foreigners assess not only the interest rate offered on financial securities, but also their total wealth, the risk on the security, and their future expenditure needs. Additionally, foreign investors alter their investment decisions as financial conditions in their home countries change relative to the U.S. economy and the exchange rate of their country's currency changes vis-à-vis the U.S. dollar (see Chapter 19). For example, during the recent financial crisis, investors worldwide, searching for a safe haven for their funds, invested huge amounts of funds in U.S. Treasury securities. The amount of money invested in Treasury bills was so large that the yield on the three-month Treasury bill went below zero for the first time ever; investors were essentially paying the U.S. government to borrow money.

Demand for Loanable Funds

The *demand for loanable funds* is a term used to describe the total net demand for funds by fund users. In general, the quantity of loanable funds demanded is higher as interest rates fall. Figure 6.10 also illustrates the demand curve for loanable funds. Other factors held constant, more funds are demanded as interest rates decrease (the cost of borrowing funds is lower).

Households (although they are net suppliers of funds) also borrow funds in financial markets ($16.79 trillion in 2020). The demand for loanable funds by households reflects the demand for financing purchases of homes (with mortgage loans), durable goods (e.g., car loans, appliance loans), and nondurable goods (e.g., education loans, medical loans). Additional nonprice conditions and requirements (discussed below) also affect a household's demand for loanable funds at every level of interest rates.

Businesses demand funds to finance investments in long-term (fixed) assets (e.g., plant and equipment) and for short-term working capital needs (e.g., inventory and accounts receivable) usually by issuing debt and other financial instruments ($40.68 trillion for nonfinancial businesses and $108.85 trillion for financial businesses in 2020). When interest rates are high (i.e., the cost of loanable funds is high), businesses prefer to finance investments with internally generated funds (e.g., retained earnings) rather than through borrowed funds.

Further, the greater the number of profitable projects available to businesses, or the better the overall economic conditions, the greater the demand for loanable funds.

Governments also borrow heavily in the markets for loanable funds ($34.29 trillion in 2020). For example, state and local governments often issue debt instruments to finance temporary imbalances between operating revenues (e.g., taxes) and budgeted expenditures (e.g., road improvements, school construction). Higher interest rates can cause state and local governments to postpone borrowings and thus capital expenditures. Similar to households and businesses, governments' demand for funds varies with general economic conditions. The federal government is also a large borrower partly to finance current budget deficits (expenditures greater than taxes) and partly to finance past deficits. The cumulative sum of past deficits is called the national debt, which in the United States in 2020 stood at $27.5 trillion. Thus, the national debt and especially the interest payments on the national debt have to be financed in large part by additional government borrowing.

Finally, foreign participants (households, businesses, and governments) also borrow in U.S. financial markets ($14.65 trillion in 2020). Foreign borrowers look for the cheapest source of dollar funds globally. Most foreign borrowing in U.S. financial markets comes from the business sector. In addition to interest costs, foreign borrowers consider nonprice terms on loanable funds as well as economic conditions in their home country and the general attractiveness of the U.S. dollar relative to their domestic currency (e.g., the euro or the yen). In Chapter 19, we examine how economic growth in domestic versus foreign countries affects foreign exchange rates and foreign investors' demand and supply for funds.

Equilibrium Interest Rate LG6-5

The aggregate supply of loanable funds is the sum of the quantity supplied by the separate fund-supplying sectors (e.g., households, businesses, governments, foreign agents) discussed above. Similarly, the aggregate demand for loanable funds is the sum of the quantity demanded by the separate fund-demanding sectors. As illustrated in Figure 6.11, the aggregate quantity of funds supplied is positively related to interest rates, while the aggregate quantity of funds demanded is inversely related to interest rates. As long as competitive forces are allowed to operate freely in a financial system, the interest rate that equates the aggregate quantity of loanable funds supplied with the aggregate quantity of loanable funds demanded for a financial security, Q^*, is the equilibrium interest rate for that security, i^*, point E in Figure 6.11. For example, whenever the rate of interest is set higher than the equilibrium rate, such as i^H, the financial system has a surplus of loanable funds. As a result, some suppliers of funds will lower the interest rate at which they are willing to lend and the demanders of funds will absorb the loanable funds surplus. In contrast, when the rate of interest is lower than the equilibrium interest rate, such as i^L, there is a shortage of loanable funds in the financial system. Some borrowers will be unable to obtain the funds they need at current rates. As a result, interest rates will increase, causing more suppliers of loanable funds to enter the market and some demanders of funds to leave the market. These competitive forces will cause the quantity of funds supplied to increase and the quantity of funds demanded to decrease until a shortage of funds no longer exists.

Factors That Cause the Supply and Demand Curves for Loanable Funds to Shift

While we have alluded to the fundamental factors that cause the supply and demand curves for loanable funds to shift, in this section we formally summarize these factors. We then examine how shifts in the supply and demand curves for loanable funds

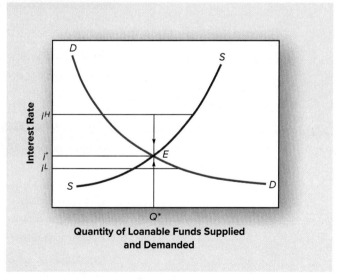

▼**FIGURE 6.11** Determination of Equilibrium Interest Rates

Interest rates always move toward the equilibrium.

determine the equilibrium interest rate on a specific financial instrument. A shift in the supply or demand curve occurs when the quantity of a financial security supplied or demanded changes at every given interest rate in response to a change in another factor besides the interest rate. In either case, a change in the supply or demand curve for loanable funds causes interest rates to move. Table 6.5 recaps the factors that affect the supply and demand for loanable funds discussed in this section, their impact on the supply of and demand for loanable funds for a specific security, and the impact on the market clearing (or equilibrium) interest rates holding all other factors constant.

Supply of Funds
We have already described the positive relation between interest rates and the supply of loanable funds along the loanable funds supply curve. Factors that cause the supply curve of loanable funds to shift, at any given interest rate, include the wealth of fund suppliers, the risk of the financial security, near-term spending needs, monetary policy objectives, and economic conditions.

Wealth As the total wealth of financial market participants (households, businesses, etc.) increases, the absolute dollar value available for investment purposes increases. Accordingly, at every interest rate, the supply of loanable funds increases, or the supply curve shifts down and to the right. For example, as the U.S. economy grew in the 2010s, total wealth of U.S. investors increased as well. Consequently, the supply of funds available for investing (e.g., in stock and bond markets) increased at every available interest rate. We show this shift (increase) in the supply curve in Figure 6.12(a) as a move from SS to SS''. The shift in the supply curve creates a disequilibrium between demand and supply. To eliminate the imbalance or disequilibrium in this financial market, the equilibrium interest rate falls, from $i*$ to $i*''$, which is associated with an increase in the quantity of funds loaned between fund suppliers and fund demanders, from $Q*$ to $Q*''$.

Conversely, as the total wealth of financial market participants decreases, the absolute dollar value available for investment purposes decreases. Accordingly, at every interest rate, the supply of loanable funds decreases, or the supply curve shifts up and to the left. The decrease in the supply of funds due to a decrease in the total wealth of market participants results in an increase in the equilibrium interest rate and a decrease in the equilibrium quantity of funds loaned (traded).

▼ **TABLE 6.5** Factors That Affect the Supply of and Demand for Loanable Funds for a Financial Security

Panel A: The Supply of Funds Factor	Impact on Supply of Funds	Impact on Equilibrium Interest Rate*
Interest rate	Movement along supply curve	Direct
Total wealth	Shift supply curve	Inverse
Risk of financial security	Shift supply curve	Direct
Near-term spending needs	Shift supply curve	Direct
Monetary expansion	Shift supply curve	Inverse
Economic conditions	Shift supply curve	Inverse

Panel B: The Demand for Funds Factor	Impact on Supply of Funds	Impact on Equilibrium Interest Rate
Interest rate	Movement along demand curve	Inverse
Utility derived from asset purchased with borrowed funds	Shift demand curve	Direct
Restrictiveness of nonprice conditions	Shift demand curve	Inverse
Economic conditions	Shift demand curve	Direct

*A "direct" impact on equilibrium interest rates means that as the "factor" increases (decreases), the equilibrium interest rate increases (decreases). An "inverse" impact means that as the factor increases (decreases), the equilibrium interest rate decreases (increases).

Risk As the risk of a financial security decreases (e.g., the probability that the issuer of the security will default on promised repayments of the funds borrowed), it becomes more attractive to suppliers of funds. At every interest rate, the supply of loanable funds increases, or the supply curve shifts down and to the right, from SS to SS'' in Figure 6.12(a). Holding all other factors constant, the increase in the supply of funds, due to a decrease in the risk of the financial security, results in a decrease in the equilibrium interest rate, from i^* to $i^{*''}$, and an increase in the equilibrium quantity of funds traded, from Q^* to $Q^{*''}$.

Conversely, as the risk of a financial security increases, it becomes less attractive to suppliers of funds. Accordingly, at every interest rate, the supply of loanable funds decreases, or the supply curve shifts up and to the left. Holding all other factors constant, the decrease in the supply of funds due to an increase in the financial security's risk results in an increase in the equilibrium interest rate and a decrease in the equilibrium quantity of funds loaned (or traded).

Near-Term Spending Needs When financial market participants have few near-term spending needs, the absolute dollar value of funds available to invest increases. For example, when a family's son or daughter moves out of the family home to live on his or her own, current spending needs of the family decrease and the supply of available funds (for investing) increases. At every interest rate, the supply of loanable funds increases, or the supply curve shifts down and to the right. The financial market, holding all other factors constant, reacts to this increased supply of funds by decreasing the equilibrium interest rate and increasing the equilibrium quantity of funds traded.

Conversely, when financial market participants have increased near-term spending needs, the absolute dollar value of funds available to invest decreases. At every interest rate, the supply of loanable funds decreases, or the supply curve shifts up and to the left. The shift in the supply curve creates a disequilibrium in the financial market that results in an increase in the equilibrium interest rate and a decrease in the equilibrium quantity of funds loaned (or traded).

Monetary Expansion One method used by the Federal Reserve to implement monetary policy is to alter the availability of funds, the growth in the money supply, and thus the rate of economic expansion of the economy.

When monetary policy objectives are to allow the economy to expand (as was the case in the late 2000s, during the financial crisis, in the early 2010s, and during the 2020/2021 pandemic), the Federal Reserve increases the supply of funds available in the financial markets. At every interest rate, the supply of loanable funds increases, the supply curve shifts down and to the right, and the equilibrium interest rate falls, while the equilibrium quantity of funds traded increases.

Conversely, when monetary policy objectives are to restrict the rate of economic expansion (and thus inflation), the Federal Reserve decreases the supply of funds available in the financial markets. At every interest rate, the supply of loanable funds decreases, the supply curve shifts up and to the left, and the equilibrium interest rate rises, while the equilibrium quantity of funds loaned or traded decreases.

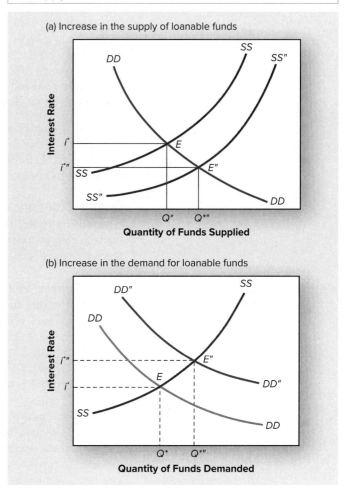

▼**FIGURE 6.12** The Effect on Interest Rates from a Shift in the Supply Curve or Demand Curve for Loanable Funds

(a) Increase in the supply of loanable funds

(b) Increase in the demand for loanable funds

Changes in the supply of and demand for loanable funds have varying effects.

Economic Conditions Finally, as the underlying economic conditions themselves (e.g., the inflation rate, unemployment rate, economic growth) improve in a country relative to other countries, the flow of funds to that country increases. This reflects the lower risk (country or sovereign risk) that the country, in the guise of its government, will default on its obligation to repay funds borrowed. For example, the severe economic crisis in Greece in the 2010s resulted in a decrease in the supply of funds to that country. An increased inflow of foreign funds to U.S. financial markets increases the supply of loanable funds at every interest rate and the supply curve shifts down and to the right. Accordingly, the equilibrium interest rate falls and the equilibrium quantity of funds loaned or traded increases.

Conversely, when economic conditions in foreign countries improve, domestic and foreign investors take their funds out of domestic financial markets (e.g., the United States) and invest abroad. Thus, the supply of funds available in the financial markets decreases and the equilibrium interest rate rises, while the equilibrium quantity of funds traded decreases.

Demand for Funds

We explained above that the quantity of loanable funds demanded is negatively related to interest rates. Factors that cause the demand curve for loanable funds to shift include the utility derived from assets purchased with borrowed funds, the restrictiveness of nonprice conditions on borrowing, and economic conditions.

Utility Derived from Assets Purchased with Borrowed Funds As the utility (i.e., satisfaction or pleasure) derived from an asset purchased with borrowed funds increases, the willingness of market participants (households, businesses, etc.) to borrow increases and the absolute dollar value borrowed increases. Accordingly, at every interest rate, the demand for loanable funds increases, or the demand curve shifts up and to the right. For example, suppose a change in jobs takes an individual from Arizona to Minnesota. The individual currently has a convertible automobile. Given the move to Minnesota, the individual's utility from the convertible decreases, while it would increase for a car with heated seats. Thus, with a potential increased utility from the purchase of a new car, the individual's demand for funds in the form of an auto loan increases. We show this shift (increase) in the demand curve in Figure 6.12(b) as a move from DD to DD''. The shift in the demand curve creates a disequilibrium in this financial market. Holding all other factors constant, the increase in the demand for funds due to an increase in the utility from the purchased asset results in an increase in the equilibrium interest rate, from $i*$ to $i*''$, and an increase in the equilibrium quantity of funds traded, from $Q*$ to $Q*''$.

Conversely, as the utility derived from an asset purchased with borrowed funds decreases, the willingness of market participants (households, businesses, etc.) to borrow decreases and the absolute dollar amount borrowed decreases. Accordingly, at every interest rate, the demand for loanable funds decreases, or the demand curve shifts down and to the left. The shift in the demand curve again creates a disequilibrium in this financial market. As competitive forces adjust, and holding all other factors constant, the decrease in the demand for funds due to a decrease in the utility from the purchased asset results in a decrease in the equilibrium interest rate and a decrease in the equilibrium quantity of funds loaned or traded.

Restrictiveness of Nonprice Conditions on Borrowed Funds As the nonprice restrictions put on borrowers as a condition of borrowing decrease, the willingness of market participants to borrow increases and the absolute dollar value borrowed increases. Such nonprice conditions may include fees or collateral. The lack of such restrictions makes the loan more desirable to the user of funds. Accordingly, at every interest rate, the demand for loanable funds increases, or the demand curve shifts up and to the right, from DD to DD''. As competitive forces adjust, and holding all other factors constant, the increase in the demand for funds due to a decrease in the restrictive conditions on the borrowed funds results in an increase in the equilibrium interest rate, from $i*$ to $i*''$, and an increase in the equilibrium quantity of funds traded, from $Q*$ to $Q*''$. Conversely, as the nonprice restrictions put on borrowers as a condition of borrowing increase, market participants' willingness to borrow decreases, and the absolute dollar value borrowed decreases. Accordingly, the demand curve shifts down and to the left. The shift in the demand curve results in a decrease in the equilibrium interest rate and a decrease in the equilibrium quantity of funds traded.

Economic Conditions When the domestic economy experiences a period of growth, such as that in the United States in the mid-2000s and 2010s, market participants are willing to borrow more heavily. For example, state and local governments are more likely to repair and improve decaying infrastructure when the local economy is strong. Accordingly, the demand curve for funds shifts up and to the right. Holding all other factors constant, the increase in the demand for funds due to economic growth results in an increase in the equilibrium interest rate and an increase in the equilibrium quantity of funds traded. Conversely, when domestic economic growth is stagnant, market participants reduce their demand for funds. Accordingly, the demand curve shifts down and to the left, resulting in a decrease in the equilibrium interest rate and a decrease in the equilibrium quantity of funds traded.

Movement of Interest Rates over Time

As discussed in the previous section of this chapter, the loanable funds theory of interest rates is based on the supply of and demand for loanable funds as functions of interest rates. The equilibrium interest rate (point E in Figure 6.12) is only a temporary equilibrium. Changes in underlying factors that determine the demand and supply of loanable funds can cause continuous shifts in the supply and/or demand curves for loanable funds. Market forces will react to the resulting disequilibrium with factors that influence a change in the equilibrium interest rate and quantity of funds traded in that market. Refer again to Figure 6.12(a), which shows the effects of an *increase in the supply curve* for loanable funds, from SS to SS'' (and the resulting *decrease in the equilibrium interest rate*, from $i*$ to $i*''$), while Figure 6.12(b) shows the effects of an *increase in the demand curve* for loanable funds, from DD to DD'' (and the resulting *increase in the equilibrium interest rate*, from $i*$ to $i*''$).

6.4 • FACTORS THAT INFLUENCE INTEREST RATES FOR INDIVIDUAL SECURITIES LG6-6

So far we have looked at the general determination of equilibrium (nominal) interest rates for financial securities in the context of the loanable demand and supply theory of the flow of funds. In this section, we examine the specific factors that affect differences in interest rates across the range of real-world financial markets (i.e., differences among interest rates on individual securities, given the underlying level of interest rates determined by the demand for and supply of loanable funds). These factors include

- Inflation.
- The real risk-free rate.
- Default risk.
- Liquidity risk.
- Special provisions regarding the use of funds raised by a particular security issuer.
- The security's term to maturity.

We will discuss each of these factors after summarizing them in Table 6.6.

time **out!**

6-7 Who are the main suppliers and demanders of loanable funds?

6-8 What happens to the equilibrium interest rate when the demand for (supply of) loanable funds increases?

6-9 How do supply and demand together determine interest rates?

Inflation

The first factor that influences interest rates is the economy-wide *actual or expected inflation rate*. Specifically, the higher the level of actual or expected inflation, the higher will be the level of interest rates. We define **inflation** of the general price index of goods and services (or the inflation premium, IP) as the (percentage) increase in the price of a standardized basket of goods and services over a given period of time. The U.S. Department of Commerce measures inflation using indexes such as the consumer price index (CPI) and the producer price index (PPI). For example, the annual inflation rate using the CPI index between years t and $t + 1$ would be equal to

$$IP = \frac{CPI_{t+1} - CPI_t}{CPI_t} \times 100 \qquad (6\text{-}1)$$

The positive relationship between interest rates and inflation rates is fairly intuitive: When inflation raises the general price level, investors who buy financial assets must earn a higher interest rate (or inflation premium) to compensate for continuing to hold the investment. Holding on to their investments means that they incur higher costs of forgoing consumption of real goods and services today, only to have to buy these same goods and services at higher prices in the future. In other words, the higher the rate of inflation, the more expensive the same basket of goods and services will be in the future.

Real Risk-Free Rate

A **real risk-free rate** is the rate that a risk-free security would pay if no inflation were expected over its holding period (e.g., a year). As such, it measures only society's relative time preference for consuming today rather than tomorrow. The higher society's preference to consume today (i.e., the higher its time value of money or rate of time preference), the higher the real risk-free rate will be.

Fisher Effect Economists often refer to the relationship among real risk-free rates (RFR), expected inflation (expected IP), and nominal risk-free rates (*i*), described previously, as the Fisher effect, named for Irving Fisher, who identified these economic relationships early last century. The Fisher effect theorizes that nominal risk-free rates that we observe in financial markets (e.g., the one-year Treasury bill rate) must compensate investors for

- Any inflation-related reduction in purchasing power lost on funds lent or principal due.

- An additional premium above the expected rate of inflation for forgoing present consumption (which reflects the real risk-free rate issue discussed previously).

$$i = \text{Expected } IP + RFR \qquad (6\text{-}2)$$

Thus, the nominal risk-free rate will equal the real risk-free rate only when market participants expect inflation to be zero: Expected $IP = 0$. Similarly, the nominal risk-free rate

▼ **TABLE 6.6** Factors Affecting Nominal Interest Rates

Inflation: A continual increase in the price level of a standardized basket of goods and services throughout the economy as a whole.

Real risk-free rate: Risk-free rate adjusted for inflation; generally lower than nominal risk-free rate at any particular time.

Default risk: Risk that a security issuer will miss an interest or principal payment or continue to miss such payments.

Liquidity risk: Risk that a security cannot be sold at a price relatively close to its fair-market value with low transaction costs on short notice.

Special provisions: Provisions (e.g., taxability, convertibility, and callability) that impact a security holder beneficially or adversely and as such are reflected in the interest rates on securities that contain such provisions.

Time to maturity: Length of time until a security is repaid; used in debt securities as the date upon which the security holders get their principal back.

EXAMPLE 6-1

For interactive versions of this example, log in to Connect or go to mhhe.com/Cornett6e.

Calculating Real Risk-Free Rates LG6-6

One-year Treasury bill rates in 2007 averaged 4.53 percent and inflation (measured by the consumer price index) for the year was 4.10 percent. If investors had expected the same inflation rate as that actually realized, calculate the real risk-free rate for 2007 according to the Fisher effect.

SOLUTION:

$$4.53\% - 4.10\% = 0.43\%$$

Similar to Problems 6-1, 6-2, Self-Test Problem 1

will equal the expected inflation rate only when the real risk-free rate is zero. We can rearrange the nominal risk-free rate equation to show what determines the real interest rate:[1]

$$RFR = i - \text{Expected } IP \qquad (6\text{-}3)$$

It needs to be noted that the expected inflation rate is difficult to estimate accurately, so the real risk-free rate can be difficult to measure accurately. Investors' expectations are not always realized either.

The one-year T-bill rate in 2020 was 0.12 percent, while the CPI for the year was 0.64 percent, which implies a real risk-free rate of −0.52 percent—that is, the real risk-free rate was actually negative. Thus, the real value of investments actually decreased in that year.

Figure 6.13 shows the nominal risk-free rate (one-year T-bill rate) versus the change in the CPI from 1962 through 2018. Note that, generally, the T-bill rate is greater than the CPI;

▼**FIGURE 6.13** Nominal Interest Rates versus Inflation

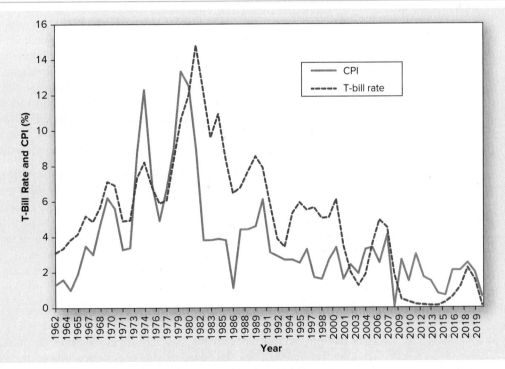

Notice the difference between the nominal risk-free rate and the change in CPI over the last several decades.

Source: Federal Reserve Board and U.S. Department of Labor websites, various dates. www.federalreserve.gov and www.dol.gov.

that is, the real risk-free rate earned on securities is positive. It is during periods of economic slowdowns that the T-bill rate is less than the CPI; that is, real risk-free rates are negative.

Default or Credit Risk

Default risk is the risk that a security issuer may fail to make its promised interest and principal payments to its bondholders (or its dividend in the case of stockholders). The higher the default risk, the higher the interest rate that security buyers will demand to compensate them for this default (or credit) risk relative to default-risk-free U.S. Treasury securities. Because the U.S. government has taxation powers and can print currency, the risk of its defaulting on debt payments is practically zero. But some borrowers, such as corporations or individuals, have less predictable cash flows (and no powers to tax anyone to raise funds immediately). So investors must charge issuers other than the U.S. government a premium for any perceived probability of default and the cost of potentially recovering the amount loaned built into their regular interest rate premium. The difference between a quoted interest rate on a security (security j) and a Treasury security with similar maturity, liquidity, tax, and other features is called a *default* or *credit risk premium (DRP$_j$)*. That is,

$$DRP_j = i_{jt} - i_{Tt} \qquad (6\text{-}4)$$

where i_{jt} = Interest rate on a security issued by a non–Treasury issuer (issuer j) of maturity m at time t.

i_{Tt} = Interest rate on a security issued by the U.S. Treasury of maturity m at time t.

Various rating agencies, including Moody's and Standard & Poor's, evaluate and categorize the potential default risk on many corporate bonds, some state and municipal bonds, and some stocks. We cover these ratings in more detail in Chapter 8. For example, in 2020, the 10-year Treasury rate was 0.87 percent. Moody's Aaa-rated and Baa-rated corporate debt carried interest rates of 2.30 percent and 3.31 percent, respectively. Thus, the average default risk premiums on the Aaa-rated and Baa-rated corporate debt were

$$DRP_{Aaa} = 2.30\% - 0.87\% = 1.43\%$$
$$DRP_{Baa} = 3.31\% - 0.87\% = 2.44\%$$

Figure 6.14 presents these risk premiums for the stated creditworthiness categories of bonds from 1977 through 2020. Notice from this figure and Figure 6.13 that default risk premiums tend to increase when the economy is contracting and decrease when the economy is expanding. For example, from 2007 to 2008, real risk-free rates (T-bills—CPI in Figure 6.13) increased from 0.43 percent to 1.73 percent. Over the same period, default risk premiums on Aaa-rated bonds increased from 1.39 percent to 1.97 percent. Baa-rated bonds showed a default risk premium increase from 2.55 percent to 3.78 percent.

Liquidity Risk

A highly liquid asset can be sold at a predictable price with low transaction costs. That is, the holder can convert the asset at its fair market value on short notice. The interest rate on a security reflects its relative liquidity, with highly liquid assets carrying the lowest interest rates (all other characteristics remaining the same). Likewise, if a security is illiquid, investors add a **liquidity risk** premium (LRP) to the interest rate on the security. In the United States, most government securities sell in liquid markets, as do large corporations' stocks and bonds. Securities issued by smaller companies trade in relatively less liquid markets.

A different type of liquidity risk premium may also exist if investors dislike long-term securities because their prices (present values, as discussed below and in Chapters 4 and 7) react more to interest rate changes than short-term securities do. In this case, a higher liquidity risk premium may be added to a security with a longer maturity because of its greater exposure to price risk (loss of capital value) on the longer-term security as interest rates change.

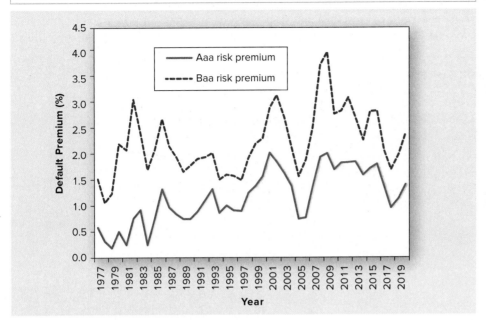

Source: Federal Reserve Board website, various dates. www.federalreserve.gov.

> **term structure of interest rates** A comparison of market yields on securities, assuming all characteristics except maturity are the same.

Special Provisions or Covenants

Sometimes a security's issuing party attaches special provisions or covenants to the security issued. Such provisions affect the interest rates on these securities relative to securities without such provisions attached to them. Some of these special provisions include the security's taxability, convertibility, and callability. For example, investors pay no federal taxes on interest payments received from municipal securities. The Tax Cuts and Jobs Act of 2017 capped the tax deduction at $10,000. Thus, up to this limit, a municipal bondholder may demand a lower interest rate than that demanded on a comparable taxable bond—such as a Treasury bond (which is taxable at the federal level but not at the state or local levels) or a corporate bond (the interest on which is taxable at the state, local, and federal levels).

Another special covenant is convertibility: A convertible bond offers the holder the opportunity to exchange the bond for another type of the issuer's securities—usually preferred or common stock—at a preset price (see Chapter 7). This conversion option can be valuable to purchasers, so convertible security buyers require lower interest rates than a comparable nonconvertible security holder would require (all else equal). In general, special provisions that benefit security holders (e.g., tax-free status and convertibility) bring with them lower interest rates, and special provisions that benefit security issuers (e.g., callability, by which an issuer has the option to retire, or call, the security prior to maturity at a preset price) require higher interest rates to encourage purchase.

Term to Maturity

Interest rates also change—sometimes daily—because of a bond's term to maturity. Financial professionals refer to this daily or even hourly changeability in interest rates as the **term structure of interest rates,** or the yield curve. The shape of the yield curve derives directly from time value of money principles. The term structure of interest rates compares interest rates on debt securities based on their time to maturity, assuming that all other characteristics (i.e., default risk, liquidity risk) are equal. Interest rates change as the maturity of a debt security changes; in general, the longer the term to maturity, the higher the required interest rate buyers will demand. This addition to the required interest rate is the maturity premium (MP). The MP, which is the difference between the required yield on long- versus short-term securities of the same characteristics except maturity, can be positive, negative, or zero.

The financial industry most often reports and analyzes the yield curve for U.S. Treasury securities. The yield curve for U.S. Treasury securities has taken many shapes over the years, but the three most common shapes appear in Figure 6.15. In graph (a), the yield curve on May 11, 2018, yields rise steadily with maturity when the yield curve slopes

FIGURE 6.15 Common Shapes for Yield Curves on Treasury Securities

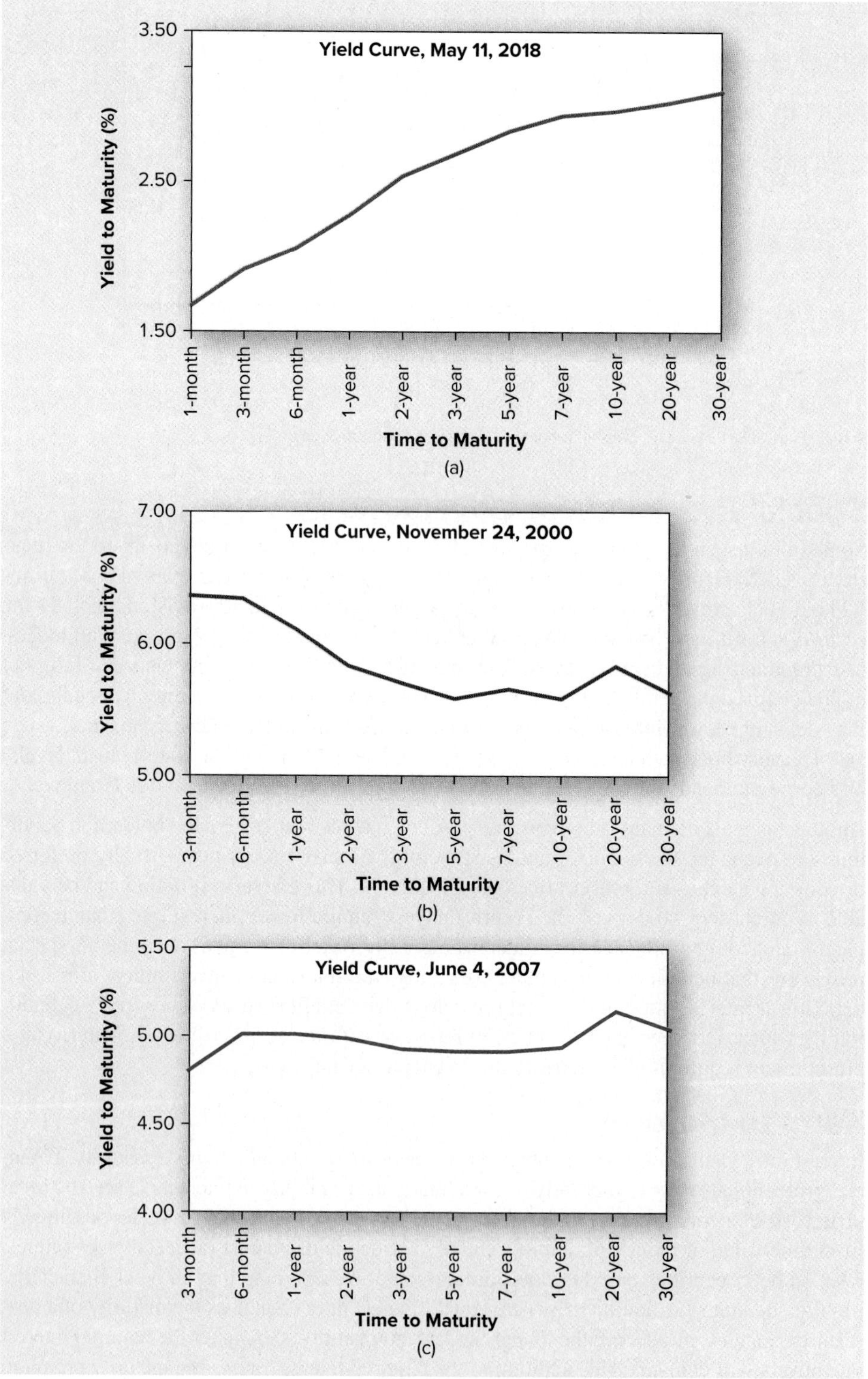

Three common yield curve shapes are (a) upward sloping, (b) downward sloping, and (c) a flat slope.

Source: U.S. Treasury, Office of Debt Management, Daily Treasury Yield Curves, various dates. www.ustreas.gov.

EXAMPLE 6-2

For interactive versions of this example, log in to Connect or go to mhhe.com/Cornett6e.

Determinants of Interest Rates for Individual Securities LG6-6

Morningstar Corp.'s eight-year bonds are currently yielding a return of 6.85 percent. The expected inflation premium is 1.15 percent annually and the real risk-free rate is expected to be 2.25 percent annually over the next eight years. The default risk premium on Morningstar's bonds is 1.35 percent. The maturity risk premium is 0.50 percent on two-year securities and increases by 0.05 percent for each additional year to maturity. Calculate the liquidity risk premium on Morningstar's eight-year bonds.

SOLUTION:

$$6.85\% = 1.15\% + 2.25\% + 1.35\% + LRP + [0.50\% + (0.05\% \times 6)]$$

$$=> DRP = 6.85\% - [1.15\% + 2.25\% + 1.35\% + (0.50\% + [0.05\% \times 6])] = 1.30\%$$

Similar to Problems 6-3, 6-4, Self-Test Problem 2

upward. This is the most common yield curve. On average, the MP is positive, as you might expect. Graph (b) shows an inverted, or downward-sloping, yield curve, reported on November 24, 2000, in which yields decline as maturity increases. Inverted yield curves do not generally last very long. In this case, the yield curve inverted as the U.S. Treasury began retiring long-term (30-year) bonds as the country began to pay off the national debt. Finally, graph (c) shows a flat yield curve, reported on June 4, 2007, when the yield to maturity is virtually unaffected by the term to maturity.

Putting together the factors that affect interest rates in different markets, we can use the following general equation to note the influence of the factors that functionally impact the fair interest rate—the rate necessary to compensate investors for all security risks—(i_j^*) on an individual (jth) financial security.

$$i_j^* = f(IP, RFR, DRP_j, LRP_j, SCP_j, MP_j) \tag{6-5}$$

where

IP = Inflation premium.

RFR = Real risk-free rate.

DRP_j = Default risk premium on the jth security.

LRP_j = Liquidity risk premiumon the jth security.

SCP_j = Special covenant premium on the jth security.

MP_j = Maturity premium on the jth security.

The first two factors, IP and RFR, are common to all financial securities, while the other factors can uniquely influence the price of a single security.

time out!

6-10 What is the difference between nominal and real risk-free rates?

6-11 What does "the term structure of interest rates" mean?

6-12 What shape does the term structure usually take? Why?

6.5 • THEORIES EXPLAINING THE SHAPE OF THE TERM STRUCTURE OF INTEREST RATES[2] LG6-7

We just explained the necessity of a maturity premium, the relationship between a security's interest rate and its remaining term to maturity. We can illustrate these issues by showing that the term structure of interest rates can take a number of different shapes. As you might expect, economists and financial theorists with various viewpoints differ among

FIGURE 6.16 Unbiased Expectations Theory of the Term Structure of Interest Rates

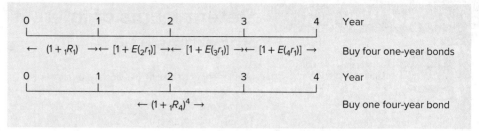

Return from buying four one-year maturity bonds versus buying one four-year maturity bond.

themselves in theorizing why the yield curve takes different shapes. Explanations for the yield curve's shape fall predominantly into three categories:

1. The unbiased expectations theory.

2. The liquidity premium theory.

3. The market segmentation theory.

Look again at Figure 6.15(a), which presents the Treasury yield curve as of May 11, 2018. We see that the yield curve on this date reflected the normal upward-sloping relationship between yield and maturity. Now let's turn to explanations for this shape based on the three predominant theories noted above.

Unbiased Expectations Theory

According to the unbiased expectations theory of the term structure of interest rates, at any given point in time, the yield curve reflects the *market's current expectations of future short-term rates*. As illustrated in Figure 6.16, the intuition behind the unbiased expectations theory is this: If investors have a four-year investment horizon, they could either buy current four-year bonds and earn the current (or spot) yield on a four-year bond ($_1R_4$, if held to maturity) each year, or they could invest in four successive one-year bonds [of which they know only the current one-year spot rate ($_1R_1$)]. But investors also expect what the unknown future one-year rates [$E(_2r_1)$, $E(_3r_1)$, and $E(_4r_1)$] will be. Note that each interest rate term has two subscripts, for example, $_1R_4$. The first subscript indicates the period in which the security is bought, so that 1 represents the purchase of a security in period 1. The second subscript indicates the maturity on the security. Thus, 4 represents the purchase of a security with a four-year life. Similarly, $E(_3r_1)$ is the expected return on a security with a one-year life purchased in period 3.

According to the unbiased expectations theory, the return for holding a four-year bond to maturity should equal the expected return for investing in four successive one-year bonds (as long as the market is in equilibrium). If this equality does not hold, an arbitrage opportunity exists. That is, if investors

the
Math Coach on...

66 When putting interest rates into the equation, enter them in decimal format, not percentage format.

Correct: $(1 + 0.0294)$

Not correct: $(1 + 2.94)$ 99

EXAMPLE 6-3

Calculating Yield Curves LG6-7

Suppose that the current one-year rate (one-year spot rate) and expected one-year T-bond rates over the following three years (i.e., years 2, 3, and 4, respectively) are as follows:

$$_1R_1 = 2.94\%, \quad E(_2r_1) = 4\%, \quad E(_3r_1) = 4.74\%, \quad E(_4r_1) = 5.10\%$$

Construct a yield curve using the unbiased expectations theory.

SOLUTION:

Using the unbiased expectations theory, current (or today's) rates for one-, two-, three-, and four-year maturity Treasury securities should be

$_1R_1 = 2.94\%$ (Expected return of security with one-year life purchased in period 1)

$_1R_2 = [(1 + 0.0294)(1 + 0.04)]^{1/2} - 1 = 3.47\%$

$_1R_3 = [(1 + 0.0294)(1 + 0.04)(1 + 0.0474)]^{1/3} - 1 = 3.89\%$

$_1R_4 = [(1 + 0.0294)(1 + 0.04)(1 + 0.0474)(1 + 0.051)]^{1/4} - 1 = 4.19\%$

and the current yield to maturity curve will be upward sloping as shown:

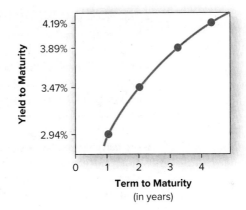

This upward-sloping yield curve reflects the market's expectation of persistently rising one-year (short-term) interest rates over the future horizon.[3]

The spreadsheet solution is:

	A	B	C	D	E	F
1	$_1R_1 =$	2.94%				
2	$E(_2r_1) =$	4.00%		$_1R_2 =$	3.47%	=((1+B1)*(1+B2))^0.5-1
3	$E(_3r_1) =$	4.74%		$_1R_3 =$	3.89%	=((1+B1)*(1+B2)*(1+B3))^(1/3)-1
4	$E(_4r_1) =$	5.10%		$_1R_4 =$	4.19%	=((1+E3)^3*(1+B4))^(1/4)-1

Microsoft Excel

Similar to Problems 6-5, 6-6, 6-9, Self-Test Problem 3

could earn more on the one-year bond investments, they could short (or sell) the four-year bond, use the proceeds to buy the four successive one-year bonds, and earn a guaranteed profit over the four-year investment horizon. So, according to the unbiased expectations theory, if the market expects future one-year rates to rise each successive year into the future, then the yield curve will slope upward. Specifically, the current four-year T-bond rate or return will exceed the three-year bond rate, which will exceed the two-year bond rate, and so on. Similarly, if the market expects future one-year rates to remain constant each successive year into the future, then the four-year bond rate will equal the three-year bond rate. That is, the term structure of interest rates will remain constant (flat) over the relevant time period. Specifically, the unbiased expectation theory states that current long-term interest rates are geometric averages of current and expected *future* short-term interest rates. The mathematical equation representing this relationship is

$$(1 + {}_1R_N)^N = (1 + {}_1R_1)[1 + E({}_2r_1)] \ldots [1 + E({}_Nr_1)] \tag{6-6}$$

Therefore,

$${}_1R_N = \{[1 + {}_1R_1][1 + E({}_2r_1)] \ldots [1 + E({}_Nr_1)]\}^{1/N} - 1 \tag{6-7}$$

where ${}_1R_N$ = Actual N-period rate today (i.e., the first day of year 1).

     N = Term to maturity.

     ${}_1R_1$ = Actual one-year rate today.

     $E({}_ir_1)$ = Expected one-year rates for years 2, 3, 4, . . . , N in the furure.

Notice that uppercase interest rate terms, ${}_1R_t$, are the actual current interest rates on securities purchased today with a maturity of t years. Lowercase interest rate terms, ${}_tr_1$, represent estimates of future one-year interest rates starting t years into the future.

Liquidity Premium Theory

The second popular explanation—the liquidity premium theory of the term structure of interest rates—builds on the unbiased expectations theory. The liquidity premium idea is as follows: Investors will hold long-term maturities only if these securities with longer-term maturities are offered at a premium to compensate for future uncertainty in the security's value. Of course, uncertainty or risk increases with an asset's maturity. This theory is thus consistent with our discussions of market risk and liquidity risk, above. Specifically, in a world of uncertainty, short-term securities provide greater marketability (due to their more active secondary markets) and have less price risk than long-term securities do. As a result (due to smaller price fluctuations for a given change in interest rates), investors will prefer to hold shorter-term securities because this kind of investment can be converted into cash with little market risk. Said another way, investors face little risk of a capital loss, that is, a fall in the price of the security below its original purchase price. So, investors must be offered a liquidity premium to buy longer-term securities that carry higher capital loss risk. This difference in market and liquidity risk can be directly related to the fact that longer-term securities are more sensitive to interest rate changes in the market than are shorter-term securities—Chapter 7 discusses bond interest rate sensitivity and the link to a bond's maturity. Because longer maturities on securities mean greater market and liquidity risk, the liquidity premium increases as maturity increases.

The liquidity premium theory states that long-term rates are equal to geometric averages of current and expected short-term rates (like the unbiased expectations theory), plus liquidity risk premiums that increase with the security's maturity (this is the extension of the liquidity premium added to the unbiased expectations theory). Figure 6.17 illustrates the differences in the shape of the yield curve under the unbiased expectations theory versus the liquidity premium theory. For example, according to the liquidity premium theory, an upward-sloping yield curve may reflect investors' expectations that future short-term rates will be flat, but because liquidity premiums increase with maturity, the yield curve will nevertheless slope upward. Indeed, an upward-sloping yield curve may reflect expectations that future interest rates will rise, be flat, or even fall as long as the liquidity premium increases with maturity fast enough to produce an upward-sloping yield curve. The liquidity premium theory can be mathematically represented as

$${}_1R_N = \{[1 + {}_1R_1][1 + E({}_2r_1) + L_2] \ldots [1 + E({}_Nr_1) + L_N]\}^{1/N} - 1 \tag{6-8}$$

where L_t = Liquidity premium for a period t and $L_2 < L_3 < L_N$.

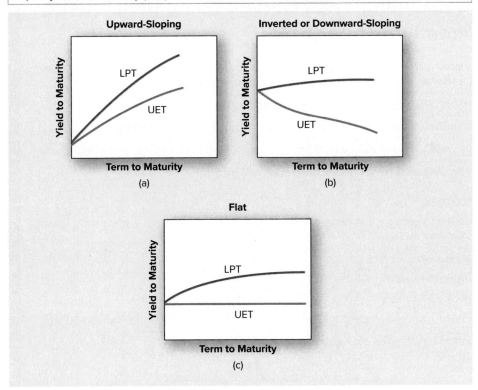

Notice the differences in the shape of the yield curve under the UET and the LPT.

Let's compare the yield curves in Examples 6-3 (using the unbiased expectations theory) and 6-4. Notice that the liquidity premium in year 2 ($L_2 = 0.10\%$) produces a 0.05 ($= 3.52\% - 3.47\%$) percent premium on the yield to maturity on a two-year T-note, the liquidity premium for year 3 ($L_3 = 0.20\%$) produces a 0.10 ($= 3.99\% - 3.89\%$) percent premium on the yield to maturity on the three-year T-note, and the liquidity premium for year 4 ($L_4 = 0.30\%$) produces a 0.15 ($= 4.34\% - 4.19\%$) percent premium on the yield to maturity on the four-year T-note.

Market Segmentation Theory

The market segmentation theory does not build on the unbiased expectations theory or the liquidity premium theory but rather argues that individual investors and FIs have specific maturity preferences, and convincing them to hold securities with maturities other than their most preferred requires a higher interest rate (maturity premium). The main thrust of the market segmentation theory is that investors do not consider securities with different maturities as perfect substitutes. Rather, individual investors and FIs have distinctly pre-ferred investment horizons dictated by the dates when their liabilities will come due. For example, banks might prefer to hold relatively short-term U.S. Treasury bonds because their deposit liabilities also tend to be short term—recall that bank customers can access their funds on demand. Insurance companies, on the other hand, may prefer to hold long-term U.S. Treasury bonds because life insurance contracts usually expose insurance firms to long-term liabilities. Accordingly, distinct supply and demand conditions within a par-ticular maturity segment—such as the short end and long end of the bond market—deter-mine interest rates under the market segmentation theory.

The market segmentation theory assumes that investors and borrowers generally do not want to shift from one maturity sector to another without adequate compensation—that

EXAMPLE 6-4

For interactive versions
of this example, log
in to Connect or go to
mhhe.com/Cornett6e.

Calculating Yield Curves Using the Liquidity Premium Theory LG6-7

Suppose that the current one-year rate (one-year spot rate) and expected one-year T-bond rates over the following three years (i.e., years 2, 3, and 4, respectively) are as follows:

$$_1R_1 = 2.94\%, \quad E(_2r_1) = 4.00\%, \quad E(_3r_1) = 4.74\%, \quad E(_4r_1) = 5.10\%$$

In addition, investors charge a liquidity premium on longer-term securities such that

$$L_2 = 0.10\%, \quad L_3 = 0.20\%, \quad L_4 = 0.30\%$$

Using the liquidity premium theory, construct the yield curve.

SOLUTION:

Using the liquidity premium theory, current rates for one-, two-, three-, and four-year maturity Treasury securities should be

$$_1R_1 = 2.94\%$$
$$_1R_2 = [(1 + 0.0294)(1 + 0.04 + 0.001)]^{1/2} - 1 = 3.52\%$$
$$_1R_3 = [(1 + 0.0294)(1 + 0.04 + 0.001)(1 + 0.0474 + 0.002)]^{1/3} - 1 = 3.99\%$$
$$_1R_4 = [(1 + 0.0294)(1 + 0.04 + 0.001)(1 + 0.0474 + 0.002)(1 + 0.051 + 0.003)]^{1/4} - 1 = 4.34\%$$

and the current yield to maturity curve will be upward sloping as shown:

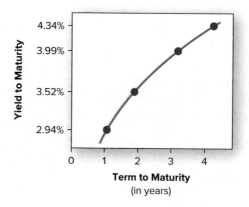

The spreadsheet solution is:

	A	B	C	D	E	F
1	$_1R_1 =$	2.94%				
2	$E(_2r_1) =$	4.00%		$_1R_2 =$	3.52%	=((1+B1)*(1+B2+0.001))^0.5-1
3	$E(_3r_1) =$	4.74%		$_1R_3 =$	3.99%	=((1+B1)*(1+B2+0.001)*(1+B3+0.002))^(1/3)-1
4	$E(_4r_1) =$	5.10%		$_1R_4 =$	4.34%	=((1+E3)^3*(1+B4+0.003))^(1/4)-1

Microsoft Corporation

Similar to Problems 6-7, Self-Test Problem 3

is, an interest rate premium. Figure 6.18 demonstrates how changes in supply for short- versus long-term bond market segments result in changing shapes of the yield to maturity curve. Specifically, as shown in Figure 6.18, the higher the demand for securities is, the higher the yield on those securities is.[4] Further, as the supply of securities decreases in the short-term market and increases in the long-term market, the slope of the yield curve

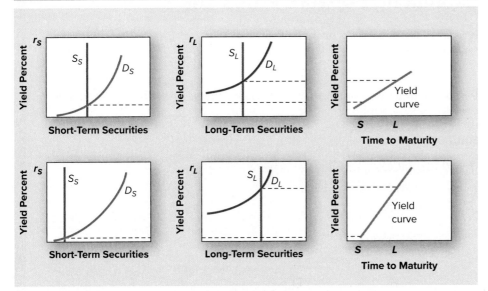

The higher the demand for securities, the higher the yield on those securities.

becomes steeper. If the supply of short-term securities had increased while the supply of long-term securities had decreased, the yield curve would have a flatter slope and might even have sloped downward. Indeed, the U.S. Treasury's large-scale repurchase of long-term Treasury bonds (i.e., reductions in supply) in early 2000 has been viewed as the major cause of the inverted yield curve that appeared in February 2000.

6.6 • FORECASTING INTEREST RATES[5] LG6-8

We noted in the time value of money (TVM) chapters (Chapters 4 and 5) that as interest rates change, so do the values of financial securities. Accordingly, both individual investors and public corporations want to be able to predict or forecast interest rates if they wish to trade profitably. For example, if interest rates rise, the value of investment portfolios of individuals and corporations will fall, resulting in a loss of wealth. So, interest rate forecasts are extremely important for the financial wealth of both public corporations and individuals.

Recall our discussion of the unbiased expectations theory in the previous section of this chapter. That theory indicates that the market's expectation of future short-term interest rates determines the shape of the yield curve. For example, an upward-sloping yield curve implies that the market expects future short-term interest rates to rise. So, we can use the unbiased expectations theory to forecast (short-term) interest rates in the future (i.e., forward one-year interest rates). A **forward rate** is an expected, or implied, rate on a short-term security that will originate at some point in the future. Using the equations in the unbiased expectations theory, we can directly derive the market's expectation of forward rates from existing or actual rates on spot market securities.

To find an implied forward rate on a one-year security to be issued one year from today, we can rewrite the unbiased expectations theory equation as follows:

$$_1R_2 = [(1 + _1R_1)(1 + _2f_1)]^{1/2} - 1 \qquad (6\text{-}9)$$

where $_2f_1$ = expected one-year rate for year 2, or the implied forward one-year rate for the next year.

time **out!**

6-13 What three theories explain the shape of the yield curve?

6-14 Explain how arbitrage plays a role in the unbiased expectations explanation of the shape of the yield curve.

forward rate An expected rate (quoted today) on a security that originates at some point in the future.

EXAMPLE 6-5   Estimating Forward Rates   LG6-8

In the late-2010s, the existing or current (spot) one-, two-, three-, and four-year zero coupon Treasury security rates were as follows:

$$_1R_1 = 2.30\%, \ _1R_2 = 2.57\%, \ _1R_3 = 2.70\%, \ _1R_4 = 2.80\%$$

Using the unbiased expectations theory, calculate one-year forward rates on zero coupon Treasury bonds for years 2, 3, and 4.

SOLUTION:

$$_2f_1 = \left[(1.0257)^2/(1.0230)\right] - 1 = 2.84\%$$

$$_3f_1 = \left[(1.0270)^3/(1.0257)^2\right] - 1 = 2.96\%$$

$$_4f_1 = \left[(1.0280)^4/(1.0270)^3\right] - 1 = 3.10\%$$

The spreadsheet solution is

	A	B	C	D	E	F
1	$_1R_1 =$	2.30%				
2	$_1R_2 =$	2.57%		$_2f_1 =$	2.84%	=(1+B2)^2/(1+B1)-1
3	$_1R_3 =$	2.70%		$_3f_1 =$	2.96%	=(1+B3)^3/(1+B2)^2-1
4	$_1R_4 =$	2.80%		$_4f_1 =$	3.10%	=(1+B4)^4/(1+B3)^3-1

Microsoft Corporation

Similar to Problems 6-13, 6-14, Self-Test Problem 4

time out!

6-15 What is a forward rate?

6-16 How can we obtain an implied forward rate from current short- and long-term interest rates?

6-17 Why is it useful to calculate forward rates?

Saying that $_2f_1$ is the expected one-year rate for year 2 is the same as saying that, once we isolate the $_2f_1$ term, the equation will give us the market's estimate of the expected one-year rate for year 2. Solving for $_2f_1$ we get

$$_2f_1 = \left[(1 + {_1R_2})^2/(1 + {_1R_1})\right] - 1 \qquad (6\text{-}10)$$

In general, we can find the forward rate for any year, N, into the future using the following generalized equation derived from the unbiased expectations theory:

$$_Nf_1 = \left[(1 + {_1R_N})^N/(1 + {_1R_{N-1}})^{N-1}\right] - 1 \qquad (6\text{-}11)$$

Get Online

mhhe.com/CornettM6e

for study materials including

quizzes, iPod downloads,

and video

Your Turn...

Questions

1. Classify the following transactions as taking place in the primary or secondary markets *(LG6-1):*

   a. IBM issues $200 million of new common stock.

   b. The New Company issues $50 million of common stock in an IPO.

   c. IBM sells $5 million of GM preferred stock out of its marketable securities portfolio.

   d. The Magellan Fund buys $100 million of previously issued IBM bonds.

   e. Prudential Insurance Co. sells $10 million of GM common stock.

2. Classify the following financial instruments as money market securities or capital market securities *(LG6-2):*

   a. Federal funds.

   b. Common stock.

   c. Corporate bonds.

   d. Mortgages.

   e. Negotiable certificates of deposit.

   f. U.S. Treasury bills.

   g. U.S. Treasury notes.

   h. U.S. Treasury bonds.

   i. State and government bonds.

3. What are the different types of financial institutions? Include a description of the main services offered by each. *(LG6-3)*

4. How would economic transactions between suppliers of funds (e.g., households) and users of funds (e.g., corporations) occur in a world without FIs? *(LG6-3)*

5. Why would a world limited to the direct transfer of funds from suppliers of funds to users of funds likely result in quite low levels of fund flows? *(LG6-3)*

6. How do FIs reduce monitoring costs associated with the flow of funds from fund suppliers to fund users? *(LG6-3)*

7. How do FIs alleviate the problem of liquidity risk faced by investors wishing to invest in securities of corporations? *(LG6-3)*

8. Who are the suppliers of loanable funds? *(LG6-4)*

9. Who are the demanders of loanable funds? *(LG6-4)*

10. What factors cause the supply of funds curve to shift? *(LG6-5)*

11. What factors cause the demand for funds curve to shift? *(LG6-5)*

12. What are six factors that determine the nominal interest rate on a security? *(LG6-6)*

13. What should happen to a security's equilibrium interest rate as the security's liquidity risk increases? *(LG6-6)*

14. Discuss and compare the three explanations for the shape of the yield curve. *(LG6-7)*

15. Are the unbiased expectations and liquidity premium theories explanations for the shape of the yield curve completely independent theories? Explain why or why not. *(LG6-7)*

16. What is a forward interest rate? *(LG6-8)*

17. If we observe a one-year Treasury security rate that is higher than the two-year Treasury security rate, what can we infer about the one-year rate expected one year from now? *(LG6-8)*

Problems

BASIC PROBLEMS

6-1 **Determinants of Interest Rates for Individual Securities** A particular security's default risk premium is 2 percent. For all securities, the inflation risk premium is 1.75 percent and the real risk-free rate is 3.50 percent. The security's liquidity risk premium is 0.25 percent and the maturity risk premium is 0.85 percent. The security has no special covenants. Calculate the security's equilibrium rate of return. *(LG6-6)*

6-2 **Determinants of Interest Rates for Individual Securities** You are considering an investment in 30-year bonds issued by Moore Corporation. The bonds have no special covenants. *The Wall Street Journal* reports that one-year T-bills are currently earning 1.25 percent. Your broker has determined the following information about economic activity and Moore Corporation bonds:

Real risk-free rate = 0.75%

Default risk premium = 1.15%

Liquidity risk premium = 0.50%

Maturity risk premium = 1.75%

a. What is the inflation premium? *(LG6-6)*

b. What is the fair interest rate on Moore Corporation's 30-year bonds? *(LG6-6)*

6-3 **Determinants of Interest Rates for Individual Securities** Dakota Corporation 15-year bonds have an equilibrium rate of return of 8 percent. For all securities, the inflation risk premium is 1.75 percent and the real risk-free rate is 3.50 percent. The security's liquidity risk premium is 0.25 percent and the maturity risk premium is 0.85 percent. The security has no special covenants. Calculate the bond's default risk premium. *(LG6-6)*

6-4 **Determinants of Interest Rates for Individual Securities** A two-year Treasury security currently earns 1.94 percent. Over the next two years, the real risk-free rate is expected to be 1.00 percent per year and the inflation premium is expected to be 0.50 percent per year. Calculate the maturity risk premium on the two-year Treasury security. *(LG6-6)*

6-5 **Unbiased Expectations Theory** Suppose that the current one-year rate (one-year spot rate) and expected one-year T-bill rates over the following three years (i.e., years 2, 3, and 4, respectively) are as follows:

$$_1R_1 = 6\%, \quad E(_2r_1) = 7\%, \quad E(_3r_1) = 7.5\%, \quad E(_4r_1) = 7.85\%$$

Using the unbiased expectations theory, calculate the current (long-term) rates for one-, two-, three-, and four-year-maturity Treasury securities. Plot the resulting yield curve. *(LG6-7)*

6-6 **Unbiased Expectations Theory** One-year Treasury bills currently earn 1.45 percent. You expect that one year from now, one-year Treasury bill rates will increase to 1.65 percent. If the unbiased expectations theory is correct, what should the current rate be on two-year Treasury securities? *(LG6-7)*

6-7 **Liquidity Premium Theory** One-year Treasury bills currently earn 3.45 percent. You expect that one year from now, one-year Treasury bill rates will increase to 3.65 percent. The liquidity premium on two-year securities is 0.05 percent. If the liquidity premium theory is correct, what should the current rate be on two-year Treasury securities? *(LG6-7)*

6-8 **Liquidity Premium Theory** Based on economists' forecasts and analysis, one-year Treasury bill rates and liquidity premiums for the next four years are expected to be as follows:

$$R_1 = 0.65\%$$
$$E(_2r_1) = 1.75\% \qquad L_2 = 0.05\%$$
$$E(_3r_1) = 1.85\% \qquad L_3 = 0.10\%$$
$$E(_4r_1) = 2.15\% \qquad L_4 = 0.12\%$$

Using the liquidity premium theory, plot the current yield curve. Make sure you label the axes on the graph and identify the four annual rates on the curve both on the axes and on the yield curve itself. *(LG6-7)*

6-9 **Spreadsheet Problem: Unbiased Expectations Theory** Suppose that the current one-year rate (one-year spot rate) and expected one-year T-bill rates over the following three years (i.e., years 2, 3, and 4, respectively) are as follows:

$$_1R_1 = 1\%, \quad E(_2r_1) = 3.75\%, \quad E(_3r_1) = 4.25\%, \quad E(_4r_1) = 5.75\%$$

Using the unbiased expectations theory, calculate the current (long-term) rates for one-, two-, three-, and four-year-maturity Treasury securities. Plot the resulting yield curve. *(LG6-7)*

6-10 **Spreadsheet Problem: Liquidity Premium Theory** Based on economists' forecasts and analysis, one-year Treasury bill rates and liquidity premiums for the next four years are expected to be as follows:

$$R_1 \quad = 1.25\%$$
$$E(_2r_1) = 2.15\% \qquad L_2 = 0.08\%$$
$$E(_3r_1) = 2.55\% \qquad L_3 = 0.10\%$$
$$E(_4r_1) = 3.00\% \qquad L_4 = 0.15\%$$

Using the liquidity premium theory, plot the current yield curve. Make sure you label the axes on the graph and identify the four annual rates on the curve both on the axes and on the yield curve itself. *(LG6-7)*

6-11 **Determinants of Interest Rates for Individual Securities** Tom and Sue's Flowers, Inc.'s 15-year bonds are currently yielding a return of 8.25 percent. The expected inflation premium is 2.25 percent annually and the real risk-free rate is expected to be 3.50 percent annually over the next 15 years. The default risk premium on Tom and Sue's Flowers' bonds is 0.80 percent. The maturity risk premium is 0.75 percent on five-year securities and increases by 0.04 percent for each additional year to maturity. Calculate the liquidity risk premium on Tom and Sue's Flowers, Inc.'s 15-year bonds. *(LG6-6)*

6-12 **Determinants of Interest Rates for Individual Securities** NikkiG's Corporation's 10-year bonds are currently yielding a return of 6.05 percent. The expected inflation premium is 1.00 percent annually and the real risk-free rate is expected to be 2.10 percent annually over the next 10 years. The liquidity risk premium on NikkiG's bonds is 0.25 percent. The maturity risk premium is 0.10 percent on two-year securities and increases by 0.05 percent for each additional year to maturity. Calculate the default risk premium on NikkiG's 10-year bonds. *(LG6-6)*

6-13 **Unbiased Expectations Theory** Suppose we observe the following rates: $_1R_1 = 8\%$, $_1R_2 = 10\%$. If the unbiased expectations theory of the term structure of interest rates holds, what is the one-year interest rate expected one year from now, $E(_2r_1)$? *(LG6-7)*

6-14 **Unbiased Expectations Theory** *The Wall Street Journal* reports that the rate on four-year Treasury securities is 1.60 percent and the rate on five-year Treasury securities is 2.15 percent. According to the unbiased expectations theory, what does the market expect the one-year Treasury rate to be four years from today, $E(_5r_1)$? *(LG6-7)*

6-15 **Liquidity Premium Theory** *The Wall Street Journal* reports that the rate on three-year Treasury securities is 5.25 percent and the rate on four-year Treasury securities is 5.50 percent. The one-year interest rate expected in three years, $E(_4r_1)$, is 6.10 percent. According to the liquidity premium hypothesis, what is the liquidity premium on the four-year Treasury security, L_4? *(LG6-7)*

6-16 **Liquidity Premium Theory** Suppose we observe the following rates: $_1R_1 = 0.75\%$, $_1R_2 = 1.20\%$, and $E(_2r_1) = 0.907\%$. If the liquidity premium theory of the term structure of interest rates holds, what is the liquidity premium for year 2, L_2? *(LG6-7)*

6-17 **Forecasting Interest Rates** You note the following yield curve in *The Wall Street Journal*. According to the unbiased expectations theory, what is the one-year forward rate for the period beginning one year from today, $_2f_1$? *(LG6-8)*

Maturity	Yield
One day	2.00%
One year	5.50
Two years	6.50
Three years	9.00

6-18 **Spreadsheet Problem: Forecasting Interest Rates** On March 11, 20XX, the existing or current *(spot)* one-, two-, three-, and four-year zero coupon Treasury security rates were as follows:

◢	A	B	C	D
1	$_1R_1 =$	0.75%		
2	$_1R_2 =$	1.35%		$_2f_1 =$
3	$_1R_3 =$	1.75%		$_3f_1 =$
4	$_1R_4 =$	1.90%		$_4f_1 =$

Microsoft Excel

Using the unbiased expectations theory, calculate the one-year forward rates on zero coupon Treasury bonds for years 2, 3, and 4 as of March 11, 20XX. *(LG6-8)*

ADVANCED PROBLEMS

6-19 **Determinants of Interest Rates for Individual Securities** *The Wall Street Journal* reports that the current rate on 10-year Treasury bonds is 7.25 percent, on 20-year Treasury bonds is 7.85 percent, and on a 20-year corporate bond issued by MHM Corp. is 8.75 percent. Assume that the maturity risk premium is zero. If the default risk premium and the liquidity risk premium on a 10-year corporate bond issued by MHM Corp. are the same as those on the 20-year corporate bond, calculate the current rate on MHM Corp.'s 10-year corporate bond. *(LG6-6)*

6-20 **Determinants of Interest Rates for Individual Securities** *The Wall Street Journal* reports that the current rate on five-year Treasury bonds is 1.85 percent and on 10-year Treasury bonds is 3.35 percent. Assume that the maturity risk premium is zero. Calculate the expected rate on a five-year Treasury bond purchased five years from today, $E(_5r_5)$. *(LG6-6)*

6-21 **Unbiased Expectations Theory** Suppose we observe the three-year Treasury security rate ($_1R_3$) to be 8 percent, the expected one-year rate next year— $E(_2r_1)$—to be 4 percent, and the expected one-year rate the following year— $E(_3r_1)$—to be 6 percent. If the unbiased expectations theory of the term structure of interest rates holds, what is the one-year Treasury security rate, $_1R_1$? *(LG6-7)*

6-22 **Forecasting Interest Rates** Assume the current interest rate on a one-year Treasury bond ($_1R_1$)is 4.50 percent, the current rate on a two-year Treasury bond ($_1R_2$) is 5.25 percent, and the current rate on a three-year Treasury bond ($_1R_3$) is 6.50 percent. If the unbiased expectations theory of the term structure of interest rates is correct, what is the one-year forward rate expected on Treasury bills during year 3, $_3f_1$? *(LG6-8)*

6-23 **Forecasting Interest Rates** A recent edition of *The Wall Street Journal* reported interest rates of 1.25 percent, 1.60 percent, 1.98 percent, and 2.25 percent for three-, four-, five-, and six-year Treasury security yields, respectively. According to the unbiased expectation theory of the term structure of interest rates, what are the expected one-year forward rates for years 4, 5, and 6? *(LG6-8)*

6-24 Spreadsheet Problem: Unbiased Expectations Theory and Liquidity Premium Theory Suppose that the current one-year rate (one-year spot rate) and expected one-year T-bill rates over the following three years (i.e., years 2, 3, and 4, respectively), along with the associated liquidity premiums, are as follows:

	A	B
1	$_1R_1 =$	0.94%
2	$E(_2r_1) =$	1.55%
3	$E(_3r_1) =$	2.64%
4	$E(_4r_1) =$	3.31%
5		
6	$L_2 =$	0.05%
7	$L_2 =$	0.12%
8	$L_2 =$	0.18%

Microsoft Excel

Using both the unbiased expectations theory and liquidity premium theory, calculate the current (long-term) rates for one-, two-, three-, and four-year-maturity Treasury securities. Plot both resulting yield curves on one graph. *(LG6-7)*

Notes

CHAPTER 6

1. Often the Fisher effect formula is written as $(1 + i) = (1 + IP) \times (1 + RFR)$, which, when solved for i, becomes: $i =$ Expected $IP + RFR +$ (Expected $IP \times RFR$), where Expected $IP \times RFR$ is the inflation premium for the loss of purchasing power on the promised nominal interest rate payments due to inflation. For small values of Expected IP and RFR, this term is negligible. The approximation formula used here assumes these values are small.

2. This section, which contains more technical details, may be included or dropped from the chapter reading, depending on the rigor of the course.

3. That is, $E(_4r_1) > E(_3r_1) > E(_2r_1) > {}_1R_1$.

4. In general, the price and yield on a bond are inversely related. Thus, as the price of a bond falls (becomes cheaper), the demand for the bond will rise. This is the same as saying that as the yield on a bond rises, it becomes cheaper and the demand for it increases. See Chapter 7.

5. This section, which contains more technical details, may be included in or dropped from the chapter reading depending on the rigor of the course.

Design elements: (Clock) Floortje/Getty Images; (Referee) Richard Ransier/Getty Images

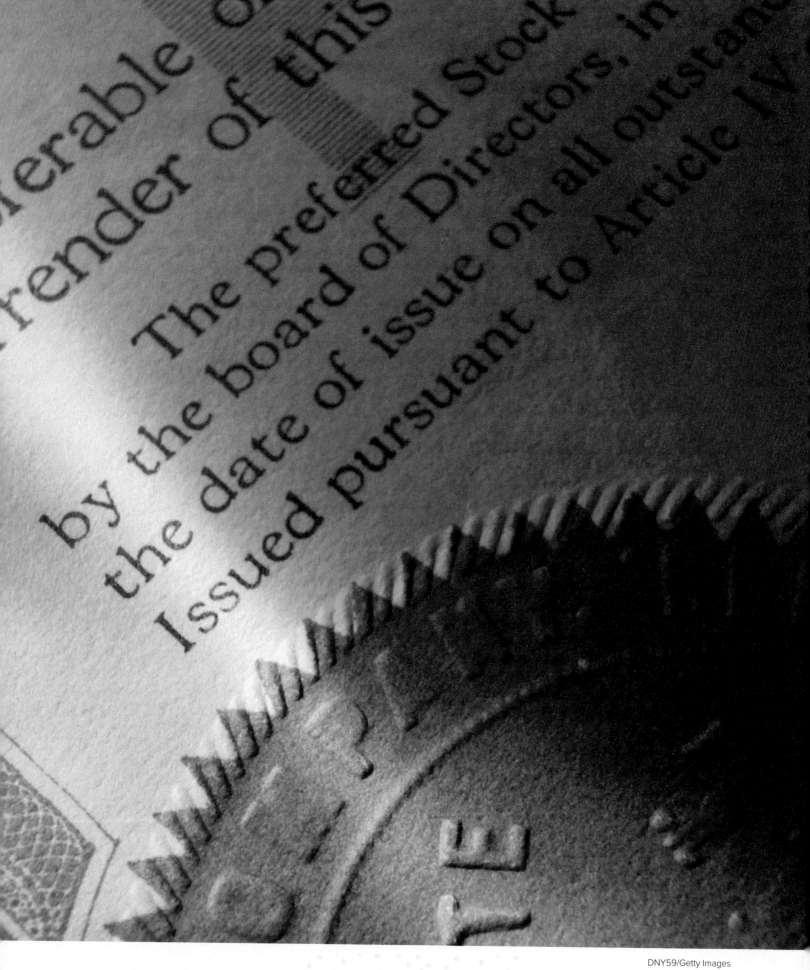

valuing
bonds

H ow important are bonds and the bond market to a capitalist economy? Those unfamiliar with the financial markets may have the impression that the stock market dominates capital markets in the United States and in other countries. Stock market performance appears constantly on 24-hour TV news channels and on the evening news. By contrast, we seldom hear any mention of the bond market. While bonds may not generate the same excitement that stocks do, they are an even more important capital source for companies, governments, and other organizations. The bond market is actually larger than the stock market. At the end of 2020, the U.S. bond market represented over $50 trillion in outstanding debt obligations. At the same time, the market value of all common stock issues was worth much less than the value of the bond market, at roughly $38 trillion.

Bonds also trade in great volume and frequency. During 2020, the total average daily trading in all types of U.S. bonds reached over $965 billion. Investors are often attracted to the stock market because it offers the potential for high investor returns—but great risks come with that high

continued on p. 192

LEARNING GOALS

LG7-1 Describe bond characteristics.

LG7-2 Identify various bond issuers and their motivation for issuing debt.

LG7-3 Read and interpret bond quotes.

LG7-4 Compute bond prices using present value concepts.

LG7-5 Explain the relationship between bond prices and interest rates.

LG7-6 Compute bond yields.

LG7-7 Find bond ratings and assess credit risk's effects on bond yields.

LG7-8 Assess bond market performance.

»viewpoints

bond Publicly traded form of debt.

fixed-income securities Any securities that make fixed payments.

principal Face amount, or par value, of debt.

indenture agreement Legal contract describing the bond characteristics and the bondholder and issuer rights.

maturity date The calendar date on which the bond principal comes due.

par value Amount of debt borrowed to be repaid; face value.

time to maturity The length of time (in years) until the bond matures and the issuer repays the par value.

continued from p. 191

potential return. While some bonds offer safer and more stable returns than stocks, other bonds also offer high potential rewards and, consequently, higher risk.

In this chapter, we will explore bond characteristics and their price dynamics. You will see that bond pricing uses many time value of money principles that we've used in the preceding chapters. ∎

7.1 • BOND MARKET OVERVIEW LG7-1

Bond Characteristics

Bonds are debt obligation securities that corporations, the federal government or its agencies, or states and local governments issue to fund various projects or operations. All of these organizations periodically need to raise capital for various reasons, which was formally discussed in Chapter 6. Bonds are also known as **fixed-income securities** because bondholders (investors) know both how much they will receive in interest payments and when their principal will be returned. From the bond issuer's point of view, the bond is a loan that requires regular interest payments and an eventual repayment of the borrowed **principal.** Investors—often pension funds, banks, and mutual funds—buy bonds to earn investment returns. Most bonds follow a relatively standard structure. A legal contract called the **indenture agreement** outlines the precise terms between the issuer and the bondholders. Any bond's main characteristics include:

- The date the principal will be repaid (the **maturity date**).
- The **par value,** or face value, of each bond, which is the principal loan amount that the borrower must repay.
- The coupon (interest) rate.
- A description of any property to be pledged as collateral.
- Steps that the bondholder can take in the event that the issuer fails to pay the interest or principal.

Table 7.1 describes par value and other bond characteristics. Most bonds have a par value of $1,000. This is the amount of principal the issuer has promised to repay. Bonds have fixed lives. The bond's life ends when the issuer repays the par value to the buyer on the bond's maturity date. Although a bond will mature on a specific calendar date, the bond is usually referenced by its **time to maturity,** that is, 2 years, 5 years, 20 years, and so on. In fact, the market groups bonds together by their time to maturity and classifies them as short-term bonds, medium-term bonds, or long-term bonds, regardless of issuer. Long-term bonds carry 20 or 30 years to maturity. Of course, over time, the 30-year bond

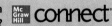
becomes a 20-year bond, 10-year bond, and eventually matures. But other time periods to maturity do exist. For example, in 2011, the railroad company Norfolk Southern Corp. issued $400 million of bonds with 100 years to maturity. The bonds have a coupon (interest) rate of 6 percent and mature in 2111.

When interest rates economywide fall several percentage points (which often takes several years), homeowners everywhere seek to refinance their home mortgages. They want to make lower interest payments (and sometimes want to pay down their mortgage principal) every month. Corporations that have outstanding bond debt will also want to refinance those bonds. Sometimes the indenture contract (the legal contract between a bond issuer and bondholders) allows companies to do so; sometimes the indenture prohibits refinancing. Bonds that can be refinanced have a **call** feature, which means that the issuer can "call" the bonds back and repay the principal before the maturity date. To compensate the bondholders for getting the bond called, the issuer pays the principal and a **call premium.** The most common call premium is one year's worth of interest payments. In some indentures, the call premium declines over time.

The bond's **coupon rate** determines the dollar amount of interest paid to bondholders. The coupon rate appears on the bond and is listed as a percentage of the par value. So a 5 percent coupon rate means that the issuer will pay 5 percent of $1,000, or $50, in interest every year, usually divided into two equal semiannual payments. So a 5 percent coupon bond will pay $25 every six months. Companies set the coupon rate as the prevailing market interest rate at the time of bond issue. The name *coupon* is a holdover from the past, when bonds were actually issued with a coupon book. Every six months a bondholder would tear out a coupon and mail it to the issuer, who would then make the interest payment. These are sometimes

call An issuer redeeming the bond before the scheduled maturity date.

call premium The amount in addition to the par value paid by the issuer when calling a bond.

coupon rate The annual amount of interest paid expressed as a percentage of the bond's par value.

▼ **TABLE 7.1** Typical Bond Features

Characteristic	Description	Common Values
Par value	The amount of the loan to be repaid. This is often referred to as the *principal* of the bond.	$ 1,000
Time to maturity	The number of years left until the maturity date.	1 year to 30 years
Call	The opportunity for the issuer to repay the principal before the maturity date, usually because interest rates have fallen or issuer's circumstances have changed. When calling a bond, the issuer commonly pays the principal and one year of interest payments.	Many bonds are not callable. For those that are, a common feature is that the bond can be called any time after 10 years of issuance.
Coupon rate	The interest rate used to compute the bond's interest payment each year. Listed as a percentage of par value, the actual payments usually are paid twice per year.	2 to 10 percent
Bond price	The bond's market price reported as a percentage of par value.	80 to 120 percent of par value

the
Math Coach on...
Percent-to-Decimal Conversions

❝ When discussing interest rates or using them in calculator or spreadsheet time value of money functions, the value should be in percent (%) form, like 2.5%, 7%, and 11%. When using interest rates in formulas, the value needs to be in decimal form, like 0.025, 0.07, and 0.11.

To convert between the two forms of representing an interest rate, use

$$\text{Decimal} = \frac{\text{Percent(\%)}}{100}$$ ❞

referred to as *bearer bonds* (often a feature of spy or mystery movies) because whoever held the coupon book could receive the payments. Nowadays, issuers register bond owners and automatically wire interest payments to the owner's bank or brokerage account. Nevertheless, the term *coupon* persists today.

At original issue, bonds typically sell at par value, unless interest rates are very volatile. Bondholders recoup the par value on the bond's maturity date.

However, at all times in between these two dates, bonds might trade among investors in the secondary bond market. The **bond's price** as it trades in the secondary market will not likely be the par value. Bonds trade for higher and lower prices than their par values. We'll thoroughly demonstrate the reasons for bond pricing in a later section of this chapter. Bond prices are quoted in terms of percent of par value rather than in dollar terms. Sources of trading information list a bond that traded at $1,150 as 115, and a bond that traded for $870 as 87.

Bond Issuers LG7-2

For many years, bonds were considered stodgy, overly conservative investments. Not anymore! The fixed-income industry has seen tremendous innovation in the past couple of decades. The financial industry has created and issued many new types of bonds and fixed-income securities, some with odd-sounding acronyms, like TIGRs, CATS, COUGRs, and PINEs, all of which are securities based on U.S. Treasuries. Even with all the innovation, the traditional three main bond issuers remain U.S. Treasury bonds, corporate bonds, and municipal bonds. Figure 7.1 shows the amount of money that these bond issuers have raised each year.

Treasury Bonds Treasury bonds carry the "full-faith-and-credit" backing of the U.S. government and investors have long considered them among the safest fixed-income investments in the world. The federal government sells Treasury securities through public auctions to finance the federal deficit. When the deficit is large, more bonds come to auction. In addition, the Federal Reserve System (the Fed) uses Treasury securities to implement monetary policy. Technically, Treasury securities issued with 1 to 10 years until maturity

> **bond price** Current price that the bond sells for in the bond market.

EXAMPLE 7-1

For interactive versions of this example, log in to Connect or go to mhhe.com/Cornett6e.

Bond Characteristics LG7-1

Consider a bond issued 10 years ago with an at-issue time to maturity of 30 years. The bond's coupon rate is 8 percent and it currently trades in the bond market for 109. Assuming a par value of $1,000, what are the bond's current time to maturity, semiannual interest payment, and bond price in dollars?

Time to maturity = 30 years − 10 years = 20 years
Annual payment = 0.08 × $1,000 = $80, so semiannual payment is $40
Bond price = 1.09 × 1,000 = $1,090

Similar to Problems 7-1, 7-2, Self-Test Problem 1

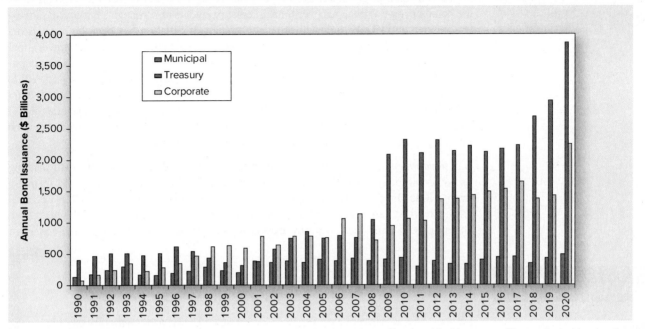

Local or municipal governments, the U.S. Treasury, and corporations have issued many new types of bonds and fixed-income securities over the past two decades.

Source: Securities Industry and Financial Markets Association.

are Treasury notes. Securities issued with 10 to 30 years until maturity are Treasury bonds. Figure 7.1 shows that the number of new Treasuries being offered actually declined in the late 1990s as the federal budget deficit declined. However, this reversed in 2002 and then dramatically accelerated in 2009 after the global financial crisis and during the years of the Fed's quantitative easing programs. The U.S. government's 2020 pandemic relief spending also required a dramatic increase in Treasury offerings to fund them.

> **Treasury Inflation-Protected Securities** TIPS are U.S. government bonds where the par value changes with inflation.

Corporate Bonds Corporations raise capital to finance investments in inventory, plant and equipment, research and development, and general business expansion. As managers decide how to raise capital, corporations can issue debt, equity (stocks), or a mixture of both. The driving force behind a corporation's financing strategy is the desire to minimize its total capital costs. Through much of the 1990s, corporations tended to issue equity (stocks) to raise capital. Beginning in 1998 and through 2020, corporations switched to raising capital by issuing bonds to take advantage of low interest rates and issued $25.3 trillion in new bonds during the period. You can see this rise in capital issuance reflected in Figure 7.1.

Municipal Bonds State and local governments borrow money to build, repair, or improve streets, highways, hospitals, schools, sewer systems, and so on. The interest and principal on these municipal bonds are repaid in two ways. Projects that benefit the entire community, such as courthouses, schools, and municipal office buildings, are typically funded by general obligation bonds and repaid using tax revenues. Projects that benefit only certain groups of people, such as toll roads and airports, are typically funded by revenue bonds and repaid from user fees. Interest payments paid to municipal bondholders are not taxed at the federal level, or by the state for which the bond is issued.

Other Bonds and Bond-Based Securities

Treasury Inflation-Protected Securities (TIPS) have proved one of the most successful recent innovations in the bond market. The U.S. Treasury began issuing this new type of Treasury bond, which is indexed to inflation, in 1997. TIPS have fixed coupon rates like traditional Treasuries. The new aspect is that the federal government adjusts the par value

agency bonds Bonds issued by U.S. government agencies.

of the TIPS bond for inflation. Specifically, it increases at the rate of inflation (measured by the consumer price index, CPI, not seasonally adjusted and lagged three months). As the bond's par value changes over time, interest payments also change. At maturity, investors receive an inflation-adjusted principal amount. If inflation has been high, investors will expect that the adjusted principal amount will be substantially higher than the original $1,000. Consider a 10-year TIPS issued on January 15, 2015, that pays a 0.25 percent coupon. The reference CPI for these bonds is 237.433. Six years later (on January 15, 2021) the reference CPI was 260.388. So the par value of the TIPS in early 2021 was $1,096.68 (=$1,000 × 260.388 ÷ 237.433). Therefore, the 0.25 percent coupon (paid semiannually) would be $1.37 = (0.0025 × $1,096.68 ÷ 2). A TIPS' total return comes from both the interest payments and the inflation adjustment to the par value.

U.S. government agency securities are debt securities issued to provide low-cost financing for desirable private-sector activities such as home ownership, education, and farming. Fannie Mae, Freddie Mac, Student Loan Marketing Association (Sallie Mae), Federal Farm Credit System, Federal Home Loan Banks, and the Small Business Administration, among others, issue these **agency bonds** to support particular sectors of the economy.

EXAMPLE 7-2

For interactive versions of this example, log in to Connect or go to mhhe.com/Cornett6e.

TIPS Payments LG7-2

Consider a TIPS bond issued on January 15, 2014, that pays a 0.625 percent coupon. The reference CPI at issue was 233.916. The reference CPI for the following interest payments was

January 2017	242.839
July 2017	244.786
January 2018	247.867

Given these numbers, what is the par value and interest payment of the TIPS on the three interest-payment dates? What is the total return from January 2017 to January 2018?

SOLUTION:

Compute the TIPS index ratio for each period as current CPI divided by the at-issue CPI. The par value for January 2017 is $1,000 × 242.839 ÷ 233.916 = $1,038.15, so the interest payment is 0.00625 × $1,038.15 ÷ 2 = $3.24. The answers for the next two dates are:

July 2017	Par value = $1,046.47	Interest Payment = $3.27
July 2018	Par value = $1,059.64	Interest Payment = $3.31

The capital gain between January 2017 and January 2018 is $1,059.64 − $1,038.15 = $21.49. Adding the two interest payments together results in $6.58(=$3.27 + $3.31). Thus, the total return is 2.70% = ($21.49 + $6.58)/$1,046.47.

The spreadsheet solution is:

	A	B	C	D	E	F	G
1	Reference CPI	233.916					
2				Par Value		Interest	
3	January-17	242.839		$ 1,038.15	=B3/$B$1*1000	$ 3.24	=0.00625*D3/2
4	July-17	244.786		$ 1,046.47	=B4/$B$1*1000	$ 3.27	=0.00625*D4/2
5	January-18	247.867		$ 1,059.64	=B5/$B$1*1000	$ 3.31	=0.00625*D5/2
6							
7	Capital Gain	$ 21.49	=D5-D3				
8	Interest Payments	$ 6.58	=F4+F5				
9	Total Return	$ 28.08	=B7+B8				
10	Pct Return	2.70%	=B9/D3				

Microsoft Excel

Similar to Problems 7-4, 7-10, 7-20

finance at work //:personal finance

Agency securities do not carry the federal government's full-faith-and-credit guarantee, but the government has never let one of its agencies fail. Because investors believe that the federal government will continue in this watchdog role, agency bonds are thought to be very safe and may provide a slightly higher return than Treasury securities do.

U.S. government agencies invented one popular type of debt security: **mortgage-backed securities** (MBSs). Fannie Mae and Freddie Mac offer subsidies or mortgage guarantees for people who wouldn't otherwise qualify for mortgages, especially first-time homeowners. Fannie Mae started out as a government-owned enterprise in 1938 and became a publicly held corporation in 1968. Freddie Mac was chartered as a publicly held corporation at its inception in 1970. Since 2008, both have been in government conservatorship and run by the Federal Housing Finance Agency. To increase the amount of money available (liquidity) for the home mortgage market, Fannie Mae and Freddie Mac purchase home mortgages from banks, credit unions, and other lenders. They combine the mortgages into diversified portfolios of such loans and then issue to investors mortgage-backed securities, which represent a share in the mortgage debt. As homeowners pay off or refinance the underlying portfolio of mortgage loans, MBS investors receive interest and principal payments. After selling mortgages to Fannie Mae or Freddie Mac, mortgage lenders have "new" cash to provide more mortgage loans. This process worked well for decades until the late 2000s, when subprime mortgages were given to people who couldn't afford them. As you know, defaults on these loans were the underpinnings of the financial crisis.

mortgage-backed securities
Securities that represent a claim against the cash flows from a pool of mortgage loans.

finance at work //:markets

asset-backed securities Debt securities whose payments originate from other loans, such as credit card debt, auto loans, and home equity loans.

convertible bond A debt security that can be converted to shares of stock or another type of security.

We could apply the same concept to any type of loan; indeed, the financial markets have already invented many such pooled-debt securities. Typical examples include credit card debt, auto loans, home equity loans, and equipment leases. Like mortgage-backed securities, investors receive interest and principal from **asset-backed securities** as borrowers pay off their consumer loans. The asset-backed securities market is one of the fastest-growing areas in the financial services sector.

On the bond's maturity date, the bondholder receives the par value, which is typically $1,000. However, some corporate bonds give the bondholder a choice between the par value and a specified number of shares of stock. This type of bond is referred to as a **convertible bond** because it can be converted to company stock. The number of shares of stock for which the bond can be converted is specified when the bond is originally issued. Thus, the bondholder will want to receive the shares when the stock price has risen since bond issuance, and they will want the $1,000 when the stock has declined in value. Although the bondholder can convert to the stock shares anytime, investors tend to wait until the maturity date when the interest payments from the bond exceed the dividends that would be paid from the stock shares.

Reading Bond Quotes LG7-3

To those familiar with bond terminology, bond quotes provide all of the information needed to make informed investment decisions. The volume of Treasury securities traded each day is substantial. Treasury bonds and notes average more than a half billion dollars in trading daily. Investors exhibit much less enthusiasm for corporate or municipal bonds, perhaps because the markets for each particular bond or bonds with the same maturity, coupon rate, and credit ratings are much thinner and, therefore, less liquid. Most bond quote tables report only a small fraction of the outstanding bonds on any given day. Bond quotes and data can be found in *The Wall Street Journal* and online at places like Yahoo! Finance (finance.yahoo.com). Table 7.2 shows three bond quote examples.

A typical listing for Treasury bonds appears first. Here, this Treasury bond pays bondholders a coupon of 1.250 percent. On a $1,000 par value bond, this interest income would be $12.50 annually, paid as $6.25 every six months per bond. The bond will mature in August of 2024—since this is fairly soon, the bond is considered a short-term bond. Both the bid and the ask quotes for the bond appear, expressed as percentages of the bond's par value of $1,000. The bid price is the price at which investors can sell the bond. A bid of 103.236 means that an investor could sell for $1,032.36. Investors can buy this bond at the ask price of 103.242, or $1,032.42. Since the price is higher than the par value of the bond, the bond is selling at a premium to par and its coupon rate is higher than current rates. Thus, investors call this kind of security a **premium bond.**

Notice that the ask price is higher than the bid price. The difference is known as the bid-ask spread. Investors buy at the higher price and sell at the lower price. The bid-ask spread is thus the cost of actively trading bonds. Investors buy and sell with a bond dealer. Since the bond dealer takes the opposite side of the transaction, the dealer buys at the low price and sells at the higher price. The bid-ask spread is part of the dealer's compensation for taking on risk. An investor who bought this bond and held it to maturity would experience a $32.42(=$1,032.42 − $1,000) capital loss (−3.14 percent[= −$32.42/$1,032.42]). The bond gained 0.0060 percent of its value during the day's trading—a change of $0.060 for a $1,000 par value bond. Last, the bond is offering investors who purchase it at the ask price and hold it to maturity a 0.221 percent annual return.

Corporate bond quotes provide similar information. The table shows the quote for a Boeing bond that offers bondholders a coupon of 2.80 percent, or $14.00 semiannually (= $1,000 × 0.028 ÷ 2). The bond would be considered a midterm bond (usually five years to maturity) since it matures in the year 2027. Corporate bonds are also quoted in percentage of par value. The price quote of 97.380 indicates that the last trade occurred at a price of $973.80 per bond. Since the bond is selling for a price lower than its $1,000 par value, it's called a **discount bond.** An investor who bought this bond would reap a

premium bond A bond selling for greater than its par value.

discount bond A bond selling for lower than its par value.

▼ **TABLE 7.2** Bond Quote Examples

Treasury Securities					
COUPON RATE	MO/YR	BID	ASKED	CHG	ASK YLD
1.250	Aug 24	103.236	103.242	0.0060	0.221

Corporate Bond				
COMPANY	COUPON	MATURITY	LAST PRICE	YIELD
Boeing Co	2.80	March 2027	97.380	3.26

Municipal Bond				
ISSUE	COUPON	MATURITY	PRICE	BID YLD
Breck Mnt Metro	3.150	12/01/45	107.995	1.70

$26.20 (= \$1,000 - \$973.80)$ capital gain if the bond were held to maturity. The Boeing bond represents an annual return of 3.26 percent for the investor who purchases the bond at \$976.80.

Companies set a bond's coupon rate when they originally issue the bond. A number of factors determine that coupon rate:

- The amount of uncertainty about whether the company will be able to make all the payments.
- The term of the loan.
- The level of interest rates in the overall economy at the time.

Bonds from different companies carry different coupon rates because some, or all, of these determining factors differ. Even a single company that has raised capital through bond issues many times may carry very different coupon rates on its various issues because the bond issues would be offered in different years when the overall economic conditions and interest rates differ.

Table 7.2 also shows a quote for a municipal bond issued by Breckenridge Mountain Metropolitan District Colorado Refunding and Improvement. This city government district

EXAMPLE 7-3

For interactive versions of this example, log in to Connect or go to mhhe.com/Cornett6e.

Bond Quotes LG7-3

You note the following bond quotes and wish to determine each bond's price, term, and interest payments.

Treasury Securities					
MATURITY RATE	MO/YR	BID	ASKED	CHG	ASK YLD
2.75	Feb 25	110.074	110.080	0.0040	0.275

Corporate Bond				
COMPANY	COUPON	MATURITY	LAST PRICE	LAST YIELD
Apple Inc	2.40	Aug 8, 2050	102.38	2.287

Municipal Bond				
ISSUE	COUPON	MATURITY	PRICE	YLD TO MAT
N Olmsted Ohio School Facilities Improvements	4.00	Dec 1, 2048	109.42	0.736

SOLUTION:

The Treasury bond matures in February of 2025 and pays 2.75 percent interest. Investors receive cash interest payment of $13.75 (= 0.0275 \times \$1,000 \div 2)$ semiannually. Since the bond matures in less than 10 years but more than 1 year, we would consider it a midterm bond. Since no "n" appears next to the maturity date, we can also tell that the security was issued as a bond that would mature in 30 years. Investors could sell this bond for $\$1,100.74 (= 1.10074 \times \$1,000)$ and buy it for $\$1,100.80$ $(= 1.10080 \times \$1,000)$. The price increases on this particular day by $\$0.40 (= 0.0040 \times \$1,000)$. The dealer earned $\$0.06 (= \$1,100.80 - \$1,100.74)$ on each trade of these premium bonds.

The Apple Inc. corporate bond pays a semiannual interest payment of $\$12.00 (= 0.0240 \times \$1,000 \div 2)$ and its price is $\$1,023.80 (= 1.0238 \times \$1,000)$. This premium bond's 2.40 percent rate is above market rates, which is why an investor would be willing to pay a premium for it.

The city of Olmsted in Ohio issued the muni bond to fund school facility improvements. With a \$5,000 par value, the interest payments are $\$100 (= 0.04 \times \$5,000 \div 2)$ every six months. The bonds are priced at $\$5,471.00 (= 1.0942 \times \$5,000)$.

Similar to Problem 7-5, Self-Test Problem 1

has raised capital by issuing municipal bonds to fund various infrastructure projects in the Breckenridge, Colorado, area. The bond pays a 3.150 percent coupon, and since it matures in 2045, it's considered a long-term bond. According to Table 7.2, the bond is trading at a price above par value—107.995 percent. Most municipal bonds, unlike other bonds, feature a $5,000 face value rather than the typical par value of $1,000. So, the 107.995 percent price quote represents a dollar amount of $5,399.75 (=1.0799.50 × $5,000). The low rate of return has an explanation. Municipal bondholders do not have to pay federal income taxes on the interest payments that they receive from those securities. We explore this (sometimes) substantial advantage further in a later section of this chapter.

7.2 • BOND VALUATION LG7-4

Present Value of Bond Cash Flows

Any bond's value computation directly applies time value of money concepts. Bondholders know the interest payments that they are scheduled to receive and the repayment of the par value at maturity. The current price of a bond is, therefore, the *present value of these future cash flows discounted at the prevailing market interest rate.* The prevailing market interest rate will depend on the bond's term to maturity, credit quality, and tax status.

The simplest type of bond for time value of money calculations is a **zero coupon bond.** As you might guess from its name, a zero coupon bond makes no interest payments. Instead, the bond pays only the par value payment at its maturity date. So a zero-coupon bond sells at a substantial discount from its par value. For example, a bond with a par value of $1,000, maturing in 20 years, and priced to yield 6 percent might be purchased for about $306.56. At the end of 20 years, the bond investor will receive $1,000. The difference between $1,000 and $306.56 (which is $693.44) represents the interest income received over the 20 years based upon the discount rate of 6 percent. The time line for this zero-coupon bond valuation appears as

Period	0	5	6%	10	15	20 years
Cash flow	PV = ?					1,000

We compute the zero's price by finding the present value of the $1,000 cash flow received in 20 years. However, to be consistent with regular coupon-paying bonds, zero coupon bonds are priced using semiannual compounding. So the formula and calculator valuation would use 40 semiannual periods at a 3 percent interest rate rather than 20 periods at 6 percent. Using the present value equation of Chapter 4 results in

$$PV = \frac{FV_N}{(1 + i)^N} = \frac{\$1,000}{1.03^{40}} = \frac{\$1,000}{3.262} = \$306.56$$

So the zero-coupon bond's price is indeed a steep discount to its par value. This makes sense because investors would only buy a security that pays $1,000 in many years for a price that is much lower to make enough profit to make up for the forgone semiannual interest payments. For comparison's sake, instead of the 20-year zero, consider a 20-year bond with a 7 percent coupon. So this 20-year maturity bond pays $35 in interest payments every six months. We can think of these interest payments as an annuity stream. If the market discount rate is 6 percent annually, the time line appears as

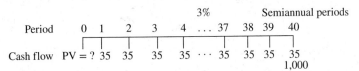

The time line shows the 40 semiannual payments (with the accompanying semiannual interest rate at 3 percent) of $35 and the par value payment at the bond's maturity.

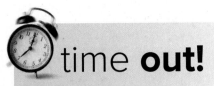

time out!

7-1 Describe the different reasons that the U.S. government, local governments, and corporations would issue bonds.

7-2 What is the following bond's price and what dollar amount will the bond pay for its semi-annual interest payment?

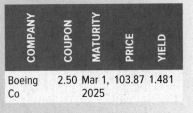

COMPANY	COUPON	MATURITY	PRICE	YIELD
Boeing Co	2.50	Mar 1, 2025	103.87	1.481

zero coupon bond A bond that does not make interest payments but generally sells at a deep discount and then pays the par value at the maturity date.

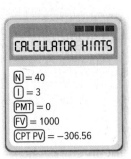

CALCULATOR HINTS

N = 40
I = 3
PMT = 0
FV = 1000
CPT PV = −306.56

Think through this: When bonds pay semiannual payments, the discount rate must be a semiannual rate. Thus, the 6 percent annual rate becomes a 3 percent semiannual rate. So we then compute the price of this bond by adding the present value of the interest payment annuity cash flow to the present value of the future par value. A combination of the present value equations for the annuity cash flows and the value of the par redemption appear in the bond valuation equation 7-1:

$$\underset{\text{bond}}{\text{Present value of}} = \underset{\text{interest payments}}{\text{Present value of}} + \underset{\text{of par value}}{\text{Present value}}$$

$$= PMT \times \left[\frac{1 - \frac{1}{(1 + i)^N}}{i} \right] + \frac{\$1{,}000}{(1 + i)^N} \tag{7-1}$$

where PMT is the interest payment, N is the number of periods until maturity, and i is the market interest rate per period on securities with the same bond characteristics. If this bond paid interest annually, then these variables would take yearly period values. Since this bond pays semiannually, PMT, N, and i are all denoted in semiannual periods. The price of this coupon bond should be

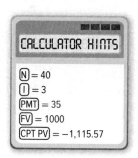

CALCULATOR HINTS

$N = 40$
$I = 3$
$PMT = 35$
$FV = 1000$
$CPT\ PV = -1{,}115.57$

$$\text{Bond price} = \$35 \times \left[\frac{1 - \frac{1}{(1 + 0.03)^{40}}}{0.03} \right] + \frac{\$1{,}000}{(1 + 0.03)^{40}}$$

$$= \$809.017 + \$306.557 = \$1{,}115.57$$

Of the $1,115.57 bond price, most of the value comes from the semiannual $35 coupon payments ($809.017) and not the value from the future par value payment ($306.557).

EXAMPLE 7-4

LG7-4

For interactive versions of this example, log in to Connect or go to mhhe.com/Cornett6e.

Consider a 15-year bond that has a 5.5 percent coupon, paid semiannually. If the current market interest rate is 6.5 percent, and the bond is priced at $940, should you buy this bond?

SOLUTION:

Compute the value of the bond using equation 7-1. Use semiannual compounding ($N = 2 \times 15 = 30$, $i = 6.5 \div 2 = 3.25$, and $PMT = 0.055 \times \$1{,}000 \div 2 = \$27.50$) as

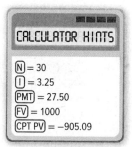

CALCULATOR HINTS

$N = 30$
$I = 3.25$
$PMT = 27.50$
$FV = 1000$
$CPT\ PV = -905.09$

$$\text{Bond value} = \$27.50 \times \left[\frac{1 - \frac{1}{1 + (0.0325)^{30}}}{0.0325} \right] + \frac{\$1{,}000}{(1 + 0.0325)^{30}} = \$522.00 + \$383.09 = \$905.09$$

So this bond's value is $905.09, which is less than the $940 price. The bond is overvalued in the market and you should not buy it.

The spreadsheet solution uses the PV function:

	A	B	C	D
1	**I**	**N**	**PMT**	**FV**
2	6.50%	15	55	1000
3				
4	Value =	$905.09	< $940	
5		=PV(A2/2,B2*2,-C2/2,-D2)		

Microsoft Excel

Similar to Problems 7-11, 7-12, Self-Test Problem 1

the
Math Coach on...
Bond Pricing and Periods

Because equation 7-1 is quite complex, we usually compute bond prices using a financial calculator or computer program. An investor would compute the bond value using a financial calculator by entering N = 40, I = 3, PMT = 35, FV = 1000, and computing the present value (PV). The calculator solution is $1,115.57.[1]

> **interest rate risk** The chance of a capital loss due to interest rate fluctuations.

To compute a bond price using a spreadsheet, use the present value function detailed in Chapter 5, PV(.03,40,−35,−1000) = $1,115.57.

Bond Prices and Interest Rate Risk LG7-5

At the time of purchase, the bond's interest payments and par value expected at maturity are fixed and known. Over time, economywide interest rates change, but the bond's coupon rate remains fixed. A rise in prevailing interest rates (also called *increasing the discount rate*) reduces all bonds' values. If interest rates fall, all bonds will enjoy rising values. Consider that when interest rates rise, newly issued bonds offer to pay higher interest rates than the rates offered on existing bonds. So to sell an existing bond with its lower coupon rate, its market price must fall so that the buyer can expect a profit similar to that offered by newly issued bonds. Similarly, when prevailing interest rates fall, market prices for outstanding bonds rise to bring the offered return on older bonds with higher coupon rates into line with new issues. So market interest rates and bond prices are *inversely* related. That is, they move in opposite directions.

Figure 7.2 demonstrates how the price of a 30-year Treasury bond may change over time. The 8.19 percent coupon exactly matched prevailing interest rates when the bond was issued in February of 1991. Consequently, the bond sells for its par value of $1,000. For the next two and a half years, interest rates declined to just under 6 percent. As interest rates declined, bond prices rose. Then interest rates reversed direction and rose back to nearly 8 percent. Thus, bond prices declined. For the next 25 years, interest progressed on a prolonged descent to lows not seen for decades. Note that while a bond is issued at $1,000 and returns $1,000 at maturity, its price can vary a great deal in between. Bond investors must be aware that bond prices fluctuate on a day-to-day basis as interest rates fluctuate. Note that since the bond will only pay $1,000 when it matures, the price must converge to $1,000 at the end. The determinants of market interest rate levels and changes are discussed in Chapter 6. Bondholders can incur large capital gains or capital losses.

The fact that, as prevailing interest rates change, the prices of existing bonds will change has a specific name in the financial industry—interest rate risk. **Interest rate risk** means that during periods when interest rates change substantially (and quickly), bondholders experience distinct gains and losses in their bond inventories. But interest rate risk does not affect all bonds exactly the same. Very short-term bonds experience little or no fluctuation

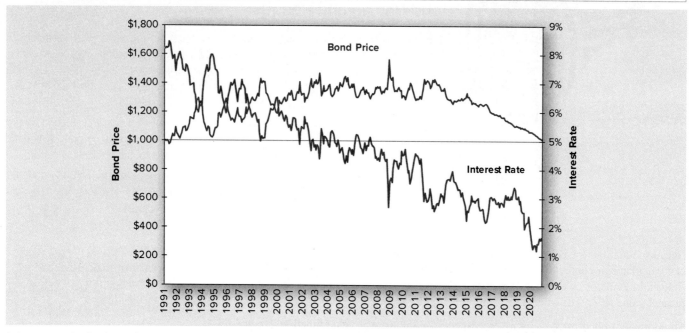

As interest rates rise, bond prices fall. Here you can see great variance in the economy over 30 years. Long-term bondholders experience substantial interest rate risk.

Source: Yahoo! Finance, finance.yahoo.com.

in their prices, and thus expose the bondholder to little interest rate risk. Long-term bondholders experience substantial interest rate risk. Table 7.3 illustrates the impact of interest rate risk on bonds with different coupons and times to maturity.

The first four rows show the prices and price changes for 30-year bonds with different coupon rates. Notice that the bonds with higher coupon rates also have higher prices. Bondholders as a rule find it more valuable to receive the large annuity payments. Also notice that a

▼ **TABLE 7.3** Interest Rate Risk

	A	B	C	D	E
1	**Time to Maturity**	**Coupon**	**Price at 6%**	**Price at 7%**	**Change**
2					
3			**THE IMPACT OF THE COUPON RATE ON PRICE**		
4	30 years	0%	$ 169.73	$ 126.93	−25.2%
5	30 years	5	861.62	750.55	−12.9
6	30 years	7	1,138.38	1,000.00	−12.2
7	30 years	10	1,553.51	1,374.32	−11.5
8					
9			**THE IMPACT OF TIME TO MATURITY ON PRICE**		
10	20 years	5	884.43	786.45	−11.1
11	10 years	5	925.61	857.88	−7.3
12	5 years	5	957.35	916.83	−4.2
13	2 years	5	981.41	963.27	−1.8
14					
15	=PV(0.06/2,2*5,−B12*10/2,−1000)			=(D12−C12)/C12	

Microsoft Excel

1 percent increase in interest rates from 6 percent to 7 percent causes bond prices to fall. Bondholders with higher coupon bonds are not affected as much by interest rate increases because they can take the large coupon payments and reinvest those cash flows in new bonds that offer higher returns.

The price decline is greater for bonds with lower coupons because of **reinvestment rate risk.** When interest rates increase, bondholders' cash flows—both periodic payments and final payoff at maturity—are discounted at a higher rate, decreasing a bond's value. Because the cash flows from low-coupon bonds are smaller, the holder of such bonds will have less money available from interest payments to buy the new, higher coupon bonds. Thus, bondholders of lower coupon bonds have their capital tied up in assets that are not making them as much money. They face a bad dilemma: They can sell their lower coupon bonds and take a greater capital loss, using the (smaller) proceeds to buy new bonds with higher coupon rates. Or they can continue to receive the small income payments and hold

> **reinvestment rate risk**
> The chance that future interest payments will have to be reinvested at a lower interest rate.

EXAMPLE 7-5

Capital Gains in the Bond Market LG7-5

For interactive versions of this example, log in to Connect or go to mhhe.com/Cornett6e.

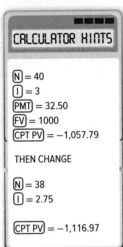

CALCULATOR HINTS

$N = 40$
$I = 3$
$PMT = 32.50$
$FV = 1000$
$CPT\ PV = -1,057.79$

THEN CHANGE

$N = 38$
$I = 2.75$

$CPT\ PV = -1,116.97$

Say that you anticipate falling long-term interest rates from 6 percent to 5.5 percent during the next year. If this occurs, what will be the total return for a 20-year, 6.5 percent coupon bond through the interest rate decline?

SOLUTION:

To determine the total return, compute the capital gain or loss and the interest paid over the year. The capital gain or loss is determined from the change in price. The current bond price is

$$\text{Bond price} = \$32.50 \times \left[\frac{1 - \frac{1}{(1 + 0.03)^{40}}}{0.03} \right] + \frac{\$1,000}{(1 + 0.03)^{40}} = \$751.230 + \$306.557 = \$1,057.79$$

The price in one year would be

$$\text{Bond price} = \$32.50 \times \left[\frac{1 - \frac{1}{(1 + 0.0275)^{38}}}{0.0275} \right] + \frac{\$1,000}{(1 + 0.0275)^{38}} = \$760.276 + \$356.690 = \$1,116.97$$

So, the capital gain is $59.18 (= $1,116.97 − $1,057.79). The interest payment during the year is $65 (= 0.065 × $1,000). If interest rates fall to 5.5 percent, then this bond should provide a total return of $124.18, which would be an 11.74 percent return (= $124.18 ÷ $1,057.79). Of course, this is only an anticipated interest rate change and it may not occur.

The spreadsheet solution is:

	A	B	C	D
1	I	N	PMT	FV
2	6.00%	20	65	1000
3	5.50%	19	65	1000
4				
5	Pre-Value =	$1,057.79		
6		=PV(A2/2,B2*2,-C2/2,-D2)		
7	Post-Value =	$1,116.97		
8		=PV(A3/2,B3*2,-C3/2,-D3)		
9				
10	Capital gain =	$59.18	=B7-B5	
11	Interest paid =	$65.00	=C2	
12	Total return =	$124.18	=B10+B11	
13	Percent return =	11.74%	=B12/B5	

Microsoft Excel

Similar to Problems 7-13, 7-17, 7-21, Self-Test Problem 5

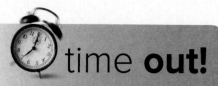

7-3 Show the time line and compute the present value for an 8.5 percent coupon bond (paid semiannually) with 12 years left to maturity and a market interest rate of 7.5 percent.

7-4 Describe the relationship between interest rate changes and bond prices.

current yield Return from interest payments; computed as the annual interest payment divided by the current bond price.

yield to maturity The total return the bond offers if purchased at the current price and held to maturity.

their lower coupon bonds to maturity to avoid locking in the capital loss. Either way, they lose money relative to those bondholders with higher coupon rates. You can see this illustrated in the 30-year bonds shown in Table 7.3. Reinvestment rates tend to help partially offset changing discount rates for higher-coupon-paying bonds.

Another factor that influences the amount of reinvestment risk bondholders face is their bonds' time to maturity. The last four bonds in the table all have a 5 percent coupon but have different times to maturity. Note that when interest rates increase, the bond prices of longer-term bonds decline more than those of shorter-term bonds. Thus, the 100-year bond Disney issued in 1993, referred to as the Sleeping Beauty bond, would have interest rate risk due to its long time to maturity. This shows that bonds with longer maturities and lower coupons have the highest interest rate risk. Short-term bonds with high coupons have the lowest interest rate risk. High interest rate risk bonds experience considerable price declines when interest rates are rising. However, these bonds also experience dramatic capital gains when interest rates are falling. While a 1 percent change in market interest rates is not commonly seen on a daily or monthly basis, such a change is not unusual over the course of several months or a year.

7.3 • BOND YIELDS LG7-6

Current Yield

Although we speak about "the prevailing interest rate," bond relationships reflect many interest rates (also called *yields*). Some rates are difficult to calculate but accurately reflect the return the bond is offering. Others, like the **current yield,** are easy to compute but only approximate the bond's true return. A bond's current yield is defined as the bond's annual coupon rate divided by the bond's current market price. Current yield measures the rate of return a bondholder would earn annually from the coupon interest payments alone if the bond were purchased at a stated price. Current yield does not measure the total expected return because it does not account for any capital gains or losses that will occur from purchasing the bond at a discount or premium to par.

Yield to Maturity

Yield to maturity is a more meaningful equation for investors than the simple current yield calculation. The yield to maturity calculation tells bond investors the total rate of return that they might expect if the bond were bought at a particular price and held to maturity. While the yield to maturity calculation provides more information than the current yield calculation, it's also more difficult to compute because we must compute the bond's cash flows' internal rate of return. This calculation seeks to equate the bond's current market price with the value of all anticipated future interest and par value payments. In other words, it is the discount rate that equates the present value of all future cash flows with the current price of the bond. To calculate yield to maturity, investors must solve for the interest rate, i, in equation 7-2, or solve for i in

$$\text{Bond price} = PV \text{ of annuity } (PMT, i, N) + PV(FV, i, N) \qquad (7\text{-}2)$$

Investors commonly compute the yield to maturity using financial calculators. For example, consider a 7 percent coupon bond (paid semiannually) with eight years to maturity and a current price of $1,150. The return that the bond offers investors, the yield to maturity, is computed as $N = 16$, $PV = -1150$, $PMT = 35$, and $FV = 1000$. Computing the interest rate (i) gives us 2.363 percent. We must remember, however, that 2.363 percent is only the return for six months because the bond pays semiannually. Yield to maturity always means an annual return. So, this bond's yield to maturity is 4.73 percent (2×2.363 percent).

To solve for the yield to maturity using a spreadsheet, use the RATE function from Chapter 5, which is RATE(nper,pmt,pv,[fv],[type],[guess]). For this example, the function would

the
Math Coach on...
Bond Yields and Financial Calculators

❝ People computing a bond's yield to maturity make three common mistakes. To avoid the first mistake, ensure that the bond price (PV) is a different sign than the interest and par value cash flows (PMT and FV). The second mistake: People forget to make the number of periods (N) and the per-period interest payment (PMT) consistent. Both should be in semiannual terms if the coupon payment is paid semiannually. Last, many people forget to multiply the resulting calculator interest rate (I) output by 2 to convert the semiannual rate back to an annual rate. ❞

produce RATE(16,35,−1150,1000) = 2.363 percent. Again, the bond's yield to maturity is double this value, or 4.726 percent.

Notice the link between a bond's yield to maturity and the prevailing market interest rates used to determine a bond's price, as we discussed in the previous section. We use the market interest rate to compute the bond's value. We use the actual bond price to compute its yield to maturity. If the bond is correctly priced at its economic value, then the market interest rate will equal the yield to maturity. Thus, the relationship that we previously identified between bond prices and market interest rates applies to yields as well. This shows the inverse relationship between bond prices and bond yields. As a bond's price falls, its

EXAMPLE 7-6

For interactive versions of this example, log in to Connect or go to mhhe.com/Cornett6e.

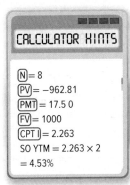

CALCULATOR HINTS

$\boxed{N} = 8$
$\boxed{PV} = -962.81$
$\boxed{PMT} = 17.50$
$\boxed{FV} = 1000$
$\boxed{CPT\ I} = 2.263$
SO YTM = 2.263 × 2
= 4.53%

Computing Current Yield and Yield to Maturity LG7-6

You have identified a 3.5 percent Treasury bond with four years left to maturity and a quoted price of 96.281. Calculate the bond's current yield and yield to maturity.

SOLUTION:

(1) First, identify that the bond's price is $962.81 (= 96.281% × $1,000 = 0.96281 × $1,000).
(2) The annual $35 in interest payments is paid in two $17.50 semiannual payments. Therefore, the current yield of the bond is 3.64 percent (= $35 ÷ $962.81).
(3) The yield to maturity is computed using equation 7-2 and the financial calculator as N = 8, PV = −962.81, PMT = 17.50, and FV = 1,000. Computing the interest rate (I) results in 2.263 percent, and multiplying by 2 gives the yield to maturity of 4.53 percent.
(4) Note that the current yield is less than the yield to maturity because it does not account for the capital gain to be earned if held to maturity.

The spreadsheet solution is:

	A	B	C	D	E	F
1	Quoted Price	Coupon Rate	Maturity			
2	96.281	3.5000	4			
3						
4		Price	Payment			
5	Treasury	$ 962.81	$ 17.50			
6						
7	Current Yield	3.64%	=B2/100*1000/B5			
8	Yield to Maturity	4.53%	=RATE(C2*2,B2/100*1000/2,-B5,1000)*2			

Microsoft Excel

Similar to Problems 7-7, 7-14, 7-18, Self-Test Problem 2

yield to maturity increases, and a rising bond price accompanies a falling yield. Look back at Figure 7.2 and you will see this relationship clearly.

Yield to Call

The yield to maturity computation assumes that the bondholder will hold the bond to its maturity. But remember that some bonds have call provisions that allow the issuers to repay the bondholder's par value prior to its scheduled maturity. Issuers often call bonds after large drops in market interest rates. In such cases, issuers commonly pay bondholders the bond's par value plus one year of interest payments. The reasons behind early bond redemptions are obvious. When interest rates fall, issuers can sell new bonds at lower interest rates. Companies want to refinance their debt—just as homeowners do—to reduce their interest payments.

Issuers gain important advantages with call provisions because they allow refinancing opportunities. Of course, the same provisions are disadvantages for bond investors. When bonds are called, investors receive the par value and call premium, but then investors must seek equally profitable bonds to buy with the proceeds. You will recall that investors can face reinvestment risk—the available bonds aren't as profitable because interest rates have declined. Bonds are called away at the worst time for investors. In addition, bond prices will rise as market interest rates fall, which could provide issuers opportunities to sell the bonds at a profit. But the price increases will be limited by the fact that the bond will likely be called early. As partial compensation, bond investors receive the call price, which is the par value of the bond plus the call premium (typically one year of interest payments). The possibility that bonds can be called early dampens their upside price potential. We can even compute the price of a bond that's likely to be called from the equation

$$\frac{\text{Price of a}}{\text{callable bond}} = \frac{\text{Present value of interest}}{\text{payments to call date}} + \frac{\text{Present value}}{\text{of call price}}$$

$$= PMT \times \left[\frac{1 - \frac{1}{(1+i)^N}}{i} \right] + \frac{\text{Call price}}{(1+i)^N} \qquad (7\text{-}3)$$

In this case, N is the number of periods until the bond can be called and i is the prevailing market rate. The prevailing market interest rate will probably differ from the rate for a noncallable bond. The previous section demonstrated via the yield curve that bonds with different maturities have different yields. A bond that matures in 20 years, but is likely to be called in five years, will carry a yield appropriate for a five-year bond.

Now, reconsider the 20-year bond with a 7 percent coupon that we discussed previously. If the bond can be called in five years with a call price of $1,070, the appropriate discount rate happens to be 5.75 percent annually at that time (instead of the 6 percent in the original problem). This time line would be

							2.875%			Semiannual periods
Period	0	1	2	3	4	... 7	8	9	10	
Cash flow	PV=?	35	35	35	35	··· 35	35	35	35 1,070	

The changes in this time line are only 10 semiannual payments of $35 (rather than 40 such semiannual payments), a 2.875 percent semiannual discount rate, and the call price payment of $1,070. The price of this callable bond would be

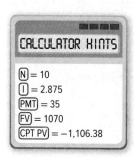

CALCULATOR HINTS

$\boxed{N} = 10$
$\boxed{I} = 2.875$
$\boxed{PMT} = 35$
$\boxed{FV} = 1070$
$\boxed{\text{CPT PV}} = -1,106.38$

$$\text{Bond price} = \$35 \times \left[\frac{1 - \frac{1}{(1+0.02875)^{10}}}{0.02875} \right] + \frac{\$1,070}{(1+0.02875)^{10}}$$

$$= \$300.47 + \$805.91 = \$1,106.38$$

In this example, the callable bond would be priced at $1,106.38, which is slightly lower than an identical bond that was not callable, priced at $1,115.57.

If a bond is likely to be called, then the yield to maturity calculation does not give investors a good estimate of their return. Bondholders can use instead a **yield to call** calculation, which differs from the yield to maturity only in that its calculation assumes that the investor will receive the par value and call premium at the earliest call date. For example, reconsider the 7 percent coupon bond (paid semiannually) with eight years to maturity, which we examined previously. The current bond price is $1,130 (which is slightly lower than the yield to maturity bond price of $1,150). If the bond can be called in three years at a specific call price of the par value plus one annual coupon, then what is the yield to call? The yield to call is computed as $N = 6$, $PV = -1130$, $PMT = 35$, and $FV = 1070$. The resulting interest rate (i) is 2.26 percent. The yield to call for this bond is thus 4.52 percent ($= 2 \times 2.26\%$).

Municipal Bonds and Yield

Municipal bonds (munis) seem to offer low yields to maturity compared to the return that corporate bonds and Treasury securities offer. Munis offer lower rates because the interest income they generate for investors is tax-exempt—at least at the federal level.[2] Specifically, income from municipal bonds is not subject to taxation by the federal government or the state government where the bonds are issued. As a result, municipal bond investors willingly accept lower yields than those they can obtain from taxable bonds. Generally speaking, investors compare the after-tax interest income earned on taxable bonds against the return earned on municipal bonds. For example, suppose an investor in the 35 percent *marginal* income tax bracket has $100,000 to invest in either corporate or municipal bonds. The $100,000 investment would earn a taxable $7,000 annually from 7 percent corporate bonds or $5,000 from tax-exempt 5 percent municipal bonds. After taxes, the corporate bond leaves the investor with $4,550 [$= (1 - 0.35) \times \$7,000$]. Obviously, this is less than the tax-free income of $5,000 generated by the muni bond.

A common way to compare yields from muni bonds versus those from taxable bonds is to convert the yield to maturity of the muni to a **taxable equivalent yield,** as shown in equation 7-4.

$$\text{Equivalent taxable yield} = \frac{\text{Muni yield}}{1 - \text{Tax rate}} \qquad (7\text{-}4)$$

For high-income investors (in the 35 percent marginal tax bracket), a 5 percent muni bond has an equivalent taxable yield of 7.69 percent [$= 0.05 \div (1 - 0.35)$]. The 5 percent muni is more attractive for this investor than a 7 percent corporate bond. However, for an investor with lower income (in the 24 percent marginal tax bracket), the equivalent taxable yield is only 6.58 percent. The corporate bond provides more after-tax profit than the muni for this investor. It's easy to see why muni bonds are popular among high-income investors (those with substantial marginal tax rates).

Summarizing Yields

In this section, we have presented several different types of interest rates, or yields, associated with bonds. See a summary in Table 7.4. Many of these yields relate to one another. Consider the bonds and associated yields reported in Table 7.5. Treasury bonds (1) to (3) show how coupon rates, current yield, and yield to maturity relate. When a bond trades at its par value (usually $1,000), then the coupon rate, current yield, and yield to maturity are all the same. When that bond is priced at a premium (bond 2), then both the current yield and the yield to maturity will be lower than the coupon rate. They are both higher than the coupon rate when the bond trades at a discount. Notice that yield to maturity is higher than current yield for discount bonds, and that yield to maturity is lower than current yield for premium bonds. In other words, the current yield always lies between the coupon rate and the yield to maturity. Both the current yield and the yield to maturity move in the opposite direction to the bond's price.

yield to call The total return that the bond offers if purchased at the current price and held until the bond is called.

taxable equivalent yield Modification of a municipal bond's yield to maturity used to compare muni bond yields to taxable bond yields.

EXAMPLE 7-7

For interactive versions of this example, log in to Connect or go to mhhe.com/Cornett6e.

Which Bond Has a Better After-Tax Yield? LG7-6

Imagine a time when you have a high income, placing you in the 32 percent marginal tax bracket. You are interested in investing some money in a bond issue and have three alternatives. The first is a corporate bond with a 6.4 percent yield to maturity. The second bond is a Treasury that offers a 5.7 percent yield. The third choice is a municipal bond priced at a yield to maturity of 4.0 percent. Which bond gives you the highest after-tax yield?

SOLUTION:

The Treasury and corporate bonds are both taxable, so we can compare them directly with each other. The yield of 6.4 percent on the corporate is clearly higher than the 5.7 percent yield offered by the Treasury bond. To include a comparison with the nontaxable municipal bond, compute its equivalent taxable yield as in equation 7-4:

$$\text{Equivalent taxable yield} = \frac{4.0\%}{1 - 0.32} = 5.88\%$$

The municipal bond's equivalent taxable yield of 5.88 percent is higher than the Treasury's yield but lower than that of the corporate bond.

Similar to Problems 7-8, 7-16, 7-22, Self-Test Problem 3

▼ **TABLE 7.4** Summary of Interest Rates

Interest Rate	Purpose	Description
Coupon rate	Compute bond cash interest payments	The coupon rate is reported as a bond characteristic. It is reported as a percentage and is multiplied by the par value of the bond to determine the annual cash interest payment. The coupon rate will not change through the life of the bond.
Current yield	Quick assessment of the interest rate a bond is offering	Computed as the annual interest payment divided by the current price of the bond. It measures the return to be expected from just the interest payments if the bond was purchased at the current price. Because the bond price may change daily, the current yield will change daily.
Yield to maturity	Accurate measurement of the interest rate a bond is offering	The return offered by the bond if purchased at the current price. This return includes both the expected income and capital gain/loss if held to the maturity date. The yield to maturity will change daily as the bond price changes.
Yield to call	Interest rate obtained if the bond is called	Same as the yield to maturity except that it is assumed that the bond will be called at the earliest date it can be called.
Taxable equivalent yield	Comparison of nontaxable bond yields to taxable bond yields	Investors must pay taxes on most types of bonds. However, municipal bonds are tax free. To compare the muni's nontaxable yield to maturity to that of taxable bonds, divide the yield by one minus the investor's marginal tax rate.
Market interest rate	Comparison of prices of all bonds	The interest rate determined by the bond prices of actual trades between buyers and sellers. The market interest rate will be different for bonds of different times to maturity and different levels of risk.
Total return	Determine realized performance of an investment	Realized return that includes both income and capital gain/loss profits.

Bonds (4) to (6) are callable corporate bonds. Recall that all the yields (current yield, yield to maturity, and yield to call) are identical when the bond trades at par value. When interest rates fall and bond prices increase, as with bond (5), the issuing corporation has a strong incentive to call the bond after five years, as allowed in the indenture agreement. So investors should base their purchase decisions on the yield to call. When interest rates

	A	B	C	D	E	F	G
1		Price	Coupon Rate	Current Yield	Yield to Maturity	Yield to Call (in 5 Years)	Taxable Equivalent Yield (35% Tax Rate)
2	(1) Treasury	$1,000	5.00%	5.00%	5.00%		5.00%
3	(2) Treasury	1,100	5.00	4.55	3.79		3.79
4	(3) Treasury	900	5.00	5.56	6.37		6.37
5	(4) Corporate	1,000	6.00	6.00	6.00	6%	6.00
6	(5) Corporate	1,100	6.00	5.41	4.61	4.59	4.61
7	(6) Corporate	900	6.00	6.67	7.44	9.52	7.44
8	(7) Muni	1,000	4.00	4.00	4.00		6.15
9	(8) Muni	1,100	4.00	3.64	2.84		4.37
10	(9) Muni	900	4.00	4.44	5.30		8.15
11							
12		=C3*10/B3		=2*RATE(10,C7*10/2,−B7,1000+C7*10)			=E10/(1−0.35)
13					=2*RATE(10,C7*10/2,−B7,1000+C7*10)		
14							

Call price = Par value + One year's interest

Microsoft Excel

increase, bond prices decline (as bond (6) shows). In this case, investors could compute the yield to call (as shown), but the information isn't useful because the company will not likely call the bond while interest rates are high.

The last three bonds shown in the table are municipal bonds. Recall that these bonds typically offer lower yields because the income from munis is tax exempt. It is easier to compare municipal bonds with Treasuries and corporate bonds if you compute the municipal bond's taxable equivalent yield first. Here, we use a marginal tax rate of 35 percent in the calculation. The last column of the table shows that the taxable equivalent yield of the municipal bonds is really quite competitive with corporate bond yields. Any investor with income taxed at the 35 percent marginal tax bracket would prefer the municipal bond over the corporate bond if the muni's taxable equivalent yield is higher than the yield to maturity (or yield to call) of the corporate bond.

The table also shows that Treasury securities offer lower yields than corporate bonds with similar terms to maturity. The difference (or spread) between Treasury and corporate yields gives rise to a discussion of bond credit risk, which follows.

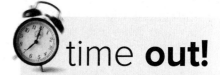

time out!

7-5 Calculate the yield to maturity for a zero-coupon bond with a price of $525 and 10 years left to maturity.

7-6 Which is higher for a discount bond, the yield to maturity or the coupon rate? Why?

7.4 • CREDIT RISK LG7-7

Bond Ratings

Will a bond issuer make the promised interest and par value payments over the next 10, 20, or even 30 years? **Credit quality risk** is the chance that the bond issuer will not be able to make timely payments. To assess this risk, independent **bond rating** agencies, such as Moody's and Standard & Poor's, monitor corporate, U.S. agency, or municipal developments during the bond's lifetime and report their findings as a grade or rating. The U.S. government issues the highest credit quality debt, though that consensus has recently come into doubt as the U.S. debt and budget deficit have ballooned.

The primary "big three" bond credit rating agencies in the United States include Moody's Investors Service, Standard & Poor's Corporation, and Fitch IBCA Inc. Each of these

credit quality risk The chance that the issuer will not make timely interest payments or may even default.

bond rating A grade of credit quality as reported by credit rating agencies.

▼ **TABLE 7.6** Standard & Poor's Bond Credit Ratings

Credit Risk	Credit Rating	Description
Investment Grade		
Highest quality	AAA	The obligor's (issuer's) capacity to meet its financial commitment on the obligation is extremely strong.
High quality	AA	The obligor's capacity to meet its financial commitment on the obligation is very strong.
Upper medium grade	A	The obligor's capacity to meet its financial commitment on the obligation is still strong, though somewhat susceptible to the adverse effects of changes in circumstances and economic conditions.
Medium grade	BBB	The obligor exhibits adequate protection. However, adverse economic conditions or changing circumstances are more likely to lead to a weakened capacity to meet its financial commitment.
Below Investment Grade		
Somewhat speculative	BB	Faces major ongoing uncertainties or exposure to adverse business, financial, or economic conditions that could lead to the obligor's inadequate capacity to meet its financial commitment.
Speculative	B	Adverse business, financial, or economic conditions will likely impair the obligor's capacity or willingness to meet its financial commitment.
Highly speculative	CCC	Currently vulnerable to nonpayment, and is dependent upon favorable business, financial, and economic conditions for the obligor to meet its financial commitment.
Most speculative	CC	Currently highly vulnerable to nonpayment.
Imminent default	C	Bankruptcy petition has been filed or similar action taken, but payments on this obligation are being continued.
Default	D	Obligations are in default or the filing of a bankruptcy petition has occurred and payments are jeopardized.

Source: Standard & Poor's web page.

investment grade High credit quality corporate bonds.

junk bonds Low credit quality corporate bonds, also called speculative bonds or high-yield bonds.

unsecured corporate bonds Corporate debt not secured by collateral such as land, buildings, or equipment.

debentures Unsecured bonds.

credit analysis firms assigns similar ratings based on detailed analyses of issuers' financial condition, general economic and credit market conditions, and the economic value of any underlying collateral. The Standard & Poor's ratings are shown in Table 7.6. Their highest credit quality rating is AAA. Bonds rated AAA, AA, A, or BBB are considered **investment grade** bonds. The issuers of these securities have the highest chance of making all interest and par value payments promised in the indenture agreement.

The investment community considers bonds rated BB and below to be below-investment-grade bonds, and some investors, such as pension funds or other fiduciaries, cannot purchase these securities for their portfolios. These bonds are considered to be speculative because they carry a significant risk that the issuer will not make current or future payments. Speculative bonds are sometimes called **junk bonds** because of this risk. In order to attract buyers, issuers sell these bonds at a considerable discount from par and a high associated yield to maturity. Agencies often enhance ratings from "AA" to "CCC" with the addition of a plus (+) or minus (−) sign to show relative standing within the major rating categories. The pandemic in 2020 caused many companies to be less financially secure, which led them to see their bonds downgraded. For example, Boeing saw its bonds downgraded from BBB to BBB− by Standard & Poor's. Other well-known companies were downgraded as well, like Marriott, Carnival, Ford Motor, Delta, ExxonMobil, and more. However, the same day, Standard and Poor's downgraded Pier 1 Imports Inc. to B−. On the other hand, Tesla debt was upgraded by Moody's to B2 from B3. These rating changes impact not only the current prices of these bonds, but also the interest rate these companies would have to pay if they issued new bonds.

Rating agencies signal when they are considering a rating change by changing the outlook of a bond issue, or all of a given issuer's bonds, between negative, stable, and positive. For example, a month before Boeing debt was downgraded, rating agency Fitch placed Boeing bonds on its Ratings Watch Negative list. Rating agencies make their ratings information available to the public through their ratings information desks. In addition to published reports, ratings are made available in many public libraries and over the Internet.

Credit rating agencies conduct general economic analyses of companies' business and analyze firms' specific financial situations. A single company may carry several outstanding bond issues. If these issues feature fundamental differences, then they may have different credit level risks. For example, **unsecured corporate bonds,** or **debentures,** are backed only by the reputation and financial stability of the corporation. A **senior bond** has a priority claim over junior (more recently issued) securities in the event of default or bankruptcy. So, senior bonds carry less credit risk than junior bonds. Some bonds are secured with collateral. When you buy a car using a loan, the car is collateral for that loan. If you don't make the loan payments, the bank will repossess the car. Companies can also offer collateral when issuing bonds. When a firm uses collateral such as real estate or factory equipment, the bonds are called **mortgage bonds** or **equipment trust certificates,** respectively. Bonds issued with no collateral generally carry higher credit risk.

Credit Risk and Yield

Investors will only purchase higher risk bonds if those securities offer higher returns. Therefore, issuers price bonds with high credit risk to offer high yields to maturity. So another common name for junk bonds is **high-yield bonds.** Differences in credit risk are a prime source of differences in yields between government and various corporate bonds. Figure 7.3 shows the historical average annual yields for long-term Treasury bonds and corporate bonds with credit ratings of Aaa and Baa since 1980. Riskier low-quality bonds always offer a higher yield than the higher-quality bonds. However, the yield spread between high- and low-quality bonds varies substantially over time. The yield difference between Baa bonds and Treasuries was as high as 3.7 percent and 3.3 percent in 1982 and 2003, respectively. The spread has been as narrow as 1.3 percent and 1.4 percent in 1994 and 2006, respectively.

How do some corporations' debt obligations become junk bonds? Some companies that aren't economically sound or those that use a high degree of financial leverage issue junk bonds. In other cases, financially strong companies issue investment grade bonds and then, over time, begin to have trouble. Eventually a company's bonds can be downgraded to junk status. For example, General Motors (GM) bonds were considered of the highest quality from the 1950s through the 1980s and much of the 1990s. On May 9, 2005, Standard & Poor's downgraded GM bonds to junk status. Junk bonds that were originally issued at investment grade status are called *fallen angels*. GM eventually filed for bankruptcy protection in June 2009. By 2018, its credit rating was at the lowest end of investment grade (BBB). The pandemic in 2020 caused it to be downgraded even further.

Bonds that experience credit-rating downgrades must offer a higher yield. As all the future cash flows are fixed, the bond price must fall to create a higher yield to maturity.

senior bonds Older bonds that carry a higher claim to the issuer's assets.

mortgage bonds Bonds secured with real estate as collateral.

equipment trust certificates Bonds secured with factory and equipment as collateral.

high-yield bonds Bonds with low credit quality that offer a high yield to maturity, also called junk bonds.

▼**FIGURE 7.3** Yield to Maturity on Long-Term Bonds of Different Credit Risk, 1980–2020

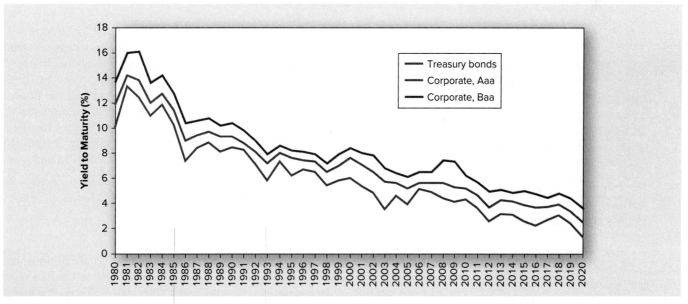

Looking at the historical yields for long-term Treasury and corporate bonds, notice how the yield spread between high- and low-quality bonds varies substantially over time.

finance at work //: personal finance

COVID-19 and the Credit Market

The COVID-19 pandemic caused a global economic recession. The travel and hospitality industries were hit particularly hard. With the resulting lower levels of travel, oil demand dropped and oil prices declined. This hit the oil and petroleum industry hard, as well as many countries that rely on oil exports to fund large portions of the national budget, like Russia and Saudi Arabia. Because of the substantial decline in revenue, the bonds of many companies and countries were downgraded.

Through mid-December of 2020, S&P Global Rating took 236 rating actions for the banking industry alone. These actions include credit downgrades, negative outlook revisions, and negative CreditWatch placements. They announced 193 rating actions for the energy sector and 60 for sovereign issuers. More actions were taken for speculative grade issues than investment grade issues. However, some of the actions for investment grade bonds downgraded them to junk-bond status. For example, Ford Motor, Nordstrom Inc., NOVA Chemicals, Speedway Motorsports, Renault, Mitsubishi Motors, and more, were downgraded to BB+ from investment grade.

The pandemic sent shockwaves through the credit markets in March of 2020. As illustrated, credit ratings and outlooks became much more negative and credit spreads ballooned. The investment grade corporate yield spread versus Treasury yield is a good measure of expected economic risk: The higher the spread, the higher the risk. The spread swelled from 1.02 percent on February 19, 2020, to a peak of 4.01 percent only four weeks later. However, by the end of 2020, the credit markets had normalized. The spread

Max shen/Getty Images

was back down to 1.07 percent. It was a similar story in the high-yield and emerging-market corporate bond spreads versus Treasuries. While the beginning of 2021 still held much uncertainty, the credit markets were signaling confidence that global economies would regain their footing.

Want to know more?

Key Words to Search for Updates: **COVID, Treasury yields, pandemic credit risk**

Further Reading: S&P Global Ratings, "COVID-19- and Oil Price-Related Public Rating Actions on Corporations, Sovereigns, International Public Finance, and Project Finance to Date," December 15, 2020. https://www.spglobal.com/ratings/en/research/articles/200318-covid-19-coronavirus-related-public-rating-actions-on-non-financial-corporations-to-date-11393186?.

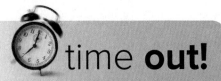

time out!

7-7 Explain why a change in a bond's credit rating will cause its price to change.

7-8 One company has issued two bond classes. One issue is a mortgage bond and the other is a debenture. Which issue will have a higher bond rating, and which will offer a higher yield?

Alternatively, bonds that are upgraded experience price increases and yield decreases. Bond upgrades often occur during strong economic periods because corporate issuers tend to perform better financially at these times. In a weak economy, high-yield bonds lose their luster because the default risk rises. More credit downgrades occur during economic recessions. In general, any event that impacts the likelihood of a firm paying back the interest payments and principal it owes will impact its credit risk. Credit risk is a determinant of the discount rate. The discount rate is also influenced by macroeconomic factors, like decisions by the Federal Reserve Board. A change in the discount rate directly changes the value of the bond. Therefore, company performance, strength of the economy, and monetary policy all affect bond values.

7.5 • BOND MARKETS LG7-8

The majority of trading volume in the bond market occurs in a decentralized, over-the-counter market. Most trades occur between bond dealers and large institutions (like mutual funds, pension funds, and insurance companies). Dealers bid for bonds that investors seek to sell and offer bonds from their own inventory when investors want to buy.

This is especially true for the very active Treasury securities market. However, a small number of corporate bonds are listed on centralized exchanges.

The NYSE operates the largest centralized U.S. bond market. The majority of bond volume at the NYSE is in corporate debt. However, corporate bonds experience relatively low trading volume. The largest price and yield changes for investment grade bonds and high-yield bonds for the day are shown in Figure 7.4. Note that some of the bonds traded are

▾**FIGURE 7.4** Corporate Bond Trading, December 29, 2020

Corporate Debt

Prices of firms' bonds reflect factors including investors' economic, sectoral and company-specific expectation

Investment grade spreads that tightened the most...

Issuer	Symbol	Coupon(%)	Yield(%)	Maturity	Spread', in basis points		
					Current	One-day change	Last week
HSBC Holdings	HSBC	4.375	1.64	Nov.23,'26	126	−6	132
Toyota Motor Credit	...	2.900	0.32	March 30,'23	15	−5	9
Verizon Communications	VZ	4.125	2.90	Aug.15,'46	120	−3	112
American International	AIG	4.125	0.67	Feb.15,'24	29	−1	34

...And spreads that widened the most

Citigroup	C	3.700	0.93	Jan.12,'26	57	6	n.a.
Wells Fargo	WFC	4.750	0.32	Dec. 7,'46	138	5	138
Svenska Handelsbanken AB	...	3.900	2.90	Nov.20,'23	17	1	20

High-yield issues with the biggest price increases ...

Issuer	Symbol	Coupon(%)	Yield(%)	Maturity	Bond Price as % of face value		
					Current	One-day change	Last week
Teva Pharmaceutical Finace Netherlands Iii Bv*	...	2.800	3.00	July 21,'23	99.500	0.88	98.625
Hughes Satellite Systems	...	6.625	4.19	Aug. 1,'26	112.030	0.75	110.500
Netflix	NFLX	4.375	2.26	Nov.15,'26	111.550	0.65	110.625
Ford Motor	F	4.750	4.57	Jan.15,'43	102.529	0.53	101.000
Sprint	S	7.125	1.87	June 15,'24	117.530	0.30	116.000
GrafTech Finance	...	4.625	4.46	Dec. 15,'28	101.125	0.15	101.250

...And with the biggest price decreases

Bombardier	...	7.450	9.16	May 1,'34	87.000	−0.50	87.000
Intesa Sanpaolo S.p.A.	...	5.017	1.91	June 26,'24	110.453	−0.14	109.372

'Estimated spread over 2-year, 3-year, 5-year, 10-year or 30-year hot-run Treasury, 100 basis points=one percentage; change in spread shown is for Z-spread.

Note: Data are for the most active issue of bonds with maturities of two years or more.

This is an example of the largest corporate bond price and yield changes for a given day.

Source: The Wall Street Journal, December 29, 2020.

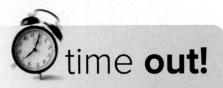

time out!

7-9 Why can we use various interest rates to describe the performance of the entire bond market?

7-10 What bond segments are measured by which bond indexes?

short-term, like Toyota Motor Credit and Sprint. Other bonds have many years to maturity, like the Verizon Communications bond that matures in August 2046.

Following the Bond Market

The entire bond market encompasses a wide variety of securities with varying credit quality from different issuers. Large differences also arise among bonds in terms of their characteristics such as term to maturity and size of the coupon. The biggest factor associated with changes in bond prices is changes in interest rates. So, one common way to describe the direction of bond prices is simply to report the change in interest rates because we know that interest rate changes will affect all bonds the same way. The interest rate referenced is the yield to maturity and daily yield change for the 10-year Treasury. Knowing how this interest rate changed today gives bond investors a good idea of the general price movement of all types of bonds.

Bond indexes track specific segments of the bond market. Various securities firms, such as Bloomberg Barclays and J.P. Morgan, maintain these indexes that capture bond price and yield changes in particular segments. You can find information about major bond indexes on the Internet and in publications like *The Wall Street Journal* (both in print and online). Figure 7.5 shows indexes that track bonds by type of issuer (corporation, U.S. Agency, Mortgage-Backed, Global Government, etc.) and time to maturity (short, intermediate, and long).

▼FIGURE 7.5 Major Bond Indexes as Reported in The Wall Street Journal and on the Internet, December 30, 2020

Tracking Bond Benchmarks

Return on investment and spreads over Treasurys and/or yields paid to investors compared with 52-week highs and lows for different types of bonds

Total return close	YTD total return(%)	Index	Yield(%) Latest	Yield(%) Low	Yield(%) High	Total return close	YTD total return(%)	Index	Yield(%) Latest	Yield(%) Low	Yield(%) High
Broad Market Bloomberg Barclays						**Mortgage-Backed** Bloomberg Barclays					
2288.26	7.3	U.S. Aggregate	1.140	1.020	2.310	2230.58	3.8	Mortgage-Backed	1.290	0.930	2.690
U.S. Corporate Indexes Bloomberg Barclays						2177.94	3.7	Ginnie Mae(GNMA)	0.760	0.290	2.660
3450.43	9.6	U.S. Corporate	1.770	1.770	4.580	1317.30	3.9	Fannie mae(FNMA)	1.470	1.110	2.690
3109.41	7.3	Intermediate	1.110	1.110	4.400	2021.81	3.9	FreddieMac(FHLMC)	1.450	1.080	2.710
5166.45	13.4	Long term	2.810	2.730	4.930	595.66	5.3	Muni Master	0.863	0.838	3.441
701.05	8.7	Double-A-rated	1.420	1.300	3.360	421.61	5.7	7-12 year	0.843	0.771	3.447
920.15	9.6	Triple-B-rated	2.030	2.030	5.350	482.35	6.5	12-22 year	1.257	1.224	3.690
High Yield Bonds ICE BofA						468.50	6.3	22-plus year	1.894	1.765	4.123
494.76	5.9	High Yield Contrained	4.257	4.257	11.400	**Global Government** J.P. Morgan'					
455.62	4.1	Triple-C-rated	8.391	8.375	19.071	614.63	5.4	Global Government	0.560	0.390	1.060
3324.38	4.1	High Yield 100	3.568	3.568	10.740	861.52	7.2	Canada	0.850	0.590	1.740
446.94	6.0	Global High Yield Constrained	4.264	4.264	11.310	420.69	5.1	EMUS	0.048	0.010	0.794
337.57	2.7	Europe High Yield Constrained	2.847	2.464	8.183	793.28	4.5	France	−0.110	−0.150	0.430
U.S. Agency Bloomberg Barclays						552.38	3.1	Germany	−0.470	−0.740	−0.050
1866.47	5.4	U.S. Agency	0.490	0.460	1.880	295.25	−1.0	Japan	0.290	0.040	0.320
1626.93	4.1	10-20 years	0.380	0.340	1.760	618.38	3.7	Netherlands	−0.390	−0.540	−0.080
4265.50	11.8	20-plus years	1.650	1.170	2.450	1092.22	8.7	U.K.	0.570	0.390	1.140
2931.25	7.2	Yankee	1.380	1.380	3.500	931.81	5.7	Emerging Markets"	4.345	4.345	7.480

*Constrained indexes limit individual issuer concentrations to 2% the High Yield 100 are the 100 largest bonds
**EMBI Global Index

In local currency & Euro-zone bonds
Sources: ICE Data Services; Bloomberg Barclays J.P.Morgan

Here are indexes that track bonds by type of issuer (corporation, U.S. Agency, Mortgage-Backed, Global Government, etc.) and time to maturity (short, intermediate, and long).
Source: The Wall Street Journal Online, December 30, 2020, page B7.

Get Online

mhhe.com/CornettM6e

for study materials including
quizzes, iPod downloads,
and video

Your Turn...

Questions

1. What does a call provision allow issuers to do, and why would they do it? *(LG7-1)*

2. List the differences between the new TIPS and traditional Treasury bonds. *(LG7-2)*

3. Explain how mortgage-backed securities work. *(LG7-2)*

4. Provide the definitions of a discount bond and a premium bond. Give examples. *(LG7-3)*

5. Describe the differences in interest payments and bond price between a 5 percent coupon bond and a zero-coupon bond. *(LG7-4)*

6. All else equal, which bond's price is more affected by a change in interest rates, a short-term bond or a longer-term bond? Why? *(LG7-5)*

7. All else equal, which bond's price is more affected by a change in interest rates, a bond with a large coupon or a small coupon? Why? *(LG7-5)*

8. Explain how a bond's interest rate can change over time even if interest rates in the economy do not change. *(LG7-5)*

9. Compare and contrast the advantages and disadvantages of the current yield computation versus yield to maturity calculations. *(LG7-6)*

10. What is the yield to call and why is it important to a bond investor? *(LG7-6)*

11. What is the purpose of computing the equivalent taxable yield of a municipal bond? *(LG7-6)*

12. Explain why high-income and wealthy people are more likely to buy a municipal bond than a corporate bond. *(LG7-6)*

13. Why does a Treasury bond offer a lower yield than a corporate bond with the same time to maturity? Could a corporate bond with a different time to maturity offer a lower yield? Explain. *(LG7-7)*

14. Describe the difference between a bond issued as a high-yield bond and one that has become a "fallen angel." *(LG7-7)*

15. What is the difference in the trading volume between Treasury bonds and corporate bonds? Give examples and/or evidence. *(LG7-8)*

Problems

BASIC PROBLEMS

7-1 **Interest Payments** Determine the interest payment for the following three bonds: 3½ percent coupon corporate bond *(paid semiannually),* 4.25 percent coupon Treasury note, and a corporate zero-coupon bond maturing in 10 years. (Assume a $1,000 par value.) *(LG7-1)*

7-2 **Time to Maturity** A bond issued by Ford on May 15, 1997, is scheduled to mature on May 15, 2097. If today is November 16, 2014, what is this bond's time to maturity? *(LG7-1)*

7-3 **Call Premium** A 6 percent corporate coupon bond is callable in five years for a call premium of one year of coupon payments. Assuming a par value of $1,000, what is the price paid to the bondholder if the issuer calls the bond? *(LG7-1)*

7-4 **TIPS Interest and Par Value** A 2¾ percent TIPS has an original reference CPI of 185.4. If the current CPI is 210.7, what are the current interest payment and par value of the TIPS? *(LG7-2)*

7-5 **Bond Quotes** Consider the following three bond quotes: a Treasury note quoted at 97.844, a corporate bond quoted at 103.25, and a municipal bond quoted at 101.90. If the Treasury and corporate bonds have a par value of $1,000 and the municipal bond has a par value of $5,000, what are the prices of these three bonds in dollars? *(LG7-3)*

7-6 **Zero-Coupon Bond Price** Calculate the price of a zero-coupon bond that matures in 20 years if the market interest rate is 3.8 percent. *(LG7-4)*

7-7 **Current Yield** What's the current yield of a 3.8 percent coupon corporate bond quoted at a price of 102.08? *(LG7-6)*

7-8 **Taxable Equivalent Yield** What's the taxable equivalent yield on a municipal bond with a yield to maturity of 3.5 percent for an investor in the 33 percent marginal tax bracket? *(LG7-6)*

7-9 **Credit Risk and Yield** Rank from highest credit risk to lowest risk the following bonds, with the same time to maturity, by their yield to maturity: Treasury bond with yield of 5.55 percent, IBM bond with yield of 7.49 percent, Trump Casino bond with yield of 8.76 percent, and Banc One bond with a yield of 5.99 percent. *(LG7-7)*

INTERMEDIATE PROBLEMS

7-10 **TIPS Capital Return** Consider a 3.5 percent TIPS with an issue CPI reference of 185.6. At the beginning of this year, the CPI was 193.5 and was at 199.6 at the end of the year. What was the capital gain of the TIPS in dollars and in percentage terms? *(LG7-2)*

7-11 **Compute Bond Price** Compute the price of a 3.8 percent coupon bond with 15 years left to maturity and a market interest rate of 6.8 percent. *(Assume interest payments are semiannual.)* Is this a discount or premium bond? *(LG7-4)*

7-12 **Compute Bond Price** Calculate the price of a 5.2 percent coupon bond with 18 years left to maturity and a market interest rate of 4.6 percent. *(Assume interest payments are semiannual.)* Is this a discount or premium bond? *(LG7-4)*

7-13 **Bond Prices and Interest Rate Changes** A 5.75 percent coupon bond with 10 years left to maturity is priced to offer a 6.5 percent yield to maturity. You believe that in one year, the yield to maturity will be 5.8 percent. What is the change in price the bond will experience in dollars? *(LG7-5)*

7-14 **Yield to Maturity** A 5.65 percent coupon bond with 18 years left to maturity is offered for sale at $1,035.25. What yield to maturity is the bond offering? *(Assume interest payments are semiannual.)* *(LG7-6)*

7-15 **Yield to Call** A 6.75 percent coupon bond with 26 years left to maturity can be called in 6 years. The call premium is one year of coupon payments. It is offered for sale at $1,135.25. What is the yield to call of the bond? *(Assume interest payments are semiannual.)* *(LG7-6)*

7-16 **Comparing Bond Yields** A client in the 39 percent marginal tax bracket is comparing a municipal bond that offers a 4.5 percent yield to maturity and a similar-risk corporate bond that offers a 6.45 percent yield. Which bond will give the client more profit after taxes? *(LG7-6)*

7-17 **Spreadsheet Problem: Bond Prices and Interest Rate Changes** A 6.5 percent coupon bond with 14 years left to maturity is priced to offer a 7.2 percent yield to maturity. You believe that in one year, the yield to maturity will be 6.8 percent. What is the change in price the bond will experience in dollars? *(LG7-5)*

7-18 **Spreadsheet Problem: Yield to Maturity** A 4.30 percent coupon bond with 14 years left to maturity is offered for sale at $943.22. What yield to maturity is the bond offering? *(Assume interest payments are semiannual.)* *(LG7-6)*

7-19 **Spreadsheet Problem: Yield to Call** A 5.25 percent coupon bond with 14 years left to maturity can be called in four years. The call premium is one year of coupon payments. It is offered for sale at $1,075.50. What is the yield to call of the bond? *(Assume interest payments are semiannual.)* *(LG7-6)*

ADVANCED PROBLEMS

7-20 **TIPS Total Return** Reconsider the 3.5 percent TIPS discussed in problem 7-10. It was issued with CPI reference of 185.6. The bond is purchased at the beginning of the year *(after the interest payment),* when the CPI was 193.5. For the interest payment in the middle of the year, the CPI was 195.1. Now, at the end of the year, the CPI is 199.6 and the interest payment has been made. What is the total return of the TIPS in dollars and in percentage terms for the year? *(LG7-2)*

7-21 **Bond Prices and Interest Rate Changes** A 6.25 percent coupon bond with 22 years left to maturity is priced to offer a 5.5 percent yield to maturity. You believe that in one year, the yield to maturity will be 6.0 percent. If this occurs, what would be the total return of the bond in dollars and percent? *(LG7-5)*

7-22 **Yields of a Bond** A 2.50 percent coupon municipal bond has 12 years left to maturity and has a price quote of 98.45. The bond can be called in four years. The call premium is one year of coupon payments. Compute and discuss the bond's current yield, yield to maturity, taxable equivalent yield *(for an investor in the 35 percent marginal tax bracket),* and yield to call. (Assume interest payments are semiannual and it has a par value of $5,000.) *(LG7-6)*

7-23 Bond Ratings and Prices A corporate bond with a 6.5 percent coupon has 15 years left to maturity. It has had a credit rating of BBB and a yield to maturity of 7.2 percent. The firm has recently gotten into some trouble and the rating agency is downgrading the bonds to BB. The new appropriate discount rate will be 8.5 percent. What will be the change in the bond's price in dollars and percentage terms? *(Assume interest payments are semiannual.) (LG7-7)*

7-24 Spreadsheet Problem: Bond Ratings and Prices A corporate bond with a 6.75 percent coupon has 10 years left to maturity. It has had a credit rating of BB and a yield to maturity of 8.2 percent. The firm has recently become more financially stable and the rating agency is upgrading the bonds to BBB. The new appropriate discount rate will be 7.1 percent. What will be the change in the bond's price in dollars and percentage terms? *(Assume interest payments are semiannual.) (LG7-7)*

7-25 Spreadsheet Problem: Bond Ratings and Interest Rate Changes Say that in June of this year, a company issued bonds that are scheduled to mature three years from now in June. The coupon rate is 5.75 percent and is paid semiannually. The bond issue was rated AAA. *(LG7-7)*

a. Build a spreadsheet that shows how much money the firm pays for each interest rate payment and when those payments will occur if the bond issue sells 50,000 bonds.

b. If the bond issue rating would have been BBB, then the coupon rate would have been 6.30 percent. Show the interest payments with this rating. Explain why bond ratings are important to firms issuing capital debt.

c. Consider that interest rates in the economy increased in the first half of this year. If the firm would have issued the bonds in January of this year, then the coupon rate would have only been 5.40 percent. How much extra money per year is the firm paying because it issued the bonds in June instead of January?

7-26 Spreadsheet Problem: Interest Rate Changes and Maturity You have a portfolio of three bonds. The long bond will mature in 19 years and has a 5.5 percent coupon rate. The midterm bond matures in 9 years and has a 6.6 percent coupon rate. The short bond matures in only 2 years and has a 4 percent coupon rate. *(LG7-5)*

a. Construct a spreadsheet that shows the value of these three bonds and the portfolio when the discount rate is 5 percent. The spreadsheet can look something like this:

	A	B	C	D	E
1					
2	Settlement date	11/15/2011	=DATE(2011,11,15)		
3	Maturity date	11/15/2026	=DATE(2026,11,15)		
4	Coupon Rate	5.50%			
5	Interest rate (Yld)	6.50%			
6	Redemption	100			
7	Frequency	2			
8					
9	Bond price (per $100 par value) =	$90.51	=PRICE(B2,B3,B4,B5,B6,B7,1)		
10	Bond price (per $1000 par value) =	$905.09	=10*B9		

Microsoft Excel

b. Illustrate what happens when the discount rate increases by 0.5 percent. What do you notice about the changes in price between the three bonds?

c. Show the bond prices when the discount rate decreases by 0.5 percent from the discount rate in part a. What do you notice about the price change between parts b and c?

Notes

CHAPTER 7

1. In order to focus on the valuation concepts, we present these examples with the full six months until the bond's next interest payment. However, bonds can be sold anytime between interest payments. When this occurs, we simply add the interest accrued since the last payment to the price.

2. States have differing rules about whether they tax the income from a particular municipal bond—they will generally tax income from munis issued out of state. Further, capital gains arising from municipal bond sales may be taxed, and the income from municipal bonds must be added to overall income when determining the alternative minimum tax consequences.

Design elements: (Clock) Floortje/Getty Images; (Referee) Richard Ransier/Getty Images

eight

valuing
stocks

B usinesses need capital to start up operations, expand product lines and services, and serve new markets. In the last chapter, we discussed debt, which is one source of financial capital upon which businesses can draw. Their other source of capital is called *equity,* or *business ownership*. Business ownership comes in different forms that depend on its organizational structure. Chapter 1 discusses the advantages and disadvantages of business forms like sole proprietor, partnerships, and corporations. This chapter focuses on the common business form for large companies, the C corporation, otherwise referred to as a public corporation. Indeed, anyone can buy the stock of these companies. This contrasts with S corporations, which are limited to 100 investors and whose stock does not sell on the public stock exchanges. Public corporations share business ownership and raise money by issuing stocks to investors. When the company sells this form of equity ownership to raise money, it gives up some ownership—and thus some control—over the business. Investors buy stock to receive the benefits of business ownership.

continued on p. 224

LEARNING GOALS

LG8-1 Understand the rights and returns that come with common stock ownership.

LG8-2 Explain how stock exchanges function.

LG8-3 Track the wider stock market with stock indexes and differentiate among the kinds of information each index provides.

LG8-4 Recognize the terminology of stock trading.

LG8-5 Compute stock values using dividend discount and constant-growth models.

LG8-6 Calculate the stock value of a variable-growth-rate company.

LG8-7 Assess relative stock values using the P/E ratio model.

»viewpoints

business APPLICATION

As CEO of your firm, Dawa Tech, which makes computer components, you have been able to grow its dividends by 8 percent per year to a recent $2 per share. You expect this growth to continue. As a result, the stock price has risen to $65 and has a P/E ratio of 16.25.

Tomorrow, you are scheduled to meet with some stockholders and financial analysts. To prepare for the meeting, you should know what return the shareholders seem to expect and estimate where the Dawa stock price may be in three years. How will you go about preparing for this meeting? **(See the solution at the end of the chapter.)**

continued from p. 223

Most citizens do not have the time or expertise to operate their own businesses. Buying stock allows them to participate in the profits of economic activities. Access to equity capital has allowed entrepreneurs like Bill Gates of Microsoft and Larry Page of Google to take their companies public so that their businesses can become large corporations. Both the company founders and the new owners (stock investors) have amassed much wealth over the years under this arrangement. One very important reason that investors are willing to buy company stock as an investment is that they know that they can sell the stock during any trading day. Investors buy and sell stocks among themselves in stock markets. Well-functioning stock markets are critical to any capitalistic economy. In this chapter, we'll discuss stock market operations and stock valuation. ■

common stock An ownership stake in a corporation.

residual claimants Ownership of cash flows and value after other claimants are paid.

8.1 • COMMON STOCK LG8-1

Equity securities (stocks) represent ownership shares in a corporation. **Common stock** offers buyers the potential for current income from dividends and capital appreciation from any stock price increases. Over time, some corporate profits are reinvested in the firm, which increases the value of each shareholder's stake in the business. At any point in time, the market value of a firm's common stock depends on many factors, including

- The company's profitability.
- Growth prospects for the future.
- Current market interest rates.
- Conditions in the overall stock market.

Over periods of 30 to 40 years, stocks have offered investors the best opportunities to increase wealth. Since stocks are also susceptible to price declines and stock price fluctuations can be very volatile over short periods of time, stock investing requires a longer-term outlook.

Virtually any business firm that is organized as a corporation (see Chapter 1) may choose to issue publicly traded stock. Common stockholders vote to elect the board of directors; they also vote on various other proposals requested by other shareholders or the management team. As owners of the firm, common stockholders are considered to be **residual claimants.** This means that common stockholders have the right to claim any cash flows or value after all other claimants have received what they are owed. As a company earns cash flows, it must pay suppliers, employees, expenses, taxes, and debt interest payments.

You are impressed with the news and entertainment firm CBC Newscorp. The per-share dividends have increased from $1.25 per year three years ago to the recent $1.68 annual dividend. Then you discover that 15 analysts are following the firm and that their mean growth estimate for the future is 10.1 percent. Now you want to know if the current selling price of $54 seems like a good deal if the appropriate required return for the stock is 13.5 percent. **(See the solution at the end of the chapter.)**

Who are these "analysts," and where can you find their opinions?

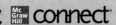

Stockholders claim the leftover (or residual) cash flow. These profits can be used to reinvest in the firm to foster growth, pay dividends to shareholders, or a combination of the two.

Stocks of growing firms are valuable. Stocks in firms that pay dividends to shareholders are also valuable. Stocks issued by firms that have greater amounts of residual cash flow are more valuable. The value is reflected in the stock price. *Therefore, stock price values arise from the company's underlying business success.* Many different investors and analysts may estimate a stock's fundamental value based upon some outlook or theory. But the actual stock price is determined on stock exchanges when investors seek to trade with one another. Let's discuss this trading process and then explore how stocks are valued.

> **New York Stock Exchange (NYSE)** Large and prestigious stock exchange with a trading floor.
>
> **trading posts** Trading location on the floor of a stock exchange.

8.2 • STOCK MARKETS LG8-2

In general, people will invest significant amounts of their wealth in stocks only if they know that they can convert their shares into cash at any time. Stock exchanges provide this liquidity, allowing buyers and sellers the means to transact stock trades with each other. This liquidity gives many people the confidence to invest in the first place and makes stocks (as well as bonds) attractive investments relative to less-liquid assets like real estate or fine collectibles—which can be difficult to sell quickly at full value.

The most well-known stock exchange in the world is the **New York Stock Exchange (NYSE).** The NYSE, located in New York City on the corner of Wall Street and Broad Street, is the largest U.S. stock exchange as measured by the value of companies listed and the dollar value of trading activity. The NYSE is the largest equities marketplace in the world and is home to more than 2,800 companies (many with multiple securities listed). While other exchanges may boast more companies listed, many of the largest companies in the world tend to list in New York. The holding company that owns the NYSE, Intercontinental Exchange, also operates stock exchanges and futures exchanges throughout the world. For decades, the American Stock Exchange, located just down the street, competed with the NYSE. However, in 2008, the NYSE acquired this exchange. Now, smaller companies trade at this location, which is referred to as NYSE American.

Much of the stock buying and selling at the NYSE occurs at physical stations, called **trading posts,** on the trading floor.

The NYSE trades millions upon millions of stock shares in a given day.
Tetra Images/Brand X Pictures/Getty Images

Each post is staffed by a designated market maker, who oversees the orderly trading of the specific stocks assigned to that post. **Brokers,** located around the perimeter of the floor, act as agents for those buying and selling stocks. Brokers execute orders by matching buy and sell orders. Once the buy and sell orders match, the transaction is completed and the trade appears on trading screens viewed by people all over the world.

Consider this scenario. You decide to buy shares of McDonald's stock because of new menu items and other initiatives. You place a buy order for 100 shares with your broker—either with a simple phone call or through an online brokerage service. The broker then sends the order to the NYSE electronically to the trading post assigned for McDonald's stock. At the trading post, the designated market maker ensures the transaction is executed in a fair and orderly manner. Your buy order competes with other orders at the point of sale for the best price and an on-floor broker executes your purchase. You will receive a trade confirmation from your broker describing the trade and noting the exact amount you owe for the 100 shares of McDonald's plus any applicable commissions. The NYSE reports the transaction and it appears within seconds on displays across the country and around the world. Note that buy and sell orders are electronically routed from all over the world to the NYSE, which then routes trade results back. Since most of the trade orders are already in electronic form, why not electronically match buy and sell orders and bypass any human intervention in floor trading? Indeed, the NYSE has joined many other exchanges in becoming increasingly electronic. Some floor market-maker firms can see a time when no human intervention will be a part of floor trading at the NYSE.

The NYSE will trade millions of McDonald's stock shares in a given day. A stock quote for McDonald's stock, **ticker symbol** MCD, is shown in Figure 8.1. On December 30, 2020,

▼FIGURE 8.1 Read a Stock Quote, December 30, 2020, McDonald's Corp

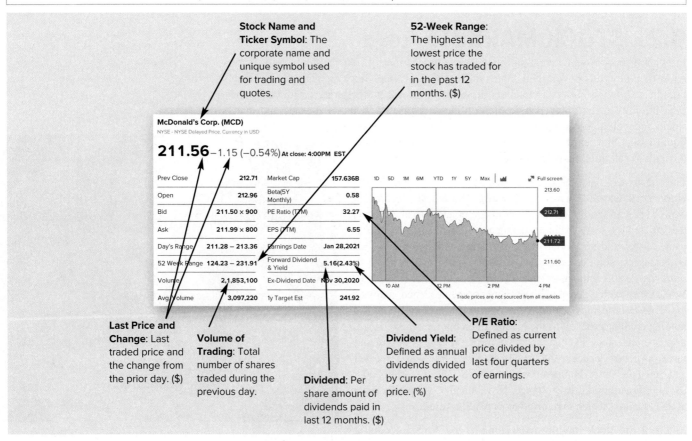

If you know what to look for, reading a stock quote is not as complicated as it first may appear.

more than 1.8 million McDonald's shares traded. That is a slow day for this stock, as it averages nearly 3.1 million shares per day. The stock closed at $211.56 per share, which was $1.15 lower than the closing price of the previous day. At this price, McDonald's stock is currently in the upper half of its 52-week price range that has a high of $231.23 and a low of $124.23.

To list its stock on the NYSE, a company must meet minimum requirements for its

- Total number of stockholders.
- Level of trading volume.
- Corporate earnings.
- Firm size.

The exchange also charges an initial list fee and an annual fee. Listing standards and fees are higher for the NYSE than for other stock exchanges, so many firms cannot (or choose not to) list their stocks there.

Another popular stock trading system is the **NASDAQ Stock Market,** an electronic stock market without a physical trading floor. Today, NASDAQ features many of the big-name high-tech companies investors have come to know, like Apple Inc. (ticker: AAPL), Intel (ticker: INTC), Microsoft (ticker: MSFT), and Qualcomm (ticker: QCOM). Many newer high-tech companies like Google (ticker: GOOG), Netflix (ticker: NFLX), and Amazon. com Inc. (ticker: AMZN) are also listed on NASDAQ. NASDAQ ranks second, behind the NYSE, among the world's equity markets in terms of total dollar volume. NASDAQ lists approximately 3,300 domestic and foreign companies and operates a U.S. stock exchange and eight European exchanges.

Instead of having a trading floor, NASDAQ uses a vast electronic trading system that executes trades via computer rather than in person. Instead of one designated market maker overseeing the process for an individual stock on a trading floor, Nasdaq's system uses multiple **market makers,** or **dealers.** Market makers use their own stock inventory and capital to compete with other dealers to buy and sell the stocks they represent. When an investor places an order through a stockbroker for a NASDAQ-listed stock, the electronic system routes the order and the investor buys shares from the dealer offering the best (lowest) price. Typical NASDAQ stocks support 10 market makers actively competing with one another for investor trades.

Table 8.1 shows trading activity on the two main stock exchanges for one day in December 2020. Note that the combined number of shares traded was more than 6 billion shares during the day.

The business of providing platforms or forums for investors and speculators to trade stocks and other financial assets has been changing rapidly. Many exchanges that previously used physical floor trading systems with specialists and open outcry to establish stock

NASDAQ Stock Market Large electronic stock exchange.

market makers Dealers and specialists who oversee an orderly trading process.

dealers NASDAQ market makers who use their own capital to trade with investors.

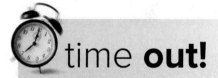

time out!

8-1 What are three primary stock exchanges in the United States, and where are they located? For which of the exchanges does physical location matter? Why?

8-2 Describe differences in trading procedures on the NYSE versus the NASDAQ. Which do you think is most fair to investors? Why?

▼ **TABLE 8.1** Trading on the NYSE and NASDAQ, December 22, 2020

	NYSE	NASDAQ
Advancing issues	1,335 (41%)	2,052 (53%)
Declining issues	1,812 (56%)	1,701 (44%)
Unchanged issues	100 (3%)	89 (3%)
New highs	296	433
New lows	4	12
Total volume	909,070,552	5,682,590,404

Source: *The Wall Street Journal.*

prices are shifting to electronic systems with no trading floors. Long-standing, traditional exchanges are also merging with other domestic and international exchanges to create fewer, but larger, forums that focus not just on U.S. securities but on many more internationally focused financial assets. The wider range of represented securities allows traders new opportunities to explore trading relationships among securities traded across the world. This worldwide trading will establish economically sound prices and additional financial stability around the world.

Tracking the Stock Market LG8-3

With thousands of stocks trading every minute, many stock prices rise while others fall. Table 8.1 also shows that, throughout the trading day, 1,335 stocks increased in price on the NYSE while 1,812 stocks decreased in price. The NASDAQ saw more advances than declines. In addition to the number of stocks advancing and declining, the table also shows the number of stocks that hit new 52-week price highs (296 listed on the NYSE) and new lows (4 on the NYSE) on that day. So, was this a good day or a bad day in the stock market?

To say anything about the *general* direction of the stock market, **stock indexes** are useful. Dozens of stock indexes are designed to track the overall market; many more track different market segments. The three most recognized indexes are the **Dow Jones Industrial Average (DJIA)**, the **Standard & Poor's 500 Index (S&P 500)**, and the **NASDAQ Composite Index.**

Charles H. Dow invented the first stock average in 1884. At the turn of the 20th century, railroads were the first major corporations. So he began with 11 stocks, mostly railroads. Dow created a price average by simply adding up 11 stock prices and dividing by the number 11. Two years later, Dow began tracking a 12-stock industrial average. This industrial average would eventually evolve into the modern DJIA, which is a price average of 30 large, industry-leading stocks that together represent roughly 30 percent of the total stock value of all U.S. equities. DJIA level changes describe how the largest companies that participate in the stock market performed over a given period. The DJIA closed at 30,015.51, a change of −200.94 (or −0.66 percent), on the day illustrated in Table 8.1.

The Standard & Poor's Corp. introduced its 500-stock index in 1957. Standard & Poor's chooses companies to include in the S&P 500 Index to represent the 10 sectors of the economy:

1. Financial
2. Information technology
3. Health care
4. Industrials
5. Consumer discretionary
6. Consumer staples
7. Energy
8. Telecom services
9. Utilities
10. Materials

Investors consider the NASDAQ to be a reflection of the tech sector's general performance.
TongRo Image Stock/Alamy Stock Photo

S&P uses **market capitalization** (a measure of company size using stock price times shares outstanding), not just stock prices, of the largest 500 U.S. firms to compute the index. These 500 firms represent roughly 80 percent of the overall stock market capitalization (number of shares times share price).

Although the DJIA is a long-time favorite with the media and individual investors, the S&P 500 is much preferred in the investment industry because of its broader representation of the market as a whole. S&P 500 performance provides a standard against which most U.S. money managers and pension plan sponsors can compare their investment performance. During trading on December 22, 2020, the S&P 500 lost 7.66 (−0.21 percent) to close at 3,687.26.

The NASDAQ Composite Index measures the market capitalization of all common stocks listed on the NASDAQ stock exchange. Because the NASDAQ lists so many large, technology-oriented companies, many investors and analysts consider this index to reflect the tech sector performance more than that of the overall stock market. The NASDAQ Composite gained 28.13 to close at 12,807.92 on December 22, 2020, a gain of 0.51 percent. It was a bit of an unusual trading day because the DJIA was down, the S&P 500 was slightly down, and the NASDAQ was up.

Figure 8.2 shows the levels of all these stock indexes since 1980. The DJIA (red line) level appears on the left-hand axis. Both the S&P 500 (blue line) and the NASDAQ Composite (orange line) run from the right-hand axis. The rapid price appreciation for NASDAQ stocks during the late 1990s—the tech boom years—is unprecedented for such a large and widely followed market index. The NASDAQ Composite soared from 817 in March 1995 to peak on March 10, 2000, at 5,048.62, for a 518 percent total return in only five years—a 43.9 percent annual rate of share-price appreciation for NASDAQ stocks. The NASDAQ index performed much better than did the DJIA (19.0 percent per year) or the S&P 500 (22.7 percent per year). The NASDAQ "price bubble" set the stage for one of the most dramatic stock price declines in history: The NASDAQ Composite Index plunged to 1,114.11 on October 9, 2002, losing 78 percent of its value. The other index values also fell during this period, albeit not as sharply. Note that the DJIA did not climb back to its 2000 high until March 2006. The S&P 500 Index finally recovered in May 2007. The NASDAQ Composite did not exceed its 2000 high until April 22, 2015. The stock market has been very volatile during the past two decades.

time out!

8-3 Discuss why the day's market return may be different when measured by the DJIA, S&P 500 Index, and NASDAQ Composite taken separately.

8-4 Why might the "market bubble" phenomenon appear more dramatic because it occurred in the NASDAQ Composite rather than with the DJIA or S&P 500 Index?

8-5 If you followed the market regularly, to which index would you give the most credence? Why?

▼**FIGURE 8.2** Stock Market Index Levels since 1980

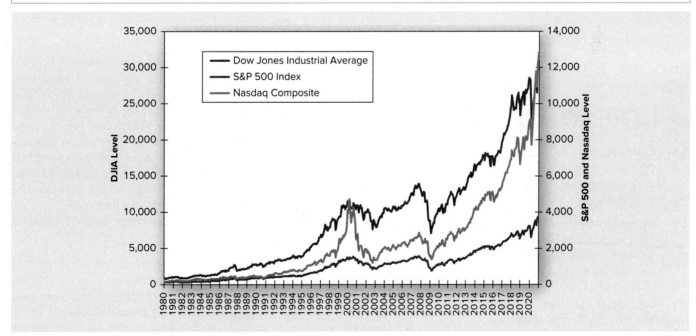

This graph comparing the DJIA, S&P 500, and NASDAQ Composite indexes gives you a picture of their magnitude, as well as their patterns.

The figure also shows the stock market reaction to the financial crisis that began in 2008. There were sharp declines in all three indexes. After closing at a new high of 14,093.08 on October 12, 2007, the DJIA then fell to close at only 6,547.05 on March 9, 2009. The DJIA fully recovered in early 2013 and closed above 15,000 for the first time on May 7, 2013, and above 18,000 on February 13, 2015. This massive stock market rise coincides with the quantitative easing programs implemented by the U.S. Federal Reserve. Lastly, in 2020, COVID-19 severely impacted the stock markets in the spring. The S&P 500 Index fell from 3,380.16 on February 14, 2020, to a session low of 2,191.86 during trading on March 23, a decline of 35 percent in only five weeks. However, the impact was short-lived as the S&P 500 Index returned to 3,380 on August 12 and closed 2020 at a high of 3,732.04.

Trading Stocks LG8-4

People who wish to buy and sell stocks need to open stock brokerage accounts. Traditional, full-service stockbrokers (e.g., Morgan Stanley Wealth Management, Merrill Lynch, UBS, Edward Jones) provide clients with research and advice in addition to executing trades. Their clients pay for this research and advice: Commission fees for these services may run well over $100 per trade. Discount brokerage firms (e.g., Charles Schwab, E-trade, TD Ameritrade) charge a much lower commission, $5 to $30 per trade, but do not provide the additional services. Investors at discount brokerages usually place trades through the brokerage's Internet sites. Recently, the Robinhood Financial trading app and website have become popular because it does not charge a commission for stock and option trades. Other new securities trading platforms are TradeStation, M1 Finance, Moomoo, and Betterment.

Buy and sell orders go through the brokerage firm to a market maker (a dealer or a specialist) at a stock exchange. The quoted **bid** is the highest price at which the market maker offers to pay for the stock. Investors have little choice but to accept this selling price because regardless of the broker used, the market maker offers the only place to sell the stock. The quoted **ask** price is the lowest price at which a market maker will sell a stock—so investors buy at the ask price. The difference between the bid and the ask price may be only $0.01 for high-volume stocks and can be as high as $0.20 for less-often-traded companies. The spread between the bid and the ask price is a cost to the investor and a profit for the market maker. This profit compensates the market maker for providing a market and liquidity for that stock.

Investors can place a buy or sell **market order.** A market order to buy stock will be filled immediately at the current ask price when routed to the stock exchange. A sell market order will be filled at the current bid price. The advantage of a market order is that it executes immediately at the best available price. The disadvantage of a market order is that the investor does not know in advance what that fill price will be. Investors can name their own prices by using **limit orders,** in which investors specify the price at which they are willing to execute the buy or sell order. With a buy limit order, a trade is executed if the ask quote is at or below the price target. For a sell limit order, a trade is executed if the bid quote moves through the specified price. If the current quote does not meet the price cited in the limit order, the trade is not executed. The advantage of a limit order is that the investor makes the trade at the desired price; the disadvantage is that the trade might not be executed at all.

Consider a quote of McDonald's stock with a bid price of $211.50 and an ask price of $211.99. An investor placing a market buy order would purchase the stock at $211.99. A market sell order would execute as the price rises through $211.50. Note that an investor who simultaneously bought and sold 100 shares would pay $21,199 and receive $21,150—losing $49. An investor who places a buy limit order at $211.70 will only purchase the shares if the ask price falls to $211.70 or lower. If the ask price does not fall, the order will not execute. Bid and ask prices tell investors at what prices the stock can currently be

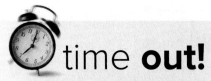

finance at work //:behavioral

Investor Psychology

Investing and trading are different. Investing involves buying and holding securities for an extended time period. Trading focuses on short-term buying and selling to capture short-term price fluctuations. The short-term focus of trading enhances one's emotions and behavioral biases. This typically leads to losses, which is especially true during the mania of price bubbles.

In a "main street versus Wall Street" narrative, Reddit's WallStreetBets discussion board advocated purchasing GameStop stock to torpedo hedge funds' short bets. A short sale tries to profit from a drop in stock price. Someone borrows the stock from the broker and sells it. If the stock price goes down, the short seller can purchase the stock at the new lower price and use it to repay the stock loan. A short seller loses money when the price goes up. Thus, the discussion board advocated buying GameStop to force the price higher so that short sellers would lose money. GameStop, a physical retailer of games, was losing money before the pandemic, which exacerbated the losses. This situation encouraged hedge funds to short the stock. The short interest in most stocks is typically far less than 5% of the shares outstanding, but in early February of 2021, the short interest in GameStop was 122%.

At the end of 2020, GameStop stock closed at $18.84. The attention by individual investors caused the stock price to dramatically rise, passing $100, $200, and even $300 by January 27, 2021. Throughout this quick meteoric increase in price, the media reported hedge fund losses in the hundreds of millions of dollars. The news spurred even more buying. The price reached an intraday high of $483 on January 28 before collapsing to under $50 in early February. As with all price bubbles, those who get in late lose most of their money. While some of the Wall Street investors lost money, the media reported that most of the main street investors did too.

Many of the individual investors purchased shares through the broker app Robinhood. Robinhood was criticized for the gamification of its trading platform, which encourages one's emotions as in a casino. The GameStop episode is not the first instance in which a stock price rocketed to an absurd level and then crashed, leaving massive losses in its wake. Nor will it be the last.

katjen/Shutterstock

Seemingly irrational behavior does not just occur during highly emotional periods of a price bubble. Recently, a growing recognition has arisen that "normal" investors often behave in a way that might not be described as fully rational. Investors, being human, are subject to cognitive biases and emotions. Studies of investor behavior have discovered that investors commonly succumb to psychological biases and

- Trade too much.

- Sell winners too soon.

- Refuse to realize losses.

- Become overconfident—especially when trading online.

- Seek stocks that have already increased in price—perhaps up to their full potential price.

- Consider and react to what's happening with each stock in isolation, rather than remembering the purpose for forming an overall portfolio.

Investors who succeed in the long run are those who learn to avoid these psychological biases.

Want to know more?

Key Words to Search for Updates: **irrational exuberance, price bubble, mania**

---

traded in general. But being able to buy at the ask price does not guarantee that the stock should be *valued* at that price. We'll discuss various ways to arrive at reasonable per-share stock values in the next section.

8.3 • BASIC STOCK VALUATION   LG8-5

Cash Flows

In the previous chapter, we showed how we value bonds by finding the present value of the future interest payments and the future par value. Stock valuation uses the same concept of finding the present value of future dividends and the future selling price. But, of course, uncertainty about both price appreciation and future dividend payment streams complicates stock valuation. Consider the simple case of valuing a stock to be held for one year shown in the time line.

Period	0	i	1 years
Cash flow	PV = ?		$D_1 + P_1$

The value of such a stock today, P_0, is the present value of the dividend to be received in the first year, D_1, plus the present value of the expected sales price in one year, P_1. The interest rate used to discount the cash flows is shown as i. Using the present value equation from Chapter 4 results in

Today's value = Present value of next year's dividend and price

$$P_0 = \frac{D_1 + P_1}{1 + i} \qquad (8\text{-}1)$$

Coca-Cola's dividend growth seems fairly stable and predictable.
Jill Braaten/McGraw-Hill

Whenever investors deal with future stock prices and future dividend payments, they must use expected values, not certain ones. Companies rarely decrease their dividends; most companies' dividends either remain constant or slowly grow. Examining a firm's dividend history over the past few years will give clues to that company's future dividend policy. For example, The Coca-Cola Company (ticker: KO) paid a $0.155 per share dividend for each quarter in 2006. The firm then raised the quarterly dividend to $0.17 for each quarterly dividend in 2007. The company paid quarterly dividends in 2008, 2009, 2010, 2011, and 2012 of $0.19, $0.205, $0.22, $0.235, and $0.255, respectively. For 2013 through 2015, Coca-Cola raised its quarterly dividend 2.5 cents every year. So the quarterly dividend was $0.33 in 2015, for an annual dividend of $1.32. It raised the quarterly dividend 2 cents in 2016, 2017, and 2018 to $0.39 per share. Coca-Cola raised the quarterly dividend 1 cent per share in each of 2019 and 2020 to an annual amount of $1.64. This dividend growth seems fairly stable and predictable.

Stock prices, though, show much more volatility than dividend histories do. We face much uncertainty in trying to predict stock prices in the short term. Using a longer holding period to estimate stock value reduces *some,* but by no means all, of the uncertainty. A two-year holding period appears like this:

Period	0	i	1	2 years
Cash flow	PV = ?		D_1	$D_2 + P_2$

The present value of the cash flows in years 1 and 2 is today's stock value:

Today's value = Present value of next year's dividend,
the second year's dividend, and the future price

$$P_0 = \frac{D_1}{1 + i} + \frac{D_2 + P_2}{(1 + i)^2} \qquad (8\text{-}2)$$

Notice that the divisor for the second term on the right-hand side of equation 8-2 is raised to the second power. This reflects the two years over which those cash flows must be discounted. You can do this analysis over any holding period. For a holding period of n years, the value of a stock is measured by the present value of dividends over the n years, and the eventual sale price, P_n.

P_0 = Sum of the present value of each payment received

$$P_0 = \frac{D_1}{1+i} + \frac{D_2}{(1+i)_2} + \ldots + \frac{D_n + P_n}{(1+i)_n} \qquad (8\text{-}3)$$

This formula incorporates both dividend income and capital appreciation or capital loss. It fully includes both major components of the investor's total return from investment. Note that equation 8-3 uses future dividends and a future stock price. There are many ways to estimate these future cash flows. One common method for estimating future dividends is to use an appropriate growth rate, g. Then use the future value equation in Chapter 4; for example, $D_2 = D_1 \times (1 + g)$. Some firms seem to increase their dividend by the same amount each year. Their future dividends are easy to predict. There are also different methods for estimating the future price. Later sections of this chapter illustrate variable growth rate and P/E model approaches.

As is often the case in finance, implementing equation 8-3 presents problems for some firms in practical terms. What will the future dividends of the firm be? What will the stock price be in 3, 5, or 10 years? While it seems that the dividend growth of Coca-Cola will

EXAMPLE 8-1

For interactive versions of this example, log in to Connect or go to mhhe.com/Cornett6e.

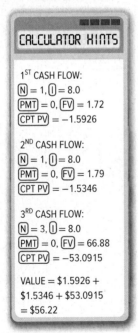

CALCULATOR HINTS

1ST CASH FLOW:
$\boxed{N} = 1, \boxed{I} = 8.0$
$\boxed{PMT} = 0, \boxed{FV} = 1.72$
$\boxed{CPT\ PV} = -1.5926$

2ND CASH FLOW:
$\boxed{N} = 1, \boxed{I} = 8.0$
$\boxed{PMT} = 0, \boxed{FV} = 1.79$
$\boxed{CPT\ PV} = -1.5346$

3RD CASH FLOW:
$\boxed{N} = 3, \boxed{I} = 8.0$
$\boxed{PMT} = 0, \boxed{FV} = 66.88$
$\boxed{CPT\ PV} = -53.0915$

VALUE = $1.5926 +
$1.5346 + $53.0915
= $56.22

Valuing Coca-Cola Stock LG8-5

At the beginning of 2021, you are valuing Coca-Cola stock to compare its value to its market price. The current market price is $54.84. Given the history of Coca-Cola's dividends, you believe that the company will pay total dividends in 2021 of $1.72 (= 4 × $0.43). Your analysis indicates that the total dividends in 2022 and 2023 will be $1.79 and $1.88, respectively. In addition, you believe that the price of Coca-Cola stock at the end of 2023 will be $65.00 per share. If the appropriate discount rate is 8.0 percent, what is the value of Coca-Cola stock?

SOLUTION:

To organize your data, you first create the following time line:

Period	0	8.0%	1	2	3 years
Cash flow	PV = ?		$1.72	$1.79	$1.88 + $65.00

Using equation 8-3, you compute the stock value as

$$P_0 = \frac{\$1.72}{1+0.08} + \frac{\$1.79}{(1+0.08)^2} + \frac{\$1.88 + \$65.00}{(1+0.08)^3} = \$1.5926 + \$5346 + \$53.0915 = \$56.22$$

The spreadsheet solution is:

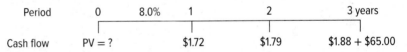

	A	B	C	D	E	F
1	D1 =	$1.72		Discount Rate =	8.00%	
2	D2 =	$1.79				
3	D3 =	$1.88		P0 =	$56.22	
4					=NPV(E1,B1,B2,B3+B5)	
5	P3 =	$65				

Microsoft Excel

Since your analysis shows that Coca-Cola's stock should be valued at $56.22 while it's selling for $54.84, the stock appears to be slightly undervalued. You believe that this might be a good time to buy some Coca-Cola stock.

Similar to Problems 8-8, 8-14, 8-15, Self-Test Problem 1

McDonald's changed to the more common quarterly dividend.
John Flournoy/McGraw-Hill Education

be constant, consider the actual dividends and stock price of McDonald's Corp. since 2000, shown in Figure 8.3.

McDonald's paid an annual dividend from 2000 to 2007. Some increases were small, like the $0.01 increase from 2000 to 2001 and again to 2002. Other increases were quite large, like the $0.50 increase between 2006 and 2007. Then McDonald's changed to the more common quarterly dividend in 2008. Since the change to quarterly payments, McDonald's dividend growth has been more stable and predictable into 2020. The figure also shows that McDonald's stock price has been very volatile. The price fell from a split-adjusted $25 in 2000 to $9.50 in 2003 and then steadily climbed to $45 in 2007. The stock went sideways during the financial crisis and then shot up to $88 in late 2011. The stock again went mostly sideways from 2012 to 2014 and then shot up again in 2015. McDonald's stock price experienced a lot of volatility from 2018 to 2020. An investor in 2000 would have had a very difficult time accurately forecasting these future dividends and stock prices. Indeed, short-term stock price changes seem almost random. Stock valuation can really only be viewed from a long-term perspective. Because predicting future dividends is uncertain at best, it's better to project valuation as a likely range of prices under reasonable assumptions rather than as a single price. After all, this computed price is an estimate of the firm's intrinsic value. This intrinsic value may differ from the stock price trading in the market. This possibility is discussed as a market efficiency topic in Chapter 10.

▼FIGURE 8.3 Dividends and Stock Price of McDonald's since 2000

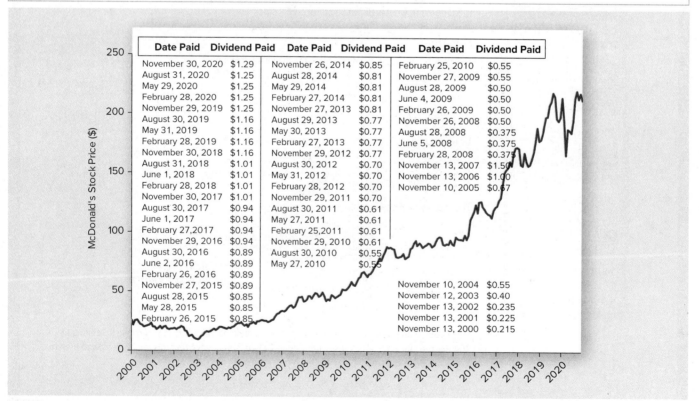

Date Paid	Dividend Paid	Date Paid	Dividend Paid	Date Paid	Dividend Paid
November 30, 2020	$1.29	November 26, 2014	$0.85	February 25, 2010	$0.55
August 31, 2020	$1.25	August 28, 2014	$0.81	November 27, 2009	$0.55
May 29, 2020	$1.25	May 29, 2014	$0.81	August 28, 2009	$0.50
February 28, 2020	$1.25	February 27, 2014	$0.81	June 4, 2009	$0.50
November 29, 2019	$1.25	November 27, 2013	$0.81	February 26, 2009	$0.50
August 30, 2019	$1.16	August 29, 2013	$0.77	November 26, 2008	$0.50
May 31, 2019	$1.16	May 30, 2013	$0.77	August 28, 2008	$0.375
February 28, 2019	$1.16	February 27, 2013	$0.77	June 5, 2008	$0.375
November 30, 2018	$1.16	November 29, 2012	$0.77	February 28, 2008	$0.375
August 31, 2018	$1.01	August 30, 2012	$0.70	November 13, 2007	$1.50
June 1, 2018	$1.01	May 31, 2012	$0.70	November 13, 2006	$1.00
February 28, 2018	$1.01	February 28, 2012	$0.70	November 10, 2005	$0.67
November 30, 2017	$1.01	November 29, 2011	$0.70		
August 30, 2017	$0.94	August 30, 2011	$0.61		
June 1, 2017	$0.94	May 27, 2011	$0.61		
February 27, 2017	$0.94	February 25, 2011	$0.61		
November 29, 2016	$0.94	November 29, 2010	$0.61		
August 30, 2016	$0.89	August 30, 2010	$0.55		
June 2, 2016	$0.89	May 27, 2010	$0.55		
February 26, 2016	$0.89				
November 27, 2015	$0.89			November 10, 2004	$0.55
August 28, 2015	$0.85			November 12, 2003	$0.40
May 28, 2015	$0.85			November 13, 2002	$0.235
February 26, 2015	$0.85			November 13, 2001	$0.225
				November 13, 2000	$0.215

Dividends rarely decline, but stock prices often do!

Dividend Discount Models

We can extend the discounted cash flow approach in equation 8-3 for an infinite stream of dividends, $n \to \infty$, and no final future selling price. If stockholders receive all future cash flows as future dividends, the stock's value to the investor is the present value of all these future dividends. In other words, embedded in any stock price is the value of all future dividends. We can demonstrate this value as

$$P_0 = \frac{D_1}{1+i} + \frac{D_2}{(1+i)^2} + \frac{D_3}{(1+i)^3} + \cdots \qquad (8\text{-}4)$$

This equation shows the general case of the **dividend discount model.** The dividend discount model provides a useful theoretical basis because it illustrates the importance of dividends as a fundamental stock price determinant.

But, again, finance professionals find it difficult to apply the dividend discount model because it requires that they estimate an infinite number of future dividends. To use the model in practice, analysts make simplifying assumptions to make the model workable. One common assumption: The firm has a constant dividend growth rate, g. If this is the case, next year's dividend is simply this year's dividend that grew one year at the growth rate, that is, $D_1 = D_0 \times (1 + g)$. In fact, we can express each dividend as a function of D_0 and we can rewrite equation 8-4 as

$$P_0 = \frac{D_0(1+g)}{1+i} + \frac{D_0(1+g)^2}{(1+i)^2} + \frac{D_0(1+g)^3}{(1+i)^3} + \cdots \qquad (8\text{-}5)$$

So, with this version of the model, we need not forecast an infinite string of dividends; D_0 and g take care of that. However, we must still compute an infinite sum of numbers. Luckily, mathematicians know equations like these; they are known as power series. This power series can be simplified to the **constant-growth model,** and it assumes that the growth rate is smaller than the discount rate (i.e., for $g < i$):

$$\text{Stock value} = \text{Next year's dividend} \div (\text{Discount rate} - \text{Growth rate})$$

$$\text{Constant growth model} = P_0 = \frac{D_0(1+g)}{i-g} = \frac{D_1}{i-g} \qquad (8\text{-}6)$$

If $g \geq i$, then the denominator would be zero or negative. Economically and mathematically, this is a nonsensical result. In the short run, a firm can grow very quickly. In the long run, no company can grow faster than the overall economic growth rate forever. You may hear the constant-growth model referred to as the *Gordon growth model,* after financial economist Myron J. Gordon.

Investors use several methods to estimate a firm's growth rate for this model. They can project the dividend trend into the future and determine the implied growth rate, compute the past growth rate, or even consider a financial analyst's growth rate predictions. Consider Coca-Cola's dividend behavior. If the 2020 dividend was $1.64 and the projected dividends will grow to $1.88 in 2023, the implied projected dividend growth rate is therefore 4.66 percent (N = 3, PV = −1.64, PMT = 0, FV = 1.88, CPT I = 3.91) annually. The growth rate in dividend changes from 2014 to 2020 was 4.44 percent (N = 6, PV = −1.22, PMT = 0, FV = 1.64, CPT I = 5.05) per year. You can find analyst forecasts many places online. The Yahoo! Finance web page for Coca-Cola has an Analyst Estimates link, which shows the average analysts' forecast for the firm's growth in the next five years at 2.77 percent at the beginning of 2021.

Preferred Stock

A special case of the constant-growth model occurs when the dividend does not grow but is the same every year. This zero-growth rate case describes a **preferred stock.** The term *preferred* comes from the fact that this type of stock takes preference over common stock

> **dividend discount model** A valuation approach based on future dividend income.
>
> **constant-growth model** A valuation method based on constantly growing dividends.
>
> **preferred stock** A hybrid security that has characteristics of both long-term debt and common stock.

EXAMPLE 8-2

Constant Growth and Coca-Cola Stock LG8-3

Assume that you are valuing Coca-Cola stock again. This time you are using the constant-growth model, assuming a discount rate of 11.0 percent.

SOLUTION:

You have a choice of three growth rates to use. The implied projected dividend growth rate is 4.66 percent. Past dividend growth has been 5.05 percent, and analysts forecast a 2.77 percent growth. Compute the stock value using all three growth rates.

Using a dividend growth rate of 4.66 percent and equation 8-6, the stock value is $51.39:

$$P_0 = \frac{\$1.64 \times (1 + 0.0466)}{0.080 - 0.0466} = \$51.39$$

Using a dividend growth rate of 5.05 percent, the stock value is $58.40:

$$P_0 = \frac{\$1.64 \times (1 + 0.0505)}{0.080 - 0.0505} = \$58.40$$

Using a dividend growth rate of 2.77 percent, the stock value is $32.23:

$$P_0 = \frac{\$1.64 \times (1 + 0.0277)}{0.080 - 0.0277} = \$32.23$$

Notice how a small change in the growth rate has a large impact on the stock value in this model. At a current price of $54.84 per share, Coca-Cola could be considered undervalued or overvalued depending on the growth rate used.

Similar to Problems 8-10, 8-16, 8-17, Self-Test Problem 2

in bankruptcy proceedings. Preferred stockholders have a higher priority for receiving proceeds from bankruptcy proceedings than do common stockholders. Preferred stock is largely owned by other companies, rather than by individual investors, because its dividends are mostly nontaxable income (70 percent of the income is exempt from taxes) to other corporations. Preferred stockholders do not have voting rights like common stockholders, though, which prevents one company from controlling another through preferred stock ownership.

An interesting characteristic of preferred stock is that it pays a constant dividend. Because the dividend does not change, the preferred stock can be valued using the constant-growth-rate model with a zero growth rate expressed as $P = D/i$. What would Coca-Cola's stock be worth if its dividend stayed at $1.64 and never grew? Using the same 8.0 percent discount rate, the stock would be valued at $20.50 (= $1.64 ÷ 0.080). Given Coca-Cola's current stock price of $54.84, over 62 percent [=($54.84 − $20.50)/$54.84] of its stock value comes from the expectation that Coca-Cola's dividend will grow. In other words, investors highly value a growing firm.

the
Math Coach on...

Using the Constant-Growth-Rate Model

❝ The distinction between the recent year's dividends, D_0, and next year's dividends, D_1, can be confusing in the constant-growth-rate model. The model's equation presents two different numerators. If you are given information about dividends last year or just paid, use the $D_0(1 + g)$ version of the equation. If you have information about expected dividends or next year's dividend, use the D_1 version of the equation. ❞

Most companies issue only common stock, but nearly 1,000 preferred stock issues still exist. Table 8.2 compares the common stock and preferred stock for four firms. Many of the preferred stocks come from the finance, energy, and real estate sectors. Notice that the **dividend yield** for preferred stock is usually higher than for the common stock, because preferred stock investors should expect a return from dividend payments only. Common stockholders will also expect a return from capital appreciation over time. Common stocks also trade much more frequently than do preferred stocks.

The zero-growth-rate version of the constant-growth valuation model shows that, since dividends are fixed, a preferred stock's price changes because of changes in the discount rate, i. When interest rates throughout the economy change, the discount rate also changes. Preferred stock prices thus tend to act like bond prices. When interest rates rise, preferred stock prices fall. When interest rates decline, preferred stock prices rise. Preferred stock is usually categorized with bonds in the fixed-income security group because it acts so much like debt securities, even though a preferred stock represents equity ownership, like common stock.

Expected Return

Stock valuation models require a discount rate, i, in order to compute the present value of the future cash flows. The discount rate used should reflect the investment risk level. Higher-risk investments should be evaluated using higher interest rates. For example, the previous chapter on bonds demonstrated that higher-risk bonds, such as junk bonds, offer higher rates of return. Similarly, investors demand higher returns from higher-risk stocks than they do from lower-risk stocks. We discuss stock risk measurement and appropriate expected returns in the next section of this book.

However, one method for determining what return stock investors require from a stock is to use the constant-growth-rate model. If the current stock price fairly reflects its value, then the discount rate, i, in equation 8-6 should be the expected return for the stock. Solving for this expected return results in equation 8-7:

$$\text{Expected return} = i = \frac{D_1}{P_0} + g = \text{Dividend yield} + \text{Capital gain} \qquad (8\text{-}7)$$

Note that the expected return comes again from two sources: dividend yield and expected appreciation of the stock price, or capital gain. At the beginning of 2021, consider that Coca-Cola's 2021 expected dividend, D_1, is expected to be $1.72 per share. At a current price of $54.84, Coca-Cola offers a dividend yield of 3.14 percent (= $1.72 ÷ $54.84). Since analysts believe that the firm's stock price will grow at 2.77% percent in the future, investors expect a total return of 5.91 percent (= 3.14% + 2.77%). Dividend yield can represent a substantial portion of the profits for an investor. Many people get too enamored of high **growth stocks** that do not pay dividends and therefore miss out on an important source of stable returns.

Corporate managers conduct an important application of the expected return concept to determine the return that their shareholders expect of them. We will discuss this application in detail in Part Six: Capital Budgeting.

dividend yield Last four quarters of dividend income expressed as a percentage of the current stock price.

growth stocks Companies expected to have above-average rates of growth in revenue, earnings, and/or dividends.

time out!

8-8 Explain how valuable a firm's (and therefore its stock's) growth is. Demonstrate this with growth and no-growth examples.

8-9 What proportion of the 5.91 percent of Coca-Cola's expected return above comes from dividend yield?

▼ **TABLE 8.2** Common and Preferred Stock, December 31, 2020

		COMMON STOCK				PREFERRED STOCK		
Company	Ticker	Price	Annual Dividend (Yield%)	Volume	Ticker	Price	Annual Dividend (Yield%)	Volume
Citigroup	C	$ 61.66	$2.04 (3.3)	23,610,858	C.PRS	$25.56	$1.58 (6.2)	65,536
Goldman Sachs Group	GS	$237.00	$3.20 (1.3)	2,687,378	GS.PRA	$24.58	$0.97 (3.9)	48,456
Public Storage Inc.	PSA	$230.93	$8.00 (3.5)	833,144	PSA.PRB	$25.07	$1.35 (5.4)	28,695
Willamette Valley Vineyard	WVVI	$ 6.37	$0.00 (0.0)	6,418	WVVIP	$ 5.36	$0.88 (4.1)	738

Source: The Wall Street Journal Data Center (www.wsj.com).

finance at work //:investments

8.4 • ADDITIONAL VALUATION METHODS LG8-6

Variable-Growth Techniques

It is useful to use a variable-growth-rate technique for three kinds of companies: temporarily struggling, high growth with no current dividends, and moderately high growth. First, some firms may be temporarily struggling and have a lower growth rate than usual for a few years. Once they overcome their difficulties, they resume their normal growth. For these firms, the first-stage growth rate will be lower than the second-stage growth rate. Second, some companies grow at such a high rate that we cannot use the constant-growth-rate model to forecast their value. Indeed, these firms often need all of their cash for creating that high growth and thus do not pay a dividend. High growth rates might be sustainable for several years but cannot continue forever. Once the growth rate slows down, these firms begin paying dividends. Thus, for these firms, the first-stage dividend is zero. The second stage would model a dividend initiation and a moderate growth rate. Lastly, some firms may be temporarily growing quickly, but the growth rate will eventually decline to a more sustainable level. In this case, the first-stage growth rate will be higher than the second-stage growth rate.

Remember that the constant-growth-rate model does not work for companies where $g > i$. And, of course, we do not really expect the growth rate for these fast-growing firms to remain constant. To value these firms, we must use a **variable-growth-rate** technique. The variable-growth-rate method combines the present-value cash flow from equation 8-3 and the constant-growth-rate model from equation 8-6.

First, the investor chooses two different growth rates for two stages of the analysis. The first and higher growth rate, g_1, is the current growth rate, which we expect to last only a few years. A few years from now, we expect the firm to grow at a slower but more sustainable rate of growth, g_2. Figure 8.4 shows the cash flow time line when the first growth rate applies for the first n years, followed by the second growth rate, which applies forever.

When we analyze a variable-growth-rate stock like the one in the figure, we know the recent dividend, D_0, and the two expected growth rates. Therefore, we can calculate each of the dividends shown in general terms (i.e., D_1). For example, the dividend in the first year (D_1) is the year-zero dividend that grows at g_1, specifically $D_1 = D_0 \times (1 + g_1)$. The dividend then grows at g_1 again for the second-year dividend, $D_2 = D_0 \times (1 + g_1)^2$. The dividend continues to grow through the first stage to year n at $D_n = D_0 \times (1 + g_1)^n$. Figure 8.5 shows the first-stage dividends.

At this point, the company starts to move into Stage 2 at the more modest growth rate, g_2, and the dividends reflect that slower growth rate. So D_{n+1} is the dividend D_n that grew at the rate g_2, or $D_{n+1} = D_0 \times (1 + g_1)^n \times (1 + g_2)$. Similarly, the dividend in year $n + 2$ is $D_{n+2} = D_0 \times (1 + g_1)^n \times (1 + g_2)^2$. We can now substitute the known dividends as presented in Figure 8.5 into Figure 8.6.

Once we have calculated all of the dividends, we can begin finding the value of the variable-growth stock by focusing on Stage 2 of the problem. Assume that the dividends in Stage 2 are growing at a modest rate, g_2, forever. As long as $g_2 < i$, Stage 2 can use the constant-growth model, equation 8-6. Remember that the constant-growth model, $P_0 = D_1/(i - g)$,

variable growth rate A valuation technique used when a firm's current growth rate is expected to change some time in the future.

▼**FIGURE 8.4** Variable Dividend Growth

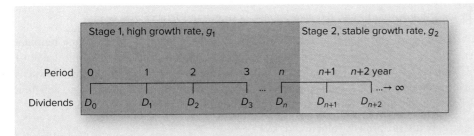

Divide into two stages at the first year of the new growth rate.

▼**FIGURE 8.5** Stage 1 Dividends

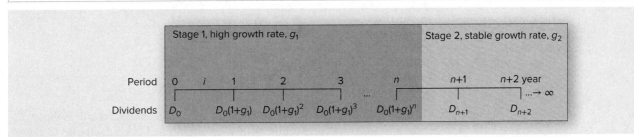

Calculate the dividends in the first stage.

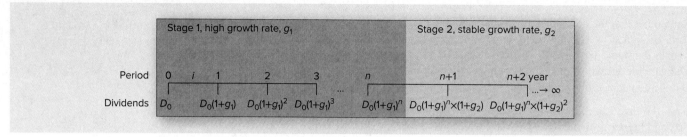

Compute the dividends in the second stage.

▼**FIGURE 8.7** New Stage 1 of the Variable-Growth Dividend Technique

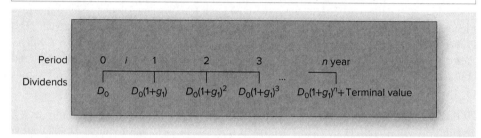

Replace all of the dividends to infinity with the price (terminal value) in year n. Stage 2 disappears.

replaces all future dividends with one value in the previous period. In previous applications, the growth began in year 1, so the value used for all future dividends came from the year 0 dividend. In this case, the change in the dividend rate occurs in year $n + 1$, so we will use the value from year n. So, using the constant-growth model, we can replace all the cash flows in Stage 2 with one value from year n, as

$$P_n = \frac{D_{n+1}}{i - g_2} = \frac{D_0(1 + g_1)^n(1 + g_2)}{i - g}$$

The cash flows from Figure 8.6 now appear as shown in Figure 8.7.

By replacing all the Stage 2 cash flows that continued indefinitely with one terminal price in year n, we reduce the problem to a fixed number of cash flows. The value of this variable-growth stock is finally computed as the present value of these cash flows, as solved with equation 8-3. Substituting the cash flows shown in Figure 8.7 into equation 8-3 gives us the general formula for finding the value of a variable-growth stock:

General two-stage growth valuation model:

Stock value = Present value of each dividend during the first growth stage
+ Present value of the second stage growth

$$P_0 = \frac{D_0(1 + g_1)}{1 + i} + \frac{D_0(1 + g_1)^2}{(1 + i)^2} + \frac{D_0(1 + g_1)^3}{(1 + i)^3} + \dots$$

$$+ \frac{D_0(1 + g_1)^n + \text{Terminal value}}{(1 + i)^n}$$

(8-8)

where Terminal value $= \dfrac{D_0(1 + g_1)^n(1 + g_2)}{i - g_2}$

The practical application of the variable-growth valuation technique requires the investor to decide how long the current high growth rate will last before declining to a more stable rate.

The constant-growth-rate model is most useful for large, mature companies that grow in a stable manner. The variable-growth-rate model is more flexible and can estimate the value of companies that are expected to change growth rates or even initiate dividends. But there are still many firms that do not fit these descriptions of firm growth. For example, many firms pay no dividends and have no plans to initiate dividend payments. To value firms with no dividends, replace the dividends in the models with cash flows. When you

EXAMPLE 8-3

For interactive versions of this example, log in to Connect or go to mhhe.com/Cornett6e.

Variable Growth and Stock Value LG8-6

Consider that a firm's dividend has grown over 6 years from $1.00 per share to $2.20. This represents an annual growth rate of 21.8 percent (N = 6, PV = −1.00, PMT = 0, FV = 220, CPT I = 21.8) You think this growth rate will continue for three years and then fall to the long-term growth rate of 10.2 percent predicted by analysts. You assume a 14 percent discount rate.

SOLUTION:

Modify equation 8-8 for a Stage 1 length of three years and then substitute $i = 0.14$, $g_1 = 0.218$, $g_2 = 0.102$, and $D_0 = \$2.20$. The valuation equation and solution become

Period	0	14.0%	1	2	3

Dividends $D_0 = \$2.20$ $D_1 = \$2.20$ $D_2 = \$2.20$ $D_3 = \$2.20$
$\times (1.218)$ $\times (1.218)^2$ $\times (1.218)^3$

$$P_3 = \$2.20 \times (1.218)^3$$
$$\times (1.102)$$
$$\div (0.14 - 0.102)$$

$$P_0 = \frac{\$2.20(1 + 0.218)}{1 + 0.14} + \frac{\$2.20(1 + 0.218)^2}{(1 + 0.14)^2} + \frac{\$2.20(1 + 0.218)^3 + \text{Terminal value}}{(1 + 0.14)^3}$$

where Terminal value $= \dfrac{\$2.20(1 + 0.218)^3 \times (1 + 0.102)}{0.14 - 0.102} = \$115.28$

$$= \$2.68 + \$3.26 + \frac{\$3.98 + \$115.28}{1.482}$$

$$= \$86.44$$

Given these parameters, the company's stock is worth $86.44 per share.

The spreadsheet solution is:

◢	A	B	C
1	D_0	$2.20	
2	Growth in years 1-3	21.8%	
3	Growth after year 3	10.20%	
4	Discount Rate	14.00%	
5			
6	D_1 =	$ 2.68	=B1*(1+B2)
7	D_2 =	$ 3.26	=B6*(1+B2)
8	D_3 =	$ 3.98	=B7*(1+B2)
9	P_3 =	$ 115.28	=B8*(1+B3)/(B4-B3)
10			
11	P_0 =	$ 86.44	=B6+B7+NPV(B4,0,0,B8+B9)

Microsoft Excel

Similar to Problem 8-18, Self-Test Problem 3

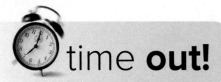

time out!

8-10 Explain how the variable-growth-rate technique could be used for a firm whose dividend is not expected to grow for three years and then will grow at 5 percent indefinitely.

8-11 Set up and solve the valuation problem of Example 8.3 assuming that the first-stage growth will last only two years.

relative value A stock's priceyness measured relative to other stocks.

price-earnings (P/E) ratio Current stock price divided by four quarters of earnings per share.

trailing P/E ratio The P/E ratio computed using the *past* four quarters of earnings per share.

do this, you are valuing the entire firm, not just the stock value, because cash flows go to both stockholders and debt holders. In the case where a firm has low or even negative cash flows, the valuation techniques in the next section can be employed.

The P/E Model LG8-7

The valuation models that we've presented thus far help investors attempt to compute a stock's fundamental value based upon its cash flows to the investor. Another common approach is to assess a stock's **relative value.** This approach compares one company's stock valuation to other firms' stock values to evaluate whether your target company's stock is appropriately priced. The price of a stock taken in isolation doesn't give us a good measure of how expensive it is. Let's use an analogy: At the grocery store, we are less concerned with the total price of a bag of sugar than we are with the price per pound. Similarly, the price of the stock matters less than its price per one dollar of earnings.

Consider one company that earned $5 per share in profits for the year. Its stock sells for $100. Another company earned $2 per share and its stock price is $50 per share. At first glance, the first stock appears to be more expensive because its price is a high $100 compared to the lower $50 price of the second stock. However, the first company generated higher per-share profits than did the second company. Buying the first stock means that you purchase $5 in earnings. The $100 stock price implies a cost of $20 for every $1 in earnings (=$100 ÷ $5) generated. The $50 price of the second stock implies a cost of $25 for every $1 in earnings (=$50 ÷ $2). So in this regard, the second company becomes more expensive. The **price-earnings (P/E) ratio** represents the most common valuation yardstick in the investment industry; it allows investors to quickly compare the cost of earnings. The P/E ratio is simply the current price of the stock divided by the last four quarters of earnings per share:

$$P/E = \frac{\text{Current stock price}}{\text{Per-share earnings for last 12 months}} \tag{8-9}$$

More accurately, this figure is the **trailing P/E ratio,** and it is often denoted as P/E_0, where the 0 subscript denotes the past (or trailing) earnings.

Figure 8.8 shows two companies' trailing P/E ratios: Coca-Cola and McDonald's, as well as the S&P 500 Index's trailing P/E ratio over a 24-year period. The P/E ratio for the S&P500 changes slowly and mostly stays in the 16 to 25 range, though the period leading up to the financial crisis is an exception. Historically, the S&P 500's P/E ratio has fallen as low as single digits and climbed to over 60. The figure also shows that the P/E ratio for McDonald's has varied less than has Index's P/E ratio. The P/E ratio for Coca-Cola has experienced wild changes—as high as 64 and as low as 7. Figure 8.8 shows that investors valued Coca-Cola more than McDonald's in the late 1990s, but valued them nearly the same by the beginning of 2008 until 2016.

Variations in P/E ratios between popular companies can be quite large. For example, in December of 2020, the P/E ratio for Amazon.com Inc. was 95.23, while the ratio for Procter & Gamble was only 26.59. Amazon stock is much more expensive than Procter & Gamble stock. But this does not mean that Procter & Gamble stock is a better deal than Amazon stock. Investors are willing to pay much more in relative terms for Amazon because they expect Amazon will grow much faster than Procter & Gamble. Indeed, analysts predict an annual growth rate of 36.35 percent per year for Amazon over the next five years, while they expect a growth rate of only 8.47 percent for Procter & Gamble. Remember that Example 8-2 shows how small changes in growth can result in large stock value changes. The large difference in expected growth between Procter & Gamble and Amazon causes a large difference in their relative value.

We can more directly see the impact that growth can have on the P/E ratio by modifying the constant-growth model. Begin with the model, $P_0 = D_1 \div (i - g)$. Dividing both sides by the firm's earnings results in $P_0/E_0 = (D_1/E_0) \div (i - g)$. Note that the dividend payout

FIGURE 8.8 Historical P/E Ratio of the S&P 500 Index, Coca-Cola, and McDonald's

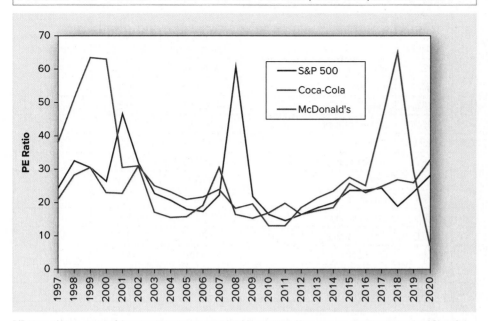

P/E ratios of large, successful companies can vary considerably over time. Here, you see that investors valued Coca-Cola over McDonald's for much of the period, but there were periods when McDonald's was valued higher.

Source: Morningstar.com.

forward P/E ratio The P/E ratio computed using the *estimated* next four quarters of earnings per share.

ratio of the firm (*D/E*), the discount rate (*i*), and the growth rate (*g*), taken together, determine the P/E ratio. All else held equal, larger growth rates will lead to larger P/E ratios. Also, firms that have higher payout ratios will have higher P/E ratios. Of course, if a firm pays out a high portion of its earnings as dividends, then it may not have the cash to fund high growth. Thus, high-dividend-payout firms tend not to be priced the same as high-growth firms.

The value of a stock, and thus its price, relates directly to its future success. Note that valuation models use estimates of future dividends and growth rates. Because of this focus on the future, many people prefer to use a P/E ratio that also looks forward rather than trailing. A **forward P/E ratio** uses analyst estimates of the earnings in the next 12 months instead of the past 12 months and can be denoted as P/E. The forward P/E ratio has the advantage over the trailing P/E ratio in that it incorporates investors' expectations of the firm's upcoming profits. A disadvantage is that expected earnings are harder to estimate and thus less accurate than past earnings. The media uses the trailing P/E ratio, while financial managers and investors use the forward P/E ratio more.

Knowledgeable investors who use the P/E ratio as a relative measure of value compare it to the firm's expected growth rate. Table 8.3 shows the forward P/E ratio and analysts' expected growth rates for the 30 Dow Jones Industrial Average firms. Investors consider companies with high P/E ratios and high growth rates to be appropriately priced. Companies with low P/E ratios and low growth also seem to be appropriately priced. Investors should be concerned about firms with high P/E ratios and only single-digit growth rates. As such, salesforce.com, Visa, Chevron, Boeing, and McDonald's, among others, may be too expensive for their expected growth rates. Many investors like to buy growth stocks. They seek companies with high growth rates. But growth stock investors are also concerned about

Investors consider the Walt Disney Company an appropriately priced stock.
Lucian Milasan/Shutterstock

▼ **TABLE 8.3** P/E Ratios and Analyst Growth Estimates of DJIA Firms, December 31, 2020

	A	B	C	D	E
1	Ticker	Company Name	Stock Price	Forward P/E Ratio	Next 5 Year's Growth (%)
2	DIS	Walt Disney	$181.18	84.03	41.57
3	WMT	Walmart	144.15	25.25	6.81
4	DOW	Dow	55.50	20.37	−6.51
5	CRM	salesforce.com	222.53	64.10	17.69
6	NKE	NIKE	141.47	51.02	34.30
7	HD	Home Depot	265.62	21.93	7.60
8	V	Visa	218.73	37.88	12.02
9	MSFT	Microsoft	222.42	33.00	14.55
10	MMM	3M Company	174.79	18.55	4.23
11	CSCO	Cisco Systems	44.75	14.33	6.14
12	KO	Coca-Cola	54.84	24.51	2.77
13	AAPL	Apple	132.69	34.01	12.64
14	HON	Honeywell International	212.70	27.10	3.02
15	JNJ	Johnson & Johnson	157.38	16.92	4.38
16	TRV	Travelers Companies	140.37	13.40	4.48
17	PG	Procter & Gamble	139.14	25.77	8.47
18	CVX	Chevron Corporation	84.45	34.60	−2.92
19	VZ	Verizon	58.75	11.79	2.37
20	CAT	Caterpillar	182.02	24.27	−2.72
21	BA	Boeing Company	214.06	90.91	12.33
22	AMGN	Amgen	229.92	13.40	6.65
23	IBM	International Business Machines	125.88	10.65	−1.09
24	AXP	American Express	120.91	17.42	9.25
25	JPM	JPMorgan Chase	127.07	13.33	−0.91
26	WBA	Walgreens Boots Alliance	39.88	8.14	6.99
27	MCD	McDonald's	214.58	24.94	5.59
28	MRK	Merck	81.80	12.41	7.48
29	GS	Goldman Sachs	263.71	10.27	10.71
30	UNH	UnitedHealth Group	350.68	18.73	12.34
31	INTC	Intel	49.82	10.42	7.94

Source: Yahoo! Finance Screener.

Microsoft Excel

paying too much for a stock. While examining growth stocks, they can use the P/E ratio to assess how expensive the stock is. On the other hand, investors consider companies with low P/E ratios and high expected growth to be undervalued, and they are often referred to as **value stocks.** American Express, UnitedHealth, and Goldman Sachs would qualify as value stocks. Many investors like to buy value stocks because they feel they are getting a bargain price for a stable company.

There are some cases when a P/E ratio is not useful for relative valuation. For example, sometimes, a firm will lose money. That is, the earnings are negative. In other cases, a firm will take a large "write-off" that will temporarily suppress earnings. In these cases, the P/E ratio would be negative or temporarily large. Therefore, other common relative value techniques are to utilize cash flow (CF) or book value (B) instead of earnings. The P/CF ratio

EXAMPLE 8-4

For interactive versions of this example, log in to Connect or go to mhhe.com/Cornett6e.

The P/E Ratio Model for Procter & Gamble LG8-7

Look at Table 8.3 and notice that the P/E ratio for Procter & Gamble seems high at 25.77 relative to the growth (8.47 percent) that analysts expect. Procter & Gamble earned $5.23 per share and paid a $3.16 dividend last year. You decide to explore this apparent anomaly and figure out what Procter & Gamble's stock price might reach in five years.

SOLUTION:

Compute the expected future price in five years under two different scenarios. The first assumption is that Procter & Gamble's P/E ratio will be the same in five years as it is today. But since this P/E ratio seems a bit high, the second scenario allows for a decline in the P/E ratio to 20. Under these two scenarios, the future price estimates are

$$P_5 = (P/E)_n \times E_0 \times (1 + g)^n = 25.77 \times \$5.23 \times (1 + 0.0847)^5 = \$202.38$$

$$P_5 = (P/E)_n \times (1 + g)^n = 20 \times \$5.23 \times (1 + 0.0847)^5 = \$157.07$$

Note that if the P/E ratio decreases from 25.77 to 20 in five years, the future price could be much lower than analysts expect without the change.

The spreadsheet solution is:

	A	B	C	D
1	P/E =	25.77		20
2	E_0 =	$5.23		$5.23
3	g =	8.47%		8.47%
4				
5	P_5 =	$202.38		$157.07
6		=B1*B2*(1+B3)^5		=D1*D2*(1+D3)^5

Microsoft Excel

Similar to Problems 8-13, 8-19, 8-20

---

is useful when firms take accounting write-offs that temporarily and dramatically impact earnings. The P/B ratio is useful in all cases but is particularly useful when a firm loses money and has negative cash flows. The book value of a firm is a very stable measure of accounting value, and it is therefore useful when earnings are volatile.

Estimating Future Stock Prices

We can often find it useful to estimate a stock's future price. Consider equation 8-3's cash flow discount valuation model. The model requires estimates of future dividends and a future price. How can investors estimate this future price? They can use the P/E ratio model for this purpose. Upon reflection, you will see that multiplying the P/E ratio by earnings results in a stock price. So, in order to estimate a future price, simply multiply the expected P/E ratio by the expected earnings. This concept is captured in the following equation:

Future price = Future P/E ratio × Future earnings per share

$$P_n = (P/E)_n \times E_n \tag{8-10}$$
$$= (P/E)_n \times E_0 \times (1 + g)^n$$

As the formula shows, we can use assumptions about the earnings growth rate to estimate earnings in year n. Many investors believe the firm's P/E ratio in year n is best estimated using today's P/E ratio. However, if today's P/E ratio seems unusual compared with similar firms or even compared with a stock index, then adjustments might be wise.

time out!

8-12 Consider two firms with the same P/E ratio. Explain how one could be described as expensive compared to the other.

8-13 From the data in Example 8-4, compute the stock price in five years if you expect the P/E ratio to decline to 18.

Get Online

mhhe.com/CornettM6e

for study materials including

quizzes, iPod downloads,

and video

JGI/Jamie Grill/Getty Images

Your Turn...

Questions

1. As owners, what rights and advantages do shareholders obtain? *(LG8-1)*

2. Describe how being a residual claimant can be very valuable. *(LG8-1)*

3. Obtain a current quote of McDonald's (MCD) from the Internet. Describe what has changed since the quote in Figure 8.1. *(LG8-2)*

4. Get the trading statistics for the three main U.S. stock exchanges. Compare the trading activity to that of Table 8.1. *(LG8-2)*

5. Why might the Standard & Poor's 500 Index be a better measure of stock market performance than the Dow Jones Industrial Average? Why is the DJIA more popular than the S&P 500? *(LG8-3)*

6. Explain how it is possible for the DJIA to increase one day while the NASDAQ Composite decreases during the same day. *(LG8-3)*

7. Which is higher, the ask quote or the bid quote? Why? *(LG8-4)*

8. Illustrate through examples how trading commission costs impact an investor's return. *(LG8-4)*

9. Describe the difference in the timing of trade execution and the certainty of trade price between market orders and limit orders. *(LG8-4)*

10. What are the differences between common stock and preferred stock? *(LG8-5)*

11. How important is growth to a stock's value? Illustrate with examples. *(LG8-5)*

12. Under what conditions would the constant-growth model *not* be appropriate? *(LG8-5)*

13. The expected return derived from the constant-growth-rate model relies on dividend yield and capital gain. Where do these two parts of the return come from? *(LG8-5)*

14. Describe, in words, how to use the variable-growth-rate technique to value a stock. *(LG8-6)*

15. Can the variable-growth-rate model be used to value a firm that has a negative growth rate in Stage 1 and a stable and positive growth in Stage 2? Explain. *(LG8-6)*

16. Explain why using the P/E relative value approach may be useful for companies that do not pay dividends. *(LG8-7)*

17. How is a firm's changing P/E ratio reflected in the stock price? Give examples. *(LG8-7)*

18. Differentiate the characteristics of growth stocks and value stocks. *(LG8-7)*

19. What's the relationship between the P/E ratio and a firm's growth rate? *(LG8-7)*

20. Describe the process for using the P/E ratio to estimate a future stock price. *(LG8-7)*

Problems

BASIC PROBLEMS

8-1   **Stock Index Performance** On March 5, 2013, the Dow Jones Industrial Average set a new high. The index closed at 14,253.77, which was up 125.95 that day. What was the return (in percent) of the stock market that day? *(LG8-3)*

8-2   **Buying Stock with Commissions** Your discount brokerage firm charges $7.95 per stock trade. How much money do you need to buy 200 shares of Pfizer, Inc. (PFE), which trades at $31.40? *(LG8-4)*

8-3   **Selling Stock with Commissions** Your full-service brokerage firm charges $140 per stock trade. How much money do you receive after selling 200 shares of Nokia Corporation (NOK), which trades at $20.13? *(LG8-4)*

8-4   **Buying Stock with a Market Order** You would like to buy shares of Sirius Satellite Radio (SIRI). The current ask and bid quotes are $3.96 and $3.93, respectively. You place a market buy order for 500 shares that executes at these quoted prices. How much money did it cost to buy these shares? *(LG8-4)*

8-5   **Selling Stock with a Limit Order** You would like to sell 200 shares of Xenith Bankshares, Inc. (XBKS). The current ask and bid quotes are $4.66 and $4.62, respectively. You place a limit sell order at $4.65. If the trade executes, how much money do you receive from the buyer? *(LG8-4)*

8-6   **Value of a Preferred Stock** A preferred stock from Duquesne Light Company (DQUPRA) pays $3.55 in annual dividends. If the required return on the preferred stock is 6.7 percent, what's the value of the stock? *(LG8-5)*

8-7   **P/E Ratio and Stock Price** Ultra Petroleum (UPL) has earnings per share of $1.56 and a P/E ratio of 32.48. What's the stock price? *(LG8-7)*

INTERMEDIATE PROBLEMS

8-8   **Value of Dividends and Future Price** A firm is expected to pay a dividend of $1.35 next year and $1.50 the following year. Financial analysts believe the stock will be at their price target of $68 in two years. Compute the value of this stock with a required return of 10 percent. *(LG8-5)*

8-9 **Dividend Growth** Annual dividends of ATTA Corp. grew from $0.96 in 2005 to $1.76 in 2017. What was the annual growth rate? *(LG8-5)*

8-10 **Value a Constant-Growth Stock** Financial analysts forecast Safeco Corp.'s (SAF) growth rate for the future to be 8 percent. Safeco's recent dividend was $0.88. What is the value of Safeco stock when the required return is 12 percent? *(LG8-5)*

8-11 **Expected Return** Ecolap Inc. (ECL) recently paid a $0.46 dividend. The dividend is expected to grow at a 14.5 percent rate. At a current stock price of $44.12, what is the return shareholders are expecting? *(LG8-5)*

8-12 **Dividend Initiation and Stock Value** A firm does not pay a dividend. It is expected to pay its first dividend of $0.20 per share in three years. This dividend will grow at 11 percent indefinitely. Using a 12 percent discount rate, compute the value of this stock. *(LG8-6)*

8-13 **P/E Ratio Model and Future Price** Kellogg Co. (K) recently earned a profit of $2.52 earnings per share and has a P/E ratio of 13.5. The dividend has been growing at a 5 percent rate over the past few years. If this growth rate continues, what would be the stock price in five years if the P/E ratio remained unchanged? What would the price be if the P/E ratio declined to 12 in five years? *(LG8-7)*

 8-14 **Spreadsheet Problem: Value of Dividends and Future Price** A firm is expected to pay a dividend of $2.05 next year. In the next four years, dividends are expected to be $2.20, $2.40, $2.65, and $2.95, respectively. Financial analysts believe the stock will be at their price target of $140 in five years. Compute the value of this stock with a required return of 9 percent. *(LG8-5)*

ADVANCED PROBLEMS

8-15 **Value of Future Cash Flows** A firm recently paid a $0.45 annual dividend. The dividend is expected to increase by 10 percent in each of the next four years. In the fourth year, the stock price is expected to be $80. If the required return for this stock is 13.5 percent, what is its value? *(LG8-5)*

8-16 **Constant Growth Stock Valuation** Waller Co. paid a $0.137 dividend per share in 2000, which grew to $0.55 in 2012. This growth is expected to continue. What is the value of this stock at the beginning of 2013 when the required return is 13.7 percent? *(LG8-5)*

8-17 **Changes in Growth and Stock Valuation** Consider a firm that had been priced using a 10 percent growth rate and a 12 percent required return. The firm recently paid a $1.20 dividend. The firm just announced that because of a new joint venture, it will likely grow at a 10.5 percent rate. How much should the stock price change (in dollars and percentage)? *(LG8-5)*

8-18 **Variable Growth** A fast-growing firm recently paid a dividend of $0.35 per share. The dividend is expected to increase at a 20 percent rate for the next three years. Afterward, a more stable 12 percent growth rate can be assumed. If a 13 percent discount rate is appropriate for this stock, what is its value? *(LG8-6)*

8-19 **P/E Model and Cash Flow Valuation** Suppose that a firm's recent earnings per share and dividend per share are $2.50 and $1.30, respectively. Both are expected to grow at 8 percent. However, the firm's current P/E ratio of 22 seems high for this growth rate. The P/E ratio is expected to fall to 18 within five years. Compute a value for this stock by first estimating the dividends over the next five years and the stock price in five years. Then discount these cash flows using a 10 percent required rate. *(LG8-5, LG8-7)*

 8-20 **Spreadsheet Problem: P/E Model and Cash Flow Valuation** Suppose that a firm's recent earnings per share and dividend per share are $2.75 and $1.60, respectively. Both are expected to grow at 9 percent. However, the firm's current P/E ratio of 23 seems high for this growth rate. The P/E ratio is expected to fall to 19 within five years. Compute a value for this stock by first estimating the dividends over the next five years and the stock price in five years. Then discount these cash flows using an 11 percent required rate. *(LG8-5, LG8-7)*

8-21 **Spreadsheet Problem: Variable Growth** Spreadsheets are especially useful for computing stock value under different assumptions. Consider a firm that is expected to pay the following dividends:

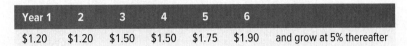

Year 1	2	3	4	5	6	
$1.20	$1.20	$1.50	$1.50	$1.75	$1.90	and grow at 5% thereafter

a. Using an 11 percent discount rate, what would be the value of this stock?

b. What is the value of the stock using a 10 percent discount rate? A 12 percent discount rate?

c. What would the value be using a 6 percent growth rate after year 6 instead of the 5 percent rate using each of these three discount rates?

d. What do you conclude about stock valuation and its assumptions?

8-22 **Spreadsheet Problem: Variable Growth** Design a spreadsheet similar to the one below to compute the value of a variable growth rate firm over a five-year horizon.

	A	B	C	D	E	F
1	**Inputs**					
2	Current dividend =					
3	First-stage growth =					
4	Second-stage growth =					
5	Discount rate =					
6						
7	**Year**	**1**	**2**	**3**	**4**	**5**
8	Projected dividend					
9					Terminal price =	
10	Present value =				Terminal price =	

Microsoft Excel

a. What is the value of the stock if the current dividend is $1.30, the first-stage growth is 18 percent, the second-stage growth is 9 percent, and the discount rate is 11 percent?

b. What is the value of the stock if the current dividend is $1.30, the first-stage growth is 2 percent, the second-stage growth is 8 percent, and the discount rate is 9.5 percent?

c. What is the value of the stock if the current dividend is $2.50, the first-stage growth is 15 percent, the second-stage growth is 7 percent, and the discount rate is 10 percent?

characterizing
risk and return

You can invest your money very safely by opening a savings account at a bank or by buying Treasury bills. So why would you invest your money in risky stocks and bonds if you can take advantage of low-risk opportunities? The answer: Very-low-risk investments also provide a very low return. Investors take on higher risk investments in expectation of earning higher returns. Likewise, businesses also take on risky capital investments only if they expect to earn higher returns that at least cover their costs, including investors' required return. Both investor and business sentiments create a positive relationship between risk and expected return. Of course, taking risk means that you get no guarantee that you will recoup your investment. In the short run, higher risk investments often significantly underperform lower risk investments. In addition, not all forms of risk are rewarded. In this chapter, you'll see how the risk–return relationship fundamentally affects finance theory. We focus on using historical information to characterize past

continued on p. 252

LEARNING GOALS

LG9-1 Compute an investment's dollar and percentage return.

LG9-2 Find information about the historical returns and volatility for the stock, bond, and cash markets.

LG9-3 Measure and evaluate the total risk of an investment using several methods.

LG9-4 Recognize the risk–return relationship and its implications.

LG9-5 Plan investments that take advantage of diversification and its impact on total risk.

LG9-6 Find efficient and optimal portfolios.

LG9-7 Compute a portfolio's return.

»viewpoints

business APPLICATION

Managers from the production and marketing departments have proposed some risky new business projects for your firm. These new ideas appear to be riskier than the firm's current business operations.

You know that diversifying the firm's product offerings could reduce the firm's overall risk. However, you are concerned that taking on these new projects will make the firm's stock too risky. How can you determine whether these project ideas would make the firm's stock riskier or less risky? **(See the solution at the end of the book.)**

continued from p. 251

> **dollar return** The amount of profit or loss from an investment denoted in dollars.

returns and risks. We show how you can diversify to eliminate some risk and expect the highest return possible for your desired risk level. In Chapter 10, we'll turn to estimating the risks and returns you should expect in the future. ■

9.1 • HISTORICAL RETURNS LG9-1

Let's begin our discussion of risk and return by characterizing the concept of return. First, we need a method for calculating returns. After computing a return, investors need to assess whether it was a good, average, or bad investment return. Examining returns from the past gives us a general idea of what we might expect to see in the future. We should think in terms of return for the long run because a return for any one year can be quite different from the average returns from the past couple of decades.

Computing Returns

How much have you earned on each of your investments? Two ways to determine this are to compute the actual dollar return or compute the dollar return as a percentage of the money invested.

Dollar Return The **dollar return** earned includes any capital gain (or loss) that occurred as well as any income that you received over the period. Equation 9-1 illustrates the dollar return calculation:

$$\text{Dollar return} = \text{Capital gain or loss} + \text{Income}$$
$$= (\text{Ending value} - \text{Beginning value}) + \text{Income}$$

(9-1)

For example, say you held 50 shares of Alphabet (GOOG), the parent company of Google. The stock price had a market price of $1,337.02 per share at the end of 2019. Alphabet paid no dividends during 2020. At the end of 2020, Alphabet's stock price was $1,751.88. For the whole of 2020, you earned a capital gain of ($1,751.88 − $1,337.02) × 50 shares, or $20,743.

In Alphabet's case, the stock price increased, so you experienced a capital gain. On the other hand, the company General Electric (GE) started the year at $11.16 per share, paid $0.04 in dividends, and ended 2020 at $10.80. If you owned 2,000 shares of GE, you would have experienced a capital loss of −$720 (= [$10.80 − $11.16 × 2,000 shares]). This loss would have been partially offset by the $80 of dividends received. However, the total dollar return would still have been −$640 (= −$720 + $80). Stock prices can fluctuate substantially and cause large positive or negative dollar returns.

Suppose an investor owns a portfolio invested 100 percent in long-term Treasury bonds because the owner prefers low risk. The investor has avoided owning stocks because of their high volatility.

The investor's stockbroker claims that putting 10 percent of the portfolio in stocks would actually reduce total risk and increase the portfolio's expected return. The investor knows that stocks are riskier than bonds. How can adding the risky stocks to the bond portfolio reduce the risk level? **(See the solution at the end of the book.)**

Is there such a thing as a high reward, zero-risk investment?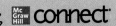

Does your dollar return depend on whether you continue to hold the Alphabet and GE stock or sell it? No. In general, finance deals with *market* values. Alphabet stock was worth $1,751.88 at the end of 2020 regardless of whether you held the stock or sold it. If you sell it, then we refer to your gains as "realized" gains. If you continue to hold the stock, the gains are "unrealized" gains.

percentage return The dollar return characterized as a percentage of money invested.

average returns A measure summarizing the past performance of an investment.

Percentage Return We usually find it more useful to characterize investment earnings as **percentage returns** so that we can easily compare one investment's return to other alternatives' returns. We calculate percentage return by dividing the dollar return by the investment's value at the beginning of the time period.

$$\text{Percentage return} = \frac{\text{Ending value} - \text{Beginning value} + \text{Income}}{\text{Beginning value}} \times 100\% \qquad (9\text{-}2)$$

Because it's standardized, we can use percentage returns for almost any type of investment. We can use beginning and ending values for stock positions, bond prices, real estate values, and so on. Investment income may be stock dividends, bond interest payments, or other receipts. The percentage return for holding the GE stock during calendar year 2020 was −2.87 percent, computed as

$$\text{GE percentage return} = \frac{(\$10.80 \times 2,000) - (\$11.16 \times 2,000) + (\$0.04 \times 2,000)}{\$11.16 \times 2,000}$$

$$= -0.0287, \text{ or } -2.87\%$$

The return for the Alphabet position during the same period was a whopping 31.03 percent:

$$\text{Alphabet percentage return} = \frac{(\$1,751.88 \times 50) - (\$1,337.02 \times 50)}{\$1,337.02 \times 50}$$

$$= 0.3103, \text{ or } 31.03\%$$

Both firms belong to the S&P 500 Index, which earned a total return of 18.40 percent in 2020.

Are one-year returns typical for expectations in the long run? We look to **average returns** to examine performance over time. The arithmetic average return provides an estimate for how the investment has performed over longer periods of time. The formula for the average return is

$$\text{Average return} = \text{Sum of all returns} \div \text{Number of returns}$$

$$= \frac{\sum\limits_{i=1}^{N} \text{Return}_t}{N} \qquad (9\text{-}3)$$

EXAMPLE 9-1

Computing Returns LG9-1

You are evaluating a stock's short-term performance. At the end of October 2017, the chip maker Qualcomm's stock was trading at $51.01. In early November, Broadcom offered to buy Qualcomm for $70 per share. Qualcomm traded as high as $69.28 in November. But the management of Qualcomm rejected the takeover attempt. In February 2018, Broadcom increased its offer to $82 per share. However, the market did not seem to believe the offer would be accepted, as the stock's price was only $65 at the end of February. Indeed, by the end of March, Broadcom had withdrawn its offer and the stock's price had fallen to $55.41 per share. What are the dollar return and percentage return of 300 shares of Qualcomm from its closing price in October 2017 to its highest price in November? What were the returns during March of 2018?

SOLUTION:

No dividends were paid during these two periods. For November 2017, the dollar return is $5,481 = 300 × ($69.28 − $51.01) + 0 and the percent return is 35.82% = $5,481 ÷ (300 × $51.01).

For March 2018, the dollar return is −$2,877 = 300 × ($55.41 − $65.00) + 0 and the percent return is −14.75% = $2,877 ÷ (300 × $65.00).

Many Qualcomm shareholders were upset with their management that the shares were trading at $55 when they could have received $82.

The spreadsheet solution is:

	A	B	C	D	E	F	G
1	Price at Beginning of November	$51.01			Price at Beginning of March	$65.00	
2	Price at End of November	$69.28			Price at End of March	$55.41	
3	Dividend	$0.00			Dividend	$0.00	
4	Number of Shares	300			Number of Shares	300	
5	Dollar Return =	$5,481.00	=B4*(B2-B1+B3)		Dollar Return =	-$2,877.00	=F4*(F2-F1+F3)
6	Percent Return =	35.82%	=B5/(B1*B4)		Percent Return =	-14.75%	=F5/(F1*F4)

Microsoft Excel

Similar to Problems 9-1, 9-2, Self-Test Problem 1

Boeing's stock returns have ranged from −50.1 percent to 94.7 percent.
McGraw-Hill Education/Andy Resek

where the return for each subperiod is summed up and divided by the number of subperiods. You can state the returns in either percentage or decimal format.

Alphabet has only been a public company for a relatively brief period, so it will not have a long history of returns. Thus, Table 9.1 shows the annual returns for airplane manufacturer Boeing and Bank of America (BAC) from 1991 to 2020. First, notice that over time, the returns are quite varied for both firms. The stock return for Boeing has ranged from a low of −50.1 percent in 2008 to a high of 94.7 percent in 2017. BAC's stock return varied between −63.4 percent (2008) and 109.6 percent (2012). Also note that the returns appear unpredictable or random. Sometimes a large negative return is followed by another bad year, like Boeing's returns in 2001 and 2002. Other times, a poor year is followed by a very good year, like 2008 and 2009 for Boeing. The table also reports average annual returns for Boeing and Bank of America of 15.0 percent and 15.6 percent, respectively. Over the years, the annual returns for these stocks have been quite different from their average returns.

▼ TABLE 9.1 Annual and Average Returns for Boeing and Bank of America, 1991 to 2020

	A	B	C	D	E	F
1		**Boeing**	**Bank of America**		**Boeing**	**Bank of America**
2	1991	7.4%	86.0%	2006	28.4%	20.7%
3	1992	−13.9%	32.0%	2007	−0.1%	−20.0%
4	1993	10.7%	−1.4%	2008	−50.1%	−63.4%
5	1994	11.2%	−4.4%	2009	31.8%	9.9%
6	1995	69.7%	77.9%	2010	23.6%	−11.2%
7	1996	37.6%	43.5%	2011	15.2%	−58.1%
8	1997	−7.1%	27.3%	2012	5.2%	109.6%
9	1998	−32.5%	1.2%	2013	84.7%	34.6%
10	1999	28.7%	−14.1%	2014	−2.6%	15.5%
11	2000	61.2%	−3.7%	2015	14.1%	−4.8%
12	2001	−40.4%	41.3%	2016	12.2%	39.7%
13	2002	−13.4%	14.6%	2017	94.7%	39.9%
14	2003	30.4%	20.0%	2018	11.5%	−15.5%
15	2004	24.9%	21.6%	2019	3.3%	46.2%
16	2005	37.9%	3.4%	2020	−33.9%	−11.7%
17				**Average =**	**15.0%**	**15.6%**

Note the range of returns. Few annual returns are close to the average return.

Source: Yahoo! Finance.
Microsoft Excel

The average returns shown in this chapter are more precisely called arithmetic average returns. These average returns are appropriate for statistical analysis. However, they do not accurately illustrate the historical performance of a stock or portfolio. To see this, consider the $100 stock that earned a 50 percent return one year (to $150) and then earned a −50 percent return the next year (to $75). The arithmetic average return is therefore (50% + −50%) ÷ 2 = 0%. Do you believe the average return was zero percent per year? If you started with a $100 stock and ended with a $75 stock, did you earn zero percent? No, you lost money. A measure of that performance should illustrate a negative return. The accurate measure to be used in performance analysis is called the **geometric mean return,** or the mean return computed by finding the equivalent return that is compounded for N periods. In this example, the mean return is $[(1 + 0.50) \times (1 + -0.50)]^{1/2} - 1 = -0.134$, or −13.4 percent. Given the loss of $25 over two years, this −13.4 percent per year mean return seems more reasonable than the zero percent average return.

> **geometric mean return** The mean return computed by finding the equivalent return that is compounded for N periods.

The general formula for the geometric mean return is

$$\text{Geometric mean return} = \left[\prod_{t=1}^{N} \left(1 + \frac{\text{Return}_t}{100} \right) \right]^{\frac{1}{N}} - 1 \qquad (9\text{-}4)$$

Note that equation 9-4 shows Return being divided by 100. This simply means that the return needs to be in the decimal format; that is, use 0.05 rather than 5 percent. A spreadsheet can easily compute the geometric mean return with the GEOMEAN(number1, [number2], . . .) function.

Performance of Asset Classes LG9-2

During any given year, the stock market may perform better than the bond market, or it may perform worse. Over longer time periods, how do stocks, bonds, or cash securities perform? Historically, stocks have performed better than either bonds or cash. Table 9.2 shows the average returns for these three asset classes over the period 1950 to 2019, as well as over various subperiods. Over the entire period, stocks (as measured by the S&P 500 Index) earned

time **out!**

9-1 How important were dividend payments to the total returns that Boeing and Bank of America offered investors?

9-2 Using the average returns shown in Table 9.2, compute how much a $10,000 investment made in each asset class at the beginning of each decade would become at the end of each decade.

▼ **TABLE 9.2** Annual and Average Returns for Stocks, Bonds, and T-Bills, 1950 to 2019

	A	B	C	D	E
1			**Stocks**	**Long-Term Treasury Bonds**	**T-Bills**
2	1950 to 2019	Average	12.7%	6.6%	4.2%
3	1950 to 1959	Average	20.9%	0.0%	2.0%
4	1960 to 1969	Average	8.7%	1.6%	4.0%
5	1970 to 1979	Average	7.5%	5.7%	6.3%
6	1980 to 1989	Average	18.2%	13.5%	8.9%
7	1990 to 1999	Average	19.0%	9.5%	4.9%
8	2000 to 2009	Average	0.9%	8.0%	2.7%
9	2010	Annual Return	15.1%	9.4%	0.01%
10	2011	Annual Return	2.1%	29.9%	0.02%
11	2012	Annual Return	16.0%	3.6%	0.02%
12	2013	Annual Return	32.4%	−12.7%	0.07%
13	2014	Annual Return	13.7%	25.1%	0.05%
14	2015	Annual Return	1.4%	−1.2%	0.21%
15	2016	Annual Return	12.0%	1.2%	0.51%
16	2017	Annual Return	21.8%	8.4%	1.39%
17	2018	Annual Return	−4.4%	−1.8%	1.94%
18	2019	Annual Return	31.5%	14.8%	2.06%
19	2010 to 2019	Average	14.2%	7.7%	0.63%

Returns have been very different among decades.

Microsoft Excel

an average 12.7 percent return per year. This is nearly double the 6.6 percent return earned by long-term Treasury bonds. Cash securities, measured by U.S. Treasury bills, earned an average 4.2 percent return.

The table also shows each asset class's average return for each decade since 1950. The best decade for the stock market was the 1950s, when stocks earned an average 20.9 percent per year. The 1990s ran a close second with a 19 percent per year return. The best decade for the bond market was the 1980s, when it earned an average 13.5 percent per year return due to capital gains as interest rates fell. Stocks have outperformed bonds in every decade since 1950 except the recent 2000s. Notice that the average return in the stock and bond markets has not been negative during any decade since 1950. But average stock returns do not really paint a very accurate picture of annual returns. Individual annual returns can vary strongly and be quite negative in any particular year. Indeed, this annual variability defines risk. The stock market return in 2008 was particularly poor because of the financial crisis. However, not all stocks fell the same amount. Notice that Boeing and Bank of America declined by 50.1 percent and 63.4 percent while the stock market in general declined 35.5 percent. Financial company stocks fell the most during the crisis.

9.2 • HISTORICAL RISKS LG9-3

When you purchase a U.S. Treasury bill, you know exactly what your dollar and percentage return are going to be. Many people find comfort in the certainty from this safe investment. On the other hand, when you purchase a stock, you do not know what your return is going to be—either in the short term or in the long run. This uncertainty is precisely what makes stock investing risky. It's useful to evaluate this uncertainty quantitatively so that we can compare risk among different stocks and asset classes.

Computing Volatility

Financial theory suggests that investors should look at an investment's historical returns to assess how much uncertainty to expect in the future. If you see high variability in historical returns, you should expect a high degree of future uncertainty. Table 9.2 shows that between 2010 and 2019, the stock market experienced a range of −4.4 percent return in 2018 to a 32.4 percent return in 2013. Bonds also experienced variability:−12.7 percent return in 2013 to 29.9 percent return in 2011. Examining the range of historical returns provides just one way to express the return volatility that we can expect. In practical terms, the finance industry uses a statistical return volatility measure known as the **standard deviation** of percentage returns. We calculate standard deviation as the square root of the variance, and this figure represents the security's or portfolio's **total risk.** We'll discuss other risk measurements in the next chapter.

standard deviation A measure of past return volatility, or risk, of an investment.

total risk The volatility of an investment, which includes current portions of firm-specific risk and market risk.

Our process of computing standard deviation starts with the average return over the period. The average annual return for the stock market since 1950 is 12.7 percent. How much can the return in any given year deviate from this average? We compute the actual annual deviation by subtracting the return each year from this average return: Return_{1950} − Average return, $\text{Return}_{(1951)}$ − Average return, $\text{Return}_{(1952)}$ − Average return, and so on. Note that many of these deviations will be negative (from a lower-than-average return that year) and others will be positive (from a higher-than-average return). If we computed the *average* of these return deviations, our result would be zero. Large positive deviations cancel out large negative deviations and hide the variability. To really see the size of the variations without the distractions that come with including a positive or negative sign, we square each deviation before adding them up. Dividing by the number of returns in the sample minus one provides the return *variance.*[1] The square root of the return variance is the standard deviation:

$$\text{Standard deviation} = \text{Square root of the average squared deviation of returns}$$

$$= \sqrt{\frac{\sum\limits_{t=1}^{N} \left(\text{Return}_t - \text{Average return}\right)^2}{N-1}} \tag{9-5}$$

Note that this equation provides an estimate of the true population standard deviation using a specific historical sample. A large standard deviation indicates greater return volatility—or high risk. Table 9.3 shows the standard deviations of Boeing stock returns over 30 years. The Deviation column shows the annual return minus Boeing's average return of 18.0 percent. The last column squares each deviation. Then we sum up these squared deviations and divide the result by the number of observations less one (29) to compute the return variance. If we want to use a measure that makes sense in the real world (how would you interpret a squared percentage, anyway?), we take the square root of the variance to get the standard deviation. Boeing's standard deviation of returns during this sample period comes to 33.9 percent. In comparison, the standard deviation of Bank of America's stock returns for this same period is 37.0 percent. Because Bank of America's standard deviation is higher, its stock features more total risk than does Boeing's stock.

Although analysts and investors use a stock return's standard deviation as an important and common measure of risk, it's laborious to compute by hand. Most people use a spreadsheet or statistical software to calculate stock return standard deviations.

Because Bank of America's standard deviation is higher, its stock features more total risk.
Tero Vesalainen/Shutterstock

▼ TABLE 9.3 Computation of Boeing Stock Return Standard Deviation

	A	B	C	D
1		**Boeing Return**	**Deviation**	**Squared Deviation**
2	1991	7.4%	−7.6%	0.6%
3	1992	−13.9%	−28.9%	8.4%
4	1993	10.7%	−4.3%	0.2%
5	1994	11.2%	−3.8%	0.1%
6	1995	69.7%	54.7%	29.9%
7	1996	37.6%	22.6%	5.1%
8	1997	−7.1%	−22.1%	4.9%
9	1998	−32.5%	−47.5%	22.6%
10	1999	28.7%	13.7%	1.9%
11	2000	61.2%	46.2%	21.3%
12	2001	−40.4%	−55.4%	30.7%
13	2002	−13.4%	−28.4%	8.1%
14	2003	30.4%	15.4%	2.4%
15	2004	24.9%	9.9%	1.0%
16	2005	37.9%	22.9%	5.2%
17	2006	28.4%	13.4%	1.8%
18	2007	−0.1%	−15.1%	2.3%
19	2008	−50.1%	−65.1%	42.4%
20	2009	31.8%	16.8%	2.8%
21	2010	23.6%	8.6%	0.7%
22	2011	15.2%	0.1%	0.0%
23	2012	5.2%	−9.8%	1.0%
24	2013	84.7%	69.7%	48.6%
25	2014	−2.6%	−17.6%	3.1%
26	2015	14.1%	−0.9%	0.0%
27	2016	12.2%	−2.8%	0.1%
28	2017	94.7%	79.7%	63.5%
29	2018	11.5%	−3.5%	0.1%
30	2019	3.3%	−11.7%	1.4%
31	2020	−33.9%	−48.9%	23.9%
32	**Average =**	**15.0%**	**Sum =**	**334.0%**
33			**Variance =**	**11.5%**
34			**Std Dev =**	**33.9%**
35	=AVERAGE(B2:B31)			
36			=VAR.S(B2:B31)	
37				=STDEV.S(B2:B31)

Investors use standard deviation as a measure of risk; the higher the standard deviation, the riskier the asset.

Source: Yahoo! Finance.

Microsoft Excel

Risk of Asset Classes LG9-2

We report the standard deviations of return for stocks, bonds, and T-bills in Table 9.4 for 1950 to 2019 and for each decade since 1950. Over the entire sample, the stock market returns' standard deviation is 17.1 percent. As we would expect, stock market volatility is

258 PART 5 | Risk and Return

Risk and Return LG9-1, LG9-3

Find the average return and risk (as measured by standard deviation) for Boeing since 2011. Table 9.3 shows the annual returns for years 2011 to 2020.

SOLUTION:

First, compute the average annual return for the period. Using equation 9-3:

$$\frac{15.2\% + 5.2\% + 84.7\% - 2.6\% + 14.1\% + 12.2\% + 94.7\% + 11.5\% + 3.3\% - 33.9\%}{10}$$

$$= \frac{204.4\%}{10}$$

$$= 20.4\%$$

Boeing has averaged a 20.4 percent return per year since 2011. To compute the risk, use the standard deviation equation 9-5. First, find the deviations of return for each year:

Year 2011	2012	2013	2014	2015	2016	2017	2018	2019	2020
15.2% − 20.4%	5.2% − 20.4%	84.7% − 20.4%	−2.6% − 20.4%	14.1% − 20.4%	12.2% − 20.4%	94.7% − 20.4%	11.5% − 20.4%	3.3% − 20.4%	−33.9% − 20.4%

Square those deviations:

Year 2011	2012	2013	2014	2015	2016	2ç017	2018	2019	2020
$(15.2\% - 20.4\%)^2$	$(5.2\% - 20.4\%)^2$	$(84.7\% - 20.4\%)^2$	$(-2.6\% - 20.4\%)^2$	$(14.1\% - 20.4\%)^2$	$(12.2\% - 20.4\%)^2$	$(94.7\% - 20.4\%)^2$	$(11.5\% - 20.4\%)^2$	$(3.3\% - 20.4\%)^2$	$(-33.9\% - 20.4\%)^2$

Then add them up, divide by $n - 1$, and take the square root:

$$= \sqrt{\frac{28.0 + 231.8 + 4131.4 + 528.7 + 40.6 + 68.5 + 5516.9 + 80.0 + 292.6 + 2953.3}{9}}$$

$$= \sqrt{1541.3} = 39.3\%$$

Boeing stock has averaged a 20.4 percent return with a standard deviation of 39.3 percent since 2011.

The spreadsheet solution is much easier:

	A	B	C
1	2011	15.2%	
2	2012	5.2%	
3	2013	84.7%	
4	2014	-2.6%	
5	2015	14.1%	
6	2016	12.2%	
7	2017	94.7%	
8	2018	11.5%	
9	2019	3.3%	
10	2020	-33.9%	
11			
12	Average Return =	20.44%	=AVERAGE(B1:B10)
13	Standard Deviation =	39.26%	=STDEV.S(B1:B10)

Microsoft Excel

Similar to Problems 9-19, 9-10, 9-15, 9-21, 9-22, Self-Test Problem 2

higher than bond market volatility (10.9 percent) or for T-bills (3.0 percent). These volatility estimates are consistent with our previously stated position that the stock market carries more risk than the bond or cash markets do. Every decade since 1950 has seen a lot of stock market volatility. The bond market has experienced the most volatility in the 1980s as interest rates varied dramatically.

▼ TABLE 9.4 Annual Standard Deviation of Returns for Stocks, Bonds, and T-Bills, 1950 to 2019

	Stocks	Long-Term Treasury Bonds	T-Bills
1950 to 2019	17.1%	10.9%	3.0%
1950 to 1959	19.8	4.9	0.8
1960 to 1969	14.4	6.2	1.3
1970 to 1979	19.2	6.8	1.8
1980 to 1989	12.7	15.1	2.6
1990 to 1999	14.2	12.8	1.2
2000 to 2009	20.4	10.3	1.9
2010 to 2019	12.3	12.9	0.8

Some decades experience higher risk than others in each asset class.
Microsoft Excel

coefficient of variation A measure of risk to reward (standard deviation divided by average return) earned by an investment over a specific period of time.

You will recall from Chapter 7 that because any bond's par value and coupon rate are fixed, bond prices must fluctuate to adjust for changes in interest rates. Bond prices respond inversely to interest rate changes: As interest rates rise, bond prices fall, and if interest rates fall, bond prices rise. T-bill returns have experienced very low volatility over each decade. Indeed, T-bills are commonly considered to be one of the only risk-free assets. Higher-risk investments offer higher returns over time. But short-term fluctuations in the value of higher-risk investments can be substantial. The stock market is risky—while it has offered a good annual return of 12.7 percent, that return comes with volatility of 17.1 percent standard deviation. Many investors may intellectually understand that this high risk means that they may receive very poor returns in the short term. Investors really felt the full force of this risk when the stock market declined three years in a row (2000 to 2002) during the bear market associated with the dot-com bubble. Some investors even decided that this was too much risk for them, and they sold out of the stock market before the 2003 rally. The standard deviation of stock returns was very high in the decade of the 2000s, 20.4 percent, because the decade experienced two major bear markets. The first was the dot-com bubble and the second was the financial crisis. Market volatility can cause investors to make emotionally based decisions—selling at low prices.

The stock market returns' standard deviations that appear in Table 9.4 are all considerably lower than the standard deviations of Boeing and of Bank of America stocks (33.9 percent and 37.0 percent, respectively). In this case, we measure stock market return and standard deviation using the S&P 500 Index. Boeing and Bank of America are both included in the S&P 500 Index. Why do these two large firms have measures of total risk—standard deviations—that are at least twice as large as the standard deviations on the stock market returns? Are Boeing and Bank of America just two of the most risky firms in the Index? Actually, no. The differences in standard deviations between these individual companies and the entire market have much more to do with *diversification*. Owning 500 companies, such as all of those included in the S&P 500 Index, generates much less risk than owning just one company. This phenomenon appears in the standard deviation measure. We'll discuss the effects of diversification in detail later in this chapter.

Risk versus Return LG9-4

Investors can buy very safe T-bills. Or they can take some risk to seek higher returns. How much extra return can you expect for taking more risk? This is known as the *trade-off between risk and return*. The **coefficient of variation** (CoV) is a common *relative* measure of this risk-versus-reward relationship. The equation for the coefficient of variation is

EXAMPLE 9-3

For interactive versions of this example, log in to Connect or go to mhhe.com/Cornett6e.

Risk versus Return LG9-4

You are interested in the risk–return relationship of stocks in each decade since 1950. Obtain the average returns and risks in Table 9.2 and Table 9.4.

SOLUTION:

Using the average return and standard deviation of return, compute the coefficient of variation for the following risk–return relationships:

$$CoV_{1950s} = \frac{19.8\%}{20.9\%} = 0.95 \quad CoV_{1960s} = \frac{14.4\%}{8.7\%} = 1.66$$

$$CoV_{1970s} = \frac{19.2\%}{7.5\%} = 2.56 \quad CoV_{1980s} = \frac{12.7\%}{18.2\%} = 0.70$$

$$CoV_{1990s} = \frac{14.2\%}{19.0\%} = 0.75 \quad CoV_{2000s} = \frac{20.4\%}{0.9\%} = 22.67$$

$$CoV_{2010s} = \frac{12.3\%}{14.2\%} = 0.87$$

Note that over short time periods, the stock risk–return relationship varies significantly. The coefficient of variation was unusually high during the 2000s because that decade experienced the dot-com crash and the financial crisis, which both drove average returns down and volatility up.

Similar to Problems 9-4, 9-11, 9-21, 9-22, Self-Test Problem 3

---

simply the standard deviation divided by average return. It is interpreted as the amount of risk (measured by volatility) per unit of return:

$$\text{Coefficient of variation} = \text{Amount of risk} \div \text{Return}$$
$$= \frac{\text{Standard deviation}}{\text{Average return}} \quad (9\text{-}6)$$

As an investor, you would want to receive a very high return (the denominator in the equation) with a very low risk (the numerator). So, a smaller CoV indicates a better risk–reward relationship. Since the average return and standard deviation for Boeing stock are 15.0 percent and 33.9 percent, respectively, its CoV is 2.26 (= 33.9 ÷ 15.0). This is a little better than Bank of America's CoV of 2.37 (= 37.0 ÷ 15.6). For all asset classes for the period 1950 to 2019, the stock market earned a higher return than bonds and was also riskier. But which one had a better risk–return relationship? The CoV for common stock is 1.35 (= 17.1 ÷ 12.7). For Treasury bonds, the coefficient of variation is 1.65 (= 10.9 ÷ 6.6). Even though stocks are riskier than bonds, they involve a somewhat better risk–reward trade-off.

9.3 • FORMING PORTFOLIOS LG9-5

As we noted previously, Boeing and Bank of America stocks' risk as measured by their standard deviations appear quite high compared to the standard deviation of the S&P 500 Index. This is by no means a coincidence. Combining stocks into **portfolios** can reduce many sources of stock risk. **Diversification** reduces risk. The S&P 500 Index, for example, tracks 500 companies, which allows for a great deal of diversification. Indeed, what if you could easily buy all 500 of the S&P 500 Index companies? Actually you can. Instead of buying the stock of all 500 companies individually, you can buy the stock of the SPDR S&P 500

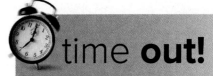

time out!

9-3 What volatility measure can we use to evaluate and compare risk among different investment alternatives?

9-4 Explain why the coefficients of variation for Boeing and Bank of America are so much higher than the CoV for the stock market as a whole.

portfolio A combination of investment assets held by an investor.

diversification The process of putting money in different types of investments for the purpose of reducing the overall risk of the portfolio.

Diversification reduces risk.
Dimitri Vervitsiotis/Getty Images

Exchange Traded Fund (ETF), ticker SPY. With the SPY ETF and other index ETFs, you can easily become fully diversified. That is why ETFs became very popular during the 2000s and still are today. On some days, several ETFs are among the most actively traded stocks in the stock market.

Diversifying to Reduce Risk

Think about a stock's total risk as having two components. The first component includes risks that are both specific to that company and common to other companies in the same industry. We call this risk **firm-specific risk.** The stock's other risk component is general risk that all firms—and all individuals, for that matter—face based upon economic strength both domestically and globally. We call this type of risk **market risk.** These risks appear in the equation

$$\text{Total risk} = \text{Firm-specific risk} + \text{Market risk} \tag{9-7}$$

Standard deviations measure total risk. Individual stocks are subject to many firm-specific risks. We can reduce firm-specific risk by combining stocks into a portfolio. Since we can reduce firm-specific risk by diversifying, this risk is sometimes referred to as **diversifiable risk.** If Bank of America announces lower-than-expected profits, its stock price will decline. However, since this news is *specific* to Bank of America, the news should not affect Boeing's stock price. On the other hand, if the government announces a change in unemployment, both stocks' prices will change to some degree. Macroeconomic events represent market risks because such events—unemployment claims, interest rate changes, national budget deficits, or surpluses—affect all companies.

Suppose that you own only Boeing stock and have earned the annual returns shown in Table 9.5. Then someone suggests that you add Bank of America to your Boeing stock to form a two-stock portfolio. Both Boeing and Bank of America stocks carry a lot of total risk. But look at the risk and return characteristics of a portfolio consisting of 50 percent Bank of America stock and 50 percent Boeing stock. You start with Boeing stock, which provided an average return of 15.0 percent with a risk of 33.9 percent. The Bank of America stock you are adding has more risk than Boeing. The two-stock portfolio earns an average 15.3 percent return with a standard deviation of only 28.0 percent. You added a higher-risk stock to a high-risk stock and you ended up with a portfolio with lower risk and a higher return! This is the objective of forming properly diversified portfolios, which reduce firm-specific risks overall.

Next, add IBM stock to your Boeing and Bank of America stock portfolio. Figure 9.1 shows that the total risk of this three-stock portfolio declines to 21.4 percent. Note that adding General Electric, Newmont Corporation, and Disney also reduces the total risk of the stock portfolio. As you add more stocks, the firm-specific risk portion of the total portfolio risk declines. The total risk falls rapidly as we add the first few stocks. Diversification's power to reduce firm-specific risk weakens for the later stocks added to the portfolio because we have already eliminated much of the firm-specific risk. We could continue to add stocks until the portfolio comprises all S&P 500 Index firms, in which case the standard deviation of the portfolio would be 17.1 percent. At this point, virtually all of the firm-specific risk has been purged and the portfolio carries only market risk, which is sometimes called **nondiversifiable risk.**

Modern Portfolio Theory LG9-6

The concept that diversification reduces risk was formalized in the early 1950s by Harry Markowitz, who eventually won the Nobel Prize in Economics for his work. Markowitz's **modern portfolio theory** shows how risk reduction occurs when securities are combined.

	A	B	C	D
1		**Boeing**	**Bank of America**	**Portfolio of Boeing and Bank of America**
2	1991	7.4%	86.0%	46.7%
3	1992	−13.9%	32.0%	9.1%
4	1993	10.7%	−1.4%	4.7%
5	1994	11.2%	4.4%	3.4%
6	1995	69.7%	77.9%	73.8%
7	1996	37.6%	43.5%	40.6%
8	1997	−7.1%	27.3%	10.1%
9	1998	−32.5%	1.2%	−15.6%
10	1999	28.7%	−14.1%	7.3%
11	2000	61.2%	−3.7%	28.8%
12	2001	−40.4%	41.3%	0.4%
13	2002	−13.4%	14.6%	0.6%
14	2003	30.4%	20.0%	25.2%
15	2004	24.9%	21.6%	23.2%
16	2005	37.9%	3.4%	20.7%
17	2006	28.4%	20.7%	24.5%
18	2007	−0.1%	−20.0%	−10.1%
19	2008	−50.1%	−63.4%	−56.7%
20	2009	31.8%	9.9%	20.8%
21	2010	23.6%	−11.2%	6.2%
22	2011	15.2%	−58.1%	−21.5%
23	2012	5.2%	109.6%	57.4%
24	2013	84.7%	34.6%	59.6%
25	2014	−2.6%	15.5%	6.5%
26	2015	14.1%	−4.8%	4.7%
27	2016	12.2%	39.7%	26.0%
28	2017	94.7%	29.9%	62.3%
29	2018	11.5%	−15.5%	−2.0%
30	2019	3.3%	46.2%	24.8%
31	2020	−33.9%	−11.7%	−22.8%
32				
33	**Average =**	**15.0%**	**15.6%**	**15.3%**
34	**Std Dev =**	**33.9%**	**37.0%**	**28.0%**
35				
36	=AVERAGE(B2:B31)			=0.5*B31+0.5*C31
37			=STDEV(C2:C31)	

The risk-reducing power of diversification! Note that the risk of the portfolio is lower than the risk of the two stocks individually.

Source: Yahoo! Finance.

Microsoft Excel

finance at work //:personal

optimal portfolio The best portfolio of securities for the investor's level of risk aversion.

The theory also describes how to combine stocks to achieve the lowest total risk possible for a given expected return. Or, said differently, it describes how to achieve the highest expected return for the desired risk level. The combination of securities that achieves the highest expected return for a person's desired level of risk is called the investor's **optimal portfolio.**

In our Boeing and Bank of America portfolio example, we allocated 50 percent of the portfolio to Boeing and 50 percent to Bank of America. Is this the best allocation for the portfolio? Consider the different allocations shown in Figure 9.2 for the two stocks. The graph shows the expected return (computed as average return) and risk (computed as standard deviation) of various portfolios. It would be terrific if you could find a portfolio located in the upper left-hand corner. That is, investors would like a high expected return with low risk. One large dot shows the risk–return point for owning only Boeing. The other large dot shows owning only Bank of America. The smaller diamonds show 10/90, 25/75, 40/60, 50/50, 60/40, 75/25, and 90/10 allocations of Boeing/Bank of America stocks.

While all these portfolios are possible, not all are desirable. For example, the portfolio of 75 percent Boeing and 25 percent Bank of America is not desirable. Other portfolios provide *both* higher return and lower risk. We say that one portfolio dominates the other if it has higher expected return for the same (or less) risk, or the same (or higher) expected return with lower risk. The dominating portfolios appear higher and to the left in the figure. One such portfolio consists of 25 percent Boeing stock and 75 percent Bank of America stock.

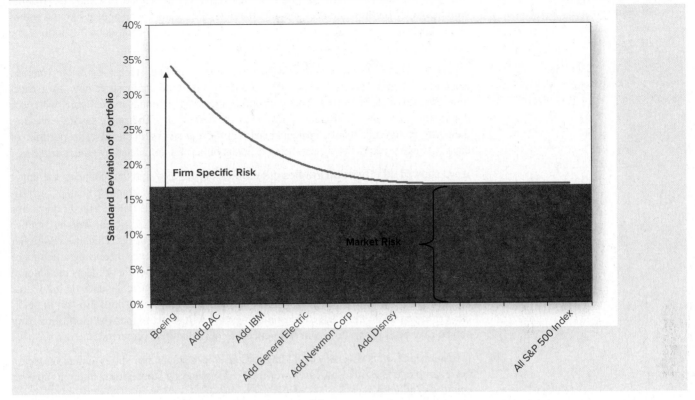

The total portfolio risk is greatly reduced by adding the first few stocks to a portfolio.

▼ **FIGURE 9.2** Risk and Return Ramifications of Portfolio Allocations to Boeing and Bank of America (BAC)

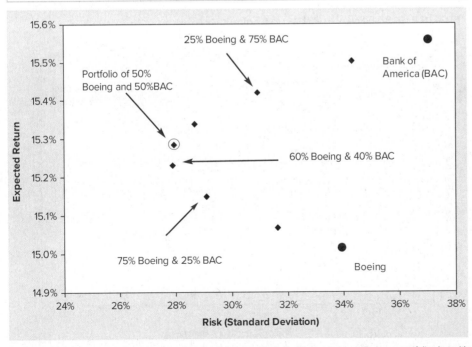

Investors only value the portfolios at the top of the graph because they offer the same risk as the lower portfolios but with higher expected return!

The 50/50 portfolio (circled in the figure) is also better than the 75/25 portfolio. Portfolios with the highest return possible for each risk level are called **efficient portfolios.** Notice that if you drew a line connecting the dots, the figure would appear like the end of a bullet. The portfolios on the top of the bullet dominate the portfolios on the bottom; the top portfolio dots show the efficient portfolios for these two stocks.

Figure 9.3 shows efficient portfolios for combining the four stocks: Bank of America, Boeing, IBM, and General Electric. We used this portfolio to demonstrate how diversification reduces risk in Figure 9.1. These portfolios appear as diamonds in the figure, with each diamond representing a different allocation of the four stocks. The single square represents the portfolio that consists of 25 percent in each of the four stocks. In this case, the portfolio of equally weighted stocks is close to being efficient but is still dominated by other portfolios.

If we showed all efficient portfolios, they would appear as a line that connects the upper side of the bullet shape. If we added all available securities to the graph, then all of the efficient portfolios of those securities form the **efficient frontier.** Efficient frontier portfolios dominate all other possible stock portfolios. The shape of the efficient frontier implies that diminishing returns apply to risk-taking in the investment world. To gain ever-higher expected rates of return, investors must be willing to take on ever-increasing amounts of risk. The optimal portfolio for you is one on the efficient frontier that reflects the amount of risk that you're willing to take. Clearly, optimal portfolio choice depends on individual risk preferences. Highly risk-averse investors will select low-risk portfolios on the efficient frontier, while more adventuresome investors will select higher-risk portfolios. Any choice may be appropriate, given differences in individual risk preferences.

Investors can further diversify by adding foreign stocks and commodities to their portfolio. For example, a U.S. investor can lower total risk by adding stocks from emerging market countries and gold.

How Does Diversification Work? LG9-5 Will combining any two stocks greatly reduce total risk as much as combining Boeing and Bank of America did? The answer is no. If two stocks are subject to exactly the same kinds of events such

▼FIGURE 9.3 Efficient Portfolios from Four Stocks

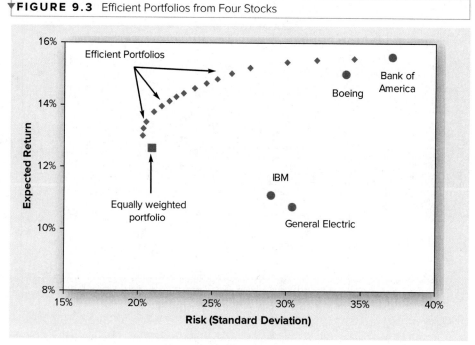

The efficient portfolios dominate all of the individual stocks.

that their returns always behave the same way over time, then we have no need to own both stocks—simply pick the one that performs better. Diversification comes when two stocks are subject to different kinds of events such that their returns differ over time.

Consider the illustration in Figure 9.4. You own Stock A in Panel A of the figure. The stock features risk, as demonstrated by its price volatility over time. You would like to reduce the risk by combining your position in Stock A with an equal position in Stock B. In this case, the alternative stock, Stock B, moves the same way over time as Stock A does. When Stock A goes up, so does Stock B. They also decline together. A portfolio of both stocks is illustrated. Notice how the portfolio has the same volatility as Stocks A and B separately. Combining these two stocks did not reduce volatility, or total risk.

Now consider Stock C, shown in Panel B. Stock C has the same volatility as Stock A, but its price moves in different directions than does the price of Stock A. When Stock A's

▼FIGURE 9.4 Efficient Portfolios from Four Stocks

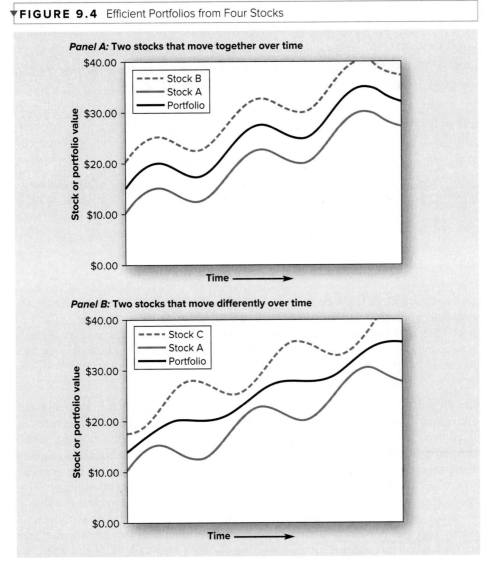

Combining stocks that move together over time does not offer much risk reduction. Combining stocks that do not move together provides a lot of risk reduction.

Correlation shows that some stocks move together and some do not.

finance at work //: markets

International Opportunities for Diversification

The U.S. stock market represents nearly 47 percent of all stock value worldwide. Japanese and U.K. stock markets represent 11 percent and 8 percent of the worldwide stock market value, respectively. Many investment and diversification opportunities present themselves internationally! However, most people allocate very little or none of their portfolios to international securities. If worldwide opportunities can create greater diversification, then those who don't invest in international stocks miss out on an important opportunity to reduce risk in their portfolios.

MSCI Barra is the leading provider of global stock market indexes. Some MSCI Barra indexes follow individual countries. In addition, MSCI Barra compiles composite indexes for groups of companies in developed markets, emerging markets, and frontier markets, and by geographic regions. Investment managers use the MSCI World Index, the MSCI EAFE (Europe, Australasia, Far East) Index, and the MSCI Emerging Markets Index as premier benchmarks to measure global stock market performance.

The following table shows the average annual returns and standard deviations for the U.S. stock market, Treasury bonds, and the MSCI EAFE and MSCI Emerging Markets indexes for the period 1991 to 2020. Note that both the EAFE and the Emerging Markets indexes feature higher risk than the S&P 500 Index. The Emerging Markets return has been high, but the EAFE return has been low compared to the U.S. stock and bond markets.

	S&P 500	Bonds	EAFE	Emerging Markets
Average	12.1%	8.8%	6.3%	12.1%
Std. Deviation	17.1	11.7	18.4	31.4

The correlations among these markets appear as follows:

	S&P 500	Bonds	EAFE	Emerging Markets
S&P 500	1			
Bonds	−0.13	1		
EAFE	0.77	−0.37	1	
Emerging Markets	0.45	−0.32	0.75	1

The correlation between the S&P 500 Index and the MSCI EAFE is 0.77 and between the S&P 500 and the Emerging Markets is 0.45. These correlations indicate that diversification might work. Even better diversification appears to be possible between the U.S. Treasury Bond Market and the EAFE and Emerging Markets indexes—look at the negative correlations!

Want to know more?

Key Words to Search for Updates: **international diversification, global asset allocation**

Source: www.msci.com

---

correlation A measurement of the co-movement between two variables that range between −1 and +1.

price increases, Stock C's price increases sometimes and decreases sometimes. As shown, a portfolio of Stock A and Stock C features much lower volatility than either Stock A or Stock C alone. Combining Stocks A and C reduces risk because their price movements often counteract one another. In short, combining stocks with similar characteristics does not provide much diversification and thus risk reduction. Combining stocks with many differences does provide diversification and thus lowers risk.

The ways that stocks co-move over time determines how much diversification and thus risk reduction we can achieve by combining them. So what we need is some measure of co-movement to help investors form diversified portfolios. That measure, called **correlation,** is denoted by the Greek letter ρ (rho). Correlation is a statistical measure with some very useful characteristics that makes it easy to interpret. Its value is bounded between −1 and +1. A correlation value of +1 means that returns from two different securities move perfectly in sync. They change lock-step up and down together. A value of −1 means that returns from two securities are perfectly inversely correlated—they move exactly opposite. A value of 0 means that the movements of the two returns over time are unrelated to one another. Investors seeking diversification look for stocks where the returns have low or negative correlations with each other.

What return correlations are common between stocks? Panel A of Table 9.6 shows the correlations between many companies. One high correlation shown is the 0.665 correlation between Citigroup and the Bank of America. This shouldn't be surprising because these are two similar firms in the same industry. Combining these two stocks wouldn't reduce risk very much in a portfolio. The largest negative correlation is the correlation of −0.147 between Newmont Corporation and Disney. These firms participate in very different industries and provide large risk-reduction possibilities. Note that the correlation between Bank of America and Boeing is 0.240. This low correlation gives us an answer to the question of why total risk (in the form of standard deviations) fell so much when we combined the two stocks relative to their individual standard deviations as shown in Figure 9.2. Most of the correlations in Table 9.6 are positive. Because most stocks are positively correlated, we typically add many stocks together to fully eliminate all the firm-specific risk in the portfolio, as we showed in Figure 9.1.

> 66 When computing portfolio returns, use the decimal format for the portfolio weights and the percentage format for the security returns. The result of equation 9-8 will then be in percentage format. 99

the
Math Coach on...

LG9-2

Panel B of Table 9.6 shows correlations between stocks, bonds, and T-bills. At −0.004, the correlation between stocks and bonds is negligible. The small correlation allows for the possibility of good risk reduction by adding bonds to a stock portfolio. Therefore, a well-diversified portfolio will contain both stocks and bonds.

Portfolio Return LG9-7 A portfolio's return calculation is straightforward. A portfolio's return comes directly from the returns of the portfolio securities and the proportion of the portfolio invested in each security. For example, consider that General Electric stock earned −1.9 percent and Newmont Corp. earned 17.3 percent over the same period. If you

▼ **TABLE 9.6** Correlation between Various Stocks and Asset Classes

	PANEL A: COMPANY ANNUAL RETURNS, 1991 TO 2020					
	Bank of America	**Boeing**	**IBM**	**Newmont Corp.**	**Disney**	**General Electric**
Bank of America	1					
Boeing	0.240	1				
IBM	0.088	−0.015	1			
Newmont Corp.	0.037	−0.035	−0.017	1		
Disney	0.426	0.338	0.090	−0.147	1	
General Electric	0.412	0.170	0.452	−0.012	0.500	1
Citigroup	0.665	0.393	0.115	0.121	0.408	0.713
	PANEL B: ASSET CLASS ANNUAL RETURNS, 1950 TO 2020					
	Stocks			**Long-Term Treasury Bonds**		
Stocks	1					
Long-Term Treasury bonds	−0.004			1		
T-bills	−0.072			0.118		

Computing Portfolio Returns LG9-7

For interactive versions
of this example, log
in to Connect or go to
mhhe.com/Cornett6e.

At the beginning of the year, you owned $5,000 of Disney stock, $10,000 of Bank of New York stock, and $15,000 of IBM stock. During the year, Disney, Bank of New York, and IBM returned −4.8 percent, 19.4 percent, and 12.8 percent, respectively. What is your portfolio's return?

SOLUTION:

First determine your portfolio weights. The three stocks make up a $30,000 portfolio. Disney makes up a 16.67 percent (= $5,000 ÷ $30,000) portion of the portfolio. Bank of New York stock makes up a 33.33 percent (= $10,000 ÷ $30,000) portion, and IBM a 50.0 percent (= $15,000 ÷ $30,000) portion. The portfolio return can now be computed as

$$R_p = (0.1667 \times -4.8\%) + (0.3333 \times 19.4\%) + (0.50 \times 12.8\%) = -0.80\% + 6.47\% + 6.40\% = 12.07\%$$

The spreadsheet solution can use the equation as shown in the first answer, or use the Excel SUMPRODUCT function that returns the sum of the products of corresponding arrays and is shown in the second answer.

	A	B	C	D
1		Boeing	Bank of America	Portfolio of Boeing and Bank of America
2	1991	7.4%	86.0%	46.7%
3	1992	-13.9%	32.0%	9.1%
4	1993	10.7%	-1.4%	4.7%
5	1994	11.2%	-4.4%	3.4%
6	1995	69.7%	77.9%	73.8%
7	1996	37.6%	43.5%	40.6%
8	1997	-7.1%	27.3%	10.1%
9	1998	-32.5%	1.2%	-15.6%
10	1999	28.7%	-14.1%	7.3%
11	2000	61.2%	-3.7%	28.8%
12	2001	-40.4%	41.3%	0.4%
13	2002	-13.4%	14.6%	0.6%
14	2003	30.4%	20.0%	25.2%
15	2004	24.9%	21.6%	23.2%
16	2005	37.9%	3.4%	20.7%
17	2006	28.4%	20.7%	24.5%
18	2007	-0.1%	-20.0%	-10.1%
19	2008	-50.1%	-63.4%	-56.7%
20	2009	31.8%	9.9%	20.8%
21	2010	23.6%	-11.2%	6.2%
22	2011	15.2%	-58.1%	-21.5%
23	2012	5.2%	109.6%	57.4%
24	2013	84.7%	34.6%	59.6%
25	2014	-2.6%	15.5%	6.5%
26	2015	14.1%	-4.8%	4.7%
27	2016	12.2%	39.7%	26.0%
28	2017	94.7%	29.9%	62.3%
29	2018	11.5%	-15.5%	-2.0%
30	2019	3.3%	46.2%	24.8%
31	2020	-33.9%	-11.7%	-22.8%
32				
33	Average =	15.0%	15.6%	15.3%
34	Std Dev =	33.9%	37.0%	28.0%
35				
36	=AVERAGE(B2:B31)			=0.5*B31+0.5*C31
37			=STDEV.S(C2:C31)	

Microsoft Excel

Similar to Problems 9-6, 9-7, 9-8, 9-13, 9-14, 9-16, 9-17, 9-19, 9-20, Self-Test Problem 1

had invested a quarter of your money in General Electric stock and three-quarters of it in Newmont Corp. stock, then your portfolio return would be

Return contribution from GE + Contribution from NEM
$$= (0.25 \times -1.9\%) + (0.75 \times 17.3\%) = 12.50\%$$

To calculate the return on a three-stock portfolio, you will need the proportion of each stock in the portfolio and each stock's return. We typically call these proportions *weights,* signified by *w.* So, a portfolio with *n* securities will have a return of

$$R_p = \text{(Proportion of portfolio in first stock} \times \text{That stock's return)}$$
$$+ \text{(Second stock portion} \times \text{Second stock return)} + \ldots \quad (9\text{-}8)$$
$$= (w_1 \times R_1) + (w_2 \times R_2) + (w_3 \times R_3) + \ldots + (w_n \times R_n) = \sum_{i=1}^{n} w_i R_i$$

where the sum of the weights, *w,* must equal one.

The portfolio's rate of return is a simple weighted sum of the returns of each stock in the portfolio. Investors choose portfolio weights by determining how much of each stock they want in their portfolios. Ideally, investors will choose weights for their portfolios located on the efficient frontier (shown in Figure 9.3).

time out!

9-5 Describe characteristics of companies that would be good to combine into a portfolio.

9-6 Explain why one portfolio made up of the same companies (but not in the same proportions) as another portfolio can be undesirable in comparison.

9-7 Combining which two companies in Table 9.6 would reduce risk the most? Combining which two would create the least diversification?

Get Online

mhhe.com/CornettM6e

for study materials including
quizzes, iPod downloads,
and video

JGI/Jamie Grill/Getty Images

Your Turn...

Questions

1. Why is the percentage return a more useful measure than the dollar return? *(LG9-1)*

2. Characterize the historical return, risk, and risk–return relationship of the stock, bond, and cash markets. *(LG9-2)*

3. How do we define risk in this chapter, and how do we measure it? *(LG9-3)*

4. What are the two components of total risk? Which component is part of the risk–return relationship? Why? *(LG9-3)*

5. What's the source of firm-specific risk? What's the source of market risk? *(LG9-3)*

6. Which company is likely to have lower total risk, General Electric or Coca-Cola? Why? *(LG9-3)*

7. Can a company change its total risk level over time? How? *(LG9-3)*

8. What does the coefficient of variation measure? Why is a lower value better for the investor? *(LG9-4)*

9. You receive an investment newsletter advertisement in the mail. The letter claims that you should invest in a stock that has doubled the return of the S&P 500 Index over the last three months. It also claims that this stock is a surefire safe bet for the future. Explain how these two claims are inconsistent with finance theory. *(LG9-4)*

10. What does diversification do to the risk and return characteristics of a portfolio? *(LG9-5)*

11. Describe the diversification potential of two assets with a −0.8 correlation. What's the potential if the correlation is +0.8? *(LG9-5)*

12. You are a risk-averse investor with a low-risk portfolio of bonds. How is it possible that adding some stocks (which are riskier than bonds) to the portfolio can lower the total risk of the portfolio? *(LG9-5)*

13. You own only two stocks in your portfolio but want to add more. When you add a third stock, the total risk of your portfolio declines. When you add a tenth stock to the portfolio, the total risk declines. Adding which stock, the third or the tenth, likely reduced the total risk more? Why? *(LG9-5)*

14. Many employees believe that their employer's stock is less likely to lose half of its value than a well-diversified portfolio of stocks. Explain why this belief is erroneous. *(LG9-5)*

15. Explain what we mean when we say that one portfolio dominates another portfolio. *(LG9-6)*

16. Explain what the efficient frontier is and why it is important to investors. *(LG9-6)*

17. If an investor's desired risk level changes over time, should the investor change the composition of his or her portfolio? How? *(LG9-6)*

18. Say you own 200 shares of Boeing and 100 shares of Bank of America. Would your portfolio return be different if you instead owned 100 shares of Boeing and 200 shares of Bank of America? Why? *(LG9-7)*

Problems

BASIC PROBLEMS

9-1 **Investment Return** FedEx Corp. stock ended the previous year at $103.39 per share. It paid a $0.35 per share dividend last year. It ended last year at $106.69. If you owned 200 shares of FedEx, what were your dollar return and percent return? *(LG9-1)*

9-2 **Investment Return** A corporate bond that you own at the beginning of the year is worth $975. During the year, it pays $35 in interest payments and ends the year valued at $965. What were your dollar return and percent return? *(LG9-1)*

9-3 **Total Risk** Rank the following three stocks by their level of total risk, highest to lowest. Rail Haul has an average return of 12 percent and standard deviation of 25 percent. The average return and standard deviation of Idol Staff are 15 percent and 35 percent, respectively; and for Poker-R-Us they are 9 percent and 20 percent, respectively. *(LG9-3)*

9-4 **Risk versus Return** Rank the following three stocks by their risk–return relationship, best to worst. Rail Haul has an average return of 12 percent and standard deviation of 25 percent. The average return and standard deviation of Idol Staff are 15 percent and 35 percent, respectively, and of Poker-R-Us are 9 percent and 20 percent, respectively. *(LG9-4)*

9-5 **Dominant Portfolios** Determine which one of these three portfolios dominates another. Name the dominated portfolio and the portfolio that dominates it. Portfolio Blue has an expected return of 12 percent and risk of 18 percent. The expected return and risk of portfolio Yellow are 15 percent and 17 percent, respectively, and for the Purple portfolio they are 14 percent and 21 percent surefire safe. *(LG9-6)*

9-6 **Portfolio Weights** An investor owns $6,000 of Adobe Systems stock, $5,000 of Dow Chemical, and $5,000 of Office Depot. What are the portfolio weights of each stock? *(LG9-7)*

9-7 **Portfolio Return** Year-to-date, Oracle had earned a −1.34 percent return. During the same time period, Valero Energy earned 7.96 percent and McDonald's earned 0.88 percent. If you have a portfolio made up of 30 percent Oracle, 25 percent Valero Energy, and 45 percent McDonald's, what is your portfolio return? *(LG9-7)*

9-8 **Spreadsheet Problem: Portfolio Return** Consider the year-to-date returns of Yum Brands, Raytheon, and Coca-Cola. If you have a portfolio made up of the weights shown below, what is your portfolio return? *(LG9-7)*?

	A	B	C	D
1		Yum Brands	Raytheon	Coca-Cola
2	Return	3.80%	4.26%	-0.46%
3	Weight	0.3	0.3	0.4

Microsoft Excel

INTERMEDIATE PROBLEMS

9-9 **Average Return** The past five monthly returns for Kohls are 4.11 percent, 3.62 percent, −1.68 percent, 9.25 percent, and −2.56 percent. What is the average monthly return? *(LG9-1)*

9-10 **Standard Deviation** Compute the standard deviation of Kohls' monthly returns shown in problem 9-15. *(LG9-3)*

9-11 **Risk versus Return in Bonds** Assess the risk–return relationship of the bond market (see Tables 9.2 and 9.4) during each decade since 1950. *(LG9-2, LG9-4)*

9-12 **Diversifying** Consider the characteristics of the following three stocks:

	Expected Return	Standard Deviation
Thumb Devices	13%	23%
Air Comfort	10	19
Sport Garb	10	17

The correlation between Thumb Devices and Air Comfort is −0.12. The correlation between Thumb Devices and Sport Garb is −0.21. The correlation between Air Comfort and Sport Garb is 0.77. If you can pick only two stocks for your portfolio, which would you pick? Why? *(LG9-4, LG9-5)*

9-13 Portfolio Return At the beginning of the month, you owned $5,500 of General Dynamics, $7,500 of Starbucks, and $8,000 of Nike. The monthly returns for General Dynamics, Starbucks, and Nike were 7.44 percent, −1.36 percent, and −0.54 percent, respectively. What is your portfolio return? *(LG9-7)*

9-14 Portfolio Weights If you own 200 shares of Alaska Air at $42.88, 350 shares of Best Buy at $51.32, and 250 shares of Ford Motor at $8.51, what are the portfolio weights of each stock? *(LG9-7)*

9-15 Spreadsheet Problem: Standard Deviation and Variance Compute the standard deviation and variance of the following monthly returns. *(LG9-3)*

	A	B	C	D	E	F	G	H
1	Date	TSLA						
2	Jul-10	-16.32%	Mar-13	8.79%	Nov-15	11.27%	Jul-18	-13.07%
3	Aug-10	-2.31%	Apr-13	42.49%	Dec-15	4.23%	Aug-18	1.18%
4	Sep-10	4.77%	May-13	81.07%	Jan-16	-20.34%	Sep-18	-12.23%
5	Oct-10	7.01%	Jun-13	9.82%	Feb-16	0.38%	Oct-18	27.40%
6	Nov-10	61.77%	Jul-13	25.07%	Mar-16	19.72%	Nov-18	3.90%
7	Dec-10	-24.62%	Aug-13	25.86%	Apr-16	4.78%	Dec-18	-5.04%
8	Jan-11	-9.50%	Sep-13	14.42%	May-16	-7.28%	Jan-19	-7.75%
9	Feb-11	-0.87%	Oct-13	-17.29%	Jun-16	-4.91%	Feb-19	4.19%
10	Mar-11	16.16%	Nov-13	-20.42%	Jul-16	10.60%	Mar-19	-12.51%
11	Apr-11	-0.54%	Dec-13	18.19%	Aug-16	-9.70%	Apr-19	-14.71%
12	May-11	9.20%	Jan-14	20.59%	Sep-16	-3.76%	May-19	-22.43%
13	Jun-11	-3.35%	Feb-14	34.95%	Oct-16	-3.09%	Jun-19	20.68%
14	Jul-11	-3.30%	Mar-14	-14.85%	Nov-16	-4.21%	Jul-19	8.12%
15	Aug-11	-12.18%	Apr-14	-0.27%	Dec-16	12.82%	Aug-19	-6.62%
16	Sep-11	-1.41%	May-14	-0.06%	Jan-17	17.90%	Sep-19	6.76%
17	Oct-11	20.42%	Jun-14	15.54%	Feb-17	-0.77%	Oct-19	30.74%
18	Nov-11	11.47%	Jul-14	-6.98%	Mar-17	11.32%	Nov-19	4.77%
19	Dec-11	-12.77%	Aug-14	20.78%	Apr-17	12.85%	Dec-19	26.79%
20	Jan-12	1.79%	Sep-14	-10.02%	May-17	8.58%	Jan-20	55.52%
21	Feb-12	14.93%	Oct-14	-0.40%	Jun-17	6.04%	Feb-20	2.68%
22	Mar-12	11.46%	Nov-14	1.17%	Jul-17	-10.55%	Mar-20	-21.56%
23	Apr-12	-11.04%	Dec-14	-9.04%	Aug-17	10.03%	Apr-20	49.21%
24	May-12	-10.96%	Jan-15	-8.46%	Sep-17	-4.16%	May-20	6.79%
25	Jun-12	6.07%	Feb-15	-0.13%	Oct-17	-2.81%	Jun-20	29.32%
26	Jul-12	-12.37%	Mar-15	-7.17%	Nov-17	-6.84%	Jul-20	32.50%
27	Aug-12	4.01%	Apr-15	19.75%	Dec-17	0.81%	Aug-20	74.15%
28	Sep-12	2.66%	May-15	10.95%	Jan-18	13.80%	Sep-20	-13.91%
29	Oct-12	-3.93%	Jun-15	6.96%	Feb-18	-3.18%	Oct-20	-9.55%
30	Nov-12	20.23%	Jul-15	-0.79%	Mar-18	-22.42%	Nov-20	46.27%
31	Dec-12	0.15%	Aug-15	-6.42%	Apr-18	10.43%	Dec-20	24.33%
32	Jan-13	10.75%	Sep-15	-0.26%	May-18	-3.12%		
33	Feb-13	-7.14%	Oct-15	-16.69%	Jun-18	20.45%		

Microsoft Excel

9-16 Spreadsheet Problem: Portfolio Weights If you own 400 shares of Xerox at $17.34, 500 shares of Qwest at $8.15, and 350 shares of Liz Claiborne at $44.73, what are the portfolio weights of each stock? *(LG9-7)*

	A	B	C	D
1		Xerox	Qwest	Liz Claiborne
2	Shares	400	500	350
3	Price	$17.34	$8.15	$44.73

Microsoft Excel

9-17 Spreadsheet Problem: Portfolio Return At the beginning of the month, you owned $6,000 of News Corp, $5,000 of First Data, and $8,500 of Whirlpool. The monthly returns for News Corp, First Data, and Whirlpool were 8.24 percent, −2.59 percent, and 10.13 percent, respectively. What's your portfolio return? *(LG9-7)*

◢	A	B	C	D
1		News Corp	First Data	Whirlpool
2	Value	$6,000	$5,000	$8,500
3	Return	8.24%	-2.59%	10.13%

Microsoft Excel

ADVANCED PROBLEMS

9-18 Asset Allocation You have a portfolio with an asset allocation of 50 percent stocks, 40 percent long-term Treasury bonds, and 10 percent T-bills. Use these weights and the returns in Table 9.2 to compute the return of the portfolio in the year 2010 and each year since. Then compute the average annual return and standard deviation of the portfolio and compare them with the risk and return profile of each individual asset class. *(LG9-2, LG9-5)*

9-19 Portfolio Weights You have $15,000 to invest. You want to purchase shares of Alaska Air at $42.88, Best Buy at $51.32, and Ford Motor at $8.51. How many shares of each company should you purchase so that your portfolio consists of 30 percent Alaska Air, 40 percent Best Buy, and 30 percent Ford Motor? Report only whole stock shares. *(LG9-7)*

9-20 Portfolio Return The following table shows your stock positions at the beginning of the year, the dividends that each stock paid during the year, and the stock prices at the end of the year. What are your portfolio dollar return and percentage return? *(LG9-7)*

Company	Shares	Beginning-of-Year Price	Dividend per Share	End-of-Year Price
US Bank	300	$43.50	$2.06	$43.43
PepsiCo	200	59.08	1.16	62.55
JDS Uniphase	500	18.88		16.66
Duke Energy	250	27.45	1.26	33.21

9-21 Risk, Return, and Their Relationship Consider the following annual returns of Estee Lauder and Lowe's Companies:

	Estee Lauder	Lowe's Companies
Year 1	23.4%	−26.0
Year 2	−26.0	16.1
Year 3	17.6	4.2
Year 4	49.9	48.0
Year 5	−16.8	−19.0

Compute each stock's average return, standard deviation, and coefficient of variation. Which stock appears better? Why? *(LG9-3, LG9-4)*

9-22 Spreadsheet Problem: Risk, Return, and Their Relationship Consider the following annual returns of Clearwater Beer and Bed & Bath Corp.

	A	B	C
1		**Clearwater Beer**	**Bed & Bath**
2	Year 1	16.3%	4.5%
3	Year 2	-9.7%	-17.5%
4	Year 3	36.5%	-0.2%
5	Year 4	-6.9%	26.6%
6	Year 5	16.2%	-11.1%
7	Year 6	7.2%	6.5%
8	Year 7	9.4%	11.1%
9	Year 8	-2.5%	6.8%
10	Year 9	9.6%	8.5%
11	Year 10	15.3%	4.2%

Microsoft Excel

Compute each stock's average return, standard deviation, and coefficient of variation. Which stock appears better? Why? *(LG9-3, LG9-4)*

9-23 Spreadsheet Problem: Returns and Risks Following are the monthly returns for January 2016 to December 2020 of three international stock indices: All Ordinaries of Australia, Nikkei 225 of Japan, and Euronext of Europe. *(LG9-3, LG9-4)*

a. Compute and compare each index's monthly average return and standard deviation.

b. Compute the correlation between (1) All Ordinaries and Nikkei 225, (2) All Ordinaries and Euronext, and (3) Nikkei 225 and Euronext, and compare them.

c. Form a portfolio consisting of one-third of each of the indexes and show the portfolio return each year, and the portfolio's return and standard deviation.

	A	B	C	D	E	F	G	H
1	Date	All Ordinaries	NIKKEI 225	Euronext	Date	All Ordinaries	NIKKEI 225	Euronext
2	December-20	1.61%	3.82%	1.36%	June-18	2.71%	0.46%	-0.41%
3	November-20	9.93%	15.04%	16.95%	May-18	0.85%	-1.18%	-1.36%
4	October-20	2.06%	-0.90%	-2.93%	April-18	3.45%	4.72%	5.12%
5	September-20	-3.79%	0.20%	-2.14%	March-18	-4.06%	-2.78%	-1.62%
6	August-20	3.10%	6.59%	2.69%	February-18	-0.48%	-4.46%	-3.26%
7	July-20	0.95%	-2.59%	-2.28%	January-18	-0.34%	1.46%	2.93%
8	June-20	2.20%	1.88%	4.98%	December-17	2.39%	0.18%	-0.64%
9	May-20	4.90%	8.34%	3.38%	November-17	0.79%	3.24%	-2.70%
10	April-20	9.53%	6.75%	4.87%	October-17	4.03%	8.13%	3.06%
11	March-20	-21.51%	-10.53%	-16.03%	September-17	-0.54%	3.61%	4.53%
12	February-20	-8.56%	-8.89%	-8.77%	August-17	0.04%	-1.40%	-0.42%
13	January-20	4.69%	-1.91%	-2.11%	July-17	0.17%	-0.54%	0.97%
14	December-19	-2.10%	1.56%	1.28%	June-17	0.05%	1.95%	-3.31%
15	November-19	2.59%	1.60%	2.92%	May-17	-3.13%	2.36%	0.90%
16	October-19	-0.41%	5.38%	-0.12%	April-17	0.74%	1.52%	2.50%
17	September-19	1.53%	5.08%	3.30%	March-17	2.48%	-1.10%	4.59%
18	August-19	-2.88%	-3.80%	-1.57%	February-17	1.52%	0.41%	2.87%
19	July-19	2.95%	1.15%	0.90%	January-17	-0.77%	-0.38%	-1.84%
20	June-19	3.19%	3.28%	4.83%	December-16	3.94%	4.40%	5.57%
21	May-19	1.14%	-7.45%	-5.94%	November-16	1.85%	5.07%	0.32%
22	April-19	2.50%	4.97%	4.23%	October-16	-2.22%	5.93%	0.04%
23	March-19	0.14%	-0.84%	2.27%	September-16	-0.08%	-2.59%	0.63%
24	February-19	5.31%	2.94%	4.75%	August-16	-2.03%	1.92%	-0.01%
25	January-19	3.99%	3.79%	6.16%	July-16	6.28%	6.38%	3.49%
26	December-18	-0.69%	-10.45%	-5.81%	June-16	-2.52%	-9.63%	-4.26%
27	November-18	-2.77%	1.96%	-1.26%	May-16	2.48%	3.41%	1.64%
28	October-18	-6.52%	-9.12%	-7.09%	April-16	3.19%	-0.55%	0.63%
29	September-18	-1.59%	5.49%	0.21%	March-16	4.12%	4.57%	1.70%
30	August-18	0.97%	1.38%	-1.80%	February-16	-2.15%	-8.51%	-2.79%
31	July-18	1.22%	1.12%	3.19%	January-16	-5.39%	-7.96%	-3.53%

Microsoft Excel

9-24 Spreadsheet Problem: Portfolio Returns and Weights

a. Create a spreadsheet like the one shown below. The spreadsheet should use the returns for assets A and B to form a portfolio return using the weights for each asset shown in cells E1 and E2. The average portfolio return and standard deviation should compute at the bottom of the column of portfolio returns. When you change the weights, the portfolio returns, average, and standard deviation should recalculate.

	A	B	C	D	E	F
1	**A**	**B**		Weight A =	0.50	**Portfolio**
2	−9.1%	20.11%		Weight B =	0.50	5.51%
3	11.9%	4.56%		Sum =	1	8.23%
4	−22.1%	7.17%				−7.47%
5	28.7%	2.06%				15.38%
6	10.9%	7.70%				9.30%
7	4.9%	−6.50%				−0.80%
8	15.8%	1.85%				8.82%
9	3.5%	9.81%				6.66%
10	−5.5%	22.7%				8.60%
11	23.45%	−12.19%				5.63%
12	15.06%	9.38%				12.22%
13	2.11%	29.93%				16.02%
14	16.00%	3.56%				9.78%
15	32.39%	−12.66%				9.87%
16	13.69%	15.07%				14.38%
17						
18	**9.4%**	**6.8%**	= Average		Average =	**8.1%**
19	**14.41%**	**12.04%**	= StDev		StDev =	**6.07%**

Microsoft Excel

b. Use the Solver function to find the weights that provide the highest return for a standard deviation of 6 percent, 7.5 percent, 9 percent, 10.5 percent, 12 percent, and 13.5 percent. Report the weights and the return for each of these portfolio standard deviations. The Solver function is found in the Data tab. (*You may have to enable the function through the File tab, then Options, then Add-ins.*) The Solver image illustrates the maximizing of the average return for the specific constraints. The constraints are that the weights must be between 0 and 1, inclusive, and must sum to 1. Lastly, set the standard deviation constraint to the desired level. (*LG9-5, LG9-6, LG9-7*)

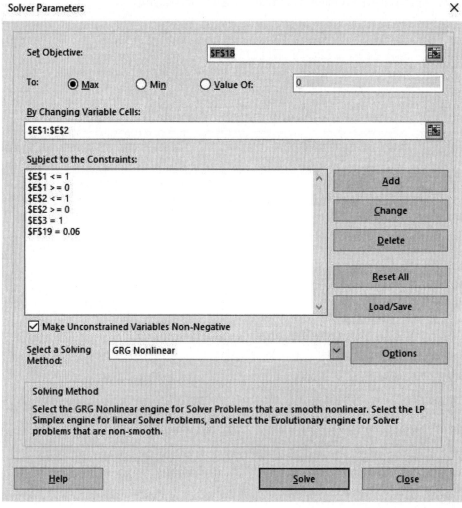

Microsoft Excel

Notes

CHAPTER 9

1. We use the denominator of $N - 1$ to compute a sample's standard deviation, which is the most common for finance applications. We would divide the standard deviation of a population simply by N.

Design elements: (Clock) Floortje/Getty Images; (Referee) Richard Ransier/Getty Images

chapter ten

estimating
risk and return

I s it possible for investors to know the exact risk they have to take? In Chapters 9 and 10, we explore methods to find the return that individual or institutional investors require to make a particular investment attractive. In the previous chapter, we established a positive relationship between risk and return using historical data. Risk and return play an undeniable role as investors seek the best return for the least risk. But until there's some way to forecast the future, financial managers and investors must make investment decisions armed only with their *expectations* about future risk and return. We need an exact specification that shows directly the amount of reward required for investors to take the level of risk in a given firm's stock or portfolio of securities. In this chapter we will also see how investors get the information they need to make risk-reward decisions.

Investors need to know how much risk they have to take to confidently expect a 10 percent return. Managers also want to know what return shareholders require so that they can decide how to meet those expectations. In Chapter 11, we'll explore how managers conduct financial analysis to find the shareholders' required return. If we want to specify the exact risk–return relationship, we need to develop a better measure of *risk* for individuals and institutional investors. As we saw in Chapter 9, any firm's total risk is specific to that particular firm. But the market doesn't reward firm-specific risk

continued on p. 282

LEARNING GOALS

LG10-1 Compute forward-looking expected return and risk.

LG10-2 Understand risk premiums.

LG10-3 Explain and apply the capital asset pricing model (CAPM).

LG10-4 Calculate and apply beta, a measure of market risk.

LG10-5 Differentiate among the different levels of market efficiency and their implications.

LG10-6 Calculate and explain investors' required return and risk.

LG10-7 Use the constant-growth model to compute required return.

»viewpoints

Consider that you work in the finance department of a large corporation. Your team is analyzing several new projects the firm can pursue. To complete the analysis, the team needs to know what return stockholders require from the firm.

You are to estimate this required return. Shareholders' expected return will depend on your company's risk level. What information do you need to gather and how might you compute this return? **(See the solution at the end of the book.)**

continued from p. 281

because investors can easily diversify away any single firm's specific risks by owning other offsetting firms' stocks to create a portfolio subject only to market or undiversifiable risk. So, we need to find just the market risk portion of total risk for investors. The theory to find the market risk portion of stock ownership extends modern portfolio theory. Our search to find market risk will lead us to the capital asset pricing model (CAPM), which utilizes a measure of market risk called beta. CAPM's risk–return specification provides us a powerful tool to make better investment decisions.

Corporate finance managers and investment professionals commonly use the beta measure. But like any theory, CAPM has its limitations. We'll discuss the CAPM's limitations and concerns about beta and propose an alternate required return measure. Whether beta or any other risk–return specification is useful relies in part on whether a stock's price represents a fair estimate of the true company value. Stock price validity and reliability—their general correctness—are vitally important to both investors and corporate managers. ■

10.1 • EXPECTED RETURNS LG10-1

In the previous chapter, we characterized risk and return in historical terms. We defined a stock's return as the actual profit realized while holding the stock or the average return over a longer period. We described risk simply as the standard deviation of those returns—a term already familiar to you from your statistics classes. So, we did a good job describing the risk and return that the stock experienced *in the past*. But do those risk and return figures hold into the future? Firms can quite possibly change their stocks' risk level by substantially changing their business. If a firm takes on riskier new projects over time, or changes the nature of its business, the firm itself will become riskier. Similarly, firms can reduce their risk level—and, hence, their stock's riskiness—by choosing low-risk new projects. Both investors and firms find *expected return,* a forward-looking return calculation that includes risk measures, very useful to estimate future stock performance.

Expected Return and Risk

We can attribute a company's business success over a year partly to its management talent, strategies, and other firm-specific activities, but overall economic conditions will also affect a firm's level of success or failure. Consider a steel manufacturer—Nucor Corp. The steel business closely follows economic trends. In a good economy, demand for steel

You have just started your first job in the corporate world and need to make some retirement plan decisions. The company's 401(k) retirement plan offers three investment choices: a stock portfolio with a beta of 1, a bond portfolio with a beta of 0.18, and a money market account. For your allocation, you decide to contribute $200 per month to the stock portfolio, $100 to the bond portfolio, and $50 to the money market account.

If the expected return to the market portfolio is 11 percent, what risk level are you taking in your retirement portfolio and what return should you expect over the long run? **(See the solution at the end of the book.)**

Investing mainly in my own company's stock is safer, right? Maybe not . . .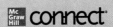

is strong as builders and manufacturers step up building and production. During economic recessions, demand for steel falls off quickly. So, if we want to assess Nucor's probabilities for success next year, we know that we must look partly at Nucor's managerial ability and partly at the economic outlook.

Unfortunately, we cannot accurately predict what the economy will be like next year. Predicting economic activity is like predicting the weather—forecasts give the **probability** of rain or sunshine. Economists cannot say for sure whether the economy will be good or bad next year. Instead, they may forecast a 70 percent chance that the economy will be good and a 30 percent chance of a recession. Similarly, analysts might say that given Nucor's managerial talent, if the economy is good, Nucor will perform well and the stock will increase 20 percent. If the economy goes into a recession, then Nucor's stock will fall 10 percent. So what return do you expect from Nucor? The return still depends on the state of the economy.

A company's success depends partly on management talent, strategies, and other activities.
Robert Nicholas/AGE Fotostock

This leads us directly to a key concept: **expected return.** We compute expected return by multiplying each possible return by the probability, *p*, of that return occurring. We then sum them (recall that all probabilities must add to one). Let's place Nucor in an economy with only two states: good and recession. In this scenario, Nucor's expected return would be 11 percent [=(0.7 × 20%) + (0.3 × −10%)]. Of course, nothing is quite that simple. Economists seldom predict simple two-state views of the economy as in the previous example. Rather, economists give much more detailed forecasts (such as three states: red-hot economy, average expansion, and recession). So our general equation for a stock's expected return with S different conditions of the economy is

probability The likelihood of occurrence.

expected return The average of the possible returns weighted by the likelihood of those returns occurring.

probability distribution The set of probabilities for all possible occurrences.

$$\text{Expected return} = \text{Sum of (Each return} \times \text{Probability of that return)}$$
$$= (p_1 \times \text{Return}_1) + (p_2 \times \text{Return}_2) + (p_3 \times \text{Return}_3) \qquad \text{(10-1)}$$
$$+ \cdots + (p_s \times \text{Return}_s) = \sum_{j=1}^{s} p_j \times \text{Return}_j$$

The result of this expected return calculation has some interesting properties. First, the expected return figure expresses what the average return would be over time if the probabilistic states of the economy occur as predicted. For example, the 70/30 **probability distribution** for good/recession economic states suggests that the economy will be good in 7 of the next 10 years, earning Nucor shareholders a 20 percent return in each of those years. Shareholders would lose 10 percent in each of the three recession years.

required return The level of total return needed to be compensated for the risk taken. It is made up of a risk-free rate and a risk premium.

So the *average return* over those 10 years would be 11 percent, the same as the expected return. The second interesting property: The expected return itself will not likely occur during any one year. Remember that Nucor will earn a return of either 20 percent or −10 percent. Yet its expected return is 11 percent, a value that it cannot earn because we have no economic condition for which the return is 11 percent. Again, this illustration seems extreme because we used only two economic states. Any real economic forecast would instead include a probability distribution of many potential economic conditions.

We can also characterize risk via this expected return figure. The expected return procedure shows potential return possibilities, but we don't know which one will actually occur, so we face uncertainty. In the last chapter, we measured risk using the standard deviation of returns over time. We can use the same principle to measure risk for expected returns. What range of different expected returns will Nucor exhibit from the expected return of 11 percent? In our two-state description of the economy, the deviation could be either 9 percent (=20% − 11%) or −21 percent (= − 10% − 11%). We compute the standard deviation of expected returns the same way we did for historical returns. We square the deviations, then multiply by the probability of that deviation occurring, and then sum them all up. So Nucor's return variance is $189.0[= (0.7 \times 9^2) + (0.3 \times -21^2)]$. As a final step, we take the square root of our result to put the figure back into sensible terms. The standard deviation for Nucor is 13.75 percent $(= \sqrt{189})$. The general equation for the standard deviation of S different economic states is

$$
\begin{aligned}
\text{Standard deviation} &= \begin{array}{l}\text{Square root of the sum of (Probability of a return}\\ \times \text{ Each return''s squared deviation from the average)}\end{array}\\
&= \sqrt{\begin{array}{l} p_1 \times (\text{Return}_1 - \text{Expected return})^2 + p_2 \\ \times (\text{Return}_2 - \text{Expected return})^2 + ... \end{array}} \\
&= \sqrt{\sum_{j=1}^{s} p_j \times (\text{Return}_j - \text{Expected return})^2}
\end{aligned}
$$

(10-2)

the
Math Coach on...

Expected Return and Standard Deviation

❝ When you compute expected return and standard deviation, you'll find it helpful to use the decimal format for the probability of the economic state and percentages to state the return in each state. ❞

Risk Premiums LG10-2

Throughout the book, we have mentioned the positive relationship between expected return and risk. Consider this key question: You have a risk-less investment available to you. The short-term government debt security, the T-bill, offers you a low return with no risk. Why would you invest in anything risky, when you could simply buy T-bills? The answer, of course, is that some investors want a higher return and are willing to take some risk to raise their returns. Investors who take on a little risk should expect a slightly higher return than the T-bill rate. People who take on higher risk levels should expect higher returns. Indeed, it's only logical that investors require this extra return to willingly take the added risk.

The expected return of an investment is often expressed in two parts, a risk-free return and a risky contribution. The return investors require for the risk level they take is called the **required return**:

$$\text{Required return} = \text{Risk-free rate} + \text{Return premium} \qquad (10\text{-}3)$$

The *risk-free rate* is typically considered the return on U.S. government bonds and bills and equals the real interest rate and the expected inflation premium that we discussed

EXAMPLE 10-1

Expected Return and Risk LG10-1

Bailey has a probability distribution for four possible states of the economy, as shown below. She has also calculated the return that Motor Music stock would earn in each state. Given this information, what are Motor Music's expected return and risk?

Economic State	Probability	Return
Fast growth	0.15	25%
Slow growth	0.60	15
Recession	0.20	−5
Depression	0.05	−20

SOLUTION:

Bailey can compute the expected return using equation 10-1:

$$\text{Expected return} = (0.15 \times 25\%) + (0.60 \times 15\%) + (0.20 \times -5\%) + (0.05 \times -20\%) = 10.75\%$$

Then Bailey can compute the expected return by computing the standard deviation using equation 10-2:

$$\text{Standard deviation} = \sqrt{\begin{array}{l} 0.15 \times (25\% - 10.75\%)^2 + 0.60 \times (15\% - 10.75\%)^2 + 0.20 \\ \times (-5\% - 10.75\%)^2 + 0.05 \times (-20\% - 10.75\%)^2 \end{array}}$$

$$= \sqrt{30.46 + 10.84 + 49.61 + 47.28} = 11.76\%$$

The expected return and standard deviation are 10.75 percent and 11.76 percent, respectively. The spreadsheet solution requires the SQRT function:

▲	A	B	C	D	E	F	G	H
1	Probability	Return						
2	0.15	25%						
3	0.60	15%						
4	0.20	-5%						
5	0.05	-20%						
6								
7	Expected Return =	10.75%	=SUMPRODUCT(A2:A5,B2:B5)					
8	Standard Deviation =	11.76%	=SQRT(A2*(B2-B7)^2+A3*(B3-B7)^2+A4*(B4-B7)^2+A5*(B5-B7)^2)					

Microsoft Excel

Similar to Problems 10-1, 10-10, 10-13, 10-15, Self-Test Problem 1

in Chapter 6. The **risk premium** is the reward investors require for taking risk. How large are the rewards for taking risk? As we discussed in the previous chapter, the market doesn't reward all risks. The firm-specific portion of total risk for any stock can be diversified away, and since the investor takes on such risk out of ignorance or by mistake, an efficient market will not reward anyone for taking on this "superfluous" risk. So as we examine historical risk premiums, we do so with a diversified portfolio that contains no firm-specific risk.

Table 10.1 shows the average annual return on the S&P 500 Index minus the T-bill rate for different time periods. The remainder after we subtract the T-bill rate is the risk premium; in this case, it's the **market risk premium**—the reward for taking general (unsystematic) stock market risk. Since 1950, the average market risk premium has been 8.6 percent per year. Over the long run, this is the reward for taking stock market risk. The actual, realized risk premium during particular decades has varied. The average risk premium has been as high as 18.8 percent for the 1950s and as low as −1.8 percent during the 2000s.

risk premium The portion of the required return that represents the reward for taking risk.

market risk premium The return on the market portfolio minus the risk-free rate. Risk premiums for specific firms are based on the market risk premium.

	1950 to 2019	1950 to 1959	1960 to 1969	1970 to 1979	1980 to 1989	1990 to 1999	2000 to 2009	2010 to 2019
Risk premium	8.6%	18.8%	4.7%	1.2%	9.3%	14.1%	−1.8%	13.5%

Realized risk premiums were very different in each decade. The 2000s even had a negative risk premium!

Source: S&P 500 Index and T-bill rate data.

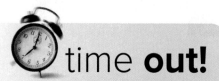

time out!

10-1 Describe the similarities between computing average return and expected return. Also, describe the similarities between expected return risk and historical risk.

10-2 Why would people take risks by investing their hard-earned money?

asset pricing The process of directly specifying the relationship between required return and risk.

capital asset pricing model (CAPM) An asset pricing theory based on a beta, a measure of market risk.

capital market line (CML) The line on a graph of return and risk (standard deviation) from the risk-free rate through the market portfolio.

market portfolio In theory, the market portfolio is the combination of securities that places the portfolio on the efficient frontier and on a line tangent from the risk-free rate. In practice, the S&P 500 Index is used to proxy for the market portfolio.

The performance in the 2000s is unusual; the stock market return has been so poor that it has not beaten the risk-free rate. Investors require a risk premium for taking on market risk. But taking that risk also means that they will periodically experience poor returns.

10.2 • MARKET RISK LG10-3

How much risk should you take to achieve the return you want over time? In the previous chapter, we demonstrated that individual stocks and different portfolios exhibit different levels of total risk. Recall that the rewards for carrying risk apply only to the market risk (or undiversifiable) portion of total risk. But how do investors know how much of the 33.9 percent standard deviation of returns for Boeing is firm-specific risk and how much of that deviation is market risk? The answer to this important question will determine how much of a risk premium investors should require for Boeing. The attempt to specify an equation that relates a stock's required return to an appropriate risk premium is known as **asset pricing.**

The Market Portfolio

The best-known asset pricing equation is the **capital asset pricing model,** typically referred to as **CAPM.** Though many theorists formulated theories that, in the end, supported the CAPM's effectiveness, credit for the model goes to William Sharpe and John Lintner. Sharpe eventually won a Nobel Prize for his work in 1990. (Lintner died in 1983, and Nobel Prizes are not awarded posthumously.) Today, both investors and corporate finance professionals use CAPM widely. In developing the CAPM, Lintner and Sharpe sought to emphasize the individual investor's best strategy to maximize returns for a given amount of market risk.

CAPM starts with modern portfolio theory. Remember from the previous chapter that when you combine securities into a portfolio, you can find a set of portfolios that dominate all others. The best combinations possible use all the risky securities available (but not the risk-free asset) to create efficient frontier portfolios, which would lie along a curved line in risk/return space, as shown in Figure 10.1, panel A. These portfolios represent combinations of various risky securities that give the highest expected return for each potential level of risk (i.e., they lie the furthest "up and to the left" that we can achieve when considering all possible combinations of the available risky securities).

The idea of a risk premium in equation 10-3 implies a risk-free investment, like T-bills. Panel B shows where the risk-free asset would appear on the **capital market line (CML).** The risk-free asset must lie on the y-axis precisely because it carries no risk. Now we draw a line from the risk-free security to a point tangent to the efficient frontier. The CML relationship appears as a line because investments show a direct risk-reward relationship. You may recall from your economics classes that only one tangency point will be possible between this kind of curve and a straight line. The spot where the tangency occurs is called the **market portfolio,** which has a special significance. The market portfolio represents ownership in all traded assets in the economy, so this portfolio provides maximum diversification. You can locate your optimal portfolio on this line by owning various combinations of the risk-free security and the market portfolio. If most of your money is invested in the market portfolio, then you will have a portfolio on the line that lies just to the left of the market portfolio dot in the graph. If you own just a little of the market portfolio and hold mostly risk-free securities, then your portfolio will lie on the line near the risk-free security dot. For your investments to lie on the line to the right of the market portfolio, you would have to invest all your money in the market portfolio, then borrow more money at the risk-free rate and invest these additional funds in the market portfolio. Borrowing money to invest is known as using **financial leverage.** Using financial leverage increases the overall risk of the portfolio, which is illustrated in this figure as a higher standard deviation.

Notice that if you had a portfolio on the efficient frontier (labeled "old portfolio"), you could do better. Instead of owning the old portfolio, you can put some of your money in the market portfolio and some in the risk-free security to obtain the "new portfolio." See how the new portfolio dominates that old one? It carries the same risk level but offers a higher return. In fact, notice that the line drawn between the risk-free investment and the market portfolio dominates all of the efficient frontier portfolios (except the market portfolio itself). All portfolio allocations between the risk-free security and the market portfolio constitute the capital market line. All investors should want to locate their portfolios on the CML, rather than the efficient frontier. Portfolios on the CML offer the highest expected return for any level of desired risk, which the investor controls by deciding how much of the market portfolio and how much of the risk-free asset to hold. Risk-averse investors can put more of their money in T-bills and less into the market portfolio. Investors willing to take on higher risk for larger returns can put more of their money in the market portfolio.

Beta, a Measure of Market Risk LG10-4

The CML demonstrates that the market portfolio is crucial. Indeed, its return less the risk-free rate represents the expected average market risk premium. The market portfolio features no firm-specific risk; all such risk is diversified away. So the market portfolio carries only market risk. Thus, the market portfolio's risk factor allows us to compute a measure of firm-specific risk for any individual stock or portfolio. We can now examine the question posed at the beginning of this section: "How much of Boeing's total risk is attributable to market risk?" The standard deviation of returns includes all of Boeing stock's risk—it quantifies how much the stock price rises and falls. The market risk portion will rise and fall along with the market portfolio. If we subtract the market risk portion from the total risk measure, we're left with firm-specific risk. This part of risk rises and falls in ways unrelated to market changes.

Remember that portfolio theory describes a measure—correlation—that measures how two stocks move together through time. Instead of measuring how any two stocks or portfolios move together, we now want to know how a stock or portfolio moves relative to market portfolio movements. This measure is known as **beta (β).** Beta measures the comovement between a stock and the market portfolio.

If Boeing's total risk level is measured by its standard deviation, σ_{Boeing}, then we can find the portion of this risk that is attributable to the market in general by multiplying Boeing's total risk by its correlation with the market

financial leverage The extent to which debt securities are used by a firm.

beta (β) A measure of the sensitivity of a stock or portfolio to market risk.

▼**FIGURE 10.1** Maximizing Expected Return

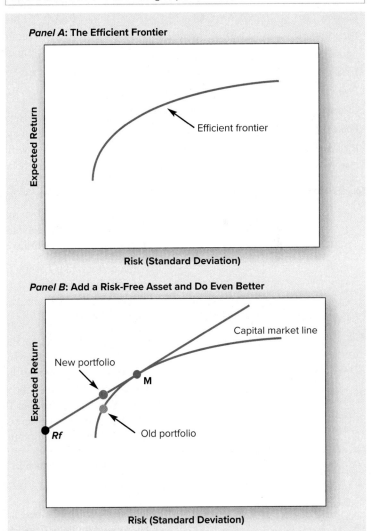

Panel A: **The Efficient Frontier**

Panel B: **Add a Risk-Free Asset and Do Even Better**

In MPT, investors want to be on the efficient frontier (Panel A) because it gives them the highest expected return for each level of risk. However, after adding a riskless asset (Panel B), investors can then get portfolios on the straight line (shown), which offers a higher expected return for each level of risk than the efficient frontier.

portfolio, $\sigma_{\text{Boeing}} \times \rho_{\text{Boeing, Market}}$. The beta computation is scaled so that the market portfolio itself has a beta of one. The scaling is done by dividing by the standard deviation of the market portfolio: $\sigma_{\text{Boeing}} \times \rho_{\text{Boeing, Market}} \div \sigma_{\text{Market}}$.[1] Stocks with betas larger than one are considered riskier than the market portfolio, while betas of less than one indicate lower risk. Boeing has a beta of 1.66, meaning that Boeing has high sensitivity to market risk. When the market portfolio moves, you can expect Boeing stock to move in the same direction. Technically, you should expect Boeing's realized risk premium to be 66 percent more than the realized market risk premium.

▼ **TABLE 10.2** Dow Jones Industrial Average Stock Betas

Company	Beta	Company	Beta
3M Company	0.92	Intel	0.73
American Express	1.36	Johnson & Johnson	0.70
Amgen	0.76	JPMorgan Chase	1.22
Apple	1.28	McDonald's	0.58
Boeing	1.66	Merck	0.44
Caterpillar	0.96	Microsoft	0.83
Chevron	1.32	Nike	0.84
Cisco Systems	0.94	Procter & Gamble	0.38
Coca-Cola	0.58	salesforce.com	1.17
Disney	1.20	Travelers	0.78
Dow	1.39	UnitedHealth Group	0.74
Goldman Sachs	1.50	Verizon Communications	0.40
Home Depot	1.03	Visa	0.96
Honeywell	1.15	Walgreens	0.54
IBM	1.24	Walmart Stores	0.42

Source: Yahoo! Finance, January 15, 2021.

Table 10.2 shows the beta for each of the 30 companies in the Dow Jones Industrial Average. Note that Boeing is considered the riskiest of the DJIA stocks with a $\beta = 1.66$. The next highest beta firm is Dow. These firms' stocks carry high market risk because the demand for their products is very sensitive to the overall economy's strength. Investors consider other companies safe bets with low risk, like Procter & Gamble (0.38), Verizon (0.40), and Walmart (0.42). Many lower-beta firms sell consumer goods that we consider the necessities of life, which we will buy whether the economy is in recession or expansion. The demand for these products is price inelastic and not sensitive to economic conditions. Some companies have nearly the same risk as the market portfolio, like Home Depot (1.03), Caterpillar (0.96), and Visa (0.96).

The Security Market Line LG10-3

Beta indicates the market risk that each stock represents to investors. So the higher the beta, the higher the risk premium investors will demand to undertake that security's market risk. Since beta sums up precisely what investors want to know about risk, we often replace the standard deviation risk measure shown in Figure 10.1 with beta. Figure 10.2 shows required return versus beta risk. We call the line in this figure the **security market line (SML),** which illustrates how required return relates to risk at any particular time, all else held equal. The SML also shows the market portfolio's risk premium or any stock's risk premium.

When a stock like Disney carries a beta greater than one, then its risk premium must be larger than the market risk premium. A stock like Johnson & Johnson carries a lower beta than does the overall market; therefore, Johnson & Johnson would offer a lower risk premium to investors.

We can use the SML to show the relationship between risk and return for any stock or portfolio. To precisely quantify this relationship, we need the equation for the SML. The equation of any line can be defined as $y = b + mx$, where b is the intercept and m is the slope. In this case, the y-axis is required return and the x-axis is beta. The intercept is R_f. You may remember that the slope is the "rise over run" between two points on the line. The rise between the risk-free security and the market portfolio is $R_M - R_f$ and the run is $1 - 0$. Substituting into the line equation results in the CAPM:

$$\text{Expected return} = \text{Risk-free rate} + \text{Beta} \times \text{Market risk premium}$$
$$= R_f + \beta(R_M - R_f) \tag{10-4}$$

So, we have determined a way to estimate any stock's required return once we have determined its beta. Consider this: We expect the market portfolio to earn 12 percent and T-bill yields are 5 percent. Then Disney's required return, with a $\beta = 1.20$, is $5\% + 1.20 \times (12\% - 5\%) = 13.40$ percent. Table 10.3 shows the 30 Dow Jones Industrial Average stocks' required returns, using these same market and risk-free rate assumptions. Higher-risk companies have higher betas and thus require higher returns.

FIGURE 10.2 The Security Market Line Uses Beta as the Risk Measure

portfolio beta The combination of the individual company betas in an investor's portfolio.

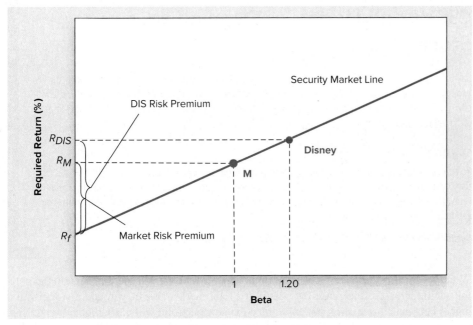

Disney has higher risk than the overall stock market, so it should require a higher return.

Portfolio Beta

As you might expect, a stock **portfolio's beta** is the weighted average of the portfolio stocks' betas. The portfolio beta equation resembles equation 9-7, which gives the return of a portfolio:

$$\beta_p = \text{Sum of the beta of each stock} \times \text{Its weight in the portfolio}$$

$$= (w_1 \times \beta_1) + (w_2 \times \beta_2) + (w_3 \times \beta_3) + \ldots + (w_n \times \beta_n) = \sum_{j=1}^{n} w_j \beta_j \qquad (10\text{-}5)$$

▼ **TABLE 10.3** Required Returns for DJIA Stocks

Company	Required Return	Company	Required Return
3M Company	11.44%	Intel	10.11%
American Express	14.52	Johnson & Johnson	9.9
Amgen	10.32	JPMorgan Chase	13.54
Apple	13.96	McDonald's	9.06
Boeing	16.62	Merck	8.08
Caterpillar	11.72	Microsoft	10.81
Chevron	14.24	Nike	10.88
Cisco Systems	11.58	Proctor & Gamble	7.66
Coca-Cola	9.06	salesforce.com	13.19
Disney	13.40	Travelers	10.46
Dow	14.73	UnitedHealth Group	10.18
Goldman Sachs	15.50	Verizon Communications	7.80
Home Depot	12.21	Visa	11.72
Honeywell	13.05	Walgreens	8.78
IBM	13.68	Walmart Stores	7.94

Higher beta stocks require higher expected returns.

Assumptions: market return = 12% and risk-free rate = 5%.

Source: Yahoo! Finance, January 15, 2021.

CAPM and Under- or Overvalued Stock LG10-3

Say that you are a corporate CFO. You know that the risk-free rate is currently 4.5 percent and you expect the market to earn 11 percent this year. Through your own analysis of the firm, you think it will earn a 13.5 percent return this year. If the beta of the company is 1.2, should you consider the firm undervalued or overvalued?

SOLUTION:

You can compute shareholders' required return with CAPM as $4.5\% + 1.2 \times (11\% - 4.5\%) = 12.3\%$. Since you think the firm will actually earn more than this required return, the firm appears to be currently undervalued. That is, its price must rise more than predicted by CAPM to obtain the return you estimated in your original analysis.

Similar to Problems 10-4, 10-11, Self-Test Problem 3

With this equation, you can easily determine whether adding a particular stock to the portfolio will increase or decrease the portfolio's total market risk. If you add a stock with a higher beta than the existing portfolio, then the new portfolio will carry higher market risk than the old one did. Although we can find the effects on total portfolio risk of adding particular stocks using beta, the same is not necessarily true if we use standard deviations as our risk measure. The new stock, however risky, might have low correlations with the other stocks in the portfolio—offsetting (negative) correlations would reduce total risk.

Finding Beta LG10-4

The CAPM is an elegant explanation that relates the return you should require for taking on various levels of market risk. Although CAPM provides many practical applications, you need a company's beta to use those applications. Where or how can you obtain a beta? You have two ways. First, given the returns of the company and the market portfolio, you

Portfolio Beta LG10-4

You have a portfolio consisting of 20 percent Boeing stock ($\beta = 1.66$), 40 percent Amgen stock ($\beta = 0.76$), and 40 percent McDonald's stock ($\beta = 0.58$). How much market risk does the portfolio have?

SOLUTION:

Compute a beta for the portfolio. Using equation 10-5, the portfolio beta is $0.2 \times 1.66 + 0.4 \times 0.76 + 0.4 \times 0.58 = 0.87$. Note that this portfolio carries 13 percent less market risk than the general market does.

The spreadsheet solution is

▲	A	B	C	D	E
1		Beta	Weight		
2	Boeing	1.66	20%		
3	Amgen	0.76	40%		
4	McDonald's	0.58	40%		
5					
6	Portfolio Beta =	0.87	=SUMPRODUCT(B2:B4,C2:C4)		

Microsoft Excel

Similar to Problems 10-6, 10-9, 10-12, 10-14, 10-17, Self-Test Problem 2

can compute the beta yourself. Second, you can find the beta that others have computed through financial information data providers.

Many financial outlets publish company betas. Websites that provide company betas for free include MarketWatch, MSN Money, and Yahoo! Finance, to name just a few. For example, in January 2021, the beta these websites listed for Disney were 0.96 (MarketWatch), 1.19 (MSN Money), and 1.20 (Yahoo! Finance). Note that these reported betas have some differences. To know why differences might arise, consider how you would go about gathering information and computing beta yourself.

To compute your own beta, first obtain historical returns for the company of interest and of the market portfolio. Then, run a regression of the company return as the dependent variable and the market portfolio return as the independent variable. The resulting market portfolio return coefficient is beta. Many important questions may come to mind. First, what do you use as the market portfolio? People typically use a major stock index like the

▼ **TABLE 10.4** Compute Beta Using a Spreadsheet

	A	B	C	D	E
1	Date	Stock Return	Market Return		
2	Apr	−4.13%	−1.01%		
3	Mar	0.84	3.60	beta =	
4	Feb	−0.46	1.11	= SLOPE(B2:B61,C2:C61) =	0.83
5	Jan	5.83	5.04		
6	Dec	−0.47	0.71		
7	Nov	8.23	0.28		
8	Oct	−8.43	−1.98		
9	Sep	2.44	2.42		
10	Aug	6.42	1.98		
11	Jul	2.17	1.26		
12	Jun	7.25	3.96		
13	May	−8.19	−6.27		
14	Apr	14.51	−0.75		
15	Mar	12.70	3.13		
16	Feb	−7.59	4.06		
17	Jan	12.33	4.36		
18	Dec	−9.98	0.85		
19	Nov	−9.94	−0.51		
20	Oct	−1.26	10.77		
21	Sep	0.46	−7.18		
22	Aug	−3.28	−5.68		
⋮	⋮	⋮	⋮	⋮	⋮
49	May	−3.14	5.31		
50	Apr	9.64	9.39		
51	Mar	13.35	8.54		
52	Feb	10.15	−10.99		
53	Jan	14.70	−8.57		
54	Dec	20.09	0.78		
55	Nov	−25.40	−7.48		
56	Oct	−21.33	−16.94		
57	Sep	−9.96	−9.08		
58	Aug	5.86	1.22		
59	Jul	4.10	−0.99		
60	Jun	−10.16	−8.60		
61	May	3.80	1.07		

The spreadsheet function SLOPE() finds the statistical relationship between a stock's return and the market return.
Considering these monthly returns for a stock and a market index, the beta of this stock is 0.83.

Microsoft Excel

finance at work //:markets

Are Stocks Really Good or Bad?

One of the basic financial theories tells us how we should view the relationship between risk and expected returns. In a nutshell, risk and expected return are positively related. A high-risk investment needs to have a high expected return, or no one would want to buy that investment. With this lack of demand, the investment's price would drop until it offers new buyers a high expected return for the future. The higher return is the reward for taking the extra risk. Similarly, low-risk investments offer low expected returns.

To quantify risk, the finance industry tends to use two measures: volatility of returns and beta. The volatility, measured by variance or standard deviation, tells us how much a return can deviate from the average return. Beta tells us how much market risk an investment has. These measures are very useful in assessing the risk of an investment or portfolio and what return premium should be expected for taking risk.

However, people do not naturally think of risk within this financial theory framework. First, investors care less about how an investment's return deviates from expectations and more about how the return may be lower than expected. In other words, a higher return than expected is not considered risky, only a lower return, or even, gulp, a loss, is viewed as risk.

Also, real people do not think in terms of the high risk/return versus the low risk/return scale. Instead, people think in terms of better or worse. For example, three financial economists ran an experiment in which they asked high-net-worth individuals for either their expected return predictions or their risk assessment (both on a 0 to 10 scale) of over 200 of the Fortune 500 companies. When they compiled all the responses, they found the relationship in the figure shown below. Notice anything odd? This shows that firms with low risk are expected to earn a high return. People act as if expected return and risk are negatively related! This is the

Beliefs about Performance and Risk of Fortune 500 Firms

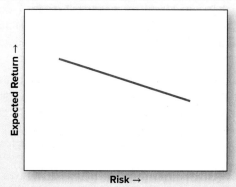

opposite of financial theory. Instead of evaluating firms within the framework that high expected return goes with high risk and low return goes with low risk, people seem to think in terms of good versus bad stocks. What are the characteristics of a "good" stock? Characteristics that seem good are high expected return and low risk. When an investor feels a stock is good, then it is attributed with high return and low risk. When an investor feels the stock is bad, then it is attributed with low return and high risk. Psychologists call this perception or belief an "affect."

Unfortunately, thinking about risk and return from the affect framework causes investors to misunderstand the underlying dynamics of actual expected return and risk. Thus, they may make poor decisions regarding risk and return.

Want to know more?

Key Words to Search for Updates: **affect, measuring investment risk, risk and behavioral finance**

Source: Meir Statman, Kenneth L. Fisher, and Deniz Anginer, "Affect in a Behavioral Asset-Pricing Model," *Financial Analysts Journal,* March/April 2008, Figure 3: Relationship between Expected Return Scores and Risk Scores.

S&P 500 Index to proxy for the market portfolio. Second, what time frame should you use? You can use daily, weekly, monthly, or even annual returns. Using monthly returns is the most common. How long a time series is needed? As you will recall, statistical estimates become more reliable and valid as more data are used. But you will have to weigh those statistical advantages against the fact that companies change their business enterprises and thus their risk levels over time. Using data from too long ago reflects risks that may no longer apply. Generally speaking, using time series data of three to five years is common. Whatever decisions you make to address these questions, be consistent by making the same decisions for all the company betas you compute.

Table 10.4 shows the spreadsheet of a stock's beta calculation. In this case, monthly returns from five years are used for the stock return and a market index. The SLOPE() function of the spreadsheet directly computes the regression coefficient of interest. The beta estimation using the spreadsheet function is 0.83.

Concerns about Beta

Consider the estimation choices just mentioned. Say you estimate a firm's beta using monthly data for five years and the Dow Jones Industrial Average return as the market portfolio. Suppose that the result is a beta of 1.3. Then you try again using weekly returns for three years and the return from the S&P 500 Index as the market portfolio's yield, resulting in a beta of 0.9. These estimates are quite different and would create a large variation in required return if you plugged them into the CAPM. So, which is the more accurate estimate? Unfortunately, we may not be able to determine which is most representative, or "true." In general, you may estimate a little different beta using different market portfolio proxies, different return intervals (like monthly returns versus annual returns), and different time periods.

In addition to these estimation problems, a company can change its risk level, and thus its beta, by changing the way it operates within its business, by expanding into new businesses, and/or by changing its debt load. So even if beta is an accurate measure of what the firm's risk level was in the past, does it apply to the future? Beta's applicability will depend on the firm's future plans.

Both financial managers and investors share these concerns about beta. In the end, beta's usefulness depends on its reliability. Unfortunately, beta's empirical record is not as good as we would like. We should expect that companies with high betas yield higher returns than companies with low betas. On average, though, this does not turn out to be the case. A company's beta does not appear to predict its future return very well. Since characterizing the risk–return relationship is so important, finance researchers have introduced other asset pricing models. One promising model adds more risk factors to the predictive relationship other than just market risk. Firm size and book-to-market ratio have had some success predicting returns, so new models often include factors derived from these characteristics along with beta as a measure of market risk.

10.3 • CAPITAL MARKET EFFICIENCY LG10-5

The risk and return relationship rests on an underlying assumption that stock prices are generally "correct"—they are not predictably too high or too low. Imagine having a system that identified undervalued stocks with low risks (i.e., relatively high returns with a low beta). Because those stocks are undervalued, they will earn you a high return, on average, as their stock prices rise to their correct value. Note that the CAPM's risk–return relationship would be incorrect. You would be consistently getting high returns with low risk. On the other hand, if you consistently picked overvalued stocks, you wouldn't be earning enough return to compensate you for the risks you are taking. Investors move their money to the best alternatives by selling overvalued stocks and buying undervalued stocks. This causes the prices of the overvalued stocks to drop and the prices of the undervalued stocks to rise until both stocks' returns stand more in line with their riskiness. Thus, the risk–return relationship relies on the idea that prices are generally accurate.

What conditions are necessary for an **efficient market?** Efficient, or perfectly competitive, markets feature

- Many buyers and sellers.
- No prohibitively high barriers to entry.
- Free and readily available information available to all participants.
- Low trading or transaction costs.

efficient market A securities market in which prices fully reflect available information on each security.

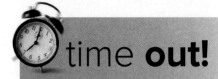

time out!

10-3 Explain why portfolios that lie on the capital market line offer better risk–return trade-offs than those that lie on the efficient frontier.

10-4 Examine the betas in Table 10.2. Which seem about right to you and which seem to indicate too much or too little risk for that firm?

penny stocks The stocks of small companies that are priced below $1 per share.

efficient market hypothesis (EMH) A theory that describes what types of information are reflected in current stock prices.

public information The set of information that has been publicly released. Public information includes data on past stock prices and volume, financial statements, corporate news, analyst opinions, etc.

privately held information The set of information that has not been released to the public but is known by few individuals, likely company insiders.

Are these conditions met for the U.S. stock market? Certainly millions of stock investors trade every day, buying and selling securities. With discount brokers and online traders, the costs to trade are fairly minimal and present no real barriers to enter the market. Information is increasingly accessible from many sources and trading philosophies, and commission costs and bid–ask spreads have steadily declined. With millions of the larger companies' shares (say the S&P 500) of stock trading every day, the U.S. stock exchanges appear to meet efficiency conditions. But other segments of the market, like those exchanges that trade in **penny stocks,** feature very thin trading. The prices of these very small companies' stock may not be fair, and these equities may be manipulated in fraudulent scams. In the 1970s and 1980s, penny stock king Meyer Blinder and his firm Blinder-Robinson were known as "blind 'em and rob 'em" as they practiced penny stock price manipulation to rob many small investors of their entire investments in these small markets. These days, penny stock price manipulation is typically conducted through e-mail and web posting scams.

Efficient Market Hypothesis

Our concept of market efficiency provides a good framework for understanding how stock prices change over time. This theory is described in the **efficient market hypothesis (EMH),** which states that *security prices fully reflect all available information.* At any point in time, the price for any stock or bond reflects the collective wisdom of market participants about the company's future prospects. Security prices change as new information becomes available. Since we cannot predict whether new information about a company will be good news or bad news, we cannot predict whether its stock price will go up or go down. This makes short-term stock-price movements unpredictable. But in the longer run, stock prices will adjust to their proper level as market participants gather and digest all available information.

The EMH brings us to the question of what type of information is embedded within current stock prices. Segmenting information into three categories leads to the three basic levels of market efficiency, described as:

1. Weak-form efficiency—current prices reflect all information derived from trading. This stock market information generally includes current and past stock prices and trading volume.

2. Semistrong-form efficiency—current prices reflect all **public information.** This includes all information that has already been revealed to the public, like financial statements, news, analyst opinions, and so on.

3. Strong-form efficiency—current prices reflect *all* information. In addition to public information, prices reflect the **privately held information** that has not yet been released to the public, but may be known to some people, like managers, accountants, auditors, and so on.

Each of the EMH's three forms rests on different assumptions regarding the extent of information that is incorporated into stock prices at any point in time. A fourth possibility—that markets may not be efficient and prices may not reflect all the information known about a company—also arises.

The *weak-form* efficiency level involves the lowest information hurdle, stating that stock prices reflect all past price and trading volume activity. If true, this level of efficiency would have important ramifications. A segment of the investment industry uses price and volume charts to make investment timing decisions. Technical analysis has a large following and its own vocabulary of patterns and trends (resistance, support, breakout, momentum, etc.). If the market is at least weak-form efficient, then prices already reflect this information and these activities would not result in useful predictions about future price changes, and thus would be a waste of time. Indeed, the people who make the most money from price charting services are the people who sell the services, not the investors who buy and use those services.

The *semistrong-form* efficiency level assumes that stock prices include all public information. Notice that past stock prices and volumes are publicly available information, so this level includes the weak form as a subset. Important investment implications arise if markets are efficient to public information. Many investors conduct security analysis in which they obtain financial data and other public information to assess whether a company's stock is undervalued or overvalued. But in a semistrong-form efficient market, stock prices already reflect this information and are thus "correct." Using only public information, you would not be able to determine whether a stock is misvalued because that information is already reflected in the price.

If prices reflect all public information, then those prices will react as traders hear new (or private) information. Consider a company that announces surprisingly good quarterly profits. Traders and investors will have factored the old profit expectations into the stock price. As they incorporate the new information, the stock price will quickly rise to a new and accurate price as shown in the solid black line in Figure 10.3. Note that the stock price was $35 before the announcement and $40 immediately following. If you tried to buy the stock after hearing the news, then you would have bought at $40 and not received

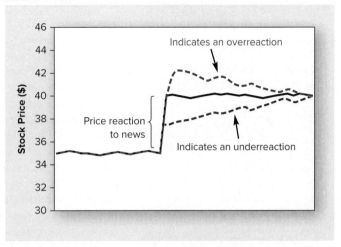

Stock prices react quickly to news, but do they react accurately?

any benefit of the good quarterly profit news. On the other hand, if the market is not semistrong-form efficient, then the price might react quickly, but not accurately. The dashed red line shows a reaction in a non-semistrong efficient market where the price continues to drift up well after the announcement. This gradual drift to the "correct" price indicates that the market initially underreacted to the news. In this case, you could have bought the stock after the announcement and still earned a profit. The dashed blue line shows an overreaction to the firm's better-than-expected profits announcement. If markets either consistently underreact or consistently overreact to announcements that would change stock prices (earnings, stock split, dividend, etc.), then we would believe that the market is not semistrong efficient.

The *strong-form* market efficiency level presents the highest hurdle to test market reaction to information. The strong-form level includes information considered by the weak-form, the semistrong-form, as well as privately known information. People within firms, like CEOs and CFOs, know information that has not yet been released to the public. They may trade on this privately held, or insider, information and their trading may cause stock prices to change as it reflects that private information. In this way, stock prices could reflect even privately known information. Note that the firm managers, accountants, and auditors know several days in advance that a firm has earned unexpectedly high quarterly profits. If the stock price already incorporated this closely held private knowledge, then the big price reaction shown in Figure 10.3 would not occur.

So, is the stock market efficient? If it is, at what level? This has been a hotly debated topic for decades and continues to be. It is not likely that the market is strong-form efficient. Since insider trading is punished, insider information must be valuable. However, much evidence suggests that the market could be weak-form or semistrong-form efficient. Of course, we also have evidence that the market is not efficient at any of the three levels. We will explore this more in the following section.

Behavioral Finance

The argument for the market being efficient works as follows: Many individual and professional investors constantly look for mispriced stocks. If they find a stock that is undervalued, they will buy it and drive up its price until it's correctly priced.

The technology sector fell victim to a stock market bubble in 2000.
Ingram Publishing/SuperStock

Likewise, investors would sell an overpriced stock, driving down its price until it's correctly valued. With so many investors looking for market "mistakes," it's unlikely that any mispriced stock opportunities will be left in the market.

The argument against the market being efficient is equally convincing. The market comprises many people transacting with one another. When someone makes trading decisions influenced by emotion or psychological bias, those decisions may not seem rational. When many people fall under such influences, their trading decisions may actually drive stock prices away from the correct price as emotion carries the traders away from rationality. For example, many people believe that investors were "irrationally exuberant" about technology stocks in the late 1990s—and that their buying excitement drove prices to an artificially high level. In 2000, the excitement wore off and tech stock prices plummeted. Whenever a set of stock prices go unnaturally high and subsequently crash down, the market experiences what we call a **stock market bubble.** The stock market can also be seemingly driven by fear and experience a temporary dramatic decline. In 2020, as the world watched the COVID-19 pandemic spread, the S&P 500 Index fell 34 percent from a February record high to bottom in March. Despite that the pandemic impacted the economy longer than many anticipated, the stock market was back in new record highs by August and ended 2020 at its peak for the year.

In the past couple of decades, finance researchers have studied **behavioral finance** and found that people often behave in ways that are very likely "irrational." At times, investors appear to be too optimistic, as though they are looking through rose-colored glasses. At other times they appear to be too pessimistic. Common investment decisions aren't necessarily optimal ones, which flies in the face of the economist's expectation of rational economic actors. Perhaps, then, capital markets don't represent perfectly competitive or efficient markets if buyers and sellers do not always make rational choices.

It may take many biased investors to move a stock's price enough that it would be considered a pricing mistake. However, the important decisions in a company are typically made by just one CEO or a management team. Thus, their biases can have a direct impact on decisions involving hundreds of millions, or even billions, of dollars. In other words, the contribution of behavioral finance to economic decision making is likely to be even more important in corporate behavior than market behavior. For example, consider the psychological concept of **overconfidence.** One of the most pervasive biases, overconfidence describes a tendency for people to overestimate the accuracy of their knowledge and underestimate the risks of a decision. These problems can adversely affect important decisions of investment (i.e., acquiring other firms) and financing (i.e., issuing new stock or bonds).

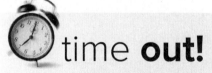

time out!

10.4 • IMPLICATIONS FOR FINANCIAL MANAGERS LG10-6

Financial managers must understand the crucial relationship between risk and return for several reasons. First, while the relationship between risk and return is demonstrated here using the capital markets, it equally applies to many business decisions. A firm's product mix, marketing campaign combination, and research and development programs all entail risk and potential rewards. Being able to understand and characterize these decisions within a risk and return framework can help managers make better decisions. In addition, managers must understand what return their stockholders require at various times of firm operations. After all, a firm must receive enough revenue from its variously risky activities to pay its business and debt costs and reward the owners (the stockholders). Managers must thus include the return to shareholders when they analyze new business opportunities.

finance at work //:markets

Bubble Trouble

Many professionals criticize the EMH because the overall market sometimes seems too high or too low. A very dramatic example of the market level being artificially high is the market bubble. During a market bubble, the market quickly inflates on rampant speculation and subsequently crashes. Investors who buy near the peak of the bubble risk losing nearly all their investment.

One of the United States' earliest stock market bubbles was the bubble and crash of 1929. Note from the figure that the DJIA started in 1927 at around 160. By October 1929, the DJIA had reached nearly 400 and then crashed. By mid-1932, the DJIA had fallen to the 40s. The sustained fall coincided with an economic depression. Panel A of the figure also shows a price bubble in gold. The price of gold was $230 per ounce in January 1979. The late 1970s and early 1980s saw double-digit inflation throughout the economy, and many investors felt that gold represented a safe and inflation-proof investment. Just one year later, the price had skyrocketed to $870. It then fell below $300 in less than two and a half years.

See the spectacular tech bubble during the 1990s? The NASDAQ 100, which started in 1985 at 250, soared to a peak of 4,816.35 on March 24, 2000. It then fell to less than 1,000 in two and a half years. The rise and fall of the NASDAQ 100 seem much more pronounced than the Japanese stock bubble of the 1980s. From January 2, 1985, start at 11,543, the Nikkei 225 soared to a closing high of 38,916 on December 29, 1989. The bubble then burst and the Japanese stock market plummeted.

EMH critics do not believe that the entire stock market, or a substantial segment of it, can be correctly valued before, during, or after a bubble. It certainly appears to be overvalued during the time the bubble is inflating.

Want to know more?

Key Words to Search for Updates: **stock bubble, irrational exuberance**

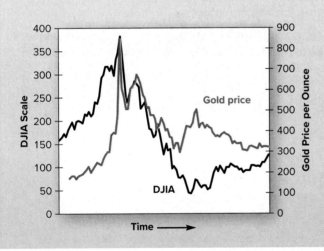

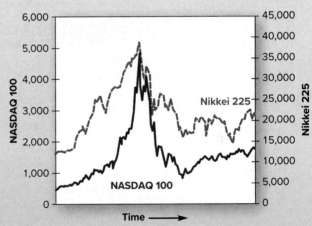

Firms and capital markets also interact directly. For example, a good understanding of market efficiency helps managers understand how their stock prices will react to different types of decisions (like dividend changes) and news announcements (like unexpectedly high or low profitability). In fact, many managers own company stock and are thus compensated through programs that rely on the stock price, like **restricted stock** and **executive stock options.** Companies also periodically issue (sell) additional shares of stock to raise more capital, and these sales depend upon market efficiency assumptions. The firm would not want to sell additional shares if the stock price is too low (i.e., undervalued). They *would* want to sell more shares at any time that they thought their shares are overvalued. Other times, firms repurchase (buy back) shares of stock. The firm might want to do this if its shares were undervalued, but not if its shares were overvalued. Of course, valuation is not an issue if security markets are efficient.

restricted stock A special type of stock that is not transferable from the current holder to others until specific conditions are satisfied.

executive stock options Special rights given to corporate executives to buy a specific number of shares of the company stock at a fixed price during a specific period of time.

Using the Constant-Growth Model for Required Return LG10-7

For decades, financial managers have used the CAPM to compute shareholders' required return. Given recent concerns about beta's limitations, many see the CAPM as a less useful model for calculating appropriate returns. Some have turned instead to another model useful for computing required return—the constant-growth model discussed in Chapter 8. We can arrange the terms of that model as

$$i = \text{Dividend yield} + \text{Constant growth}$$
$$= \frac{D_1}{P_0} + g \tag{10-6}$$

Of course, this model assumes that the stock is efficiently priced. This model holds an advantage in that it uses current firm data (dividend, D_1, and price, P_0) and a simple forward estimate (growth, g) to assess what investors currently expect the stock to return, i.

EXAMPLE 10-4

For interactive versions of this example, log in to Connect or go to mhhe.com/Cornett6e.

Required Return LG10-7

Consider that the required returns for 3M, Apple, and McDonald's are 11.44 percent, 13.96 percent, and 9.06 percent, respectively. These expectations may seem quite far apart, considering that all three firms are in the DJIA and are leaders in their market sectors. Use the following information to compute the constant-growth model estimate of the required return:

	Expected Dividend	Current Price	Analyst Growth Estimate
3M Company	$6.16	$165.55	4.70%
Apple	0.88	127.14	12.92
McDonald's	5.26	209.91	5.50

SOLUTION:

You can now use equation 10-6 to find each company's required return as

3M required return = ($6.16 ÷ $165.55) + 0.0470 = 8.42%

Apple required return = ($0.88 ÷ $127.14) + 0.1292 = 13.61%

McDonald's required return = ($5.26 ÷ $209.91) + 0.0550 = 8.01%

The Apple estimates using CAPM and the constant-growth model are similar. The constant-growth model estimate is 3 percentage points lower than the CAPM estimate for Caterpillar, but only 1 percentage point lower for McDonald's.

The spreadsheet solution is:

1		Expected Dividend	Current Price	Growth Estimate
2	3M	$ 6.16	$ 165.55	4.70%
3	Apple	$ 0.88	$ 127.14	12.92%
4	McDonald's	$ 5.26	$ 209.91	5.50%
5				
6		Required Returns		
7	3M	8.42%	=B2/C2+D2	
8	Apple	13.61%	=B3/C3+D3	
9	McDonald's	8.01%	=B4/C4+D4	

Microsoft Excel

Similar to Problems 10-8, 10-18, 10-19, Self-Test Problem 3

For example, Table 10.2 shows Walmart's beta as 0.42. Using this beta, Table 10.3 shows that shareholders require only 7.94 percent return to hold Walmart's stock, given its low-risk profile. You may find it hard to believe that Walmart's owners (the shareholders) expect such a low return from one of the world's most profitable firms. So perhaps this is a case in which the CAPM result isn't very useful. Applying the constant-growth model looks something like this: Walmart is expected to pay a $2.20 dividend this year and the stock price currently stands at $144.64 per share. Financial analysts believe Walmart will grow at 6.93 percent per year for the next five years. The constant-growth model suggests that Walmart's shareholders expect an 8.45 percent return [=($2.20 ÷ $144.64) + 0.0693]. So, which required return seems more likely, the 7.94 percent computed from CAPM or the 8.45 percent suggested by the constant-growth model? It is likely that Walmart's investors are expecting the higher return or even more.

Financial managers need an estimate of their shareholders' required return in order to make appropriate decisions about their companies' future growth. Good financial managers will compute shareholders' required return using as many methods as they can to determine the most realistic value possible.

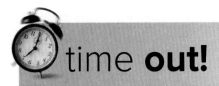

time out!

10-7 Why is the shareholders' required return important to corporate managers?

Get Online

mhhe.com/CornettM6e

for study materials including
quizzes, iPod downloads,
and video

JGI/Jamie Grill/Getty Images

Your Turn...

Questions

1. Consider an asset that provides the same return no matter what economic state occurs. What would be the standard deviation (or risk) of this asset? Explain. *(LG10-1)*

2. Why is expected return considered "forward-looking"? What are the challenges for practitioners to utilize expected return? *(LG10-1)*

3. In 2000, the S&P 500 Index earned −9.1 percent while the T-bill yield was 5.9 percent. Does this mean the market risk premium was negative? Explain. *(LG10-2)*

4. How might the magnitude of the market risk premium impact people's desire to buy stocks? *(LG10-2)*

5. Describe how adding a risk-free security to modern portfolio theory allows investors to do better than the efficient frontier. *(LG10-3)*

6. Show on a graph like Figure 10.2 where a stock with a beta of 1.3 would be located on the security market line. Then show where that stock would be located if it is undervalued. *(LG10-3)*

7. Consider that you have three stocks in your portfolio and wish to add a fourth. You want to know if the fourth stock will make the portfolio riskier or less risky. Compare and contrast how this would be assessed using standard deviation versus market risk (beta) as the measure of risk. *(LG10-3)*

8. Describe how different allocations between the risk-free security and the market portfolio can achieve any level of market risk desired. Give examples of a portfolio from a person who is very risk averse and a portfolio for someone who is not so averse to taking risk. *(LG10-3)*

9. Cisco Systems has a beta of 1.25. Does this mean that you should expect Cisco to earn a return 25 percent higher than the S&P 500 Index return? Explain. *(LG10-4)*

10. Note from Table 10.2 that some technology-oriented firms (Apple) in the Dow Jones Industrial Average have high market risk while others (Intel and Verizon) have low market risk. How do you explain this? *(LG10-4)*

11. Find a beta estimate from three different sources for General Electric (GE). Compare these three values. Why might they be different? *(LG10-4)*

12. If you were to compute beta yourself, what choices would you make regarding the market portfolio, the holding period for the returns (daily, weekly, etc.), and the number of returns? Justify your choices. *(LG10-4)*

13. Explain how the concept of a positive risk–return relationship breaks down if you can systematically find stocks that are overvalued and undervalued. *(LG10-5)*

14. Determine what level of market efficiency is consistent with each of the following events: *(LG10-5)*

    a. Immediately after an earnings announcement, the stock price jumps and then stays at the new level.

    b. The CEO buys 50,000 shares of his company and the stock price does not change.

    c. The stock price immediately jumps when a stock split is announced, but then retraces half of the gain over the next day.

    d. An investor analyzes company quarterly and annual balance sheets and income statements looking for undervalued stocks. The investor earns about the same return as the S&P 500 Index.

15. Why do most investment scams conducted over the Internet and e-mail involve penny stocks instead of S&P 500 Index stocks? *(LG10-5)*

16. Describe a stock market bubble. Can a bubble occur in a single stock? *(LG10-5)*

17. If stock prices are not strong-form efficient, what might be the price reaction to a firm announcing a stock buyback? Explain. *(LG10-6)*

18. Compare and contrast the assumptions that need to be made to compute a required return using CAPM and the constant-growth model. *(LG10-7)*

19. How should you handle a case where required return computations from CAPM and the constant-growth model are very different? *(LG10-7)*

Problems

BASIC PROBLEMS

10-1 **Expected Return** Compute the expected return given these three economic states, their likelihoods, and the potential returns: *(LG10-1)*

Economic State	Probability	Return
Fast growth	0.3	40%
Slow growth	0.4	10
Recession	0.3	−25

10-2 **Required Return** If the risk-free rate is 3 percent and the risk premium is 5 percent, what is the required return? *(LG10-2)*

10-3 **Risk Premium** The average annual return on the S&P 500 Index from 1986 to 1995 was 15.8 percent. The average annual T-bill yield during the same period was 5.6 percent. What was the market risk premium during these 10 years? *(LG10-2)*

10-4 **CAPM Required Return** Hastings Entertainment has a beta of 0.65. If the market return is expected to be 11 percent and the risk-free rate is 4 percent, what is Hastings' required return? *(LG10-3)*

10-5 **Company Risk Premium** Netflix, Inc., has a beta of 3.61. If the market return is expected to be 13 percent and the risk-free rate is 3 percent, what is Netflix's risk premium? *(LG10-3)*

10-6 **Portfolio Beta** You have a portfolio with a beta of 1.35. What will be the new portfolio beta if you keep 85 percent of your money in the old portfolio and 15 percent in a stock with a beta of 0.78? *(LG10-3)*

10-7 **Stock Market Bubble** The NASDAQ stock market bubble peaked at 4,816 in 2000. Two and a half years later it had fallen to 1,000. What was the percentage decline? *(LG10-5)*

10-8 **Required Return** Paccars' current stock price is $48.20, and it is likely to pay an $0.80 dividend next year. Because analysts estimate Paccar will have an 8.8 percent growth rate, what is its required return? *(LG10-7)*

10-9 **Spreadsheet Problem: Portfolio Beta** You have a portfolio of six stocks. The portfolio weights of each stock and each stock's beta are shown below. What is your portfolio beta? *(LG10-3)*

	A	B	C
1		Beta	Weight
2	Wingbat	1.22	21%
3	Flow Exchange	0.95	16%
4	Mega Metalurgy	0.58	13%
5	Fly by Cart	1.15	18%
6	Zip Tripper	1.88	13%
7	Alphabet Now	0.86	19%

Microsoft Excel

10-10 Expected Return Risk For the same economic state probability distribution in problem 10-1, determine the standard deviation of the expected return. *(LG10-1)*

Economic State	Probability	Return
Fast growth	0.3	40%
Slow growth	0.4	10
Recession	0.3	−25

10-11 Undervalued/Overvalued Stock A manager believes his firm will earn a 14 percent return next year. His firm has a beta of 1.5, the expected return on the market is 12 percent, and the risk-free rate is 4 percent. Compute the return the firm should earn given its level of risk and determine whether the manager is saying the firm is undervalued or overvalued. *(LG10-3)*

10-12 Portfolio Beta You own $10,000 of Olympic Steel stock that has a beta of 2.2. You also own $7,000 of Rent-a-Center (beta = 1.5) and $8,000 of Lincoln Educational (beta = 0.5). What is the beta of your portfolio? *(LG10-3)*

10-13 Spreadsheet Problem: Expected Return and Risk For the following economic state probability distribution, determine the expected return and the standard deviation of the expected return. *(LG10-1)*

	A	B	C
1		Probability	Return
2	Fast growth	0.08	38%
3	Slow growth	0.40	14%
4	No growth	0.34	6%
5	Recession	0.16	-16%
6	Depression	0.02	-30%

Microsoft Excel

10-14 Spreadsheet Problem: Portfolio Beta and Return You own the portfolio of five stocks shown below. Given the amount owned of each stock and their respective betas, what is the beta of your portfolio? If the market return is expected to be 9.5 percent and the risk-free rate is 2 percent, what is the required rate of return for the portfolio? *(LG10-3)*

	A	B	C
1		Value	Beta
2	Human Genome	$7,000	0.94
3	Frozen Food Express	$8,500	1.34
4	Molecular Devices	$4,200	1.22
5	Pandemic Busters	$6,600	1.27
6	Zoom Technologies	$11,500	0.57

Microsoft Excel

10-15 Expected Return and Risk Compute the expected return and standard deviation given these four economic states, their likelihoods, and the potential returns: *(LG10-1)*

Economic State	Probability	Return
Fast growth	0.30	60%
Slow growth	0.50	13
Recession	0.15	−15
Depression	0.05	−45

10-16 Risk Premiums You own $10,000 of Dennys Corp. stock that has a beta of 2.9. You also own $15,000 of Qwest Communications (beta = 1.5) and $5,000 of Southwest Airlines (beta = 0.7). Assume that the market return will be 11.5 percent and the risk-free rate is 4.5 percent. What is the market risk premium? What is the risk premium of each stock? What is the risk premium of the portfolio? *(LG10-3)*

10-17 Portfolio Beta and Required Return You hold the positions in the following table. What is the beta of your portfolio? If you expect the market to earn 12 percent and the risk-free rate is 3.5 percent, what is the required return of the portfolio? *(LG10-3)*

	Price	Shares	Beta
Amazon.com	$40.80	100	3.8
Family Dollar Stores	30.10	150	1.2
McKesson Corp.	57.40	75	0.4
Schering-Plough Corp.	23.80	200	0.5

10-18 Required Return Using the information in the table, compute the required return for each company using both CAPM and the constant-growth model. Compare and discuss the results. Assume that the market portfolio will earn 12 percent and the risk-free rate is 3.5 percent. *(LG10-3, LG10-7)*

	Price	Upcoming Dividend	Growth	Beta
US Bancorp	$36.55	$1.60	10.0%	1.8
Praxair	64.75	1.12	11.0	2.4
Eastman Kodak	24.95	1.00	4.5	0.5

10-19 Spreadsheet Problem: Required Return Using the information in the table, compute the required return for each company using both CAPM and the constant-growth model. Compare and discuss the results. Assume that the market portfolio will earn 11 percent and the risk-free rate is 4 percent. *(LG10-3, LG10-7)*

	A	B	C	D	E
1		Expected Dividend	Current Price	Growth Estimate	Beta
2	Ester Lauder	$ 0.60	$ 47.40	11.7%	0.75
3	Kimbo Realty	$ 1.54	$ 52.10	8.0%	1.3
4	Nordstream	$ 0.50	$ 5.25	14.6%	2.2

Microsoft Excel

10-20 Spreadsheet Problem As discussed in the text, beta estimates for one firm will vary depending on various factors such as the time over which the estimation is conducted, the market portfolio proxy, and the return intervals. You will demonstrate this variation using returns for Microsoft. *(LG10-4)*

  a. Using all 45 monthly returns for Microsoft and the two stock market indexes, compute Microsoft's beta using the S&P 500 Index as the market proxy. Then compute the beta using the NASDAQ index as the market portfolio proxy. Compare the two beta estimates.

	A	B	C	D	E	F	G	H	I	J	K	L
1	Date	MSFT	S&P500	Nasdaq	Date	MSFT	S&P500	Nasdaq	Date	MSFT	S&P500	Nasdaq
2	Dec 20	4.17%	3.71%	5.65%	Sep 2019	1.18%	1.72%	0.46%	Jun 2018	0.20%	0.48%	0.92%
3	Nov 20	5.73%	10.75%	11.80%	Aug 2019	1.17%	-1.81%	-2.60%	May 2018	5.69%	2.16%	5.32%
4	Oct 20	-3.74%	-2.77%	-2.29%	Jul 2019	1.72%	1.31%	2.11%	Apr 2018	2.47%	0.27%	0.04%
5	Sep 20	-6.51%	-3.92%	-5.16%	Jun 2019	8.71%	6.89%	7.42%	Mar 2018	-2.21%	-2.69%	-2.88%
6	Aug 20	10.01%	7.01%	9.59%	May 2019	-5.30%	-6.58%	-7.93%	Feb 2018	-1.31%	-3.89%	-1.87%
7	Jul 20	0.74%	5.51%	6.82%	Apr 2019	10.73%	3.93%	4.74%	Jan 2018	11.07%	5.62%	7.36%
8	Jun 20	11.37%	1.84%	5.99%	Mar 2019	5.72%	1.79%	2.61%	Dec 2017	2.14%	3.43%	0.43%
9	May 20	2.25%	4.53%	6.75%	Feb 2019	7.28%	2.97%	3.44%	Nov 2017	1.19%	0.37%	2.17%
10	Apr 20	13.63%	12.68%	15.45%	Jan 2019	2.82%	7.87%	9.74%	Oct 2017	11.67%	2.22%	3.57%
11	Mar 20	-2.39%	-12.51%	-10.12%	Dec 2018	-8.01%	-9.18%	-9.48%	Sep 2017	0.16%	1.93%	1.05%
12	Feb 20	-4.83%	-8.41%	-6.38%	Nov 2018	3.82%	1.79%	0.34%	Aug 2017	2.85%	0.05%	1.27%
13	Jan 20	7.95%	-0.16%	1.99%	Oct 2018	-6.61%	-6.94%	-9.20%	Jul 2017	5.47%	1.93%	3.38%
14	Dec 19	4.53%	2.86%	3.54%	Sep 2018	2.21%	0.43%	-0.78%	Jun 2017	-0.74%	0.48%	-0.94%
15	Nov 19	5.59%	3.40%	4.50%	Aug 2018	5.89%	3.03%	5.71%	May 2017	2.02%	1.16%	2.50%
16	Oct 19	3.12%	2.04%	3.66%	Jul 2018	7.58%	3.60%	2.15%	Apr 2017	3.95%	0.91%	2.30%

Microsoft Excel

b. Now estimate the beta using only the most recent 30 monthly returns and the S&P 500 Index. Compare the beta estimate to the estimate in part (a) when using the S&P 500 Index and all 45 monthly returns.

c. Estimate Microsoft's beta using the following quarterly returns. Compare the estimate to the ones from parts (a) and (b).

	A	B	C
1	Date	MSFT	S&P500
2	Q4 2020	6.02%	11.69%
3	Q3 2020	3.60%	8.47%
4	Q2 2020	29.40%	19.95%
5	Q1 2020	0.28%	-20.00%
6	Q4 2019	13.81%	8.53%
7	Q3 2019	4.13%	1.19%
8	Q2 2019	14.00%	3.79%
9	Q1 2019	16.61%	13.07%
10	Q4 2018	-10.81%	-13.97%
11	Q3 2018	16.43%	7.20%
12	Q2 2018	8.51%	2.93%
13	Q1 2018	7.20%	-1.22%
14	Q4 2017	15.41%	6.12%
15	Q3 2017	8.64%	3.96%

Microsoft Excel

 10-21 Spreadsheet Problem Build a spreadsheet that automatically computes the expected market return and risk for different assumptions about the state of the economy. *(LG10-1)*

a. First, create a spreadsheet like the one shown below and compute the expected return and standard deviation.

	A	B	C
1	State of Economy	Probability of State	Expected Market Return
2	Fast Growth	0.13	35%
3	Slow Growth	0.42	17%
4	No Growth	0.25	3%
5	Recession	0.18	-15%
6	Depression	0.02	-30%
7			
8	Sum =	1.00	

Microsoft Excel

b. Compute the expected return and risk for the following two scenarios:

	A	B	C
1	State of Economy	Probability of State	Expected Market Return
2	Fast Growth	0.13	30%
3	Slow Growth	0.33	15%
4	No Growth	0.30	2%
5	Recession	0.20	-18%
6	Depression	0.04	-25%
7			
8	Sum =	1.00	

Microsoft Excel

	A	B	C
1	State of Economy	Probability of State	Expected Market Return
2	Fast Growth	0.15	40%
3	Slow Growth	0.35	18%
4	No Growth	0.34	4%
5	Recession	0.15	-20%
6	Depression	0.01	-35%
7			
8	Sum =	1.00	

Microsoft Excel

Notes

CHAPTER 10

1. A mathematically equivalent equation for beta is $\beta = \text{cov}(R_S, R_M)/\text{var}(R^M)$, where cov() is the covariance between the stock and market portfolio returns, and var() is the variance of the market portfolio.

Design elements: (Clock) Floortje/Getty Images; (Referee) Richard Ransier/Getty Images

I n the previous two chapters, we discussed investors' required return given a particular risk profile. In this chapter, we examine the question from the firm's point of view: How much must the firm pay to finance its operations and expansions using debt and equity sources? Firms use a combination of debt and equity sources to fund their operations, projects, and any expansions they may undertake. In Chapter 14, we'll explore the factors that managers consider as they choose the optimal capital structure mix. For now, we'll assume that management has chosen the optimal mix for us, and that it's our job to implement it.

LG11-1   As we've seen in previous chapters, investors face different kinds of risks associated with debt, preferred stock, and equity. As a result, their required rates of return for each debt or equity source differ as well. So, as the firm uses a combination of different financing sources, we must calculate the investors' *average* required rate of return to use as the *cost of capital* for evaluating decisions about investing the firm's capital. Since firms seldom use equal amounts of debt and equity capital sources, we will need to calculate this as a *weighted* average, with weights based on the proportion of debt and equity capital used.

calculating the
cost of capital

As we'll see, we can measure such a **weighted-average cost of capital (WACC)** in a variety of situations and for a number of purposes. For example, if we're interested in determining the average rate of return that the firm must earn from existing operations when we don't expect the firm's capital structure to change, we can calculate the WACC using the firm's *current* capital structure and *existing* **component costs;** however, if we're trying to determine the average rate of return that we would need to earn from a new project in order for it to add value to the firm, we would want to use the project's *proposed* capital structure and *its* component costs.

One important point about the component costs to be used in the firm's computation of the average required rate of return is that dividends paid to either common or preferred stockholders are *not* tax deductible, but interest paid to debt holders *is* tax deductible, up to a certain point.

continued on p. 308

LEARNING GOALS

LG11-1 Understand the relationship of cost of capital to the investor's required return.

LG11-2 Use the weighted-average cost of capital (WACC) formula to calculate a project's cost of capital.

LG11-3 Explain how the firm chooses among estimating costs of equity, preferred stock, and debt.

LG11-4 Calculate the weights used for WACC projections.

LG11-5 Identify which elements of WACC are used to calculate a project-specific WACC.

LG11-6 Evaluate trade-offs between a firmwide WACC and a divisional cost of capital approach.

LG11-7 Distinguish subjective and objective approaches to divisional cost of capital.

LG11-8 Demonstrate how to adjust the WACC to reflect flotation costs.

Stream Devices, Inc., is about to launch a new project to create and market a combination streaming music-video projector. Stream Devices currently uses a particular mixture of debt, common stock, and preferred shares in its capital structure, but the firm is thinking of using the launch of the new project as an opportunity to change that capital structure.

The new project will be funded with 40 percent debt, 10 percent preferred stock, and 50 percent common stock. Stream Devices currently has 10 million shares of common stock outstanding, selling at $18.75 per share, and expects to pay an annual dividend of $1.35 one year from now, after which future dividends are expected to grow at a constant 6 percent rate. Stream's current debt consists of 20-year, 10 percent annual coupon bonds with a face value of $150 million and a market value of $165 million, and the company's capital mix also includes 100,000 shares of 10 percent preferred stock selling at par.

If Stream Devices faces a marginal tax rate of 21 percent, and estimates that it can take full advantage of the interest tax shields on debt, what weighted average cost of capital should it use as it evaluates this project? **(See the solution at the end of the book.)**

continued from p. 307

We will go into more detail later in this chapter concerning when and how much debt interest is tax deductible, but, for now, the important point is this: since at least a portion of the firm's payments to its debt holders is tax deductible, those payments are, in effect, being at least partially subsidized by the government: If the firm hadn't paid out that interest rate to the debt holders, it would have had to have paid out taxes to the government on the money it used to pay the interest. And, to the extent that subsidy on debt means that it's a relatively cheap source of capital, firms should, and will, take advantage of it. ■

weighted-average cost of capital (WACC) The weighted-average after-tax cost of the capital used by a firm, with weights set equal to the relative percentage of each type of capital used.

component costs The individual costs of each type of capital—bonds, preferred stock, and common stock.

11.1 • THE WACC FORMULA LG11-2

Until recently, calculating the average cost per dollar of capital raised, referred to as the weighted average cost of capital (WACC), was a fairly simple proposition. However, the Tax Cut and Jobs Act (TCJA) of 2017, discussed previously, had significant direct and indirect effects on the calculation of the WACC, which make the calculation a little more complicated than it was before.

First, the reduction of corporate tax rates to a flat 21 percent rate means that the after-tax cost of debt, even though still subsidized through the deductibility of interest for most firms, is not *as subsidized* as it previously was. That is, debt is still cheap relative to equity and preferred stock, but it's not *as* relatively cheap as it used to be.

In addition, the TCJA also placed constraints on when firms can deduct those interest payments. Previously, any interest paid on a firm's debt was generally completely deductible. However, starting with tax years beginning after December 31, 2017, businesses with revenues of more that $25 million are only allowed to deduct for tax purposes interest expenses totaling up to 30 percent of "adjustable taxable income." For tax years ending in 2018–2021, adjustable taxable income is defined as income with allowable deductions for depreciation, amortization, and depletion added back in (i.e., EBITDA); for tax years ending in 2022 and later, adjustable taxable income will be set equal to EBIT.

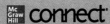
Any business interest expense that is disallowed under this limitation in a particular tax year can still be carried forward as an expense in subsequent tax years, but "pushing back" the tax deductibility of such interest payments is obviously going to reduce the present value of those tax deductions and, potentially, change exactly how much debt the firm decides to use.

Together, these new rules present us with three possible scenarios concerning how debt interest will be treated:

1. The *unconstrained* scenario: For most firms, including those with revenues less than $25 million per year, and the vast majority of healthy, publicly traded firms, we think that interest on all their debt will be fully tax deductible.

2. The fully *constrained* scenario: For firms that have so much debt that at least 30 percent of their EBITDA or EBIT (as appropriate) is already claimed by existing debt issues for the foreseeable future, the likelihood of being able to take advantage of the interest tax shield on a new debt issue for such firms is either so low or so far away in the future that it might as well not even exist.

3. The *uncertain* scenario: For firms that more or less fall in the middle of the other two scenarios, being unable to immediately take full advantage of the tax interest shields during the period when the interest payments are made, but also being expected to be able to use those interest tax shields at some near-term time in the future, means that the impact of the interest tax shields will fall somewhere in the middle between the first two scenarios.

Of these three scenarios, the third, uncertain, one is the one most difficult to model, as questions concerning exactly how long the delays between each interest payment and the firm being able to use the tax shield are, what the expected future EBITDA or EBIT levels are, and so forth, make finding a closed-form solution for the impact of the cumulative tax shields on the WACC beyond the focus of this discussion.

Accordingly, we will leave the discussion of the third scenario to more advanced texts, and will instead focus on analyzing the first two situations. The WACC for the unconstrained scenario, where firms *can* make full and immediate use of the interest tax shields as soon as the interest payments are made, is shown below in equation 11-1, while the formula for the full constrained scenario, for firms that *cannot* make use of any of the interest tax shields, is shown below in equation 11-2:

$$WACC_{\text{Unconstrained}} = \text{Percentage of equity} \times \text{Cost of equity}$$
$$+ \text{Percentage of preferred stock} \times \text{Cost of preferred stock} \qquad (11\text{-}1)$$
$$+ \text{Percentage of debt} \times \text{After-tax cost of dept}$$
$$= \frac{E}{E+P+D} \times i_E + \frac{P}{E+P+D} \times i_P \times \frac{D}{E+P+D} \times i_D(1-T_c)$$

$$WACC_{\text{Constrained}} = \text{Percentage of equity} \times \text{Cost of equity}$$
$$+ \text{Percentage of preferred stock} \times \text{Cost of preferred stock}$$
$$+ \text{Percentage of debt} \times \text{After-tax cost of debt} \qquad (11\text{-}2)$$
$$= \frac{E}{E+P+D} \times i_E + \frac{P}{E+P+D} \times i_P + \frac{D}{E+P+D} \times i_D$$

where

E = Market value of equity used in financing the relevant project or firm.
P = Market value of preferred stock used.
D = Market value of debt used.
$\dfrac{E}{E+P+D}$ = Percentage of financing that is equity.
$\dfrac{E}{E+P+D}$ = Percentage of financing that is preferred stock.
$\dfrac{P}{E+P+D}$ = Percentage of financing that is debt.
i_E = Cost of equity.
i_P = Cost of preferred stock.
i_D = Before-tax cost of debt.
T_c = The marginal corporate tax rate.

Notice that we use weights based on *market* values rather than *book* values because market values reflect investors' assessment of what they *would* be willing to pay for the various types of securities, while book values would reflect what *was* paid for such securities at varying times in the past. Since we're interested in coming up with the cost of capital for new investments in the firm or its projects, using market values here makes more sense.

Calculating the Component Cost of Equity LG11-3

We could calculate i_E using the capital asset pricing model, as discussed in Chapter 10:

$$i_E = R_f + \beta(R_M - R_f) \qquad (11\text{-}3)$$

Or we can assume that the equity in question is a constant-growth stock such as the ones we modeled in Chapter 8. Under this assumption, we can solve the constant-growth model for i_E:

$$i_E = \frac{D_1}{P_0} + g \qquad (11\text{-}4)$$

Which way is better? Well, theoretically, both should give us the same answer, but depending on the situation, some pragmatic reasons may dictate your choice.

1. In situations where you do not have sufficient historic observations to estimate β (i.e., when the stock is fairly new), or when you suspect that the *past* level of the stock's systematic (or market) risk might not be a good indicator of the future risk, you do not want to use the CAPM. Using calculated *historic* systematic risk when it is not a good estimate of β_E, estimated *future* systematic risk, will not work too well.

EXAMPLE 11-1

For interactive versions of this example, log in to Connect or go to mhhe.com/Cornett6e.

Cost of Equity LG11-2

ADK Industries' common shares sell for $32.75 per share. ADK expects to set its next annual dividend at $1.54 per share. If ADK expects future dividends to grow by 6 percent per year, indefinitely, the current risk-free rate is 3 percent, the expected return on the market is 9 percent, and the stock has a beta of 1.3, what should be the firm's cost of equity?

SOLUTION:

The cost of equity using the CAPM will be

$$i_E = R_r + \beta(R_M - R_r)$$
$$= 0.03 + 1.3[0.09 - 0.03]$$
$$= 0.1080, \text{ or } 10.80\%$$

The cost of equity using the constant-growth model will be

$$i_E = \frac{D_1}{P_0} + g$$
$$= \frac{\$1.54}{\$32.75} + 0.06$$
$$= 0.1070, \text{ or } 10.70\%$$

Our best estimate of ADKs equity would therefore be $\dfrac{10.70\% + 10.80\%}{2} = 10.75\%$

The spreadsheet solution is:

	A	B	C
1			
2	Price	$ 32.75	
3	D_1	$ 1.54	
4	Growth	6.00%	
5	Risk-Free Rate	3.00%	
6	Return on Market	9.00%	
7	Beta	1.3	
8			
9	CAPM Cost of Equity	10.80%	=B5+B7*(B6-B5)
10	Constant-Growth Cost of Equity	10.70%	=B3/B2+B4
11			
12	Average Cost of Equity	10.75%	=AVERAGE(B9:B10)

Microsoft Excel

As shown, calculating the cost of equity when we have enough information to use both CAPM and the constant-growth approach simply involves calculating both, then taking the average of the two.

Similar to Problem 11-1

2. In situations where you can expect constant dividend growth, the constant-growth model is appropriate. But although you can try to adjust the model for stocks without constant dividend growth, doing so may introduce potentially sizable errors, so it is not the best choice for stocks that increase their dividends irregularly.

Overall, we should expect that the CAPM approach to estimating i_E will apply more accurately in most cases. However, if you do encounter a situation in which the constant-growth model applies, then you can certainly use it. If we are really fortunate and happen to have enough information to use both approaches, then we should probably *use* both, taking an average of the resulting estimates of i_E.[1]

EXAMPLE 11-2

Cost of Preferred Stock LG11-3

Suppose that ADK also has 1 million shares of 7 percent preferred stock outstanding, trading at $72 per share. What is ADK's component cost for preferred equity?

SOLUTION:

The cost of the preferred stock will equal

$$i_P = \frac{D_1}{P_0}$$

$$= \frac{\$7}{\$72}$$

$$= 0.0972, \text{ or } 9.72\%$$

The spreadsheet solution is:

▲	A	B	C
1			
2	Price	$ 72.00	
3	Dividend	$ 7.00	
4			
5	Cost of Preferred Equity	9.72%	=B3/B2

Microsoft Excel

There is no built-in function in Excel for calculating the cost of preferred equity, but since the rate of return on preferred equity will be equal to the dividend divided by the price, this is easy to calculate in Excel.

Similar to Problem 11-4

Calculating the Component Cost of Preferred Stock

As we discussed in Chapter 8, preferred stock represents a special case of the constant-growth model, wherein *g* equals zero. So we can estimate preferred stocks' component cost using a simplified version of equation 11-4:

the
Math Coach on...

Preferred Stock Dividends

❝ The assumed par value of preferred stock is $100. So, a 7 percent preferred stock pays $7 a year in dividends. ❞

$$i_P = \frac{D_1}{P_0} \qquad (11\text{-}5)$$

Calculating the Component Cost of Debt

Because of the potential tax deductibility of debt interest for the firm, computing the component cost of debt actually has two parts. We must first estimate the before-tax cost of debt, i_D, and then apply the correct version of the WACC, either equation 11-1 or equation 11-2, as appropriate, to convert i_D to the appropriate after-tax rate of return.

To estimate i_D, we need to solve for the yield to maturity (YTM) on the firm's existing debt

$$\text{Solve} \left\{ PV = PMT \times \left[\dfrac{1 - \dfrac{1}{(1 + i_D)^N}}{i_D} \right] + \dfrac{FV}{(1 + i_D)^N} \right\} \text{ for } i_D \qquad (11\text{-}6)$$

Cost of Debt with No Restriction on Interest Deductions LG11-3

For interactive versions of this example, log in to Connect or go to mhhe.com/Cornett6e.

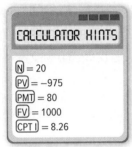

CALCULATOR HINTS

N = 20
PV = −975
PMT = 80
FV = 1000
CPT I = 8.26

ADK has 30,000 20-year, 8 percent annual coupon bonds outstanding; expects annual revenues of approximately $18 million per year for the life of the bonds; and anticipates EBIT to be at least $8 million per year. If the bonds currently sell for 97.5 percent of par and the firm pays an average tax rate of 21 percent and can take full advantage of the interest tax shields, what will be the before-tax and after-tax component costs for debt it expects revenues of $5 million per year?

SOLUTION:

The before-tax cost of debt will be the solution to

$$\text{Solve} \left\{ \$975 = \$80 \times \left[\dfrac{1 - \dfrac{1}{(1 + i_D)^{20}}}{i_D} \right] + \dfrac{\$1,000}{(1 + i_D)^{20}} \right\} \text{ for } i_D$$

which will equal 8.26 percent. Multiplying this by one minus the tax rate will yield the after-tax cost of debt: $0.0826 \times (1 - 0.21) = 0.0653$, or 6.53 percent.

The spreadsheet solution is:

⊿	A	B	C
1			
2	Maturity	20	
3	Coupon Rate	8.00%	
4	Price Quote	97.50	
5	Tax Rate	21.00%	
6	Coupons per Year	1	
7			
8	Before-Tax Cost of Debt	8.26%	=B6*RATE(B2*B6,B3*1000/B6,-B4/100*1000,1000)
9	After-Tax Cost of Debt	6.53%	=B8*(1-B5)

Microsoft Excel

The best way to calculate the before-tax cost of debt in Excel is to use the RATE(nper,pmt,pv,[fv], [type],[guess]) function, which takes the present value (price), payment amounts, future value (face value), and number of coupon payments and uses it to calculate the rate per coupon period that makes the TVM equation work out. The [type] is the default value, as payments occur at the end of the periods, and you can enter a [guess] for the interest rate if you wish to tell it where to start its search for the actual rate, but it's usually not necessary.

The one thing you do have to be careful about, though, is that, assuming that rates will be entered and read as nominal annual rates, you need to make sure that you adjust all of the relevant arguments for the number of payments per year. As shown in cell B8, this involves multiplying the maturity in years by the number of payments per year (cell B6), dividing the annual payment by the number of payments per year, and multiplying the result of the RATE() function by the number of payments per year, as well, to get your answer on a nominal annual basis if required.

Lastly, we take the before-tax cost of debt (cell B8) and multiply it by one minus the tax rate to get the after-tax cost of debt (cell B9).

Similar to Problem 11-2

Solve for the interest rate that makes the price equal to the sum of the present values of the coupons and the face value of the bond, as discussed in Chapter 7.

Intuitively, by using the price on the firm's existing debt in equation 11-6, we are calculating the rate of return expected by investors currently buying the firm's existing bonds. As discussed later when we cover how to calculate project-specific WACCs, the fact that *all* of the firms' bonds get their interest paid out of *all* the firm's cash flows before any of the firm's shareholders get anything implies that this expected rate of return on existing firm debt should also be a good proxy for the rate of return that potential investors would demand on any *new* debt issued by the firm, as well.

Finally, if we think of the YTM as the rate that bond investors expect to *get* for investing in the bond, then we need to adjust it for any possible tax deductibility of debt interest to convert this to a measure of how much it actually costs the firm to *pay* that YTM.

As per our discussion above, our decision as to which version of the WACC formula to use, the one in equation 11-1 or the one in equation 11-2, will boil down to a determination of whether the firm can or cannot take immediate advantage of the interest tax shields when the debt payments are made: If they can, we will use equation 11-1, which will set the after-tax cost of debt equal to $i_D \times (1 - T_C)$; if they cannot, we will use equation 11-2, treating the after-tax cost of debt as being equal to the before-tax cost of debt.

For example, if a firm pays a 10 percent coupon on $1 million in debt while it is subject to a 21 percent tax rate, then each coupon payment will be equal to $0.10 \times \$1,000,000 = \$100,000$, but that $100,000 in interest, being potentially tax deductible, may reduce the firm's tax bill.

If the firm can take advantage of the tax shields, each $100,000 interest payment will be immediately deductible, allowing the firm to lower each year's tax by $0.21 \times \$100,000 = \$21,000$. So, paying $100,000 in interest saves the firm $21,000 in taxes, making the effective after-tax cost of debt equal to $\$100,000 - \$21,000 = \$79,000$ and the effective after-tax interest rate equal to $10\% \times (1 - 0.21) = 7.9\%$.

However, if the same firm was not able to take advantage of the interest tax shields, then the effective after-tax cost of debt would be equal to the before-tax cost, 10 percent.

Calculating the Weights LG11-4

Calculating the weights to be used in the WACC formula is mathematically very simple: We just calculate the percentages of the funding that come from equity, preferred stock, and debt, respectively.

Sounds easy, right? Well, the tricky part to this lies in determining what we mean by "the funding": If we are calculating WACC for a firm, then "the funding" encompasses all the capital in the firm, and *E, P,* and *D* will be determined by computing the total market value of the firm's common stock, preferred stock, and debt, respectively. However, if we

EXAMPLE 11-4

For interactive versions of this example, log in to Connect or go to mhhe.com/Cornett6e.

Cost of Debt LG11-3

Continuing the previous example, suppose that ADK expects its debt ratio to be so high that it will not be able to take advantage of the interest tax shelter on this bond issue for the foreseeable future. What, then, would be the appropriate after-tax interest rate to be used for the debt component of ADK's WACC?

SOLUTION:

The after-tax interest rate would simply be equal to the before-tax interest rate of 8.26 percent.

EXAMPLE 11-5

Capital Structure Weights and WACC LG11-4

For interactive versions of this example, log in to Connect or go to mhhe.com/Cornett6e.

Let us continue the previous examples but roll back to assuming that ADK can take full advantage of the interest tax shields. Suppose that ADK has issued 3 million shares of common stock, 1 million shares of preferred stock, and the previously mentioned 30,000 bonds outstanding. What will ADK's WACC be, considering ADK as a firm?

SOLUTION:

Using the securities' prices given in previous examples, ADK's equity, preferred stock, and debt will have the following total market values:

- Equity: 3m × $32.75 = $98.25m
- Preferred stock: 1m × $72 = $72m
- Debt: 30,000 × $975 = $29.25m

The total combined market value for all three capital sources is $199.5 million. The applicable weights for each capital source will therefore be

For common equity: $\dfrac{E}{E+P+D} = \dfrac{\$98.25m}{\$199.5m} = 0.4925$, or 49.25%

For preferred stock: $\dfrac{P}{E+P+D} = \dfrac{\$72m}{\$199.5m} = 0.3609$, or 36.09%

For debt: $\dfrac{D}{E+P+D} = \dfrac{\$29.25m}{\$199.5n} = 0.1466$, or 14.66%

Tying this all together with the answers from the previous examples, ADK will have a WACC of

$$WACC = \frac{E}{E+P+D} \times i_E + \frac{P}{E+P+D} \times i_P + \frac{D}{E+P+D} \times i_D \times (1 - T_C)$$

$$= (0.4925 \times 0.1075) + (0.3609 \times 0.0972) + (0.1466 \times 0.0653)$$

$$= 0.0976, \text{ or } 9.76\%$$

The spreadsheet solution is:

	A	B	C
1			
2	Cost of Equity	10.75%	
3	Cost of Preferred Stock	9.72%	
4	Cost of Debt	8.26%	
5	Tax Rate	21%	
6			
7	Shares of Common	3,000,000	
8	Price of Common	$ 32.75	
9	Shares of Preferred	1,000,000	
10	Price of Preferred	$ 72.00	
11	Number of Bonds	30,000	
12	Price of Bonds	$ 975.00	
13			
14	Equity	$ 98,250,000.00	=B7*B8
15	Preferred Stock	$ 72,000,000.00	=B9*B10
16	Debt	$ 29,250,000.00	=B11*B12
17			
18	E/(E+P+D)	49.25%	=B14/(SUM($B$14:$B$16))
19	P/(E+P+D)	36.09%	=B15/(SUM($B$14:$B$16))
20	D/(E+P+D)	14.66%	=B16/(SUM($B$14:$B$16))
21			
22	WACC	9.76%	=B2*B18+B3*B19+B4*(1-B5)*B20

Microsoft Excel

This is where the template that we showed you before comes in. We enter the costs of equity, preferred stock, and debt, as well as the tax rate, then we enter enough information about each source of capital to calculate the total market value of each source: namely, how many shares/bonds are outstanding, and what their respective prices are. This allows us to calculate the total market value of all outstanding common shares, preferred stock, and debt, as shown in cells B14 through B16. The sum of the three is then the total market capitalization of the firm, which we use as the divisor underneath each type of asset's market value to get the weights in cells B18 through B20. Finally, we multiply these weights times the relevant costs of each type (remembering to multiply the before-tax cost of debt by one minus the tax rate to get the after-tax cost of debt) and then add all the results up to get the WACC, shown in cell B22.

Similar to Problems 11-5 to 11-7, 11-11, Self-Test Problem 1

time out!

11-1 Explain why we multiply the component cost of debt by a factor containing the marginal tax rate, T_D, but don't do so for the component costs of equity or preferred stock.

11-2 How would we compute i_D if a company had multiple bond issues outstanding?

are computing WACC for a *project,* then "the funding" will only include the financing for that project, and *E, P,* and *D* will be equal to the amount of each used in the financing of that project.[2]

If you think about this for a second, you will realize that this means that projects can wind up having different WACCs than their firm. That is not just OK, it is also exactly right because, as we will see in a later chapter, the firm is like a diversified portfolio of different projects, all with different risks and returns. And one of the things that can contribute to the risk of a project is the choice of how much common stock, preferred stock, and debt are used to finance it.

11.2 • FIRM WACC VERSUS PROJECT WACC LG11-5

So far, we have been defining the WACC as a weighted-average cost across the firm's different financing sources. If we think of the firm as a portfolio of different projects and products, we see that the WACC will be a weighted-average cost of capital across the items in that portfolio, too. This way it represents the cost of capital for the "typical" project that the firm is currently undertaking. However, firms grow by taking on new projects. So now the question is: Can managers use our firmwide WACC, calculated previously, to evaluate the firm's *newly* proposed projects?

The answer is: *It depends.* If a new project is similar enough to existing projects, then yes, managers can use the firm's WACC as the new project's cost of capital. But say that your firm is contemplating undertaking a significantly different project—one far different from any project that the firm is already engaged in. What then? Then we cannot expect the firm's overall WACC to appropriately measure the new project's cost of capital.

Let your intuition work on this for a second: If the new project is *riskier* than the firm's existing projects, then it should be "charged" a *higher* cost of capital; if it's *safer,* then the firm should assign the new project a *lower* cost of capital. That seems only fair, right?

Consider a U.S. firm—let's call it GassUp—that currently owns a chain of gas stations. Firm management is considering a new project: opening up a series of gourmet coffee shops inside its existing gas stations. Given the demand for upscale coffee in the United States, as well as the historically volatile oil markets, it's probably difficult to say exactly whether the coffee shops will be *more* or *less* risky than gas stations. We can probably say, though, that the two enterprises will face *different* risks. For example, one could argue that at least a certain amount of gas is a necessity, while gourmet coffee is more of a luxury good, so it makes sense that the two "parts" of the new, expanded product line

Ingram Publishing/SuperStock

Even if GassUp's coffee venture fails, the firm's creditors would likely still collect payments from gas station operations.
Tetra Images/Alamy Stock Photo

for GassUp will perform differently in boom or bust periods. Likewise, what if the coffee shops are located within the busiest and most stable gas stations—say the ones that lie along freeways? Then the firm faces remodeling existing buildings, rather than starting from scratch, and can pick and choose to put gourmet coffee facilities in the gas stations that have the volume to support them, which likely means that the risks of adding the facilities for gourmet coffee to those stations will be lower than building new facilities from scratch.

So, this means that GassUp probably should not use the same WACC for the new line of gourmet coffee expansions to its gas stations as it does for the gas stations themselves; that is, the WACC for the new expansion projects should not be equal to the WACC of the firm as it currently exists.

However, does this mean that *all the components* of WACC for each new gourmet coffee expansion should be different for every store? Well, not exactly. As we'll discuss, some inputs to WACC should be project-specific, but others should be consistent with the firm-wide values used in calculating a firmwide WACC.

Project Cost Numbers to Take from the Firm

It is tempting to argue that all component inputs for a project-specific WACC should be based on the specific project attributes, but if we created all project-specific numbers, what fundamental issue related to bonds and preferred stock would we be ignoring? That both bonds and preferred stocks create claims on the *firm*, not on any particular group of projects within that firm. Furthermore, debt claims are superior to those of common stockholders. So if the new project *does* significantly increase the firm's overall risk, the increased risk will be borne disproportionately by common stockholders. Debt holders and preferred stockholders will likely face minimal impact on the risk and return that their investments give them, no matter what new project the firm undertakes—even if those claimants own bonds or preferred shares that the firm issued to fund the new project.

business risk The risk of a project arising from the line of business it is in; the variability of a firm's or division's cash flows.

For example, suppose GassUp decides to build entirely separate facilities for its coffee shops, which it will name "Bottoms Up." Furthermore, suppose GassUp partially finances its expansion into coffee shops with debt, and that the project turns out to be more like "Bottoms Down"—far less successful than the firm had hoped. Though this would be an unfortunate turn of events for GassUp's common shareholders, the firm's creditors and preferred shareholders would likely still collect their usual interest and dividend payments from GassUp's gross revenues from gas station operations.

Creditors understand that their repayment probably comes from continuing operations and take current cash flows into account when a firm comes seeking funds. For example, if a small firm approaches a bank for a loan to finance an expansion, the bank will normally spend more time analyzing *current* cash flows to determine the probability that it will recoup its loan than it will analyzing the potential new cash flows from the proposed expansion.

Note that this situation holds true only as long as the new projects represent fairly small investments compared to ongoing operations. As new projects become *large* relative to ongoing cash-flow-producing activities, creditors will have to examine the likelihood of being repaid from the new projects much more closely. New projects, however great their potential, inherently carry more risk than do established current operations. Changes in the proportion of new projects relative to ongoing operations will thus translate into increased risk for the creditor, who will ask for a higher rate of return to offset the risk.

Since most firms tend to grow incrementally, we will assume (unless otherwise indicated) that we're examining situations in which the number of new projects is small relative to ongoing operations. We can therefore also assume that using the firm's existing, pre-project component costs of debt and preferred stock to calculate WACC is appropriate.

Project Cost Numbers to Find Elsewhere: The Pure-Play Approach

Since we have decided not to adjust the firmwide costs of debt or preferred stock for the risk of a project, where *should* we account for the new project risk brought to the firm overall? As with several other questions associated with risk and profit-sharing that we'll discuss in Chapter 16, the answer lies with *equity*.

The firm's risk changes when it takes on a project that is noticeably different from its existing lines of business. Debt holders and preferred stockholders will not bear much of this change in risk; rather, when it takes on a new project, the firm instead creates risk for its common stockholders that is disproportionately large compared to the amount of stockholder capital used to finance the project.

In response to such a change in the firm's risk profile, stockholders adjust their required rate of return to adjust for the new risk level. Absent any alteration to the firm's capital structure,[3] changes in the firm's risk profile are due to differences in the firm's **business risks** based on the mix of the new and existing product lines. The stock's beta reflects those differences in each product line.

Obviously, no proposed new project will have a history of previous returns. Without such data, neither analysts nor investors can calculate a project-specific beta. So what data can we use? To the extent that we can find other firms engaged in the proposed new line of business, we can use their betas as proxies to estimate the project's risk. Ideally, the other firms would be engaged *only* in the proposed new line of business; such monothemed firms are usually referred to as *pure plays,* with this term also in turn being applied to this approach to estimating a project's beta.

An average of *n* such **proxy betas** will give us a fairly accurate estimate of what the new project's beta will be.[4]

$$i_E = r_f + \beta_{\text{AVg}}\left[E(r_M) - r_f\right]$$

where

$$\beta_{\text{AVg}} = \frac{\sum\limits_{j=1}^{N} \beta_j}{n} \tag{11-7}$$

This average will be an estimate, in the strictest statistical sense of the word. You might recall from your statistics classes that we will need to be careful to get as large a sample as possible if we want to get as much statistical power for our estimate as possible. Ideally, we would like to find at least three or four companies from which to draw proxy betas, called *pure-play proxies,* to ensure that we have a large enough sample size to safely make meaningful inferences. In reality, however, two proxies (or even one) might represent a suitable sample if their business line resembles the proposed new project closely enough. In particular, we may want to use betas from industry front-runners, and rely less on betas of any firms that the company really doesn't want to emulate.

What shall we do if we cannot find *any* pure-play proxies? Well, in that case, we may want to use firms that, while not *solely* in the same business as the proposed project's venture, have a sizable proportion of revenues from that line. We may then be able to "back out" the impact of their other lines of business from their firm's beta to leave us with a good enough estimate of what the new project's beta might be.

Be sure to use weights based on the *project's* sources of capital, and not necessarily the *firm's* capital structure. If the new project is going to use more or less debt than the firm's existing projects do, then the risk and reward-sharing are going to vary across the different types of capital (as discussed in Chapter 16), and we will want to recognize this in our WACC computation.

Finally, we need to consider the appropriate corporate tax rate to use in calculating the WACC for a project. Since all corporate tax rates are now 21 percent, the appropriate tax rate to compute the project's WACC will also be 21 percent.

To summarize, the component costs and weights to compute a project-specific WACC should be as shown in equation 11-8 (for firms that *can* take full advantage of the interest tax shields) or in equation 11-9 (for firms that *cannot* take advantage of the interest tax shields), with the source of each part indicated by the appropriate subscript:

$$
\begin{aligned}
WACC_{\text{Uconstrained, Project}} = {} & \frac{E_{\text{Project}}}{E_{\text{Project}} + P_{\text{Project}} + D_{\text{Project}}} \times i_{E,\text{ Project}} \\
& + \frac{P_{\text{Project}}}{E_{\text{Project}} + P_{\text{Project}} + D_{\text{Project}}} \times i_{P,\text{ Firm}} \\
& + \frac{D_{\text{Project}}}{E_{\text{Project}} + P_{\text{Project}} + D_{\text{Project}}} \times i_{P,\text{ Firm}} \times (1 - T_C)
\end{aligned}
\tag{11-8}
$$

$$
\begin{aligned}
WACC_{\text{Constrained, Project}} = {} & \frac{E_{\text{Project}}}{E_{\text{Project}} + P_{\text{Project}} + D_{\text{Project}}} \times i_{E,\text{ Project}} \\
& + \frac{P_{\text{Project}}}{E_{\text{Project}} + P_{\text{Project}} + D_{\text{Project}}} \times i_{P,\text{ Firm}} \\
& + \frac{D_{\text{Project}}}{E_{\text{Project}} + P_{\text{Project}} + D_{\text{Project}}} \times i_{D,\text{ Firm}}
\end{aligned}
\tag{11-9}
$$

time out!

11-3 For computing a project WACC, why do we take some component costs from the firm but compute others that are specific for the project being considered?

11-4 It is usually much easier to find proxy firms that are engaged in multiple lines of business than it is to find pure-play proxies. Explain how such firms can be used to estimate the beta for a new project.

EXAMPLE 11-6

Calculation of Project WACC LG11-5

For interactive versions of this example, log in to Connect or go to mhhe.com/Cornett6e.

Suppose that Evita's Subs, a local shipyard, is considering opening up a chain of sandwich shops. Evita's capital structure currently consists of 2 million outstanding shares of common stock, selling for $83 per share, and a $50 million bond issue, selling at 103 percent of par. Evita's stock has a beta of 0.72, the expected market risk premium is 7 percent, and the current risk-free rate is 4.5 percent. The bonds pay a 9 percent annual coupon and mature in 20 years. The current operations of the firm produce EBIT of $100 million per year, and the new sandwich operations would add only an expected $12 million per year to that. Also, suppose that Evita's management has done some research on the sandwich shop industry and discovered that such firms have an average beta of 1.23. If the new project will be funded for $110 million consisting of 50 percent debt and 50 percent equity, and Evita's faces a marginal tax rate of 21 percent and can make full use of the tax shield on new debt, what should be the WACC for this new project?

SOLUTION:

First, note that Evita's currently doesn't have any outstanding preferred stock and doesn't plan on using any to finance the new project, so that makes our job a little simpler. Also note that, though we are given enough information to calculate the firm's current capital structure weights and component cost of equity, we will use the new project's capital structure to calculate the weights instead, as it differs from the existing capital structure. And we already know the capital structure weights for the new project (50 percent debt and 50 percent equity), so we just need to calculate the appropriate component costs.

For equity, the appropriate cost will be based upon the average risk of sandwich shops:

$$i_E = R_r + \beta_{Project}(R_M - R_r)$$
$$= 0.045 + 1.23[0.07]$$
$$= 0.1311, \text{ or } 13.11\%$$

Since the new sandwich project appears to be small relative to the firm's existing line of business, we will assume that the new bondholders will expect to be repaid out of cash flows to the existing shipyards, and the YTM on the new bonds issued to finance this project will be the same as the YTM on the existing bonds:

$$\text{Solve} \left\{ \$1,030 = \$90 \times \left[\frac{1 - \frac{1}{\{1 + i_D\}^{20}}}{i_D} \right] + \frac{\$1,000}{\{1 + i_D\}^{20}} \right\} \text{ for } i_D$$

which gives us an i_D of 8.68 percent.

Now, since we are told that the firm currently has EBIT of $100 million and that the new project is expected to add $12 million, we expect total EBIT with the new project to be $112 million. Since EBIT must be less than or equal to EBITDA, it doesn't really matter which year it is: If total interest expenditures are less than 30 percent of EBIT, they will also be less than 30 percent of EBITDA.

Since the firm can be expected to price the new $55 million in debt with a coupon of 8.86 percent so it will sell at face value, and since it pays a coupon of 9 percent on the currently outstanding $50 million in debt already in the capital structure, total interest payments with the new project funded should be equal to 8.68% × $55million + 9% × $50million = $9,373,000, which is only 8.37 percent of the $112 million expected yearly EBIT. Therefore, the after-tax cost of debt will be equal to $i_D \times (1 - T_C) = 0.0886 \times (1 - 0.21) = .0700$, or 7 percent.

Therefore, the WACC of the new project will be

CALCULATOR HINTS

$N = 20$
$PV = -1030$
$PMT = 90$
$FV = 1000$
$CPT\ I = 8.68$

$$WACC_{Project} = \frac{E_{Project}}{E_{Project} + P_{Project} + D_{Project}} \times i_{E,\ Project} + \frac{D_{Project}}{E_{Project} + P_{Project} + D_{Project}} \times i_{D,\ Firm} \times (1 - T_C)$$
$$= 0.5 \times 0.1311 + 0.5 \times .0868 \times (1 - 0.21)$$
$$= 0.0998, \text{ or } 9.98\%$$

The spreadsheet solution is:

	A	B	C
1			
2	Beta	1.23	
3	Market Risk Premium	7.00%	
4	Risk-Free Rate	4.50%	
5			
6	Bond Coupon Rate	9%	
7	Bond Maturity	20	
8	Bond Price	$ 1,030.00	
9			
10	Cost of Equity	13.11%	=B4+B2*B3
11	Cost of Preferred Stock	0.00%	
12	Cost of Debt	8.68%	=RATE(B7,B6*1000,-B8,1000)
13	Tax Rate	21.00%	
14			
15			
16	E/(E+P+D)	50.00%	
17	P/(E+P+D)	0.00%	
18	D/(E+P+D)	50.00%	
19			
20	WACC	9.98%	=B10*B16+B11*B17+B12*(1-B13)*B18

Microsoft Excel

This calculation of WACC can be accomplished using the same template that we used in the last example (albeit without any preferred stock, which we indicate by setting both the cost and weight of preferred stock to zero in the template). The only thing we have to take care with is to ensure that we use the beta and weights for the new project rather than the existing firm.

Similar to Problems 11-8 to 11-11, Self-Test Problem 2

11.3 • DIVISIONAL WACC LG11-6

> **divisional WACC** An estimated WACC computed using some sort of proxy for the average equity risk of the projects in a particular division.

Do firms calculate risk-appropriate WACC for *every* new project they consider? While this would be ideal, pragmatically it just is not always feasible. In large corporations, managers evaluate dozens or even hundreds of proposed new projects each year. The costs in terms of time and effort of estimating project-specific WACCs individually for each project are simply prohibitive. Instead, large firms often take a middle-of-the-road approach that can achieve many of the results of using project-specific WACC calculations with much less time and resources. The key to this approach is to calculate **divisional WACCs** for each product line of the company based on that line's, but *not* each individual product's, risk profile.

Pros and Cons of a Divisional WACC

As with most choices in life as well as finance, there are pros and cons to using the divisional WACC approach. Let's first consider the disadvantage of using a firm's WACC to evaluate new, risk-heterogeneous projects. To make things simple, let's assume that we are looking at a firm that uses only equity finance, so that WACC is simply equal to i_E, and let's further assume that all the proposed new projects are in the same product line as each other and as the firm's existing projects, so that the divisional WACC would be equal to the firm's existing WACC.

Take a look at Figure 11.1. Similar to our discussion of the security market line in Chapter 10, required rates of return for projects with varying degrees of risk would lie along the sloped line shown in the figure. We could then evaluate projects with various degrees of risk based on the relationship between their expected rate of return and the required rate of return for that risk level. Turning to Figure 11.2, you can see that using risk-appropriate WACCs, projects A and B would be accepted because their *expected* rates of return would be higher than their respective *required* rates of return. Projects C and D would be rejected since our simple scheme shows that these projects are not expected to return enough to cover market-required returns, given the projects' riskiness.

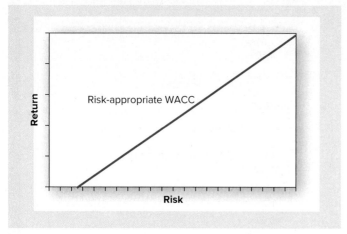

▼FIGURE 11.1 Risk-Appropriate WACCs

Return (vertical axis) / *Risk* (horizontal axis)

Risk-appropriate WACC

In an all-equity firm, WACC is theoretically equal to *iE* for each proposed project, which will increase as the risk (i.e., *β*) of the project increases.

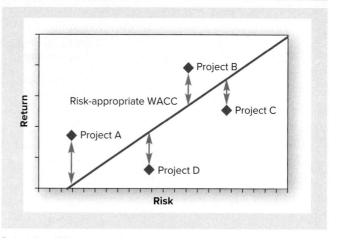

▼FIGURE 11.2 Sample Projects versus Risk-Sensitive WACC

Return (vertical axis) / *Risk* (horizontal axis)

Risk-appropriate WACC

Project B
Project C
Project A
Project D

Projects A and B have expected returns *greater than* their risk-appropriate WACCs. Projects C and D have expected returns *less than* their risk-appropriate WACCs.

However, using a firmwide WACC would result in a comparison of the project's expected rates of return to a single, flat, firmwide cost of capital, as Figure 11.3 shows. Using a simple firmwide WACC to evaluate new projects would give an unfair advantage to projects that present more risk than the firm's average beta. Using a firmwide WACC would also work against projects that involved less risk than the firm's average beta. Looking at the same sample projects as before, we see that Project A would now be rejected, while Project C would be accepted.

Using a firmwide WACC in this way, as an inappropriate benchmark for projects of differing risk from the firm's current operations, will result in quite a few incorrect decisions. In fact, the use of a firmwide WACC to evaluate *any* projects with risk-return coordinates lying in the two shaded triangles shown in Figure 11.4 will result in an incorrect accept/reject decision.

▼FIGURE 11.4 Incorrect Decisions Caused by Inappropriate Use of Firmwide WACC

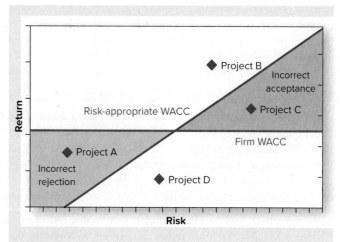

Return (vertical axis) / *Risk* (horizontal axis)

Risk-appropriate WACC
Firm WACC
Project B
Incorrect acceptance
Project C
Project A
Incorrect rejection
Project D

The gold-shaded triangle on the lower left contains projects such as Project A, which is *incorrectly rejected* by a firm. It has risk *less than* the average risk of the firm. Its expected rate of return is *greater than* its correctly calculated risk-appropriate WACC but *less than* an inappropriately calculated firmwide WACC. The pink-shaded triangle on the upper right contains projects such as Project C, which is *incorrectly accepted* by a firm. It has risk *greater than* the average risk of the firm. Its expected rate of return is *less than* a correctly calculated risk-appropriate WACC but *greater than* an inappropriately calculated firmwide WACC.

▼FIGURE 11.3 Sample Project versus Firmwide WACC

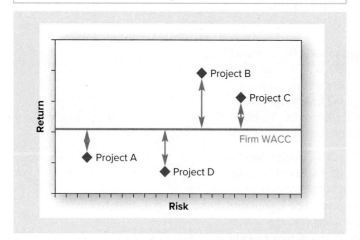

Return (vertical axis) / *Risk* (horizontal axis)

Project B
Project C
Firm WACC
Project A
Project D

If we were to mistakenly compare projects bearing different risks to this single firmwide WACC, we would conclude that projects A and D have expected rates of return *less than* the firmwide WACC and Projects B and C have expected returns *greater than* the firmwide WACC.

▼FIGURE 11.5 Divisional WACCs

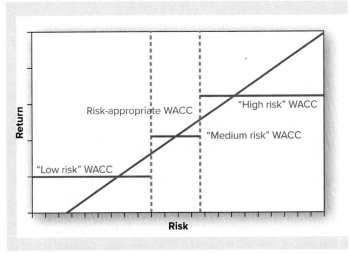

Instead of calculating a single firmwide WACC based on the average risk of all projects in the firm, assume that the firm calculates division-specific WACCs based on the average risk of the projects in each respective division.

▼FIGURE 11.6 Divisional WACC Errors

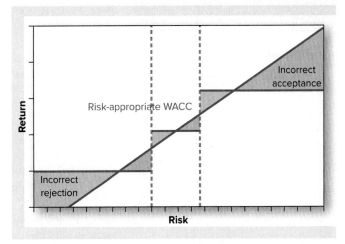

Total incorrect acceptances/rejections turn out to be less when divisional WACCs are used.

Computing a few "risk aware" divisional WACCs instead of just one "risk insensitive" firmwide WACC can greatly reduce the number of projects that get incorrectly accepted or rejected this way. To do so, we divide the firm's existing projects into divisions, where the different divisions proxy for systematically different average project risk levels. Calculating WACCs for each division separately, as Figure 11.5 shows, greatly reduces the problem of basing decisions on inaccurate results from using firmwide WACC for all projects.

Using divisional WACCs like this will not *eliminate* problems of incorrect acceptance and incorrect rejection, but it will greatly reduce their frequency. Instead of making errors corresponding to the two large triangular areas indicated in Figure 11.4, we will instead have six smaller areas of error shown in Figure 11.6. More acceptance/rejection regions will result in fewer errors.

For example, let's consider our four sample projects from before. Suppose that, instead of assigning the proposed new projects to the same firmwide division we had previously assumed, the firm divides its operations into "low-risk," "mid-risk," and "high-risk" product lines and decides that, based on their associated products and risk profiles, Project A should be assigned to the "low-risk" division, Project D to the "mid-risk" division, and projects B and C to the "high-risk" division. If we were to now evaluate them using divisional WACCs as shown in Figure 11.7, we would correctly accept both projects A and B and correctly reject projects C and D.

Subjective versus Objective Approaches LG11-7

We can form divisional WACCs subjectively by simply considering the project's risk relative to the firm's existing lines of business and then, if the project is riskier (safer) than the firm average, adjust the firm WACC upward (downward) to account for our subjective opinion of project riskiness. The biggest disadvantage to this approach is that the adjustments

▼FIGURE 11.7 Example Decisions Using Divisional WACCs

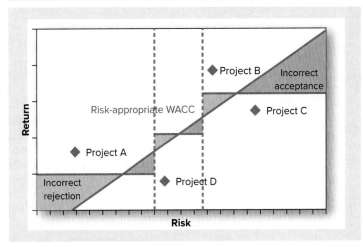

Projects A and B here are *correctly accepted,* while projects C and D are *correctly rejected.*

EXAMPLE 11-7

Divisional Costs of Capital LG11-7

For interactive versions of this example, log in to Connect or go to mhhe.com/Cornett6e.

Assume that BF, Inc., an all-equity firm, has a firmwide WACC of 10 percent and that the firm is broken into three divisions: Textiles, Accessories, and Miscellaneous. The average Textiles project has a beta of 0.7, the average Accessories project has a beta of 1.3, and the average Miscellaneous project has a beta of 1.1.

The firm is currently considering the projects shown in the table below. The current approach is to use the firm's WACC to evaluate all projects, but management sees the wisdom in adopting a subjective divisional cost of capital approach. Firm management is thus considering a divisional cost of capital scheme in which it will use the firm's WACC for Miscellaneous projects, the firm's WACC minus 1 percent for Textiles projects, and the firm's WACC plus 3 percent for Accessories projects. The current expected return to the market is 12 percent, and the current risk-free rate is 5.75 percent.

For this group of projects, how much better would its accept/reject decisions be if it used this approach rather than if it continued to use the firm's WACC to evaluate all projects? Would switching to an objective divisional cost of capital approach, where the WACC for each division is based on that division's average beta, improve its accept/reject criteria any further?

Project	Division	Expected i_E	Beta
A	$\beta_{Accessories}$	17.00%	1.3
B	$\beta_{Accessories}$	15.00	1.2
C	$\beta_{Miscellaneous}$	13.00	1.3
D	$\beta_{Miscellaneous}$	11.00	0.7
E	$\beta_{Textiles}$	9.00	0.8
F	$\beta_{Textiles}$	7.00	0.5

SOLUTION:

Determine the required rates of return for each project assuming that the firm uses the firmwide WACC and adds the subjective adjustments to construct divisional WACCs. The objective computation of divisional WACCs using each division's average beta and the iE computed using each project's specific beta is indicated in the following table. In each case, project acceptances appear in blue print, and project rejections appear in red print.

Project	Division	Expected i_E	Beta	Firm WACC	Subjective i_E	Objective i_E	Specific i_E
A	$\beta_{Accessories}$	17.00%	1.3	10.00%	13.00%	13.88%	13.88%
B	$\beta_{Accessories}$	15.00	1.2	10.00	13.00	13.88	13.25
C	$\beta_{Miscellaneous}$	13.00	1.3	10.00	10.00	12.63	13.88
D	$\beta_{Miscellaneous}$	11.00	0.7	10.00	10.00	12.63	10.13
E	$\beta_{Textiles}$	9.00	0.8	10.00	9.00	10.13	10.75
F	$\beta_{Textiles}$	7.00	0.5	10.00	9.00	10.13	8.88

Using the "Specific i_E" yields the "correct" accept/reject decision; that is, these accept/reject decisions would be generated exactly the same if the firm had the time and resources to compute i_E on a project-by-project basis. In this particular situation, using the firm WACC as a benchmark for all the projects would result in projects E and F being rejected since they both will return expected rates less than the firm's 10 percent required rate of return. By comparison to the results using the Specific iE, both of these rejections are appropriate. We would prefer that the accept/reject criteria took account of risk; that is, both projects would be rejected because their expected returns (9 percent and 7 percent, respectively) are less than the required returns (10.75 percent and 8.88 percent, respectively) based on their specific levels of project risk rather than assuming that both projects carry the same risk as the firm's overall risk. However, using the firm's WACC incorrectly accepts project C.

Using the subjectively adjusted approach to calculating i_E results in required rates of return of 13 percent for Accessories projects, 10 percent for Miscellaneous projects, and 9 percent for Textiles projects. The associated accept/reject decisions actually incorrectly accept projects C and E, making the subjectively adjusted WACC approach worse (in this specific example) than simply using the firmwide WACC.

Finally, using the objective approach to constructing divisional costs of capital, along with the three divisions' average betas given above, results in required rates of return for the three divisions of

$$i_E = R_f + \beta(R_M - 11.3R_f)$$

$$i_{E,\ Accessories} = 0.0575 + 1.3[0.12 - 0.0575] = 0.1388, \text{ or } 13.88\%$$

$$i_{E,\ Miscellaneous} = 0.0575 + 1.1[0.12 - 0.0575] = 0.1263, \text{ or } 12.63\%$$

$$i_{E,\ Textiles} = 0.0575 + 0.7[0.12 - 0.0575] = 0.1013, \text{ or } 10.13\%$$

As these solutions show, using these divisional costs of capital figures as required rates of return for each project results in correct rejections of projects E and F, but also results in an incorrect rejection of project D and an incorrect acceptance of project C relative to computing i_E on a project-by-project basis.

Overall, using either the objective or subjective approaches to calculating divisional costs of capital will not be as precise as using project-specific WACCs: We will wind up incorrectly accepting and/or rejecting some projects. Making incorrect decisions on some of our project choices may be worth it if the projects in question aren't large enough for project-specific calculations to be cost-effective.

The spreadsheet solution is:

	A	B	C	D	E	F	G
1							
2	Project	Division	Expected i_E	Beta	Firm WACC	Subjective	
3	A	Accessories	17.00%	1.3	10%	13%	=E3+B14
4	B	Accessories	15.00%	1.2	10%	13%	=E4+B14
5	C	Miscellaneous	13.00%	1.3	10%	10%	=E5+B15
6	D	Miscellaneous	11.00%	0.7	10%	10%	=E6+B15
7	E	Textiles	9.00%	0.8	10%	9%	=E7+B16
8	F	Textiles	7.00%	0.5	10%	9%	=E8+B16
9							
10	$\beta_{Accessories}$	1.30				Objective	
11	$\beta_{Miscellaneous}$	1.10				13.88%	=$B$19+B10*($B$18-$B$19)
12	$\beta_{Textiles}$	0.70				13.88%	=F11
13						12.63%	=$B$19+B11*($B$18-$B$19)
14	Subjective Adj - Accessories	3.00%				12.63%	=F13
15	Subjective Adj - Miscellaneous	0.00%				10.13%	=$B$19+B12*($B$18-$B$19)
16	Subjective Adj - Textiles	-1.00%				10.13%	=F15
17							
18	Market Expected Return	12.00%				Project-Specific	
19	Risk-Free Rate	5.75%				13.88%	=$B$19+D3*($B$18-$B$19)
20						13.25%	=$B$19+D4*($B$18-$B$19)
21						13.88%	=$B$19+D5*($B$18-$B$19)
22						10.13%	=$B$19+D6*($B$18-$B$19)
23						10.75%	=$B$19+D7*($B$18-$B$19)
24						8.88%	=$B$19+D8*($B$18-$B$19)

Microsoft Excel

In reality, it is probably pretty unlikely that a firm would need to calculate firm WACC, subjective divisional costs of capital, objective divisional costs of capital, and firm-specific divisional costs of capital. However, this is exactly the type of situation with highly repetitive reuses of inputs for which Excel really shines.

In the given spreadsheet, we've used conditional formatting to show accept/reject decisions, setting a computed value to green if the expected return from a project would be greater than the cost of capital (and therefore accepted) using a particular approach, and to red if it would be less than the cost of capital (and therefore rejected).

For the firm WACCs in cells E3 through E8, we merely entered 10 percent manually.

For the subjective costs of capital in cells F3 through F8, we added the project's division's subjective adjustment from cells B14 through B16, as appropriate, to the firm WACC.

For the objective costs of capital in cells F11 through F16, we used the CAPM formula but referenced the appropriate divisional beta in cells B10 through B12.

Finally, for the calculation of the project-specific costs of capital in cells F19 through F24, we again used the CAPM, but this time referenced each project's specific beta in cells D3 through D8.

Similar to Problems 11-14, 11-15

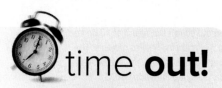

11-5 Divisions of a corporation are not usually formed based explicitly on differences in risk between the projects in different divisions. Rather, they are normally formed along product-type or geographic differences. Explain how this division scheme may still result in divisions that *do* differ among themselves by average risk. Also explain why calculating divisional WACCs in such a situation will still improve decision making over simply using a firmwide WACC for project acceptance or rejection.

11-6 Explain why, in Example 11-7, using objectively computed divisional WACCs still resulted in an incorrect accept/reject decision for project D.

---

flotation costs Fees paid by firms to investment banks for issuing new securities.

separation principle Theory maintaining that the sources and uses of capital should be decided upon independently.

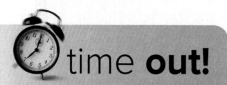
11-7 Why should we expect the flotation costs for debt to be significantly lower than those for equity?

11-8 Explain how we should go about computing the WACC for a project that uses both retained earnings and a new equity issue.

▼ **TABLE 11.1** Subjective Divisional WACCs

Risk Level	Discount Rate
Very low risk	Firm WACC − 5%
Low risk	Firm WACC − 2%
Same risk as firm	Firm WACC
High risk	Firm WACC + 3%
Very high risk	Firm WACC + 7%

are pretty much picked out of thin air and created just for the project at hand. For example, consider the sample subjective divisional WACCs in Table 11.1. Both the project assignments to the divisions and then the WACC adjustments for the very low risk, low risk, high risk, and very high risk are fairly arbitrary.

An objective approach would be to compute the average beta per division, use these figures in the CAPM formula to calculate i_E for each division, and then, in turn, use divisional estimates of i_E to construct divisional WACCs. Though the objective approach would usually be more precise, resulting in fewer incorrect accept/reject decisions, the subjective approach is more frequently used because it is easier to implement.

11.4 • FLOTATION COSTS LG11-8

We know that firms use varied sources of funding. Until now, our calculations have been assuming that we were using retained earnings to fund projects. What if a firm funds a project by issuing externally generated new capital—additional stock, bonds, and so on? Then the firm has to pay the costs of printing the new stock or bond certificates, commissions to the underwriters helping the firm to sell the stocks and bonds, government registration fees, and other associated costs. So to figure project WACCs, we must integrate these **flotation costs** into our component costs as well.

We can approach the commission costs in two basic ways. We can either increase the project's WACC to incorporate the flotation costs' impact as a percentage of WACC, or we can leave the WACC alone and adjust the project's initial investment upward to reflect the "true" cost of the project. Both approaches have advantages and disadvantages. The first approach tends to understate the component cost of new equity, and the latter approach violates the **separation principle** of capital budgeting, which states that the calculations of cash flows should remain independent of financing. We will discuss the separation principle and the second approach in the next chapter.

Adjusting the WACC

The first approach to adjusting for flotation costs is to adjust the issue price of new securities by subtracting flotation cost, F, to reflect the net security price. Then use this net price to calculate the component cost of capital. For equity, this approach is most commonly applied to the constant-growth model:

$$i_E = \frac{D_1}{P_0 - F} + g \qquad (11\text{-}10)$$

If we instead want to apply this approach to the cost of equity obtained from the CAPM formula, we would adjust it upward by an equivalent amount.

EXAMPLE 11-8

Flotation-Adjusted Cost of Equity LG11-8

For interactive versions
of this example, log
in to Connect or go to
mhhe.com/Cornett6e.

Suppose that, as in Example 11-1, ADK Industries' common shares are selling for $32.75 per share, and the company expects to set its next annual dividend at $1.54 per share. All future dividends are expected to grow by 6 percent per year indefinitely. In addition, let us suppose that ADK faces a flotation cost of 20 percent on new equity issues. Calculate the flotation-adjusted cost of equity.

SOLUTION:

Twenty percent of $32.75 will be $6.55, so the flotation-adjusted cost of equity will be

$$i_E = \frac{D_1}{P_0 - F} + g$$

$$= \frac{\$1.54}{\$32.75 - \$6.55} + 0.66$$

$$= 0.1188, \text{ or } 11.88\%$$

Notice that the result is 1.18 percent above the non-flotation-adjusted cost of equity, 10.70 percent, computed using the constant-growth model in Example 11-1. If we instead wanted to use the CAPM estimate, we would take the non-flotation-adjusted CAPM estimate from the same example, 10.80 percent, and add the same differential of 1.18 percent to it to get the flotation-adjusted value:

$$i_E = 0.1080 + 0.0118 = 0.1198, \text{ or } 11.98\%$$

The adjustments for the component costs of preferred stock and debt will be similar:

$$i_P = \frac{D_1}{P_o - F} \tag{11-11}$$

$$\text{Solve} \left\{ PV - F = PMT \times \left[\frac{1 - \dfrac{1}{(1 + i_D)^N}}{i_D} \right] + \frac{FV}{(1 + i_D)^N} \right\} \text{ for } i_D \tag{11-12}$$

The spreadsheet solution is:

	A	B	C
1			
2	Price	$ 32.75	
3	D1	$ 1.54	
4	g	6%	
5	F	20%	
6			
7	F	$ 6.55	=B2*B5
8			
9	i_E	11.88%	=B3/(B2-B7)+B4

Microsoft Excel

To calculate the flotation-adjusted cost of equity, we first calculate the dollar flotation cost per share, shown in cell B7. This is then used to calculate the rate of return on a perpetuity, but it substitutes the amount the firm actually raises from selling each share (selling price minus flotation cost, or cell B2 minus cell B7) in cell B9.

Similar to Problems 11-23, 11-24

Your Turn . . .

Questions

1. How would you handle calculating the cost of capital if a firm were planning to issue two different classes of common stock? *(LG11-1)*

2. Expressing WACC in terms of i_E, i_P, and i_D, what is the theoretical minimum for the WACC? *(LG11-2)*

3. Under what situations would you want to use the CAPM approach for estimating the component cost of equity? The constant-growth model? *(LG11-3)*

4. Could you calculate the component cost of equity for a stock with nonconstant expected growth rates in dividends if you didn't have the information necessary to compute the component cost using the CAPM? Why or why not? *(LG11-3)*

5. Why do we use market-based weights instead of book-value-based weights when computing the WACC? *(LG11-4)*

6. Suppose your firm wanted to expand into a new line of business quickly, and that management anticipated that the new line of business would constitute over 80 percent of your firm's operations within three years. If the expansion was going to be financed partially with debt, would it still make sense to use the firm's existing cost of debt, or should you compute a new rate of return for debt based on the new line of business? *(LG11-5)*

7. Explain why the divisional cost of capital approach may cause problems if new projects are assigned to the wrong division. *(LG11-6)*

8. When will the subjective approach to forming divisional WACCs be better than using the firmwide WACC to evaluate all projects? *(LG11-7)*

9. Suppose a new project was going to be financed partially with retained earnings. What flotation costs should you use for retained earnings? *(LG11-8)*

Problems

BASIC PROBLEMS

11-1 **Cost of Equity** Diddy Corp. stock has a beta of 1.2, the current risk-free rate is 5 percent, and the expected return on the market is 13.5 percent. What is Diddy's cost of equity? *(LG11-3)*

11-2 **Spreadsheet Problem: Cost of Debt** Oberon, Inc., has a $20 million *(face value)* 10-year bond issue selling for 97 percent of par that pays an annual coupon of 8.25 percent. What would be Oberon's before-tax component cost of debt? *(LG11-3)*

11-3 **Tax Rate** Suppose that LilyMac Photography expects EBIT to be approximately $200,000 per year for the foreseeable future, and that it has 1,000 10-year, 9 percent annual coupon bonds outstanding. What would the appropriate tax rate be for use in the calculation of the debt component of LilyMac's WACC? *(LG11-3)*

11-4 **Cost of Preferred Stock** ILK has preferred stock selling for 97 percent of par that pays an 8 percent annual coupon. What would be ILK's component cost of preferred stock? *(LG11-3)*

11-5 **Spreadsheet Problem: Weight of Equity** FarCry Industries, a maker of telecommunications equipment, has 2 million shares of common stock outstanding, 1 million shares of preferred stock outstanding, and 10,000 bonds. If the common shares are selling for $27 per share, the preferred shares are selling for $14.50 per share, and the bonds are selling for 98 percent of par, what would be the weight used for equity in the computation of FarCry's WACC? *(LG11-4)*

11-6 **Spreadsheet Problem: Weight of Debt** FarCry Industries, a maker of telecommunications equipment, has 2 million shares of common stock outstanding, 1 million shares of preferred stock outstanding, and 10,000 bonds. If the common shares are selling for $27 per share, the preferred shares are selling for $14.50 per share, and the bonds are selling for 98 percent of par, what weight should you use for debt in the computation of FarCry's WACC? *(LG11-4)*

11-7 **Spreadsheet Problem: Weight of Preferred Stock** FarCry Industries, a maker of telecommunications equipment, has 2 million shares of common stock outstanding, 1 million shares of preferred stock outstanding, and 10,000 bonds. If the common shares sell for $27 per share, the preferred shares sell for $14.50 per share, and the bonds sell for 98 percent of par, what weight should you use for preferred stock in the computation of FarCry's WACC? *(LG11-4)*

INTERMEDIATE PROBLEMS

11-8 **WACC** Suppose that TapDance, Inc.'s, capital structure features 65 percent equity and 35 percent debt, and that its before-tax cost of debt is 8 percent, while its cost of equity is 13 percent. If the appropriate weighted average tax rate is 21 percent and TapDance estimates it *cannot* make any use of the interest tax shield in the foreseeable future, what will be TapDance's WACC? *(LG11-2)*

11-9 **WACC** Suppose that MNINK Industries' capital structure features 63 percent equity, 7 percent preferred stock, and 30 percent debt. If the before-tax component costs of equity, preferred stock, and debt are 11.60 percent, 9.5 percent, and 9 percent, respectively, what is MNINK's WACC if the firm faces an average tax rate of 21 percent and can make full use of the interest tax shield? *(LG11-2)*

11-10 Spreadsheet Problem: WACC Johnny Cake Ltd. has 10 million shares of stock outstanding selling at $23 per share and an issue of $50 million in 9 percent annual coupon bonds with a maturity of 17 years, selling at 93.5 percent of par. If Johnny Cake's weighted average tax rate is 21 percent, it *cannot* make use of interest tax shields for the foreseeable future, its next dividend is expected to be $3 per share, and all future dividends are expected to grow at 6 percent per year, indefinitely, what is its WACC? *(LG11-3)*

11-11 Spreadsheet Problem: WACC Weights BetterPie Industries has 3 million shares of common stock outstanding, 2 million shares of preferred stock outstanding, and 10,000 bonds. If the common shares are selling for $47 per share, the preferred shares are selling for $24.50 per share, and the bonds are selling for 99 percent of par, what would be the weights used in the calculation of BetterPie's WACC? *(LG11-4)*

11-12 Spreadsheet Problem: Flotation Cost Suppose that Brown-Murphies' common shares sell for $19.50 per share, that the firm is expected to set their next annual dividend at $0.57 per share, and that all future dividends are expected to grow by 4 percent per year, indefinitely. If Brown-Murphies faces a flotation cost of 13 percent on new equity issues, what will be the flotation-adjusted cost of equity? *(LG11-8)*

ADVANCED PROBLEMS

11-13 Flotation Cost A firm is considering a project that will generate perpetual after-tax cash flows of $15,000 per year beginning next year. The project has the same risk as the firm's overall operations and must be financed externally. Equity flotation costs 14 percent and debt issues cost 4 percent on an after-tax basis. The firm's D/E ratio is 0.8. What is the most the firm can pay for the project and still earn its required return? *(LG11-2)*

11-14 Spreadsheet Problem: Firmwide versus Project-Specific WACCs An all-equity firm is considering the projects shown below. The T-bill rate is 4 percent and the market risk premium is 7 percent. If the firm uses its current WACC of 12 percent to evaluate these projects, which project(s), if any, will be incorrectly rejected? *(LG11-6)*

Project	Expected Return	Beta
A	8.0%	0.5
B	19.0	1.2
C	13.0	1.4
D	17.0	1.6

11-15 Spreadsheet Problem: Divisional WACCs Suppose your firm has decided to use a divisional WACC approach to analyze projects. The firm currently has four divisions, A through D, with average betas for each division of 0.6, 1.0, 1.3, and 1.6, respectively. If all current and future projects will be financed with half debt and half equity, and if the current cost of equity (based on an average firm beta of 1.0 and a current risk-free rate of 7 percent) is 13 percent and the after-tax yield on the company's bonds is 8 percent, what will the WACCs be for each division? *(LG11-7)*

Notes

CHAPTER 11

1. Think of taking such an average as being intuitively the same as diversifying our "portfolio" of data across the two different estimation techniques, thereby reducing the average amount of estimation error. Taking this average is intuitively the same as diversifying your portfolio of data across two different estimation techniques. These options allow you to reduce your average amount of estimation error.

2. We'll discuss more about calculating WACC for a project later in the chapter.

3. In reality, new projects are often financed with different proportions of equity, debt, and preferred stock than were used to fund the firm's existing operations. As we will discuss in Chapter 16, such a change in capital structure will result in a change in **financial risk** with increased leverage magnifying β.

4. As we will also discuss in Chapter 16, we will be able to take a straight average of the proxy firms' betas as the estimate of our beta only if the capital structures of all the proxies are identical to each other and to that of our proposed new project. If not, we will need to adjust the proxies' estimated betas for differences in capital structures before averaging them. Then we will need to readjust the average beta for our project's capital structure before using the estimate.

To evaluate capital budgeting projects, we have to estimate how much cash outflow each project will need and how much cash inflow it will generate, as well as exactly when such outflows and inflows will occur. Estimating these cash flows isn't difficult, but it is *complicated*, as there are lots of little details to keep track of. Accordingly, as you look

twelve

estimating cash flows on
capital budgeting projects

through this chapter's examples, questions, and problems, you'll notice that these types of problems involve a lot more information than those you've seen elsewhere in the text, such as

- The particular new product or service's costs and revenues.
- The likely impact that the new service or product will have on the firm's existing products' costs and revenues.
- The impact of using existing assets or employees already employed elsewhere in the firm.
- How to handle charges such as the research and development costs incurred to develop the new product.

One of the keys to this chapter will be making sure that we have a systematic approach to handling and arranging details. In the next few sections, we're going to construct a process that, if we follow it faithfully, will guide us in considering factors such as those listed.

continued on p. 334

LEARNING GOALS

LG12-1 Explain why we use pro forma statements to analyze project cash flows.

LG12-2 Identify which cash flows we can incrementally apply to a project and which ones we cannot.

LG12-3 Calculate a project's expected cash flows using the free cash flow approach.

LG12-4 Explain how accelerated depreciation affects project cash flows.

LG12-5 Calculate free cash flows for replacement equipment.

LG12-6 Calculate cash flows associated with cost-cutting proposals.

LG12-7 Demonstrate the EAC approach to choosing among alternative cash streams for recurring projects.

LG12-8 Adjust initial project investments to account for flotation costs.

>>viewpoints

Suppose that McDonald's is considering introducing the McTurkey Dinner (MTD). The company anticipates that the MTD will have unit sales, prices, and cost figures as shown in the following table for the next five years, after which the firm will retire the MTD. Introducing the MTD will require $7 million in new assets, which is eligible for 100 percent bonus depreciation, and McDonald's has enough net income from other operations to take full advantage of the bonus depreciation. McDonald's expects the necessary assets to be worth $2 million in market value at the end of the project life. In addition, the company expects that NWC requirements at the beginning of each year will be approximately 13 percent of the projected sales throughout the coming year and fixed costs will be $2 million per year. McDonald's uses an 11 percent cost of capital for similar projects and is subject to a 21 percent marginal tax rate. What will be this project's expected cash flows? **(See the solution at the end of the book.)**

McTURKEY DINNER PROJECTIONS

Year	Estimated Unit Sales	Estimated Selling Price per Unit	Estimated Variable Cost per Unit
1	400,000	$7.00	$3.35
2	1,000,000	7.21	3.52
3	1,000,000	7.43	3.70
4	1,000,000	7.65	3.89
5	500,000	7.88	4.08

continued from p. 333

> **pro forma analysis** Process of estimating expected future cash flows of a project using only the relevant parts of the balance sheet and income statements.

The exact process that we're going to use is more formally referred to as **pro forma analysis,** which estimates expected future cash flows of a project using only the necessary parts of the balance sheet and income statements; if a part of either financial statement doesn't change because of the new project, we'll ignore it. This approach will allow us to focus on the question, "What will be this project's impact on the firm's total cash flows if we go forward?" ■

LG12-1

12.1 • SAMPLE PROJECT DESCRIPTION LG12-1

Let's suppose that we are working for a game development company, First Strike Software (FSS). FSS is considering leasing a new plant in Gatlinburg, Tennessee, which it will use to produce copies of its new console game "FinProf," a role-playing game where the player battles aliens invading a local college's finance department.

FSS will price this game at $39.99, and the firm estimates sales for each of the next three years as shown in Table 12.1. Given buyers' rapidly changing tastes in console games, FSS does not expect to be able to sell any more copies after year 3.

Variable costs per game are low ($4.25), and FSS expects fixed costs to total $150,000 per year, including rent. Start-up costs include $75,000 for the purchase of a software-duplicating machine, plus an additional $2,000 in shipping and installation costs. For our

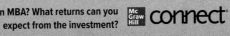
first stab at analyzing this project, we will assume that the duplicating machine will be straight-line depreciated to an estimated ending **salvage value** of $5,000 over the life of the project. However, due to the rapidly declining market for such machines (many of FSS's competitors are switching to download-only games), we are also estimating that we'll only be able to sell the machine for $2,000 after we're done using it.

FinProf is an updated version of an older game sold by FSS, MktProf. FSS intends to keep selling MktProf but anticipates that FinProf will decrease sales of MktProf by 2,000 units per year throughout the life of the new game. MktProf sells for $19.99 and has variable costs of $3.50 per unit. The decrease in MktProf sales will not affect either NWC or fixed assets.

Development costs totaled $150,000 throughout the creation of the game, and First Strike estimates its NWC requirements at the beginning of each year will be approximately 10 percent of the projected sales during the coming year. First Strike is in the 21 percent tax bracket and uses a discount rate of 15 percent on projects with risk profiles such as this. The relevant question: Should FSS put FinProf into production or not?

> **salvage value** The estimated amount for tax purposes that a company will receive when it disposes of an asset at the end of the asset's usable life.
>
> **incremental cash flows** Cash flows directly attributable to the adoption of a new project.

12.2 • GUIDING PRINCIPLES FOR CASH FLOW ESTIMATION LG12-2

When we calculate a project's expected cash flows, we must ensure that we cover all **incremental cash flows;** that is, the cash flow changes that we would expect *throughout* the entire firm, for both this project and for everything else the firm is already doing, *because of* the new project coming on board. Some incremental cash flow effects are fairly obvious. For example, suppose a firm has to buy a new asset to support a new project but would not be buying the asset if the project were not adopted. Clearly, the cash associated with buying the asset is due to the project, and we should therefore count it when we calculate the cash flows associated with that project. But we can hardly expect *all* incremental cash flows to be so obvious. Other incremental cash flows, as discussed in the following sections, are more subtle, and we'll have to watch for them very carefully.

▼ **TABLE 12.1** Sample Project Projected Unit Sales

Year	Unit Sales
1	15,000
2	27,000
3	5,000

Opportunity Costs

As you likely remember from your microeconomics classes, an **opportunity cost** exists whenever a firm has to choose how to allocate scarce resources. If those resources go into project A, the firm must forgo using them in any other way. Those forgone choices represent lost opportunities, and we have to account for them when calculating cash flows attributable to project A.

For example, suppose that FSS already owned the piece of software-duplicating machinery discussed previously. If the machinery was already being fully utilized by another project within the company, then obviously switching it over to the FinProf game would require that other project to find another source of software duplication. Therefore, to be fair, the FinProf project should be charged for the use of the machinery.

Even if the machinery was not currently being used in any other projects, it could still possibly have an opportunity cost associated with using it in the FinProf project. If FSS could potentially sell the machinery on the open market for $75,000, the company would have to give up receiving that $75,000 in order to use the piece of machinery for the FinProf game. In the end, it would not really matter whether the firm had to buy the asset from outside sources or not; either way, the project will be tying up $75,000 worth of capital, and it should be charged for doing so.

The underlying concept behind charging the project for the opportunity cost of using an asset also applies to expenses other than those associated with capital assets such as machinery: Overall, we should charge any new project for any assets used by that project *as well as any wages and benefits paid to employees working on it.* Even if the firm was already employing those people prior to starting work on the new project, they are no longer available to work on any existing projects; and if the firm did not have any new projects, it could have laid those employees off, saving their wages and benefits.

In the FSS project, wages and benefits to employees would constitute part of the variable costs we were quoted earlier. Just as with the software-duplicating machinery, whether these employees were previously working for FSS on another project would be irrelevant; if FSS is going to use these employees on this project, the project should be charged for them.

Sunk Costs

If a firm has already paid an expense in the past or is obligated to pay one in the future (i.e., there's no way out of paying it), regardless of whether a particular project is undertaken, that expense is a **sunk cost.** A firm should *never* count sunk costs in project cash flows. Intuitively, if you have to pay the expense regardless of your decision concerning the project, it doesn't meet the definition of being "incremental."

For example, we are told that FSS incurred $150,000 in development costs as it developed the game. Development costs would presumably include items such as the salaries of the game's programmers, market research costs, and so forth. Since we are not told otherwise, we can sensibly assume that this money is gone and that FSS will never recoup the money, even if it decides not to go ahead with publishing the game. Thus, those costs are sunk, and FSS should not even consider them as part of its decision about whether to move forward with putting the FinProf game into production.

Substitutionary and Complementary Effects

If a new product or service will either reduce or increase sales, costs, or necessary assets for other, *already existing* products or services, then those changes to the cash flows of the other projects are incremental to the new project and should rightfully be included in the new project's cash flows.

For example, consider how FSS's FinProf game may affect the existing MktProf game. The gross sales and variable cost figures for the new game might be as shown in Table 12.2.

However, FSS also expects the MktProf game to *lose* yearly sales of $2,000 \times \$19.99 = \$39,980$ when the FinProf game starts selling. Partially offsetting this, the decrease in sales of MktProf will also result in a decrease in yearly variable costs for MktProf of $2,000 \times \$3.50 = \$7,000$ in savings (i.e., forgone costs) per year. So the net incremental sales and variable cost figures for the project will be as shown in Table 12.3.

As we see, we have to reduce FinProf's sales each year by the $39,980 reduction in MktProf sales attributable to the Finprof game existing, but we also get to reduce FinProf's costs by $7,000 each year due to the cost savings of not having to make so many copies of MktProf. Technically speaking, we are seeing a reduction in both sales and variable costs because FinProf is a partial **substitute** for MktProf. If the new game had been a **complement** (i.e., if we had sold *more* of the MktProf game due to the rollout of FinProf), then both sales and variable costs of the existing product would have increased instead.

Stock Dividends and Bond Interest

One final, important note concerning incremental project cash flows: We will never count any **financing costs,** including dividends paid on stock or interest paid on debt, as expenses of the project. The costs of capital are already included as component costs in the weighted-average cost of capital (WACC) that we will be using to discount these cash flows in the next chapter. If we were to include them in the cash flow figures as well, we would be double-counting them.

▼ **TABLE 12.2** Gross Sales and Variable Costs for FinProf

Year	Sales	Variable Costs
1	$15,000 \times \$39.99 = \$599,850$	$15,000 \times \$4.25 = \$63,750$
2	$27,000 \times \$39.99 = \$1,079,730$	$27,000 \times \$4.25 = \$114,750$
3	$5,000 \times \$39.99 = \$199,950$	$5,000 \times \$4.25 = \$21.250$

▼ **TABLE 12.3** Net Incremental and Variable Costs for FinProf

Year	Sales	Variable Costs
1	$\$599,850 - \$39,980 = \$559,870$	$\$63,750 - \$7,000 = \$56,750$
2	$\$1,079,730 - \$39,980 = \$1,039,750$	$\$114,750 - \$7,000 = \$107,750$
3	$\$199,950 - \$39,980 = \$159,970$	$\$21,250 - \$7,000 = \$14,250$

12.3 • TOTAL PROJECT CASH FLOW LG12-3

In Chapter 2, we discussed the concept of free cash flow (FCF), which we defined as

$$FCF = \text{Operating cash flow} - \text{Investment in operating capital}$$
$$= [EBIT(1 - \text{Tax rate}) + \text{Depreciation}] \quad (12\text{-}1)$$
$$- [\Delta\text{Gross fixed assets} + \Delta\text{Net operating working capital}]$$

In this chapter, we are going to use this variable again as a measure of the total amount of available cash flow from a project. However, we will observe two important differences from how we used it in Chapter 2. First, since we will be considering potential projects rather than a particular firm's actual, historic activities, the FCF numbers we calculate will be, frankly, guesses—informed guesses, surely, but still guesses. Since we will be "calculating" guesses, we will introduce possible estimation error into our capital budgeting decision statistics, but we will hold off on discussing that until the next chapter.

Second, we will now calculate FCF on potential projects *individually,* rather than across the firm as a whole as we did in Chapter 2. In some ways, calculating FCF on individual projects will make our job much easier since we don't have to worry about estimating an entire set of balance sheets for the firm. Instead, we will only have to be concerned with the limited subset of pro forma statements necessary to keep track of the assets, expense categories, and so on, that a new project will affect. Unfortunately, the elements of that limited set will vary from situation to situation, and the hard part will be identifying which parts of the balance sheets are necessary and which are not.

Calculating Depreciation

Expected depreciation on equipment used during the life of the project will affect both the operating cash flows and the change in gross fixed assets that will occur at the end of the project when we sell or abandon them, so let's start our organizing there.

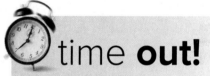
time **out!**

12-1 Suppose that your manager will be devoting half of her time to a new project, with the other half devoted to currently existing projects. How would you reflect this in your calculation of the incremental cash flows of the project?

12-2 Could a new product have both substitutionary and complementary effects on existing products?

For First Strike's proposed FinProf project, let's first assume the firm will depreciate capital assets such as the software-duplicating machine using the straight-line method to an ending book value of $5,000. To calculate the annual depreciation amount, First Strike will first need to compute the machinery's **depreciable basis.** According to the Internal Revenue Service's (IRS) Publication 946, the depreciable basis for real property is the sum of:

- Its cost.

- Amounts paid for items such as sales tax.

- Freight charges.

- Installation and testing fees.

We aren't told anything about sales tax on the machinery, so the depreciable basis for the new project's software-duplicating machine will be the $75,000 purchase price plus the $2,000 shipping and installation cost, for a total depreciable basis of $77,000.

Under straight-line depreciation, the annual depreciation for each year will be equal to the depreciable basis minus the projected ending book value, all over the number of years in the life of the asset:

$$\text{Depreciation} = \frac{\text{Depreciable basis} - \text{Ending book value}}{\text{Life of asset}}$$

$$= \frac{\$77,000 - \$5,000}{3 \text{ years}} \qquad (12\text{-}2)$$

$$= \$24,000 \text{ per year}$$

We'll discuss later in the chapter why this depreciation assumption is far too simple, and why other, more complicated depreciation methods can be much more advantageous to the company. For now, though, this straight-line depreciation approach will suffice for our initial go at calculating the project's cash flows.

Calculating Operating Cash Flow

We defined operating cash flow (OCF) in Chapter 2 as EBIT × (1 − Tax rate) + Depreciation. We will still calculate OCF as being mathematically equal to EBIT × (1 − Tax rate) + Depreciation. But remember that we will be constructing the FCF components ourselves instead of taking them off an income statement that someone else has already produced. So we will usually find it most helpful to conduct this calculation by using what we will call a "quasi-income statement" that leaves out some components that don't matter for project cash flows, such as interest deductions. (Note that the process of leaving out any interest deduction is exactly in line with our discussion of not counting interest on debt as an expense of the project, but the resulting financial statement would *not* make an accountant happy.)

Such a statement is shown in Table 12.4 for First Strike's proposed project. The primary benefit of calculating OCF this way instead of as an algebraic formula is that with this format, we have space to expand subcalculations, such as the impact of FinProf being a partial substitute for the MktProf product.

Before we move on, notice that not only is EBIT negative in year 3 of the OCF calculations, but we also assume that this negative EBIT, in turn, generates a "negative tax bill" (i.e., a tax credit, when we subtract the negative tax amount of −$5,939 from the negative EBIT). How, and when, can we get away with making this assumption?

Well, the rule for handling negative EBIT is that when calculating the cash flows for a single project for a firm, we assume that any loss by *this* project in a particular period can be applied against

The depreciable basis for real property includes freight charges.
Steve Boyko/Shutterstock

	YEAR 1		YEAR 2		YEAR 3	
Sales of FinProf	$599,850		$1,079,730		$199,950	
Less: Reduced sales of MktProf	39,980		39,980		39,980	
Net incremental sales		$559,870		$1,039,750		$159,970
Variable costs of FinProf	$ 63,750		$ 114,750		$ 21,250	
Less: Reduced costs of MktProf	7,000		7,000		7,000	
Less: Incremental variable costs		56,750		107,750		14,250
Less: Fixed costs		150,000		150,000		150,000
Less: Depreciation		24,000		24,000		24,000
Earnings before interest and taxes		$329,120		$ 758,000		-$ 28,280
Less: Taxes		69,115		159,180		-5,939
Net income		$260,005		$ 598,820		-$ 22,341
Plus: Depreciation		24,000		24,000		24,000
Operating cash flow		$284,005		$ 622,820		$ 1,659

assumed before-tax profits made by the *rest* of the firm in that period. So, while our project is expected to have a loss of $28,280 before taxes during year 3, the assumed ability of the firm to use that loss to shelter $28,280 in before-tax profits *elsewhere* in the firm means that the incremental after-tax net income for this project during year 3 is expected to be $-\$28,280 - (-\$5,939) = -\$22,341$. This is still negative, but less negative than the EBIT because of this tax-sheltering effect.

What would we do if we expected a negative EBIT during a particular year and this was the only project the firm was undertaking, or if this project was so big that a negative EBIT would overshadow any potential profits elsewhere in the firm? Long story short, we would not get to take the tax credit during that year . . . but we will leave the discussion of just exactly when we *would* get to take it to a more advanced text.

Calculating Changes in Gross Fixed Assets

Gross fixed assets will change in almost every project at both the beginning (when assets are usually *purchased*) and at the end (when assets are usually *sold*). First Strike's proposed project is no exception.

Calculating the change in gross fixed assets at the beginning of the project is fairly straightforward—it will simply equal the asset's depreciable basis. So, for FSS's project, we will increase gross fixed assets by $77,000 at time zero.

At the end of a project, the change in gross fixed assets is a little more complicated because whenever a firm sells any asset, it has to consider the tax consequences of that sale. The IRS treats any sale of assets for *more* than depreciated book value as a taxable *gain* and any sale for *less* than book value as a taxable *loss*. In either event, we can calculate the after-tax cash flow (ATCF) from the sale of an asset using the following formula, where T_C is the same appropriate corporate tax rate discussed in the previous chapter.

$$ATCF = \text{Market value} - (\text{Market value} - \text{Book value}) \times T_C \qquad (12\text{-}3)$$

Since the machinery for FSS's project will be depreciated down to $5,000 but is expected to sell for only $2,000, the ATCF for that asset's sale will equal

$$ATCF = \$2,000 - (\$2,000 - \$5,000) \times 0.21$$
$$= \$2,630$$

ATCF for an Asset Sold at a Gain LG12-3

Suppose that a firm facing a marginal tax rate of 21 percent sells an asset for $4,000 when its depreciated book value is $2,000. What will be the ATCF from the sale of this asset?

SOLUTION:

The ATCF will equal

$$ATCF = \$4,000 - (\$4,000 - \$2,000) \times 0.21$$
$$= \$3,580$$

Similar to Problems 12-1 and 12-8

Although it may be a little difficult to wrap your brain around the idea of reducing the $5,000, we were "supposed to get" (at least, according to the IRS) from the sale of the machinery at the end of the project by only 66 percent of the shortfall from that amount we actually *expect* to happen (i.e., $5,000 − $2,000 = $3,000), that's exactly what we're doing. "Losing" $3,000 of the $5,000 expected book value when we sell the machinery will let us hide $3,000 in revenues elsewhere from the tax man, so we get credit for shielding $3,000 from our 21 percent tax rate loss (i.e., $3,000 × 21% = $630) in addition to estimating that we'll be able to sell the machinery for $2,000 cash.

If this really is making your brain hurt, just realize that, as long as you faithfully and precisely apply the formula for ATCF, it will give you the net cash flow from the sale of the asset. In particular, note that this formula would work equally well on an asset sold at a gain.

Calculating Changes in Net Working Capital

We can make several different assumptions concerning the NWC level necessary to support a project. The most straightforward of these would be to simply assume that we add NWC at the beginning of the project and subtract it at the end. This assumption would be valid if the project is expected to have steady sales throughout its life, or if variations in NWC do not affect the project much.

FSS's proposed project, however, features a more typical product life cycle. Its unit sales will follow an approximate bell-shaped curve, starting out low at the beginning, peaking in the middle of the project, and then dropping off again at the end. When sales are timed in this way, FSS needs to give a little more thought to exactly *when* the firm needs to set aside net working capital to support high sales volumes and when it can reduce NWC as sales drop off.

The assumption that First Strike's NWC at any particular time will be a function of the *next* year's sales might seem odd at first glance. But a little thought about how we measure balance sheet numbers (such as NWC) and income statement items (such as sales) will show that, really, this assumption makes a lot of sense.

Since income statements (and our quasi-income statement discussed previously) measure what happens *during* a period, the sales show up on the statement at the end of the year, even though they actually start accumulating at the *beginning* of the year. The balance sheet "snapshots," on the other hand, capture how much capital sits in NWC accounts *at a particular point in time*. So, for example, the sales figures from our quasi-income statement for year 1 that are used in the OCF calculation for year 1 must be supported when they *start* occurring, which would be at the start of year 1. But remember, timelines are funny things: The start of year 1 is actually year 0, so we have to plan to have the NWC shown on the year 0 balance sheet reflect capital earmarked for NWC that will be supporting year 1 sales.

Of course, this same line of reasoning can be generalized for all other time periods, too: Any sales figure that appears in a time N OCF calculation needs NWC support at the *beginning* of year N, which is actually time $N - 1$. So NWC at time $N - 1$ should vary with time N sales. Therefore, the assumption that First Strike's NWC at any particular time will be a function of the *next* year's sales isn't as crazy as we first thought.

Also, note that it is just the *changes* in the level of NWC, not the levels themselves, that will affect our cash flows. To explain why, we need to throw a little more intuition into the pot here.

First, we have to admit that we do not really care about the changes in NWC, either, at least not for their own sake; instead, what we are actually measuring is the *investment* in capital necessary to make those changes happen. (And that's why there is a negative sign in front of NWC in our formula for free cash flow: It *costs* us money to make NWC bigger, and vice versa.)

Second, we need to think a little about exactly *what* we are measuring when we talk about using NWC to support sales. Since NWC equals current assets minus current liabilities, it's probably easier to think of it as being composed of cash, accounts receivable, and inventory, net of current liabilities. Do these types of assets get used up? Sure, when cash is used to make change, or when someone pays off an account receivable, or when we sell finished goods out of inventory, the respective asset account will go down. But those accounts go down *because we are bringing in money*, and some of that money can be used to "restock the shelves," so to speak; that is, when someone buys one of our products out of inventory, we assume that part of the purchase price goes toward replenishing the inventory we just sold, and when someone pays off an account receivable, we assume that allows us to turn around and lend that money to someone else and so forth.

The basic point here is that cash, once invested in NWC, pretty much replenishes itself until we manually take it back out. So when we are looking at the levels of NWC throughout the life of a project, it is the *changes* in those levels that we have to finance, not the levels themselves. Once we put a million dollars into inventory, it sort of stays there because of this idea of replenishment, even when we sell some of the inventory. And if we are keeping track of the amount of money that we have to invest in inventory or some other type of NWC account, we will find investment necessary only when we need to *grow* NWC by adding to that million dollars (or when we decide to take some of it back out).

First Strike's NWC at any time will be a function of next year's sales.
Don Carstens/Brand X Pictures

So, we can use the given information for the First Strike project to compute the NWC necessary to support sales throughout the project's life, and then in turn use NWC levels to compute the necessary changes in NWC, as shown in Table 12.5. Notice that the NWC level at each time is simply 10 percent of the following year's sales figures from Table 12.4.

This method for computing changes in NWC levels has several appealing features:

- The *changes* in NWC at the beginning of a project will always equal the *level* at time 0, as NWC will be going from a presumed zero level before the project starts up to that new, nonzero level.

- Allowing NWC to vary as a percentage of coming sales like this allows FSS to add NWC during periods when it expects sales to increase (e.g., years 0 and 1 in this example) and to decrease NWC when it expects sales to fall off (e.g., years 2 and 3 in this example). NWC levels fall off the last two years of this project precisely *because* FSS expects sales to fall off and is adjusting NWC to compensate.

- Finally, one especially nice feature of this approach is that it will always automatically bring NWC back down to a zero level when the project ends. Since sales in the year *after* the project ends are always zero, 10 percent of zero will also be zero. This corresponds to what we would expect to see in the real world: When a project ends, the firm sells off inventory, collects from customers, pays off accounts receivable, and so forth.

Bringing It All Together

Using the numbers that we calculated for OCF, change in gross fixed assets, and change in NWC, First Strike's expected total cash flows from the new project would be as shown in Table 12.6.

Note, in particular, that correct use of the after-tax cash flow from selling the machinery at the end of the project requires that we change the cash flow's sign to negative when we enter it for year 3. Why? Because the ATCF formula shown in equation 12-3 does a little *too* much work for us. It computes cash flow effects of selling the asset, while the formula we are using for FCF wants us to enter the *change in fixed assets*. Or, to put it another way, cash flow at the end of the project should go up *because* fixed assets decrease. We subtract that decrease in our $FCF = OCF - (\Delta FA + \Delta NWC)$ calculation, which has the effect of "subtracting a minus." Eventually, then, we increase the final year's FCF above that which we would have generated by just combining OCF with the cash freed up from decreasing NWC.

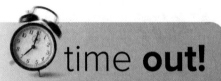

time out!

12-3 Explain why an increase in NWC is treated as a cash outflow rather than as an inflow.

12-4 Will OCF typically be larger or smaller than net income? Why?

▼ **TABLE 12.5** Change in NWC

Year:	0	1	2	3
Level of NWC	$59,985	$107,973	$19,995	$0
$NWC_t - NWC_{T-1}$	$59,985 – $0	$107,973 – $59,985	$19,995 – $107,973	$0 – $19,995
$= \Delta NWC_t$	= $59,985	= $47,988	= –$87,978	= –$19,995

▼ **TABLE 12.6** Total Cash Flows

Year:	0		1		2		3	
OCF		$ 0		$284,005		$622,820		$ 1,659
FA	$77,000		$ 0		$ 0		–$2,630	
NWC	59,985		47,988		–87,978		–19,995	
Less: IOC		136,985		47,988		–87,978		–22,625
FCF		–$136,985		$236,017		$710,798		$24,284

12.4 • ACCELERATED DEPRECIATION AND THE HALF-YEAR CONVENTION LG12-4

class life The number of years of assumed usage for an asset to be used in the calculation of depreciation.

Our FCF calculation in the previous section was complete, but we used a rather simplistic assumption concerning depreciation in the calculations. In reality, the IRS requires that depreciation be calculated in one of several (much more complicated) ways.

Even if a firm does use straight-line depreciation, it must be calculated using the *half-year convention,* which basically says that all property placed in service during a given period is assumed to be placed in service at the midpoint of that period.[1] By implication, three years of asset life, such as the machinery in the First Strike example, will extend over *four* calendar years of the firm, starting a half-year before the project starts and ending a half-year after it ends.

Just to make things a little more confusing, the IRS names an asset's **class life** in its depreciation tables according to how long the asset will *live,* not according to how many of the firm's calendar years the depreciation will *stretch across.* For example, Table 12.7 shows an excerpt from the IRS depreciation table for straight-line depreciation using the half-year convention.

Note that assets falling in, for example, the three-year class life (denoted by the column headings along the top) get depreciation taken during the first *four* calendar years after purchase, with the percentage figures in the relevant column denoting how much of the asset's depreciable basis may be deducted in each respective firm calendar year. For example, an asset with a depreciable basis of $100,000 falling into the three-year class life would be depreciated $100,000 × 0.1667 = $16,670 during the first calendar year the firm owned it, $33,330 during the second and third years of ownership, and another $16,670 during the fourth year of ownership.

▼ **TABLE 12.7** Excerpt of Straight-Line Depreciation Table with Half-Year Convention

Year	Normal Recovery Period				
	2.5	3	3.5	4	5
1	20.00%	16.67%	14.29%	12.50%	10.00%
2	40.00	33.33	28.57	25.00	20.00
3	40.00	33.33	28.57	25.00	20.00
4	0.00	16.67	28.57	25.00	20.00
5	0.00	0.00	0.00	12.50	20.00
6	0.00	0.00	0.00	0.00	10.00

The IRS provides guidance on which categories various assets fall into, so it's usually pretty easy to figure out which column to use. For this text, we will assume that we are always told which column to use.

Note that the IRS's interpretation of the half-year convention is not as direct as simply taking one-half of the first year's depreciation and moving it to the end of the asset's life. For example, the column for 3.5-year depreciation shows that such an asset would have 14.29 percent of its value depreciated during the first year and 28.57 percent during each of the second, third, and fourth years. So, rather than using a formula to compute the depreciation percentage, it's preferable to look the percentages up from the appropriate IRS table. A copy of the entire table for straight-line depreciation using the half-year convention appears as Appendix 12A at the end of this chapter.

MACRS Depreciation Calculation

Though the IRS allows firms to use the straight-line method with the half-year convention to depreciate assets, most businesses probably benefit from using some form of *accelerated depreciation.* Accelerated depreciation allows firms to expense more of an asset's cost earlier in the asset's life. An example of this is the double-declining-balance (DDB or 200 percent declining balance) depreciation method, under which the depreciation rate is double that used in the straight-line method.

To make all of this completely confusing, the IRS also uses the half-year convention with DDB depreciation and tends to switch back and forth between DDB and SL depreciation methods *in the same table,* depending upon which method is more advantageous to the taxpayer.

For example, MACRS (modified accelerated cost recovery system) depreciation tables use DDB for 3- to 10-year property, the 150 percent declining balance method for 15- to

20-year property, and straight-line depreciation whenever it becomes more advantageous to the taxpayer. But for real estate, MACRS uses straight-line depreciation and the mid-month convention for all asset classes.

This all can be more than enough to make you want to cry, but the good news is that the applicable depreciation percentages are provided for you in the MACRS depreciation tables compiled by the IRS. We have provided this for you in Appendix 12A. An excerpt of the DDB section of the MACRS table appears as Table 12.8. MACRS is generally the depreciation method of choice for firms since it provides the most advantageous method of depreciation.

Bonus Depreciation and Section 179 Deductions

In certain circumstances, we can accelerate asset expensing even further by expensing assets immediately in the year of purchase rather than having to depreciate them over time.

Before 2017, businesses were allowed to speed up the depreciation of many new business assets by immediately deducting 50 percent of the purchase price for MACRS-eligible assets. The Tax Cuts and Jobs Act (TCJA) increased this immediate deduction to 100 percent bonus depreciation (i.e., immediate expensing) on *qualified property* placed in service after September 27, 2017, and before January 1, 2023. **Qualified property,** which had previously been restricted to new real assets, was also expanded to include any tangible personal property with a recovery period of 20 years or less, including used property. The inclusion of used property, in particular, is a significant, and favorable, change from previous bonus depreciation rules.

As of the writing of this edition of the textbook, bonus depreciation for most types of assets is scheduled to be retired via the schedule shown in Table 12.9.

▼ **TABLE 12.8** DDB Depreciation with Half-Year Convention

	Normal Recovery Period			
Year	3	5	7	10
1	33.33%	20.00%	14.29%	10.00%
2	44.45	32.00	24.49	18.00
3	14.81	19.20	17.49	14.40
4	7.41	11.52	12.49	11.52
5	0.00	11.52	8.93	9.22
6	0.00	5.76	8.92	7.37
7	0.00	0.00	8.93	6.55
8	0.00	0.00	4.46	6.55
9	0.00	0.00	0.00	6.56
10	0.00	0.00	0.00	6.55
11	0.00	0.00	0.00	3.28
12	0.00	0.00	0.00	0.00
13	0.00	0.00	0.00	0.00
14	0.00	0.00	0.00	0.00
15	0.00	0.00	0.00	0.00
16	0.00	0.00	0.00	0.00
17	0.00	0.00	0.00	0.00
18	0.00	0.00	0.00	0.00
19	0.00	0.00	0.00	0.00
20	0.00	0.00	0.00	0.00
21	0.00	0.00	0.00	0.00

In addition to using bonus depreciation, the IRS also allows most businesses to immediately pass through to shareholders or partners in the business expenses up to $1,000,000 per year of property placed in service each year under what is referred to as a **Section 179 deduction.** The Section 179 deduction is obviously targeted at helping small businesses, so it places an annual limit on the amount of deductible property. If the cost of qualifying Section 179 property you put into service in a single tax year exceeds the current statutory base of $2.5 million (as of the 2018 tax year), then you cannot take the full deduction. The maximum deduction is also limited to the annual taxable income from the active conduct of the business.

For example, consider a manufacturer who completely re-equips his facility in 2022, at a cost of $2.6 million. This is $100,000 more than allowed, so he must reduce his eligible deductible limit to $900,000, which is the current $1,000,000 expensing limit minus the $100,000 excess over the current statutory base limit. To take this deduction, the firm must have at least $900,000 of taxable income for the year. A company that spent $3.5 million (= $2.5 million + $1,000,000) or more on qualifying Section 179 property would not be able to take the deduction at all, regardless of its taxable income. However, property that does not qualify for a Section 179 deduction could still be eligible for bonus depreciation or, at worst, depreciated using MACRS.

Property eligible for a Section 179 deduction includes

- Machinery and equipment.
- Furniture and fixtures.
- Most storage facilities.

- Single-purpose agricultural or horticultural structures.

- Off-the-shelf computer software.

- Certain qualified real property (limited to $250,000 of the $500,000 expensing limit).

- Certain depreciable tangible personal property used primarily to furnish lodging (or in connection with furnishing lodging).

- Improvements made to nonresidential real property: roofs; heating, ventilation, and air-conditioning property; fire protection; and alarm and security systems.

Ineligible property includes

- Buildings and their structural components (unless specifically qualified).

- Income-producing property (investment or rental property).

- Property held by an estate or trust.

- Property acquired by gift or inheritance.

- Property used in a passive activity.

- Property purchased from related parties.

- Property used outside of the United States.

Like many IRS deductions, there are several terms and conditions that apply, so be sure to get all the facts if you intend to use this method of depreciation.

Impact of Accelerated Depreciation

So, let's return to our FSS example and FinProf. Remember that our initial, simplistic view of depreciation had us taking $24,000 per year in depreciation for each of the three years of the project's life. If the software reproduction machinery fell into the three-year life class and we were not eligible to use either bonus depreciation or Section 179 expensing, we could instead have taken the following depreciation amounts by using either the straight-line or DDB approaches, as shown in Table 12.10.

If First Strike could take advantage of bonus depreciation or the Section 179 deduction, that would probably be the most advantageous way to deduct the cost of the new machinery—it could deduct the entire $77,000 in year 1. If FSS could not use either bonus depreciation or a Section 179 deduction, the DDB depreciation available under MACRS would result in the next quickest recovery of the tax breaks associated with the machinery purchase.

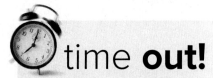

time out!

12-5 Explain why, under MACRS, "five-year" depreciation is actually spread over six years, six-year depreciation spreads into seven years, and so forth.

12-6 If the IRS wanted to encourage businesses to invest in certain types of assets, would it put them into shorter or longer MACRS life-class categories?

▼ **TABLE 12.9** Bonus Depreciation Schedule

Placed-in-Service Period (Year)	Bonus Depreciation Percentage
September 28, 2017–December 31, 2022	100%
2023	80%
2024	60%
2025	40%
2026	20%
2027 and thereafter	0%

▼ **TABLE 12.10** FSS's Yearly Depreciation and Ending Book Values under Alternative Depreciation

	Year 1	Year 2	Year 3	Ending BV
Straight-line	$77,000 − 16.67%	$77,000 − 33.33%	$77,000 − 33.33%	$12,835.90
	= $12,835.90	= $25,664.10	= $25,664.10	
	$77,000 − 33.33%	$77,000 − 44.45%	$77,000 − 14.81%	
DDB	= $25,664.10	= $34,226.50	= $11,403.70	$ 5,705.70

Machinery is eligible for a Section 179 deduction.
©Brand X Pictures/PunchStock

And why is it better to depreciate the cost of an asset as quickly as possible? Well, taking the depreciation over a longer time span doesn't get you more dollars of depreciation tax shield; it just stretches the same total amount of dollars over that longer time span. So, think about it in the context of time value of money: The present value of $X of total income tax shield will be highest when we get the $X as soon as possible.

12.5 • "SPECIAL" CASES AREN'T REALLY THAT SPECIAL LG12-5

As long as we are consistent in using incremental FCF to calculate total project cash flows, we can handle many project types that are habitually viewed as "special" cases requiring extraordinary treatment with some relatively simple revisions to the methods we used for valuing First Strike's proposed new project.

EXAMPLE 12-2

For interactive versions of this example, log in to Connect or go to mhhe.com/Cornett6e.

Replacement Problem LG12-5

Suppose that Just-in-Time Donuts is considering replacing one of its existing ovens. The original oven cost $100,000 when purchased five years ago and has been depreciated by $9,000 per year since then. Just-in-Time thinks that it can sell the old machine for $65,000 if it sells today, and for $10,000 by waiting another five years until the oven's anticipated life is over. Just-in-Time is considering replacing this oven with a new one, which costs $150,000, partly because the new oven will save $50,000 in costs per year relative to the old oven. The new oven will be subject to three-year class life DDB depreciation under MACRS, with an anticipated useful life of five years, but is ineligible for either bonus depreciation or Section 179 expensing. At the end of the five years, Just-in-Time will abandon the oven as worthless. If Just-in-Time faces a marginal tax rate of 21 percent, what will be the total project cash flows if it replaces the oven?

SOLUTION:

If Just-in-Time sells the old oven today for $65,000 when it has a remaining book value of $55,000 ($100,000 purchase price − 5 years of $9,000-per-year depreciation), then the ATCF from its sale will equal

$$ATCF = \text{Market value} - (\text{Market value} - \text{Book value}) \times T_C$$
$$= \$65,000 - (\$65,000 - \$55,000) \times 0.21$$
$$= \$62,900$$

In return for selling the old oven today, however, Just-in-Time will have to forgo both the yearly depreciation that the company would have received for it over the next five years and the $10,000 that it could get for selling it at the end of the five years. We must reflect both of these factors in our calculation of incremental FCFs so that we are reckoning the true costs of the project. In addition, switching from the old oven to the new one would apparently alter neither sales nor NWC requirements across the five-year life of the new oven (see Table 12.10).

	Year 0	Year 1	Year 2	Year 3	Year 4	Year 5
Net incremental sales		$ 0	$ 0	$ 0	$ 0	$ 0
Less: Net incremental variable costs		−50,000	−50,000	−50,000	−50,000	−50,000
Depreciation on new oven		$ 49,995	$ 66,675	$ 22,215	$ 11,115	$ 0
Forgone depreciation on old oven		−9,000	−9,000	−9,000	−9,000	−9,000
Less: Incremental depreciation		40,995	57,675	13,215	2,115	−9,000
EBIT		$ 9,005	−$7,675	$36,785	$47,885	$59,000
Less: Taxes		1,891	−1,612	7,725	10,056	12,390
"Net income"		$ 7,114	−$6,063	$29,060	$37,829	$46,610
Plus: Depreciation		40,995	57,675	13,215	2,115	−9,000
OCF		$ 48,109	$51,612	$42,275	$39,944	$37,610
ΔFA for new oven	$150,000					$ 0
ΔFA for old oven	−62,900					10,000
ΔFA	$ 87,100					$10,000
ΔNWC	0					0
Less: Investment in operating capital	$87,100	0	0	0	0	10,000
FCF = OCF − IOC	−$87,100	$ 48,109	$ 51,612	$42,275	$39,944	$27,610

We usually think that a positive value for ΔFA is associated with the purchase of FA. But note that in this circumstance, the $10,000 for the *forgone sale* of the old oven at time 5 is *not* an investment in fixed assets, but rather the opportunity cost of not getting to sell the old oven at that time.

Similar to Problem 12-13

EXAMPLE 12-3

Cost-Cutting Problem LG12-6

For interactive versions of this example, log in to Connect or go to mhhe.com/Cornett6e.

Your company is considering a new computer system that will initially cost $1 million. It will save your firm $300,000 a year in inventory and receivables management costs. The system is expected to last for five years and will be depreciated using three-year MACRS, and bonus depreciation and Section 179 expensing cannot be used. The firm expects that the system will have a salvage value of $50,000 at the end of year 5. This purchase does not affect net working capital; the marginal tax rate is 21 percent, and the required return is 8 percent. What will be the total project cash flows if this cost-cutting proposal is implemented?

SOLUTION:

Since the new computer falls into the three-year MACRS category, it will be fully depreciated when the project ends five years from now. As a result, the ATCF from the sale of the computer will be

$$ATCF = MV - (MV - BV) \times T_C$$
$$= \$50,000 - (\$50,000 - \$0) \times 0.21$$
$$= \$39,500$$

And the FCFs for the cost-cutting proposal will be equal to

Year	Year 0	Year 1	Year 2	Year 3	Year 4	Year 5
Net incremental sales		$ 0	$ 0	$ 0	$ 0	$ 0
Less: Incremental variable costs		−300,000	−300,000	−300,000	−300,000	$ 0 −300,000
Less: Incremental depreciation		333,300	444,500	148,100	74,100	0
EBIT		−$33,300	−$144,500	$151,900	$225,900	$300,000
Less: Taxes		−6,993	−30,345	31,899	47,439	63,000
"Net income"		−$26,307	−$114,155	$120,001	$178,461	$237,000
Plus: Depreciation		333,300	444,500	148,100	74,100	0
OCF		$306,993	$ 330,345	$268,101	$252,561	$237,000
ΔFA	$1,000,000				−$39,500	
ΔNWC	0				0	
Less: Investment in operating capital	$ 1,000,000	0	0	0	0	−39,500
FCF = OCF − IOC	−$1,000,000	$306,993	$ 330,345	$268,101	$252,561	$276,500

Similar to Problem 12-9

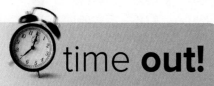

time out!

12-7 Explain why, in Example 12-2, the investment in operating capital in the last year of the project was positive instead of negative.

12-8 Would it ever be possible to have a project that generated net positive cash flows across all years of a project's life just by buying and depreciating assets?

12.6 • CHOOSING BETWEEN ALTERNATIVE ASSETS WITH DIFFERING LIVES: EAC LG12-7

One type of problem that also deserves special mention involves situations where we're asked to choose between two different assets that can be used for the same purpose. Such a problem does not usually require the computation of incremental FCF, but instead will require you to take the two alternative sets of incremental cash flows associated with the two assets and restructure them so that they can be compared to each other.

For example, suppose a company has decided to go ahead with a project but needs to choose between two alternative assets, where

- Both assets will result in the same sales.
- Both assets may have different costs and recurring expenses.
- Assets will last different lengths of time.
- When the chosen asset wears out, it will be replaced with an identical machine.

In such a situation, the firm cannot really compare one iteration of each machine to the other since they last different lengths of time. The key here is to use the fact that, since the firm will replace each machine with another identical machine when it wears out, it is really being asked to choose between two *sets* of infinite, but systematically varying, cash flows. To handle such a situation, we need to "smooth out" the variation in each set of cash flows so that each becomes a perpetuity. Then the company can choose between the two machines based on which will generate the highest present value of cash flows.

Since the decision will involve only a subset of a project's cash flows—the purchase of one of a choice of assets—that present value will probably be negative. If the firm were to look at all the benefits deriving from the choice of which asset to use, including expected sales and so forth, the present value of all cash flows would need to be positive for the entire project to be attractive. We will discuss this in much greater depth in the next chapter when we cover the net present value (NPV) rule for capital budgeting decisions.

The basic concept behind the EAC approach is to use TVM to turn each iteration of each project into an annuity. Once we have done that, then we can think of the stream of iterations of

---

EAC Approach LG12-7

For interactive versions of this example, log in to Connect or go to mhhe.com/Cornett6e.

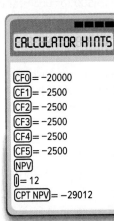

CALCULATOR HINTS

CF0	= −20000
CF1	= −2500
CF2	= −2500
CF3	= −2500
CF4	= −2500
CF5	= −2500
NPV	
I	= 12
CPT NPV	= −29012

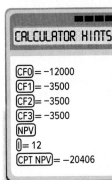

CALCULATOR HINTS

CF0	= −12000
CF1	= −3500
CF2	= −3500
CF3	= −3500
NPV	
I	= 12
CPT NPV	= −20406

Suppose that your company has won a bid for a new project—painting highway signs for the local highway department. Based on past experience, you are pretty sure that your company will have the contract for the foreseeable future, and now you have to decide whether to use machine A or machine B to paint the signs: Machine A costs $20,000, lasts five years, and will generate annual after-tax net expenses of $2,500. Machine B costs $12,000, lasts three years, and will have after-tax net expenses of $3,500 per year. Assume that, in either case, each machine will simply be junked at the end of its useful life, and the firm faces a cost of capital of 12 percent. Which machine should you choose?

SOLUTION:

One iteration of each machine will consist of the sets of cash flows shown below:

Year	Year 0	Year 1	Year 2	Year 3	Year 4	Year 5
Machine A CFs	−$20,000	−$2,500	−$2,500	−$2,500	−$2,500	−$2,500
Machine B CFs	−12,000	−3,500	−3,500	−3,500		

The sum of the present values of machine A's cash flows will be

$$\sum_{t=0}^{5} \frac{CF_t}{(1+i)^t} = \frac{CF_0}{(1+i)^0} + \frac{CF_1}{(1+i)^1} + \frac{CF_2}{(1+i)^2} + \frac{CF_3}{(1+i)^3} + \frac{CF_4}{(1+i)^4} + \frac{CF_5}{(1+i)^5}$$

$$= \frac{-\$20,000}{(1.12)^0} + \frac{-\$2,500}{(1.12)^1} + \frac{-\$2,500}{(1.12)^2} + \frac{-\$2,500}{(1.12)^3} + \frac{-\$2,500}{(1.12)^4} + \frac{-\$2,500}{(1.12)^5}$$

$$= -\$29,012$$

Treating this as the present value of a five-period annuity, setting *i* to 12 percent, and solving for payment will yield a payment of −$8,048, which is machine A's EAC.
The sum of the present values of machine B's cash flows will be

$$\sum_{t=0}^{3} \frac{CF_t}{(1+i)^t} = \frac{CF_0}{(1+i)^0} + \frac{CF_1}{(1+i)^1} + \frac{CF_2}{(1+i)^2} + \frac{CF_3}{(1+i)^3}$$

$$= \frac{-\$12,000}{(1.12)^0} + \frac{-\$3,500}{(1.12)^1} + \frac{-\$3,500}{(1.12)^2} + \frac{-\$3,500}{(1.12)^3}$$

$$= -\$20,406$$

Treating this as the present value of a three-period annuity, setting *i* to 12 percent, and solving for payment will yield a payment of −$8,496, which is machine B's EAC.
Since machine A's EAC is less negative than machine B's, your firm should choose machine A.
Similar to Problems 12-3 to 12-5, Self-Test Problem 3

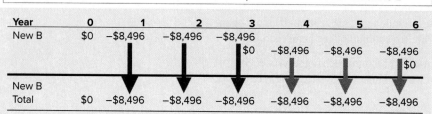

▼FIGURE 12.1 Cash Flows of Repeated Purchases of Machine B

Year	0	1	2	3	4	5	6
B	−$12,000	−$3,500	−$3,500	−$3,500			
				−$12,000	−$3,500	−$3,500	−$3,500
							−$12,000
B Total	−$12,000	−$3,500	−$3,500	−$15,500	−$3,500	−$3,500	−$15,500

▼FIGURE 12.2 Converted Cash Flows of Repeated Purchases of Machine B

Year	0	1	2	3	4	5	6
New B	$0	−$8,496	−$8,496	−$8,496			
				$0	−$8,496	−$8,496	−$8,496
							$0
New B Total	$0	−$8,496	−$8,496	−$8,496	−$8,496	−$8,496	−$8,496

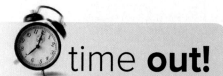

time out!

12-9 Explain how the EAC approach turns uneven cash flows for infinitely repeated asset purchases into perpetuities.

12-10 What if two alternative assets lasted the same length of time: Would the EAC approach still work?

doing that project again and again as a stream of annuities, all with equal payments—or, to put it another way, as a perpetuity.

To compute and use the EACs of two or more alternative assets

1. Find the sum of the present values of the cash flows (the net present value, or NPV, which we will cover in great detail in the next chapter) for one iteration of A and one iteration of B.

2. Treat each sum as the present value of an annuity with life equal to the life of the respective asset, and solve for each asset's EAC (i.e., payment).

3. Choose the asset with the highest (i.e., least negative) EAC.

It may seem that we have just done exactly what we said we should not do: compare the cash flows from one machine A to those from one machine B. In fact, the comparison we just did is actually much broader than that, though it will take a little explanation to see.

Visualize the cash flows to the infinitely repeated purchases of machine B (chosen simply because it has a short life, so it will be easier to see multiple iterations on a time line in the following discussion) as shown in Figure 12.1.

Notice that, after the initial purchase of the first machine B, the cash flows exhibit a systematic cycle: −$3,500 for two years, followed by −$15,500 for one year (when the next machine B is purchased), repeating this way forever. This systematic cycle, which we don't have a formula for valuing, makes it necessary to convert these cash flows into a perpetuity, which we *can* value.

When we computed the NPV of one iteration of machine B, we basically "squished" that machine's cash flows down to a single lump sum at one point in time (i.e., the purchase point for that particular machine), and when we treated that as the present value of an annuity and solved for the payments, we were effectively taking that same value and spreading it evenly across the life of the first machine B. Furthermore, since subsequent machine B purchases will be identical to this first one, we can visualize doing the exact same thing to *every* machine B's cash flow. Turning each machine B's cash flow into an annuity in this manner has the net effect of turning all the machine B's cash flows into a perpetuity, as shown in Figure 12.2.

In the process, we also turn the repeated purchase of machine A into a perpetuity. We *could* calculate the present values of these two perpetuities and then compare them, which is what we're really interested in doing:

$$PV_{\text{Perpetuity of Infinitely Repeated As}} \text{ vs. } PV_{\text{Perpetuity of Infinitely Repeated Bs}}$$

$$\frac{-\$8,048}{0.12} \text{ vs. } \frac{-\$8,496}{0.12}$$

But do we really need to? No. The relationship between these two present values of the respective perpetuities is really the same as the relationship between their payment amounts[2]—each machine's respective EAC.

12.7 • FLOTATION COSTS REVISITED LG12-8

In the previous chapter, we talked about how to take flotation costs into account by adjusting the WACC upwards, incorporating flotation costs directly into the issue prices of the

EXAMPLE 12-5

Adjusting CF_0 for Flotation Cost LG12-8

For interactive versions of this example, log in to Connect or go to mhhe.com/Cornett6e.

Your company is considering a project that will cost $1 million. The project will generate after-tax cash flows of $375,000 per year for five years. The WACC is 15 percent and the firm's target D/A ratio is 0.375. The flotation cost for equity is 5 percent, the flotation cost for debt is 3 percent, and your firm does not plan on issuing any preferred stock within its capital structure. If your firm follows the practice of incorporating flotation costs into the project's initial investment, what will the flotation-adjusted cash flows for this project be?

SOLUTION:

Since the D/A is 0.375, the E/A ratio will be equal to $1 - 0.375 = 0.625$, and the weighted-average flotation cost for the firm will be

$$f_A = \frac{E}{E+P+D} f_E + \frac{P}{E+P+D} f_P + \frac{D}{E+P+D} f_D$$

$$= (0.625 \times 0.05) + (0.375 \times 0.03)$$

$$= 0.0425, \text{ or } 4.25\%$$

Using this, the adjusted CF_0 for the project will be

$$\text{Adjusted } CF_0 = \frac{CF_0}{1 - f_A}$$

$$= \frac{-\$1,000,000}{1 - 0.0425}$$

$$= -\$1,044,386$$

So the flotation-adjusted cash flows for the project will be

Year	0	1	2	3	4	5
Cash Flow	−$1,044,386	$375,000	$375,000	$375,000	$375,000	$375,000

securities used to fund projects. Another way that we can account for flotation costs is to adjust the project's initial cash flow so that it will reflect the flotation costs of raising capital for the project as well as the necessary investment in assets.

In this approach, we will

1. Compute the weighted-average flotation cost, f_A, using the firm's target capital weights (because the firm will issue securities in these percentages over the long term):

$$f_A = \frac{E}{E+P+D} f_E + \frac{P}{E+P+D} f_P + \frac{D}{E+P+D} f_D \qquad (12\text{-}4)$$

where f_E, f_P, and f_D are the percentage flotation costs for new equity, preferred stock, and debt, respectively.

2. Compute the flotation-adjusted initial investment, CF_0, using

$$\text{Adjusted } CF_0 = \frac{CF_0}{1 - f_A} \qquad (12\text{-}5)$$

As we discussed in the previous chapter, this approach to adjusting for flotation costs violates the spirit of the separation principle of capital budgeting, which states that the calculations of cash flows should remain independent of the choice of financing. On the other hand, the approach we used in the last chapter, increasing the project's WACC to incorporate the flotation costs' impact, tends to understate the component cost of new equity. So, which approach is better? Well, even though most practitioners have historically taken the approach of adjusting the WACC upward, it is intuitively a little "distasteful"; it burdens the capital raised to finance a project with a higher required rate of return from then on, even though those flotation costs are actually a one-time thing. So, ideally, we would handle flotation costs as we've done in this chapter, by adjusting the project's initial cash flow to account for them. Pragmatically, however, it is not unusual for firms to use either approach based on what they find the most intuitively appealing.

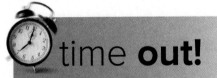

time out!

12-11 How would you compute the equity flotation cost if a firm were going to use a mixture of retained earnings and new equity to finance a project?

12-12 Why do we divide the initial cash flow by $(1 - f_A)$ instead of multiplying it by $(1 + f_A)$?

Get Online

mhhe.com/CornettM6e

for study materials including quizzes,
iPod downloads, and video

JGI/Jamie Grill/Getty Images

Your Turn...

Questions

1. How is the pro forma statement we used in this chapter for computing OCF different from an accountant's income statement? *(LG12-1)*

2. Suppose you paid your old college finance professor to evaluate a project for you. If you would pay him regardless of your decision concerning whether to proceed with the project, should his fee for evaluating the project be included in the project's incremental cash flows? *(LG12-2)*

3. Why does a decrease in NWC result in a cash inflow to the firm? *(LG12-3)*

4. Everything else held constant, would you rather depreciate a project with straight-line depreciation or with DDB? *(LG12-3)*

5. Everything else held constant, would you rather depreciate a project with DDB depreciation or deduct it under a Section 179 deduction? *(LG12-4)*

6. In a replacement problem, would we ever see changes in NWC? *(LG12-5)*

7. In a replacement problem, will incremental net depreciation always be less than the gross depreciation on the new piece of equipment? *(LG12-5)*

8. In a cost-cutting proposal, what might cause you to sometimes have negative EBIT? *(LG12-6)*

9. How many TVM formulas do you use every time you calculate EAC for a project? *(LG12-7)*

10. Will an increase in flotation costs increase or decrease the initial cash flow for a project? *(LG12-8)*

Problems

12-1 **After-Tax Cash Flow from Sale of Assets** Suppose you sell a fixed asset for $109,000 when its book value is $129,000. If your company's marginal tax rate is 21 percent, what will be the effect on cash flows of this sale (i.e., what will be the after-tax cash flow of this sale)? *(LG12-3)*

12-2 **Spreadsheet Problem: PV of Depreciation Tax Benefits** Your company is considering a new project that will require $1 million of new equipment at the start of the project. The equipment will have a depreciable life of 10 years and will be depreciated to a book value of $150,000 using straight-line depreciation. Neither bonus depreciation nor Section 179 expensing will be used. The cost of capital is 13 percent, and the firm's tax rate is 21 percent. Estimate the present value of the tax benefits from depreciation. *(LG12-4)*

12-3 **Spreadsheet Problem: EAC Approach** You are trying to pick the least-expensive car for your new delivery service. You have two choices: the Kia Rio, which will cost $14,000 to purchase and which will have OCF of −$1,200 annually throughout the vehicle's expected life of three years as a delivery vehicle; and the Toyota Prius, which will cost $20,000 to purchase and which will have OCF of −$650 annually throughout that vehicle's expected four-year life. Both cars will be worthless at the end of their life. If you intend to replace whichever type of car you choose with the same thing when its life runs out, again and again out into the foreseeable future, and if your business has a cost of capital of 12 percent, which one should you choose? *(LG12-7)*

12-4 **Spreadsheet Problem: EAC Approach** You are evaluating two different cookie-baking ovens. The Pillsbury 707 costs $57,000, has a five-year life, and has an annual OCF (after tax) of −$10,000 per year. The Keebler CookieMunster costs $90,000, has a seven-year life, and has an annual OCF (after tax) of −$8,000 per year. If your discount rate is 12 percent, what is each machine's EAC? *(LG12-8)*

12-5 **Spreadsheet Problem: EAC Approach** You are considering the purchase of one of two machines used in your manufacturing plant. Machine A has a life of two years, costs $80 initially, and then requires $125 per year in maintenance costs. Machine B costs $150 initially, has a life of three years, and requires $100 in annual maintenance costs. Either machine must be replaced at the end of its life with an equivalent machine. Which is the better machine for the firm? The discount rate is 12 percent and the tax rate is zero. *(LG12-8)*

12-6 **Spreadsheet Problem: Project Cash Flows** KADS, Inc., has spent $400,000 on research to develop a new computer game. The firm is planning to spend $200,000 on a machine to produce the new game. Shipping and installation costs of the machine will be capitalized and depreciated using bonus depreciation; they total $50,000. The machine has an expected life of three years and a $75,000 estimated resale value. Revenue from the new game is expected to be $600,000 per year, with costs of $250,000 per year. The firm has a tax rate of 21 percent, has an opportunity cost of capital of 15 percent, and expects net working capital to increase by $100,000 at the beginning of the project. What will the cash flows for this project be? *(LG12-3)*

12-7 **Spreadsheet Problem: Depreciation Tax Shield** Your firm needs a computerized machine tool lathe that costs $50,000 and requires $12,000 in maintenance for each year of its three-year life. After three years, this machine will be replaced. The machine falls into the MACRS three-year class life category, and neither bonus depreciation nor Section 179 expensing can be used. Assume a tax rate of 21 percent and a discount rate of 12 percent. Calculate the depreciation tax shield for this project in year 3. *(LG12-4)*

12-8 **After-Tax Cash Flow from Sale of Assets** If the lathe in the previous problem can be sold for $5,000 at the end of year 3, what is the after-tax salvage value? *(LG12-4)*

12-9 **Spreadsheet Problem: Project Cash Flows** You have been asked by the president of your company to evaluate the proposed acquisition of a new special-purpose truck for $60,000. The truck falls into the MACRS three-year class, is not eligible for either bonus depreciation or Section 179 expensing, and will be sold after three years for $20,000. Use of the truck will require an increase in NWC (spare parts inventory) of $2,000. The truck will have no effect on revenues, but it is expected to save the firm $20,000 per year in before-tax operating costs, mainly labor. The firm's marginal tax rate is 21 percent. What will the cash flows for this project be? *(LG12-6)*

ADVANCED PROBLEMS

12-10 **Change in NWC** You are evaluating a project for The Farstroke golf club, guaranteed to correct that nasty slice. You estimate the sales price of The Farstroke to be $400 per unit and sales volume to be 1,000 units in year 1; 1,500 units in year 2; and 1,325 units in year 3. The project has a three-year life. Variable costs amount to $225 per unit and fixed costs are $100,000 per year. The project requires an initial investment of $165,000 in assets, which can be depreciated using bonus depreciation. The actual market value of these assets at the end of year 3 is expected to be $35,000. NWC requirements at the beginning of each year will be approximately 20 percent of the projected sales during the coming year. The tax rate is 21 percent and the required return on the project is 10 percent. What change in NWC occurs at the end of year 1? *(LG12-3)*

12-11 **Operating Cash Flow** Continuing the previous problem, what is the operating cash flow for the project in year 2? *(LG12-3)*

12-12 **Project Cash Flows** Your highly successful software company is considering adding a new software title to your list. If you add the new product, it will use the full capacity of your disk duplicating machines that you had planned on using for your flagship product, "Battlin' Bobby." You had previously planned on using the unused capacity to start selling "BB" on the West Coast in two years. Eventually, you would have had to purchase additional duplicating machines 10 years from today, but since your new product will use up the extra capacity, this will require moving this purchase up to two years from today. If the new machines will cost $100,000 and can be expensed under Section 179, your marginal tax rate is 21 percent, and your cost of capital is 12 percent, what is the opportunity cost associated with using the unused capacity for the new product? *(LG12-3)*

12-13 **Spreadsheet Problem: Project Cash Flows** You are evaluating a project for The Ultimate recreational tennis racket, guaranteed to correct that wimpy backhand. You estimate the sales price of The Ultimate to be $400 per unit and sales volume to be 1,000 units in year 1; 1,250 units in year 2; and 1,325 units in year 3. The project has a three-year life. Variable costs amount to $225 per unit and fixed costs are $100,000 per year. The project requires an initial investment of $165,000 in assets, which can be depreciated using bonus depreciation. The actual market value of these assets at the end of year 3 is expected to be $35,000. NWC requirements at the beginning of each year will be approximately 20 percent of the projected sales during the coming year. The tax rate is 21 percent and the required return on the project is 10 percent. What will the cash flows for this project be? *(LG12-3)*

12-14 Spreadsheet Problem: Project Cash Flows Mom's Cookies, Inc., is considering the purchase of a new cookie oven. The original cost of the old oven was $30,000; it is now five years old and has a current market value of $13,333.33. The old oven is being depreciated over a 10-year life toward a zero estimated salvage value on a straight-line basis, resulting in a current book value of $15,000 and an annual depreciation expense of $3,000. The old oven can be used for six more years but has no market value after its depreciable life is over. Management is contemplating the purchase of a new oven whose cost is $25,000 and whose estimated salvage value is zero. Expected before-tax cash savings from the new oven are $4,000 a year over its full life, you can use bonus depreciation on the oven, and the cost of capital is 10 percent. Assume a 21 percent tax rate. What will the cash flows for this project be? *(LG12-5)*

12-15 Spreadsheet Problem: Project Cash Flows Your company is contemplating replacing its current fleet of delivery vehicles with Nissan NV vans. You will be replacing five fully depreciated vans, which you think you can sell for $3,000 each and which you could probably use for another two years if you chose not to replace them. The NV vans will cost $29,850 each in the configuration you want them and can be depreciated using MACRS over a five-year life, but you are unable to make use of either bonus depreciation or Section 179 expensing. Expected yearly before-tax cash savings due to acquiring the new vans amounts to about $3,700 each. If your cost of capital is 8 percent and your firm faces a 21 percent tax rate, what will the cash flows for this project be? *(LG12-5)*

Notes

CHAPTER 12

1. There are also midmonth and midquarter conventions, which apply in special circumstances. Please refer to IRS Publication 946 for details.

2. Because the two perpetuities have the same interest rate and the same periodicity (i.e., length between payments), the only possible source of difference in their present values would be the respective payment amounts.

twelve
appendix 12A

MACRS Depreciation Tables

▼ **MACRS DEPRECIATION**

| | Normal Recovery Period | | | | | | Real Estate | | |
| | | | | | | | Residential | Nonresidential | |
Year	3	5	7	10	15	20	27.5	31.5	39
1	33.33%	20.00%	14.29%	10.00%	5.00%	3.750%	3.485%	3.042%	2.461%
2	44.45	32.00	24.49	18.00	9.50	7.219	3.636	3.175	2.564
3	14.81	19.20	17.49	14.40	8.55	6.677	3.636	3.175	2.564
4	7.41	11.52	12.49	11.52	7.70	6.177	3.636	3.175	2.564
5	0.00	11.52	8.93	9.22	6.93	5.713	3.636	3.175	2.564
6	0.00	5.76	8.92	7.37	6.23	5.285	3.636	3.175	2.564
7	0.00	0.00	8.93	6.55	5.90	4.888	3.636	3.175	2.564
8	0.00	0.00	4.46	6.55	5.90	4.522	3.636	3.175	2.564
9	0.00	0.00	0.00	6.56	5.91	4.462	3.636	3.174	2.564
10	0.00	0.00	0.00	6.55	5.90	4.461	3.637	3.175	2.564
11	0.00	0.00	0.00	3.28	5.91	4.462	3.636	3.174	2.564
12	0.00	0.00	0.00	0.00	5.90	4.461	3.637	3.175	2.564
13	0.00	0.00	0.00	0.00	5.91	4.462	3.636	3.174	2.564
14	0.00	0.00	0.00	0.00	5.90	4.461	3.637	3.175	2.564
15	0.00	0.00	0.00	0.00	5.91	4.462	3.636	3.174	2.564
16	0.00	0.00	0.00	0.00	2.95	4.461	3.637	3.175	2.564
17	0.00	0.00	0.00	0.00	0.00	4.462	3.636	3.174	2.564
18	0.00	0.00	0.00	0.00	0.00	4.461	3.637	3.175	2.564
19	0.00	0.00	0.00	0.00	0.00	4.462	3.636	3.174	2.564
20	0.00	0.00	0.00	0.00	0.00	4.461	3.637	3.175	2.564
21	0.00	0.00	0.00	0.00	0.00	2.231	3.636	3.174	2.564
22	0.00	0.00	0.00	0.00	0.00	0.00	3.637	3.175	2.564
23	0.00	0.00	0.00	0.00	0.00	0.00	3.636	3.174	2.564
24	0.00	0.00	0.00	0.00	0.00	0.00	3.637	3.175	2.564
25	0.00	0.00	0.00	0.00	0.00	0.00	3.636	3.174	2.564
26	0.00	0.00	0.00	0.00	0.00	0.00	3.637	3.175	2.564
27	0.00	0.00	0.00	0.00	0.00	0.00	3.636	3.174	2.564
28	0.00	0.00	0.00	0.00	0.00	0.00	1.970	3.175	2.564
29	0.00	0.00	0.00	0.00	0.00	0.00	0.00	3.174	2.564
30	0.00	0.00	0.00	0.00	0.00	0.00	0.00	3.175	2.564

| | | Normal Recovery Period | | | | | | Real Estate | | |
| | | | | | | | | Residential | Nonresidential | |
Year	3	5	7	10	15	20	27.5	31.5	39
31	0.00	0.00	0.00	0.00	0.00	0.00	0.00	3.174	2.564
32	0.00	0.00	0.00	0.00	0.00	0.00	0.00	1.720	2.564
33	0.00	0.00	0.00	0.00	0.00	0.00	0.00	0.00	2.564
34	0.00	0.00	0.00	0.00	0.00	0.00	0.00	0.00	2.564
35	0.00	0.00	0.00	0.00	0.00	0.00	0.00	0.00	2.564
36	0.00	0.00	0.00	0.00	0.00	0.00	0.00	0.00	2.564
37	0.00	0.00	0.00	0.00	0.00	0.00	0.00	0.00	2.564
38	0.00	0.00	0.00	0.00	0.00	0.00	0.00	0.00	2.564
39	0.00	0.00	0.00	0.00	0.00	0.00	0.00	0.00	2.564
40	0.00	0.00	0.00	0.00	0.00	0.00	0.00	0.00	0.107
41	0.00	0.00	0.00	0.00	0.00	0.00	0.00	0.00	0.000

▼ SL DEPRECIATION

| | Normal Recovery Period | | | | | | | | | | | |
Year	2.5	3	3.5	4	5	6	6.5	7	7.5	8	8.5	9
1	20.00%	16.67%	14.29%	12.50%	10.00%	8.33%	7.69%	7.14%	6.67%	6.25%	5.88%	5.56%
2	40.00	33.33	28.57	25.00	20.00	16.67	15.39	14.29	13.33	12.50	11.77	11.11
3	40.00	33.33	28.57	25.00	20.00	16.67	15.38	14.29	13.33	12.50	11.76	11.11
4	0.00	16.67	28.57	25.00	20.00	16.67	15.39	14.28	13.33	12.50	11.77	11.11
5	0.00	0.00	0.00	12.50	20.00	16.66	15.38	14.29	13.34	12.50	11.76	11.11
6	0.00	0.00	0.00	0.00	10.00	16.67	15.39	14.28	13.33	12.50	11.77	11.11
7	0.00	0.00	0.00	0.00	0.00	8.33	15.38	14.29	13.34	12.50	11.76	11.11
8	0.00	0.00	0.00	0.00	0.00	0.00	0.00	7.14	13.33	12.50	11.77	11.11
9	0.00	0.00	0.00	0.00	0.00	0.00	0.00	0.00	0.00	6.25	11.76	11.11
10	0.00	0.00	0.00	0.00	0.00	0.00	0.00	0.00	0.00	0.00	0.00	5.56
11	0.00	0.00	0.00	0.00	0.00	0.00	0.00	0.00	0.00	0.00	0.00	0.00
12	0.00	0.00	0.00	0.00	0.00	0.00	0.00	0.00	0.00	0.00	0.00	0.00
13	0.00	0.00	0.00	0.00	0.00	0.00	0.00	0.00	0.00	0.00	0.00	0.00
14	0.00	0.00	0.00	0.00	0.00	0.00	0.00	0.00	0.00	0.00	0.00	0.00
15	0.00	0.00	0.00	0.00	0.00	0.00	0.00	0.00	0.00	0.00	0.00	0.00
16	0.00	0.00	0.00	0.00	0.00	0.00	0.00	0.00	0.00	0.00	0.00	0.00
17	0.00	0.00	0.00	0.00	0.00	0.00	0.00	0.00	0.00	0.00	0.00	0.00
18	0.00	0.00	0.00	0.00	0.00	0.00	0.00	0.00	0.00	0.00	0.00	0.00
19	0.00	0.00	0.00	0.00	0.00	0.00	0.00	0.00	0.00	0.00	0.00	0.00
20	0.00	0.00	0.00	0.00	0.00	0.00	0.00	0.00	0.00	0.00	0.00	0.00
21	0.00	0.00	0.00	0.00	0.00	0.00	0.00	0.00	0.00	0.00	0.00	0.00
22	0.00	0.00	0.00	0.00	0.00	0.00	0.00	0.00	0.00	0.00	0.00	0.00
23	0.00	0.00	0.00	0.00	0.00	0.00	0.00	0.00	0.00	0.00	0.00	0.00
24	0.00	0.00	0.00	0.00	0.00	0.00	0.00	0.00	0.00	0.00	0.00	0.00
25	0.00	0.00	0.00	0.00	0.00	0.00	0.00	0.00	0.00	0.00	0.00	0.00

Year	2.5	3	3.5	4	5	6	6.5	7	7.5	8	8.5	9
						Normal Recovery Period						
26	0.00	0.00	0.00	0.00	0.00	0.00	0.00	0.00	0.00	0.00	0.00	0.00
27	0.00	0.00	0.00	0.00	0.00	0.00	0.00	0.00	0.00	0.00	0.00	0.00
28	0.00	0.00	0.00	0.00	0.00	0.00	0.00	0.00	0.00	0.00	0.00	0.00
29	0.00	0.00	0.00	0.00	0.00	0.00	0.00	0.00	0.00	0.00	0.00	0.00
30	0.00	0.00	0.00	0.00	0.00	0.00	0.00	0.00	0.00	0.00	0.00	0.00
31	0.00	0.00	0.00	0.00	0.00	0.00	0.00	0.00	0.00	0.00	0.00	0.00
32	0.00	0.00	0.00	0.00	0.00	0.00	0.00	0.00	0.00	0.00	0.00	0.00
33	0.00	0.00	0.00	0.00	0.00	0.00	0.00	0.00	0.00	0.00	0.00	0.00
34	0.00	0.00	0.00	0.00	0.00	0.00	0.00	0.00	0.00	0.00	0.00	0.00
35	0.00	0.00	0.00	0.00	0.00	0.00	0.00	0.00	0.00	0.00	0.00	0.00
36	0.00	0.00	0.00	0.00	0.00	0.00	0.00	0.00	0.00	0.00	0.00	0.00
37	0.00	0.00	0.00	0.00	0.00	0.00	0.00	0.00	0.00	0.00	0.00	0.00
38	0.00	0.00	0.00	0.00	0.00	0.00	0.00	0.00	0.00	0.00	0.00	0.00
39	0.00	0.00	0.00	0.00	0.00	0.00	0.00	0.00	0.00	0.00	0.00	0.00
40	0.00	0.00	0.00	0.00	0.00	0.00	0.00	0.00	0.00	0.00	0.00	0.00
41	0.00	0.00	0.00	0.00	0.00	0.00	0.00	0.00	0.00	0.00	0.00	0.00
42	0.00	0.00	0.00	0.00	0.00	0.00	0.00	0.00	0.00	0.00	0.00	0.00
43	0.00	0.00	0.00	0.00	0.00	0.00	0.00	0.00	0.00	0.00	0.00	0.00
44	0.00	0.00	0.00	0.00	0.00	0.00	0.00	0.00	0.00	0.00	0.00	0.00
45	0.00	0.00	0.00	0.00	0.00	0.00	0.00	0.00	0.00	0.00	0.00	0.00
46	0.00	0.00	0.00	0.00	0.00	0.00	0.00	0.00	0.00	0.00	0.00	0.00
47	0.00	0.00	0.00	0.00	0.00	0.00	0.00	0.00	0.00	0.00	0.00	0.00
48	0.00	0.00	0.00	0.00	0.00	0.00	0.00	0.00	0.00	0.00	0.00	0.00
49	0.00	0.00	0.00	0.00	0.00	0.00	0.00	0.00	0.00	0.00	0.00	0.00
50	0.00	0.00	0.00	0.00	0.00	0.00	0.00	0.00	0.00	0.00	0.00	0.00
51	0.00	0.00	0.00	0.00	0.00	0.00	0.00	0.00	0.00	0.00	0.00	0.00
52	0.00	0.00	0.00	0.00	0.00	0.00	0.00	0.00	0.00	0.00	0.00	0.00

▼ SL DEPRECIATION

Year	9.5	10	10.5	11	11.5	12	12.5	13	13.5	14	15	16	16.5
							Normal Recovery Period						
1	5.26%	5.00%	4.76%	4.55%	4.35%	4.17%	4.00%	3.85%	3.70%	3.57%	3.33%	3.13%	3.03%
2	10.53	10.00	9.52	9.09	8.70	8.33	8.00	7.69	7.41	7.14	6.67	6.25	6.06
3	10.53	10.00	9.52	9.09	8.70	8.33	8.00	7.69	7.41	7.14	6.67	6.25	6.06
4	10.53	10.00	9.53	9.09	8.69	8.33	8.00	7.69	7.41	7.14	6.67	6.25	6.06
5	10.52	10.00	9.52	9.09	8.70	8.33	8.00	7.69	7.41	7.14	6.67	6.25	6.06
6	10.53	10.00	9.53	9.09	8.69	8.33	8.00	7.69	7.41	7.14	6.67	6.25	6.06
7	10.52	10.00	9.52	9.09	8.70	8.34	8.00	7.69	7.41	7.14	6.67	6.25	6.06
8	10.53	10.00	9.53	9.09	8.69	8.33	8.00	7.69	7.41	7.15	6.66	6.25	6.06
9	10.52	10.00	9.52	9.09	8.70	8.34	8.00	7.69	7.41	7.14	6.67	6.25	6.06
10	10.53	10.00	9.53	9.09	8.69	8.33	8.00	7.70	7.40	7.15	6.66	6.25	6.06

	Normal Recovery Period												
Year	9.5	10	10.5	11	11.5	12	12.5	13	13.5	14	15	16	16.5
11	0.00	5.00	9.52	9.09	8.70	8.34	8.00	7.69	7.41	7.14	6.67	6.25	6.06
12	0.00	0.00	0.00	4.55	8.69	8.33	8.00	7.70	7.40	7.15	6.66	6.25	6.06
13	0.00	0.00	0.00	0.00	0.00	4.17	8.00	7.69	7.41	7.14	6.67	6.25	6.06
14	0.00	0.00	0.00	0.00	0.00	0.00	0.00	3.85	7.40	7.15	6.66	6.25	6.06
15	0.00	0.00	0.00	0.00	0.00	0.00	0.00	0.00	0.00	3.57	6.67	6.25	6.06
16	0.00	0.00	0.00	0.00	0.00	0.00	0.00	0.00	0.00	0.00	3.33	6.25	6.06
17	0.00	0.00	0.00	0.00	0.00	0.00	0.00	0.00	0.00	0.00	0.00	3.12	6.07
18	0.00	0.00	0.00	0.00	0.00	0.00	0.00	0.00	0.00	0.00	0.00	0.00	0.00
19	0.00	0.00	0.00	0.00	0.00	0.00	0.00	0.00	0.00	0.00	0.00	0.00	0.00
20	0.00	0.00	0.00	0.00	0.00	0.00	0.00	0.00	0.00	0.00	0.00	0.00	0.00
21	0.00	0.00	0.00	0.00	0.00	0.00	0.00	0.00	0.00	0.00	0.00	0.00	0.00
22	0.00	0.00	0.00	0.00	0.00	0.00	0.00	0.00	0.00	0.00	0.00	0.00	0.00
23	0.00	0.00	0.00	0.00	0.00	0.00	0.00	0.00	0.00	0.00	0.00	0.00	0.00
24	0.00	0.00	0.00	0.00	0.00	0.00	0.00	0.00	0.00	0.00	0.00	0.00	0.00
25	0.00	0.00	0.00	0.00	0.00	0.00	0.00	0.00	0.00	0.00	0.00	0.00	0.00
26	0.00	0.00	0.00	0.00	0.00	0.00	0.00	0.00	0.00	0.00	0.00	0.00	0.00
27	0.00	0.00	0.00	0.00	0.00	0.00	0.00	0.00	0.00	0.00	0.00	0.00	0.00
28	0.00	0.00	0.00	0.00	0.00	0.00	0.00	0.00	0.00	0.00	0.00	0.00	0.00
29	0.00	0.00	0.00	0.00	0.00	0.00	0.00	0.00	0.00	0.00	0.00	0.00	0.00
30	0.00	0.00	0.00	0.00	0.00	0.00	0.00	0.00	0.00	0.00	0.00	0.00	0.00
31	0.00	0.00	0.00	0.00	0.00	0.00	0.00	0.00	0.00	0.00	0.00	0.00	0.00
32	0.00	0.00	0.00	0.00	0.00	0.00	0.00	0.00	0.00	0.00	0.00	0.00	0.00
33	0.00	0.00	0.00	0.00	0.00	0.00	0.00	0.00	0.00	0.00	0.00	0.00	0.00
34	0.00	0.00	0.00	0.00	0.00	0.00	0.00	0.00	0.00	0.00	0.00	0.00	0.00
35	0.00	0.00	0.00	0.00	0.00	0.00	0.00	0.00	0.00	0.00	0.00	0.00	0.00
36	0.00	0.00	0.00	0.00	0.00	0.00	0.00	0.00	0.00	0.00	0.00	0.00	0.00
37	0.00	0.00	0.00	0.00	0.00	0.00	0.00	0.00	0.00	0.00	0.00	0.00	0.00
38	0.00	0.00	0.00	0.00	0.00	0.00	0.00	0.00	0.00	0.00	0.00	0.00	0.00
39	0.00	0.00	0.00	0.00	0.00	0.00	0.00	0.00	0.00	0.00	0.00	0.00	0.00
40	0.00	0.00	0.00	0.00	0.00	0.00	0.00	0.00	0.00	0.00	0.00	0.00	0.00
41	0.00	0.00	0.00	0.00	0.00	0.00	0.00	0.00	0.00	0.00	0.00	0.00	0.00
42	0.00	0.00	0.00	0.00	0.00	0.00	0.00	0.00	0.00	0.00	0.00	0.00	0.00
43	0.00	0.00	0.00	0.00	0.00	0.00	0.00	0.00	0.00	0.00	0.00	0.00	0.00
44	0.00	0.00	0.00	0.00	0.00	0.00	0.00	0.00	0.00	0.00	0.00	0.00	0.00
45	0.00	0.00	0.00	0.00	0.00	0.00	0.00	0.00	0.00	0.00	0.00	0.00	0.00
46	0.00	0.00	0.00	0.00	0.00	0.00	0.00	0.00	0.00	0.00	0.00	0.00	0.00
47	0.00	0.00	0.00	0.00	0.00	0.00	0.00	0.00	0.00	0.00	0.00	0.00	0.00
48	0.00	0.00	0.00	0.00	0.00	0.00	0.00	0.00	0.00	0.00	0.00	0.00	0.00
49	0.00	0.00	0.00	0.00	0.00	0.00	0.00	0.00	0.00	0.00	0.00	0.00	0.00
50	0.00	0.00	0.00	0.00	0.00	0.00	0.00	0.00	0.00	0.00	0.00	0.00	0.00
51	0.00	0.00	0.00	0.00	0.00	0.00	0.00	0.00	0.00	0.00	0.00	0.00	0.00
52	0.00	0.00	0.00	0.00	0.00	0.00	0.00	0.00	0.00	0.00	0.00	0.00	0.00

▼ SL DEPRECIATION

	Normal Recovery Period													
Year	17	18	19	20	22	24	25	26.5	28	30	35	40	45	50
1	2.94%	2.78%	2.63%	2.50%	2.273%	2.083%	2.00%	1.887%	1.786%	1.667%	1.429%	1.25%	1.111%	1.00%
2	5.88	5.56	5.26	5.00	4.545	4.167	4.00	3.774	3.571	3.333	2.857	2.50	2.222	2.00
3	5.88	5.56	5.26	5.00	4.545	4.167	4.00	3.774	3.571	3.333	2.857	2.50	2.222	2.00
4	5.88	5.55	5.26	5.00	4.545	4.167	4.00	3.774	3.571	3.333	2.857	2.50	2.222	2.00
5	5.88	5.56	5.26	5.00	4.546	4.167	4.00	3.774	3.571	3.333	2.857	2.50	2.222	2.00
6	5.88	5.55	5.26	5.00	4.545	4.167	4.00	3.774	3.571	3.333	2.857	2.50	2.222	2.00
7	5.88	5.56	5.26	5.00	4.546	4.167	4.00	3.773	3.572	3.333	2.857	2.50	2.222	2.00
8	5.88	5.55	5.26	5.00	4.545	4.167	4.00	3.774	3.571	3.333	2.857	2.50	2.222	2.00
9	5.88	5.56	5.27	5.00	4.546	4.167	4.00	3.773	3.572	3.333	2.857	2.50	2.222	2.00
10	5.88	5.55	5.26	5.00	4.545	4.167	4.00	3.774	3.571	3.333	2.857	2.50	2.222	2.00
11	5.89	5.56	5.27	5.00	4.546	4.166	4.00	3.773	3.572	3.333	2.857	2.50	2.222	2.00
12	5.88	5.55	5.26	5.00	4.545	4.167	4.00	3.774	3.571	3.333	2.857	2.50	2.222	2.00
13	5.89	5.56	5.27	5.00	4.546	4.166	4.00	3.773	3.572	3.334	2.857	2.50	2.222	2.00
14	5.88	5.55	5.26	5.00	4.545	4.167	4.00	3.773	3.571	3.333	2.857	2.50	2.222	2.00
15	5.89	5.56	5.27	5.00	4.546	4.166	4.00	3.774	3.572	3.334	2.857	2.50	2.222	2.00
16	5.88	5.55	5.26	5.00	4.545	4.167	4.00	3.773	3.571	3.333	2.857	2.50	2.222	2.00
17	5.89	5.56	5.27	5.00	4.546	4.166	4.00	3.774	3.572	3.334	2.857	2.50	2.222	2.00
18	2.94	5.55	5.26	5.00	4.545	4.167	4.00	3.773	3.571	3.333	2.857	2.50	2.222	2.00
19	0.00	2.78	5.27	5.00	4.546	4.166	4.00	3.774	3.572	3.334	2.857	2.50	2.222	2.00
20	0.00	0.00	2.63	5.00	4.545	4.167	4.00	3.773	3.571	3.333	2.857	2.50	2.222	2.00
21	0.00	0.00	0.00	2.50	4.546	4.166	4.00	3.774	3.572	3.334	2.857	2.50	2.222	2.00
22	0.00	0.00	0.00	0.00	4.545	4.167	4.00	3.773	3.571	3.333	2.857	2.50	2.222	2.00
23	0.00	0.00	0.00	0.00	2.273	4.166	4.00	3.774	3.572	3.334	2.857	2.50	2.222	2.00
24	0.00	0.00	0.00	0.00	0.000	4.167	4.00	3.773	3.571	3.333	2.857	2.50	2.222	2.00
25	0.00	0.00	0.00	0.00	0.000	2.083	4.00	3.774	3.572	3.334	2.857	2.50	2.222	2.00
26	0.00	0.00	0.00	0.00	0.000	0.000	2.00	3.773	3.571	3.333	2.857	2.50	2.222	2.00
27	0.00	0.00	0.00	0.00	0.000	0.000	0.00	3.774	3.572	3.334	2.857	2.50	2.222	2.00
28	0.00	0.00	0.00	0.00	0.000	0.000	0.00	0.000	3.571	3.333	2.858	2.50	2.222	2.00
29	0.00	0.00	0.00	0.00	0.000	0.000	0.00	0.000	1.786	3.334	2.857	2.50	2.223	2.00
30	0.00	0.00	0.00	0.00	0.000	0.000	0.00	0.000	0.000	3.333	2.858	2.50	2.222	2.00
31	0.00	0.00	0.00	0.00	0.000	0.000	0.00	0.000	0.000	1.667	2.857	2.50	2.223	2.00
32	0.00	0.00	0.00	0.00	0.000	0.000	0.00	0.000	0.000	0.000	2.858	2.50	2.222	2.00
33	0.00	0.00	0.00	0.00	0.000	0.000	0.00	0.000	0.000	0.000	2.857	2.50	2.223	2.00
34	0.00	0.00	0.00	0.00	0.000	0.000	0.00	0.000	0.000	0.000	2.858	2.50	2.222	2.00
35	0.00	0.00	0.00	0.00	0.000	0.000	0.00	0.000	0.000	0.000	2.857	2.50	2.223	2.00
36	0.00	0.00	0.00	0.00	0.000	0.000	0.00	0.000	0.000	0.000	1.429	2.50	2.222	2.00
37	0.00	0.00	0.00	0.00	0.000	0.000	0.00	0.000	0.000	0.000	0.000	2.50	2.223	2.00
38	0.00	0.00	0.00	0.00	0.000	0.000	0.00	0.000	0.000	0.000	0.000	2.50	2.222	2.00
39	0.00	0.00	0.00	0.00	0.000	0.000	0.00	0.000	0.000	0.000	0.000	2.50	2.223	2.00
40	0.00	0.00	0.00	0.00	0.000	0.000	0.00	0.000	0.000	0.000	0.000	2.50	2.222	2.00

	Normal Recovery Period													
Year	17	18	19	20	22	24	25	26.5	28	30	35	40	45	50
41	0.00	0.00	0.00	0.00	0.000	0.000	0.00	0.000	0.000	0.000	0.000	1.25	2.223	2.00
42	0.00	0.00	0.00	0.00	0.000	0.000	0.00	0.000	0.000	0.000	0.000	0.00	2.222	2.00
43	0.00	0.00	0.00	0.00	0.000	0.000	0.00	0.000	0.000	0.000	0.000	0.00	2.223	2.00
44	0.00	0.00	0.00	0.00	0.000	0.000	0.00	0.000	0.000	0.000	0.000	0.00	2.222	2.00
45	0.00	0.00	0.00	0.00	0.000	0.000	0.00	0.000	0.000	0.000	0.000	0.00	2.223	2.00
46	0.00	0.00	0.00	0.00	0.000	0.000	0.00	0.000	0.000	0.000	0.000	0.00	1.111	2.00
47	0.00	0.00	0.00	0.00	0.000	0.000	0.00	0.000	0.000	0.000	0.000	0.00	0.000	2.00
48	0.00	0.00	0.00	0.00	0.000	0.000	0.00	0.000	0.000	0.000	0.000	0.00	0.000	2.00
49	0.00	0.00	0.00	0.00	0.000	0.000	0.00	0.000	0.000	0.000	0.000	0.00	0.000	2.00
50	0.00	0.00	0.00	0.00	0.000	0.000	0.00	0.000	0.000	0.000	0.000	0.00	0.000	2.00
51	0.00	0.00	0.00	0.00	0.000	0.000	0.00	0.000	0.000	0.000	0.000	0.00	0.000	1.00
52	0.00	0.00	0.00	0.00	0.000	0.000	0.00	0.000	0.000	0.000	0.000	0.00	0.000	0.00

Stockbyte/Getty Images

thirteen

weighing net present value and other capital budgeting criteria

O nce you have calculated the cost of capital for a project and estimated its cash flows, deciding whether to invest in that project basically boils down to asking the question "Is the project worth more or less than it costs?" To answer this question, we will, not surprisingly, turn once again to the time value of money (TVM) formulas we used to value stocks, bonds, loans, and other marketable securities in Chapters 7 and 8. But first, a caveat: Though the *mechanics* of using the TVM formulas will be the same, the *intuition* underlying our analysis of investment criteria will be very different in this chapter. And this shift in intuition will be signaled by a seemingly minor thing. You will recall that when we used the pricing equations for marketable securities such as stocks, bonds, and other instruments, they all had "=" signs. In this chapter, we're going to see that most capital budgeting decision rules that we will encounter will have ">" or "<" signs.

Even though it seems like a small thing, this switch from an assumption of equality in all our previous TVM equations to one of inequality in those used in this chapter reflects a dramatic shift

continued on p. 364

LEARNING GOALS

LG13-1 Analyze the logic underlying capital budgeting decision techniques.

LG13-2 Calculate and use the payback (PB) and discounted payback (DPB) methods for valuing capital investment opportunities.

LG13-3 Calculate and use the net present value (NPV) method for evaluating capital investment opportunities.

LG13-4 Calculate and use the internal rate of return (IRR) and the modified internal rate of return (MIRR) methods for evaluating capital investment opportunities.

LG13-5 Use NPV profiles to reconcile sources of conflict between NPV and IRR methods.

LG13-6 Compute and use the profitability index (PI).

»viewpoints

ADK Industries, a startup firm in the online social networking industry, has run into capacity constraints with its Internet bandwidth provider. ADK management is considering building its own dedicated web server farm at a cost of $5 million. In return, the firm expects that the increased bandwidth will generate higher demand for its services, resulting in increased cash flows of $1.2 million in the first year, $1.6 million in the second year, $2.3 million in the third year, and $2.8 million in the fourth year, for a total of $7.9 million over the next four years. At that point, the firm will scrap the server farm as obsolete. If ADK estimates that its target rate of return on such projects is 14 percent, should ADK go ahead with the project? **(See the solution at the end of the book.)**

continued from p. 363

in both the investment environment we are operating in and our assessment of what types of returns are possible in that environment. This difference arises because the marketable securities valued in all the previous chapters are *financial* assets that trade in competitive financial markets, while the capital budgeting projects that we consider in this chapter usually involve investment in *real* assets (such as land, machinery, and so forth), which typically trade in much less competitive markets. In this context, "less competitive" basically means that we will be operating in an environment where these real assets associated with a project will convey at least some monopoly power (and the associated monopolistic revenues) to us if we undertake the project.

To see this difference, consider two situations: In one, an investor is deciding whether to buy a share of stock in a company that only has one class of common stock, while in the other, a restaurant chain is deciding whether to purchase a particular corner lot as a location for one of its restaurants. The stock purchase decision will focus on the cash flows expected to be received back from the stock, but which *particular* share of stock is purchased won't really matter; all shares of stock will get the same cash flows and, as long as the stock markets are reasonably efficient, you'll pay about the same price and commission regardless of which particular share of stock you buy.

The restaurant purchase decision, though, will be different from the stock purchase decision on a couple of levels. First, real estate markets are nowhere near as efficient as stock markets, so the fees paid in the form of commissions, closing costs, etc., will represent a far higher percentage of the purchase price of the restaurant than the commission rate on the stock purchase does. Even more important, though, is that, if the restaurant chain does buy a particular piece of land, *no one else can buy that exact piece of land.* So its asset will be unique, and no one else will be able to *perfectly* compete with a restaurant built there. Oh, its competitors might try to build on plots of land that are as close as possible (there's a reason that you will often see competing restaurant chains clustered on corner lots around the same intersection, or across the road from each other), but if this particular lot has the best traffic flow potential . . . you get the picture.

In sum, uses of TVM equations in previous chapters were dealing with assets trading in financial markets where "what you get is what you pay for," that is, where the present value of the

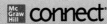
expected future cash flows should just equal what you have to pay for it, taking into account the risks associated with those cash flows, as well as the going rate for compensating the purchaser for bearing those risks. In this chapter, we're going to be using TVM to value real assets, a situation where it is possible to expect to earn returns *above and beyond* those necessary to compensate us for the associated risks (a situation sometimes referred to as earning *economic profits*). In other words, the name of the game in this chapter is to always look for projects that are worth *more* than they cost, even after we take risks into account. ∎

13.1 • THE SET OF CAPITAL BUDGETING TECHNIQUES LG13-1

So, now we are going to apply what we have learned in the preceding two chapters about the cost of capital and cash flows that result from capital budgeting decisions to choose the projects that most deserve to be funded using the firm's scarce capital—that is, to determine which projects promise the best expected returns to the company. Commonly used capital budgeting techniques for doing this include

- NPV (net present value).
- IRR (internal rate of return).
- PB (payback).
- DPB (discounted payback).
- MIRR (modified internal rate of return).
- PI (profitability index).

As we discuss each of these techniques in this chapter, you will find that, while the net present value (NPV) technique is the preferred one for most project evaluations, in some cases using one of the other decision rules, either in lieu of NPV or in conjunction with it, makes sense. For example, a company or person faced with a time constraint to repay the initial capital for a project may be more worried about a project's payback (PB) statistic, while a firm facing capital constraints might prefer to use one of the interest-rate-based

Technique	Unit of Measurement	Benchmark	Uses TVM	Works Well With Non-Normal Cash Flows	Works Well for Choosing Among Projects
PB (payback)	Time	Varies	No	No	No
DPB (discounted payback)	Time	Varies	Yes	No	No
NPV (net present value)	Dollars	$0	Yes	Yes	Yes
IRR (internal rate of return)	Rate	Cost of capital	Yes	No	No
MIRR (modified internal rate of return)	Rate	Cost of capital	Yes	Yes	No
PI (profitability index)	Rate	1	Yes	Yes	No

decision statistics, such as the profitability index (PI), to prioritize its project choices. Choosing a capital budgeting technique or techniques to use is affected by five subchoices:

1. The statistical format you choose.

2. The benchmark you compare it to.

3. Whether you compute it with TVM.

4. Whether non-normal cash flows are a factor.

5. What other projects you may or may not have to decide among.

Table 13.1 details the implicit subchoices associated with each of the capital budgeting techniques.

13.2 • THE CHOICE OF DECISION STATISTIC FORMAT LG13-1

Managers tend to focus on three general measurement units for financial decisions: currency, time, and rate of return. Of these three types, rate-based statistics can potentially be the trickiest to use. Computing these statistics usually involves summarizing the relationship between cash inflows and cash outflows across the project's lifetime through the use of a ratio. Any time we use a ratio to create a summary statistic like this, some (crucial) information is lost along the way.

In particular, although rate-based decision statistics tell us the rate of return *per dollar* invested, they don't reflect the *amount* of the investment on which that return is based.

Image Source/Cadalpe

Image Source, all rights reserved.

imageshop/PunchStock

Among currency, time, and rate of return, managers usually prefer rate-based statistics.

Payback Benchmark

The payback method shows an additional weakness in that its benchmark must be exogenously specified: In other words, it is not always the same value, nor is it determined by the required rate of return or any other input variable. Ideally, the maximum allowable PB for a project should be set based on some relevant external constraint, such as the number of periods until capital providers need their money back, or the time available until a project would violate a bond issue's protective covenants. As you might suspect, in real life managers often indicate the maximum allowable payback—that is, set the exogenous specification—arbitrarily.

Let us assume that we have been told that the maximum allowable payback for this project is three years. With this decision rule, we want to accept projects that show a calculated statistic less than the benchmark of three years:

Accept project if PB $\leq$ Maximum allowable PB

Reject project if PB > Maximum allowable PB

(13-2)

discounted payback (DPB) A capital budgeting method that generates decision rules and associated metrics that choose projects based on how quickly they return their initial investment plus interest.

Discounted Payback Statistic

Yet another problem that arises when we use the payback technique is that it does not recognize or incorporate the time value of money. To compensate for this exclusion, we often calculate the **discounted payback (DPB)** statistic instead, using the following formula:

$$0 = \sum_{n=0}^{DPB} \frac{CF_n}{(1+i)^n}$$

(13-3)

Notice that all we are doing here is summing the *present values* of the cash flows until we get a cumulative sum of zero, instead of summing the cash flows themselves as we did for the PB statistic. Other than that, we follow all the steps in the computation of DPB just as we did for the PB statistic.

EXAMPLE 13-1

For interactive versions of this example, log in to Connect or go to mhhe.com/Cornett6e.

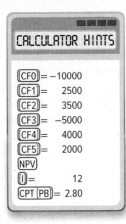

CALCULATOR HINTS

$\boxed{\text{CF0}} = -10000$
$\boxed{\text{CF1}} = 2500$
$\boxed{\text{CF2}} = 3500$
$\boxed{\text{CF3}} = -5000$
$\boxed{\text{CF4}} = 4000$
$\boxed{\text{CF5}} = 2000$
$\boxed{\text{NPV}}$
$\boxed{\text{I}} = 12$
$\boxed{\text{CPT } \boxed{\text{PB}}} = 2.80$

Payback Calculation LG13-2

Consider the sample project with the cash flows shown in Table 13.2. Should this project be accepted based on payback if the maximum allowable payback period is three years?

▼ **TABLE 13.2** Payback Calculation on Sample Project with Normal Cash Flows

Year:	0	1	2	3	4	5
Cash flow	−$10,000	$2,500	$3,500	$5,000	$4,000	$2,000
Cumulative cash flow	−10,000	−7,500	−4,000	1,000		

SOLUTION:

To calculate this project's payback, we would first calculate the cumulative cash flows until they went from negative to positive. From this first step, we know that payback occurs somewhere between periods 2 and 3. To determine the exact statistic, we note that if the magnitude of the last negative cumulative cash flow represents how much cash flow we *need* during year 3 to achieve payback, then the marginal cash flow for year 3 represents how much we will *get* over the course of the entire third year. By linear interpolation, our exact statistic is therefore where we start (year 2) plus what we need (the absolute value of the last negative cumulative cash flow, −$4,000) over what we are going to get during that year:

$$PB = 2 + \frac{\$4,000}{\$5,000} = 2.8 \text{ years}$$

Since our calculated payback is 2.8 years and the maximum allowable payback period is three years, we should accept the project based on the payback rule.

(continued)

The spreadsheet solution is:

	A	B	C	D	E	F
1	Year	Cash Flow	Cumulative Cash Flow		Payback	
2	0	-$10,000	-$10,000 =B2			=IF(AND(C2<0,C3>=0),A2+ABS(C2/B3),"")
3	1	$2,500	-$7,500 =C2+B3			=IF(AND(C3<0,C4>=0),A3+ABS(C3/B4),"")
4	2	$3,500	-$4,000 =C3+B4		2.8	=IF(AND(C4<0,C5>=0),A4+ABS(C4/B5),"")
5	3	$5,000	$1,000 =C4+B5			=IF(AND(C5<0,C6>=0),A5+ABS(C5/B6),"")
6	4	$4,000	$5,000 =C5+B6			=IF(AND(C6<0,C7>=0),A6+ABS(C6/B7),"")
7	5	$2,000	$7,000 =C6+B7			=IF(AND(C7<0,C8>=0),A7+ABS(C7/B8),"")

Microsoft Excel

Unfortunately, there is no built-in function in Excel for calculating PB directly. However, we can implement the formula shown in Equation 13-1 through a combination of (a) calculating the cumulative running subtotal of cash flows at each time, (b) using an IF(logical_test, [value_if_true], [value_if_false]) function to determine if that cumulative running subtotal has passed 0 (zero) for the first time, and, if so, then (c) calculating the total PB statistic as the sum of the last year in which the cumulative running subtotal was negative plus the ratio of the amount of cash flow needed that last year to reach a cumulative subtotal of 0 divided by the amount of cash flow during the year the cumulative subtotal went from negative to positive.

While this sounds complex, the individual calculations are fairly simple and easily copied and pasted from one year to the next.

Similar to Problems 13-3, 13-9, Self-Test Problem 1

Discounted Payback Benchmark

We may be tempted to assume that we should simply use the same maximum allowable payback benchmark for DPB that we used for PB. If we did so, then we would obviously have to reject this project because its calculated DPB is 3.56 years (Example 13-2) versus a stated maximum allowable time of only three years. However, we should be very cautious about applying the same benchmark to DPB that we did to PB. To see why, recall that payback calculations only make sense when applied to normal cash flows, so we would assume that we will be dealing with normal cash flows here. But think about *which* cash flows are affected when we switch from calculating payback to discounted payback: Only the ones in the future will fall to lower values because the present value of the time 0 cash flow will always be the same as its nominal value. And if the future cash flows are all positive and the initial cash flow is negative, then it is only the positive cash flows that will be affected by switching to cumulative present value for DPB.

In other words, we would expect the calculated DPB statistic to always be larger than the "regular" PB statistic because DPB incorporates the interest you must pay until you reach the benchmark. Said another way, DPB will always take longer to achieve payback if you are "chipping away" at the same-sized initial cash outflow with the present values of a bunch of positive cash inflows rather than their simple nominal values. Therefore, it probably is not fair to hold the DPB statistic up to the same benchmark we use for the PB statistic.

What benchmark should we use? Well, as with PB, management will set the DPB maximum allowable payback exogenously and, once again, often arbitrarily. Let us assume that we are told that senior management has set the maximum allowable payback for DPB as 3.5 years.

Accept project if calculated DPB ≤ Maximum allowable discounted payback

Reject project if calculated DPB > Maximum allowable discount payback

(13-4)

EXAMPLE 13-2

Discounted Payback Calculation LG13-2

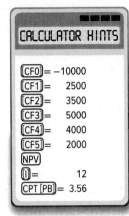

CALCULATOR HINTS

CF0 =	−10000
CF1 =	2500
CF2 =	3500
CF3 =	5000
CF4 =	4000
CF5 =	2000
NPV	
I =	12
CPT PB =	3.56

Consider the same project from Example 13-1. To calculate this project's discounted payback, we would first need to calculate the PV of each cash flow separately. Assuming a 12 percent interest rate, we would calculate these values as shown in Table 13.3.

▼ **TABLE 13.3** Discounted Payback Calculation: Present Values of Cash Flows

Year:	0	1	2	3	4	5
Cash flow	−$10,000.00	$2,500.00	$3,500.00	$5,000.00	$4,000.00	$2,000.00
Cash flow present value	−10,000.00	2,232.14	2,790.18	3,558.90	2,542.07	1,134.85

In Table 13.4 we calculate the cumulative present value of the cash flows until they switch from negative to positive:

▼ **TABLE 13.4** Discounted Payback Calculation on Sample Project with Normal Cash Flows

Year:	0	1	2	3	4	5
Cash flow	−$10,000.00	$2,500.00	$3,500.00	$5,000.00	$4,000.00	$2,000.00
Cash flow present value	−10,000.00	2,232.14	2,790.18	3,558.90	2,542.07	1,134.85
Cumulative cash flow PV	−10,000.00	−7,767.86	−4,977.68	−1,418.78	1,123.29	

SOLUTION:

As before, we can stop once the cumulative values go from negative to positive. In this case, linear interpolation will give us a DPB statistic of

$$DPB = 3 + \frac{\$1,418.78}{\$2,542.07} = 3.56 \text{ years}$$

Since our calculated DPB is 3.56 years and the maximum allowable amount is 3.5 years, we should reject the project.
The spreadsheet solution is:

	A	B	C	D	E	F	G	H
1	Interest	12%						
2	Year	Cash Flow	Present Value of CF		Cumulative PV of CF		Discounted Payback	
3	0	-$10,000	-$10,000.00	=PV($B$1,A3,,-B3)	-$10,000.00	=C3		=IF(AND(E3<0,E4>=0),A3+ABS(E3/C4),"")
4	1	$2,500	$2,232.14	=PV($B$1,A4,,-B4)	-$7,767.86	=E3+C4		=IF(AND(E4<0,E5>=0),A4+ABS(E4/C5),"")
5	2	$3,500	$2,790.18	=PV($B$1,A5,,-B5)	-$4,977.68	=E4+C5		=IF(AND(E5<0,E6>=0),A5+ABS(E5/C6),"")
6	3	$5,000	$3,558.90	=PV($B$1,A6,,-B6)	-$1,418.78	=E5+C6	3.56	=IF(AND(E6<0,E7>=0),A6+ABS(E6/C7),"")
7	4	$4,000	$2,542.07	=PV($B$1,A7,,-B7)	$1,123.29	=E6+C7		=IF(AND(E7<0,E8>=0),A7+ABS(E7/C8),"")
8	5	$2,000	$1,134.85	=PV($B$1,A8,,-B8)	$2,258.15	=E7+C8		=IF(AND(E8<0,E9>=0),A8+ABS(E8/C9),"")

Microsoft Excel

Just as with the PB statistic, there is also no built-in function in Excel for calculating DPB directly. However, steps necessary, illustrated in Example 13-2, are very similar to those for PB, with the exception of calculating the cumulative PV of cash flows rather than the cumulative cash flows themselves.

Similar to Problems 13-4, 13-10, Self-Test Problem 1

the Math Coach on...

Payback And Discounted Payback Using Financial Calculators And Spreadsheet Programs

❝ Most financial calculators and spreadsheet programs (with the notable exception of Texas Instrument's BA II Plus Professional) will not compute PB or DPB for you. Instead, you have to go through the process of cumulating cash flows or the PV of cash flows noted in Examples 13-1, 13-2, and 13-3. **❞**

Payback and Discounted Payback Strengths and Weaknesses LG13-1

A common criticism of PB is that it does not account for the time value of money. The use of PV formulas in computing DPB compensates for TVM, but DPB is not intended to really replace PB, but rather to complement it, providing additional information to analyze capital budgeting decisions.

For example, if we consider a typical, normal payback statistic based on a set of cash flows as a loan problem in which the company borrows the money for the initial investment and then pays it off over time, then the PB statistic will intuitively equal the amount of time necessary to repay just principal on the loan, and the DPB statistic will indicate the time necessary to repay principal plus interest. But, as discussed above, there is no way to impose a correspondingly logical relationship between the *benchmarks* used with each of these statistics due to their exogenously specified nature.

Both PB and DPB have another, potentially even more serious, flaw. Both decision statistics completely ignore any cash flows that accrue *after* the project reaches its respective payback benchmark. Ignoring this vital information can have serious implications when managers choose between two mutually exclusive projects that have very similar paybacks but very different cash flows after payback is achieved.

time out!

13-1 Which should we expect to be larger: a project's payback statistic or its discounted payback statistic?

13-2 If the discount rate is increased, will a project's discounted payback period increase or decrease?

EXAMPLE 13-3

For interactive versions of this example, log in to Connect or go to mhhe.com/Cornett6e.

Payback Calculation for Alternative Project LG13-2

Consider once again the sample project shown in Table 13.2. As we calculated in Example 13-1, that project has a PB statistic of 2.8 years. Now, compare that project to the one shown in Table 13.5.

▼ TABLE 13.5 Payback Calculation on Alternative Sample Project with Normal Cash Flows

Year:	0	1	2	3	4	5
Cash flow	−$10,000	$2,500	$3,500	$4,000	$104,000	$102,000
Cash flow present value	−10,000	−7,500	−4,000	0	0	0

SOLUTION:

This project would have a slightly higher PB statistic of 3.0. Given that it still achieves payback in exactly the maximum allowable three years, it should be highly favored over the first project due to the large positive cash flows that will accrue in the later years. But managers who ignore this aspect of the PB rule and who focus only on the PB statistics of these two projects will likely incorrectly choose the first project due to its lower PB statistic.

Note that NPV will *not* suffer from this problem. Since the NPV statistic takes all of a project's cash flows into account, there aren't "remaining" cash flows to get left out of the statistic as there are with PB and DPB.

Similar to Problems 13-3, 13-4

13.5 • NET PRESENT VALUE LG13-1

At its heart, **net present value (NPV)** represents the "purest" of capital budgeting rules, measuring exactly the value we are interested in: the amount of wealth increase we expect from accepting a project. As we cover in more detail below, the NPV method measures this expected wealth increase by computing the difference between the present values of a project's cash inflows and outflows. Since this calculation includes the necessary capital expenditures and other startup costs of the project as cash outflows, a positive value indicates that the project is desirable—that it more than covers all of the necessary resource costs to do the project.

net present value (NPV)
A technique that generates a decision rule and associated metric for choosing projects based on the total discounted value of their cash flows.

NPV Statistic LG13-3

We actually already know how to calculate the NPV statistic. In fact, we used a very similar approach in developing bond and stock pricing equations. The NPV statistic is simply the sum of all the cash flows' present values:

the
Math Coach on...

Financial Calculators Versus Spreadsheet Programs

66 While financial calculators expect to be told CF0 when being asked to compute NPV, the NPV functions in spreadsheet programs such as Microsoft Excel usually *don't* want to be told CF0. Instead, they expect you to handle the inclusion of CF0 in the calculation of the NPV statistic outside the NPV function. For example, if you wanted to find the NPV of the cash flows in Example 13-4 using Excel, the function would look like "= NPV(12, 2500, 3500, 5000, 4000, 2000) − 10000". 99

$$NPV = \frac{CF_0}{(1+i)^0} + \frac{CF_1}{(1+i)^1} + \ldots + \frac{CF_N}{(1+i)^N}$$

$$= \sum_{n=0}^{N} \frac{CF_n}{(1+i)^n}$$

(13-5)

NPV Benchmark

NPV analysis includes all of the cash flows—both inflows and outflows. This inclusion implies that any required investment in the project is already factored in, so any NPV greater than zero represents value *above and beyond* that investment. Accordingly, the NPV decision rule is

Accept project if NPV ≥ 0
Reject project if NVP < 0

(13-6)

EXAMPLE 13-4

For interactive versions of this example, log in to Connect or go to mhhe.com/Cornett6e.

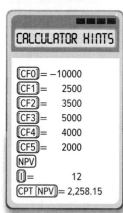

CALCULATOR HINTS

CF0 =	−10000
CF1 =	2500
CF2 =	3500
CF3 =	5000
CF4 =	4000
CF5 =	2000
NPV	
I =	12
CPT NPV =	2,258.15

NPV for a Normal Set of Cash Flows LG13-2

A company is evaluating a project with a set of normal cash flows using a risk-appropriate discount rate of 12 percent, as shown in Table 13.6. Compute the NPV to determine whether the company should undertake the project.

▼ **TABLE 13.6** Sample Project with Normal Cash Flows

Year:	0	1	2	3	4	5
Cash flow	−$10,000	$2,500	$3,500	$5,000	$4,000	$2,000

SOLUTION:

The NPV statistic for this project will be

$$NPV = \frac{-\$10,000}{(1.12)^0} + \frac{\$2,500}{(1.12)^1} + \frac{\$3,500}{(1.12)^2} + \frac{\$5,000}{(1.12)^3} + \frac{\$4,000}{(12.1)^4} + \frac{\$2,000}{(1.12)^5}$$
$$= \$2,258.15 > 0$$

The NPV decision will be to accept the project.

When you first start calculating NPV, it is easy to miss its deeper meaning. A relatively small NPV, such as the $2,258.15 figure in this example, raises the question of whether $2,258.15 is "worth it," in this sense: Will the project cover the opportunity cost of using the $10,000 of necessary capital? The point, of course, is that the $2,258.15 is above and beyond the recovery of that opportunity cost, so, *yes, it's worth it.*

The spreadsheet solution is:

	A	B	C
1	Interest	12%	
2	Year	Cash Flow	
3	0	-$10,000	
4	1	$2,500	
5	2	$3,500	
6	3	$5,000	
7	4	$4,000	
8	5	$2,000	
9			
10	NPV	$2,258.15	=NPV(B1,B4:B8)+B3

Microsoft Excel

Luckily, there is a built-in function in Excel, NPV(rate, value1, [value2], . . .), designed expressly for calculating the net present value of multiple cash flows. The cash flows passed to the NPV() function can be passed either one at a time or as a range with a colon (":") between the addresses of the cells at the beginning and end of the range. For example:

Note that we have to remember to keep CF0 out of the NPV() function and to "manually" add it in to calculate the NPV statistic, as Excel's NPV() function is constructed with the assumption that cash flows that don't need to be moved (i.e., those at time 0) won't be passed through the function.

Similar to Problems 13-1, 13-13, Self-Test Problem 1

the
Math Coach on...

Using a Financial Calculator–Part 2 (Revisited)

The TVM worksheet present in most financial calculators has been fine, so far, for the types of TVM problems we've been solving. Sometimes we had to use the worksheet two or three times for a single problem, but that was usually because we needed an intermediate calculation to input into another TVM equation.

In this chapter, we will generally be using simpler TVM equations (i.e., PV and FV), but we'll find ourselves having to use them repeatedly, making only small variations in inputs over and over again within the same problem. We're also going to run up against the problem of cash flow inconsistencies in most projects. If you thought the cash flows of stocks jumped around a lot, wait until you see what project cash flows do! If we stick with the TVM worksheet, these inconsistent cash flows will be a problem for us. If we want to solve for a "common" *i* or *N* value, the TVM worksheet won't let us enter multiple cash flows unless we're solving an annuity problem. (The one notable exception to this has been when we used the TVM worksheet to simultaneously solve the annuity/lump-sum problems that arise with bonds. If you recall, those problems require agreement between the inputs to the annuity and the lump-sum problems. This kind of agreement is highly unlikely to occur in other circumstances.)

Remember that most financial calculators also have built-in worksheets specifically designed for computing NPV in problems with multiple non-constant cash flows. In many cases, they will also calculate most of the other decision rule statistics that we're going to be discussing.

Here is what we already know: To make calculator worksheets as flexible as possible, they are usually divided into two parts—one for input, which we'll refer to as the CF (cash flow) worksheet, and one or more for calculating decision statistics. We'll go over the conventions concerning the CF worksheet here. The CF worksheet is usually designed to handle inputting sets of multiple cash flows as quickly as possible. As a result, it normally consists of two sets of variables or cells—one for the cash flows and one to hold a set of frequency counts for the cash flows, so that we can tell it we have seven $1,500 cash flows in a row instead of having to enter $1,500 seven times.

Using the frequency counts to reduce the number of inputs is handy, but you must take care. Frequency counts are only good for embedded annuities of identical cash flows. You have to ensure that you don't mistake another kind of cash flow for an annuity.

Also, using frequency counts will usually affect the way that the calculator counts time periods. As an example, let's talk about how we would put the set of cash flows shown here into a CF worksheet:

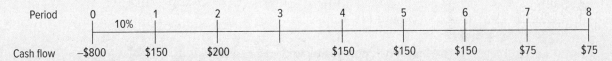

Period	0	1	2	3	4	5	6	7	8
		10%							
Cash flow	–$800	$150	$200		$150	$150	$150	$75	$75

To designate which particular value we'll place into each particular cash flow cell in this worksheet, we'll note the value and the cell identifier, such as CF0, CF1, and so forth. We'll do the same for the frequency cells, using F1, F2, etc., to identify which CF cell the frequency cell goes with. (Note that in most calculators, CF0 is treated as a unique value with an unalterable frequency of 1; we're going to make the same assumption here so you'll never see a listing for F0.) For this sample timeline, our inputs would be

–$800	[CF0]		
$150	[CF1]	1	[F1]
$200	[CF2]	1	[F2]
$0	[CF3]	1	[F3]
$150	[CF4]	3	[F4]
$75	[CF5]	2	[F5]

Then, on the NPV worksheet, you would simply need to enter the interest rate and solve for the NPV:

10%	[I]
[CPT]	[NPV] = –$144.61

Note a few important things about this example:

1. We had to manually enter a value of $0 for CF3: If we hadn't, the calculator wouldn't have known about it and would have implicitly assumed that CF4 came one period after CF2.

2. Once we use a frequency cell for one cash flow, all numbering on any subsequent cash flows that we enter into the calculator is going to be messed up, at least from our point of view. For instance, the first $75 isn't what we would call "CF5," is it? We'd call it "CF7" because it comes at time period 7; but calculators usually treat CF5 as "the fifth set of cash flows," so we'll just have to try to do the same to be consistent.

3. If we really don't need to use frequency cells, we will usually just leave them out of the guidance instructions in this chapter to save space.

EXAMPLE 13-5

For interactive versions of this example, log in to Connect or go to mhhe.com/Cornett6e.

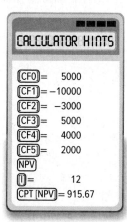

CALCULATOR HINTS

CF0	=	5000
CF1	=	−10000
CF2	=	−3000
CF3	=	5000
CF4	=	4000
CF5	=	2000
NPV		
I	=	12
CPT NPV	=	915.67

NPV for a Non-normal Set of Cash Flows LG13-3

Note that the NPV rule works equally well with non-normal cash flows, such as those for the project shown in Table 13.7. Compute the NPV for this project to determine whether it should be accepted. Use a 12 percent discount rate.

▼ **TABLE 13.7** Sample Project with Normal Cash Flows

Year:	0	1	2	3	4	5
Cash flow	$5,000	−$10,000	−$3,000	$5,000	$4,000	$2,000

SOLUTION:

The NPV statistic will be

$$NPV = \frac{\$5,000}{(1.12)^0} + \frac{-\$10,000}{(1.12)^1} + \frac{-\$3,00}{(1.12)^2} + \frac{\$5,000}{(1.12)^3} + \frac{\$4,000}{(12.1)^4} + \frac{\$2,000}{(1.12)^5}$$

$$= \$915.67 > 0$$

Based on this NPV, the project should be accepted.

The spreadsheet solution is:

	A	B	C
1	Interest	12%	
2	Year	Cash Flow	
3	0	$5,000	
4	1	-$10,000	
5	2	-$3,000	
6	3	$5,000	
7	4	$4,000	
8	5	$2,000	
9			
10	NPV	$915.67	=NPV(B1,B4:B8)+B3

Microsoft Excel

As long as we are consistent about keeping outflows as negative and inflows as positive, the NPV() function will give consistent answers.

Similar to Problem 13-2

NPV Strengths and Weaknesses

One strength of the NPV rule is that the statistic is *not* a ratio as with the rate-based decision statistics. It works equally well for independent projects and for choosing among mutually exclusive projects. In the latter case, the mutually exclusive project with the highest NPV should add the most wealth to the firm, and so management should accept it over any competing projects.

Unfortunately, this ability to choose among projects stems from exactly what gives it its greatest weakness—the format of the statistic. Since the NPV statistic is a dollar figure, it accurately reflects the net effect of any differences in timing or scale of two projects' expected cash flows. It thus allows comparisons of two projects' NPV statistics to fully incorporate those differences. However, this same currency format often results in confusion for uninformed decision makers: Managers not completely familiar with how the NPV statistic works often insist on comparing the NPV to the *cost* of the project, not understanding that the cost is already incorporated into the NPV.

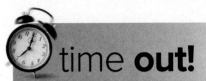
13.6 • INTERNAL RATE OF RETURN AND MODIFIED INTERNAL RATE OF RETURN LG13-1

The **internal rate of return (IRR)** technique is, by far, the most popular rate-based capital budgeting technique. The main reason for its popularity is that, if you are considering a project with normal cash flows that is independent of other projects, the IRR statistic will give exactly the same accept/reject decision as the NPV rule does. This is due to the fact that NPV and IRR are very closely related. NPV is the sum of the present values of the cash flows at a particular interest rate (usually the firm's cost of capital), whereas IRR is the interest rate that will cause the NPV to be equal to zero.

internal rate of return (IRR) A capital budgeting technique that generates decision rules and associated metrics for choosing projects based on the implicit expected geometric average of a project's rate of return.

Solve for NPV:

$$NPV = \sum_{n=0}^{N} \frac{CF_n}{(1+i)^n}$$

Solve for IRR:

versus $$0 = \sum_{n=0}^{N} \frac{CF_n}{(1+IRR)^n}$$ (13-7)

As long as the cash flows of a project are normal, the NPV calculated in the equation on the left will be greater than zero if and only if the IRR calculated in the equation on the right is greater than *i*.

However, IRR runs into a lot of problems if project cash flows are not normal or if you are using this statistic to decide among mutually exclusive projects. As we will show, we can correct for the non-normal cash flows, but all of the rate-based decision statistics will exhibit the problem of choosing between multiple projects that we discussed above.

Internal Rate of Return Statistic LG13-4

To solve for the IRR statistic, we simply solve the NPV formula for the interest rate that will make NPV equal zero:

$$0 = \sum_{n=0}^{N} \frac{CF_n}{(1+IRR)^n}$$ (13-8)

Unfortunately, we cannot solve directly for the interest rate that will set NPV equal to zero. We either have to use trial and error to determine the appropriate rate, or we have to rely on a calculator or computer, both of which use much the same approach.

Internal Rate of Return Benchmark

Once we calculate the IRR, we must then compare the decision statistic to the relevant cost of capital for the project—the average rate of return necessary to pay back the project's capital providers, given the risk that the project represents:

$$\text{Accept project if IRR} \geq \text{Cost of capital}$$
$$\text{Reject project if IRR} < \text{Cost of capital}$$

(13-9)

EXAMPLE 13-6

For interactive versions of this example, log in to Connect or go to mhhe.com/Cornett6e.

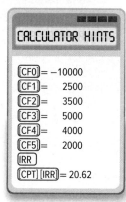

CALCULATOR HINTS

[CF0] =	−10000
[CF1] =	2500
[CF2] =	3500
[CF3] =	5000
[CF4] =	4000
[CF5] =	2000
[IRR]	
[CPT] [IRR] =	20.62

IRR Calculation LG13-4

Looking once again at our sample set of normal cash flows from Table 13.6, IRR will be the solution to

$$0 = \frac{-\$10{,}000}{(1 + IRR)^0} + \frac{\$2{,}500}{(1 + IRR)^1} + \frac{\$3{,}500}{(1 + IRR)^2} + \frac{\$5{,}000}{(1 + IRR)^3} + \frac{\$4{,}000}{(1 + IRR)^4} + \frac{\$2{,}000}{(1 + IRR)^5}$$

$IRR = 0.2062$, or 20.62%

The spreadsheet solution is:

	A	B	C
1	Interest	12%	
2	Year	Cash Flow	
3	0	-$10,000	
4	1	$2,500	
5	2	$3,500	
6	3	$5,000	
7	4	$4,000	
8	5	$2,000	
9			
10	IRR	20.62%	=IRR(B3:B8)

Microsoft Excel

Excel's IRR(values, [guess]) function uses a type of "educated search methodology" to repeatedly try different values for Interest rate, computing the NPV at a starting rate, then using the result to adjust its guess about the rate with the goal of finding the rate that will cause the NPV statistic for the set of cash flows you pass it to be as close to 0 (zero) as it can get.

Luckily, it performs this repeated guessing quite quickly, so we don't have to sit through the process of watching it repeatedly guess and refine its guesses; normally, we simply type in the equation, and literally quicker than the eye can detect, it has settled on an answer and displays that to us.

However, there is one downside to the methodology that the Excel IRR() function uses: It finds a solution, but not necessarily the only solution. That is the main reason that there is also an allowance for us to enter an optional parameter for a "starting guess": If there actually were multiple interest rates that could lead to an NPV of zero for a given set of cash flows, starting at different rates might allow us to guide Excel in finding those multiple rates. We present an example of this below in our discussion of some of the potential problems with IRR.

Similar to Problems 13-5, 13-11, Self-Test Problem 1

At this point, you may find yourself getting a little confused about which rate is *the* interest rate. The IRR statistic will equal the expected rate of return, which incorporates risk (as probabilities). We will compare that expected rate of return to the cost of capital, which is often called the *required rate of return.* Up until this chapter, we have been using all of these phrases interchangeably for *"the"* interest rate. We have been able to get away with doing so to this point because stocks, bonds, and all other types of financial assets trade in relatively liquid, competitive financial markets. In liquid markets, the rate of return you expect to earn is pretty much equal to the rate of return you require for taking on that particular security's risk. In such an environment, it makes sense to assume that we are not going to be able to earn any "extra" return or economic profit above and beyond what is appropriate for the amount of risk we are bearing.

Remember, though, that in this chapter, we are no longer talking about *financial* assets, but *real* assets such as land, factories with inventories, and production lines. These types of assets do not generally trade in perfectly competitive markets. Instead, they trade in quite illiquid markets in which an individual or a firm can gain at least some amount of market or monopoly power by virtue of technological, legal, or marketing expertise.

We noted this difference at the beginning of this chapter when we differentiated between formulas for financial assets such as stocks and bonds and the equations we are using in this chapter to value projects. The formulas we used to value stocks and bonds use "=" signs because those assets trade in nearly perfectly competitive markets, where what you get is (approximately, at least) equal to what you paid for it. Here, on the other hand, we examine situations in which companies seek to choose projects that are worth *more* than what they pay for them—leaving room for economic profit. That is why all of these capital budgeting rules use ">" and "<" signs.

Real assets like production lines don't trade in perfectly competitive markets.
Digital Vision/Getty Images

So, when we deal with physical asset projects, we have to expect that two different rates of return will arise. The best way to think of these two rates is as the *expected* rate of return (IRR) and the *required* rate of return (i). We only want to invest in projects where the rate we expect to get (IRR) is larger than the rate investors require (i) based on the project's expected return, including risk.[1]

Problems with Internal Rate of Return

As we mentioned previously, IRR will give the same accept/reject decision as NPV if two conditions hold true:

1. The project has normal cash flows.

2. We are evaluating the project independently of other projects—that is, we are not considering mutually exclusive projects.

To see the problems that arise if these conditions do *not* hold, we will make use of a tool called the **NPV profile.** This is simply a graph of a project's NPV as a function of possible capital costs. The NPV profile for our sample project with normal cash flows from Table 13.6 appears as Figure 13.1.

LG13-5

NPV profile A graph of a project's NPV as a function of the cost of capital.

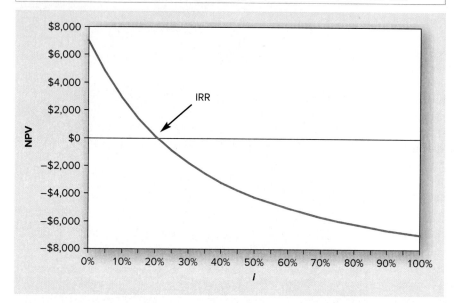

▼FIGURE 13.1 NPV Profile for Sample Normal Cash Flows

This graph presents our sample project's NPV profile, using the normal cash flows listed in Table 13.6.

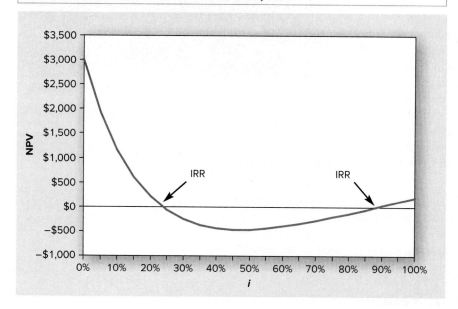

▼FIGURE 13.2 NPV Profile for Sample Non-normal Cash Flows

Notice how the graph shows two valid IRRs. Which one should you use?

As you can see, the NPV profile for this normal set of cash flows slopes downward. As we noted previously concerning the relationship between the PB and DPB statistics, increasing values of *i* with a normal set of cash flows affect the present value of positive cash flows, but not that of negative cash flows. All sets of normal cash flows will therefore share this general, downward-sloping shape.

Note that IRR appears on this graph as the intersection of the NPV profile with the *x*-axis (horizontal)—the intersection will represent the interest rate where NPV equals exactly zero. With normal cash flows such as these, the constant downward slope of the NPV profile dictates that only one such intersection will exist for each project.

IRR and NPV Profiles with Non-normal Cash Flows

But let us revisit what happens to the NPV profile if cash flows are *not* normal. The NPV profile will not necessarily slope continually downward and thus may cross over the *x*-axis at more than one interest rate. In this case we may find more than one valid IRR for which NPV equals zero. An example of such an NPV profile, constructed from the cash flows in Table 13.7, appears in Figure 13.2.

In this instance, the project shows two valid IRRs: one at 23.62 percent and another at 88.62 percent. Which of these two should we use as "the" statistic? Well, it depends on what the firm pays as the actual cost of capital. If the firm pays 12 percent for capital, then using either of these two IRR values would generate a correct "accept" decision, as the project *does* have a positive NPV at *i* = 12 percent. But what if the firm paid a relatively high cost of capital, for example, 30 percent? Then the IRR rule would have us accept the project if we used the higher value (88.62 percent) as the project's statistic but reject it if we used the lower IRR (23.62 percent). Of course, since the project generates a negative NPV if *i* is 30 percent, we would actually want to reject the project.

Using the IRR technique requires a bit more complicated analysis if we come across more than one valid IRR like this. Perhaps the best thing to do in such a situation is to simply use a decision statistic other than IRR on projects with non-normal cash flows.

If you (or, more likely, upper management) insist on using IRR with non-normal cash flows, you are going to need to use some trial and error to find all the possible IRRs.

It will help to know how many there might possibly be. According to the Rule of Signs,[2] we can end up with no more different positive IRRs than the number of sign changes in the cash flows—that is, inflows to outflows or outflows to inflows. Since our non-normal cash flow set shows two sign changes (one change from positive to negative and one change from negative to positive), we know that the two IRRs we have found constitute the entire possible set.

Luckily we can solve IRR's problems associated with non-normal cash flows by using the modified internal rate of return (MIRR), which also accounts for another problem associated with IRR, that of an unrealistic reinvestment rate assumption.

Differing Reinvestment Rate Assumptions of NPV and IRR

In addition to the problems associated with non-normal cash flows and handling mutually exclusive projects discussed above, IRR also has a different assumption than NPV concerning what we do with the cash inflows once we get them back. IRR assumes that any cash inflows will be reinvested in another project with the same earning power as the first project, while NPV assumes that cash inflows will be reinvested at the cost of capital, i.

Which assumption is more reasonable? NPV's is because one way to effectively "earn" the cost of capital is to pay back your capital investors, and all companies have this option. On the other hand, IRR's assumption seems a little far-fetched: If we assume that this project beat out a bunch of other projects at step 2 of the decision process, it must have had the highest possible IRR among all the alternatives, right? But now that the cash flows are rolling in, we find another project with *the same* "highest" possible rate of return? Seems like a little too much to expect, doesn't it?

Modified Internal Rate of Return Statistic LG13-4

The name **modified internal rate of return** is a little misleading. We are going to calculate IRR the same way we did before, but we are going to *modify* the set of cash flows to account for the cost of capital before we calculate IRR. We first use the cost of capital to "move" all the negative cash flows to the initial project start date (i.e., time 0) and all the positive cash inflows to the project termination date—and only *then* will we use the regular steps to calculate IRR.

IRRs, MIRRs, and NPV Profiles with Mutually Exclusive Projects LG13-5

Even if we use the MIRR method for a project with non-normal cash flows, we can still run into problems if we're trying to use it to choose between mutually exclusive projects.

Two (or more) projects are **mutually exclusive** if management can accept one, the other, or neither, but not both, projects. As we will discuss, if we compare two mutually exclusive projects using a rate-based decision statistic, problems can arise if the projects' cash flows exhibit differences in *scale* or *timing* (i.e., the size of the initial investment in each

time out!

13-5 Is it possible for the NPV profile of a finite set of normal cash flows to never cross the *x*-axis?

13-6 Suppose a normal set of cash flows has an IRR equal to zero. Would NPV accept or reject such a project?

modified internal rate of return (MIRR) A capital budgeting method that converts a project's cash flows using a more consistent reinvestment rate prior to applying the IRR decision rule.

mutually exclusive projects Groups or pairs of projects where you can accept one but not all.

the Math Coach on...

MIRR Using Financial Calculators and Spreadsheet Programs

" Notice that we have assumed that both the positive and negative cash flows get moved using the same interest rate. In many situations, practitioners want to move the negative cash flows using one interest rate and the positive cash flows using another. Because of this, both spreadsheet programs and more advanced financial calculators allow for the use of two interest rates in exactly that way. For now, if you are using a calculator or spreadsheet program that requires two interest rates, just use the cost of capital for both rates. "

EXAMPLE 13-7

MIRR Calculation LG13-4

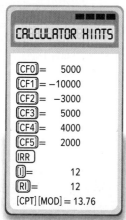

CALCULATOR HINTS

[CF0] =	5000
[CF1] =	−10000
[CF2] =	−3000
[CF3] =	5000
[CF4] =	4000
[CF5] =	2000
[IRR]	
[I] =	12
[RI] =	12
[CPT] [MOD] =	13.76

Turning once again to the sample non-normal project cash flows in Table 13.7, and assuming that the firm still faces a cost of capital of 12 percent, we convert the cash flows as shown in Table 13.8.

▼ **TABLE 13.8** MIRR Cash Flow Adjustments for Sample Project with Non-normal Cash Flows

Year:	0	1	2	3	4	5
Cash flow	$5,000.00	−$10,000.00	−$3,000.00	$5,000.00	$4,000.00	$2,000.00

SOLUTION:

Finding the PV of just the negative cash flows

Year:	0	1	2	3	4	5
Cash flow		−$10,000.00	−$3,000.00			
Present value of cash flows at 12 percent		−8,928.57	−2,391.58			
Sum of PV of cash flows	−$11,320.15					

and finding the FV of just the positive cash flows

Year:	0	1	2	3	4	5
Cash flow	$5,000.00			$5,000.00	$4,000.00	$2,000.00
Future value of cash flows at 12 percent	8,811.71			6,272.00	4,480.00	2,000.00
Sum of PV of cash flows						21,563.71

gives us the following set of modified cash flows:

Year:	0	1	2	3	4	5
Cash flow	−$11,320.15					$21,563.71

With this new set of modified cash flows, the MIRR is

$$0 = \frac{-\$11,320.15}{(1 + IRR)^0} + \frac{\$21,563.71}{(1 + IRR)^5}$$

$IRR = 0.1376$, or 13.76%

Since our MIRR decision statistic exceeds the 12 percent cost of capital, we would accept the project under the MIRR method, which uses the same benchmark as the IRR rule. Notice that, regardless of how many possible IRRs a project may have, it will only ever have one possible MIRR. When you take a bunch of cash flows and convert them into two cash flows, one negative and one positive, you will only ever see one change in sign.

The spreadsheet solution is:

	A	B	C
1	Interest	12%	
2	Year	Cash Flow	
3	0	$5,000	
4	1	-$10,000	
5	2	-$3,000	
6	3	$5,000	
7	4	$4,000	
8	5	$2,000	
9			
10	MIRR	13.76%	=MIRR(B3:B8,B1,B1)

Microsoft Excel

As noted above, the Excel MIRR(values,finance_rate,reinvest_rate) function allows for different borrowing ("finance_rate") and reinvestment rates in its calculation of the MIRR statistic. In the real world, firms often do face higher borrowing rates than the rates they can earn by reinvesting in comparable-risk marketable securities, so moving the negative cash flows to the beginning of the project using the borrowing rate and moving the positive cash flows to the end of the project at the (lower) reinvestment rate can have a conservative impact on the calculated MIRR statistic, causing it to be a little lower than it would be if the borrowing and reinvestment rates were equal.

However, for most firms, particularly large ones, the difference between the two rates is fairly small and fails to take into account the presence of any "internal" reinvestment opportunities in other projects, so we will make the assumption, unless specifically told otherwise, that the two rates are the same. This means that we will wind up having to enter the same rate twice when we use the Excel MIRR() function.

Similar to Problems 13-6, 13-12, Self-Test Problem 1

project). Over time, a "large" project that earns a slightly lower rate of return may be a better choice for the firm than a "small" project that earns a higher rate, but we will see that the rate-based decision techniques do not do well in choosing between these types of alternative projects.

What makes two or more projects mutually exclusive? Generally, mutually exclusive projects either share a common asset or target a common market, but the firm can only spare resources for one of them, or the market may only accept one product. Consider the prototypical example of mutually exclusive projects: A landowner owns two plots of land on either side of a river that people want to cross, and she is considering either building a bridge or operating a ferry for that purpose.

First, let us assume there is enough land on each lot to provide space for bridge footings or for pier pilings, but not for both. In this case, the two plots of land represent assets that the two projects cannot share, which is the first factor making the bridge and the ferry mutually exclusive projects.

Stockbyte/Getty Images

Second, even if the land provided enough room to build both ferry landing piers and bridge footings, it stands to reason that no one would take the ferry if they could simply drive across the bridge—so the two projects' inability to share a potential target market provides a second reason why the projects are mutually exclusive.

To see the problems associated with choosing between two mutually exclusive projects using a rate-based decision statistic, let us suppose that we face a choice between two mutually exclusive projects with the cash flows shown in Table 13.9.

Calculating the NPVs for these two projects across a range of possible rates as shown in Table 13.10 will yield the NPV profiles shown in Figure 13.3.

As you can see approximately (and calculate precisely), A's IRR equals 32.88 percent and B's equals 40.59 percent. You will also notice that the two NPV profiles cross each other in the first quadrant, and that intersection is exactly what is going to cause problems for us as we try to apply an IRR decision rule.

To see why, recall our discussion of the three-step decision process necessary for mutually exclusive projects, and go through that process for both NPV and IRR using a couple of not-so-arbitrary interest rates.

▼ **TABLE 13.9** Sample Mutually Exclusive Projects

Year:	0	1	2	3	4	5
Project A cash flows	−$800	$600	$500	$40	$0	$200
Project B cash flows	−400	250	200	250	50	100

▼ **TABLE 13.10** NPV Profiles

i	NPV A	NPV B
0%	$540.00	$450.00
2	487.66	409.68
4	439.15	372.48
6	394.07	338.08
8	352.09	306.22
10	312.91	276.63
12	276.27	249.12
14	241.92	223.48
16	209.67	199.54
18	179.33	177.16
20	150.75	156.20
22	123.76	136.54
24	98.25	118.07
26	74.10	100.69
28	51.21	84.32
30	29.47	68.88
32	8.80	54.30
34	−10.86	40.51
36	−29.61	27.45
38	−47.49	15.07
40	−64.56	3.33

▼**FIGURE 13.3** NPV Profiles for Sample Mutually Exclusive Projects

Notice how the two profiles cross each other in the first quadrant. How will this intersection affect how we apply an IRR decision?

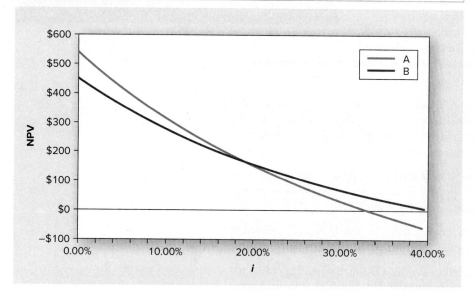

First, let us suppose that the project would be subject to a 30 percent cost of capital. In that case, as per Table 13.11, the NPV for project A would be $29.47 and the NPV for project B would be $68.88. This means that project B would win the runoff. Since its NPV is greater than zero, the NPV decision rule would have us also accept project B.

Likewise, if we were using IRR in the same situation, project B's IRR of 40.59 percent would win the runoff over project A's IRR of 32.88 percent. Since 40.59 percent is greater than the 30 percent cost of capital, IRR would also have us accept project B. These results appear in Table 13.11.

Now let's see what happens if the cost of capital is, say, 10 percent. In that case, as per Table 13.10, the NPV for project A would be $312.91 and the NPV for project B would be $276.63. This means that project A would now win the runoff and, ultimately, would be accepted under the NPV statistic as well.

However, if we were using IRR in the same situation, project B's IRR of 40.59 percent would *still* win the runoff over project A's IRR of 32.88 percent, and since 40.59 percent is greater than the 30 percent cost of capital, IRR would continue to have us accept project B. These results are summarized in Table 13.12.

Why is IRR still choosing project B, despite the 30 percent cost of capital? Well, IRR's refusal to "change its mind"[3] arises from a combination of how we calculate the statistic and how we use it in the three-step decision process. Think about it this way: The NPV statistic includes the cost of capital in its calculation, so when we get to the runoff, NPV is able to make an **interest-rate-cognizant** decision. IRR does not incorporate the cost of capital in calculating its statistic. Therefore, when it reaches step 2, it will always be comparing the same two IRRs for two particular projects, no matter what the cost of capital is.

The implication here is that for any interest rate to the right of where the two NPV profiles cross, NPV and IRR will make the same accept/reject decision. For rates to the left of the crossover point, NPV will choose the right project, but IRR will choose the wrong project. So, because it is sort of important, how do we calculate the rate at which the two NPV profiles cross? Well, we mathematically manipulate each NPV profile until one comes as close to the x-axis as possible, and then figure out the rate at which they cross each other as the IRR of the other project.

It sounds complicated, but it really is not. All we have to do is subtract one project's cash flows from those of the other, period by period, to get a new set of cash flows that show the differences between the original two projects' cash flows, and then find the IRR of these differences. The values for the cash flows of "A − B," the calculated values for the

interest-rate cognizant A decision-making process that includes the cost of capital calculation.

▼ **TABLE 13.11** Decision Process for Projects A and B at *i* = 30%

NPV

1. Compute the statistic for each project.	$NPV_A = \$29.47$
2. Have a runoff between the mutually exclusive projects, choosing the one with the best statistic.	$NPV_B = \$68.88$ $NPV_B > NPV_A$
3. Compare the computed statistic for the winner of the runoff to the benchmark to decide whether to accept or reject.	$NPV_B > 0$

IRR

1. Compute the statistic for each project.	$IRR_A = 32.88\%$
2. Have a runoff between the mutually exclusive projects, choosing the one with the best statistic.	$IRR_B = 40.59\%$ $IRR_B > IRR_A$
3. Compare the computed statistic for the winner of the runoff to the benchmark to decide whether to accept or reject.	$IRR_B > 30\%$

▼ **TABLE 13.12** Decision Process for Projects A and B at *i* = 10%

NPV

1. Compute the statistic for each project.	$NPV_A = \$312.91$
2. Have a runoff between the mutually exclusive projects, choosing the one with the best statistic.	$NPV_B = \$276.63$ $NPV_A > NPV_B$
3. Compare the computed statistic for the winner of the runoff to the benchmark to decide whether to accept or reject.	$NPV_A > 0$

IRR

1. Compute the statistic for each project.	$IRR_A = 32.88\%$
2. Have a runoff between the mutually exclusive projects, choosing the one with the best statistic.	$IRR_B = 40.59\%$ $IRR_B > IRR_A$
3. Compare the computed statistic for the winner of the runoff to the benchmark to decide whether to accept or reject.	$IRR_B > 10\%$

▼**FIGURE 13.4** Translated NPV Profiles

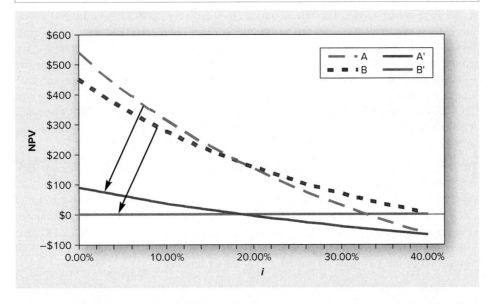

NPV profile of these differences, and the resulting translated NPV profiles appear in Table 13.13, Table 13.14, and Figure 13.4, respectively. Note that A′ will be equal to "A − B," while B′ will be the new, translated, *x*-axis.

▼ TABLE 13.14 NPV Profile, A – B

i	NPV, A – B
0%	$ 90.00
2	77.98
4	66.67
6	55.99
8	45.88
10	36.28
12	27.15
14	18.45
16	10.13
18	2.17
20	−5.45
22	−12.77
24	−19.81
26	−26.59
28	−33.12
30	−39.41
32	−45.49
34	−51.37
36	−57.06
38	−62.56
40	−67.89

▼ TABLE 13.13 Difference in Cash Flows—Sample Mutually Exclusive Projects

Year:	0	1	2	3	4	5
Project A cash flows	−$800	$600	$500	$ 40	$ 0	$200
Project B cash flows	−400	250	200	250	50	100
A – B	−400	350	300	−210	−50	100

The crossover rate will be equal to the IRR of the "A − B" cash flows:

$$0 = \frac{-\$400}{(1+IRR)^0} + \frac{\$350}{(1+IRR)^1} + \frac{\$300}{(1+IRR)^2} + \frac{-\$210}{(1+IRR)^3}$$
$$+ \frac{-\$50}{(1+IRR)^4} + \frac{\$100}{(1+IRR)^5}$$

$IRR = 0.1856$, or 18.56%

So now, IRR will give us the correct answer for these two projects if i is greater than 18.56 percent, and will choose exactly the wrong project if i is less than 18.56 percent.

You may have noticed that the set of "A − B" cash flows is *not* normal. How, then, can we feel comfortable using IRR to calculate the crossover rate given that we have previously decided not to use IRR with non-normal cash flows? Well, this is a special case: We knew that the two original projects' cash flows *were* normal. So we intuitively understood that their NPV profiles, while not exactly straight lines, at least sloped downward continually. So, if two "almost straight" lines do cross, they are probably only going to cross once. That is, we expect only one solution to the IRR problem for the "A − B" differences in cash flows.

Also notice that we have to worry about IRR giving incorrect decisions only if the NPV profiles cross in the so-called first quadrant of the graph. If they cross outside this quadrant at a rate higher than both projects' IRRs, then we do not have to worry about problems with IRR choosing the wrong project. Any cost of capital high enough for IRR to reject the project at the third step of the IRR decision process will also result in a negative NPV.[4]

MIRR Strengths and Weaknesses

As we have constructed it, the MIRR statistic explicitly corrects IRR's faulty and unreasonable reinvestment rate assumption, implicitly fixing any problems with non-normal cash flows along the way. However, it does not correct the problem of IRR choosing the wrong mutually exclusive project for a particular range of rates. For example, even if we go back to the two sample mutually exclusive projects of Table 13.9 and compute each project's MIRR (using a 12 percent rate to move the cash flows), we will still see that the MIRR of project B (23.39 percent) will *always* be greater than the MIRR of project A (18.85 percent), causing the MIRR to also choose the incorrect project to the left of the crossover rate.

There is an old joke in computer programming that gets reused every time a major software product is revised: "That's not a bug; it's a feature!" Well, this "problem" we are experiencing with IRR and MIRR, as well as NPV, truly *is* a feature. It's a feature of all rate-based decision statistics: They tend to focus on the rate of return *per dollar invested* at the expense of ignoring *how many* dollars are getting invested in each project. IRR and MIRR chose project B all the time because, even though it sometimes had a lower NPV, it was always earning a higher rate of return *per dollar invested*.

What causes this confusion? The two cash flows differ in timing and scale. Looking back at the cash flows associated with our two mutually exclusive projects again (shown again in Table 13.15) we see that project B costs only half as much as project A. Also, project B has a "flatter," less steeply sloped, indifference curve.

time out!

13-7 Suppose two projects with normal cash flows, X and Y, have exactly the same required initial investment, but X has a longer payback. Can we say anything about X's IRR versus that of Y?

13-8 Assume you are evaluating a project that requires an initial investment of $5,000 at time zero, then another investment of $4,000 in one year, after which it will have cash inflows of $3,000 per year for five years. How many IRRs could this project possibly have?

LG13-1

Year:	0	1	2	3	4	5
Project A cash flows	−$800	$600	$500	$40	$0	$200
Project B cash flows	−400	250	200	250	50	100

time **out!**

13-9 For a project with normal cash flows, what would you expect the relationship to be between its IRR and its MIRR?

13-10 Describe how you would go about calculating the IRR of a perpetuity.

13.7 • PROFITABILITY INDEX LG13-6

Another popular rate-based decision technique is the **profitability index (PI).** PI is based upon NPV, so its results will more closely resemble NPV than will those of IRR or PB/DPB. PI takes the present value of a project's future cash flows and standardizes them by simply dividing by the project's initial investment. The result: We get a decision statistic that measures "bang per buck invested." Such a measure comes in handy when the firm faces resource constraints concerning how much capital is available for new projects.

> **profitability index (PI)** A decision rule and associated methodology for converting the NPV statistic into a rate-based metric.

Profitability Index Statistic

The mathematics of computing the PI is straightforward:

$$PI = \frac{NPV + CF_0}{CF_0} \qquad (13\text{-}10)$$

EXAMPLE 13-8

For interactive versions of this example, log in to Connect or go to mhhe.com/Cornett6e.

Calculation of Profitability Index LG13-6

Turning yet again to the sample project cash flows in Table 13.6, the PI for that project will be

$$PI = \frac{\$2{,}258.15 + \$10{,}000}{\$10{,}000} = 1.23$$

The spreadsheet solution is:

	A	B	C
1	Interest	12%	
2	Year	Cash Flow	
3	0	-$10,000	
4	1	$2,500	
5	2	$3,500	
6	3	$5,000	
7	4	$4,000	
8	5	$2,000	
9			
10	PI	1.23	=NPV(B1,B4:B8)/ABS(B3)

Microsoft Excel

Calculating the PI in Excel is most easily done by computing the NPV of the future (i.e., other than time 0) cash flows and then dividing it by the absolute value of the time 0 cash flow.

Similar to Problems 13-7, 13-14

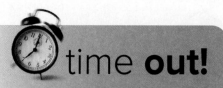

time out!

13-11 There is another version of the PI that uses the NPV as its numerator. How would you expect that version's benchmark to change from the version of PI we initially discussed?

13-12 Suppose you have a project whose discounted payback is equal to its termination date. What can you say for sure about its PI? (*Hint:* What will the project's NPV be?)

Profitability Index Benchmark

Because of its close linkage to the NPV statistic, PI's benchmark is, not surprisingly, identical to that of NPV:

$$\text{Accept project if PI} \geq 1$$
$$\text{Reject project if PI} < 1 \tag{13-11}$$

Though we might be tempted to assume that, like IRR and MIRR, we should compare the PI to the cost of capital, this is not the case. Remember that the NPV already includes the necessary investment, so any PI above zero is "found money" or the present value of expected economic profits. In this case, the PI of 1.23 is telling us that the project will, roughly speaking, earn the equivalent of a 23 percent return on the initial investment of $10,000 above and beyond the return necessary to repay the initial cost.

Your Turn...

Questions

1. Is the set of cash flows depicted below normal or non-normal? Explain. *(LG13-1)*

Time:	0	1	2	3	4	5
Cash flow	−$100	−$50	−$80	$0	$100	$100

2. Derive an accept/reject rule for IRR similar to equation 13-8 that would make the correct decision on cash flows that are non-normal, but that always have one large positive cash flow at time zero followed by a series of negative cash flows. *(LG13-1)*

Time:	0	1	2	3	4	5
Cash flow	+	−	−	−	−	−

3. Is it possible for a company to initiate two products that target the same market that are not mutually exclusive? *(LG13-1)*

4. Suppose that your company used "APV," or "All-the-Present Value-Except-CF_0," to analyze capital budgeting projects. What would this rule's benchmark value be? *(LG13-3)*

5. Under what circumstances could payback and discounted payback be equal? *(LG13-2)*

6. Could a project's MIRR ever exceed its IRR? *(LG13-4)*

7. If you had two mutually exclusive, normal-cash-flow projects whose NPV profiles crossed at all points, for which range of interest rates would IRR give the right accept/reject answer? *(LG13-5)*

8. Suppose a company wanted to double the firm's value with the next round of capital budgeting project decisions. To what would it set the PI benchmark to make this goal? *(LG13-6)*

9. Suppose a company faced different borrowing and lending rates. How would this range change the way that you would compute the MIRR statistic? *(LG13-4)*

Problems

BASIC PROBLEMS

13-1 NPV with Normal Cash Flows Compute the NPV statistic for Project Y and indicate whether the firm should accept or reject the project with the cash flows shown below if the appropriate cost of capital is 12 percent. *(LG13-3)*

Project Y					
Time:	0	1	2	3	4
Cash flow	–$8,000	$3,350	$4,180	$1,520	$300

13-2 NPV with Non-normal Cash Flows Compute the NPV statistic for Project U and recommend whether the firm should accept or reject the project with the cash flows shown below if the appropriate cost of capital is 10 percent. *(LG13-3)*

Project U						
Time:	0	1	2	3	4	5
Cash flow	–$1,000	$350	$1,480	–$520	$300	–$100

13-3 Payback Compute the payback statistic for Project B and decide whether the firm should accept or reject the project with the cash flows shown below if the appropriate cost of capital is 12 percent and the maximum allowable payback is three years. *(LG13-2)*?

Project B						
Time:	0	1	2	3	4	5
Cash flow	–$11,000	$3,350	$4,180	$1,520	$0	$1,000

13-4 Discounted Payback Compute the discounted payback statistic for Project C and recommend whether the firm should accept or reject the project with the cash flows shown below if the appropriate cost of capital is 8 percent and the maximum allowable discounted payback is three years. *(LG13-2)*

Project C						
Time:	0	1	2	3	4	5
Cash flow	–$1,000	$480	$480	$520	$300	$100

13-5 Spreadsheet Problem: IRR Compute the IRR statistic for Project F and note whether the firm should accept or reject the project with the cash flows shown below if the appropriate cost of capital is 12 percent. *(LG13-4)*

Project F					
Time:	0	1	2	3	4
Cash flow	–$11,000	$3,350	$4,180	$1,520	$2,000

13-6 Spreadsheet Problem: MIRR Compute the MIRR statistic for Project I and indicate whether to accept or reject the project with the cash flows shown below if the appropriate cost of capital is 12 percent. *(LG13-4)*

Project I					
Time:	0	1	2	3	4
Cash flow	−$11,000	$5,330	$4,480	$1,520	$2,000

13-7 **PI** Compute the PI statistic for Project Z and advise the firm whether to accept or reject the project with the cash flows shown below if the appropriate cost of capital is 8 percent. *(LG13-6)*

Project Z						
Time:	0	1	2	3	4	5
Cash flow	−$1,000	$350	$480	$650	$300	$100

13-8 **Spreadsheet Problem: Multiple IRRs** How many possible IRRs could you find for the following set of cash flows? *(LG13-1)*

Time:	0	1	2	3	4
Cash flow	−$2111,000	−$39,350	$440,180	$217,520	−$2,000

INTERMEDIATE PROBLEMS

Use this information to answer the next six questions. If you should not use a particular decision technique, indicate why.

Suppose your firm is considering investing in a project with the cash flows shown below, that the required rate of return on projects of this risk class is 11 percent, and that the maximum allowable payback and discounted payback statistics for your company are 3 and 3.5 years, respectively.

Time:	0	1	2	3	4	5
Cash flow	−$235,000	$65,800	$84,000	$141,000	$122,000	$81,200

13-9 **Spreadsheet Problem: Payback** Use the payback decision rule to evaluate this project; should it be accepted or rejected? *(LG13-2)*

13-10 **Spreadsheet Problem: Discounted Payback** Use the discounted payback decision rule to evaluate this project; should it be accepted or rejected? *(LG13-2)*

13-11 **Spreadsheet Problem: IRR** Use the IRR decision rule to evaluate this project; should it be accepted or rejected? *(LG13-4)*

13-12 **Spreadsheet Problem: MIRR** Use the MIRR decision rule to evaluate this project; should it be accepted or rejected? *(LG13-4)*

13-13 **Spreadsheet Problem: NPV** Use the NPV decision rule to evaluate this project; should it be accepted or rejected? *(LG13-3)*

13-14 **Spreadsheet Problem: PI** Use the PI decision rule to evaluate this project; should it be accepted or rejected? *(LG13-6)*

ADVANCED PROBLEMS

Use the project cash flows for the two mutually exclusive projects shown below to answer the following two questions.

Time	Project A Cash Flow	Project B Cash Flow
0	−$725	−$850
1	100	200
2	250	200
3	250	200
4	200	200
5	100	200
6	100	200
7	100	200

13-15 Spreadsheet Problem: NPV Profiles Graph the NPV profiles for both projects on a common chart, making sure that you identify all of the "crucial" points. *(LG13-5)*

 13-16 Spreadsheet Problem: IRR Applicability For what range of possible interest rates would you want to use IRR to choose between these two projects? For what range of rates would you NOT want to use IRR? *(LG13-5)*

 13-17 Spreadsheet Problem: Multiple IRRs Construct an NPV profile and determine EXACTLY how many non-negative IRRs you can find for the following set of cash flows: *(LG13-5)*

Time:	0	1	2	3	4	5	6	7
Cash flow	−$200	$400	$150	−$100	−$100	−$300	$200	−$300

Notes

CHAPTER 13

1. As explained in earlier chapters, by definition the expected rate of return incorporates risk.

2. First described by René Descartes in his 1637 manuscript *La Geometrie.*

3. You will sometimes hear this phenomenon referred to as IRR being "myopic," which is the technical name for nearsightedness.

4. Actually, in such cases the IRR rule will still choose the wrong project at step 2 of the decision process, the runoff, but the last step of the decision process, the comparison with the benchmark, will save us. The wrong project may be chosen at the runoff, but if they are both bad projects, they will be rejected anyway.

fourteen

working capital

management and policies

n this chapter, we focus on the major trade-off implicit in funding net working capital. By and large, the trade-off involves comparing the explicit costs of funding an investment in current assets with the **shortage costs** associated with the firm not having enough cash, inventory, or accounts receivable.

   As we'll see, the firm's ideal solution to providing net working capital would be to get someone else to foot the bill. Though this may be a valid approach to fund *some* of the firm's current assets, it's usually difficult to get someone else to cover the *entire* amount of net working capital necessary to run the firm efficiently. We will, however, discuss how to shift those costs elsewhere as much as possible in this chapter by covering the following topics:

1. How to determine the optimal amount of investment in current assets.
2. How to measure the portion of current assets that the firm is responsible for funding.
3. How to choose the source of funding for that portion of current assets.

continued on p. 396

LEARNING GOALS

LG14-1 Set overall objectives of a good working capital policy.

LG14-2 Discuss how net working capital serves the firm.

LG14-3 Analyze the firm's operating and cash cycles to determine what funding for current assets the firm needs.

LG14-4 Model the optimal trade-off between carrying costs and shortage costs that dictates the firm's current asset investment.

LG14-5 Compare the flexible and restrictive approaches to financing current assets.

LG14-6 Differentiate among sources of short-term financing available for funding current assets.

LG14-7 Justify the firm's need to hold cash.

LG14-8 Use the Baumol and Miller-Orr models for determining cash policy.

LG14-9 Identify sources of float and show how to control float for the firm's disbursement and collection functions.

LG14-10 Identify firms' choices for using excess cash.

LG14-11 Connect the firm's credit terms and collection policy and the amount of capital the firm has invested in accounts receivable.

LG14-12 Be able to create and interpret a cash budget.

Chewbacca Manufacturing expects sales of $32 million next year. CM's cost of goods sold normally runs at 55 percent of sales; inventory requirements are usually 10 percent of annual sales; the average accounts receivable balance is one-sixth of annual sales; and the average accounts payable balance is 5 percent of sales. If all sales are on credit, what will Chewbacca's level of net working capital and its cash cycle be? **(See the solution at the end of the book.)**

continued from p. 395

LG14-1, 14-2

shortage costs Costs associated with not having sufficient cash, inventory, or accounts receivable.

operations management The area of management concerned with designing and overseeing the process of production.

just in time (JIT) A production strategy that attempts to improve a firm's return on investment by reducing in-process inventory and associated carrying costs as much as possible.

Barabas Economic Order Quantity (EOQ) The inventory order quantity that minimizes total holding and ordering costs.

Depending on the firm's line of business and the extent to which it provides physical goods versus services, the management of portions of the current assets may come under a specialized department responsible for the firm's **operations management.** Though beyond the scope of this book, if you ever get a chance to read about the models used in operations management, you'll notice that many of the concepts we'll discuss here are directly related to the inventory management models used extensively in operations management. For example, our discussion below of flexible, restrictive, and compromise financing of current assets would fit right in with the concept of **"just in time" (JIT)** inventory management, while the Baumol model we'll be discussing for determining the target cash balance is a simple extension of the **Barabas Economic Order Quantity (EOQ)** model for minimizing total inventory holding and ordering costs. ■

14.1 • REVISITING THE BALANCE-SHEET MODEL OF THE FIRM

Recall our discussion of the balance sheet in Chapter 2. At a glance, the balance sheet brings together the firm's assets or sources of financing and its liabilities, or investments, as Table 14.1 shows. Net working capital reflects the need for the firm to generate funds to stay in business and maximize profit.

▼ **TABLE 14.1** The Basic Balance Sheet

Total Assets	Total Liabilities and Equity
Current assets	Current liabilities
Cash and marketable securities	Accrued wages and taxes
Accounts receivable	Accounts payable
Inventory	Notes payable
Fixed assets	Long-term debt
Gross plant and equipment	Stockholders' equity
Less: Depreciation	Preferred stock
Net plant and equipment	Common stock and paid-in surplus
Other long-term assets	Retained earnings

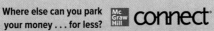
Wanda has saved enough money to go back to grad school. She is planning to put the money in a money market account where it will earn 3.5 percent. If she anticipates slowly drawing the money out over the course of her time in grad school at a constant rate of $25,000 per year but is charged a commission of $9.95 every time she sells shares, how much should she take out of the mutual fund at a time? **(See the solution at the end of the book.)**

Where else can you park your money . . . for less?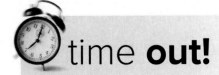

Earlier in the text, we discussed the fact that current assets, while the most liquid, are also usually less profitable than fixed assets. Because of that, many managers view net working capital as a "necessary evil," that is, as something they *have* to fund, but would really rather not.

And they *do* have to fund it: Most firms can't sell finished goods without inventory to display, or without offering to sell to customers on credit, and so forth.

But just because a firm has to fund *some* current assets does not mean that it has to fund *too much* of it. Ideally, the firm should invest in each type of current assets only up to the point where the marginal benefit of each dollar tied up by doing so just equals the marginal **opportunity cost** of not having that dollar invested in fixed assets with positive net present value (NPV).

Also, the firm normally is able to shift part of the burden of funding current assets through the judicious use of current liabilities. While we normally think of liabilities as the "bad" entries (compared to assets) on a balance sheet, from a cash flow perspective they actually act as *sources* of capital, while assets represent, in a sense, "money pits" that require us to *use* capital to fund them. To the extent that the firm can partially offset the capital they have tied up in necessary current assets by buying from suppliers on credit, or by getting employees to work for them in advance of getting paid, such *accounts payable* or *accrued wages* are actually good things.

This line of reasoning helps explain why some managers like to think of net working capital as "the net amount of current assets that the firm has to fund, above and beyond those that someone else funds for us."

14.2 • TRACING CASH AND NET WORKING CAPITAL LG14-3

To trace cash flows through the firm's operations, we must measure the **operating cycle**—the time necessary to acquire raw materials, turn them into finished goods, sell them, and receive payment for them—as well as the firm's **cash cycle.**

If we continue in the vein of thinking of net working capital as the portion of current assets that the firm must fund (above and beyond those assets funded by current liabilities), then we can similarly think of the firm's cash cycle as *the portion of the operating cycle that the firm must finance.*

time out!

14-1 Why might a firm's creditors *not* think of net working capital as a necessary evil, but rather as a good thing?

14-2 If demand for a firm's products suddenly slows down so that inventory increases while sales decrease, how will the firm's needs for net working capital react?

opportunity cost The dollar cost or forgone opportunity of using an asset already owned by the firm, or a person already employed by the firm, in a new project.

operating cycle The time required to acquire raw materials and to produce, sell, and receive payment for the finished goods.

cash cycle The operating cycle minus the average payment period.

The Operating Cycle

To measure the firm's operating cycle, we need to turn to some of the ratios that we discussed in Chapter 3:

$$\text{Operating cycle} = \text{Days' sales in inventory} + \text{Average collection period}$$
$$= \frac{\text{Inventory} \times 365}{\text{Cost of goods sold}} + \frac{\text{Accounts receivable} \times 365}{\text{Credit sales}} \qquad (14\text{-}1)$$

The Cash Cycle

The firm's cash cycle will simply be the operating cycle minus the average payment period, as shown in Figure 14.1.

▼**FIGURE 14.1** Relationship between Operating and Cash Cycles

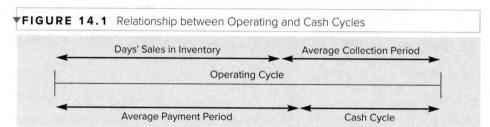

The firm's cash cycle will simply be the operating cycle minus the average payment period.

EXAMPLE 14-1

For interactive versions of this example, log in to Connect or go to mhhe.com/Cornett6e.

Calculation of Operating Cycle LG14-3

Suppose that MMK Industries has annual sales of $1 million, cost of goods sold of $650,000, average inventories of $116,000, and average accounts receivable of $150,000. Assuming that all MMK's sales are on credit, what will be the firm's operating cycle?

SOLUTION:

The operating cycle will be equal to

$$\text{Operating cycle} = \frac{\text{Inventory} \times 365}{\text{Cost of goods sold}} + \frac{\text{Accounts receivable} \times 365}{\text{Credit sales}}$$
$$= \frac{\$116,000 \times 365}{\$650,000} + \frac{\$150,000 \times 365}{\$1,000,000}$$
$$= 65.14 \text{ days} + 54.75 \text{ days}$$
$$= 119.89 \text{ days}$$

So it will take MMK almost 120 days from the time it receives raw materials to produce, market, sell, and collect the cash for the finished goods.

The spreadsheet solution is:

	A	B	C
1	Sales	$ 1,000,000	
2	CGS	$ 650,000	
3	Inventory	$ 116,000	
4	A/R	$ 150,000	
5			
6	Operating Cycle	119.89	=(B3*365)/B2+(B4*365)/B1

Microsoft Excel

Though there is no built-in function in Excel for calculating operating cycle, the formula is fairly straightforward to implement.

Similar to Problem 14-7

EXAMPLE 14-2

For interactive versions of this example, log in to Connect or go to mhhe.com/Cornett6e.

Calculation of Cash Cycle LG14-3

Extending the previous example, assume that MMK's average accounts payable balance is $120,000. What will be the firm's cash cycle?

SOLUTION:

The cash cycle will be equal to

$$\text{Cash cycle} = \text{Operating cycle} - \frac{\text{Accounts payable} \times 365}{\text{Cost of goods sold}}$$

$$= 119.89 \text{ days} - \frac{\$120,000 \times 365}{\$650,000}$$

$$= 119.89 \text{ days} - 67.38 \text{ days}$$

$$= 52.50 \text{ days}$$

The spreadsheet solution is:

	A	B	C	D	E
1	Sales	$ 1,000,000			
2	CGS	$ 650,000			
3	Inventory	$ 116,000			
4	A/R	$ 150,000		A/P	$ 120,000
5					
6	Operating Cycle	119.89	=(B3*365)/B2+(B4*365)/B1		
7					
8	Cash Cycle	52.50	=B6-(E4*365)/B2		

Microsoft Excel

Continuing the previous example, it is also straightforward to calculate the cash cycle from the operating cycle.

Similar to Problem 14-8

Translating this into a formula yields

$$\text{Cash cycle} = \text{Operating cycle} - \text{Average payment period}$$

$$= \text{Operating cycle} - \frac{\text{Accounts payable} \times 365}{\text{Cost of goods sold}} \qquad (14\text{-}2)$$

Note that even though it will take MMK almost 120 days to turn the raw materials into cash, the cash cycle indicates that the firm will have to foot the bill for its production cycle for only 52.50 days of that time. This is the crux of managing the firm's operating and cash cycles: Minimize the number of days that the firm has to pay for its production cycle.

14.3 • SOME ASPECTS OF SHORT-TERM FINANCIAL POLICY LG14-4

In the last section, we derived the cash cycle by first determining the operating cycle and then subtracting the payment cycle. This derivation suggests two obvious ways that firms can reduce their net working capital needs.

1. They can reduce their cash cycle by managing their need for current assets.
2. They can extend the payment cycle by seeking to obtain as many current liabilities as economically feasible to fund the current assets that they do need.

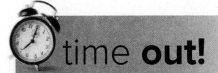

time out!

14-3 How will a firm affect its operating cycle if it can reduce inventory on hand?

14-4 When we compare two firms, will the one with the longer cash cycle tend to have more or less net working capital requirements than the one with a shorter cash cycle, everything else held equal? Why?

finance at work //: investments

carrying costs The opportunity costs associated with having capital tied up in current assets instead of more productive fixed assets and explicit costs necessary to maintain the value of the current assets.

The Size of the Current Assets Investment

Choosing the optimal level of investment in each current asset type involves a trade-off between carrying costs and shortage costs.

Carrying costs are associated with having current assets and fall into two general categories:

1. The opportunity costs associated with having capital tied up in current assets instead of more productive fixed assets.
2. Explicit costs necessary to maintain the value of the current assets.

For example, a car dealer who purchases used vehicles and keeps them in inventory would incur not only the opportunity cost of not being able to invest the money paid for the used vehicles in a more lucrative opportunity, such as new hybrid vehicles, but would also incur explicit costs consisting of rental or lease payments on the piece of property where the used cars are on display and any maintenance costs necessary to keep the cars ready to sell.

Shortage costs are the costs associated with not having enough current assets and can include opportunity costs such as sales lost due to not having enough inventory on hand, as well as any explicit transaction fees paid to replenish the particular type of current asset. For example, consider a camera shop that has a policy to reorder particular lenses from its supplier only if a customer comes in asking for them, and, even then, to order only one lens at a time. In today's business environment, most customers who are seeking an item want it *now*. If that item is out of stock at one store, the customer will probably buy it either at another store or online, resulting in lost sales to the store. If, in addition, we assume that stores pay a shipping fee for every order placed—or that they get quantity discounts if they order in bulk—then the camera shop's current policy will probably result in higher shipping fees and missed volume discounts.

▼FIGURE 14.2 Carrying and Shortage Costs

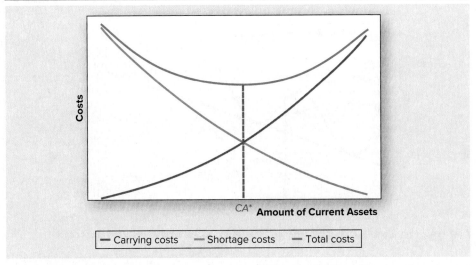

The point at which marginal carrying and shortage costs are equal (*CA**) is the optimal level of investment for each current asset category.

Carrying costs will increase, and shortage costs will decrease, as a firm buys more of any particular asset. Therefore, firms should ideally try to choose the point of an asset's lowest total cost, which occurs where marginal carrying and shortage costs are equal. This level is identified as *CA** in Figure 14.2.

Alternative Financing Policies for Current Assets LG14-5

In a perfect world, a firm would use long-term debt and equity to finance long-term (i.e., fixed) assets and short-term debt to finance current assets. Such an approach would allow the firm to maturity-match assets with their corresponding liabilities, resulting in a low or nonexistent level for net working capital. As we have previously discussed, in the real world, net working capital is usually positive for most firms. The implication: At least some portion of current assets must be financed with long-term debt, equity, or a mixture of both.

Assuming that most firms can expect to have some steady, stable need for current assets throughout their calendar year and additional demand for current assets that fluctuates on some seasonal cycle, a growing firm's total demand for assets would resemble that shown in Figure 14.3.

So, a firm in such a situation faces the basic question of whether it should finance the peaks or the valleys of total asset demand (or somewhere in between) using long-term financing. Figures 14.4, 14.5, and 14.6 illustrate some of these choices.

We usually refer to the decision to finance the peaks of asset demand with long-term debt and equity, shown in Figure 14.4, as a *flexible financing policy.* It provides the firm with a surplus of cash and marketable securities most of the time—except during peak asset demand.

On the opposite side of the continuum, we refer to a decision to finance the troughs or valleys of asset demand with long-term debt and equity, shown in Figure 14.5, as a *restrictive financing policy.* Under this policy, the firm will have to seek short-term

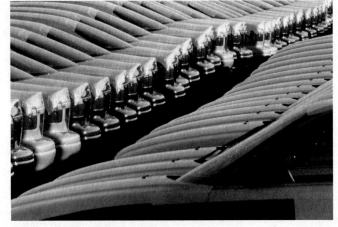

Vehicles kept in inventory incur an opportunity cost.
Comstock Images/Jupiterimages

▼FIGURE 14.3 Components of Current Assets

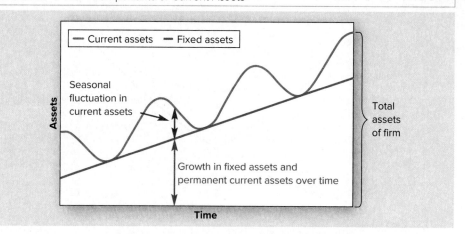

A firm makes long- or short-term financing decisions by examining the peaks and valleys of total asset demand.

▼FIGURE 14.4 Flexible Financing of Current Assets

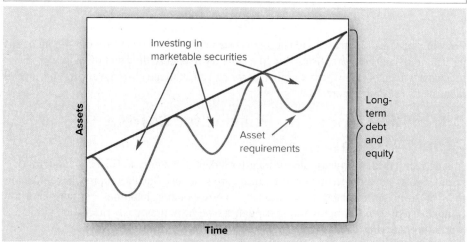

Flexible financing policy reflects the decision to finance the peaks of asset demand with long-term debt and equity.

▼FIGURE 14.5 Flexible Financing of Current Assets

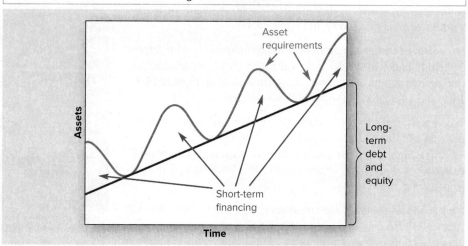

Restrictive financing policy reflects the decision to finance the troughs of asset demand with long-term debt and equity.

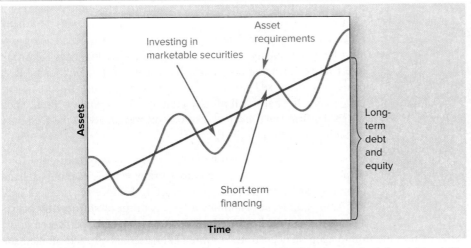

▼FIGURE 14.6 Compromise Financing of Current Assets

Compromise financing policy reflects the decision to finance the seasonally adjusted average level of asset demand with long-term debt and equity.

financing for all peak demand fluctuations for current assets, as well as for in-between demand situations. In some ways, this policy is the most "conservative"; on the other hand, it's also the least convenient for the firm, as it involves seeking some level of short-term financing almost all of the time.

A third choice is to follow a *compromise financing policy,* wherein the firm finances the seasonally adjusted average level of asset demand with long-term debt and equity. The firm uses both short-term financing and short-term investing as needed. Figure 14.6 illustrates such a policy.

Which approach works best? As is the case with almost all working capital decisions, it depends on several factors:

- Current and future expected interest rate levels. If we expect rates to rise in the future, the firm may want to lock in fixed rates for a longer time by shifting toward a flexible financing policy. With falling rates, the opposite would, of course, hold true.

- The spread between short- and long-term rates. Long-term borrowing usually costs more than short-term financing, but the "gap" (called the *spread*) between the two terms may be historically small or large, encouraging firms to shift to a more flexible or restrictive policy, respectively.

- Alternative financing availability and costs, discussed in the following sections. Firms with easy and sustained access to alternative sources will want to shift toward more restrictive policies.

14.4 • THE SHORT-TERM FINANCIAL PLAN LG14-6

Firms that follow any financing policy other than a flexible financing plan will find themselves forced to seek short-term financing at times. Depending on their industry, they may find themselves using unsecured loans, secured loans, or other sources of short-term financing.

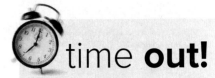

time out!

14-5 Suppose that the gap between short-term rates and long-term rates increases. Would firms tend to shift more toward flexible current asset financing policies or toward more restrictive policies?

14-6 If a firm offers longer credit terms to its customers, what will happen to its carrying costs?

Firms can also use their inventory as collateral for an inventory loan.
Brand X Pictures/PunchStock

Unsecured Loans

For most businesses—particularly smaller ones—the most common way to cover a short-term financing need is to apply at a bank for a commercial loan. The company may expect to need such short-term loans repeatedly in the future—perhaps because it is following a restrictive financing policy but faces seasonal fluctuations in asset demand, as discussed previously. If the bank deems the firm creditworthy enough, the bank will usually grant the firm a *line of credit,* upon which the firm can draw and then pay off repeatedly as the firm goes through those seasonal fluctuations.

Fees for lines of credit can be both explicit (usually taking the form of an interest rate equal to the bank's prime lending rate plus a small premium) and implicit (as a compensating balance requirement and/or a bank's up-front commitment fee). A **compensating balance** is a percentage of the borrowed money (usually 5 to 10 percent) that the bank requires the firm to keep on deposit in the firm's bank accounts. In return, the bank agrees to lend money to the firm.[1]

Commitment fees, if charged, are usually calculated as a flat percentage of the credit line. But banks also charge commitment fees based on the portion of the line of credit "taken down" (i.e., used by the firm) or even of the portion *not* taken down. The amount of fees the bank charges for a line of credit and their type will depend on whether the bank is trying to encourage the use of the line of credit or not.

Secured Loans

Asset-based loans are short-term loans secured by a company's assets. Secured loans carry lower interest rates than unsecured loans, so it is usually in the firm's best interest to provide security (or collateral) when it can. Though real estate, accounts receivable, inventory, and equipment are all sometimes used to back asset-based loans, most firms seeking such a loan to finance seasonal fluctuations in current assets will typically prefer to use inventory or accounts receivable as security for the loan, as they won't wish to encumber long-term assets such as real estate or equipment.

Accounts receivable can either be sold outright to a factor or assigned. A **factor** is an entity who will buy accounts receivable on a discounted basis before they are due, with the spread between the discounted price and the receivable's face value providing the factor with expected compensation for both the time value of money and the expected level of defaults among the accounts receivable. **Assignment** is a process whereby the firm borrows money from another entity, providing in return a lien on the accounts receivable as well as the right of **recourse** (i.e., the legal right to hold the firm responsible for payment of the debt if the accounts receivable debtors do not repay as promised).

Firms can also use their inventory as collateral for an *inventory loan,* a secured short-term loan used to purchase that inventory. Inventory loans include blanket inventory liens, trust receipts, and field warehousing financing. The major difference between the three lies with the question of who owns and keeps the inventory in question:

- Under a blanket inventory lien, the lender gets a lien against all the firm's inventory, but the firm retains ownership and possession.

- When the borrower holds the inventory in trust for the lender, with any proceeds from the sale of the inventory being the property of that lender, the document acknowledging this loan commitment is referred to as the *trust receipt.*

- In field warehousing financing, a public warehouse company takes possession and supervises the inventory for the lender.

Other Sources

Two other primary sources of short-term financing are commercial paper issues and financing through banker's acceptances. **Commercial paper,** which we explore in depth in Chapter 18, is a money-market security, issued by large banks and medium-to-large corporations, that matures in nine months or less. Since these issues have such short durations, and since firms use the proceeds only for current transactions, commercial paper (or simply *paper*) is exempt from registering as a security with the SEC. The corresponding lack of paperwork and regulations to issue short-term debt, along with the fact that commercial paper is usually issued only by firms with very high credit rankings, makes commercial paper cheaper than using a bank line of credit.

A **banker's acceptance (BA)** is a short-term promissory note issued by a corporation, bearing the unconditional guarantee (*acceptance*) of a major bank. The bank guarantee makes them very safe, and the rates are usually roughly equivalent to those charged on commercial paper.

14.5 • CASH MANAGEMENT LG14-7

One common source of confusion when we're discussing net working capital is the difference between a *cash flow* and a *cash account. Cash flows,* which we have discussed in a number of contexts within this book (such as estimating cash flows for proposed new projects in Chapter 12), are a *good* thing. A *cash account,* on the other hand, is a current asset account just like all the other current asset accounts we have been discussing, and it has exactly the same attributes of high liquidity and low profitability that inventory and accounts receivable accounts have: that is, it is, relatively speaking, a *bad* thing from a cash flow perspective.

Reasons for Holding Cash

A firm may keep part of its capital tied up in cash for three primary reasons:

1. **Transaction facilitation**: Firms need cash to pay employees' wages, taxes, suppliers' bills, interest on debts, and stock dividends. Though the firm will have cash coming in from day-to-day operations and any financing activities, the inflows and outflows are not usually perfectly synchronized, so the firm will need to keep enough cash on hand to meet reasonable transaction demands.
2. Compensating balances: As we previously discussed, firms must often keep a certain percentage of borrowed funds in their checking accounts with their lending institution. Since lenders are exempt from paying interest on corporate checking accounts, compensating balances become a cheap source of funds for the lender and represent opportunity costs for borrowing firms.
3. Investment opportunities: In some industries, investment opportunities come and go very quickly. Sometimes, this happens even too quickly for the firm to arrange a loan or seek other financing, so having excess cash on hand may allow the firm to take advantage of investment opportunities that would otherwise be impossible to transact.

To determine how much cash to keep on hand, firms must trade off the opportunity costs associated with holding too much cash against the shortage costs of not holding enough. The two standard models for calculating the trade-offs are the Baumol Model and the Miller-Orr Model.

Determining the Target Cash Balance: The Baumol Model LG14-8

An economist named William Baumol developed the first model designed to minimize the sum of the opportunity costs associated with holding cash and the trading costs associated with converting other assets to cash.[2] Baumol's model is intuitively appealing, and

time out!

14-7 If its bank started charging fees to a firm based upon the portion of a line of credit not taken down, how would the firm's financing policy for current assets likely change? Why would a bank take such a stance?

14-8 If a firm starts selling its accounts receivable to a factor, how will the firm's cash cycle change?

commercial paper An unsecured short-term promissory note issued by a public firm to raise short-term cash, often to finance working capital requirements.

banker's acceptance (BA) A short-term promissory note issued by a corporation, bearing the unconditional guarantee (*acceptance*) of a major bank.

transaction facilitation The use of cash to pay employees' wages, taxes, suppliers' bills, interest on debts, and dividends on stock.

Firms need cash to pay employees' wages and payroll taxes among other things.
Stockbyte/Punchstock Images

analysts still use it in industries for which cash outflows are fairly predictable. For other industries, its use is more problematic due to the model's rather unrealistic assumptions:

- The model assumes that the firm has a constant, perfectly predictable disbursement rate for cash. In reality, disbursement rates are much more variable and unpredictable.

- The model assumes that no cash will come in during the period in question. Since most firms hope to make more money than they pay out, and usually have cash inflows at all times, this assumption is obviously at odds with what we usually see.

- The model does not allow for any **safety stock** of extra cash to buffer the firm against an unexpectedly high demand for cash.

In Baumol's model, cash is assumed to start from a **replenishment level,** C, and then decline smoothly to a value of zero. When cash declines to zero, it can be immediately replenished by selling another C worth of marketable securities, for which the firm has to pay a trading cost of F.

Thus, the model implies that cash levels will follow a cyclical pattern throughout the year. For example, if a firm sells $20,000 worth of marketable securities each time it needs to replenish cash and disburses $5,000 in cash each week, then the cash balance would cycle every four weeks, as shown in Figure 14.7.

Notice another implication of the cash being disbursed at a constant rate. The average cash level should equal one-half of the replenishment level, $C/2$. If the firm can earn an interest rate i on marketable securities, then keeping an average cash balance of $C/2$ will impose an opportunity cost on the firm of

$$\text{Opportunity cost} = \frac{C}{2} \times i \qquad (14\text{-}3)$$

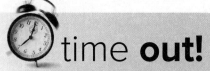

14-9 In what types of industries would firms need more cash on hand for transaction facilitation? In what industries might firms need less?

14-10 If a firm is going to take a loan with a bank that has a compensating balance requirement, how does that affect the amount of money the firm must borrow?

▼**FIGURE 14.7** Cash Flow Patterns of the Baumol Model

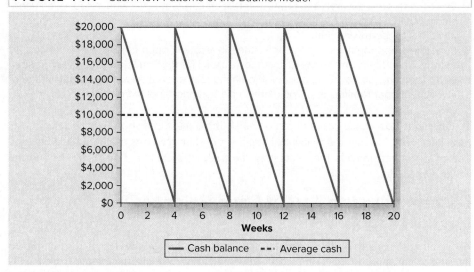

In this model, when cash declines to zero, it can be immediately replenished by selling marketable securities.

If we also assume that a particular firm faces an annual demand for cash of T, then the firm will need to sell marketable securities T/C times during the year, incurring in the process annual trading costs of

$$\text{Trading cost} = \frac{T}{C} \times F \qquad (14\text{-}4)$$

The firm's total annual costs associated with its cash management policy will therefore be

$$\text{Total cost} = \frac{C}{2} \times i + \frac{T}{C} \times F \qquad (14\text{-}5)$$

Solving this for the value of C that minimizes annual costs, C^*, yields

$$C^* = \sqrt{2TF/i} \qquad (14\text{-}6)$$

safety stock Excess amounts of a current asset kept on hand to meet unexpected shocks in demand.

replenishment level The level to which the cash account is "refilled" when marketable securities are sold to recapitalize it.

Determining the Target Cash Balance: The Miller-Orr Model

The Miller-Orr model takes a different approach to calculating the optimal cash management strategy.[3] It assumes that daily net cash flows are random but normally distributed, and allows for both cash inflows and outflows. This model bases its computations on information about

- The lower control limit, L.
- The trading cost for marketable securities per transaction, F.
- The standard deviation in net daily cash flows, σ.
- The daily interest rate on marketable securities, i_{day}.

EXAMPLE 14-3

For interactive versions of this example, log in to Connect or go to mhhe.com/Cornett6e.

Optimal Cash Replenishment under the Baumol Model LG14-8

Suppose that AFS Industries faces an annual demand for cash of $2 million, incurs transaction costs of $150 every time it sells marketable securities, and can earn 6 percent on its marketable securities. What will be the firm's optimal cash replenishment level?

SOLUTION:

The optimal cash replenishment level will be

$$
\begin{aligned}
C^* &= \sqrt{2TF/i} \\
&= \sqrt{2(\$2{,}000{,}000)(\$150)/0.06} \\
&= \$100{,}000
\end{aligned}
$$

The spreadsheet solution is:

	A	B	C
1	Annual Demand for Cash	$ 2,000,000	
2	Transaction Fee	$ 150	
3	Rate on Marketable Securities	6.00%	
4			
5	Optimal Cash Replenishment Level	$ 100,000	=SQRT(2*B1*B2/B3)

Microsoft Excel

Implementing Equation 14-6 is most easily done using the SQRT(number) function.

Similar to Problems 14-10, Self-Test Problem 4

Using their model, Miller and Orr show that the optimal cash return point, Z^*, and upper limit for cash balances, H^*, are equal to

$$Z^* = \sqrt[3]{3F\sigma^2/4\ i_{day}} + L \tag{14-7}$$

$$H^* = 3Z^* - 2L \tag{14-8}$$

Note that the firm determines L and can set it to a nonzero number to recognize the use of safety stock.

The optimal cash return point, Z^*, is analogous to the replenishment level, C^*, in Baumol's model, but with one key difference. Because Baumol's model only allowed for cash disbursements, C^* was always "replenished to" from a level of zero. In the Miller-Orr model, Z^* will be the replenishment level to which cash is replenished when the cash level hits L, but it will also be the return level that cash is brought back *down* to when cash hits H^*.

As Figure 14.8 shows, the firm will reduce cash to $126,101.72 by buying marketable securities when the cash balance gets up to $178,305.16, and it will increase cash to $126,101.72 by selling marketable securities when the cash balance gets down to $100,000.

Other Factors Influencing the Target Cash Balance

Even the Miller-Orr model, the more realistic of the two models because it deals with both cash inflows and outflows, still ignores fundamental factors that influence firms' cash management practices. First, firms also have the option of borrowing short term to meet unexpected demands for cash. Though the short-term borrowing rate faced by the firm is likely to be more expensive than the opportunity cost incurred by selling marketable securities,[4] this isn't necessarily the comparison that matters. If the probability of an unexpected demand for cash causing a firm to borrow in the short term is low enough, or if the amount of interest to be earned by investing in longer-term securities is sufficiently higher than that to be earned on marketable securities, then it might be worth it for the firm to risk occasionally paying a relatively high interest rate on short-term borrowing if it can earn a substantially higher return by investing the funds that would have been tied up in marketable securities in something more lucrative.

▼**FIGURE 14.8** Cash Flow Patterns of the Miller-Orr Model

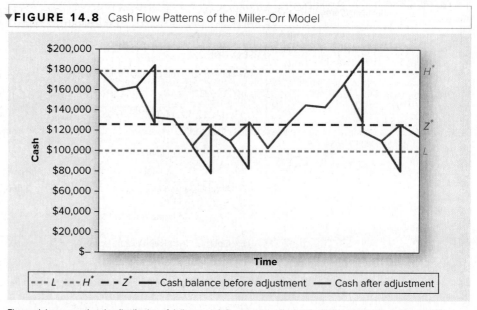

The model assumes that the distribution of daily net cash flows is normally distributed and allows for both cash inflows and outflows.

EXAMPLE 14-4	**Calculation of Optimal Return Point and Upper Limit for the Miller-Orr Model** LG14-8	

For interactive versions of this example, log in to Connect or go to mhhe.com/Cornett6e.

Suppose that Dandy Candy, Inc., would like to maintain its cash account at a minimum level of $100,000 but expects the standard deviation in net daily cash flows to be $5,000; the effective annual rate on marketable securities will be 8 percent per year, and the trading cost per sale or purchase of marketable securities will be $200 per transaction. What will be Dandy Candy's optimal cash return point and upper limit?

SOLUTION:

The daily interest rate on marketable securities will equal

$$i_{day} = \sqrt[365]{1.08} - 1 = 0.000211$$

And the optimal cash return point and upper limit will equal

$$Z^* = \sqrt[3]{3F\sigma^2/4i_{day}} + L = 0.000211$$

$$= \sqrt[3]{3(\$200)(\$5,000)^2/(4 \times 0.000211)} + \$100,000$$

$$= \$126,101.72$$

$$H^* = 3Z^* - 2L$$

$$= \$178,305.16$$

Assuming the random cash balances shown below, Dandy Candy would buy or sell securities to make adjustments as indicated:

Day	Cash Balance before Adjustment	Adjustment	Cash after Adjustment
1	$ 177,025.21		$ 177,025.21
2	$158,965.54		$158,965.54
3	$ 162,488.16		$ 162,488.16
4	$ 183,466.74	–$57,365.02	$ 126,101.72
5	$132,548.06		$132,548.06
6	$ 129,816.11		$ 129,816.11
7	$ 103,709.38		$ 103,709.38
8	$ 77,229.23	$48,872.49	$ 126,101.72
9	$ 121,483.60		$ 121,483.60
10	$ 109,309.78		$ 109,309.78
11	$ 81,609.28	$44,492.44	$ 126,101.72
12	$128,636.69		$ 128,636.69
13	$ 102,121.84		$ 102,121.84
14	$ 125,376.66		$ 125,376.66
15	$145,025.00		$145,025.00
16	$142,320.22		$ 142,320.22
17	$ 166,501.15		$ 166,501.15
18	$ 191,226.65	–$65,124.93	$ 126,101.72
19	$ 119,127.54		$ 119,127.54
20	$ 109,377.65		$ 109,377.65
21	$ 80,841.15	$45,260.57	$ 126,101.72
22	$125,476.90		$ 125,476.90
23	$ 114,416.24		$ 114,416.24

The spreadsheet solution is:

	A	B	C
1	Lower Cash Limit	$ 100,000	
2	S.D. in Daily CFs	$ 5,000	
3	EAR on Mkt Securities	8%	
4	Trading Cost per Transaction	$ 200.00	
5			
6	Daily Interest Rate	0.0211%	=NOMINAL(B3,365)/365
7			
8	Optimal Cash Return Point	$ 126,101.72	=(3*B4*B2^2/(4*B6))^(1/3)+B1
9	Upper Cash Limit	$ 178,305.16	=3*B8-2*B1

Microsoft Excel

As with the manual calculations illustrated above, the first step in calculating the optimal return point and the upper cash limit requires us to calculate the daily interest rate. In Excel, we can do this using the NOMINAL(effect_rate, npery) function to calculate a nominal annual rate based on daily compounding, which we can then divide by 365 to get the effective daily interest rate.

This rate then feeds into the formulas for both the optimal cash return point and the upper cash limit.

Similar to Problems 14-11, 14-12, Self-Test Problem 5

time out!

14-11 What effect does increasing the standard deviation in daily cash flows have on the cash return point in the Miller-Orr model?

14-12 If you were asked to adjust the Baumol model to reflect the need to keep a minimum cash balance, how would you go about doing so?

Second, the authors of both models developed their ideas when buying and selling marketable securities was a relatively expensive and time-consuming proposition. The costs and delays of trading securities have fallen dramatically since the advent of the Internet. The cost has fallen so much since then that many large firms now habitually use all or the majority of their available cash to purchase overnight securities. If trading costs are low enough that it makes sense for the firm to incur at least two sets of trading costs each day—one for selling enough marketable securities in the morning to make it through the day, and another for purchasing marketable securities at the end of the business day—then it's also probable that any unforeseen demand for cash *during* the day can probably be met fairly cheaply by selling marketable securities as needed. Or, put another way, the transaction costs associated with trading securities have fallen so dramatically relative to the opportunity costs of not having cash invested in marketable securities that keeping any "extra" money idle in cash just doesn't make sense.

Finally, both models ignore the fact that many firms must keep compensating balances in their deposit accounts as part of borrowing agreements with their banks. If the compensating balance requirement was a constant amount or percentage, then we could adjust the Miller-Orr model so that *L* included the compensating balance, but many firms must only keep a certain minimum compensating balance *on average*. This implies that an unforeseen demand for cash that causes a firm's deposit account to temporarily dip below the minimum compensating balance can be offset by keeping a corresponding amount of excess cash in the account in a later period. Even the more modern Miller-Orr model does not allow for that.

14.6 • FLOAT CONTROL: MANAGING THE COLLECTION AND DISBURSEMENT OF CASH LG14-9

The economic definition of cash includes undeposited checks, but as we all know, an undeposited check is not as liquid as the same amount of cash sitting inside your checking account. So another component of a good cash management policy involves making sure that checks clear in a timely manner.

Cash is not always liquid due to collection float.

Accelerating Collections

The period of time between when a check is written and when it clears and the funds are available for use is referred to as **float**. The checks sent to a firm experience three different types of collection float, illustrated in Figure 14.9:

1. *Mail float* is the length of time that checks are en route to the firm, either through the postal system or through some sort of electronic transfer.

2. *In-house processing float* is the length of time needed for the firm to process and deposit check payments from its customers once they have been received.

3. *Availability float* is the length of time necessary for a check to clear through the banking system once it has been deposited.

Together, these three types of float span the entire length of time between the customer sending a payment and the firm receiving cash in its account. Several different techniques can help firms reduce collection float:

- A *lockbox system* is a collection of geographically dispersed post office boxes, each maintained for the firm by a bank local to the respective box. For firms with hundreds or thousands of customers spread across a large region, the ideal situation is to have enough locations so that no customer is more than a couple of hundred miles from one of the firm's post office boxes. By having customers send their payments to the closest post office box, and then having the local bank pick up and handle the payment processing several times a day, the firm can reduce both mail float and in-house processing float.

- *Concentration banking* accelerates cash collections from customers by having funds sent to several geographically situated regional banks and then transferred to a main concentration account in another bank. The funds can be transferred through depository transfer checks and electronic transfers.

- *Wire transfers* are the fastest way of transmitting money from a local bank into the concentration bank. Banks within the United States utilize the Society for Worldwide Interbank Financial Telecommunication (SWIFT) system to make payments to banks in countries outside of the United States. Bank-to-bank transfers conducted within the United States take place over the Fedwire system, which uses the Federal Reserve System and its assignment of bank routing numbers.

Delaying Disbursements

Disbursement float is the delay between the firm sending out a payment and the money being taken out of the firm's bank account. Two legal ways to increase disbursement float involve keeping the cash available to the firm until the very last moment:

- A **zero-balance account** is a checking account that the firm sets up so that the bank agrees to automatically transfer funds from an interest-bearing account to pay off any checks presented. Since zero-balance accounts never contain excess cash, they represent one way that firms can get around regulations against corporations having interest-bearing checking accounts.

- **Drafts** resemble checks but differ in that they are payable by the firm issuing them rather than payable by a bank. When a draft is sent to the firm's bank for payment, the bank must present the draft to the firm *before* disbursing the funds.

float The period of time between when a payment is sent out and when the money is actually received by the collecting firm.

zero-balance account A corporate checking account that keeps a zero balance, automatically transferring in just enough funds to cover any checks received on the account from another interest-bearing account.

draft Similar to a check, but payable by the issuing firm rather than by its bank.

The period of time between when a check is written and when it clears is referred to as float.
jwohlfeil/iStock/Getty Images

finance at work //: global

Cultural Differences in Preferences for Paying Bills

Japan's Postal Savings Bank, the world's largest bank, has long been used as an example of the efficiencies available to both individuals and businesses of electronic transactions. Electronic transactions are instantaneous transactions that use security authentication rather than conventional check-clearing processes to transfer funds from a buyer to the seller.

However, in 2006, one of the Nikkei trade papers summarized the results of a survey among Japanese women regarding payment methods used for Internet shopping. Not surprisingly, the vast majority (56 percent) of respondents purchasing goods over the Internet reported that they used credit cards for their transactions. However, the distribution of the rest of the responses illustrates a vast difference between alternative payment pipelines that American and Japanese consumers use.

For example, 17.6 percent of Japanese respondents ordered online, then paid in cash at their local convenience store; 13.1 percent paid COD when the mail carrier delivered the goods; and 4.3 percent paid using electronic transfers from their post office savings accounts.

Though there is some anecdotal evidence that the usage of credit cards has increased slightly since 2006, the use of such alternative methods of payment in Japan is still much higher than we see elsewhere in the world.

Markus Gann/EyeEm/Getty Images

What implications does this have for the money management policies of firms doing business in Japan? Well, given that a far larger percentage of Americans probably pay for their online purchases with credit cards, and that the alternative methods of payment listed previously could be expected to have different clearing times than do payments received through a merchant's credit card account, it's something that firms seeking to do business in Japan should consider.

Want to know more?

Key Words to Search for Updates: **"Marketing Tip: Payment Methods"** **(see https://www.rapyd.net/blog/japans-payment-methods/)**

time out!

14-13 In Japan, many consumers pay their bills by electronic deduction from their checking accounts instead of using paper checks. What effect do you think this has on the collection float of Japanese firms versus that of American firms?

14-14 What's the difference between a lockbox system and concentration banking?

Ethical and Legal Questions

Using collected cash before actually receiving it, or continuing to use disbursed cash after you have sent a check out, can earn your firm higher returns, but this practice is illegal. The most extreme form of taking illegal advantage of disbursement float is a practice called *check kiting,* which is any sort of fraud that involves drawing out money from a bank account with insufficient funds to cover the check.

The Check Clearing for the 21st Century Act, which allows for transmitting electronic images of checks rather than the physical paper checks themselves, has greatly reduced the incidence of check kiting by substantially shortening the time required for a check to be cleared from one bank to another.

14.7 • INVESTING IDLE CASH LG14-10

As both the Baumol and Miller-Orr models imply, firms habitually move cash into and out of marketable securities in order to partially offset the opportunity costs of having capital tied up in current assets. Most large firms will manage their marketable securities investments themselves. Smaller firms will typically invest through an independently managed money-market fund or by letting their bank transfer all available excess funds at the end of each business day into a sweep account, which will then be invested on their behalf.

Why Firms Have Surplus Cash

Firms tend to have surplus cash available either due to seasonal fluctuations in their cash flow patterns or in preparation for planned expenditures. Seasonal fluctuations in the amount of cash on hand can occur as a result of either cyclical sales or cyclical purchases of raw materials. For example, a firm that produces swimming pool accessories will obviously experience higher sales from spring through late fall, and a firm that distributes fresh vegetables purchased on the spot market will have higher cash outflows during the harvest season.

Firms' cash balances may also temporarily increase immediately prior to a planned expenditure, either because they have been "saving up" for the expenditure or because they issued stocks or bonds in advance of the expenditure but need someplace to "park" the funds until they are needed.

What to Do with Surplus Cash

As mentioned, firms usually put surplus cash into money-market securities. As discussed in Chapter 18, these include Treasury bills, federal funds and repurchase agreements, commercial paper, negotiable certificates of deposit, and banker's acceptances.

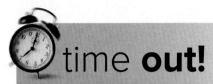

time out!

14-15 Should a firm with nonseasonal cash flows that lacks any good prospective investments keep excess cash on hand? Why or why not?

14-16 Suppose a firm has a temporary surplus of cash meant to fund an upcoming expansion project. Why might it not wish to invest these funds in capital-market (as opposed to money-market) securities?

14.8 • CREDIT MANAGEMENT LG14-11

As is the case with the firm's cash management policy, the firm's optimal credit policy will trade off the opportunity cost of lost sales (if the firm does not grant credit or is too conservative in terms of the credit it does grant) against the carrying costs associated with funding the accounts receivable plus the expected costs of default on the accounts receivable.

Credit Policy: Terms of the Sale

As a minimum, the **credit terms** of sale usually contain at least the credit period, the cash discount, and a description of the type of credit instrument. The credit period is the maturity of the credit that the firm is willing to extend, which varies based on attributes of the goods being sold and the customer purchasing the goods. For example, perishable goods will usually carry a lower credit period, regardless of who is purchasing them. Creditworthy, established customers will probably be given better credit terms than customers the firm has not dealt with before.

To encourage early repayment, firms will often offer a percentage discount if the bill is paid within a certain time period. For example, a firm that quotes customers terms of "2/10, net 30" is offering them the choice between paying the entire bill within 30 days or taking a 2 percent discount off the invoiced price if they pay within 10 days.

For most trade credit, the invoice is the only type of credit instrument involved. When the customer signs a copy upon receipt of the goods, the customer makes an implicit promise to pay under the terms listed on the invoice. If a firm wishes for a customer to make a more explicit acknowledgment of its ability and obligation to pay, a firm can ask the customer to sign a promissory note upon delivery of the goods or to furnish a commercial draft or banker's acceptance in advance of the delivery of the goods.

Credit Analysis

Before granting a customer credit, the firm may wish to engage in **credit analysis.** Such analysis involves a systematic determination of the potential borrower's ability and willingness to pay for the goods being provided on credit. A thorough credit analysis will look

credit terms A listing of the credit period, the cash discount, and the type of credit instrument to be used.

credit analysis A systematic determination of a borrower's ability and willingness to repay a potential loan.

at the potential borrower's past record and its present and forecasted future financial condition, which generally involves examining the "five C's":

1. *Capacity:* Does the borrower have the legal and economic ability to pay?

2. *Character:* Does the borrower's reputation indicate a willingness to settle debt obligations?

3. *Capital:* Having assets at risk makes it more likely that the borrower will repay as promised.

4. *Collateral:* Goods that can be seized and sold, with the proceeds being used to pay the firm in the event of bankruptcy by the borrower, also make it more likely that the customer will repay as promised.

5. *Conditions:* Any economic conditions that may affect the borrower's ability to repay the loan should also be taken into account.

Collection Policy

The firm's collection policy is aimed at collecting past-due debts from customers. The usual procedure for collecting follows a typical path of

1. Sending one or more delinquency letters informing the customer of the past-due status of the account, asking the customer to contact the firm to discuss alternative means of repayment, and pointing out what legal recourse the firm has.

2. Initiating telephone calls conveying the same information as above.

3. Employing a collection agency.

4. Taking legal action against the customer if all else fails.

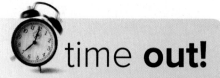

time **out!**

14-17 Why do firms offer customers discounts for paying early?

14-18 Should a firm always turn far-overdue bills from customers over to a collection agency or sue the customers? Why or why not?

To monitor and control this process, firms use a tool called an *aging schedule,* which stratifies a firm's accounts receivable by the age of each account. For example, a firm that offers terms of 2/10, net 60 to its customers might want to measure the age of accounts receivable using the categories shown in Table 14.2.

Such an aging schedule would allow the firm to see what percentage of its customers are still eligible to take the discount (i.e., those in the "0–10 days" category), how many are past due by less than 30 days (i.e., those in the "61–90 days" category), and how many are over 30 days past due (i.e., those in the "Over 90 days" category).

Firms often link their collection policies to their aging schedules. For example, the customers in Table 14.2 that fall into the "61–90 days" category might be sent a delinquency letter, while those in the "Over 90 days" category might be phoned.

▼ **TABLE 14.2** Sample Aging Schedule

Age Bracket	Percentage of AR in Bracket
0–10 days	10%
11–30 days	35
31–60 days	45
61–90 days	7
Over 90 days	3
	100

Get Online

mhhe.com/CornettM6e

for study materials including

quizzes, iPod downloads,

and video

Your Turn...

Questions

1. Is it possible for a firm to have negative net working capital? How? *(LG14-1)*

2. Would it be possible for a decision to deny credit to your customers to be value maximizing? How? *(LG14-1)*

3. Which of the following will result in an increase in net working capital? *(LG14-2)*

   a. An increase in cash.
   b. A decrease in accounts payable.
   c. An increase in notes payable.
   d. A decrease in accounts receivable.
   e. An increase in inventory.

4. Would it be possible for a firm to have a negative cash cycle? How? *(LG14-3)*

5. If a firm's inventory turnover ratio increases, what will happen to the firm's operating cycle? *(LG14-3)*

6. If a firm's inventory turnover ratio increases, what will happen to the firm's cash cycle? *(LG14-3)*

7. Everything else held constant, will an increase in the amount of inventory on hand increase or decrease the firm's profitability? *(LG14-4)*

8. Would a firm ever use short-term debt to finance permanent current assets? Why or why not? *(LG14-5)*

9. Suppose that short-term borrowing actually becomes more expensive than long-term borrowing: How would this affect the firm's choice between a flexible financing policy and a restrictive policy? *(LG14-5)*

10. If asset-backed loans are cheaper than unsecured loans, what is the disadvantage to the firm in using an asset-backed loan? *(LG14-6)*

11. Is an increase in the cash account a source of funds or a use of funds? *(LG14-7)*

12. What will be the carrying cost associated with a compensating balance requirement? *(LG14-7)*

13. What will be the shortage cost associated with a compensating balance requirement? *(LG14-7)*

14. What would be the shortage costs associated with a restaurant not having enough cash on hand to make change? *(LG14-7)*

15. If a firm needs to keep a minimum cash balance on hand and faces both cash inflows and outflows, which of the cash management models discussed in this chapter would be more appropriate for the firm to use? *(LG14-8)*

16. What effect will increasing the trading costs associated with selling marketable securities have on the optimal replenishment level in the Baumol model? Why? *(LG14-8)*

17. What effect will an increase in the standard deviation of daily cash flows have on the return point in the Miller-Orr model? Why? *(LG14-8)*

18. Could a firm ever have negative collection float? Why or why not? *(LG14-9)*

19. Could a firm ever have negative disbursement float? Why or why not? *(LG14-9)*

20. Would a draft have availability float? Why or why not? *(LG14-9)*

21. From our discussion of capital markets elsewhere in this book, why would you expect a firm to have a time delay between raising funds to finance a project and the expenditure of those funds on that project? *(LG14-9)*

22. What purpose does a discount on credit terms serve? What is the cost of such a discount to the offering firm? *(LG14-9)*

Problems

BASIC PROBLEMS

14-1 **Net Working Capital Requirements** JohnBoy Industries has a cash balance of $45,000, accounts payable of $125,000, inventory of $175,000, accounts receivable of $210,000, notes payable of $120,000, and accrued wages and taxes of $37,000. How much net working capital does the firm need to fund? *(LG14-2)*

14-2 **Days' Sales in Inventory** Dabble, Inc., has sales of $980,000 and cost of goods sold of $640,000. The firm had a beginning inventory of $36,000 and an ending inventory of $46,000. What is the length of the days' sales in inventory? *(LG14-3)*

14-3 **Average Payment Period** If a firm has a cash cycle of 67 days and an operating cycle of 104 days, what is its average payment period? *(LG14-3)*

14-4 **Payables Turnover** If a firm has a cash cycle of 73 days and an operating cycle of 127 days, what is its payables turnover? *(LG14-3)*

14-5 **Compensating Balance** Would it be worthwhile to incur a compensating balance of $10,000 in order to get a 1 percent lower interest rate on a one-year, pure discount loan of $225,000? *(LG14-7)*

14-6 **Collection Float** CM Enterprises estimates that it takes, on average, three days for customers' payments to arrive, one day for the payments to be processed and deposited by the bookkeeping department, and two more days for the checks to clear once they are deposited. What is CM's collection float? *(LG14-9)*

INTERMEDIATE PROBLEMS

14-7 **Operating Cycle** Suppose that Dunn Industries has annual sales of $2.3 million, cost of goods sold of $1,650,000, average inventories of $1,116,000, and average accounts receivable of $750,000. Assuming that all of Dunn's sales are on credit, what will be the firm's operating cycle? *(LG14-3)*

14-8 **Cash Cycle** Suppose that LilyMac Photography has annual sales of $230,000, cost of goods sold of $165,000, average inventories of $4,500, average accounts receivable of $25,000, and an average accounts payable balance of $7,000. Assuming that all of LilyMac's sales are on credit, what will be the firm's cash cycle? *(LG14-3)*

14-9 **Spreadsheet Problem: Compensating Balance Interest Rate** Suppose your firm is seeking a four-year, amortizing $200,000 loan with annual payments and your bank is offering you the choice between a $205,000 loan with a $5,000 compensating balance and a $200,000 loan without a compensating balance. If the interest rate on the $200,000 loan is 9.8 percent, how low would the interest rate on the loan with the compensating balance have to be for you to choose it? *(LG14-4)*

14-10 **Spreadsheet Problem: Optimal Cash Replenishment Level** Watkins Resources faces a smooth annual demand for cash of $1.5 million, incurs transaction costs of $75 every time the firm sells marketable securities, and can earn 3.7 percent on its marketable securities. What will be its optimal cash replenishment level? *(LG14-8)*

14-11 **Spreadsheet Problem: Optimal Cash Return Point** Veggie Burgers, Inc., would like to maintain its cash account at a minimum level of $245,000 but expects the standard deviation in net daily cash flows to be $12,000, the effective annual rate on marketable securities to be 4.7 percent per year, and the trading cost per sale or purchase of marketable securities to be $27.50 per transaction. What will be its optimal cash return point? *(LG14-8)*

14-12 **Spreadsheet Problem: Optimal Upper Cash Limit** HotFoot Shoes would like to maintain its cash account at a minimum level of $25,000 but expects the standard deviation in net daily cash flows to be $2,000, the effective annual rate on marketable securities to be 3.5 percent per year, and the trading cost per sale or purchase of marketable securities to be $200 per transaction. What will be its optimal upper cash limit? *(LG14-8)*

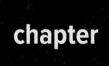

fourteen appendix 14A

the cash budget

LEARNING GOAL

LG14-12 Be able to create and interpret a cash budget.

The production and sales in many firms vary over the year. For example, a toy retailer will have many more sales in November and December than in March and April. On the other hand, consider the manufacturer of toys. That company would have to manufacture most of the toys it will sell to the retail stores before November. For the most part, all businesses have some seasonality in their sales and/or production cycle. This seasonality creates periods during the year in which the firm will generate large cash surpluses and other periods in which it will generate large cash deficits. Financial managers must plan ahead for such times so that the firm always has adequate cash to pay its liabilities. The **cash budget** is the instrument they use.

Consider the example of Yellow Jacket, Inc., a manufacturer of coats and jackets that has decided to operate its factory at a constant pace all year. Thus, inventory builds up until early fall, when it ships large amounts of its product to retailers. The coats are mostly sold in the fall, depleting inventory. This strategy allows the company to keep a few full-time workers instead of hiring many seasonal employees and then laying them off during the slow times of the year. However, incurring costs during most of the year with few sales and then selling the coats in the fall creates a serious cash flow problem that the financial manager is responsible for resolving.

Cash budgets can be created for daily, monthly, or quarterly time periods. Given the severe seasonality of Yellow Jacket's sales, its cash budget is done monthly. The cash budget begins with a projection of sales for the year. In this case, Yellow Jacket is projecting a 10 percent increase in sales each month from the same month of the previous year. The top of Table 14A.1 shows these monthly projected sales, which are quite seasonal. Many companies have sales terms like 2/10, net 45, which means that customers must pay within 45 days of the sale—but if they pay within 10 days they can take a 2 percent discount. Even with terms like this, Yellow Jacket has found that its customers take the 2 percent discount if they pay in the same month of the sale, which 30 percent do. Then 50 percent

▼ **TABLE 14A.1** Cash Collection

	A	B	C	D	E	F	G	H	I	J	K	L	M
1	($ millions)	Jan	Feb	Mar	Apr	May	Jun	Jul	Aug	Sep	Oct	Nov	Dec
2													
3	Sales	10	10	5	2	1	1	1	5	20	30	25	15
4													
5	Cash collection	14.3	10.7	8.5	5.1	2.3	1.2	1.0	2.2	8.6	19.8	26.4	22.9
6													
7													
8	_Assumptions_												
9	Collection:												
10	Month 0, 30% pay with 2% discount												
11	Month 1, 50% pay												
12	Month 2, 20% pay												
13													
14	10% increase in sales from previous year												
15													

October cash collection comes from:

30% × October sales after 2% discount = 0.3 × 0.98 × $30
plus   50% × September sales = 0.5 × $20
plus   20% × August sales = 0.2 × $5

Total = $19.8

Microsoft Excel

pay in the month after the sale, leaving the final 20 percent to pay in the following month. This is illustrated in the cash collection row of the table. Note that the firm collects only $1 million in cash payments in July while it collects as much as $26.4 million in November.

The total sales for the year are $125 million. If the company pursues the level production strategy, then it needs to produce the coats at a sale value rate of $10.42 million per month (= $125 million/12). Table 14A.2 shows the cash disbursements per month. The manufacturing costs are assumed to be materials at 50 percent of sales, while wages are 15 percent of sales. Thus, material cost payments are $5.2 million per month (= $10.42 million × 50%) and wage payments are $1.6 million per month (= $10.42 million × 15%). Other payments predicted throughout the year are those for capital investments, interest payments, and dividend payments. Yellow Jacket plans to invest in some factory upgrades for which it will pay $15 million in June. Interest payments on its bonds are semiannual (March and September), while quarterly dividends are paid in February, May, August, and November. Notice that the total cash disbursements have a high degree of variability over time. In addition, the payments do not align well with the cash collection. For example in June, the firm receives only $1.2 million in cash and expects to pay $24.5 million. On the other hand, it expects to collect $26.4 million in November and pay only $7.8 million.

The cash budget can now be completed. Table 14A.3 shows that the next step is to compute the net cash flow generated each month. This is simply the cash collection for that month minus that month's disbursement. Note that Yellow Jacket has seven months in a row (March through September) in which it generates a negative cash flow. The cumulative net cash flow row shows that the surplus of cash generated in January and February helps with the deficits from March and April. However, by May, Yellow Jacket enters a cash deficit situation that lasts the rest of the year. The deficit is increased by the fact that the firm likes to have a cash balance minimum of $2 million at all times. Finally, the cash budget shows the cash account surplus or deficit during the year. It is apparent that Yellow

time out!

14A-1 Should all cash payments and receipts made by the firm be included in the cash budget?

14A-2 Due to the nature of Yellow Jacket's business, it is likely to experience significant cash deficits each year. How is its bank likely to view this situation?

▼ **TABLE 14A.2** Cash Disbursement

	A	B	C	D	E	F	G	H	I	J	K	L	M
1	($ millions)	Jan	Feb	Mar	Apr	May	Jun	Jul	Aug	Sep	Oct	Nov	Dec
2													
3	Sales	10	10	5	2	1	1	1	5	20	30	25	15
4													
5	Cash collection	14.3	10.7	8.5	5.1	2.3	1.2	1.0	2.2	8.6	19.8	26.4	22.9
6													
7	Disbursements												
8	Materials	5.2	5.2	5.2	5.2	5.2	5.2	5.2	5.2	5.2	5.2	5.2	5.2
9	Wages, salaries & other	1.6	1.6	1.6	1.6	1.6	1.6	1.6	1.6	1.6	1.6	1.6	1.6
10	Taxes	0	0	2.7	0	0	2.7	0	0	2.7	0	0	2.7
11	Capital projects	0	0	0	0	0	15.0	0	0	0	0	0	0
12	Long-term financing	0	1.0	5.0	0	1.0	0	0	1.0	5.0	0	1.0	0
13	(interest & dividends)												
14	Total cash disbursement	6.8	7.8	14.5	6.8	7.8	24.5	6.8	7.8	14.5	6.8	7.8	9.5
15													
16													
17													
18	Assumptions												
19	Disbursement:												
20	Material is 50% of sales												
21	Wages, etc. are 15% of sales												
22	$15 million factory upgrade in June												
23	$5 million in interest, twice per year												
24	$1 million in dividends, quarterly												
25	$2.7 million in taxes, quarterly												

November cash disbursement comes from:

$5.2 million in materials purchased
+ $1.6 million in wages
+ $2.7 million in quarterly taxes paid
+ $5.0 million in semiannual interest payment on debt

$14.5 million

Microsoft Excel

▼ **TABLE 14A.3** Cash Budget

	A	B	C	D	E	F	G	H	I	J	K	L	M
1	($ millions)	Jan	Feb	Mar	Apr	May	Jun	Jul	Aug	Sep	Oct	Nov	Dec
2													
3	Sales	10	10	5	2	1	1	1	5	20	30	25	15
4													
5	Cash collection	14.3	10.7	8.5	5.1	2.3	1.2	1.0	2.2	8.6	19.8	26.4	22.9
6													
7	Disbursements												
8	Materials	5.2	5.2	5.2	5.2	5.2	5.2	5.2	5.2	5.2	5.2	5.2	5.2
9	Wages, salaries & other	1.6	1.6	1.6	1.6	1.6	1.6	1.6	1.6	1.6	1.6	1.6	1.6
10	Taxes	0	0	2.7	0	0	2.7	0	0	2.7	0	0	2.7
11	Capital projects	0	0	0	0	0	15.0	0	0	0	0	0	0
12	Long-term financing	0	1.0	5.0	0	1.0	0	0	1.0	5.0	0	1.0	0
13	(interest & dividends)												
14	Total cash disbursement	6.8	7.8	14.5	6.8	7.8	24.5	6.8	7.8	14.5	6.8	7.8	9.5
15													
16	Net cash flow	7.5	2.9	−6.0	−1.7	−5.5	−23.3	−5.8	−5.6	−5.9	13.0	18.6	13.4
17													
18	Cumulative net cash flow	7.5	10.4	4.4	2.7	−2.8	−26.1	−31.9	−37.5	−43.4	−30.4	−11.8	1.6
19													
20	Minimum cash balance	2.0	2.0	2.0	2.0	2.0	2.0	2.0	2.0	2.0	2.0	2.0	2.0
21													
22	Cash surplus or deficit	5.5	8.4	2.4	0.7	−4.8	−28.1	−33.9	−39.5	−45.4	−32.4	−13.8	−0.4
23													
24	Assumptions												
25	Minimum cash balance of $2 million												
26													
27													
28													
29													
30													

Net cash flow =
Cash collection − Total cash disbursement

Cumulative net cash flow =
Last month's cumulative cash flow +
This month's net cash flow

Cash surplus or deficit =
Cumulative net cash flow −
Minimum cash balance

Microsoft Excel

Jacket will need to obtain a bank loan or line of revolving credit that can handle a maximum of $45.4 million (September's deficit is the highest).

Note that Yellow Jacket is a profitable firm. Yet, the seasonality in the sales of coats and jackets causes severe cash deficit problems during the year. If financial managers do not plan ahead for this situation, then the firm will experience significant financial stresses that can damage its reputation and relationship with suppliers and customers. The value of building the cash budget on a spreadsheet (as shown in these tables) is that sensitivity analysis and what-if scenarios can easily be implemented.

Problems

BASIC PROBLEMS

14A-1 Cumulative Net Cash Flow The net cash flow for a firm in January, February, and March is −$2.5 million, −$3.0 million, and $2.4 million, respectively. What is the cumulative net cash flow for March? *(LG14-12)*

14A-2 Cumulative Net Cash Flow The net cash flow for a firm in January, February, and March is $3.5 million, −$1.0 million, and $1.4 million, respectively. What is the cumulative net cash flow for March? *(LG14-12)*

14A-3 Cash Disbursement The Hug-a-Bear company makes its teddy bears the month before they are sold and pays for all materials in the month of purchase. If sales of $2.5 million are expected in November and the firm pays 50 percent of sales in materials costs, then what is the materials cash disbursement in October? *(LG14-12)*

14A-4 Cash Disbursement The Snow Adventures company makes its snowboards the month before they are sold and pays for all materials in the month of purchase. If sales of $7.8 million are expected in November and the firm pays 65 percent of sales in materials costs, then what is the materials cash disbursement in October? *(LG14-12)*

INTERMEDIATE PROBLEMS

14A-5 Cash Collection Consider a company that has sales in May, June, and July of $10 million, $12 million, and $9 million, respectively. The firm is paid by 35 percent of its customers in the month of the sale, 40 percent in the following month, and 22 percent in the next month (*3 percent are bad sales and never pay*). What is the cash collected in July? *(LG14-12)*

14A-6 Cash Collection Consider a company that has sales in May, June, and July of $11 million, $10 million, and $12 million, respectively. The firm is paid by 25 percent of its customers in the month of the sale, 50 percent in the following month, and 23 percent in the next month (*2 percent are bad sales and never pay*). What is the cash collected in July? *(LG14-12)*

14A-7 Cash Surplus or Deficit A firm has estimated the two-month cash budget below. What is the cash surplus or deficit for these two months? *(LG14-12)*

($ in millions)	MAR	APR
Sales	120.0	130.0
Cash collection	84.0	90.0
Total cash disbursement	90.0	85.0
Net cash flow	−6.0	5.0
Cumulative net cash flow	−15.0	?
Minimum cash balance	10.0	10.0
Cash surplus or deficit	?	?

14A-8 Cash Surplus or Deficit A firm has estimated the two-month cash budget below. What is the cash surplus or deficit for these two months? *(LG14-12)*

($ in millions)	MAR	APR
Sales	75.0	68.0
Cash collection	63.0	65.0
Total cash disbursement	60.0	57.0
Net cash flow	3.0	8.0
Cumulative net cash flow	11.0	?
Minimum cash balance	3.0	3.0
Cash surplus or deficit	?	?

ADVANCED PROBLEM

14A-9 Cash Budget Spreadsheet Problem The company from the text, Yellow Jacket, has decided to change its production strategy. Instead of a steady production throughout the year, it will produce the coats it estimates to sell in the month prior. This will impact the materials and wage disbursements of the cash budget. (*For the December computation, assume that the following January sales will increase by 10 percent from the prior year.*) Build this cash budget. How does this impact the cash surplus/deficit of the firm? *(LG14-12)*

Notes

CHAPTER 14

1. If you are sitting there wondering why the bank doesn't just lend only 95 percent or 90 percent of the money, instead of lending it all and then asking for part of it back, the answer has to do with bank regulations. Though it's too complicated to go into great detail, the simple answer is that bank regulators see a difference between a $900,000 loan and a $1,000,000 loan with a 10 percent compensating balance requirement, though they may sound the same to us.

2. See W. S. Baumol, "The Transactions Demand for Cash: An Inventory Theoretic Approach," *Quarterly Journal of Economics* 66, no. 4 (November 1952), pp. 545–556.

3. See M. H. Miller and D. Orr, "A Model of the Demand for Money by Firms," *Quarterly Journal of Economics* 80, no. 3 (August 1966), pp. 413–435.

4. To see why, go down to your local bank or savings and loan and see which is higher: the rate it pays on savings accounts or the rate it charges on short-term borrowing.

Chapter One

BUSINESS APPLICATION SOLUTION

Because Caleb is a sole proprietor of a small business, he will have trouble getting loans for large amounts of money if he wants to expand. Caleb should consider the following options.

First, Caleb can expand slowly. He can get a small loan or self-fund an expansion into one other mall. Once the new juice stand is making a profit, he can expand again. The advantage of this slow expansion is that he retains full ownership and control of his business. One significant risk is that others may copy his idea and open their own stands, thus taking the prime spots in malls before he gets there.

In order to obtain the capital to expand more quickly, Caleb may have to take on a partner. Forming a partnership with an angel investor or a venture capitalist who can provide business expertise and substantial amounts of capital would allow for much faster expansion. The disadvantage of this option is that Caleb will have to give up some ownership of his business.

PERSONAL APPLICATION SOLUTION

Dagmar should know that the market gives no guarantees against losing money investing in company stocks. These companies failed for different reasons (declining sales in the case of CPK, debt load in the case of CHKAQ, and both of these factors in the case of JCP), but all of them cited the COVID-19 pandemic as a primary cause of their bankruptcies. At the start of 2021, all of them either have or are on the verge of reemerging from bankruptcy, but prior equity holders lost their entire investments in all three.

Dagmar should also know that the collapse of firms does occasionally occur. On the other hand, the companies that competed with these failed firms did very well. There are definitely winners and losers in capitalism. Nevertheless, she can minimize her loss from a corporate bankruptcy by not putting all her "eggs in one basket." Diversification is a finance principle discussed in detail later in this book.

Chapter Two

BUSINESS APPLICATION SOLUTION

If the managers of DPH Tree Farm increase the firm's fixed assets by $27 million and net working capital by $8 million in 2025, the balance sheet would look like the one below (Table 2.5). That is, gross fixed assets increase by $27 million, to $395 million; cash, accounts receivable, and inventory would increase by $1 million, $5 million, and $6 million, respectively. DPH Tree Farm's total assets will thus grow by $39 million to $609 million by year-end 2025. This growth in assets would be financed with $4 million in accounts payable, and the remaining $35 million will be financed with 40 percent long-term debt (0.4 × $35m = $14m) and 60 percent with common stock (0.6 × $35m = $21m).

PERSONAL APPLICATION SOLUTION

As Chris Ryan examines the 2024 financial statements for DPH Tree Farm, Inc., she needs to remember that the balance sheet reports a firm's assets, liabilities, and equity at a particular point in time, the income statement reports the total revenues and expenses over a specific period of time, the statement of cash flows shows the firm's cash flows over a period of time, and the statement of retained earnings reconciles net income earned during a given period and any cash dividends paid with the change in retained earnings over the period.

▼ **TABLE 2.5** Revised Balance Sheet for DPH Tree Farm, Inc.

DPH TREE FARM, INC. Balance Sheet as of December 31, 2022 (in millions of dollars)					
Assets	**2025**		**Liabilities and Equity**	**2025**	
Current assets:			Current liabilities:		
Cash	$ 25	($24 + $1)	Accrued wages and taxes	$ 20	
Accounts receivable	75	($70 + $5)	Accounts payable	59	($55 + $4)
Inventory	117	($111 + $6)	Notes payable	45	
Total	$217		Total	$124	
Fixed assets:					
Gross plant and equipment	$395	($368 + $27)	Long-term debt:	209	[$195 + 0.4($39 − $4)]
Less: Accumulated depreciation	53		Stockholders' equity:		
Net plant and equipment	$342		Preferred stock (5 million shares)	$ 5	
			Common stock and paid-in surplus (20 million shares)	61	[$40 + 0.6($39 − $4)]
Other long-term assets	50		Retained earnings	210	
Total	$392		Total	$276	
Total assets	$609	($570 + $39)	Total liabilities and equity	$609	($570 + $39)

GAAP procedures dictate how each financial statement is prepared. GAAP requires that the firm recognizes revenue when the firm sells the product, which is not necessarily when the firm receives the cash. Likewise, under GAAP, expenses appear on the income statement as they match sales. That is, the income statement recognizes production and other expenses associated with sales when the firm sells the product. Again, the actual cash outflow associated with producing the goods may actually occur at a very different time than that reported. In addition, the income statement contains several noncash items, the largest of which is depreciation. As a result, figures shown on an income statement may not be representative of the actual cash inflows and outflows for a firm during any particular period.

For investors like Chris Ryan, the actual cash flows are often more important than the accounting profit listed on the income statement. Cash, not accounting profit, is needed to pay the firm's obligations as they come due: to fund the firm's operations and growth and to compensate the firm's owners. So Chris is more likely to find the answers she seeks in the statement of cash flows, which shows the firm's cash flows over a given period of time. The statement of cash flows reports the amounts of cash generated and cash distributed by a firm during the time period analyzed.

Finally, Chris must remember that firms are required to prepare their financial statements according to GAAP. GAAP allows managers to have significant discretion over their reported earnings, in other words, to manage earnings. Indeed, managers can report their results in a way that indicates to investors that the firm's assets are growing more steadily than may really be the case. Similarly, the choice of depreciation method—straight-line or MACRS—for fixed assets may make two firms with identical fixed assets appear to have very different results. Thus, Chris may need to delve more deeply into research about this firm's—or any firm's—financial condition before she makes any final investment decision.

Chapter Three

BUSINESS APPLICATION SOLUTION

The managers of DPH Tree Farm, Inc., have stated that its performance surpasses that of other firms in the industry. Particularly strong are the firm's liquidity and asset management positions. The superior performance in these areas has resulted in superior overall returns for the stockholders of DPH Tree Farm, Inc., according to DPH management. Having analyzed the financial statements using ratio analysis, we could conclude that these statements are partially true. All three liquidity ratios show that DPH Tree Farm holds more liquidity on its balance sheet than the industry average. Thus, DPH Tree Farm has more cash and other liquid assets (or current assets) available to pay its bills (or current liabilities) as they come due than the average firm in the tree farm industry. In all cases, the asset management ratios show that DPH Tree Farm, Inc., is outperforming the industry average in its asset management. The firm is turning over its inventory faster than the average firm in the tree farm industry, thus producing more dollars of sales per dollar of inventory. It is also collecting its accounts receivable faster and paying its accounts

payable slower than the average firm. Further, DPH Tree Farm is producing more sales per dollar of fixed assets, working capital, and total assets than the average firm in the industry. The profitability ratios show that DPH Tree Farm, Inc., is more profitable than the average firm in the tree farm industry. The profit margin, BEP, and ROA are all higher than the industry ratios. Despite this, the ROE for DPH Tree Farm is much lower than the average for the industry.

What the managers do not state is that the debt management ratios show that DPH Tree Farm, Inc., holds less debt on its balance sheet than the average firm in the tree farm industry. This is a good sign in that this lack of financial leverage decreases the firm's potential for financial distress and even failure. If the firm has a bad year, it has promised relatively few payments to debt holders. Thus, the risk of bankruptcy is small. Further, the firm has more dollars of operating earnings and cash available to meet each dollar of interest obligations on the firm's debt.

However, low levels of debt will lead to a dilution of the return to stockholders due to increased use of equity as well as to not taking advantage of the tax deductibility of interest expense. This dilution of profit is likely to upset common stockholders of the firm.

PERSONAL APPLICATION SOLUTION

To evaluate DPH Tree Farm, Inc.'s, financial statements, Chris Ryan would want to perform ratio analysis in which she uses the financial statements to calculate the most commonly used ratios. These include liquidity ratios, asset management ratios, debt management ratios, profitability ratios, and market value ratios. The value of these ratios for DPH Tree Farms and the tree farming industry are presented in Table 3.1. Chris might also want to spread the financial statements. These calculations yield common-size, easily compared financial statements that can be used to identify changes in corporate performance as well as how DPH Tree Farm compares to other firms in the industry. Having calculated these ratios, Chris can identify any interrelationships in the ratios by performing a detailed analysis of ROA and ROE using the DuPont system of analysis. A critical part of performance analysis lies in the interpretation of these numbers against some benchmark. To interpret the financial ratios, Chris will also want to evaluate the performance of the firm over time (time series analysis) and the performance of the firm against one or more companies in the same industry (cross-sectional analysis). Finally, Chris needs to exercise some cautions when reviewing data from financial statements. For example, the financial statement data are historical and may not be representative of future performance. Further, she needs to know what accounting rules DPH Tree Farm uses before making any comparisons or conclusions about its performance from ratio analysis. Finally, DPH Tree Farm's managers may have window-dressed their financial statements to make them look better.

Chapter Four

BUSINESS APPLICATION SOLUTION

You must compare the cash flows of buying the wire now at a discount, or waiting one year. The cost of the wire should include both the supplier's bill and the storage cost, for a total of $452,000. What interest rate is implied by a $452,000 cash flow today versus $500,000 in one year? Using equation 4-2:

$$FV_N = PV \times (1 + i)^N$$
$$\$500,000 = \$452,000 \times (1 + i)^1$$
$$i = \$500,000/\$452,000 - 1$$
$$= 0.1062, \text{ or } 10.62\%$$

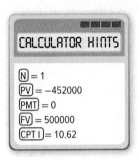

Whether your company should purchase the wire today depends on the cost of the firm's capital (discussed in Chapter 11). If it costs the firm less than 10.6 percent to obtain cash, then you should purchase the wire today. Otherwise, you should not.

PERSONAL APPLICATION SOLUTION

Since Anthony's loan of $300 requires an immediate $50 payment, the actual cash flow is $250 (= $300 − $50). He then must repay the full $300. Use equation 4-2 to compute the interest rate you pay for the period:

$$FV_N = PV \times (1 + i)^N$$
$$\$300 = \$250 \times (1 + i)^1$$
$$i = \$300/\$250 - 1$$
$$= 0.20, \text{ or } 20\%$$

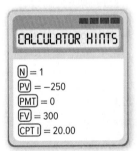

Anthony is paying 20 percent for a loan of only two weeks! This is equivalent to paying 11,348 percent per year (this is shown in Chapter 5). He will never be able to build wealth if he continues to pay interest rates like this. Indeed, many people get trapped in a continuing cycle, obtaining one payday loan after another.

WARNING: Payday loans are almost always terrible deals for the borrower!

Chapter Five

BUSINESS APPLICATION SOLUTION

Walkabout Music, Inc., pays $700,000 (= $20 million × 0.07 ÷ 2) in interest every six months on its existing debt. The new debt would require payments of $600,000 (= $20 million × 0.06 ÷ 2) every six months, which represents a $100,000 savings semiannually.

The present value of these savings over the next 20 years is computed using 40 semiannual periods and a 3 percent interest rate per period:

$$PVA_N = \$100,000 \times \left[\frac{1 - \frac{1}{(1 + 0.03)^{40}}}{0.03} \right] = \$2,311,477.20$$

The spreadsheet solution uses the PV function as
=PV(0.03,40,−100000.0) and produces the answer of $2,311,477.20.

Since this savings is less than the $2.6 million cost of refinancing, the CFO should not refinance the old debt at this time. The company should wait until it can find more favorable terms.

PERSONAL APPLICATION SOLUTION

Should you switch to a new home mortgage with a lower interest rate? To answer this question, first find the monthly savings with the new mortgage. Then compare the present value of the savings to the cost of getting the new mortgage.

The current monthly mortgage payments are

$$PMT_N = \$150,000 \times \left[\frac{0.00667}{1 - \frac{1}{(1 + 0.00667)^{360}}} \right] = \$1,100.65$$

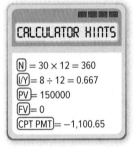 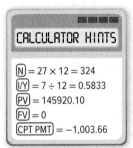

The new mortgage payments would be

$$PMT_N = \$145,920.10 \times \left[\frac{0.00583}{1 - \frac{1}{(1 + 0.00583)^{324}}} \right] = \$1,003.66$$

The new mortgage would save you $96.99 per month for the next 27 years.

The present value of these savings at the current 7 percent interest rate is

$$PVA_N = \$96.99 \times \left[\frac{1 - \frac{1}{(1 + 0.00583)^{324}}}{0.00583} \right] = \$14,101.18$$

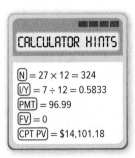

The spreadsheet solution is:

	A	B	C	D	E	F
1	**Current Mortgage Payments**					
2	i	N	PV		PMT	
3	8%	30	$150,000		$1,100.65	
4					=PMT(A3/12,B3*12,-C3,0)	
5	**New Mortgage Payments**					
6	i	N	PV		PMT	
7	7%	27	$145,920		$1,003.66	
8					=PMT(A7/12,B7*12,-C7,0)	
9	**Present Value of Monthly Savings**					
10	i	N	PMT		PV	
11	7%	27	$96.99		$14,101.18	
12					=PV(A11/12,B11*12,-C11,0)	

Microsoft Excel

Since the present value of the monthly savings is greater than the $1,000 broker fee, you should refinance the mortgage.

Chapter Six

BUSINESS APPLICATION SOLUTION

In deciding when to issue new debt, DPH Corporation needs to consider two main factors. First, what might happen to specific factors that affect interest rates on any debt the firm may issue? Such specific factors include changes in the firm's default risk, liquidity risk, any special provisions regarding the use of funds raised by the firm's security issuance, and the debt's term to maturity. An increase (decrease) in any of these risks over the next two years would increase (decrease) the rate of interest DPH Corp. would be required to pay to holders of the new debt and would potentially make the debt issue in two years less (more) attractive. Second, what might happen to the general level of interest rates in the U.S. economy over the next two years? This involves an analysis of any changes in inflation or the real risk-free rate. DPH can estimate how interest rates may change by examining the term structure of interest rates or the current yield curve. In addition to any internal analysis of these factors, DPH Corp. can get expert advice about the timing of its debt issue and get the new debt to the capital market with help from an investment bank. These financial institutions underwrite securities and engage in related activities, such as making a market in which securities can trade.

PERSONAL APPLICATION SOLUTION

In deciding which corporate bond to buy, John Adams needs to consider specific factors that affect differences in interest rates on debt. These specific factors include the general level of inflation and the real risk-free rate in the U.S. economy, as well as the default risk, liquidity risk, any special provisions regarding the use of funds raised by a security issuance, and the term to maturity of the two debt issues. While one bond earns more (10.00 percent) than the other (8.00 percent), it may be that the higher-yielding bond has more default, liquidity, or other risk than the lower-yielding bond. Thus, the higher yield brings with it more risk. John Adams must consider whether he is willing to incur higher risk to get higher returns. In addition to his own analysis of these factors, John Adams can get expert advice about

which bond to buy and then buy the bond with a securities firm's help. These financial institutions engage in activities such as securities brokerage, securities trading, and making markets in which securities can trade.

Chapter Seven

BUSINESS APPLICATION SOLUTION

To raise $150 million, Beach Sand Resorts would need to issue 150,000 bonds at the customary $1,000 par value (= $150 million ÷ $1,000). The bonds will have to offer a 7 percent coupon. This means that Beach Sand Resorts will pay $35 in interest every six months for each bond issued (= 0.07 × $1,000 ÷ 2). So for all 150,000 bonds, they will pay $5.25 million semiannually (= $35 × 150,000).

PERSONAL APPLICATION SOLUTION

You can calculate that buying 10 of the Trust Media bonds at the quoted price of 96.21 will cost $9,621 (= 0.9621 × $1,000 × 10) and would generate $285 (= 0.057 × $1,000 × 10 ÷ 2) in interest payments every six months. Buying the bond six years before maturity, it is priced to offer a 6.47 percent yield to maturity. Ten of the Abalon bonds would cost $10,194 (= 1.0194 × $1,000 × 10) and pay $268.75 (= 0.05375 × $1,000 × 10 ÷ 2) in interest payments every six months. This bond is priced to offer a 5.0 percent yield to maturity. The Trust bonds cost less to purchase, pay more in interest, and offer a higher return than the Abalon bonds. This is because the Trust bonds have higher credit risk. You must decide if the higher return of the Trust bonds is worth taking the extra risk.

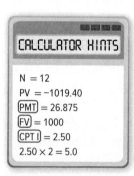

CALCULATOR HINTS

N = 12
PV = −1019.40
PMT = 26.875
FV = 1000
CPT I = 2.50
2.50 × 2 = 5.0

Chapter Eight

BUSINESS APPLICATION SOLUTION

You can compute the expected return using equation 8-7 as

$$i = \frac{\$2 \times (1 + 0.08)}{\$65} + 0.08 = 0.0332 + 0.08 = 0.1132$$

Investors expect an 11.32 percent return.

The P/E ratio of 16.25 and the stock price of $65 indicate that earnings were $4.00 per share (= $65 ÷ 16.25). If the P/E ratio of 16.25 continues, then the price of the stock in three years may be $81.88 [= 16.25 × $4 × (1.08)³]. However, a P/E ratio of 16.25 may seem a little high for a firm with an 8 percent growth rate. So the P/E ratio might decline a bit to 15. If so, the stock price in three years would be $75.58. On the other hand, P/E ratios in the stock market may increase in general, thereby inflating this firm's ratio to 17. In this case, the price would be $85.66.

You should report an expected stock price range of $75.58 to $85.66 with a target of $81.88.

PERSONAL APPLICATION SOLUTION

The information provided allows for two growth rate estimates for stock valuation. The dividend growth from $1.25 to $1.68 in three years implies a 10.36 percent historical growth rate (N = 3, PV = −1.25, PMT = 0,

FV = 1.68, CPT I = 10.36). Since analysts' mean growth estimate is 10.1 percent, you can use either, or both, rates in the constant-growthrate model using a 13.5 percent discount rate:

$$P_0 = \frac{\$1.68 \times (1 + 0.1036)}{0.135 - 0.1036} = \$59.05$$

$$P_0 = \frac{\$1.68 \times (1 + 0.101)}{0.135 - 0.101} = \$54.40$$

Both valuation estimates exceed the current price of $54. The current stock price does not appear overvalued, so you can consider the purchase.

Chapter Nine

BUSINESS APPLICATION SOLUTION

We can apply diversification concepts and modern portfolio theory to many more applications than just investment portfolios. For example, a manufacturing facility can be more efficient by producing different products during the year as demand dictates the need for one product over another. Salespeople can reduce the volatility of their commission incomes by having many different products to sell.

Although new project ideas have more risk, they could actually reduce the firm's overall risk if the projects diversify the firm's current business operations. You could evaluate this possibility by determining the correlation between the expected cash flows from each project idea with the expected cash flows of the firm's current business operations. A low or negative correlation would mean that the new projects could actually reduce risk for the firm. Note that some firms may find that their position is too conservative and that they wish to increase their risk to increase the possibility of earning a higher return.

PERSONAL APPLICATION SOLUTION

Tables 9.2 and 9.4 show that since 1950 the bond market has experienced an average return and standard deviation of 6.6 percent and 10.9 percent, respectively. Stocks earned a 12.7 percent return with a 17.1 percent standard deviation. The investor is correct in the belief that the stock market is riskier than the bond market.

However, Table 9.6 shows that the correlation between the stock and bond market is very low, at −0.004. This result allows some diversification opportunity. Indeed, a portfolio of 10 percent stocks and 90 percent bonds would have experienced an average annual return of 7.3 percent with a standard deviation of 10.0 percent since 1950. The broker is correct; adding a small portion of stocks to a bond portfolio actually reduces total risk!

Chapter Ten

BUSINESS APPLICATION SOLUTION

You need to determine the firm's level of market risk. If you can obtain a beta, then you can make a required return estimate using CAPM. To assess the result, you can use the constant-growth model to check the CAPM estimated required return for comparison's sake.

If you find the beta of the firm to be 1.8, assume a market return of 11 percent, and note a 5 percent T-bill rate, the CAPM computations would be

5% + 1.8 × (11% − 5%) = 15.8 percent

The firm will pay a $0.50 dividend next year and the current stock price is $32. Managers believe the company will grow at 13 percent per year for the foreseeable future. The constant-growth model computation gives

$0.50 ÷ $32 + 0.13 = 0.1456, or 14.56 percent

You can now take these estimates to the team.

PERSONAL APPLICATION SOLUTION

You are investing 57.1 percent (= $200 ÷ $350) of your monthly contribution in stocks. You are also contributing 28.6 percent in bonds and 14.3 percent into a money market account. The diversified stock portfolio has a beta of 1. The long-term bond portfolio has a beta of 0.18. By definition, the money market account is risk-free and thus has a beta of zero.

The beta of this portfolio is therefore

0.571 × 1 + 0.286 × 0.18 + 0.143 × 0 = 0.62

With a portfolio beta of 0.62, a market return of 11 percent, and a risk-free rate of 5 percent, you can expect a return of

5% + 0.62 × (11% − 5%) = 8.72 percent

If you want a higher expected return, you will have to take more risk. You can do that by contributing a higher proportion of your funds to the stock portfolio.

Chapter Eleven

BUSINESS APPLICATION SOLUTION

Stream Devices, Inc., faces current component costs of capital equal to

$$i_E = \frac{D_1}{P_0} + g \qquad i_P = \frac{D_1}{P_0}$$

$$= \frac{\$1.35}{\$18.75} + 0.06 \qquad = \frac{\$10}{\$100}$$

$$= 0.1320, \text{ or } 13.20\% \qquad = 0.1000, \text{ or } 10.00\%$$

$$\text{Solve} \left\{ \$1,100 = \$100 \times \left[\frac{1 - \frac{1}{(1 + i_D)^{20}}}{i_D} \right] + \frac{\$1,000}{(1 + i_D)^{20}} \right\} \text{ for } i_D$$

gives $i_D = 0.0891$, or 8.91%

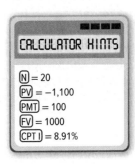

CALCULATOR HINTS

N = 20
PV = −1,100
PMT = 100
FV = 1000
CPT I = 8.91%

Stream's WACC equals

$WACC = 0.5 \times 0.1320 + 0.1 \times 0.10 + 0.4 \times 0.0891 \times [1 - 0.21]$

$= 0.1042$, or 10.42%

PERSONAL APPLICATION SOLUTION

MacKenzie can expect a total of $17,125 + $29,000 = $46,125 in student loans when she graduates from her master's program. At an 8 percent rate of interest, the yearly interest charges will be $3,690 immediately after she graduates (though they will go down once she starts paying off some of the principal). Since the yearly interest will be more than the allowable $2,500 deduction, we can express her after-tax interest rate as the following weighted average:

$$WACC = \frac{D_{Nondeductible}}{D_{Nondeductible} + D_{Deductible}} \times i_D$$

$$+ \frac{D_{Deductible}}{D_{Nondeductible} + D_{Deductible}} \times i_D \times \left(1 - T_P\right)$$

$$= \frac{\$3,690 - \$2,500}{\$3,690} \times 0.08 + \frac{\$2,500}{\$3,690} \times 0.08 \times \left(1 - 0.22\right)$$

$$= 0.3225 \times 0.08 + 0.6775 \times 0.08 \times 0.78$$

$$= 0.0681, \text{ or } 6.81\%$$

Chapter Twelve

BUSINESS APPLICATION SOLUTION

Based on the given information, the yearly sales, levels of NWC, and resulting changes in NWC for McDonald's will be:

Year	Yearly Sales	Yearly Levels of NWC	Changes in NWC
0	$ 0	$364,000	$ 364,000
1	2,800,000	937,300	573,300
2	7,210,000	965,900	28,600
3	7,430,000	994,500	28,600
4	7,650,000	512,200	−482,300
5	3,940,000	0	−512,200

OCF calculations, ΔNWC, and ΔFA for each year are shown in $ millions as follows:

(in millions)	Year 0	Year 1	Year 2	Year 3	Year 4	Year 5
Sales		$2.80	$7.21	$7.43	$7.65	$3.94
Less: Variable costs		1.34	3.52	3.70	3.89	2.04
Less: Fixed costs		2.00	2.00	2.00	2.00	2.00
Less: Depreciation		7.00	0.00	0.00	0.00	0.00
Earnings before interest and taxes		−$7.54	$1.69	$1.73	$1.76	−$0.10
Less: Taxes		−1.58	0.35	0.36	0.37	−0.02
Net income		−$5.96	$1.34	$1.37	$1.39	−$0.08
Plus: Depreciation		7.00	0.00	0.00	0.00	0.00
Operating cash flow		$1.04	$1.34	$1.37	$1.39	−$0.08
Δ Fixed assets	$7.00	$0.00	$0.00	$0.00	$0.00	−$1.58
Δ Net working capital	0.36	0.57	0.03	0.03	−0.48	−0.51
Less: Investment in operating capital	$7.36	$0.57	0.03	0.03	−0.48	−2.09
Free cash flow	−$7.36	$0.47	$1.31	$1.34	$1.87	$ 2.01

PERSONAL APPLICATION SOLUTION

Achmed's purchase of a new computer should not be counted as an incremental cash flow to getting an MBA, as he has indicated that he would be getting one anyway. Likewise, the $250 that he paid to take the GMAT is a sunk cost and should not be counted either. His tuition payments constitute an annuity due, so his incremental cash flows will equal

Years	0–3	4–23
FCF	−$15,000	$10,000

Chapter Thirteen

BUSINESS APPLICATION SOLUTION

ADK's project will have an NPV of

$$NPV = \frac{-\$5m}{(1.14)^0} + \frac{\$1.2m}{(1.14)^1} + \frac{\$1.6m}{(1.14)^2} + \frac{\$2.3m}{(1.14)^3} + \frac{\$2.8m}{(1.14)^4} = \$494,038.89 > 0$$

and an IRR of

$$NPV = \frac{-\$5m}{(1 + IRR)^0} + \frac{\$1.2m}{(1 + IRR)^1} + \frac{1.6m}{(1 + IRR)^2} + \frac{\$2.3m}{(1 + IRR)^3} + \frac{\$2.8m}{(1 + IRR)^4}$$

$$IRR = 18.09\% > 14\%$$

Both the NPV and IRR support accepting the project.

We could also calculate MIRR (16.72 percent) and PI (1.10), and these would provide additional support for accepting the project.

Finally, though we are not given maximum allowable payback or discounted payback, values of 2.96 and 3.70, respectively, would seem to be in an acceptable range, too.

PERSONAL APPLICATION SOLUTION

First, we should note that, since cash flows occur every three months, we need to convert the APR of 9 percent to a quarterly rate:

$$i_{qtr} = \left(1 + \frac{0.09}{12}\right)^3 - 1 = 0.0227$$

With these types of cash flows, our choice of decision rules is limited to NPV, MIRR, or PI; we cannot use either the payback rule or IRR because of the non-normality.

The NPV of this project will be

$$NPV = \frac{-\$5,000}{(1.0227)^0} + \frac{-\$5,000}{(1.0227)^1} + \frac{-\$10,000}{(1.0227)^2} + \ldots + \frac{30,000}{(1.0227)^{12}}$$

$$= \$3,473.72 > 0$$

This NPV indicates that the project should be accepted.

Chapter Fourteen

BUSINESS APPLICATION SOLUTION

Chewbacca's operating cycle will be equal to

$$\text{Operating cycle} = \frac{0.1 \times 365}{0.55} + \frac{0.1667 + 365}{1}$$

Their cash cycle will be equal to

$$\text{Cash cycle} = 127.20 - \frac{0.05 + 365}{0.55}$$

$$= 94.02 \text{ day}$$

Absent any other information about current assets or current liabilities, Chewbacca's net working capital will be

$$(0.10 + 0.1667 - 0.05) \times \$32 \text{ million} = \$6.93 \text{ million}$$

PERSONAL APPLICATION SOLUTION

Since Wanda will be drawing out the money smoothly from the account, she can use the Baumol model to determine the optimal replenishment level for her personal stock of cash:

$$C* = \sqrt{2(\$25,000)(\$9.95)/0.035} = \$3,770.18$$

chapter equations

chapter 2

2-1 Assets = Liabilities + Equity

2-2 Net working capital = Current assets − Current liabilities

2-3 Earnings per share $(EPS) = \dfrac{\text{Net income available to common stockholders}}{\text{Total shares of common stock outstanding}}$

2-4

Dividends per share $(DPS) = \dfrac{\text{Common stock dividends paid}}{\text{Number of shares of common stock outstanding}}$

2-5

Book value per share $(BVPS) = \dfrac{\text{Common stock + Paid-in surplus + Retained earnings}}{\text{Number of shares of common stock outstanding}}$

2-6

Market value per share $(MVPS)$ = Market price of the firm's common stock

2-7 Average tax rate $= \dfrac{\text{Tax liability}}{\text{Taxable income}}$

2-8 $FCF = [EBIT(1 - \text{Tax rate}) + \text{Depreciation}] - [\Delta\text{Gross fixed assets} + \Delta\text{Net operating working capital}]$

$= [NOPAT + \text{Depreciation}] - \text{Investment in operating capital}$

$= \text{Operating cash flow} - \text{Investment in operating capital}$

chapter 3

3-1 Current ratio $= \dfrac{\text{Current assets}}{\text{Current liabilities}}$

3-2 Quick ratio (acid-test ratio) $= \dfrac{\text{Current assets} - \text{Inventory}}{\text{Current liabilities}}$

3-3 Cash ratio $= \dfrac{\text{Cash and marketable securities}}{\text{Current liabilities}}$

3-4 Inventory turnover $= \dfrac{\text{Sales or Cost of goods sold}}{\text{Inventory}}$

3-5

Days' sales in inventory $= \dfrac{\text{Inventory} \times 365 \text{ days}}{\text{Sales or Cost of goods sold}} = \dfrac{365 \text{ days}}{\text{Inventory turnover}}$

3-6 Accounts receivable turnover $= \dfrac{\text{Credit sales}}{\text{Accounts receivable}}$

3-7 Average collection period $(ACP) = \dfrac{\text{Accounts receivable} \times 365 \text{ days}}{\text{Credit sales}}$

$= \dfrac{365 \text{ days}}{\text{Accounts receivable turnover}}$

3-8 Accounts payable turnover $= \dfrac{\text{Cost of goods sold}}{\text{Accounts payable}}$

3-9 Average payment period $(APP) = \dfrac{\text{Accounts payable} \times 365 \text{ days}}{\text{Cost of goods sold}}$

$= \dfrac{365 \text{ days}}{\text{Accounts payable turnover}}$

3-10 Fixed asset turnover $= \dfrac{\text{Sales}}{\text{Net fixed assets}}$

3-11 Sales to working capital $= \dfrac{\text{Sales}}{\text{Working capital}}$

3-12 Total asset turnover $= \dfrac{\text{Sales}}{\text{Total assets}}$

3-13 Capital intensity $= \dfrac{\text{Total assets}}{\text{Sales}}$

3-14 Debt ratio $= \dfrac{\text{Total debt}}{\text{Total assets}}$

3-15 Debt-to-equity $= \dfrac{\text{Total debt}}{\text{Total equity}}$

3-16 Equity multiplier $= \dfrac{\text{Total assets}}{\text{Total equity}}$ or $\dfrac{\text{Total assets}}{\text{Common stockholders' equity}}$

3-17 Times interest earned $= \dfrac{EBIT}{\text{Interest}}$

3-18 Fixed-charge coverage $= \dfrac{\text{Earnings available to meet fixed charges}}{\text{Fixed charges}}$

3-19 Cash coverage $= \dfrac{EBIT + \text{Depreciation}}{\text{Fixed charges}}$

3-20 Gross profit margin $= \dfrac{\text{Sales} - \text{Cost of goods sold}}{\text{Sales}}$

3-21 Operating profit margin $= \dfrac{EBIT}{\text{Sales}}$

3-22 Profit margin $= \dfrac{\text{Net income available to common stockholders}}{\text{Sales}}$

3-23 Basic earnings power $(BEP) = \dfrac{EBIT}{\text{Total assets}}$

3-24 Return on assets $(ROA) = \dfrac{\text{Net income available to common stockholders}}{\text{Total assets}}$

3-25 Return on equity $(ROE) = \dfrac{\text{Net income available to common stockholders}}{\text{Common stockholders' equity}}$

3-26 Dividend payout $= \dfrac{\text{Common stock dividends}}{\text{Net income available to common stockholders}}$

3-27 Market-to-book ratio $= \dfrac{\text{Market price per share}}{\text{Book value per share}}$

3-28 Price-earnings (PE) ratio $= \dfrac{\text{Market price per share}}{\text{Earnings per share}}$

3-29 $\underset{\dfrac{\text{Net income available to common stockholders}}{\text{Total assets}}}{ROA} = \underset{\dfrac{\text{Net income available to common stockholders}}{\text{Sales}}}{\text{Profit margin}} \times \underset{\dfrac{\text{Sales}}{\text{Total assets}}}{\text{Total asset turnover}}$

3-30 $\underset{\dfrac{\text{Net income available to common stockholders}}{\text{Common stockholders' equity}}}{ROE} = ROA \times \underset{\dfrac{\text{Total assets}}{\text{Common stockholders' equity}}}{\text{Equity multiplier}}$

3-31 $ROA = \text{Profit margin} \times \text{Total asset turnover} \times \text{Equity multiplier}$

$$\frac{\text{Net income available}}{\text{to common stockholders}}{\text{Common stockholders' equity}} = \frac{\text{Net income available}}{\text{to common stockholders}}{\text{Sales}} \times \frac{\text{Sales}}{\text{Total assets}}$$

$$\times \frac{\text{Total assets}}{\text{Common stockholders' equity}}$$

3-32 $\text{Internal growth rate} = \dfrac{ROA \times RR}{1 - (ROA \times RR)}$

3-33 $\text{Retention ratio } (RR) = \dfrac{\text{Addition to retained earnings}}{\text{Net income available to common stockholders}}$

3-34 $\text{Retention ratio} = 1 - \text{Dividend payout ratio}$

3-35 $\text{Sustainable growth rate} = \dfrac{ROE \times RR}{1 - (ROE \times RR)}$

chapter 4

4-1 $\text{Future value in 1 year} = FV_1 = PV \times (1 + i)$

4-2 $\text{Future value in } N \text{ years} = FV_N = PV \times (1 + i)^N$

4-3 $\text{Future value in } N \text{ periods} = FV_N = PV \times (1 + i_{\text{period 1}}) \times (1 + i_{\text{period 2}})$
$$\times (1 + i_{\text{period 3}}) \times \ldots \times (1 + i_{\text{period } N})$$

4-4 $\text{Present value of next period's cash flow} = PV = FV_1/(1 + i)$

4-5 $\text{Present value of cash flow made in } N \text{ years} = PV = FV_N/(1 + i)^N$

4-6 Present value with different discount rates
$$= PV = \frac{FV_N}{(1 + i_{\text{period 1}}) \times (1 + i_{\text{period 2}}) \times (1 + i_{\text{period 3}}) \times \ldots \times (1 + i_{\text{period } N})}$$

4-7 $\text{Approximate number of years to double an investment} = \dfrac{72}{\text{Interest rate}}$

chapter 5

5-1 $FV_N = \text{Future value of first cash flow}$
$+ \text{Future value of second cash flow}$
$+ \ldots + \text{Future value of last cash flow}$
$$= PMT_m \times (1 + i)^{N-m} + PMT_n \times (1 + i)^{N-n} + \cdots + PMT_p \times (1 + i)^{N-p}$$

5-2 $FVA_N = PMT \times \dfrac{(1 + i)^N - 1}{i}$

5-3
$PV = \text{Present value of first cash flow} + \text{Present value of second cash flow}$
$+ \ldots + \text{Present value of last cash flow}$

$$= \frac{PMT_m}{(1 + i)^m} + \frac{PMT_n}{(1 + i)^n} + \ldots + \frac{PMT_p}{(1 + i)^p}$$

5-4 $PVA_N = PMT \times \left[\dfrac{1 - \dfrac{1}{(1 + i)^N}}{i} \right]$

5-5 $PV \text{ of a perpetuity} = \dfrac{PMT}{i}$

5-6 $FVA_N \text{ due} = FVA_N \times (1 + i)$

5-7 $PVA_N \text{ due} = PVA_N \times (1 + i)$

5-8 $EAR = \left(1 + \dfrac{APR}{m}\right)^m - 1$

5-9 $PMT_N = PV \times \left[\dfrac{i}{1 - \dfrac{1}{(1 + i)^N}} \right]$

chapter 6

6-1 $IP = \dfrac{CPI_{t+1} - CPI_t}{CPI_t} \times 100$

6-2 $i = \text{Expected } IP + RFR$

6-3 $RFR = i - \text{Expected } IP$

6-4 $DRP_j = i_{jt} - i_{Tt}$

6-5 $i_j^* = f(IP, RFR, DRP_j, LRP_j, SCP_j, MP_j)$

6-6 $(1 + {}_1R_N)^N = (1 + {}_1R_1)[1 + E({}_2r_1)] \ldots [1 + E({}_Nr_1)]$

6-7 ${}_1R_N = \{[1 + {}_1R_1][1 + E({}_2r_1)] \ldots [1 + E({}_Nr_1)]\}^{1/N} - 1$

6-8 ${}_1R_N = \{[1 + {}_1R_1][1 + E({}_2r_1) + L_2] \ldots [1 + E({}_Nr_1) + L_N]\}^{1/N} - 1$

6-9 ${}_1R_2 = [(1 + {}_1R_1)(1 + {}_2f_1)]^{1/2} - 1$

6-10 ${}_2f_1 = [(1 + {}_1R_2)^2/(1 + {}_1R_1)] - 1$

6-11 ${}_Nf_1 = [(1 + {}_1R_N)^N/(1 + {}_1R_{N-1})^{N-1}] - 1$

chapter 7

7-1 $\text{Present value of bond} = PMT \times \left[\dfrac{1 - \dfrac{1}{(1 + i)^N}}{i} \right] + \dfrac{\$1{,}000}{(1 + i)^N}$

7-2 $\text{Bond price} = PV \text{ of annuity } (PMT, i, N) + PV(FV, i, N)$

7-3 $\text{Price of a callable bond} = PMT \times \left[\dfrac{1 - \dfrac{1}{(1 + i)^N}}{i} \right] + \dfrac{\text{Call price}}{(1 + i)^N}$

7-4 $\text{Equivalent taxable yield} = \dfrac{\text{Muni yield}}{1 - \text{Tax rate}}$

chapter 8

8-1 $P_0 = \dfrac{D_1 + P_1}{1 + i}$

8-2 $P_0 = \dfrac{D_1}{1 + i} + \dfrac{D_2 + P_2}{(1 + i)^2}$

8-3 $P_0 = \dfrac{D_1}{1 + i} + \dfrac{D_2}{(1 + i)^2} + \cdots + \dfrac{D_n + P_n}{(1 + i)^n}$

8-4 $P_0 = \dfrac{D_1}{1 + i} + \dfrac{D_2}{(1 + i)^2} + \dfrac{D_3}{(1 + i)^3} + \cdots$

8-5 $P_0 = \dfrac{D_0(1 + g)}{1 + i} + \dfrac{D_0(1 + g)^2}{(1 + i)^2} + \dfrac{D_0(1 + g)^3}{(1 + i)^3} + \cdots$

8-6 Constant-growth model $= P_0 = \dfrac{D_0(1 + g)}{i - g} = \dfrac{D_1}{i - g}$

8-7 Expected return $= i = \dfrac{D_1}{P_0} + g =$ Dividend yield + Capital gain

8-8

$$P_0 = \dfrac{D_0(1 + g_1)}{1 + i} + \dfrac{D_0(1 + g_1)^2}{(1 + i)^2} + \dfrac{D_0(1 + g_1)^3}{(1 + i)^3}$$

$$+ \cdots + \dfrac{D_0(1 + g_1)^n + \dfrac{D_0(1 + g_1)^n(1 + g_2)}{i - g_2}}{(1 + i)^n}$$

8-9 $P/E = \dfrac{\text{Current stock price}}{\text{Per-share earnings for last 12 months}}$

8-10 $P_n = (P/E)_n \times E_n$

$\qquad = (P/E)_n \times E_0 \times (1 + g)^n$

chapter 9

9-1 Dollar return = Capital gain or loss + Income

$\qquad$ = (Ending value − Beginning value) + Income

9-2 Percentage return $= \dfrac{\text{Ending value − Beginning value + Income}}{\text{Beginning value}} \times 100\%$

9-3 Average return $= \dfrac{\sum\limits_{t=1}^{N} \text{Return}_t}{N}$

9-4 Geometric mean return $= \left[\prod\limits_{t=1}^{N} \left(1 + \dfrac{\text{Return}_t}{100} \right) \right]^{\frac{1}{k}} - 1$

9-5 Standard deviation $= \sqrt{\dfrac{\sum\limits_{t=1}^{N} (\text{Return}_t - \text{Average return})^2}{N - 1}}$

9-6 Coefficient of variation $= \dfrac{\text{Standard deviation}}{\text{Average return}}$

9-7 Total risk = Firm-specific risk + Market risk

9-8 $R_p = (w_1 \times R_1) + (w_2 \times R_2) + (w_3 \times R_3) + \cdots + (w_n \times R_n) = \sum\limits_{i=1}^{n} w_i R_i$

chapter 10

10-1 Expected return $= (p_1 \times \text{Return}_1) + (p_2 \times \text{Return}_2)\,(p_3 \times \text{Return}_3)$

$\qquad + \cdots + (p_s \times \text{Return}_s) = \sum\limits_{j=1}^{s} p_j \times \text{Return}_j$

10-2 Standard deviation $= \sqrt{\begin{array}{l} p_1 \times (\text{Return}_1 - \text{Expected return})^2 + p_2 \\ \times (\text{Return}_2 - \text{Expected return})^2 + \cdots \end{array}}$

$\qquad = \sqrt{\sum\limits_{j=1}^{s} p_j \times (\text{Return}_j - \text{Expected return})^2}$

10-3 Required return = Risk-free rate + Risk premium

10-4 Expected return $= R_f + \beta(R_M - R_f)$

10-5 $\beta_\rho = (w_1 \times \beta_2) + (w_2 \times \beta_2) + (w_2 \times \beta_3) + \cdots + (w_n \times \beta_n) = \sum\limits_{j=1}^{n} w_j \beta_j$

10-6 $i =$ Dividend yield + Constant growth $= \dfrac{D_1}{P_0} + g$

chapter 11

11-1 $WACC_{\text{Unconstrained}} = \dfrac{E}{E + P + D} \times i_E + \dfrac{P}{E + P + D} \times i_P + \dfrac{D}{E + P + D} \times i_D \times (1 - T_C)$

11-2 $WACC_{\text{Constrained}} = \dfrac{E}{E + P + D} \times i_E + \dfrac{P}{E + P + D} \times i_P + \dfrac{D}{E + P + D} \times i_D$

11-3 $i_E = R_f + \beta\,(R_M - R_f)$

11-4 $i_E = \dfrac{D_1}{P_0} + g$

11-5 $i_p = \dfrac{D_1}{P_0}$

11-6 Solve $\left\{ PV = PMT \times \left[\dfrac{1 - \dfrac{1}{(1 + i_D)\,N}}{i_D} \right] + \dfrac{FV}{(1 + i_D)\,N} \right\}$ for i_D

11-7 $i_E = r_f + \beta_{\text{Avg}}[E(r_M) - r_f]$

$\qquad$ where

$\qquad \beta_{\text{Avg}} = \dfrac{\sum\limits_{j=1}^{N} \beta_j}{n}$

11-8 $WACC_{\text{Unconstrained, Project}} = \dfrac{E_{\text{Project}}}{E_{\text{Project}} + P_{\text{Project}} + D_{\text{Project}}} \times i_{E,\,\text{Project}}$

$\qquad + \dfrac{P_{\text{Project}}}{E_{\text{Project}} + P_{\text{Project}} + D_{\text{Project}}} i_{P,\,\text{Firm}}$

$\qquad + \dfrac{D_{\text{Project}}}{E_{\text{Project}} + P_{\text{Project}} + D_{\text{Project}}} i_{D,\,\text{Firm}} \times (1 + T_C)$

11-9 $WACC_{\text{Constrained, Project}} = \dfrac{E_{\text{Project}}}{E_{\text{Project}} + P_{\text{Project}} + D_{\text{Project}}} \times i_{E,\,\text{Project}}$

$\qquad + \dfrac{P_{\text{Project}}}{E_{\text{Project}} + P_{\text{Project}} + D_{\text{Project}}} i_{P,\,\text{Firm}}$

$\qquad + \dfrac{D_{\text{Project}}}{E_{\text{Project}} + P_{\text{Project}} + D_{\text{Project}}} i_{D,\,\text{Firm}}$

11-10 $i_E = \dfrac{D_1}{P_0 - F} + g$

11-11 $i_P = \dfrac{D_1}{P_0 - F}$

11-12 Solve $\left\{ PV - F = PMT \times \left[\dfrac{1 - \dfrac{1}{(1 + i_D)^N}}{i_D} \right] + \dfrac{FV}{(1 + i_D)^N} \right\}$ for i_D

12-1 FCF = Operating cash flow − Investment in operating capital
= [$EBIT$ (1 − Tax rate) + Depreciation]
− [Δ Gross fixed assets + Δ Net operating working capital]

12-2 Depreciation = $\dfrac{\text{Depreciable basis − Ending book value}}{\text{Life of asset}}$

12-3 $ATCF$ = Market value − (Market value − Book value) × T_C

12-4 $f_A = \dfrac{E}{E + P + D} f_E + \dfrac{P}{E + P + D} f_P + \dfrac{D}{E + P + D} f_D$

12-5 Adjusted $CF_0 = \dfrac{CF_0}{1 - f_A}$

13-1 Payback Statistic
$0 = \sum\limits_{n=0}^{PB} CF_n$

13-2 Payback Decision Rule
Accept project if calculated payback ≤ Maximum allowable payback
Reject project if calculated payback > Maximum allowable payback

13-3 Discounted Payback Statistic
$0 = \sum\limits_{n=0}^{DPB} \dfrac{CF_n}{(1 + i)_n}$

13-4 Discounted Payback Decision Rule
Accept project if calculated DPB ≤ Maximum allowable discounted payback
Reject project if calculated DPB > Maximum allowable discounted payback

13-5 NPV Statistic
$NPV = \dfrac{CF_0}{(1 + i)^0} + \dfrac{CF_1}{(1 + i)_1} + \ldots + \dfrac{CF_N}{(1 + i)_N}$
$= \sum\limits_{n=0}^{N} \dfrac{CF_n}{(1 + i)^n}$

13-6 NPV Decision Rule
Accept project if NPV ≥ 0
Reject project if NPV < 0

13-7 Formula Comparison (13-5 to 13-8)
Solve for NPV   Solve for IRR
$NPV = \sum\limits_{n=0}^{N} \dfrac{CF_n}{(1 + i)^n}$ versus $0 = \sum\limits_{n=0}^{N} \dfrac{CF_n}{(1 + IRR)^n}$

13-8 IRR Statistic Solve for IRR: $0 = \sum\limits_{n=0}^{N} \dfrac{CF_n}{(1 + IRR)^n}$

13-9 IRR Decision Rule
Accept project if IRR ≥ Cost of capital
Reject project if IRR < Cost of capital

13-10 Profitability Index Statistic
$PI = \dfrac{NPV + CF_0}{CF_0}$

13-11 Profitability Index Decision Rule
Accept project if PI ≥ 1
Reject project if PI < 1

14-1 Operating cycle = Days' sales in inventory + Average collection period
$= \dfrac{\text{Inventory} \times 365}{\text{Cost of goods sold}} + \dfrac{\text{Accounts receivable} \times 365}{\text{Credit sales}}$

14-2 Cash cycle = Operating cycle − Average payment period
$= \text{Operating cycle} - \dfrac{\text{Accounts payable} \times 365}{\text{Cost of good sold}}$

14-3 Opportunity cost $= \dfrac{C}{2} \times i$

14-4 Trading cost $= \dfrac{T}{C} \times F$

14-5 Total cost $= \dfrac{C}{2} \times i + \dfrac{T}{C} \times F$

14-6 $C^* = \sqrt{2TF/i}$

14-7 $Z^* = \sqrt[3]{3F\sigma^2/4 i_{\text{day}}} + L$

14-8 $H^* = 3Z^* - 2L$

Index